Fodor's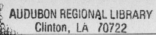

Eastern
Europe

Fodor's Travel Publications, Inc.
New York • Toronto • London • Sydney • Auckland

Portions of this book appear in *Fodor's Budapest* and *Fodor's The Czech Republic & Slovakia.*

Fodor's Eastern Europe

Editor: Christopher Billy
Contributors: Steven K. Amsterdam, Mark Baker, David Brown, Robert Cohen, William Echikson, Echo Garrett, Jaroslav Golev, Anita Guerrini, Emma Harris, Rumyana Karsteva, Alan Levy, Virginia Marsh, Bevin McLaughlin, Delia Meth-Cohn, Witold Orzechowski, Linda K. Schmidt, Mary Ellen Schultz, Julie Tomasz, Nancy van Itallie
Creative Director: Fabrizio La Rocca
Cartographer: David Lindroth
Illustrator: Karl Tanner
Cover Photograph: Scott Lynn Riley

Design: Vignelli Associates

Special Sales

Fodor's Travel Publications are available at special discounts for bulk purchases for sales promotions or premiums. Special editions, including personalized covers, excerpts of existing guides, and corporate imprints, can be created in large quantities for special needs. For more information contact your local bookseller or write to Special Markets, Fodor's Travel Publications, 201 East 50th Street, New York, NY 10022. Inquiries from Canada should be directed to your local Canadian bookseller or sent to Random House of Canada, Ltd., Marketing Department, 1265 Aerowood Drive, Mississauga, Ontario L4W 1B9. Inquiries from the United Kingdom should be sent to Fodor's Travel Publications, 20 Vauxhall Bridge Road, London, England SW1V 2SA.

Contents

Foreword   *vi*

Highlights   *ix*

Fodor's Choice   *xii*

Introduction   *xxiv*

1   Essential Information   *1*

Before You Go *2*

Government Information Offices *2*
Tours and Packages *2*
When to Go *5*
What to Pack *7*
Taking Money Abroad *8*
Getting Money from Home *9*
What It Will Cost *10*
Long-Distance Calling *10*
Passports and Visas *10*
Customs and Duties *12*
Traveling with Cameras, Camcorders, and Laptops *14*
Staying Healthy *14*
Insurance *15*
Car Rentals *17*
Rail Passes *18*
Student and Youth Travel *19*
Traveling with Children *20*
Hints for Travelers with Disabilities *21*
Hints for Older Travelers *22*
Hints for Gay and Lesbian Travelers *23*
Further Reading *24*

Arriving and Departing *24*

From North America by Plane *24*
From the United Kingdom by Plane, Car, Bus, Train, and Ferry *27*

Staying in Eastern Europe *28*

Getting Around *28*
Telephones *29*
VAT and Sales Tax *29*
Dining *29*
Lodging *30*
Credit Cards *31*

**Eastern Europe at a Glance:
A Chronology** *31*

2 Czech Republic 39

Before You Go *42*
Arriving and Departing *47*
Staying in the Czech Republic *48*
Prague *53*
Bohemia *97*
Moravia *127*

3 Slovakia 147

Before You Go *150*
Arriving and Departing *153*
Staying in Slovakia *154*
Bratislava *159*
The High Tatras *172*
Eastern Slovakia *180*

4 Hungary 193

Before You Go *196*
Arriving and Departing *200*
Staying in Hungary *201*
Budapest *206*
The Danube Bend *258*
Lake Balaton *268*
Northern Hungary and the Great Plain *287*
Transdanubia *303*

5 Poland 316

Before You Go *321*
Arriving and Departing *325*
Staying in Poland *326*
Warsaw *332*
Kraków and the South *363*
Lublin and the East *383*
Gdańsk and the Northeast *392*
Western Poland *400*

6 Bulgaria 415

Before You Go *416*
Staying in Bulgaria *419*
Sofia *423*
The Black Sea Golden Coast *431*
Inland Bulgaria *436*

7 Romania 441

Before You Go *444*
Staying in Romania *446*
Bucharest *450*
The Black Sea Coast and Danube Delta *458*
Transylvania *462*

Vocabulary 467

Index *498*

Maps

Eastern Europe *xvi–xvii*
Eastern Europe Railways *xviii–xix*
Europe *xx–xxi*
World Time Zones *xxii–xxiii*
Czech Republic *41*
Prague Metro *58*
Prague (Tours 1–4) *60–61*
Tour 5: Prague Castle (Pražský hrad) *78*
Prague Dining and Lodging *90–91*
Bohemia *100*
Moravia *131*
Brno *136*
Slovakia *149*
Slovakia Exploring *162*
Bratislava *163*
Hungary *195*
Tour 1: Castle Hill (Várhegy) *213*
Budapest (Tours 2–7) *220–221*
Budapest Dining and Lodging *244–245*
The Danube Bend *260*
Lake Balaton *271*
Northern Hungary and the Great Plain *290*
Transdanubia *305*
Poland *318–319*
Warsaw *338–339*
Warsaw Dining and Lodging *352–353*
Southeastern Poland *366*
Kraków *367*
Kraków Dining and Lodging *378*
Gdańsk and the Northeast *394*
Western Poland *403*
Bulgaria *417*
Sofia *425*
The Black Sea Golden Coast *432*
Inland Bulgaria *437*
Romania *443*
Bucharest *454–455*
The Black Sea Coast *459*

Foreword

While every care has been taken to ensure the accuracy of the information in this guide, the passage of time will always bring change, and consequently, the publisher cannot accept responsibility for errors that may occur.

All prices and opening times quoted here are based on information supplied to us at press time. Hours and admission fees may change, however, and the prudent traveler will avoid inconvenience by calling ahead.

Fodor's wants to hear about your travel experiences, both pleasant and unpleasant. When a hotel or restaurant fails to live up to its billing, let us know and we will investigate the complaint and revise our entries where the facts warrant it.

Send your letters to the editors of Fodor's Travel Publications, 201 E. 50th Street, New York, NY 10022.

Highlights and Fodor's Choice

Highlights

The Czech Republic Following the breakup of the Czechoslovak state in 1993, the new Czech Republic continues along its path of economic and cultural revitalization, with the eventual goal of incorporation into the European Union (EU) by the year 2000. Far from hurting the country, the Czech-Slovak split has freed officials to concentrate on the pressing economic problems of Bohemia and Moravia, without having to worry about Slovakia. Chief among these problems are rising prices, falling living standards, and rising unemployment. Tourism, however, remains one of the brightest sectors of the economy, and travelers will likely be unaffected by the grim economic statistics.

One tangible impact of the country's economic reforms has been an acceleration in the pace of architectural renovations. The scaffolding that has long surrounded many of Prague's historic structures is finally being dismantled, and many hotels and even family-operated inns are installing new fixtures and applying a fresh coat of paint. One of the areas to get a face-lift over the past few years is **Staroměstské náměstí** (Old Town Square), one of the jewels of the "new" Prague, lined by such landmarks as the Týn Church and the Old Town Hall.

The number of hotels keeps pace with the growing number of visitors. This is even true of Prague, which has become a major European tourist destination. At press time, an Austrian chain has reopened the **Bohemia,** an Art Nouveau jewel in the center of the city. Several other new projects are expected during the course of the year. Like the number of new large hotels, the number of smaller, privately owned hotels and pensions is also on the rise.

Events are just as exciting on the dining front. The influx of Americans and other Westerners has brought with it new restaurants offering Cajun, Mexican, vegetarian, and other exotic fare alongside the traditional ones serving pork and dumplings.

Prague's cultural life continues to thrive: New theater groups sprout up right and left, and the schedule of concerts and operas has grown each season since the revolution of 1989. The annual mid-May–early-June **Prague Spring Music Festival,** which even before the collapse of the communist government was one of the great events on the European calendar, is attracting record numbers of music lovers. One sad note: at press time, officials were planning to close the Art Nouveau Obecní Dom in 1995 for long-needed repairs.

Slovakia Europe's youngest country continues to be dogged by bad press and a bit of an identity complex. Decisions to proceed on environmental megaprojects, such as new nuclear reactors and the highly controversial Gabčikovo dam on the Danube, have been keeping officials on the defensive. Moreover, the government's unwillingness to commit to a rapid program of economic reform has some wondering (only partly in jest) whether the Communists haven't secretly regained control.

Slovakia has retained the former Czechoslovakia's policy of encouraging tourism; visitors from the United States or United Kingdom do not need visas, although those entering Slovakia from the Czech Republic should be prepared to show a passport. In addition, Czech money is no longer valid in Slovakia (and vice versa).

Changes in the hotel and restaurant scene are far less noticeable in Slovakia than in the Czech Republic. A beautiful new hotel, the **Perugia,** opened its doors in the Slovak capital, Bratislava, in 1994, bringing the number of deluxe hotels in town to three. An old Bratislava favorite, the **Carlton,** was closed for a much-needed face-lift in 1993; the hotel expects to reopen sometime in 1995. A former budget standby, the **Palace,** shut down in 1994 for renovations; it should reopen sometime in 1995, though probably not in the inexpensive category.

Elsewhere in the country, it's business as usual for the tourist sector. Hotel operators in the High Tatras report slower seasons than in the past, as the East bloc clientele on which they've relied for the past 40 years try out the more exotic destinations in Spain and France. Interest in the Tatras is sure to grow in the future, though, as West Europeans and Americans discover their charm and natural beauty.

Hungary Delta and Malev, the Hungarian national airline, joined forces in May 1994 to merge their respective direct services between Budapest and the United States. The duo now offers **daily non-stop flights** between New York City's JFK and Budapest's Ferihegy airport.

At press time, Budapest's new socialist government declared it would not support the planned **1996 World Expo,** which promoters had hoped would bring hordes of tourists to the banks of the Danube in May 1996. As a result, the $1-billion construction project involving pavilions, parks, and parking lots was put on hold pending the emergence of private investors committed to reviving the Expo.

Major chain hotels are expanding, and state-controlled hotels are going private and sprucing up. After finishing a $13-million overhaul, the **Budapest Marriott** revealed its impressive new face in June 1994. Outside the capital, a new chain of **castle hotels,** some attached to thermal spas, is preparing to open.

Travelers will find Hungary a bargain compared to western Europe, but rock-bottom prices are a thing of the past. At press time inflation was holding steady at 25%.

Poland The recently opened new terminal at Warsaw airport has greatly improved the speed and comfort of arrival at Poland's capital. Getting around within Poland is also becoming easier: new car-rental firms are popping up, and gasoline is now readily available.

The range of accommodations continues to broaden and improve. Older fine hotels are being renovated in Warsaw and there are also many new small private hotels and pensions country-wide.

Bulgaria In the next few years, Bulgaria's tourist industry will undergo a process of total privatization. International hotel chains are showing special interest in the resort areas now attracting tourists who once frequented resorts in Yugoslavia. The first hotels to go private were Hotel Sofia and Hotel Bulgaria in Sofia, and Hotel Trimontzium in Plovdiv.

During this transition period, many hotels and restaurants will be temporarily closed for reconstruction and modernization by their new owners. As a result, facilities not up to Western standards are expected to improve and acquire more individual character. At the same time, hundreds of new hotels, hostels, and taverns are mushrooming throughout the country.

Romania Having established a democratic system, Romania is now trying to build a market economy. Peasants are being given back their land, and small private enterprises are being encouraged, leading to an increasing variety in the shops and markets. A number of hotels are expected to be sold by the state to international commercial buyers.

Fodor's Choice

No two people will agree on what makes a perfect vacation, but it can be fun and helpful to know what others think. We hope you'll have a chance to experience some of Fodor's Choices yourself while visiting Eastern Europe. For detailed information on individual entries, see the relevant sections of this guidebook.

Lodging

Czech Republic
Dvořák, Karlovy Vary, Bohemia, *$$$$*

Grandhotel Pupp, Karlovy Vary, *$$$$*

U Páva, Prague, *$$$$*

Pension U Raka, Prague, *$$$*

Ruže, Český Krumlov, Bohemia, *$$$*

Černý Orel, Telč, Moravia, *$$*

Na Louži, Český Krumlov, Bohemia, *$*

Slovakia
Grand Hotel, Starý Smokovec, *$$$*

Grandhotel Praha, Tatranská Lomnica, *$$$*

Hungary
Budapest Hilton, Budapest, *$$$$*

Forum, Budapest, *$$$$*

Kempinski, Budapest, *$$$$*

Gellért, Budapest, *$$$*

Astoria, Budapest, *$$*

Savaria, Szombathely, *$*

Poland
Hotel Bristol, Warsaw, *$$$$*

Marriott, Warsaw, *$$$$*

Hotel Grand, Kraków, *$$$*

Zajazd Napoleoński, Warsaw, *$$$*

Romania
Continental, Bucharest, *$$$$*

Triumf, Bucharest, *$$*

Bulgaria
Vitosha, Sofia, *$$$$*

Grand Hotel Varna, Sveti Konstantin, *$$$*

Dining

Czech Republic
V Zátiši, Prague, *$$$$*

U Mecenáše, Prague, $$$

Lobkovická, Prague, $$$

Penguin's, Prague, $$

Slovakia Rybarský Cech, Bratislava, $$$

Koliba, Zochová Chata, Modra, $$

Hungary Alabárdos, Budapest, $$$$

Gundel, Budapest, $$$$

Légrádi Testvérek, Budapest, $$$$

Múzeum, Budapest, $$$

Aranysárkány, Szentendre, $$

Duna-Corso, Budapest, $$

Fészek, Budapest, $

Hortobágyi Csárda, Hortobágy, $

Poland Wierzynek, Kraków, $$$$

Bazyliszek, Warsaw, $$$

Pod Łososiem, Gdańsk, $$$

Zajazd Napoleoński, Warsaw, $$$

Bulgaria Budapest, Sofia, $$$

Castles and Churches

Czech Republic St. Vitus Cathedral, Hradčany, Prague

Týn Church, Staré Město, Prague

Krumlov Castle, Český Krumlov, Bohemia

St. Barbara's Cathedral, Kutná Hora, Bohemia

Villa Tugendhat, Brno, Moravia

St. Anne's Chapel, Olomouc, Moravia

Slovakia Church and Convent of the Poor Clares, Bratislava

Červený Kameň Castle, Slovakia

The wood churches off the Dukla Pass road

St. Jacob's Church, Levoča

Hungary St. Stephen's Basilica, Budapest

Matthias Church, Budapest

Esztergom Cathedral, Esztergom

Festetics Palace, Keszthely

Poland   Kościół Mariacki, Kraków

Monastery at Jasna Góra, Częstochowa

Wawel, Kraków

Puławy Palace, Puławy

Kościół Mariacki, Gdańsk

Wilanów Palace, Warsaw

Bulgaria   Hram-pametnik Alexander Neuski, Sofia

Dragalevci Monastery, near Sofia

Romania   Biserica Ortodoxă, Bucharest

Museums

Czech Republic   National Gallery, Prague

The State Jewish Museum, Prague

Theresienstadt Memorial Museum, Terezín, Bohemia

Slovakia   Šariš Icon Museum, Bardejov

Hungary   Castle District Museums, Budapest

Museum of Fine Arts, Budapest

Vasarely Museum, Pécs

Poland   Muzeum Narodowe, Warsaw

Jewish Historical Museum, Warsaw

Czartoryski Collection, Kraków

Oświęcim (Auschwitz), near Kraków

Bulgaria   Natzionalen Archeolgicheski Musei, Sofia

Romania   Muzeul Satului Romanesc, Bucharest

Muzeul de Artă al României, Bucharest

Towns and Villages

Czech Republic   Český Krumlov, Bohemia

Mariánské Lazně, Bohemia

Telč, Moravia

Slovakia   Bardejov, Eastern Slovakia

Levoča, Eastern Slovakia

Hungary   Eger, Northern Hungary

Hortobágy, Northern Hungary

Sopron, Transdanubia

Szentendre, The Danube Bend

Tihany, Lake Balaton

Poland Częstochowa, Kraków and the South

Kazimierz Dolny, Lublin and the East

Łańcut, Lublin and the East

Toruń, Western Poland

Zakopane, Kraków and the South

Bulgaria Koprivshtitsa, Inland Bulgaria

Romania Eforie Nord, Black Sea Coast and Danube Delta

Eastern Europe

Lübeck
Rostock
Hamburg
Bremen
Hannover
Słupsk Gdynia
Gdańsk
Szczecin
Gorzów Wielkopolski
Bydgoszcz
Toruń
Berlin
Poznań
RU FED
GERMANY
POLAND
Łódź
Leipzig
Erfurt
Dresden
Wrocław
Piotrków Tyrb.
Radom
Częstochowa
Wałbrzych
Prague
Plzeň
Bytom
Gliwice Sosnowiec
Katowice
Kraków
Nürnberg
CZECH REPUBLIC
Ostrava
CARPATHIANS
Brno
Kroměříž
Prešov
SLOVAKIA Košice
Munich
Linz
Vienna
Bratislava
Salzburg
AUSTRIA
Győr
Miskolc
Graz
Lake Balaton
Budapest
SLOVENIA
HUNGARY
Ljubljana
Zagreb
Pécs
Szeged
Venézia
CROATIA
Novi Sad
Tin
Re
Bologna
BOSNIA AND HERZEGOVINA
Belgrade
Sarajevo
SERBIA
ITALY
Adriatic Sea
MONTENEGRO
Rome
ALBANIA MAC

Eastern Europe Railways

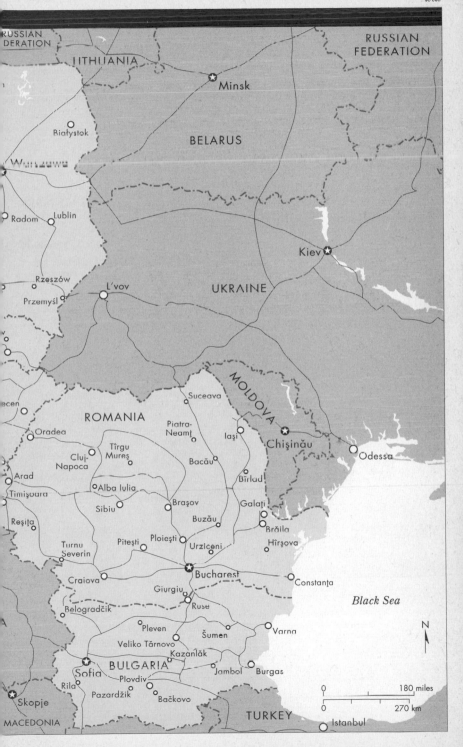

Europe

World Time Zones

MONDAY
SUNDAY

International Date Line

+12 +13

-9

-10

-7

-11

-10

+11

+12

1

2

3

4

5

6

7

8

9

10

11

12

13

14 15

16

17

18

19

20

21

22

23

24

25

-4

-3

0

-3

-7

-5 -4

-3:30

-8

-6

-4

-5

-4

-3

-3

+11   +12 -   -11   -10   -9   -8   -7   -6   -5   -4   -3   -2

Numbers below vertical bands relate each zone to Greenwich Mean Time (0 hrs.).
Local times frequently differ from these general indications,
as indicated by light-face numbers on map.

Algiers, **29**
Anchorage, **3**
Athens, **41**
Auckland, **1**
Baghdad, **46**
Bangkok, **50**
Beijing, **54**

Berlin, **34**
Bogotá, **19**
Budapest, **37**
Buenos Aires, **24**
Caracas, **22**
Chicago, **9**
Copenhagen, **33**
Dallas, **10**

Delhi, **48**
Denver, **8**
Djakarta, **53**
Dublin, **26**
Edmonton, **7**
Hong Kong, **56**
Honolulu, **2**

Istanbul, **40**
Jerusalem, **42**
Johannesburg, **44**
Lima, **20**
Lisbon, **28**
London (Greenwich), **27**
Los Angeles, **6**
Madrid, **38**
Manila, **57**

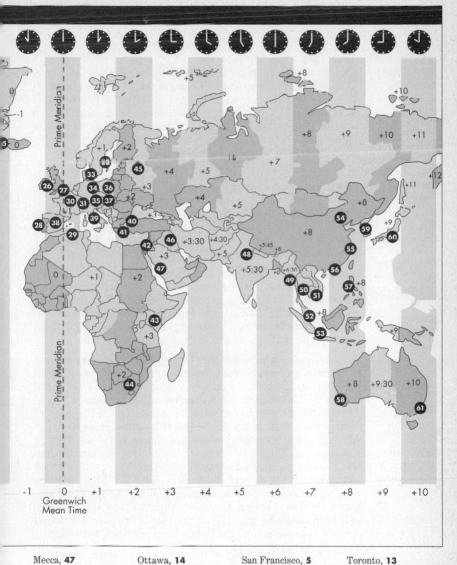

-1 0 +1 +2 +3 +4 +5 +6 +7 +8 +9 +10

Greenwich
Mean Time

Mecca, **47**
Mexico City, **12**
Miami, **18**
Montréal, **15**
Moscow, **45**
Nairobi, **43**
New Orleans, **11**
New York City, **16**

Ottawa, **14**
Paris, **30**
Perth, **58**
Reykjavík, **25**
Rio de Janeiro, **23**
Rome, **39**
Saigon (Ho Chi Minh
City), **51**

San Francisco, **5**
Santiago, **21**
Seoul, **59**
Shanghai, **55**
Singapore, **52**
Stockholm, **32**
Sydney, **61**
Tokyo, **60**

Toronto, **13**
Vancouver, **4**
Vienna, **35**
Warsaw, **36**
Washington, D.C., **17**
Yangon, **49**
Zürich, **31**

Introduction

By William Echikson

William Echikson has reported on Eastern Europe since 1985 for The Christian Science Monitor *and* The Economist. *He is the author of the book* Lighting the Night: Revolution in Eastern Europe.

Not so many years ago, heavily laden Skodas used to pour out of Prague on Friday mornings, heading to countryside cottages where Czechs puttered in privacy. But now on Saturdays and Sundays, workers such as Zdenek Burian hang shelves and paint away the drabness of four long decades of communism. "I'm making five times more than before," Burian says, "and working ten times harder."

In Warsaw, the old Communist-party headquarters houses Poland's infant stock exchange. Not far away, billboards light up the night, blaring Coca-Cola, Marlboro, and Hitachi. At one of Daniel Lewandowski's ten new L&K car washes, three woman dressed in green uniforms gloss a Mercedes sedan. "Poles are starting to buy nice cars," Lewandowski says. "Before, they owned such battered cars they didn't bother to wash them."

A short drive south of Budapest, an abandoned Russian army base has been transformed into a modern industrial park where multinational giant Philips produces video recorders, and where Ford produces its sophisticated ignition coils. "This is state-of-the art manufacturing," says a proud Ford manager John Vargha. "We don't have factories as modern in Detroit."

For a journalist who remembers the putrid smell of tear gas and the painful glare of corrupt communism on faces, returning to the liberated countries of Eastern Europe comes as a delightful surprise. Culturally, economically, and politically, East Europeans are moving fast to build democracy on the ruins of dictatorship, to move from poverty to Western-style prosperity. At every turn, the energy of reconstruction is visible. Though Romania and Bulgaria continue to lag behind, the nimble Central Europeans have sidestepped both the ethnic violence that has engulfed the former Yugoslavia, and the hyperinflation which has ravaged Russia. Despite economic and political setbacks, Hungary, Poland, the Czech Republic, and Slovakia have held free elections, guaranteed the rule of law, and permitted citizens to travel freely. Everyday life is becoming normal.

Throughout 40 years of communism, the Eastern European countries were artificially severed from their rightful place in the heart of Europe. Then, in one giant and quite unbelievable swipe, they broke the Communist party's monopoly and declared very simply, we are free. Since the turmoil of 1989 and 1990, when revolutions both violent and "velvet" captured world headlines, the abstract notions of human rights and self-determination once again have become pressing topics in Eastern Europe.

For most visitors, the stirring images associated with the collapse of communism—be it the bloodied streets of Bucharest or the former Lenin Shipyard in Gdańsk where Solidarity was born—evoke something deeper than a simple interest in contemporary politics. Like so many other Americans, my family comes from this part of the world. Fannie Wolf and Saul Gross, my mother's parents, emigrated from Vienna. My father's family came from Budapest. My father's namesake, Echikson, originated from a Jewish shtetl just outside Riga in Latvia. Arriving in Warsaw, Prague, Budapest or Bucharest, I recognize smiling, plump babushkas who resemble my grandmother. They have the same lilt in their voices, the same firm walk. I eat jellied carp, just like my grandmother's homemade gefilte fish. The men resemble my grandfather; they wear the same wide brimmed hats, the same faded tweed vests, and have the same intense, quizzical expressions. In their faces and in their mannerisms, the "world of my fathers" lives on.

Eastern Europe Divided

The region and its peoples, of course, are far from homogeneous. In ancient times as today, Europe was split between Rome and Byzantium—between the Orthodox Romanians and Bulgarians and the Roman Catholic and Protestant Poles, Czechs, Slovaks, and Magyars. The Turks long ruled present-day Romania and Bulgaria, while the Austrians, Russians, and Germans persistently took turns dominating the rest of the region. How can one compare a Czech steel worker from the industrial city of Plzen, puttering along in his locally made Skoda auto, with a Romanian peasant from the Wallachian countryside, plodding along in a horse and cart? Both are "East Europeans." But they live in two very different worlds.

Eastern Europe's profound north–south divide, coupled with a revived interest in nationalism, threatens to tear apart the more conservative and Balkanized countries of the south; the former Yugoslavia has shown what a simple thing it is to move from muted hatred to cold-blooded murder. Geographic isolation and continued dependence on trade with the former Soviet Union have delayed any economic turnaround in Bulgaria and Romania. And since its split with the Czech Republic in 1993, Slovakia has gone backwards, devaluing its currency and delaying the implementation of a free press and full-fledged democracy.

In the worst case, these slow starters will end up suffering from socialism's pain without benefiting from capitalism's prosperity. Despite Eastern Europe's economic successes, people still line up at soup kitchens. For every satellite dish that cranes upwards on old cement-and-iron balconies, there is a housewife who complains bitterly that her paycheck no longer covers food, clothing, and shelter. And for every entrepreneur driving around in a brand new Mercedes, a peasant still toils in the field with a horse and hoe.

Five years after the fall of the Berlin Wall, few are still dancing in the streets. Instead of showing solidarity, the dissidents-turned-ministers engage in party bickering; instead of offering serious plans to defend democracy, they engage in nasty innuendo. It is proving much easier to be against communism than to be "for" something. Despite the boom in private business and foreign investment, the shift to a market economy has required many painful sacrifices.

Still, democracy is more than just a bewitching catchword, and economic reform has gone farther, faster than anyone expected, even in the supposedly backward Balkans. The good news is that uncensored, opinionated newspapers proliferate, public debate flourishes, and former iron-clad borders are open for any and all—a shocking state of affairs that seemed impossible as little as five years ago. And while Soviet occupation troops complete their trek back home, East Europeans seem more worried about an invasion of Russian refugees than of Russian tanks. Although a fault line may be emerging between the fast- and slow-track reformers, an outright split is far from inevitable.

Turbulent Transitions

During my years reporting from Eastern Europe, I witnessed the world turn upside down. Communists who received me in their palatial offices in 1985 suddenly fell from the scene. Dissidents whom I first met in small, cramped apartments, suddenly became national leaders. For me, this remarkable revolution is personified in one man, Czechoslovakia's former Foreign Minister, Jiri Dienstbier.

When I first met Jiri, we went to a smoke-filled pub and ordered two beers. Over a long evening, he told how he had been a Communist party member and star foreign correspondent for the National Radio. But after Soviet tanks squashed the Prague Spring in 1968, Jiri was recalled home. He refused to sign a declaration saying that the invasion was necessary to crush a "counterrevolution." For his defiance, he and half a million others were expelled from the Party. The heart was cut out of his career and Jiri floated from job to job. In 1977, he signed the Charter 77 human rights declaration. For that "crime," he was arrested and imprisoned between 1979 and 1982, along with his best friend and confidante, playwright Vaclav Havel. Upon his release, only his old dissident friends dared stay in touch. He ended up working as a stoker, shoveling coal into a furnace for the Prague subway system.

In November 1989, Prague erupted with street protests and Jiri Dienstbier became the spokesman for the opposition, known as Civic Forum. He was brilliant in the job, charming the assembled mob of foreign correspondents in nightly press conferences at the Magic Lantern Theater. When the communist rulers finally fled their baroque medieval palaces, Jiri Dienstbier was appointed Foreign Minister. Dienstbier was amazed. He, the longtime enemy of socialism, suddenly was sitting in the beautiful baroque chambers of the Czernin Palace, directing the foreign policy of the Czechoslovak Socialist Republic. Ever the master of the witty repartee, he announced that before taking over as Foreign Minister, he would first have to find a replacement for his job as stoker.

Freedom did not come to Eastern Europe as a gift from Moscow or Washington. East Europeans always considered communism as an alien ideology, and as soon as the chance came to throw off the shackles, they pulled together. Churchmen made common cause with secular left wingers, intellectuals with workers, young with old. Together, they forged links in umbrella organizations: Czechoslovakia's Civic Forum, Poland's Solidarity, and Hungary's Democratic Opposition. Together, they experienced an intense experience of triumphant social unity. In parliamentary elections following the revolution, these broad-based coalitions usually won resounding victories.

The ensuing fall to reality, however, has been particularly painful. Today, most of the famous East European heroes catapulted from jail to power, from manual worker to minister or playwright to president, have fallen from grace. Old friends have become fierce enemies, slinging mud at each other. In Poland, for example, legendary Lech Wałesa has seen his reputation plummet. One opinion poll showed that only 20% of Poles believed he still played the role of an "arbiter" on the chaotic Polish political stage. In another survey that asked who has led Poland most effectively, Wojciech Jaruzelski, the last communist president, actually scored better than Wałesa.

In Hungary, the transition to rough and tumble post-revolutionary politics has opened the way for a fresh new generation. Polls show that Hungary's most popular political party is the Young Democrats, whose rules require members be younger than 35 years old. No one can accuse these children of the revolution either of collaborating with the Communists or of being too pure in their opposition to the old regime. "Our generation are lawyers and businessmen, pragmatic, able to translate ideas into practice," says Viktor Urban, the 30-year-old Young Democrat leader. "The old generation were intellectuals, clever but not effective."

In Prague, Dienstbier's victorious Civic Forum soon found itself torn by clashes between the anticommunist dissidents and former communist technocrats, and, worst of all, between the Czechs and Slovaks. Even though the Civic Forum won a resounding victory in the parliamentary elections of June 1989, the resulting government had trouble deciding whether to pursue a radical, free-market economic program or a slow, step-by-step plan. Dienstbier came to office harboring a lingering mistrust of capitalism and would have preferred a soft transition to some sort of Swedish-style "third way." It took time for him to realize that there was no alternative to a free market and that only rich countries can afford a welfare state like Sweden's.

Another dilemma was how to deal with the heavy bureaucracy, inherited from the Communists and filled with what he admits are scores of incompetent careerists. In typical Czech fashion, Dienstbier liked to joke about the obstacles. "Everybody's undermined by a bureaucracy," he says. "When I complained to an American manager...about how incompetent my bureaucracy was, he told me, 'Be happy! A competent bureaucracy is much worse.'"

These days Jiri Dienstbier works out of a fifth-floor walkup just off Prague's Wenceslas Square. With the election as prime minister of Vaclav Klaus, an employee of the former communist regime, most analysts think Jiri's political career is over. But this man who fought the Communists for two tumultuous decades is not the type to give up. He does not sound bitter. Yes, we lost, he says. We will do better the next time, when people desire a softer, more gentle leader than the arrogant, unfeeling Klaus. So Jiri plans to fight the next parliamentary elections with renewed vigor. "Let's look forward, not back," he urges. "I will surprise you again."

Democracy's Bitter Triumph

Poland's first free presidential elections, held in 1990, pitted Lech Wałesa, the impulsive and charismatic leader of Solidarity, against his former advisor, Tadeusz Mazowiecki, a cautious intellectual. Wałesa barnstormed Poland, working the crowds with ease. Mazowiecki made only rare campaign forays, looking stiff and ill at ease. Wałesa promised to wield "an axe" to cut through bureaucracy and sweep away former Communists. Mazowiecki offered only a solemn message that more hardships lay ahead on the long, tough road to democracy and prosperity. Constantly, insistently, Wałesa tapped the stubborn national spirit that allowed Poland to survive partitions and persecutions. "I am a full-blooded Pole," he liked to tell his audiences. Intellectuals responded that Wałesa was a dangerous demagogue ready to destroy democracy. "Lech Wałesa is unpredictable," commented Adam Michnik, a longtime Wałesa advisor turned bitter enemy. "He is irresponsible. He is incompetent."

Solidarity's split into bickering factions left the country angry and befuddled. Postcommunist politics, it seems, does not allow for the development of a coherent bloc of interests; in the postcommunist world, the easily understood divisions between left- and right-wing reformers and hard-liners, regime and opposition have vanished. Better descriptions today would be parliamentary intellectuals versus workers, country versus city, Europeans versus nationalists, and parliamentary constitutionalism versus extra-parliamentary populism.

The fragmentation is frightening: 67 parties fought in Poland's most recent general election, 74 contested Romania's. Semi-authoritarian regimes masquerade as democracies in Serbia and Romania. Czechoslovakia has split in two, despite clear public opposition in both halves, while the new Czech parliament staggers on without an upper house because of a dispute of who can sit in it. Worse still, where institutions exist, people often seem apathetic about them. In the Hungarian local elections of 1992, the turnout was a debilitating 34%. In Poland, the largest party has a mere 14% of the seats in parliament. The country has had three governments since 1991 and five changes of privatization minister since 1990.

Given such signs, many observers fear democracy is failing in Eastern Europe. They say the region lacks the deep historical traditions needed to safeguard freedom, and many predict a future of authoritarianism and anarchy. Look at how the Romanian, Bulgarian, and even the new Slovak government seem intent on installing loyal officials rather than pursuing new policies, and it is easy to imagine communism's heavy legacy leading to disaster.

But the pessimism is exaggerated. As real and dangerous as the teething pains are, democracy continues to function. Parliaments pass laws. Governments are led by prime ministers from the largest party or the main coalitions. Free elections and a free press are taken for granted. In country after country where pluralism is putting down roots, there is no deep support for presidential authoritarianism and national fascism. Fragmentation certainly exists, but most of the major parties agree on most areas of policy: all support a market economy and full membership in the European Community, and all oppose populism, both economic and political.

The Economic Big Bang

During the communist years, bespectacled Leszek Balcerowicz studied Western economics in an obscure economics institute. Confronted each day with the absurdities of a command economy, he scorned suggestions of a gradual transition from socialism to capitalism: to him, that looked like the recipe of Mikhail Gorbachev's disastrous perestroika program.

In September 1989, Balcerowicz became Poland's finance minister and four months later, he executed a monetary big bang. Prices suddenly were freed, wages capped, and strict monetary discipline imposed. For all practical purposes, similar policies have been adopted at different speeds and with varying thoroughness by the Czechs, Hungarians, Romanians, and Bulgarians.

Throughout Eastern Europe, the results have been impressive. Worthless Polish złotys, Czech crowns, and Hungarian forints suddenly became convertible into marks, pounds, and dollars. After an initial spurt of inflation, the tight fiscal and monetary policies took effect: Inflation in Poland sank from 2,000% in 1989 to 45% in 1992; in Czechoslovakia, it was less than 7% in 1992. "My big advantage over the Russians was support from the central bank," Balcerowicz says. "Every time a factory manager came to me and said, 'print more money,' I could tell him 'no,' and my word stuck."

Admittedly, the toughness exacted a price. From 1989 to 1982, real incomes and GDP fell by 30% from "pre-shock" levels. But the statistics understate the boom in private enterprise (much of which has gone unrecorded to avoid tax), and overstate the fall in the standard of living. After all, before the economic big bang, East Europeans spent hours in snail-paced queues to buy a meager selection of subsidized goods; today, long lines and empty shelves are things of the past.

In 1989 more than 75% of Eastern Europe's exports went to the Soviet Union. By 1992 the figure had fallen to about 10%, while exports to the West nearly doubled. This export boom is even more remarkable considering Western Europe's stinginess (for example, after Czech and Slovak steel exports to the EC rose by 80% in 1992, the Brussels commission blocked them). Skeptics insist that Eastern Europe's trade success remains temporary, that it has come only by taking advantage of subsidized energy prices, a low degree of environmental protection, and, above all, by selling below cost.

The criticisms, however, seem unfounded. Central Europe enjoys a long-term comparative price advantage in tough Western markets. "We're selling everything from salamis to machines," says Janos Bartha of Credit Suisse in Budapest. "This doesn't come just from selling stocks down; it comes from hard work and productivity gains."

Foreign investors are rushing to take advantage of well-trained and low-cost labor, and to fill a market of tens of millions of long-deprived consumers. Since 1989, more than $4 billion has poured into Hungary alone; in one striking move, Audi recently canceled plans for a new East German factory in favor of a Hungarian site. In 1992, more than $1.5 billion was invested in the Czech Republic. Poland, with the largest potential market of the three countries, finally is beginning to attract more foreign suitors. "Foreign investment no longer is marginal," says Andrew Rogerson, the World Bank's Budapest representative. "It's balancing the books."

The final, gigantic step needed to complete the transformation to a full market economy is privatization. Margaret Thatcher's much-heralded program involved only about 20 firms, accounting for less than 5% of the Gross Domestic Product. By comparison, the Central Europeans need to privatize anywhere from 80% to 90% of their economies. That means thousands of companies must be put into private hands, with neither an established stock market nor government subsidies.

A visible success is the massive sell off of shops and commerce. By giving old owners back their property, leasing out premises or holding outright auctions, a retail revolution has transformed both big cities and small villages. In the picturesque Bohemian hamlet of Holoubkov, population 1,500, Lubomir Belohlavek regained control of the hotel Communists confiscated from his grandfather. His Hotel Belohlavek shines from a new coat of paint; its restaurant employs half as many workers as before and is open twice as long. Says the proud new owner, "This is my family silver, and I want to polish it."

Privatization of large companies has proved slower and more difficult. The Hungarians have tried to sell companies one by one, but in four years the State Privatization Company has sold off less than two dozen firms. The Czechs and Poles have opted for mass privatization schemes, and company shares are scheduled to become tradable in Prague on a computerized over-the-counter market. But parliamentary bickering has held up the process in Poland, and everywhere privatization is plagued by disputes over how to divide property fairly and the amount of foreign involvement that should be permitted.

Many potential pitfalls still must be overcome. Frustrated by Western Europe's cautious intervention, the temptation is to close borders, not open them, especially as large chunks of East European industry begin to founder. Most experts say that about one-third of the region's public sector eventually will go bankrupt, one-third will survive, and one-third could go either way. In the very least, the Czech Republic's amazing 2.5% unemployment rate is certain to rise; unemployment in Poland and Hungary, already about 12%, could climb to 20%.

"The Balcerowicz Plan has been a disaster for us," says angry union leader Jerzy Nowak of the Ursus Tractor Factory outside Warsaw. His one factory employs 14,000 workers, down from 22,000 in 1989. Though the factory is more efficient today, every layoff increases the already high level of anger among workers. "We didn't lead the revolution against the Communists only to see our wages cut and our jobs eliminated."

Under the pressure of such criticism, free-market zealot Leszek Balcerowicz has been forced from power. He is back teaching at Warsaw University and driving a battered Lada sedan. But he remains optimistic, sure that his giant experiment has shown the way to make the daunting jump from communism to capitalism. "We are on the right path," he says. "The Russian experience shows us that once you try and hide the pain by printing money, you end up making society more hostile before the necessary shock."

Overcoming Nationalism

In their most malignant forms, Eastern Europe's new democracies have opened the way for nationalist excesses and venomous intolerance. Yugoslavia is the most disastrous example, but Central Europe has experienced its own racial and religious hate crimes, from skinhead attacks against Gypsies to anti-Semitic outbursts from a cross-section of government officials.

In Hungary, soon after Jozsef Antall became Hungary's first noncommunist prime minister in fifty years, he claimed responsibility for the fate of all Hungarians, wherever they live. Subtle shockwaves were felt throughout the Continent. In the Romanian province of Transylvania, where Romanians and the two-million-strong Hungarian minority share a bitter history of hatred, relations between the two groups simply disintegrated. Istvan Csurka, the deputy leader of Prime Minister Antall's ruling party, transformed their grievances into vicious accusations, contending that a communist-Jewish-liberal-media-capitalist conspiracy was strangling the Hungarian nation. Overtly invoking Nazi phraseology, Csurka has loudly called for Hungary to recover its lost territories and living space.

Alone among postcommunist countries and for the first time in its history, only Poland is without serious conflicts of nationality. It is not threatened with disintegration, and it is not making territorial claims on its neighbors (nor are its borders questioned by its neighbors). And yet even Poland is not immune to conflict: with Germany, over ethnic Germans living in Silesia; with Lithuania over the fate of that country's Polish minority; and with Ukraine, where relations have been soured by conflicts between the Catholic and Orthodox churches. In Poland itself, anti-Semites continue to desecrate Jewish graves.

Czechoslovakia's split shows that borders can be changed without violence. And it also shows they cannot be changed painlessly. Even as they decided to go their separate ways, polls showed that more than two-thirds of Czechs and Slovaks wished to remain in a common state. But that proved impossible as the Slovak leader Meciar, a former boxer, and the Czech leader Klaus, whose favorite sport is tennis, failed to work out a shared vision of the future. Klaus sought assurances from Meciar that the federal government would have real competence beyond the Slovak's vague notion of a "defense and economic union." Certainly the danger of a divided Czechoslovakia is not that armed confrontation might occur. Rather, it is that one potentially stable, medium-size state suddenly has become two small weaker ones—a dangerous precedent in a region that stresses homogeneity over compromise.

Of all the dangers facing Eastern Europe, nationalism is without a doubt the most explosive. For many, the longevity and bitterness of the current Balkan crisis still threaten to plunge Central and Eastern Europe into the fray: after all, the insidious, inchoate notion of "ethnic cleansing" has its adherents in Romania, Bulgaria, Poland, and beyond. Hungarian prime minister Antall has tiptoed safely through this dangerous nationalist minefield by nailing his party's colors firmly to the mast of moderation. But he can't remain idle if the large Hungarian minorities living in Serbia, Romania, and Slovakia are threatened. "So far we have been a peaceful island in a troubled neighborhood," says Miklos Jaraszti, a leader of the Hungarian Free Democrats. "Our continued success depends on keeping out of Eastern Europe's dangerous game of nationalism."

Rejoining Europe

The revolution of 1989 was one of the great, defining moments of European history. To find a year of comparable importance, we have to reach back to 1789 in France, 1917 in Russia or, above all, Europe in 1848. In that year, revolutionaries toppled repressive regimes throughout Europe. The analogy, to be sure, offers few solid assurances for the future: after the revolutionary rage had been vented, the old repressive regimes crushed the insurgents and reassumed power with a vengeance.

Yet while the task ahead is daunting for the young East European democracies, it is far from hopeless. The overall international environment looks favorable: authoritarianism is anachronistic, and the only current, viable model for growth is Western Europe. East Europeans have a clear goal: to rejoin the democratic, prosperous West. Communism was imposed upon these countries after World War II only with the backing of Moscow. In a few places—Czechoslovakia and Bulgaria, for instance—the Communists enjoyed a fair amount of support. But nowhere did they have a majority and nowhere did the Soviet-installed regimes win full legitimacy. The people of Eastern Europe always considered communism alien, associating it with the Russians whom, with their Oriental heritage, they perceived as culturally second-rate compared to their Western religious, cultural, and intellectual heritage.

Western Europeans may have ridiculed Ronald Reagan as an ignorant cowboy and George Bush as a cautious do-nothing, but in Eastern Europe both men were heroes who stood up to the Soviets. As vice president, Bush visited Warsaw and became the first Western leader after martial law to meet with Solidarity leader Lech Wałesa in public. When he returned as president, he offered little concrete aid, but the Poles didn't seem to care. They waved American flags and sang "The Star Spangled Banner," content at least to air their complaints and demands for aid.

For East Europeans the West always represented the ideal, and Westerners always have been welcomed with open arms. Visiting the region, one hears much about the dangers ahead: economic recession and narrow nationalism. Yet few question Eastern Europe's ultimate goal: joining the greater West European Common Market. European Community membership represents the great test. The East Europeans aspire above all to the kind of consumer democracy we enjoy. If they are welcome to join the West's privileged club of prosperity, that acceptance will shape their political agenda. Eastern Europe may not be ready right now for EC membership. But the principle should be made clear: the East Europeans will be welcome if they construct strong democracies and put their economies in order.

Of course, the East Europeans themselves must choose between democracy or dictatorship. I remain confident they will choose democracy. More than four decades of dictatorship have made East Europeans impatient with the give and take of democracy. But this same oppression has left another, much more hopeful legacy of resistance to the totalitarian temptation. The East Europeans did not fight so hard for freedom, only to give it up upon encountering the first difficulties. Even as the glow of the 1989 revolutions wears off, the incredible victory over the communist monolith remains intact.

One word is magic: Europe. Not Eastern Europe, not Western Europe—simply Europe. For centuries, Poles, Czechs and Slovaks, Hungarians, Romanians, and Bulgarians felt they were part of the larger European whole. When Mozart traveled from Vienna to Prague, he was not going east; physically, spiritually, and emotionally he was traveling to the west, to Europe's cultural heart. For four long decades, the artificial Iron Curtain cut East Europeans off from the rest of the Continent. Its barbed wire and machine-gun-toting guards are now gone, and the newly freed East Europeans want to rejoin their rightful place in Europe, nothing more, nothing less.

1 Essential Information

Before You Go

Government Information Offices

In the United States Čedok (10 E. 40th St., New York, NY 10016, tel. 212/689–9720, fax 212/481–0597), the Czech Republic and Slovakian travel bureau, is actually a travel agent rather than a tourist information office. It will provide hotel and travel information, tickets, and reservations, but don't expect much in the way of general information.

Hungarian Travel Bureau (IBUSZ), 1 Parker Place, Fort Lee, NJ 07024, tel. 201/592–8585, fax 201/592–8736.

Polish National Tourist Office (275 Madison Ave., Suite 1711, New York, NY 10016, tel. 212/338–9412, fax 212/338–9283), and **Orbis Polish Travel Bureau, Inc.** (342 Madison Ave., New York, NY 10173, tel. 212/867–5011, fax 212/682–4715).

Bulgarian National Tourist Office. Balkan Holidays (authorized agent), 41 E. 42nd St., Suite 508, New York, NY 10017, tel. 212/573–5530, fax 212/573–5538.

Romanian National Tourist Office, 342 Madison Ave., Suite 210, New York, NY 10173, tel. 212/697–6971, fax 212/697–6972.

U.S. Government Travel Briefings The U.S. Department of State's **Overseas Citizens Emergency Center** (Room 4811, Washington, DC 20520; enclose S.A.S.E.) issues Consular Information Sheets, which cover crime, security, political climate, and health risks as well as embassy locations, entry requirements, currency regulations, and other routine matters. (Travel Warnings, which counsel travelers to avoid a country entirely, are issued in extreme cases.) For the latest information, stop in at any U.S. passport office, consulate, or embassy; call the interactive hot line (tel. 202/647–5225, fax 202/647–3000); or, with your PC's modem, tap into the Bureau of Consular Affair's computer bulletin board (tel. 202/647–9225).

In Canada Only Hungary has a tourist office in Canada; contact the **Representative of the Hungarian Republic,** 7 Delaware Ave., Ottawa K2P 0Z2, Ontario, tel. 613/232–1549 or 613/232–1711, fax 613/232–5620. For information on the other countries, call or write any U.S. office.

In the United Kingdom **Danube Travel,** 6 Conduit St., London W1R 9TG, tel. 0171/493–0263. The Hungarian tourist bureau is a travel agency rather than a public service, but it can help with tourist information as well as reservations.

Polorbis Travel Ltd., 82 Mortimer St., London, W1N 7DE, tel. 0171/637–4971. Like Danube Travel, this is a Polish travel agency, but it should be able to provide tourist information, too.

Bulgarian National Tourist Office, 18 Princes St., London W1R 7RE, tel. 0171/499–6988.

Romanian National Tourist Office, 17 Nottingham Pl., London W1M 3RD, tel. 0171/224–3692.

Tours and Packages

Should you buy your travel arrangements to Eastern Europe packaged or do it yourself? There are advantages either way. Buying packaged arrangements saves you money, particularly if you can find a program that includes exactly the features you want. You also get a pretty good idea of what your trip will cost from the outset.

Generally you have two options: escorted tours and independent packages. Escorted tours are usually via motorcoach, with a tour director in charge. They're ideal if you don't mind having limited free time and traveling with strangers. Your baggage is handled, your time rigorously scheduled, and most meals planned. These tours are therefore the most hassle-free way to see a destination, as well as generally the least expensive. Independent packages allow plenty of flexibility. They generally include airline travel and hotels, with certain options available, such as sightseeing, car rental, and excursions. These packages are usually more expensive than escorted tours, but your time is your own.

Although you can book directly through tour operators, you will pay no more to go through a travel agent, who will be able to tell you about tours and packages from a number of operators. Whatever program you ultimately choose, be sure to find out exactly what is included: taxes, tips, transfers, meals, baggage handling, ground transportation, entertainment, excursions, sports and recreation (and rental equipment if necessary). Ask about the level of hotel used, its location, the size of its rooms, the kind of beds, and its amenities, such as pool, room service, or programs for children, if these things are important to you. Find out the operator's cancellation penalties. Nearly everyone charges them, and the only way to avoid them is to buy trip-cancellation insurance (*see* Trip Insurance, *below*). Also ask about the single supplement, a surcharge assessed to solo travelers. Some operators do not make you pay it if you agree to be matched up with a roommate of the same sex, even if one is not found by departure time. Remember that a program that has features you won't use, whether for rental sporting equipment or discounted museum admissions, may not be the most cost-wise choice for you.

Fully Escorted Tours Escorted tours are usually sold in three categories: deluxe, first class, and tourist or budget class. The most important differences are the price, of course, and the level of accommodations. Some operators specialize in one category, and others offer a range. Most itineraries are jam-packed with sightseeing, so you see a lot in a short period of time (usually one place per day). To judge just how fast-paced the tour is, review the itinerary carefully. If you are in a different hotel each night, you will be getting up early each day to head out, travel to your next destination, do some sightseeing, have dinner, and go to bed; then you'll start all over again. If you want some free time, make sure it's mentioned in the tour brochure; if you want to be escorted to every meal, confirm that any tour you consider does that. Also, when comparing programs, be sure to find out if the motorcoach is air-conditioned and has a rest room on board. Make your selection based on price and stops on the itinerary.

Contact **Abercrombie & Kent** (1520 Kensington Rd., Oak Brook, IL 60521, tel. 708/954–2944 or 800/323–7308) and **Maupintour** (Box 807, Lawrence, KS 66044, tel. 913/843–1211 or 800/255–4266) in the deluxe category; **Balkan Holidays** (41 E. 42nd St., Suite 606, New York, NY 10017, tel. 212/573–5530 or 800/852–0944), **Brendan Tours** (15137 Califa St., Van Nuys, CA 91411, tel. 818/785–9696 or 800/421–8446), **British Airways** (tel. 800/247–9297), **Caravan Tours** (401 N. Michigan Ave, Suite 3325, Chicago, IL 60611, tel. 312/321–9800 or 800/227–2826), **Cavalcade Tours** (450 Harmon Meadow Blvd., Secaucus, NJ 07096, tel. 212/617–8173 or 800/346–6314), **Cedok** (10 E. 40th St., New York, NY 10016, tel. 212/689–9720 or 800/800–8891), **Collette Tours** (162 Middle St., Pawtucket, RI 02860, tel. 401/728–3805 or 800/832–4656), **Delta Dream Vacations** (tel. 800/872–

7786), **DER Tours' Europabus division** (11933 Wilshire Blvd., Los Angeles, CA 90025, tel. 800/937–1234), **Eastern Europe Tours** (Plaza 600 Bldg., 19th Floor, Seattle, WA 98101, tel. 206/448–8400 or 800/641–3456) **Globus** (5301 S. Federal Circle, Littleton, CO 80123, tel. 303/797–2800 or 800/221–0090), **JHT Tours** (420 Lincoln Rd., Suite 448, Miami Beach, FL 33139, tel. 305/672–0729 or 800/323–2219), **ITS Tours** (1055 Texas Ave., College Station, TX 77840, tel. 409/764–9400 or 800/533–8688), **Kompas** (630 5th Ave., New York, NY 10111, tel. 212/265–8210 or 800/233–6422), **Lufthansa** (tel. 800/645–3880), **Olson-Travelworld** (Box 10066, Manhattan Beach, CA 90226, tel. 310/546–8400 or 800/421–5785), the **Orbis Polish Travel Bureau** (342 Madison Ave., New York, NY 10173, tel. 800/223–6037), **Pecum Tours** (2002 Colfax Ave. S, Minneapolis, MN 55405, tel. 612/871–8171 or 800/231–4313), **Trafalgar Tours** (21 E. 26th St., New York, NY 10010, tel. 212/689–8977 or 800/854–0103), **Travcoa** (Box 2630, Newport Beach, CA 92658, tel. 714/476–2800 or 800/992–2003), and **TWA Getaway Vacations** (tel. 800/438–2929) in the first-class category; and **Cosmos Tourama,** Globus's sister company (at the same number) in the budget category.

Independent Packages Independent packages, which travel agents call FITs (for Foreign Independent Travel), are offered by airlines, tour operators, which may also do escorted programs (*see above*), and any number of other companies from large, established firms to small, new entrepreneurs.

Delta Dream Vacations, DER Tours, Lufthansa, and **Orbis Travel** (*see above*) also offer independent packages, as do **Globetrotters** (139 Main St., Cambridge, MA 02142, tel. 617/621–9911 or 800/999–9696) and **Travel Bound** (599 Broadway, New York, NY 10012, tel. 212/334–1350 or 800/456–8656).

Their programs come in a range of prices based on levels of luxury and options—in hotel and airfare, sightseeing, car rental, transfers, admission to local attractions, and other extras. Note that when pricing different packages, it sometimes pays to purchase the same arrangements separately, as when a rock-bottom promotional airfare is being offered, for example. Again, base your choice on what's available for your budget for the destinations you wish to visit.

Special-Interest Travel Special-interest programs may be fully escorted or independent. Some require a certain amount of expertise, but most are for the average traveler with an interest and are usually hosted by experts in the subject matter. When the program is escorted it enjoys the advantages and disadvantages of all escorted programs; because your fellow travelers are apt to be passionate or knowledgeable about the subject, they can prove as enjoyable a part of your travel as the destination itself. The price range is wide, but the cost is usually higher—sometimes much higher—than that of ordinary escorted tours and packages because of the expert guidance and special activities.

General **Abercrombie & Kent** (*see above*) offers a variety of programs, including wine tasting, ballooning, and museum tours.

Bicycle Riding **Butterfield & Robinson** (70 Bond St., Toronto, Ont. M5B 1X3, tel. 416/864–1354 or 800/387–1147) travels roads between Budapest and Vienna, exploring castles, the countryside, and coffeehouses along the way. **Euro-Bike Tours** (Box 990, De Kalb, IL 60115, tel. 800/321–6060) has a two-week Eastern Europe adventure following the course of the Danube.

Cruises/Barges If your preferred mode of travel is by water, **Eurocruises** (303 W. 13th St., New York, NY 10014, tel. 212/691–2099 or 800/688–3876) has several floating tours along the Danube through the Czech Republic, Hungary, and Slovakia. Other contacts are **Le Boat, Inc.** (Box E, Maywood, NJ 07507, tel. 201/342–1838 or 800/922 0291, fax 201/342–7498), which will help you charter your own vessel if you prefer a private journey, and **KD River Cruises** (2500 Westchester Ave., Purchase, NY 10577, tel. 914/696 3600 or 800/346–6525 from the eastern U.S., and 323 Geary St., San Francisco, CA 94102, tel. 415/392–8817 or 800/858–8587 from the West).

Food and Wine **Annemarie Victory Organization** (136 E. 64th St., New York, NY 10021, tel. 212/486–0353, fax 212/751–9149) offers a gourmet exploration of the region, including a trip to Russia, with an option for extra days in Prague and/or Budapest.

History and Art **Herodot Travel** (7 S. Knoll Rd., Suite 4, Mill Valley, CA 94941, tel. 415/381–4031) specializes in educational and entertaining tours, including one with a gourmet meal in the former home of Romania's Prince Vlad the Impaler (the inspiration for Bram Stoker's *Dracula*)—try the blood sausage.

Horseback Riding **FITS Equestrian** (685 Lateen Rd., Solvang, CA 93463, tel. 805/688–9494) offers rides through horse-loving Hungary and through Czechoslovakia's magical Bohemian woods.

Nature/Ecology **Earthwatch** (680 Mount Auburn St., Watertown, MA 02272, tel. 617/926–8000) recruits volunteers to serve in its EarthCorps as short-term assistants to scientists on research expeditions such as snow-tracking red deer and Carpathian wolves in Poland, monitoring bird and beaver movements in Czechoslovakia, or mapping land use of Hungary's Lake Balaton.

Spas **Carpati International** (152 Madison Ave., Suite 1103, New York, NY 10016, tel. 212/447–1534 or 800/447–8742) leads you to the secret of a sound mind and a sound body on a variety of tours to Romania's health spas, sites of ancient Roman baths. **Health Tours** (25 W. 43rd St., New York, NY 10036, tel. 212/997–8510 or 800/443–0365) will soothe you at spas in Czechoslovakia and Hungary

Train Touring **American Museum of Natural History** (Central Park West at 79th St., New York, NY 10024, tel. 212/769–5700 or 800/462–8687 outside NY state) has an all-inclusive ride through the cities, towns, and rural landscapes of Eastern Europe on the *Red Prussian*.

Music **Daily-Thorp** (330 W. 58th St., New York, NY 10019, tel. 212/307–1555) offers a deluxe opera-and-music tour of Europe that includes Prague. **Allegro Enterprises** (900 West End Ave., Suite 12C, New York, NY 10025, tel. 212/666–6700 or 800/666–3553 outside NY) has packages to special cultural events in Eastern Europe. With **Mozart's Europe** (Deer La., Pawlet, VT, tel. and fax 802/325–3656), opera lovers can trace the composer's footsteps on tours featuring music and concert festivals in Czechoslovakia and Hungary.

When to Go

The tourist season generally runs from April or May through October; spring and fall combine good weather with a more bearable level of tourism. The ski season lasts from mid-December through March. Outside of the mountain resorts you will encounter few other visitors; you'll have the opportunity to see the region covered in snow, but many of the sights are closed, and it can get very, very cold. If you're not a skier, try visiting the Giant Mountain of Bohemia or the

High Tatras in Slovakia and Poland in late spring or fall; the colors are dazzling and you'll have the hotels and restaurants pretty much to yourself. Bear in mind that many attractions are closed November through March.

Prague and Budapest are beautiful year-round, but avoid midsummer (especially July and August) and the Christmas and Easter holidays, when the two cities are choked with visitors. Warsaw, too, suffers a heavy influx of tourists during the summer season, though not on quite the same grand scale. At the opposite end of the specturm, Bucharest and Sofia are rarely crowded, even at the height of summer. In July and August, however, the weather in these capitals sometimes borders on stifling.

Climate The following are the average daily maximum and minimum temperatures for major cities in the region.

Bratislava	Jan.	36F	2C	May	70F	21C	Sept.	72F	22C
		27	− 3		52	11		54	12
	Feb.	39F	4C	June	75F	24C	Oct.	59F	15C
		28	− 2		57	14		45	7
	Mar.	48F	9C	July	79F	26C	Nov.	46F	8C
		34	1		61	16		37	3
	Apr.	61F	16C	Aug.	79F	26C	Dec.	39F	4C
		43	6		61	16		32	0

Bucharest	Jan.	34F	1C	May	74F	23C	Sept.	78F	25C
		19	− 7		51	10		52	11
	Feb.	38F	4C	June	81F	27C	Oct.	65F	18C
		23	− 5		57	14		43	6
	Mar.	50F	10C	July	86F	30C	Nov.	49F	10C
		30	− 1		60	16		35	2
	Apr.	64F	18C	Aug.	85F	30C	Dec.	39F	4C
		41	5		59	15		26	− 3

Budapest	Jan.	34F	1C	May	72F	22C	Sept.	73F	23C
		25	− 4		52	11		54	12
	Feb.	39F	4C	June	79F	26C	Oct.	61F	16C
		28	− 2		59	15		45	7
	Mar.	50F	10C	July	82F	28C	Nov.	46F	8C
		36	2		61	16		37	3
	Apr.	63F	17C	Aug.	81F	27C	Dec.	39F	4C
		25	− 4		61	16		30	− 1

Prague	Jan.	36F	2C	May	66F	19C	Sept.	68F	20C
		25	− 4		46	8		50	10
	Feb.	37F	3C	June	72F	22C	Oct.	55F	13C
		27	− 3		52	11		41	5
	Mar.	46F	8C	July	75F	24C	Nov.	46F	8C
		32	0		55	13		36	2
	Apr.	58F	14C	Aug.	73F	23C	Dec.	37F	3C
		39	4		55	13		28	− 2

Sofia	Jan.	35F	2C	May	69F	21C	Sept.	70F	22C
		25	- 4		50	10		52	11
	Feb.	39F	4C	June	76F	24C	Oct.	63F	17C
		27	3		56	14		46	8
	Mar.	50F	10C	July	81F	27C	Nov.	48F	9C
		33	1		60	16		37	3
	Apr.	60F	16C	Aug.	79F	26C	Dec.	38F	4C
		42	5		59	15		28	- 2

Warsaw	Jan.	32F	0C	May	68F	20C	Sept.	66F	19C
		21	- 6		48	9		50	10
	Feb.	32F	0C	June	73F	23C	Oct.	55F	13C
		21	- 6		54	12		41	5
	Mar.	43F	6C	July	75F	24C	Nov.	43F	6C
		28	- 2		59	15		34	1
	Apr.	54F	12C	Aug.	73F	23C	Dec.	36F	2C
		37	3		57	14		27	- 3

Information Sources For current weather conditions and forecasts for cities in the United States and abroad, as well as the local time and helpful travel tips, call the **Weather Channel Connection** (tel. 900/932–8437; 95¢ per minute) from a touch-tone phone.

What to Pack

Clothing Don't worry about packing lots of formal clothing. Fashion was all but nonexistent under 40 years of communist rule, and Western dress of any kind is considered stylish. A sports jacket for men, and a dress or pants for women, is appropriate for an evening out. Everywhere else, you'll feel comfortable in casual corduroy or jeans.

Eastern Europe enjoys all the extremes of an inland climate, so plan accordingly. In the higher elevations winter can last until April, and even in summer the evenings will be on the cool side.

Many areas are best seen on foot, so take a pair of sturdy walking shoes and be prepared to use them. High heels will present considerable problems on the cobblestone streets of Prague and Warsaw. If you plan to visit the mountains, make sure the shoes have good traction and ankle support, as some trails can be quite challenging.

Miscellaneous Many items that you take for granted at home are occasionally unavailable or of questionable quality in Eastern Europe. Take your own toiletries and personal-hygiene products with you. Women should pack tampons or sanitary napkins, which are in chronic short supply. Few places provide sports equipment for rent; an alternative to bringing your own equipment would be to buy what you need locally and take it home with you. In general, sporting goods are relatively cheap and of good quality. Bring an extra pair of eyeglasses or contact lenses in your carry-on luggage. If you have a health problem that requires a prescription drug, pack enough of the medication to last the duration of the trip or have your doctor write a prescription using the drug's generic name, because brand names vary from one country to another. Always carry prescription drugs in their original packaging to avoid problems with customs officials. Don't pack them in luggage that you plan to check in case your bags go astray. In addition, pack a list of the offices that supply refunds for lost or stolen traveler's checks.

Electricity The electrical current in Eastern Europe is 220 volts, 50 cycles alternating current (AC); the United States runs on 110-volt, 60-cycle

AC current. Unlike wall outlets in the United States, which accept plugs with two flat prongs, outlets in Eastern Europe generally take plugs with three prongs, although some older establishments, especially in Romania, may use 110 volts.

Adapters, Converters, Transformers
To use U.S.-made electrical appliances abroad, you'll need an adapter plug. Unless the appliance is dual-voltage and made for travel, you'll also need a converter. Hotels sometimes have 110-volt outlets for low-wattage appliances marked FOR SHAVERS ONLY near the sink; don't use them for a high-wattage appliance like a blow-dryer. If you're traveling with an old laptop computer, carry a transformer. New laptop computers are auto-sensing, operating equally well on 110 and 220 volts (so you need only the appropriate adapter plug). When in doubt, consult your owner's manual or the manufacturer. Or get a copy of the free brochure "Foreign Electricity is No Deep Dark Secret," published by adapter-converter manufacturer Franzus Company (Customer Service, Dept. B50, Murtha Industrial Park, Box 142, Beacon Falls, CT 06403, tel. 203/723–6664).

Luggage Regulations
Free airline baggage allowances depend on the airline, the route, and the class of your ticket; ask in advance. In general, on domestic flights and on international flights between the United States and foreign destinations, you are entitled to check two bags—neither exceeding 62 inches, or 158 centimeters (length + width + height), or weighing more than 70 pounds (32 kilograms). A third piece may be brought aboard; its total dimensions are generally limited to less than 45 inches (114 centimeters), so it will fit easily under the seat in front of you or in the overhead compartment. In the United States, the Federal Aviation Administration gives airlines broad latitude to limit carry-on allowances and tailor them to different aircraft and operational conditions. Charges for excess, oversize, or overweight pieces vary.

If you are flying between two foreign destinations, note that baggage allowances may be determined not by piece but by weight, which generally allows 88 pounds (40 kilograms) of luggage in first class, 66 pounds (30 kilograms) in business class, and 44 pounds (20 kilograms) in economy. If your flight between two cities abroad *connects* with your transatlantic or transpacific flight, the piece method still applies.

Safeguarding Your Luggage
Before leaving home, itemize your bags' contents and their worth in case they go astray. To minimize that risk, tag them inside and out with your name, address, and phone number. (If you use your home address, cover it so that potential thieves can't see it.) Put a copy of your itinerary inside each bag so that you can be tracked easily. At check-in, make sure the tag attached by baggage handlers bears the correct three-letter code for your destination. If your bags do not arrive with you, or if you detect damage, immediately file a written report with the airline before you leave the airport.

Taking Money Abroad

Traveler's Checks
Traveler's checks are preferable in metropolitan centers, although you'll need cash in rural areas and small towns. The most widely recognized are **American Express, Citicorp, Diners Club, Thomas Cook,** and **Visa,** which are sold by major commercial banks. Both American Express and Thomas Cook issue checks that can be countersigned and used by you or your traveling companion. Typically, the issuing company or the bank at which you make your purchase charges 1% to 3% of the checks' face value as a fee. Some foreign banks charge as much as 20% of the face value as the fee for cashing traveler's checks

in a foreign currency. Buy a few checks in small denominations to cash toward the end of your trip so you won't be left with excess foreign currency. Record the numbers of checks as you spend them, and keep this list separate from the checks.

Currency Exchange Banks offer the most favorable exchange rates. If you use currency-exchange booths at airports, rail and bus stations, hotels, stores, and privately run exchange firms, you'll typically get less favorable rates, but you may find the hours more convenient.

You can get good rates and avoid long lines at airport currency-exchange booths by getting a small amount of currency at **Thomas Cook Currency Services** (630 5th Ave., New York, NY 10111, tel. 212/757–6915 or 800/223–7373 for locations in major metropolitan areas throughout the U.S.) or **Ruesch International** (tel. 800/424–2923 for locations) before you depart. Check with your travel agent to be sure that the currency of the country you will be visiting can be imported.

Getting Money from Home

Cash Machines Many automated teller machines (ATMs) are tied to international networks such as **Cirrus** and **Plus.** You can use your bank card at ATMs to withdraw money from an account and get cash advances on a credit-card account if your card has been programmed with a personal identification number, or PIN. Check in advance on limits on withdrawals and cash advances within specified periods. Ask whether your bank-card or credit-card PIN will need to be reprogrammed for use in the area you'll be visiting. Four digits are commonly used overseas. Note that Discover is accepted only in the United States. On cash advances you are charged interest from the day you receive the money from ATMs as well as from tellers. Although transaction fees for ATM withdrawals abroad may be higher than fees for withdrawals at home, Cirrus and Plus exchange rates are excellent, because they are based on wholesale rates offered only by major banks. They may also be referred to abroad as "a withdrawal from a credit account."

Plan ahead: Obtain ATM locations and the names of affiliated cash-machine networks before departure. For specific foreign Cirrus locations, call 800/424–7787; for foreign Plus locations, consult the Plus directory at your local bank.

Wiring Money You don't have to be a cardholder to send or receive an **American Express MoneyGram** for up to $10,000. Go to a MoneyGram agent in retail and convenience stores and American Express travel offices, pay up to $1,000 with a credit card and anything over that in cash. You are allowed a free long-distance call to give the transaction code to your intended recipient, who only needs to present identification and the reference number to the nearest MoneyGram agent in order to pick up the cash. MoneyGram agents are in more than 70 countries (call 800/926–9400 for locations). Fees range from 3% to 10%, depending on the amount and how you pay.

You can also use **Western Union.** To wire money, take either cash or a cashier's check to the nearest agent or call and use MasterCard or Visa. Money sent from the United States or Canada will be available for pickup at agent locations in 100 countries within minutes. Once the money is in the system it can be picked up at *any* of 25,000 locations (call 800/325–6000 for the one nearest you; tel. 800/321–2923 in Canada). Fees range from 4% to 10%, depending upon the amount you send.

What It Will Cost

Prices in Eastern Europe continue to escalate, as most countries experiment with "economic shock therapy," the radical transformation of state-controlled economies to market economies. Poland, for example, achieved a stunning 2,000% hyperinflation rate in January 1990. What all this means to the Western traveler is that quoted restaurant, hotel, and transportation costs will almost certainly have changed by the time you read this. Use the prices given as a rough and relative guide. Be advised that many hotel and other tourist-oriented enterprises in Eastern Europe list prices in deutsche marks. See the individual country chapters for more specific information.

Long-Distance Calling

AT&T, MCI, and Sprint have several services that make calling home or the office more affordable and convenient when you're on the road. Use one of them to avoid pricey hotel surcharges. **AT&T** Calling Card (tel. 800/225–5288) and the AT&T Universal Card (tel. 800/662–7759) give you access to the service. With AT&T's USA Direct (call 800/874–4000 for codes in the countries you'll be visiting), you can reach an AT&T operator with a local or toll-free call. **MCI's** call USA (MCI Customer Service, tel. 800/444–4444) accesses that service from 85 countries or from country to country via MCI WorldReach. From MCI ExpressInfo in the United States, you can get 24-hour weather, news, and stock quotes. MCI PhoneCash (tel. 800/925–0029) is available through American Express as well as through a number of convenience stores and retailers nationwide. **Sprint** Express (tel. 800/793–1153) has a toll-free number travelers abroad can dial using the WorldTraveler Foncard to reach a Sprint operator in the United States. The Sprint operator can offer international directory assistance to 224 countries worldwide. All three companies offer message-delivery services to international travelers and have added debit cards so that you don't have to fiddle with change.

Passports and Visas

If your passport is lost or stolen abroad, report the loss immediately to the nearest embassy or consulate and to the local police. If you can provide the consular officer with the information contained in the passport, you will generally be issued a new passport promptly. For this reason, it is a good idea to keep a photocopy of the data page of your passport separate from your money and traveler's checks. You should also leave a photocopy with a relative or friend at home.

U.S. Citizens

Czech Republic and Slovakia All U.S. citizens, even infants, need a valid passport to enter the Czech Republic and Slovakia for stays of up to 30 days. No visa is required to enter these countries.

Hungary A valid passport is sufficient to enter Hungary for stays of up to 90 days.

Poland U.S. citizens are required to have a passport to enter Poland only for stays of up to 90 days.

Bulgaria U.S. citizens are required to have a valid passport to enter Bulgaria for stays of up to 90 days. No visa is required.

Romania To enter Romania all U.S. citizens are required to have a valid passport as well as a visa. Conveniently, the only requirements for a visa are a passport and the fee ($31). Visas may be purchased at the border, from the Consulate of Romania (200 E. 38th St., New York, NY 10016, tel. 212/682–9120), or from the Embassy of Romania (1607 23rd St. NW, Washington, DC 20008, tel. 202/387–6902).

You can pick up new and renewal passport application forms at any of the 13 U.S. Passport Agency offices and at some post offices and courthouses. Although passports are usually mailed within four weeks of the receipt of your application, allow five weeks or more from April through summer. Call the Department of State Office of Passport Services' information line (tel. 202/647–0518) for fees, documentation requirements, and other details.

Canadian Canadian citizens are required to have a passport and a visa for
Citizens stays of up to 30 days. To obtain a visa, you must have a valid pass-
Czech Republic port, one passport-type photo, a completed application, and the C$50 fee. For applications and further information, contact the Czech Republic Embassy (541 Sussex Dr., Ottawa, Ont. K1N 6Z6, tel. 613/562–3875).

Slovakia Canadian citizens are required to have a passport and visa for stays of up to 30 days in Slovakia. As with the Czech Republic, you'll need a valid passport and passport-type photo, a completed application, and the C$50 fee. For applications and information, contact the Slovakian Embassy (50 Rideau Terr., Ottawa, Ont. K1M 2A1, tel. 613/749–4442).

Hungary Canadian citizens are required to have a passport to enter Hungary for stays of up to 90 days. No visa is required.

Poland All Canadian citizens must have a valid passport and a visa to enter Poland. To obtain a tourist visa, you must have a valid passport, two passport-type photos, and the C$50 application fee (C$40 for travelers under 24) for a single-entry visa, C$80 for a double-entry visa (C$64 for traveler under 24). Tourist visas are valid for 90 days. For applications and additional information, contact the Polish Embassy (443 Daly Ave., Ottawa, Ont. K1N 6H3, tel. 613/789–0468).

Bulgaria Canadian citizens must have a valid passport and a visa to enter Bulgaria. To obtain a tourist visa, you must have a valid passport, a passport-type photo, and a C$50 application fee. Tourist visas are valid for 90 days and can be obtained from the Consular Office of the Bulgarian Embassy (100 Adelaide St., Toronto, Ont. M5H 1F3, tel. 416/696–2420).

Romania Canadian citizens must have a valid passport and a visa to enter Romania. The only requirements for a visa are a passport and the fee (C$42); visas may be purchased at the border, from one of the **Consulates of Romania,** or from the **Embassy of Romania.** You can contact the consulates at 111 Peter Street, Suite 530, Toronto, Ontario N5V 2H1, tel. 416/585–5802 or 1111 Street Urbain, Suite M–09, Montréal, Québec H2Z 1Y6, tel. 514/876–1793; the embassy is at 655 Rideau Street, Ottawa, Ontario K1N 6A3, tel. 613/789–3709.

Canadian passport application forms are available at 23 regional passport offices as well as post offices and travel agencies. Whether applying for a first or subsequent passport, you must appear in person. Children under 16 may be included on a parent's passport but must have their own to travel alone. Passports are valid for five years and are usually mailed within two weeks of an application's receipt. For fees, documentation requirements, and other information in English or French, call the passport office (tel. 514/283–2152 or 800/567–6868).

U.K. Citizens Citizens of the United Kingdom need a valid passport to enter the
Czech Republic Czech Republic and Slovakia (cost £18 for a standard 32-page pass-
and Slovakia port). A British Visitors Passport is not acceptable. Visas are not
required.

Hungary British travelers with valid passports do not need a visa for stays of
up to 90 days.

Poland A valid passport is all that is required for stays up to 90 days in Poland.

Bulgaria Citizens of the United Kingdom must have a valid passport and a
visa to enter Bulgaria. Visas may be obtained at the border or at the
nearest embassy or consulate.

Romania Citizens of the United Kingdom must have a valid passport and a
visa to enter Romania. Visas may be obtained at the border or
through the **Consular Section of the Romanian Embassy** (4 Palace
Green, London W8, tel. 0171/937–9667).

Applications for new and renewal passports are available from main
post offices as well as at the six passport offices, located in Belfast,
Glasgow, Liverpool, London, Newport, and Peterborough. You may
apply in person at all passport offices or by mail to all except the
London office. Children under 16 may travel on an accompanying
parent's passport. All passports are valid for 10 years. Allow a
month for processing.

Customs and Duties

On Arrival You may import duty-free into the Czech Republic, Slovakia, Hungary, Poland, or Bulgaria 250 cigarettes or the equivalent in tobacco, 1 liter of spirits, and 2 liters of wine. In addition to the above, you
are permitted to import into the Czech Republic gifts valued at up to
1,000 Kčs (approximately $35) and ½ liter of perfume. You may bring
into Romania 200 cigarettes, 2 liters of spirits, 4 liters of wine or
beer, 2 cameras only and 20 rolls of film, and one small movie camera, though you may be charged duty on electronic goods.

If you are bringing into any of these countries any valuables or foreign-made equipment from home, such as cameras, it's wise to carry
the original receipts with you or register the items with U.S. Customs before you leave (Form 4457). Otherwise you could end up paying duty upon your return. When traveling to Romania, you should
declare video cameras, personal computers, and expensive jewelry
upon arrival.

Returning If you've been out of the country for at least 48 hours and haven't
Home already used the exemption, or any part of it, in the past 30 days, you
U.S. Customs may bring home $400 worth of foreign goods duty-free. So can each
member of your family, regardless of age; and your exemptions may
be pooled, so one of you can bring in more if another brings in less. A
flat 10% duty applies to the next $1,000 of goods; above $1,400, the
rate varies with the merchandise. (If the 48-hour or 30-day limits
apply, your duty-free allowance drops to $25, which may not be
pooled.) Please note that these are the *general* rules, applicable to
most countries; more generous allowances for some items, including
arts and handicrafts, are in effect for the Czech Republic, Slovakia,
Hungary, Poland, and Bulgaria, which are considered developing
countries benefiting from the Generalized System of Preferences
(GSP), but these allowances expire at the end of September 1994.
Romania is not included in the GSP program.

Travelers 21 or older may bring back 1 liter of alcohol duty-free, provided the beverage laws of the state through which they reenter the United States allow it. In addition, 100 non-Cuban cigars and 200 cigarettes are allowed, regardless of your age. Antiques and works of art more than 100 years old are duty-free.

Gifts valued at less than $50 may be mailed to the United States duty-free, with a limit of one package per day per addressee, and do not count as part of your exemption (do not send alcohol or tobacco products or perfume valued at more than $5); mark the package "Unsolicited Gift" and write the nature of the gift and its retail value on the outside. Most reputable stores will handle the mailing for you.

For a copy of "Know Before You Go," a free brochure detailing what you may and may not bring back to the United States, rates of duty, and other pointers, contact the U.S. Customs Service (Box 7407, Washington, DC 20044, tel. 202/927–6724). A copy of "GSP and the Traveler" is available from the same source.

Canadian Customs
Once per calendar year, when you've been out of Canada for at least seven days, you may bring in C$300 worth of goods duty-free. If you've been away less than seven days but more than 48 hours, the duty-free exemption drops to C$100 but can be claimed any number of times (as can a C$20 duty-free exemption for absences of 24 hours or more). You cannot combine the yearly and 48-hour exemptions, use the C$300 exemption only partially (to save the balance for a later trip), or pool exemptions with family members. Goods claimed under the C$300 exemption may follow you by mail; those claimed under the lesser exemptions must accompany you upon your return.

Acohol and tobacco products may be included in the yearly and 48-hour exemptions but not in the 24-hour exemption. If you meet the age requirements of the province through which you reenter Canada, you may bring in, duty-free, 1.14 liters (40 imperial ounces) of wine or liquor *or* two dozen 12-ounce cans or bottles of beer or ale. If you are 16 or older, you may bring in, duty-free, 200 cigarettes, 50 cigars or cigarillos, and 400 tobacco sticks or 400 grams of manufactured tobacco.

An unlimited number of gifts valued up to C$60 each may be mailed to Canada duty-free. These do not count as part of your exemption. Label the package "Unsolicited Gift—Value under $60." Alcohol and tobacco are excluded.

For more information, including details of duties on items that exceed your duty-free limit, ask the Revenue Canada Customs and Excise and Taxation Department (2265 St. Laurent Blvd. S, Ottawa, Ont., K1G 4K3, tel. 613/957–0275) for a copy of the free brochure "I Declare/Je Déclare."

U.K. Customs
From countries outside the European Community (EC), including those covered in this book, you may import, duty-free, 200 cigarettes, 100 cigarillos, 50 cigars or 250 grams of tobacco; 1 liter of spirits or 2 liters of fortified or sparkling wine; 2 liters of still table wine; 60 milliliters of perfume; 250 milliliters of toilet water; and £36 worth of other goods, including gifts and souvenirs.

For further information or a copy of "A Guide for Travellers," which details standard customs procedures as well as what you may bring into the United Kingdom from abroad, contact HM Customs and Excise (Dorset House, Stamford St., London SE1 9PY, tel. 0171/928–3344).

Traveling with Cameras, Camcorders, and Laptops

Film and Cameras If your camera is new or if you haven't used it for a while, shoot and develop a few test rolls before you leave. Store film in a cool, dry place—never in the car's glove compartment or on the shelf under the rear window.

Airport security X-rays generally aren't harmful to film with an ISO below 400. To protect your film, carry it with you in a clear plastic bag and ask for a hand inspection. Such requests are honored at U.S. airports but are up to the inspector abroad. Don't depend on a lead-lined bag to protect film in checked luggage—the airline may increase the radiation to see what's inside. Call the Kodak Information Center (tel. 800/242–2424) for details.

Camcorders Before your trip, put camcorders through their paces, invest in a skylight filter to protect the lens, and check all the batteries. Most new camcorders are equipped with batteries that can be recharged with a universal or worldwide AC adapter charger (or multivoltage converter) usable whether the voltage is 110 or 220. All that's needed is the appropriate plug.

Videotape Videotape is not damaged by X-rays, but it may be harmed by the magnetic field of a walk-through metal detector, so request a hand check. Airport security personnel may ask you to turn on the camcorder to prove that it's what it appears to be, so make sure the battery is charged. Note that instead of the National Television System Committee (NTSC) video standard used in the United States and Canada, Eastern Europe uses PAL/SECAM technology. You will not be able to view your tapes through the local TV set or view movies bought there on your home VCR. Blank tapes bought in Eastern Europe can be used for NTSC camcorder taping, but they are pricey.

Laptops Security X-rays do not harm hard-disk or floppy-disk storage, but you may request a hand check, at which point you may be asked to turn on the computer to prove that it is what is appears to be. (Check your battery before departure.) Most airlines allow you to use your laptop aloft except during takeoff and landing (to avoid interference with navigation equipment). For international travel, register your foreign-made laptop with U.S. Customs as you leave the country. If your laptop is U.S.-made, call the consulate of the country you'll be visiting to find out whether it should be registered with customs upon arrival. Before departure, find out about repair facilities at your destination, and don't forget any transformer or adapter plug you may need (*see* Electricity, *above*).

Staying Healthy

You may gain weight, but there are few other serious health hazards for the traveler in Eastern Europe. Tap water tastes bad but is generally drinkable; when it runs rusty out of the tap or the aroma of chlorine is overpowering, it might help to have some iodine tablets or bottled water handy. Milk may not be pasteurized and can make Westerners sick; stick to cheese to satisfy calcium cravings. Vegetarians and those on special diets may have a problem with the heavy local cuisine, which is based almost exclusively on pork and beef. To keep your vitamin intake above the danger levels, buy fresh fruits and vegetables at seasonal street markets—regular grocery stores often don't sell them.

No vaccinations are required for entry into any of the Eastern European countries covered in this book, but selective vaccinations are recommended by IAMAT (*see below*). Those traveling in forested areas of most Eastern European countries should consider vaccinating themselves against Central European, or tick-borne, encephalitis. Schedule vaccinations well in advance of departure because some require several doses, and others may cause uncomfortable side effects.

To avoid problems clearing customs, diabetic travelers carrying needles and syringes should have on hand a letter from their physician confirming their need for insulin injections.

Finding a Doctor The **International Association for Medical Assistance to Travellers** (IAMAT, 417 Center St., Lewiston, NY 14092, tel. 716/754–4883; 40 Regal Rd., Guelph, Ontario N1K 1B5; 57 Voirets, 1212 Grand-Lancy, Geneva, Switzerland) publishes a worldwide directory of English-speaking physicians whose qualifications meet IAMAT standards and who have agreed to treat members for a set fee. Membership is free.

Assistance Companies Pretrip medical referrals, emergency evacuation or repatriation, 24-hour telephone hot lines for medical consultation, dispatch of medical personnel, relay of medical records, cash for emergencies, and other personal and legal assistance are among the services provided by several membership organizations specializing in medical assistance to travelers. Among them are **International SOS Assistance** (Box 11568, Philadelphia, PA 19116, tel. 215/244–1500 or 800/523–8930; Box 466, Pl. Bonaventure, Montréal, Qué. H5A 1C1, tel. 514/874–7674 or 800/363–0263), **Medex Assistance Corporation** (Box 10623, Baltimore, MD 21285, tel. 410/296–2530 or 800/874–9125), **Near Services** (450 Prairie Ave., Suite 101, Calumet City, IL 60409, tel. 708/868–6700 or 800/654–6700), and **Travel Assistance International** (1133 15th St. NW, Suite 400, Washington, DC 20005, tel. 202/331–1609 or 800/821–2828). Because these companies will also sell you death-and-dismemberment, trip-cancellation, and other insurance coverage, there is some overlap with the travel-insurance policies discussed under Insurance, *below*.

Publications *The Safe Travel Book*, by Peter Savage ($12.95, Lexington Books, 866 3rd Ave., New York, NY 10022, tel. 212/702–4771 or 800/257–5755, fax 800/562–1272), is packed with handy lists and phone numbers to make your trip smooth. *Traveler's Medical Resource*, by William W. Forgey ($19.95, ICS Books, Inc., 1 Tower Plaza, 107 E. 89th Ave., Merrillville, IN 45410, tel. 800/541–7323), is also a good, authoritative guide to care overseas.

Insurance

U.S. Residents Most tour operators, travel agents, and insurance agents sell specialized health-and-accident, flight, trip-cancellation, and luggage insurance as well as comprehensive policies with some or all of these features. Before you make any purchase, review your existing health and homeowner policies to find out whether they cover expenses incurred while traveling.

Health-and-Accident Insurance Specific policy provisions of supplemental health-and-accident insurance for travelers include reimbursement for from $1,000 to $150,000 worth of medical and/or dental expenses caused by an accident or illness during a trip. The personal-accident, or death-and-dismemberment, provision pays your beneficiaries a lump sum if you die or pays you if you lose one or both limbs or your eyesight; the lump sum awarded can range from $15,000 to $500,000. The medical-assistance provision may reimburse you for the cost of referrals, evacuation, or repatriation and other services, or it may automatically enroll you as a member of a particular medical-assistance company (*see* Assistance Companies, *above*).

Flight Insurance Often bought as last-minute impulse at the airport, flight insurance pays a lump sum when a plane crashes either to a beneficiary if the insured dies or sometimes to a surviving passenger who loses his or her eyesight or a limb. Like most impulse buys, flight insurance is expensive and basically unnecessary. It supplements the airlines' coverage described in the limits-of-liability paragraphs on your ticket. Charging an airline ticket to a major credit card often automatically entitles you to coverage and may also extend to travel by bus, train, and ship.

Baggage Insurance In the event of loss, damage, or theft on international flights, the airline's liability is $20 per kilogram for checked baggage (roughly about $640 per 70-pound bag) and $400 per passenger for unchecked baggage. On domestic flights, the ceiling is $1,250 per passenger. Excess-valuation insurance can be bought directly from the airline at check-in for about $10 per $1,000 worth of coverage. However, this insurance cannot be bought at any price for the rather extensive list of excluded items shown on your airline ticket.

Trip Insurance **Trip-cancellation-and-interruption insurance** protects you in the event you are unable to undertake or finish your trip, especially if your airline ticket, cruise, or package tour does not allow changes or cancellations. The amount of coverage you purchase should equal the cost of your trip if you, a traveling companion, or a family member falls ill, forcing you to stay home, plus the nondiscounted one-way airline ticket you would need to buy if you had to return home early. Read the fine print carefully, especially sections defining "family member" and "preexisting medical conditions." **Default** or **bankruptcy insurance** protects you against a supplier's failure to deliver. Such policies often do not cover default by a travel agency, tour operator, airline, or cruise line if you bought your tour and the coverage directly from the firm in question. Tours packaged by one of the 33 members of the United States Tour Operators Association (USTOA) (211 E. 51st St., Suite 12B, New York, NY 10022, tel. 212/750-7371), which requires members to maintain $1 million each in an account to reimburse clients in case of default, are likely to present the fewest difficulties.

Comprehensive Policies Companies that supply comprehensive policies with some or all of the above features include **Access America, Inc.** (Box 90315, Richmond, VA 23230, tel. 800/284-8300); **Carefree Travel Insurance** (Box 310, 120 Mineola Blvd., Mineola, NY 11501, tel. 516/294-0220 or 800/323-3149); **Tele-Trip** (Mutual of Omaha Plaza, Box 31762, Omaha, NE 68131, tel. 800/228-9792); **The Travelers Companies** (1 Tower Sq., Hartford, CT 06183, tel. 203/277-0111 or 800/243-3174); **Travel Guard International** (1145 Clark St., Stevens Point, WI 54481, tel. 715/345-0505 or 800/826-1300); and **Wallach and Company, Inc.** (107 W. Federal St., Box 480, Middleburg, VA 22117, tel. 703/687-3166 or 800/237-6615).

U.K. Residents Most tour operators, travel agents, and insurance agents sell specialized policies covering accident, medical expenses, personal liability, trip cancellation, and loss or theft of personal property. You can also buy an annual travel-insurance policy valid for every trip (usually of less than 90 days) you make during the year in which it's purchased. Make sure you will be covered if you have a preexisting medical condition or are pregnant.

For advice by phone or a free booklet, "Holiday Insurance," that sets out what to expect from a holiday-insurance policy and gives price guidelines, contact the **Association of British Insurers** (51 Gresham St., London EC2V 7HQ, tel. 0171/600–3333; 30 Gordon St., Glasgow G1 3PU, tel. 041/226–3905; Scottish Providence, Donegall Sq. W, Belfast BT1 6JE, tel. 0232/249176; call for other locations).

Car Rentals

The big drawback here is price—rentals can rival airfare for the most expensive transport alternative. The pluses are a freewheeling itinerary and lots of luggage space. Two restrictions to keep in mind: renting a car in a Western European country and dropping it off in the East will probably be prohibited (or prohibitively expensive). Second, try to get a car that takes leaded gas, because unleaded is rare.

If you're planning to rent a car, be sure to shop around, as prices can differ greatly, and not all companies rent in all Eastern European countries. Most major car-rental companies are represented in Eastern Europe, including **Avis** (tel. 800/331–1084, 800/879–2847 in Canada); **Budget** (tel. 800/527–0700); **Hertz** (tel. 800/654–3001, 800/263–0600 in Canada); and **National** (tel. 800/227–3876), known internationally as InterRent and Europcar. At press time, Avis, Budget, Dollar, and National did not offer rentals in Romania. In the Czech Republic, the state-run **Pragocar** offers Western makes for as much as $400–$900 per week. Smaller local companies, on the other hand, can rent cars built in the former Czechoslovakia for as low as $130 per week. In Poland you can rent a car through **Orbis,** which is affiliated with Hertz; both manual and automatic transmissions are available. Rates do not include VAT in the Czech Republic and Slovakia, where it is 23%, or Poland, where it is 25%.

Requirements Your own driver's license is acceptable; British citizens need an International Driver's Permit. An International Driver's Permit, available from the American or Canadian Automobile Association, is a good idea.

Extra Charges Picking up the car in one city and leaving it in another may entail substantial drop-off charges or one-way service fees. The cost of a collision- or loss-damage waiver (*see below*) can also be high. Some rental agencies will charge you extra if you return the car *before* the time specified on the contract. Ask before making unscheduled drop-offs. Be sure the rental agent agrees *in writing* to any changes in drop-off location or other items of your rental contract. Fill the tank when you return the vehicle to avoid being charged for refueling at what you'll swear is the most expensive pump in town. In Europe, manual transmissions are standard and air-conditioning is a rarity and is often unnecessary. Asking for an automatic transmission or air-conditioning can significantly increase the cost of your rental. Find out what the standard rentals are in the country you'll be visiting and weigh that factor when making your reservation.

Cutting Costs Major international companies have programs that discount their standard rates by 15%–30% if you make the reservation before departure (anywhere from 24 hours to 14 days), rent for a minimum number of days (typically three or four), and prepay the rental. More economical rentals may come as part of fly/drive or other packages, even bare-bones deals that only combine the rental and an airline ticket (*see* Tours and Packages, *above*).

Several companies operate as wholesalers. They do not own their own fleets but rent in bulk from those that do and offer their customers advantageous rates. Rentals through such companies must be arranged and paid for before you leave the United States. Among them are **Auto Europe** (Box 7006, Portland, ME 04112, tel. 207/828–2525 or 800/223–5555, 800/458–9503 in Canada) and **The Kemwel Group** (106 Calvert St., Harrison, NY 10528, tel. 914/835–5555 or 800/678–0678). **Foremost Euro-Car** (5658 Sepulveda Blvd., Suite 201, Van Nuys, CA 91411, tel. 818/786–1960 or 800/272–3299) leases cars in Western Europe that can be driven into Eastern Europe. You won't see these wholesalers' deals advertised; they're even better in summer, when business travel is down. Always ask whether the prices are guaranteed in U.S. dollars or foreign currency and if unlimited mileage is available. Find out about any required deposits, cancellation penalties, and drop-off charges, and confirm the cost of any required insurance coverage. Wholesalers often do not serve all Eastern European countries, and there are restrictions about travel between countries; be sure to check before you rent.

Insurance and Collision-Damage Waiver Until recently, standard rental contracts included liability coverage (for damage to public property, injury to pedestrians, and so on) and coverage for the car against fire, theft, and collision damage with a deductible. Due to changes in the laws of some states and rising liability costs, however, several car-rental agencies have reduced the type of coverage they offer. Before you rent a car, find out exactly what coverage, if any, is provided by your personal auto insurer. Don't assume that you are covered. If you do want insurance from the rental company, secondary coverage may be the only type offered. You may already have secondary coverage if you charge the rental to a credit card. Only Diners Club (tel. 800/234–6377) provides primary coverage in the United States and worldwide.

In general, if you have an accident you are responsible for the automobile. Car-rental companies may offer a collision-damage waiver (CDW), which ranges in cost from $4 ot $14 a day. You should decline the CDW only if you are certain you are covered through your personal insurer or credit-card company.

Rail Passes

The **European East Pass** is good for unlimited first-class travel on the national railroads of Austria, the Czech Republic, Slovakia, Hungary, and Poland. The pass allows five days of travel within a 15-day period ($185) or 10 days of travel within 30 days ($299). Apply through your travel agent or through **Rail Europe** (226–230 Westchester Ave., White Plains, NY 10604, tel. 914/682–5172 or 800/848–7245).

The **EurailPass,** valid for unlimited first-class train travel through 17 countries, including Hungary, is an excellent value if you plan to travel around the Continent, but it does not include travel to the Czech Republic, Slovakia, Poland, Bulgaria, or Romania.

Standard Eurail passes are available for 15 days ($498), 21 days ($648), one month ($728), two months ($1,098), and three months ($1,398). **Eurail Saverpasses,** valid for 15 days, cost $430 per person, 21 days for $550, one month for $678 per person; you must do all your traveling with at least one companion (two companions from April through September). **Eurail Youthpasses,** which cover second-class travel, cost $578 for one month and $768 for two months; you must be younger than 26 on the first day you travel. **Eurail Flexipasses** allow you to travel for 5, 10, or 15 days within any two-month period. You pay $348, $560, and $740, respectively, for the Flexipass, sold for first-class travel; and $255, $398, $540, respectively, for the **Eurail Youth Flexipass**, available to those under 26 on their first day of travel and sold for second class. The **Czech Flexipass** gives you 5 days of unlimited travel within any 15-day period for $69; and the **Hungarian Flexipass** offers 5 days of unlimited travel within a 15-day period for $55 and 10 days within a month for $69. The **Polrail Pass** offers 8 days of unlimited travel for $50 in first-class and $35 in second class; 15 days for $60 and $40, respectively; 21 days for $67 and $45; and a month's travel for $75 and $50. Travelers under 26 years of age on their first day of travel can purchase this pass for $39 first-class and $26 second-class for 8 days of unlimited travel; $45 and $30 first-class and second-class, respectively, for 15 days; $51 and $34 for 21 days; and $57 and $38 for a month's travel around the country. Apply through your travel agent or through **Rail Europe** (226–230 Westchester Ave., White Plains, NY 10604, tel. 914/682–5172 or 800/848–7245, fax 800/432–1329; or 2087 Dundas E, Suite 105, Mississauga, Ont. L4X 1M2, tel. 416/602–4195); **DER Tours** (Box 1606, Des Plaines, IL 60017, tel. 800/782–2424, fax 800/282–7474); or **CIT Tours Corp.** (342 Madison Ave., Suite 207, New York, NY 10173, tel. 212/697–2104 or 800/248–8687, fax 212/697–1394; tel. 310/670–4269 or 800/248–7245 in the western U.S.). The **Polrail Pass** can also be purchased through **Orbis Polish Travel Bureau** (342 Madison Ave., New York, NY 10173, tel. 212/867–5011 or 800/233–6037).

European citizens or anyone who has lived within the EC for longer than six months can purchase an **InterRail Pass** (£249), good for one month's travel in the Eastern European countries covered in this book. The pass works just like Eurail, except that it gives only a 50% discount on train fares within the country where it was purchased. Be prepared to prove your citizenship or six months of continuous residency. InterRail is availabe only in Europe and can be purchased through local student or budget travel offices. In Great Britain you can buy InterRail at main British Rail stations and some travel agencies.

Don't make the mistake of assuming that your rail pass guarantees you seats on the trains you want to ride. Seat reservations are required on some trains, particularly high-speed trains, and are a good idea on trains that may be crowded. You will also need reservations for overnight sleeping accommodations. Rail Europe can help you determine if you need reservations and can make them for you (about $10 each, less if you purchase them in Europe at the time of travel).

Student and Youth Travel

Discount
Cards
For discounts on transportation and on museum and attractions admissions, buy the **International Student Identity Card** (ISIC) if you're a bona fide student or the **International Youth Card** (IYC) if you're under 26. In the United States the ISIC and IYC cards cost $16 each and include basic travel accident and illness coverage and a toll-free travel-assistance hot line. Apply to the **Council on International Educational Exchange** (CIEE, 205 E. 42nd St., New York, NY 10017, tel. 212/661–1450). In Canada the cards are available for $15 each from **Travel Cuts** (187 College St., Toronto, Ont. M5T 1P7, tel. 416/979–2406). In the United Kingdom they cost £5 and £4 respectively at student unions and student travel companies, includ-

ing Council Travel's London office (28A Poland St., London W1V 3DB, tel. 0171/437–7767).

Hosteling A **Hostelling International** (HI) membership card is the key to more than 5,000 hostels in 70 countries; the sex-segregated, dormitory-style sleeping quarters, including some for families, go for $7 to $20 a night per person. Membership is available in the United States through **Hostelling International-American Youth Hostels** (HI-AYH) (733 15th St. NW, Suite 840, Washington, DC 20005, tel. 202/783–6161), the U.S. link in the worldwide chain, and costs $25 for adults 18 to 54, $10 for those under 18, $15 for those 55 and over, and $35 for families. Volume 1 of the *AYH Guide to Budget Accommodation* lists hostels in Europe and the Mediterranean ($13.95, including postage). HI membership is available in Canada through **Hostelling International-Canada** (205 Catherine St. Suite 400, Ottawa, Ont. K2P 1C3, tel. 613/748–5638) for $26.75, and in the United Kingdom through the **Youth Hostel Association of England and Wales** (Trevelyan House, 8th St. Stephen's Hill, St. Albans, Herts. AL1 2DY, tel. 0727/855215) for £9.

Tour **Contiki** (300 Plaza Alicante #900, Garden Grove, CA 92640, tel. 714/
Operators 740–0808 or 800/266–8454) specializes in package tours for travelers ages 18 to 35.

Traveling with Children

Publications *Family Travel Times,* published 10 times a year by Travel with Your
Newsletter Children (TWYCH, 45 W. 18th St., New York, NY 10011, tel. 212/ 206–0688; annual subscription $55), covers destinations, types of vacations, and modes of travel. TWYCH also publishes *Cruising with Children* ($22) and *Skiing with Children* ($29).

Books *Traveling with Children—And Enjoying It,* by Arlene K. Butler ($11.95 plus $3 shipping per book; Globe Pequot Press, Box 833, 6 Business Park Rd., Old Saybrook, CT 06475, tel. 800/243–0495, or 800/962–0973 in CT), helps plan your trip with children, from toddlers to teens. *Innocents Abroad: Traveling with Kids in Europe,* by Valerie Wolf Deutsch and Laura Sutherland ($15.95 or $4.95 paperback, Penguin USA), covers child- and teen-friendly activities, food, and transportation.

The Adventures of Mickey, Taggy, Pupo, and Cica and How They Discover Budapest, by Kati Rekai (Canadian Stage Arts Publications, Toronto), is an animal fantasy story for children set in Budapest, written by a Hungarian-born author.

Tour **Grandtravel** (6900 Wisconsin Ave., Suite 706, Chevy Chase, MD
Operators 20815, tel. 301/986–0790 or 800/247–7651) offers tours for people who are traveling with their grandchildren. The catalogue, as charmingly written and illustrated as a children's book, positively invites armchair traveling with lap-sitters aboard. **Families Welcome!** (21 W. Colony Pl., Suite 140, Durham, NC 27705, tel. 919/ 489–2555 or 800/326–0724, fax 919/490–5587) packages and sells family tours.

Getting There On international flights, the fare for infants under age 2 not occupy-
Air Fares ing a seat is generally either free or 10% of the accompanying adult's fare; children ages 2 to 11 usually pay half to two-thirds of the adult fare. On domestic flights, children under two not occupying a seat travel free, and older children currently travel on the "lowest applicable" adult fare.

Baggage In general, infants paying 10% of the adult fare are allowed one carry-on bag, not to exceed 70 pounds or 45 inches (length + width + height) and a collapsible stroller; check with the airline before departure, because you may be allowed less if the flight is full. The adult baggage allowance applies for children paying half or more of the adult fare.

Safety Seats The FAA recommends the use of safety seats aloft and details approved models in the free leaflet **"Child/Infant Safety Seats Recommended for Use in Aircraft"** (available from the Federal Aviation Administration, APA–200, 800 Independence Ave. SW, Washington, DC 20591, tel. 202/267–3479; Information Hotline, tel. 800/322 7873). Airline policy varies. U.S. carriers allow FAA-approved models bearing a sticker declaring their FAA approval. Because these seats are strapped into regular passenger seats, airlines may require you to buy a ticket for an infant who would otherwise travel free. Foreign carriers may not allow infant seats, may charge the child's rather than the infant's fare for their use, or may require you to hold your baby during takeoff and landing, thus defeating the purpose of the seat.

Facilities Aloft Some airlines provide other services for children, such as children's meals and freestanding bassinets (only to those with seats at the bulkhead, where there's enough legroom). Make your request when reserving. The February issue of *Family Travel Times* details children's services on three dozen airlines ($12; *see above*). "Kids and Teens in Flight" (free from the U.S. Department of Transportation's Office of Consumer Affairs (R-25, Washington, DC 20590, tel. 202/366–2220) offers tips for children flying alone.

Lodging The **Novotel** chain (tel. 800/221–4542), which has hotels in Budapest, Warsaw and five other Polish cities, and Sofia and Plovdiv in Bulgaria, allows up to two children under 12 to stay free in their parents' room. Many Novotel properties also have playgrounds. Young visitors to the Czech Republic will enjoy staying at one of Prague's picturesque floating "botels." For further information contact **Čedok.**

Baby-Sitting Services Ask at the hotel desk or local tourist office for information on babysitters.

Hints for Travelers with Disabilities

Provisions for handicapped travelers in Eastern Europe are extremely limited; traveling with a nondisabled companion is probably the best solution. While many hotels, especially large American or international chains, offer some wheelchair-accessible rooms, special facilities at museums, restaurants, and on public transportation are difficult to find. In Poland wheelchairs are available at all airports, and most trains have special seats designated for the handicapped. Disabled visitors to Hungary may want to contact **Picknik Tours** (Pinceszerutca. 14–16, Budapest, tel. 316/1176–2722) for information on special tours, services, and accommodations.

Organizations Several organizations provide travel information for people with disabilities, usually for a membership fee, and some publish newsletters and bulletins. Among them are the **Information Center for Individuals with Disabilities** (Fort Point Pl., 27–43 Wormwood St., Boston, MA 02210, tel. 617/727–5540 or 800/462–5015 in MA between 11 AM and 4 PM, or leave a message; TTY 617/345–9743); **Mobility International USA** (Box 10767, Eugene, OR 97440, tel. and TTY 503/343–1284, fax 503/343–6812), the U.S. branch of an international organization based in Britain (*see below*) that has affiliates in 30 countries; **MossRehab Hospital Travel Information Service** (tel. 215/ 456–9603, TTY 215/456–9602); the **Travel Industry and Disabled Exchange** (TIDE) (5435 Donna Ave., Tarzana, CA 91356, tel. 818/344–3640, fax 818/344–0078); and **Travelin' Talk** (Box 3534, Clarksville, TN 37043, tel. 615/552–6670, fax 615/552–1182).

In the United Kingdom Important information sources include the **Royal Association for Disability and Rehabilitation** (RADAR) (12 City Forum, 250 City Rd., London EC1V 8AF, tel. 0171/250–3222), which publishes travel information for people with disabilities in Britain; and **Mobility International** (228 Borough High St., London SE1 1JX, tel. 0171/ 403–5688), an international clearinghouse of travel information for people with disabilities.

Travel Agencies and Tour Operators **Flying Wheels Travel** (143 W. Bridge St., Box 382, Owatonna, MN 55060, tel. 507/451–5005 or 800/535–6790) is a travel agency that specializes in domestic and worldwide cruises, tours, and independent travel itineraries for people with mobility problems. Adventurers should contact **Wilderness Inquiry** (1313 5th St. SE, Minneapolis, MN 55414, tel. and TTY 612/379–3858 or 800/728–0719), which orchestrates action-packed trips such as white-water rafting, sea kayaking, and dog sledding for people with disabilities. Tours are designed to bring together people who have disabilities with those who don't.

Publications Several free publications are available from the U.S. Consumer Information Center (Pueblo, CO 81009): "New Horizons for the Air Traveler with a Disability" (include Dept. 608Y in the address), a U.S. Department of Transportation booklet describing changes resulting from the 1986 Air Carrier Access Act and from the 1990 Americans with Disabilities Act; and the Airport Operators Council's *Access Travel: Airports* (Dept. 5804), which describes facilities and services for people with disabilities at more than 500 airports worldwide.

Travelin' Talk Directory (Box 3534, Clarksville, TN 37043, tel. 615/ 552–6670). was published in 1993. This 500-page resource book ($35 check or money order with a money-back guarantee) is packed with information for travelers with disabilities. Twin Peaks Press (Box 129, Vancouver, WA 98666, tel. 206/694–2462 or 800/637–2256) publishes the *Directory of Travel Agencies for the Disabled* ($19.95), listing more than 370 agencies worldwide. Add $2 for shipping.

Hints for Older Travelers

Organizations The **American Association of Retired Persons** (AARP, 601 E St. NW, Washington, DC 20049, tel. 202/434–2277) provides independent travelers who are members of the AARP (open to those age 50 or older; $8 per person or couple annually) with the Purchase Privilege Program, which offers discounts on lodgings, car rentals, and sightseeing, and arranges group tours, cruises, and apartment living through AARP Travel Experience from American Express (400 Pinnacle Way, Suite 450, Norcross, GA 30071, tel. 800/927–0111 or 800/745–4567).

Two other organizations offer discounts on lodgings, car rentals, and other travel products, along with such nontravel perks as magazines and newsletters: the **National Council of Senior Citizens** (1331 F St. NW, Washington, DC 20004, tel. 202/347–8800; membership $12 annually) and **Mature Outlook** (6001 N. Clark St., Chicago, IL 60660, tel. 800/336–6330; $9.95 annually).

Note: Mention your senior-citizen identification card when booking hotel reservations for reduced rates, and do so when booking, not when checking out. At restaurants, show your card before you're seated; discounts may be limited to certain menus, days, or hours. If you are renting a car, ask about promotional rates that might improve on your senior-citizen discount.

Educational Travel The nonprofit **Elderhostel** (75 Federal St., 3rd Floor, Boston, MA 02110, tel. 617/426–7788) has offered inexpensive study programs for people 60 and older since 1975. Held at more than 1,800 educational and cultural institutions, courses cover everything from marine science to Greek myths and cowboy poetry. Participants generally attend lectures in the morning and spend the afternoon sightseeing or on field trips; they live in dormitory-type lodgings. Fees for two- to three-week international trips—including room, board, and transportation from the United States—range from $1,800 to $4,500.

Interhostel (University of New Hampshire, 6 Garrison Ave., Durham, NH 03824, tel. 800/733–9753 or 603/862–1147) caters to a slightly younger clientele—50 and older—and runs programs in some 25 countries. The idea is similar to that of the Elderhostel program: Lectures and field trips mix with sightseeing, and participants stay in dormitories at cooperating educational institutions or in modest hotels. Programs usually last two weeks and cost $1,500–$2,100, excluding airfare.

Publications *The 50+ Traveler's Guidebook: Where to Go, Where to Stay, What to Do*, by Anita Williams and Merrimac Dillon ($12.95, St. Martin's Press, 175 5th Ave., New York, NY 10010), is available in bookstores and offers many useful tips. "The Mature Traveler" (Box 50820, Reno, NV 89513, tel. 702/786–7419; $29.95), a monthly newsletter, contains many travel deals.

Hints for Gay and Lesbian Travelers

Organizations The **International Gay Travel Association** (Box 4974, Key West, FL 33041, tel. 305/292–0217 or 800/999–7925 or 800/448–8550), which has 700 members, will provide you with names of travel agents and tour operators who specialize in gay travel. The **Gay & Lesbian Visitors Center of New York, Inc.** (135 W. 20th St., 3rd Floor, New York, NY 10011, tel. 212/463–9030 or 800/395–2315; $100 annually) mails a monthly newsletter, valuable coupons, and more to its members.

Tour Operators and Travel Agencies The dominant travel agency in the market is **Above and Beyond** (3568 Sacramento St., San Francisco, CA 94118, tel. 415/922–2683 or 800/397–2681). Tour operator **Olympus Vacations** (8424 Santa Monica Blvd. #721, West Hollywood, CA 90069, tel. 310/657–2220 or 800/965–9678) offers all-gay and lesbian resort holidays. **Skylink Women's Travel** (746 Ashland Ave., Santa Monica, CA 90405, tel. 310/452–0506 or 800/225–5759) handles individual travel for lesbians all over the world and conducts two international and five domestic group trips annually.

Publications The premier international travel magazine for gays and lesbians is *Our World* (1104 N. Nova Rd., Suite 251, Daytona Beach, FL 32117, tel. 904/441–5367; $35 for 10 issues). *Out & About* (tel. 203/789–8518 or 800/929–2268; $49 for 10 issues, full refund if you aren't satisfied) is a 16-page monthly newsletter with extensive information on resorts, hotels, and airlines that are gay-friendly.

Further Reading

The political changes in Eastern Europe have inspired a flurry of new books on the area. Patrick Brogan's *The Captive Nations: Eastern Europe 1945–1990* looks at recent revolutions and their aftermath and provides a historical background on eight countries as well as the Baltic republics. J.F. Brown's contribution is *Surge to Freedom: The End of Communist Rule in Eastern Europe*, and William Echikison joins in with *Revolution in Eastern Europe*. Timothy Garton Ash writes about the transformation of Poland, Czechoslovakia, Hungary, and East Germany in the 1980s in *The Uses of Adversity: Essays on the Fate of Central Europe* and also offers a fascinating personal account in *The Magic Lantern: The Revolution of '89 Witnessed in Warsaw, Budapest, Berlin, and Prague*. For more background material on the region, also consider *East Central Europe in the 19th and 20th Centuries, 1848–1945*, by Ivan T. Berend and Gyorgy Ranki.

Three highly recommended travelogues about the region are: Claudio Magris's *Danube*, which follows the river as it flows from its source in Germany to its outlet in the Black Sea; Brian Hall's *Stealing from a Deep Place*, a lively account of a solo bicycle trip through Romania and Bulgaria in 1982, followed by a stay in Budapest; and Patrick Leigh Fermor's *Between the Woods and the Water*, which relates his 1934 walk through Hungary and Romania.

The work of Romanian-born Elie Wiesel touches on several Eastern European countries. This Nobel Peace Prize winner's novels capture the horrific experience of Jews at the hands of the Nazis, as well as the anguish of those who survived and remembered, in works such as *Night* (his only directly autobiographical work), *Dawn*, *The Accident*, and *The Town Beyond the Wall*.

Enthusiasts of Slavic literature should contact **Szwede Books** (Box 1214, Palo Alto, CA 94302, tel. 415/327–5590). Its large selection includes maps and books on Poland, the Czech Republic, and Slovakia.

See individual chapters for more specific information.

Arriving and Departing

From North America by Plane

Flights are either nonstop, direct, or connecting. A **nonstop** flight requires no change of plane and makes no stops. A **direct** flight stops at least once and can involve a change of plane, although the flight number remains the same; if the first leg is late, the second waits. This is not the case with a **connecting** flight, which involves a different plane and a different flight number.

Airports and Airlines Although a number of airlines offer flights to Eastern Europe, a cheaper route might be to fly first into Western Europe or the United Kingdom, then proceed (by plane, train, bus, or auto) to your final destination. Many airlines have special fares and youth fares to Frankfurt, London, and Amsterdam, so it's often cheaper to fly into these cities and then take a train east.

Icelandair (tel. 800/223–5500) offers good rates to Luxembourg, and **KLM Royal Dutch Airlines** (tel. 800/374–7747) connects through Amsterdam to Warsaw, Prague, Budapest, Berlin, and Vienna. **British Airways** (tel. 800/247–9297), **Lufthansa German Airlines** (tel. 800/645–3880), **TWA** (tel. 800/892–4141), and **American Airlines** (tel.

800/433–7300) often offer special fares to Frankfurt, London, and Amsterdam—close enough for travelers to hop on an eastbound train.

Each Eastern European country has its own airline (right now, that is), most of which fly to the United States. Three reported bargains are **Balkan Air** (tel. 212/573–5530) flights from New York to Sofia, **LOT Polish Airways'** (tel. 800/223–0593) flights from New York or Chicago to Warsaw, and **TAROM Romanian Air Transport's** (tel. 212/687–6013) fares from New York to Vienna.

Flying Times Depending on your flight connections and layovers, flights from the West Coast to Prague will take about 19 hours and to Bucharest about 22 hours. From the East Coast you can expect travel to Prague to take about 12 hours and to Bucharest about 15 hours. Chicago–Warsaw is a 10-hour nonstop flight. Flying from Australia to Europe is a trek of about a day and a half.

Cutting Costs The Sunday travel section of most newspapers is a good source of deals. When booking, particularly through an unfamiliar company, call the Better Business Bureau and your local or state Consumer Protection Bureau to find out whether any complaints have been registered against the company, pay with a credit card if you can, and consider trip-cancellation and default insurance (*see* Insurance in Before You Go, *above*).

Promotional Less expensive fares, called promotional or discount fares, are
Airfares round-trip and involve restrictions, which vary according to the route and season. Generally you must buy the ticket—commonly called an APEX (advance purchase excursion) when it's for international travel—in advance (7, 14, or 21 days are standard), although some of the major airlines have added no-frills, cheap flights to compete with new bargain airlines on certain routes.

With the major airlines the cheaper fares generally require minimum and maximum stays (for instance, over a Saturday night or at least 7 and no more than 30 days). Airlines generally allow some return-date changes for a $25 to $50 fee, but most low-fare tickets are nonrefundable. Only a death in the family would prompt the airline to return any of your money if you canceled a nonrefundable ticket. However, you can apply an unused nonrefundable ticket toward a new ticket, again for a small fee. The lowest fare is subject to availability, and only a small percentage of the plane's total seats are sold at that price. Contact the U.S. Department of Transportation's Office of Consumer Affairs (I–25, Washington, DC 20590, tel. 202/366–2220) for a copy of "Fly-Rights: A Guide to Air Travel in the U.S." *The Official Frequent Flyer Guidebook*, by Randy Petersen (4715-C Town Center Dr., Colorado Springs, CO 80916, tel. 719/597–8899 or 800/487–8893; $14.99 plus $3 shipping and handling), yields valuable hints on getting the most for your air-travel dollars. Also new and helpful is *202 Tips Even the Best Business Travelers May Not Know*, by Christopher McGinnis, president of the Travel Skills Group (Box 52927, Atlanta, GA 30355, tel. 404/659–2855; $10 in bookstores.)

Consolidators Consolidators or bulk-fare operators—"bucket shops"—buy blocks of seats on scheduled flights that airlines anticipate they won't be able to sell. They pay wholesale prices, add a markup, and resell the seats to travel agents or directly to the public at prices that still undercut the airline's promotional or discount fares (higher than a charter ticket but lower than an APEX ticket, and usually without the advance-purchase restriction). Moreover, some consolidators sometimes give you your money back. Carefully read the fine print detailing penalties for changes and cancellations. If you doubt the reliability of a company, call the airline once you've made your booking and confirm that you do, indeed, have a reservation on the flight.

The biggest U.S. consolidator, C.L. Thomson Express, sells only to travel agents. Well-established consolidators that sell to the public include **UniTravel** (Box 12485, St. Louis, MO 63132, tel. 314/569–0900 or 800/325–2222) and **Travac** (989 6th Ave., New York, NY 10018, tel. 212/563–3303 or 800/872–8800), also a former charterer.

Discount Travel Clubs Travel clubs offer members unsold space on airplanes, cruise ships, and package tours at as much as 50% below regular prices. Membership may include a regular bulletin or access to a toll-free hot line giving details of available trips departing from three or four days to several months in the future. Most also offer 50% discounts off hotel rack rates, but double-check with the hotel to make sure it isn't offering a better promotional rate independently of the club. Clubs include **Discount Travel International** (114 Forrest Ave., Suite 203, Narberth, PA 19072, tel. 215/668–7184; $45 annually, single or family); **Entertainment Travel Editions** (Box 1014, Trumbull, CT 06611, tel. 800/445–4137; price ranges $28–$48); **Great American Traveler** (Box 27965, Salt Lake City, UT 84127, tel. 800/548–2812; $29.95 annually); **Moment's Notice Discount Travel Club** (425 Madison Ave., New York, NY 10017, tel. 212/486–0503; $45 annually, single or family); **Privilege Card** (3391 Peachtree Rd. NE, Suite 110, Atlanta, GA 30326, tel. 404/262–0222 or 800/236–9732; domestic annual membership $49.95, international, $74.95); **Travelers Advantage** (CUC Travel Service, 49 Music Sq. W, Nashville, TN 37203, tel. 800/548–1116; $49 annually, single or family); and **Worldwide Discount Travel Club** (1674 Meridian Ave., Miami Beach, FL 33139, tel. 305/534–2082; $50 annually for family, $40 single).

Publications The newsletter "Travel Smart" (40 Beechdale Rd., Dobbs Ferry, NY 10522, tel. 800/327–3633; $44 a year) has a wealth of travel deals in each monthly issue. The monthly "Consumer Reports Travel Letter" (Consumers Union, 101 Truman Ave., Yonkers, NY 10703, tel. 800/234–1970) is filled with information on travel savings and indispensable consumer tips.

Enjoying the Flight Fly at night if you're able to sleep on a plane. Because the air aloft is dry, drink plenty of fluids while on board. Drinking alcohol contributes to jet lag, as do heavy meals. Bulkhead seats, located in the front row of each cabin—usually reserved for people who have disabilities, the elderly, and those traveling with babies—provide more legroom, but trays attach awkwardly to seat armrests, and all possessions must be stowed overhead.

Smoking Since February 1990, smoking has been banned on all domestic flights of less than six hours' duration; the ban also applies to domestic segments of international flights aboard U.S. and foreign carriers. On U.S. carriers flying to Eastern Europe and other destinations abroad, a seat in a no-smoking section must be provided for every passenger who requests one, and the section must be enlarged to accommodate such passengers if necessary as long as they have complied with the airline's deadline for check-in and seat assignment. If smoking bothers you, request a seat far from the smoking section.

Foreign airlines are exempt from these rules but do provide no-smoking sections, and some nations, including Canada as of July 1, 1993, have gone as far as to ban smoking on all domestic flights; other countries may ban smoking on flights of less than a specified duration. The International Civil Aviation Organization has set July 1,

1996, as the date to ban smoking aboard airlines worldwide, but the body has no power to enforce its decisions.

From the United Kingdom by Plane, Car, Bus, Train, and Ferry

By Plane Many of the airlines listed above make stops in London en route to Eastern Europe. The list below includes other major carriers from Great Britain.

British Airways (tel. 0171/897–4000) has daily nonstop service to Prague, Warsaw, and Budapest from London (with connections to major British cities). Each Eastern European country has its own airline, which generally flies into London. Check with the appropriate Government Information Office for detailed airline information (*see* Government Information Offices in Before You Go, *above*).

By Car Theoretically it's possible to travel by car from the United Kingdom to Eastern Europe. However, unless you're planning a lengthy stay (six months or more), a combination of mass transit and rental cars should do the trick and save a lot of hassle. Bring your own car, and a mechanical failure of any kind could leave you stranded indefinitely—the chances of a local mechanic having both the parts you need and the know-how to work on your car are next to nil. If you're dead set on testing your Fiat against the serpentine roadways of Eastern Europe's many mountain ranges, make sure you don't leave any of the following back home: car registration, third-party insurance, driver's license, and (if you're not the car's owner) a notarized letter of permission from the owner. An international driver's license, although not always required, is a good idea. The vehicle must bear a country ID sticker.

The best ferry ports for Eastern Europe are Rotterdam, Holland or Ostende, Belgium, from which you drive to Cologne (Köln), Germany, and then through either Dresden or Frankfurt and on to Prague.

By Bus Unless you latch onto a real deal on airfare, a bus ticket from London's **Victoria Terminal** (tel. 0171/730–0202) is probably the cheapest transit from the United Kingdom to Eastern Europe, although it may take a little research, as regularly scheduled routes to all cities except Berlin are practically nonexistent. Check newspaper ads for eastbound passage.

By Train There are no direct trains from London. You can take a direct train from Paris via Frankfurt to Prague (daily) or from Berlin via Dresden to Prague (three times a day). Vienna is a good starting point for Prague, Brno, or Bratislava. There are three trains a day from Vienna's Franz Josefsbahnhof to Prague via Třeboň and Tábor (5½ hours) and one from the Südbahnhof (South Station) via Brno (5 hours). Bratislava can be reached from Vienna by a 67-minute shuttle service that runs every two hours during the day. You should check out times and routes before leaving. Mind-boggling timetables galore, including those for train travel to and from Eastern Europe, are in *Cook's European Timetable,* about £10 from Thomas Cook (378 Strand, London WC2 O2R, tel. 0171/836–5200, and major branches) and at some travel agencies (where looking is free). *Cook's* does not list fares, however, so ask a travel agent.

By Ferry Ferries offer a pleasant and cheap mode of transportation to Eastern Europe, although you have to be fairly close to your destination already to hop a Europe-bound ferry or hydrofoil. Flying into the appropriate hub, however, is an option. Water bookings connect Denmark and Sweden to East Germany, and Copenhagen, Denmark, to Świnoujście and Gdańsk, Poland. A hydrofoil shuttles visitors from Vienna to Bratislava, Slovakia, or Budapest, Hungary. (*See* Essential Information in the chapters for each individual country for more specific information.)

Staying in Eastern Europe

Getting Around

By Plane The airlines of the Czech Republic and Slovakia, Hungary, Poland, Bulgaria, and Romania operate an extensive network of services within the region and within their own countries. All the capitals are linked by services that operate at least twice daily. In addition to routes linking the respective capitals, there are services connecting main cities in neighboring countries—for example Kraków (Poland) and Bratislava (Slovakia).

By Train Although standards have improved during the past few years, on the whole they are far short of what is acceptable in the West. Trains are very busy and it is rare to find one running less than full or almost so. All six countries operate their own dining, buffet, and refreshment services. Always crowded, they tend to open and close at the whim of the staff. Couchette cars are second-class only and can be little more than a hard bunk without springs and adequate bed linen.

Although trains in Eastern Europe are usually crowded and aren't always comfortable, traveling by rail is very inexpensive (it's much cheaper than renting a car in this part of Europe). Rail networks in all the Eastern European countries are very extensive, though trains can be infuriatingly slow. You'll invariably enjoy interesting and friendly traveling company, however; most Eastern Europeans are eager to hear about the West and to discuss the enormous changes in their own countries.

By Bus Bus travel is generally more costly than travel by train, although this varies by country. In some instances, especially where trains are largely local (and stop seemingly every 100 feet), buses are actually speedier than rail travel. Comfort is minimal, though; roads tend to be bumpy and seats lumpy. Buses are generally tidier; train bathrooms are notoriously rank. It's a bit of a gamble; seats on buses are a rarity during prime traveling hours, and drivers don't always stop where they should, although most leave promptly on time (especially when you're still waiting in line for a ticket). Comfort and fares vary drastically by nation; *see* chapters on individual countries for more information.

By Car The plus side of driving is an itinerary free from the constraints of bus and train schedules and lots of trunk room for extra baggage. The negatives are many, however (*see* Car Rentals in Before You Go, *above*), not the least of which are shabbily maintained secondary roads, the risk of theft and vandalism, and difficulty finding gas. However, car travel does make it much easier to get to out-of-the-way monasteries and other sights not easily accessible by public transport. Good road maps are usually available.

A word of caution: If you have any alcohol whatsoever in your body, *do not* drive in Eastern Europe. Penalties are fierce, and the blood-alcohol limit is practically zero.

Roads and The main roads, usually made of macadam or concrete, are built to a
Gasoline fairly high standard. There are now quite substantial stretches of highway on main routes, and a lot of rebuilding is being done. Gas

stations are fewer than they are in the West, sited at intervals of about 48 kilometers (30 miles) along main routes and on the outskirts of large towns. Very few stations remain open after 9:30 PM. At least two grades of gasoline are sold in Eastern European countries, usually 90–93 octane (regular) and 94–98 octane (super). Lead-free gasoline is available in very few gas stations. The supply of gas to filling stations is by no means regular, so there are sometimes long lines and considerable delays. Try to get into the habit of filling your tank whenever you see a station to avoid being stranded on a long drive.

Telephones

AT&T and MCI both have direct calling programs overseas. AT&T's **USADirect** service allows you to call collect or charge calls from abroad to your AT&T calling card. Either way, you pay AT&T rates and speak to an English-speaking operator. Here are the access codes to use when dialing from within the foreign country: Czech Republic and Slovakia: tel. 00–420–00101; Hungary: tel. 00–800–01111; Poland: from Warsaw, tel. 010–480–0111, from outside Warsaw, tel. 0–010–480–0111; Romania: tel. 01–800–4288. There is no USADirect service from Bulgaria. The billing rate varies by country, and there is a $2.50 service charge for each call you make. For additional information, call 412/553–7458, ext. 314 (collect from outside the U.S.) or 800/874–4000. MCI works the same way, although at press time service was not available from Bulgaria or Romania. The MCI access code for the Czech Republic and Slovakia is 00–420–00112; for Hungary, 00–800–01411; for Poland, 0–0104–800222; the billing rate varies by country, and there is a $2 service charge for each call you make. For more information, call 800/950–5555.

VAT and Sales Tax

With the exception of Bulgaria and Romania, most Eastern European countries have some form of value-added tax (VAT); rates vary from 20% to 25%. VAT rebate rules vary by country, but you'll need to present your receipts on departure.

Dining

Eastern European cuisine, regional by nature, is suffering from an identity crisis. Until 1989, and in varying degrees, Eastern Europe suffered food shortages and rationing of even the most basic foodstuffs. In many countries, pork and potatoes became de facto replacements for the elaborate folk dishes that once graced tables from Warsaw to Sofia.

With the collapse of communism, Eastern European cuisines are on the rebound. You always could find an excellent meal in Budapest, even at the height of the Cold War; but the recent proliferation of restaurants in Budapest and throughout Eastern Europe is hopeful news, indeed. Bucharest and Sofia seem destined to lag behind, but even so, you will still be able to find quiet eateries offering excellent, modern versions of traditional recipes.

Restaurants in Eastern Europe come in all shapes and sizes. Some remain state-owned and attached to tedious cement-block hotels. Others have sprung up in abandoned warehouses or former Communist-party digs. You'll find some in the most unlikely places—in Slovakia's remote High Tatras Mountains or Romania's even more remote Danube Delta.

Restaurant standards remain high in Eastern European capitals; in Prague and Budapest, for example, you'll find everything from formal bistros to boisterous wine halls. Prices have risen dramatically since 1989, but you can still enjoy a decadent meal, even in the cities, for well under $15.

Lodging

If your experience of Eastern European hotels is limited to capital cities such as Prague and Budapest, you may be pleasantly surprised. There are Baroque mansions turned guest houses and elegant high-rise resorts, not to mention bed-and-breakfast inns presided over by matronly babushkas. Now that communism is a thing of the past, there seems to be more interest in maintaining and upgrading facilities (though, inevitably, there are exceptions).

Outside major cities, hotels and inns are more rustic than elegant. Standards of service generally do not suffer, but in most rural areas the definition of "luxury" includes little more than a television and a private bathroom. In some instances, you may have no choice but to stay in one of the cement high-rise hotels that scar skylines from Poland to the Czech Republic to Romania. It's hard to say why Communists required their hotels to be as big and impersonal as possible, but they did, and it may take a few more years to exorcise or "beautify" these ubiquitous monsters.

The good news is that room rates are reasonable in all but a handful of international chain hotels that have sprung up in Eastern Europe since 1989. During the high season it is possible to find a spacious, well-maintained double room for less than $40; in rural Eastern Europe, you may have difficulty parting with more than $20 per night for lodgings. Reservations are vital if you plan to visit Prague, Budapest, Warsaw, or most other major cities during the summer season. Reservations are a good idea but aren't imperative if you plan to strike out into the countryside.

Home Exchange You can find a house, apartment, or other vacation property to exchange for your own by becoming a member of a home-exchange organization, which then sends you its annual directories listing available exchanges and includes your own listing in at least one of them. Arrangements for the actual exchange are made by the parties involved, not by the organization. For more information, contact the **International Home Exchange Association** (IHEA, 41 Sutter St., Suite 1090, San Francisco, CA 94104, tel. 415/673–0347 or 800/788–2489). The principal clearinghouse is **Intervac International** (Box 590504, San Francisco, CA 94159, tel. 415/435–3497), which provides three annual directories; membership is $62, or $72 if you want to receive the directories but remain unlisted.

Apartment and Villa Rentals If you want a home base that's roomy enough for a family and comes with cooking facilities, a furnished rental may be the solution. It's generally cost-wise, too, although not always—some rentals are luxury properties (economical only when your party is large). Home-exchange directories do list rentals—often second homes owned by prospective house swappers—and some services search for a house or an apartment for you (even a castle if that's your fancy) and handle the paperwork. Some send an illustrated catalogue and others send photographs of specific properties, sometimes at a charge; up-front registration fees may apply.

Among the principal companies are **Europa-Let** (92 N. Main St., Ashland, OR 97520, tel. 503/482–5806 or 800/462–4486); **Interhome**

Inc. (124 Little Falls Rd., Fairfield, NJ 07004, tel. 201/882–6864); and **The Invented City** (*see* IHEA, *above*).

Credit Cards

The following credit card abbreviations are used: AE, American Express; DC, Diners Club; MC, MasterCard/Access/Barclays; V, Visa.

Eastern Europe at a Glance: A Chronology

c 400 BC Bohemia, the main region of the Czech Republic, is settled by the Celtic Boii tribe, from which the area gets its name.

AD 101–106 Trajan conquers Dacia, in what is now Romania; the victory is immortalized by the Column of Trajan in Rome.

271 Rome withdraws from Dacia; without Roman protection, the region becomes a conduit for invading tribes targeting rich lands to the south and west.

c 500 Closely related Slavic tribes begin to settle in the regions that make up the Czech Republic and Slovakia.

681 Roman emperor Constantine V Pogonatus recognizes a Bulgarian state.

c 800 Slavic tribes begin to form states in Poland. The name Poland is derived from the name of one of these tribes, the Polanie.

846–894 The great Moravian Empire under princes Ratislav and Svätopluk unites Bohemia, Moravia, and most of Slovakia, and extends into Poland and Hungary. Byzantine missionaries Cyril and Methodius—credited with the creation of the Cyrillic alphabet—translate Christian liturgy into Slavonic and convert much of the region.

864 Prince Boris of Bulgaria agrees to the mass conversion of his subjects to Christianity, helping to unify the country. The liturgy is conducted in the Slavonic language rather than in Greek or Latin.

892 German king Arnulf asks the help of the Magyars to fight Moravia. The Magyars destroy the Moravian Empire by 907 and settle in the region of modern Hungary. The name Hungary is said to derive from On-Ogur, meaning "ten arrows," by which the federation of Magyar hordes is known.

893–927 Prince Simeon the Great extends Bulgaria's borders to the Adriatic and Aegean seas. He is given the title *tsar*, equal in status with the emperors in Rome and Constantinople. Magyars begin to settle in Transylvania, and control the area a century later.

907 Slovakia is conquered by the Magyars, beginning a thousand years of subjugation by Hungary.

965 Polish prince Mieszko I marries a Czech princess, marking the start of "official" Polish history. He introduces Christianity and unifies most of Poland from the Baltic Sea to Kraków. Mieszko's son, Bolesław I the Brave, expands the empire to both Prague and Kiev.

1000 Stephen I, considered the founder of the Hungarian nation, is named the first king of Hungary by the pope. Stephen unifies the country and converts it to Christianity. Canonized in 1083, he becomes the patron saint of Hungary.

1018 Bulgaria becomes part of the Byzantine Empire.

1029 Czech princes aligned with the Holy Roman Empire shift the center of power from Moravia to Bohemia. Moravia is annexed by Bohemia.

1185–1202 A Bulgarian state is reestablished in Tŭrnovo by the brothers Petŭr and Ivan Assen. Magyars are driven out of northwest Bulgaria.

1241 Mongols invade Hungary and Transylvania and leave a trail of destruction in their wake, slaughtering about half of the population; they withdraw in 1242. Hungarian influence in Transylvania declines, and the region becomes virtually autonomous.

1290 The Romanian principality of Wallachia is formed; Moldavia, the second independent principality, is formed 60 years later.

1308 Under Charles Robert of Anjou (France), Hungary begins 600 years of almost exclusively foreign rule.

1348 Charles University, the first university in Central Europe, is built in Prague .

1355 Czech prince Charles IV, known as the "Father of the country," is named Holy Roman Emperor. Prague becomes a cultural center of Europe as well as capital of the empire.

1364 The University of Kraków, the second university in Central Europe, is founded.

1385–1572 The Jagiellonian dynasty brings a "golden age" to Poland. At the end of the 15th century its empire stretches to within a hundred miles of Moscow in the east and includes Odessa on the Black Sea as well as the areas of modern Slovakia, Hungary, Croatia, Moldavia, and Ukraine. Poland becomes a huge exporter of grain to all of Europe; its Baltic Sea port, Gdańsk, becomes the most important economic center in Eastern Europe.

1385–1396 Bulgaria falls to the Ottoman Empire. It is almost 500 years before another independent Bulgaria appears.

1415 Czech religious reformer Jan Hus is burned at the stake, but the Czech Reformation, or Hussite movement, continues.

1453–1688 Under Ottoman rule, Bulgarian culture is diminished but survives in rural areas. The decline of the Ottoman Empire is matched by a gradual rise in Bulgarian Catholic influence. Romanian trade in the Black Sea is cut off by the Turks and the eastern principalities enter a period of isolation; native princes govern Transylvania.

1526 Ferdinand I of Habsburg inherits the crown of Bohemia. Habsburgs rule the Czech region, with few brief interruptions, until 1918. Ottoman Turks destroy the Hungarian army at Mohacs. The Ottoman Empire gradually takes control of all but the westernmost region of Hungary.

1540–1690 The Reformation spreads rapidly in Transylvania. In 1571 the Transylvanian Diet approves a law guaranteeing freedom of worship, although Orthodox Christianity is not fully recognized.

1543 The book *On the Revolutions of the Heavenly Spheres* by Polish astronomer Nicolaus Copernicus shows that the earth orbits the sun and not vice versa, a discovery with implications that extend far beyond the world of science.

1569 With the Treaty of Lublin, Poland becomes a republic in which the king is elected by the nobility and must seek the nobility's approval on important issues.

1616   Copernicus's treatise is placed on the *Index of Forbidden Books* by the Roman Catholic church.

1648–1668   Under the reign of King John II Casimir Vasa, Poland collapses. Cossacks in Ukraine and the Russian army conquer much of Poland's eastern territory; Sweden attacks from the north and the Brandenburgers attack in Prussia. In 1667 Lubomirski's Rebellion in Ukraine leads Poland to cede important territory to Russia. John II Casimir abdicates in 1668 with the economy in ruins and more than a quarter of the population dead from war and disease.

1699   The Peace of Karlowitz returns to Hungary nearly all of its land conquered by the Turks. Control of Hungary falls to the Habsburgs of Austria.

1716   Czar Peter the Great defends Poland from the advances of Prussia, making Poland essentially a Russian protectorate.

1762   The monk Father Paiisi Hildenarski writes *History of Bulgarian Kings and Saints*, the first piece of modern Bulgarian literature.

1772   The First Partition of Poland grants almost a third of Polish territory to Russia, Austria, and Prussia.

1780–1790   Under Emperor Josef II's "enlightened despotism," serfs are emancipated, the Transylvanian constitution is annulled, and German is declared the official language of the Habsburg Empire.

1791   Poland adopts a liberal constitution that expands the public's role in the government and curtails the power of the nobility, culminating nearly 20 years of political and economic revival and reform.

1793   The Second Partition of Poland gives Russia vast eastern territories and Prussia a large region in the west, including Gdańsk. The Second Partition is largely a response to the Polish political reforms, and Poland is forced to abandon its new constitution, becoming a Russian puppet state.

1794   Tadeusz Kościuszko leads a revolt against the Second Partition. Kościuszko, a veteran of the American War for Independence, mobilizes a massive, poorly trained army and scores stunning victories against the Russians but is finally defeated.

1795   The Third Partition effectively wipes the Republic of Poland off the map. Prussia takes Warsaw. Austria takes Kraków and land in the southeast. Russia receives what remains of Lithuania. For 123 years there will be no independent Polish nation.

1815   The Congress Kingdom of Poland, comprised of Polish lands seized by Napoleon and then reconquered by Russia, is created. The Congress Kingdom adopts a liberal constitution and maintains its own government and army, but remains under the thumb of the Russian czars.

1828–1830   Following the Russo-Turkish War, Russian controls the eastern Romanian regions. Poland revolts against Russia. After some early successes, the Polish army is defeated in September 1831. Eighty thousand Poles are sent to Siberia. The constitution is annulled and a period of repression begins.

1846   Polish plans for another insurrection are discovered in Poznań by Prussian authorities, and Austrian troops quash an uprising in Galicia. As a result of these failures, Poland misses the wave of revolutions that sweep Europe two years later.

1848   Lajos Kossuth, a journalist, leads a revolution in Hungary. A new constitution provides for democratic reform, civil and religious rights, and Hungarian autonomy within the Austrian Empire. In early 1849 Hungary proclaims full independence, but Russian troops sent by Czar Nicholas crush the rebellion. Hungary, united with Transylvania, returns to Austrian domination. Bohemia attempts to establish an autonomous government; many of its demands are met by the emperor in April. Hapsburg emperor Ferdinand I abdicates in favor of his 18-year-old nephew Franz Josef, whose iron rule continues until 1916. Romania, with Austria's support, begins warfare against Hungary.

1859–1861 Wallachia and Moldavia are finally united when their separate assemblies elect the same man. The united principalities officially become Romania in 1861.

1862 Georgi Rakovski organizes a group of armed Bulgarians in Belgrade. He calls for armed bands to enter Bulgaria and eventually establish a Balkan Republic. The group is forcibly disbanded by the Serbs.

1864 Russia crushes yet another Polish uprising, the January Insurrection, and dissolves the kingdom. The "Czar-Liberator" Alexander II frees the serfs as they had been freed in Russia three years earlier.

1867 In response to Hungarian nationalist demands, the *Ausgleich* "compromise" creates the dual monarchy of Austria-Hungary with two parliaments and one monarch, Franz Josef. In Hungary the non-Magyar ethnic groups are pressured to adopt the Hungarian language, creating much animosity.

1876 The April Uprising in Bulgaria is crushed by Turkish forces. Twenty-nine thousand Bulgarians are killed.

1877–1879 Russia declares war on Turkey and invades the Balkans; Bulgarian and Romanian forces assist the Russian armies, driving the Ottoman army back to Constantinople. Romania is recognized as independent in 1880; Prince Charles becomes king in 1881.

1912 First Balkan War: Serbia, Bulgaria, Montenegro, and Greece form an alliance to drive Turks from the region. Bulgarian troops defeat the Turks, but Greece controls the contested area of Macedonia.

1913 Second Balkan War: Threatened by Greek and Serbian power, Bulgaria attacks both countries and is completely defeated. Macedonia is given to Serbia; Romania invades northern Bulgaria and annexes the southern region Dobruja.

1914 Archduke Ferdinand, a strong supporter of the rights of Transylvania's Romanians, is assassinated by a Bosnian Serb. Hungary and Bulgaria fight with the Central Powers—Austria and Germany—in World War I. Romania joins the war on the side of the Allies and invades Austria-Hungary.

1916 The Kingdom of Poland is reestablished by Germany and Austria in the hope of gaining Polish support in the war, but little support for the puppet kingdom materializes. Death of Franz Josef.

1917 Bolsheviks seize power in the Russian Revolution; Romania annexes Bessarabia and Bukovina from Russia.

1918 In President Woodrow Wilson's "14 points" speech, the 13th point calls for an independent Poland with access to the sea. The 10th point demands autonomy for the peoples of Austria-Hungary. The Republic of Czechoslovakia is formed; Tomaš Garrigue Masaryk, who led the independence movement, is named its first president. The Second Republic of Poland is formed, headed by Józef Piłsudski, resistance leader and political organizer. Poland is devastated: Millions are dead from war and disease, and the country's infrastructure suffers massive damage. Two more years of fighting are required to settle border disputes, most notably with the Soviet Union. Hungary is proclaimed an independent republic with Mihály Károlyi as president.

1919 Béla Kun, a Communist, takes control of Hungary's government and invades Romania. Romanian troops penetrate Hungarian lines to Budapest.

1920 Monarchy is restored in Hungary, with Miklós Horthy, a former admiral of the Austro-Hungarian navy, serving as regent. The Versailles settlement forces Hungary to give up huge areas of territory, and more than half of its prewar population. Czechoslovakia receives Slovakia and Ruthenia; Romania takes Transylvania; Croatia is given to Yugoslavia. Czechoslovakia adopts its first democratic constitution and national elections are held.

1933–1934 After the collapse of the economy, fascist Iron Guards begin to take power in Romania; the constitution is suspended. Right-wing forces take over the Bulgarian government by a military coup; the country solidifies ties with Germany and Italy.

1938 The Munich Pact formed by Germany, Italy, Britain, and France allows Hitler to annex the German-Czech border area known as Sudetenland.

1939 Slovakia led by Catholic priest Father Josef Tiso declares its independence. Two days later Slovakia becomes a protectorate of Nazi Germany and remains a semi-independent state throughout the war. Seventy thousand out of 95,000 Slovak Jews are exterminated by the end of the war. Bohemia and Moravia are proclaimed protectorates of Nazi Germany. Nazi-Soviet nonaggression pact outlines the division of Poland between the two. Germany invades in September and by the end of the month controls the country. Romania signs an economic development plan with Germany; King Carol tries to maintain neutrality, but the country soon falls to German control.

1940 Hungary agrees to an alliance with Nazi Germany under the Tripartite Pact. The Soviet Union annexes Bessarabia and northern Bukovina from Romania; Bulgaria reclaims Dobruja with German and Soviet backing. Transylvania is ceded to Hungary.

1941 Exterminations begin at the concentration camp in Oświęcim (Auschwitz). By the end of the war, 2 million Jews die in Auschwitz alone. Bulgaria declares war on Great Britain and the United States but refuses to declare war on the Soviet Union or to join Hitler's campaign against Russia. With Romanian support, Germany invades the Soviet Union and begins the march eastward.

1943 The Warsaw Ghetto uprising lasts five weeks, with poorly equipped Jews fighting against Nazi SS troops. The ghetto is destroyed; 56,000 Jews are sent to the Treblinka concentration camp.

1944 Two-hundred-fifty thousand Polish troops fight Nazi forces in the Warsaw uprising. The Poles are defeated and the city destroyed. Soviet forces enter Bulgaria and Romania and seize power.

1945 Soviet troops liberate what is left of Warsaw. Six million Poles have died during the war, 3 million of them Jews. Prague is liberated by the Soviet army, giving the Soviet Union an important political victory in Czechoslovakia.

1946 Hungary declares itself a republic. The Czechoslovak Communist party wins its first postwar national elections but does not receive a majority. The Bulgarian monarchy is dissolved; the country, under communist rule, is declared a republic. Soviet-backed Communists win rigged elections in Romania.

1947   Communists "win" elections in Poland amid widespread allegations of rigged voting. Bolestaw Beirut, an ally of Stalin, is named president. A Stalinist constitution in adopted in Bulgaria, and the country enters a period of dependence and friendship with the Soviet Union. Romania is restored to her prewar borders; the government dissolves all opposition parties.

1953   Stalin dies.

1956   Khrushchev delivers his "secret speech" denouncing Stalinism at the XXth Party Congress. A general strike is held in Poznań, Poland; 50,000 demonstrators demand government reform, and 74 are killed. Władysław Gomułka, a reform-minded Communist who was arrested in 1951 for his beliefs, is elected first secretary of the Polish Communist party, the United Workers' Party. Khrushchev arrives unannounced and enraged in Warsaw. Soviet troops are mobilized, but Gomułka convinces Khrushchev of his loyalty and remains in power for 14 years. Imre Nagy, whose attempts to reform Hungary's government as prime minister from 1953 to 1955 had resulted in his dismissal from office and the Communist party, resumes power following massive demonstrations. Nagy announces Hungary's withdrawal from the Warsaw Pact. Three days later Soviet tanks roll into Budapest. Fighting continues, strikes are held, but the movement fails. About 200,000 people flee the country. Nagy flees to Romania but is returned to Hungary and eventually executed.

1965   Nicolae Ceauçescu takes power in Romania, beginning 24 years of autocratic and repressive rule.

1968   After several years of demands for political liberalization, Slovak political reformer Alexander Dubček is named the first secretary of the Czech Communist party, ushering in the Prague Spring. Dubček tries to create "socialism with a human face," calling for multiparty democratic elections. In August, Soviet and other Warsaw Pact troops invade Czechoslovakia .

1969   Czech student Jan Palach sets himself on fire to protest the forced ending of the Prague Spring; Palach's martyrdom becomes an important source of motivation for the revolution of 1989.

1977   Czech intellectuals, including playwright Václav Havel, sign Charter 77, a declaration of grievances with the hard-line communist government.

1978   Karol Wojtyła, the Cardinal of Kraków, is elected Pope John Paul II.

1980   Electrician Lech Wałęsa leads a strike at the Lenin Shipyards in Gdańsk. The trade union *Solidarność* (Solidarity) is formed and Wałęsa is named chairman. Within a year, the organization has 10 million members.

1981–1982   General Wojciech Jaruzelski imposes martial law on Poland in response to growing demands from Solidarity for political freedom. Tanks patrol the streets of Polish cities and police break up protests around the country. Solidarity is outlawed in October 1982.

1989   Demonstrations in Prague in honor of the 20th anniversary of the death of Jan Palach lead to sweeping political and economic reforms, including free elections. Solidarity-backed candidates win nearly every contested election; voters choose not to vote at all in races that were reserved only for government-sponsored candidates. In Budapest, 200,000 people show up for the reburial of Imre Nagy, hero of Hungary's aborted 1956 revolution. Tadeusz Mazowiecki, a journalist and Solidarity activist, is chosen as the new prime minister of Poland. He becomes the first non-Communist to head an Eastern-bloc nation. Hungary's communist government and opposition groups reach an agreement, calling for multiparty elections in 1990. Czech police beat protesters at a rally in Prague and at least one student is reportedly killed. This proves to be the catalyst for the most rapid revolution in Eastern Europe. Two days later the organization Civic Forum is created by Václav Havel and others. A day after that, 200,000 people pack Wenceslas Square and demand democracy. On November 24, Alexander Dubček returns to Prague for his first public appearance there since 1969 and addresses a mass demonstration. The Communist party relinquishes its "leading role" on November 29. Václav Havel replaces Husák as president on December 29. Dubček is named speaker of the national Parliament. After a series of outdoor protests in Sofia, Bulgarian Communist-party leader Todor Zhivkov is ousted. In December, Lázló Tökés, a young minister in Timișoara, Romania, sermonizes against the lack of freedom in the country. Demonstrators take to the streets; Ceaușescu orders the use of deadly force. In Bucharest on December 21, as Ceaușescu addresses a large crowd, students unfurl anti-Ceaușescu banners. The next day the army begins to join the protesters; Ceaușescu and his wife flee but are captured and sentenced to death for "crimes against the people." They are executed on December 25.

1990   The first round of free parliamentary elections are held in Hungary. The United Democratic Front, a broad-based coalition, wins. Under pressure from Slovak nationalists, Czechoslovakia changes its name to the Czech and Slovak Federative Republic. Jozsef Antall of the center-right Democratic Forum is elected prime minister of Hungary. Solidarity sweeps local elections in Poland. Czechoslovakia holds its first free democratic elections since 1946. Civic Forum and its counterpart in Slovakia, Public Against Violence, win convincingly in races against as many as 21 parties. Lech Wałęsa is elected president of Poland, beating Polish-Canadian businessman Stanisław Tymiński. Outgoing president Jaruzelski, who introduced martial law in 1981 and outlawed Solidarity in 1982, apologizes for any harm he might have caused. Václav Havel is elected to a second two-year term as president of Czechoslovakia. Democratic elections are held in Bulgaria. Hungary becomes the first Eastern European nation to receive full membership in the Council of Europe. President Bush is the first American president to visit Prague.

1991   Czechoslovakia sends 200 troops to the Gulf War, signaling its support of the Western cause. Hungary negotiates a five-year agreement with the European Community, with the goal of full membership. The Czech Civic Forum party splits into free-market and social-democratic factions, while the leading Slovak party, Public Against Violence, splits along pro- and antiseparatist lines. The last Soviet troops leave Hungary, and the Warsaw Pact is formally dissolved on July 1. In the first postrevolutionary Polish parliamentary elections, 7,000 candidates compete for 560 seats; the top two parties are the anticommunist Democratic Union and the pro-communist Democratic Left.

1992   Parliamentary elections in Czechoslovakia lead to a deeper split between the Czech and Slovak republics. Newly elected Czech premier Václav Klaus and Slovak nationalist leader Vladimir Mečiar fail to agree on terms for a common government and direct their respective parliaments to develop guidelines for the establishment of separate governments. Unwilling to preside over the dissolution of the nation, Václav Havel resigns the presidency in July.

1993 Failing to find a compromise, Czech and Slovak leaders split the 74-year-old Czechoslovak federation on Jan. 1, 1993. The Czech Republic and Slovakia become fully sovereign and separate countries. Václav Havel is elected by Parliament to be the new Czech president; the Slovaks appoint former banker Michael Kováč.

2 The Czech Republic

By Mark Baker

Mark Baker is a freelance journalist and travel writer living in Prague.

A victim of enforced obscurity throughout much of the 20th century, the Czech Republic, comprising the provinces of Bohemia and Moravia (but no longer Slovakia), is once again in the spotlight. In a world where revolution was synonymous with violence, and in a country where truth was quashed by the tanks of Eastern bloc socialism, in November 1989 Václav Havel's sonorous voice proclaimed the victory of the "Velvet Revolution" to enthusiastic crowds on Wenceslas Square and preached the value of "living in truth." Recording the dramatic events of the time, television cameras panned across Prague's glorious skyline and fired the world's imagination with the image of political renewal superimposed on somber Gothic and voluptuous Baroque.

Travelers have rediscovered the country, and Czechs and Moravians have rediscovered the world. Not so long ago, the visitor was unhindered by crowds of tourists but had to struggle with a creeping sensation of melancholy and neglect that threatened to eclipse the city's beauty. Combined with a truly frustrating lack of services in every branch of the tourist industry, a trip to Czechoslovakia was always an adventure in the full sense of the word.

At least on the surface, the atmosphere is changing rapidly. The stagnant "normalization" of the Husák era, which froze the city out of the developments of the late 20th century, is giving way to the dynamic and the cosmopolitan. The revolution brought enthusiasm, bustle, and such conveniences as English-language newspapers, attentive hotels, and, occasionally, restaurants that will try to find a seat for you even if you don't have a reservation.

The revolution inspired one other thing: nationalism. Unable to unite on a common course of economic renewal Czechs and Slovaks peacefully agreed to dissolve their 74-year-old federal state on January 1, 1993. Though the division was greeted with sadness by outsiders, visitors to either country are not likely to notice much difference save the hassle of an extra border and the need now to change money when traveling back and forth. The chapter below covers the Czech Republic and its constituent provinces of Bohemia and Moravia. Slovakia is covered in a separate chapter (*see* Chapter 3, Slovakia).

The drab remnants of socialist reality are still omnipresent on the back roads of Bohemia and Moravia. But many of the changes made by the Communists were superficial—adding ugliness but leaving the society's core more or less intact. The colors are less jarring, not designed to attract the moneyed eye; the fittings are as they always were, not adapted to the needs of a new world.

The experience of visiting the Czech Republic still involves stepping back in time. Even in Prague, now deluged by tourists during the summer months, the sense of history—stretching back through centuries of wars, empires, and monuments to everyday life—remains uncluttered by the trappings of modernity. The peculiar melancholy of Central Europe, less tainted now by the oppressive political realities of the postwar era, still lurks in narrow streets and forgotten corners. Crumbling facades, dilapidated palaces, and treacherous cobbled streets both shock and enchant the visitor used to a world where what remains of history has been spruced up for tourist eyes.

The strange, Old World, and at times frustratingly bureaucratic atmosphere of the Czech Republic is not all a product of the communist era. Many of the small rituals that impinge on the visitor are actually remnants of the Habsburg empire and are also to be found, perhaps to a lesser degree, in Vienna and Budapest. The *šatná* (coatroom),

Czech Republic

POLAND

GERMANY

SLOVAKIA

HUNGARY

AUSTRIA

BOHEMIA

MORAVIA

Prague

N

60 miles

90 km

Bardejov · Prešov · Košice · Spišská N. Ves · Poprad · Rimavská Sobota · Liptovský Mikuláš · Ružomberok · Brezno · Banská Bystrica · Krupina · Učenec · Žilina · Čadca · Martin · Dubnica · Trenčín · Zvolen · Levice · Nové Zámky · Nitra · Nové Mesto · Piešťany · Trnava · Bratislava · Dunaj · Streda · Komárno · Vsetín · Zlín · Uherské Hradiště · Břeclav · Znojmo · Vienna

Karviná · Český Těšín · Frýdek Místek · Opava · Ostrava · Nový Jičín · Přerov · Olomouc · Prostějov · Brno · Svitavy · Havlíčkův Brod · Telč · Jihlava · Třeboň · České Budějovice · Český Krumlov

Wrocław · Opole · Görlitz · Náchod · Hradec Králové · Pardubice · Chrudim · Liberec · Jablonec · Česká Lípa · Mladá Boleslav · Kolín · Kutná Hora · Vlašim · Tábor · Milevsko · Písek · Strakonice · Klatovy

Dresden · Chemnitz · Děčín · Ústí · Litoměřice · Teplice · Most · Louny · Kladno · Beroun · Příbram · Chomutov · Karlovy Vary · Cheb · Mariánské Lázně · Plzeň

E462 · E461 · D2 · E442 · D1/E50 · E67 · E65 · E55 · E50 · E49 · E48 · E50 · E75 for example, plays a vivid role in any visit to a restaurant or theater at any time of year other than summer. Even in the coldest weather, coats must be given with a few coins to the attendant, usually an old lady with a sharp eye for ignorant or disobedient tourists. The attendant often also plays a role in controlling the rest room; the entrance fee entitles the visitor to a small roll of paper, ceremoniously kept on the attendant's table. Another odd custom, associated with this part of the world, are the *Tabák-Trafiks*, the little stores that sell two things connected for no apparent reason: tobacco products and public-transport tickets.

Outside of the capital, for those willing to put up with the inconveniences of shabby hotels and mediocre restaurants, the sense of rediscovering a neglected world is even stronger. And the range is startling, from imperial spas, with their graceful colonnades and dilapidated villas, to the hundreds of arcaded town squares, modestly displaying the passing of time with each splendid layer of once contemporary style. Gothic towers, Renaissance facades, Baroque interiors, and aging modern supermarkets merge. Between the manmade sights, the visitor is rewarded with glorious mountain ranges and fertile rolling countryside, laced with carp ponds and forests.

The key to enjoying the country is to relax. There is no point in demanding high levels of service or quality. And for the budget-conscious traveler, this is Central Europe at its most beautiful, at prices that are several times below those of Austria and even Hungary.

Before You Go

Government Tourist Offices

Čedok, the official travel bureau for the Czech Republic and Slovakia, is actually a travel agent rather than a tourist information office. It will supply you with hotel and travel information, and book air and rail tickets for travel within either country, but don't expect much in the way of general information.

In the United States: 10 E. 40th St., New York, NY 10016, tel. 212/689–9720. **In the United Kingdom:** 17–18 Old Bond St., London W1X 4RB, tel. 0171/629–6058.

Tour Groups

U.S. Tour Operators   **General Tours** (245 5th Ave., New York, NY 10016, tel. 212/685–1800 or 800/221–2216) combines Prague and Budapest on a nine-day tour that features comprehensive city sightseeing as well as excursions to Konopiště, Lidice, and the Danube Bend in Hungary.
Love Holidays/Uniworld (Box 16000 Ventura Blvd., Suite 1105, Encino, CA 91436, tel. 818/501–6868 or 800/733–7820) gives you Prague and the "Best of Czechoslovakia" in 10 days. The eight-day tour of Prague and the "Jewels of Bohemia" includes full-day excursions into the surrounding countryside.
For other operators that include Prague and the Czech Republic on their Eastern Europe itineraries, *see* Tour Groups in Chapter 1.

U.K. Tour Operators   **Čedok Tours and Holidays** (17–18 Old Bond St., London W1X 4RB, tel. 0171/629–6058) offers four- and eight-day packages to Prague, with optional sightseeing excursions to the countryside, and packages to the Prague Spring Music Festival.
Hamilton Travel Ltd. (6 Heddon St., London W1R 7LH, tel. 0171/

439–3199) offers flight/accommodation packages for one or more nights to Prague.

Page & Moy Ltd. (136–140 London Rd., Leicester LE2 1EN, tel. 0533/552251) offers a three-night package to Prague, including a city sightseeing tour and an optional visit to Karlštejn Castle.

Sovereign Cities (Groundstar House, London Road, Crawley, West Sussex RH10 2TB, tel. 0293/561444) offers three- and seven-night flight/hotel packages in the Czech Republic, with optional sightseeing excursions.

Travelscene Ltd. (Travelscene House, 11–15 St. Ann's Rd., Harrow, Middlesex HA1 1AS, tel. 0181/427–4445) offers three- and seven-night flight/hotel packages to Prague with optional excursions, and a seven-night, two-center holiday with Vienna.

When to Go

Prague is beautiful year-round, but avoid midsummer (especially July and August) and the Christmas and Easter holidays, when the city is overrun with tourists. Spring and fall generally combine good weather with a more bearable level of tourism. During the winter months you'll encounter few other visitors and have the opportunity to see Prague breathtakingly covered in snow; but many of the sights are closed, and it can get very cold. The same guidelines generally apply to traveling in the rest of Bohemia and Moravia, although even in high season (August), the number of visitors to these areas is far smaller than in Prague. The Giant Mountains of Bohemia come into their own in winter (December–February), when skiers from all over the country crowd the slopes and resorts. If you're not into skiing, try visiting the mountains in late spring (May or June) or fall, when the colors are dazzling and you'll have the hotels and restaurants pretty much to yourself. Bear in mind that many castles and museums are closed November through March.

Festivals and Seasonal Events

The Czech government publishes an annual "Calendar of Tourist Events" in English, available from Čedok or the Prague Information Service. Čedok offices can provide you with exact dates and additional information.

March: Prague City of Music Festival
April: International Consumer Goods Fair (Brno), Jazz Festival (Kroměříž)
May: Prague Spring Music Festival, International Childrens' Film Festival (Zlín)
June: Smetana National Opera Festival (Litomyšl), International Festival of Mime (Mariánské Lázně)
July: Prague Summer Culture Festival
August: Chopin Festival (Mariánské Lázně)
August–September: Brno Folklore Festival
September: Brno Engineering Goods Fair
October: Brno International Music Festival, Karlovy Vary Film Festival, Prague Marathon, International Jazz Festival (Prague)

What to Pack

In the postcommunist Czech Republic, Western dress of any kind is considered stylish, so don't bother bringing your tuxedo. A sports jacket for men, and a dress or pants for women, is appropriate for an evening out in Prague or in the better Bohemian spa towns. Everywhere else, you'll feel comfortable in casual corduroys or jeans. Most of the country is best seen on foot, so take a pair of sturdy walking shoes and be prepared to use them. Throughout Eastern Europe, high heels present a considerable problem on cobblestone streets, and Prague is no exception. If you plan to visit the mountains, make sure your shoes have good traction and ankle support, as some trails can be quite challenging. Many consumer goods are still in short supply. Be sure to bring any medications or special toiletries you may require. You will need an electrical adapter for small appliances; the voltage is 220, with 50 cycles.

Czech Currency

The unit of currency in the Czech Republic is the koruna, or crown (Kč.), which is divided into 100 haléř, or halers. There are (little-used) coins of 10, 20, and 50 halers; coins of 1, 2, 5, 10, 20, and 50 Kč., and notes of 10, 20, 50, 100, 200, 500, 1,000 Kč, and 5,000 Kč. The 100-Kč. notes are by far the most useful. The 1,000-Kč. note may not always be accepted for small purchases, because the proprietor may not have enough change.

Try to avoid exchanging money at hotels or private exchange booths, including the ubiquitous Čekobanka and Exact Change booths. They routinely take commissions of 8%–10%. The best place to exchange is at bank counters, where the commissions average 1%–3%. Although the crown is more or less convertible, you will still encounter difficulty in exchanging your money when you leave. To facilitate this process, keep your original exchange receipts so no one will think you bought your crowns on the black market. It is technically illegal to buy crowns abroad and bring them into the Czech Republic (or to take them out when you leave), although this is not strictly controlled. The black market for Western currencies is still thriving, but it's best to keep well away; such deals are strictly illegal and if caught, you risk deportation. At press time (summer 1994) the official exchange rate was around 30 Kč. to the U.S. dollar and 43 Kč. to the pound sterling. There is no longer a special exchange rate for tourists.

What It Will Cost

Despite rising inflation, the Czech Republic is still generally a bargain by Western standards. Prague remains the exception, however. Hotel prices, in particular, frequently meet or exceed the average for the U.S. and Western European—and are higher than the standard of facilities would warrant. Nevertheless, you can still find bargain private accommodations. The prices at tourist resorts outside of the capital are lower and, in the outlying areas and off the beaten track, incredibly low. Tourists can now legally pay for hotel rooms in crowns, although some hotels still insist on payment in "hard" (i.e., Western) currency.

Sample Costs   A cup of coffee will cost about 15 Kč.; museum entrance, 20 Kč.; a good theater seat, up to 100 Kč.; a cinema seat, 30 Kč.; ½ liter (pint) of beer, 15 Kč.; a 1-mile taxi ride, 60 Kč.; a bottle of Moravian wine in a good restaurant, 100 Kč.–150 Kč.; a glass (2 deciliters or 7 ounces) of wine, 25 Kč.

Passports and Visas

American and British citizens require only a valid passport for stays of up to 30 days in the Czech Republic. No visas are necessary. Canadian citizens, however, must obtain a visa (C$50) before entering the Czech Republic. For applications and information, contact the Czech Embassy (541 Sussex Dr., Ottawa, Ontario K1N 6Z6, tel. 613/562–3875). U.S. citizens can receive additional information from the Czech Embassy (3900 Linnean Ave. NW, Washington, DC, tel. 202/363–6315).

Customs and Duties

On Arrival You may import duty-free into the Czech Republic 250 cigarettes or the equivalent in tobacco, 1 liter of spirits, 2 liters of wine, and ½ liter of perfume. You may also bring up to 1,000 Kč. worth of gifts and souvenirs.

If you take into the Czech Republic any valuables or foreign-made equipment from home, such as cameras, it's wise to carry the original receipts with you or register the items with U.S. Customs before you leave (Form 4457). Otherwise you could end up paying duty upon your return.

On Departure From the Czech Republic you can take out gifts and souvenirs valued at up to 1,000 Kč., as well as goods bought at Tuzex hard-currency shops (keep the receipts). Crystal and some other items not bought at hard-currency shops may be subject to a tax of 100% of their retail price. Only antiques bought at Tuzex or specially appointed shops may be exported.

Language

Czech, a western-Slavic language, closely related to Slovak and Polish, is the official language of the Czech Republic. Learning English is popular among young people, but German is still the most useful language for tourists. Don't be surprised if you get a response in German to a question asked in English. If the idea of attempting Czech is daunting, you might consider bringing a German phrase book.

Staying Healthy

The Czech Republic poses no special health risks for visitors. Tap water tastes bad but is generally drinkable. Vegetarians and those on special diets may have a problem with the heavy local cuisine, which is based almost exclusively on pork and beef. For more information, *see* Staying Healthy in Chapter 1.

Car Rentals

There are no special requirements for renting a car in the Czech Republic, but be sure to shop around, as prices can differ greatly. **Avis** and **Hertz** offer Western makes for as much as $400–$600 per week. Smaller local companies, on the other hand, can rent Czech cars for as little as $130 per week.

The following rental agencies are based in Prague.

Avis. Opletalova 33, Nové Město, tel. 02/2422–9848.
Budget. Hotel Inter-Continental, tel. 02/2488–9995.
Esocar. Husitská 58, Prague 3, tel. 02/691–2244.
Hertz. Hotel Atrium, tel. 2484–2047; Hotel Diplomat, tel. 02/2439–4155.
Pragocar. Milevská 2, Prague 4, tel. 02/6116–1111.

Rail Passes

The **European East Pass** is good for unlimited first-class travel on the national railroads of Austria, the Czech Republic, Slovakia, Hungary, and Poland. The pass allows 5 days of travel within a 15-day period ($169) or 10 days of travel within a 30-day period ($275). Apply through your travel agent or through **Rail Europe** (226–230 Westchester Ave., White Plains, NY 10604, tel. 914/682–2999 or 800/848–7245).

The **EurailPass** and **Eurail Youthpass** are not valid for travel within the Czech Republic. The **InterRail Pass** (£249), available to European citizens only through local student or budget travel offices, is valid for one month of unlimited train travel in the Czech Republic and the other countries covered in this book. For more information, *see* Rail Passes in Chapter 1, Essential Information.

Student and Youth Travel

In the Czech Republic, **ČKM Youth Travel Service** (Žitná 12, Prague 1, tel. 02/2491–0457) provides information on student hostels and travel bargains within the Czech Republic. For general information about student identity cards, work-abroad programs, and youth hostels, *see* Student and Youth Travel in Chapter 1.

Further Reading

With the increased interest in the Czech Republic in recent years, English readers now have an excellent range of both fiction and nonfiction about the country at their disposal. The most widely read Czech author of fiction in English is probably Milan Kundera, whose well-crafted tales illuminate both the foibles of human nature and the unique tribulations of life in communist Czechoslovakia in a humorous but thought-provoking way. *The Unbearable Lightness of Being* takes a look at the 1968 invasion and its aftermath through the eyes of a strained young couple. The very entertaining *Book of Laughter and Forgetting* deals in part with the importance of memory and the cruel irony of how it fades over time. The author was no doubt coming to terms with his own forgetting as he wrote the book from his Paris exile. *The Joke*, Kundera's earliest work available in English, takes a serious look at the dire consequences of humorlessness among Communists.

Josef Škvorecký, another contemporary Czech writer, lives in exile in Canada. In his widely available *The Engineer of Human Souls*, he attempts to relate his experiences in Canada to his earlier life in Czechoslovakia under Nazi and, later, communist occupation.

Franz Kafka's *The Trial* and *The Castle* will help you feel some of the dread and mystery that he and other German writers detected beneath the 1,000 golden spires of Prague. His books were actually an indictment of the bizarre bureaucracy of the Austro-Hungarian empire, though they now seem eerily prophetic of the even crueler and more arbitrary communist system that was to come. For this reason, until recently most of his works could not be purchased in his native country.

Jaroslav Hašek's hilarious classic *The Good Soldier Schweik* concerns the antics of a good-natured boob who survives World War I in the Austro-Hungarian army. Many regard Schweik as the archetypal Czech: a guileless, downtrodden fellow who somehow always manages to get by.

As for nonfiction, the best place to start is probably *Living in Truth*, an absorbing collection of 22 inspiring essays written by President Václav Havel during his years "underground" as a dissident playwright. The first essay is an open letter to the former communist president Gustav Husák, written before the 1989 revolution, concerning the erosion of public life that occurs when the populace is forced to lip-synch empty slogans. Havel's view is that a just society is one that enables its citizens to live out their lives true to their conscience. Havel's plays are also worth seeing for a better understanding of the absurdities and pressures of life under the former communist regime.

For an excellent social and historical background on the former Czechoslovakia look to David W. Paul's *Czechoslovakia: Profile of a Socialist Republic at the Crossroads of Europe* or R. W. Seton-Watson's *The History of the Czechs and the Slovaks*.

Arriving and Departing

From North America by Plane

Airports and Airlines All international flights to the Czech Republic fly into Prague's **Ruzyně Airport**, about 20 kilometers (12 miles) northwest of downtown. The airport is small and easy to negotiate.

ČSA, (Czechoslovak Airlines), the Czech and Slovak national carrier (tel. 718/656–8439), maintains regular direct flights to Prague from New York's JFK Airport, and twice-weekly flights from Chicago, Los Angeles, and Montreal.

Several other international airlines have good connections from cities in the United States and Canada to European bases and from there to Prague. **British Airways** (tel. 800/247–9297) flies daily via London; and **SwissAir** (tel. 718/995–8400), daily via Zurich.

Flying Time From New York, a nonstop flight to Prague takes 9–10 hours; with a stopover, the journey will take at least 12–13 hours. From Montreal nonstop it is 7½ hours; from Los Angeles, 16 hours.

From the United Kingdom by Plane, Car, Bus, and Train

By Plane **British Airways** (tel. 0171/897–4000) has daily nonstop service to Prague from London (with connections to major British cities); **ČSA** (tel. 0171/255–1898) flies five times a week nonstop from London. The flight takes around three hours.

By Car The most convenient ferry ports for Prague are Hoek van Holland and Ostend. To reach Prague from either ferry port, drive first to Cologne (Köln) and then through either Dresden or Frankfurt.

By Bus There is no direct bus service from the United Kingdom to the Czech Republic; the closest you can get is Munich, and from there the train is your best bet. **International Express** (Coach Travel Center, 13 Lower Regent St., London SW1Y 4LR, tel. 0171/439–9368) operates daily in summer, leaving London's Victoria Coach Station in mid-evening and arriving in Munich about 23 hours later.

By Train There are no direct trains from London. You can take a direct train from Paris via Frankfurt to Prague (daily) or from Berlin via Dresden to Prague (three times a day). Vienna is a good starting point for Prague, Brno, or Bratislava. There are three trains a day from Vienna's Franz Josefsbahnhof to Prague via Třeboň and Tábor (5½ hours) and two from the Südbahnhof (South Station) via Brno (five hours).

Staying in the Czech Republic

Getting Around

By Plane ČSA (Czechoslovak Airlines) maintains a remarkably good internal air service linking Prague with Brno, Karlovy Vary, and Ostrava, as well as with Poprad (Tatras), Piešt'any, and Košice in Slovakia. The flights, by jet or turboprop aircraft, are relatively cheap and frequent. Reservations can be made through Čedok offices abroad or ČSA in Prague (Revoluční 1, tel. 02/2421–0132).

By Train Trains vary in speed, but it's not really worth taking anything less than an express train, marked in red on the timetable. Tickets are relatively cheap; first class is considerably more spacious and comfortable and well worth the 50% increase over standard tickets. If you don't specify "express" when you buy your ticket, you may have to pay a supplement on the train. If you haven't bought a ticket in advance at the station, it's easy to buy one on the train for a small extra charge. On timetables, departures (*odjezd*) appear on a yellow background; arrivals (*příjezd*) are on white. It is possible to book *couchettes* (sleepers) on most overnight trains, but don't expect much in the way of comfort. The European East Pass and the InterRail Pass—but not the EurailPass or Eurail Youthpass—are valid for unlimited train travel within the Czech Republic.

By Bus The Czech Republic's extremely comprehensive state-run bus service, ČSAD, is usually much quicker than the normal trains and more frequent than express trains, unless you're going to the major cities. Prices are essentially the same as those for the train. Buy your tickets from the ticket window at the bus station or directly from the driver on the bus. Long-distance buses can be full, so you might want to book a seat in advance; Čedok will help you do this. The only drawback to traveling by bus is figuring out the timetables. They are easy to read, but beware of the small letters denoting exceptions to the time given. If in doubt, inquire at the information window or ask someone for assistance.

By Car Traveling by car is the easiest and most flexible way of seeing the Czech Republic. There are few four-lane highways, but most of the roads are in reasonably good shape and traffic is usually light. The road can be poorly marked, however, so before you start out buy the excellent *Auto Atlas ČSFR* or the larger-scale *Velký Autoatlas Československá* (which also shows locations of lead-free gas pumps); both are multilingual, inexpensive, and available at any bookstore. The Czech Republic follows the usual Continental rules of the road. A right turn on red is permitted only when indicated by a green arrow. Signposts with yellow diamonds indicate a main road where drivers have the right of way. The speed limit is 110 kph (70 mph) on four-lane highways, 90 kph (55 mph) on open roads, and 60 kph (40 mph) in built-up areas. The fine for speeding is 300 Kč., payable on the spot. Seat belts are compulsory, and drinking before driving is absolutely prohibited.

Don't rent a car if you intend to visit only Prague. Most of the center of the city is closed to traffic, and you'll save yourself a lot of hassle by sticking to public transportation. If you do arrive in Prague by car, bear in mind that you can park in the center of town, including on Wenceslas Square, only if you have a voucher from one of the major hotels. If you're not staying in a hotel, a good legal solution is to park the car on one of the little streets behind the Bohemian National Museum (at the top of Wenceslas Square). This neighborhood is technically not considered part of Prague's central district, and anyone can park there.

For accidents, call the emergency number (tel. 154). In case of repair problems, get in touch with the 24-hour **Autoturist Servis** (Limuzská 12, Prague 10, tel. 02/773455). Autoturist offices throughout the Czech Republic can provide motoring information of all kinds. The Auto Atlas ČSFR has a list of emergency road-repair numbers in the various towns.

Telephones

Local Calls Coin-operated telephones take either just 1-Kč. coins or 1-, 2-, and 5-Kč. coins. Many newer public phones operate only with a special telephone card, available from newsstands and tobacconists in denominations of 100 Kč. and 190 Kč. A call within Prague costs 1 Kč. To make a call, lift the receiver and listen for the dial tone, a series of long buzzes. Dial the number. Public phones are located in metro stations and on street corners; unfortunately, they're often out of order. Try asking in a hotel if you're stuck.

International Calls To reach an English-speaking operator in the United States, dial tel. 00–420–00101 (AT&T) or tel. 00–420–00112 (MCI). The operator will connect your collect or credit-card call at standard AT&T or MCI rates. In Prague, the main post office (Hlavní pošta, Jindřišská ul. 14), open 24 hours, is the best place to make direct-dial long-distance calls. Otherwise, ask the receptionist at any hotel to put a call through for you, though beware: The more expensive the hotel, the more expensive the call will be.

Mail

Postal Rates Postcards to the United States cost 6 Kč.; letters, 11 Kč.; to Great Britain a postcard is 4 Kč.; a letter, 6 Kč. Prices are due for an increase in 1995, so check with your hotel for current rates. You can buy stamps at post offices, hotels, and shops that sell postcards.

Receiving Mail If you don't know where you'll be staying, **American Express** mail service is a great convenience, available at no charge to anyone holding an American Express credit card or carrying American Express traveler's checks. The American Express office is located on Wenceslas Square in central Prague. You can also have mail held *poste restante* (general delivery) at post offices in major towns, but the letters should be marked *Pošta 1* to designate the city's main post office. The poste restante window is No. 28 at the main post office in Prague (Jindřišská ul. 14). You will be asked for identification when you collect your mail.

Tipping

To reward good service in a restaurant, round the bill up to the nearest multiple of 10 (if the bill comes to 83 Kč., for example, give the waiter 90 Kč.); 10% is considered appropriate on very large tabs. If you have difficulty communicating the amount to the waiter, just leave the money on the table. Tip porters who bring bags to your rooms 20 Kč. For room service, a 20-Kč. tip is enough. In taxis, round the bill up by 10%. Give tour guides and helpful concierges between 20 Kč. and 30 Kč. for services rendered.

Opening and Closing Times

Though hours vary, most banks are open weekdays 8–3:30, with an hour's lunch break. Private exchange offices usually have longer hours. Museums are usually open daily except Monday (or Tuesday) 9–5; some, including many castles, are open only from May through October. Stores are open weekdays 9–6; some grocery stores open at 6 AM. Department stores often stay open until 7 PM. On Saturday, most stores close at noon. Nearly all stores are closed on Sunday.

National Holidays January 1; Easter Monday; May 1 (Labor Day); May 9 (Liberation); July 5 (Sts. Cyril and Methodius); July 6 (Jan Hus); October 28 (Independence); and December 24, 25, and 26.

Shopping

In Prague, Karlovy Vary, and elsewhere in Bohemia, look for elegant and unusual crystal and porcelain. Bohemia is also renowned for the quality and deep-red color of its garnets; keep an eye out for beautiful garnet rings and broaches, set in either gold or silver. You can also find excellent ceramics, especially in Moravia, as well as other folk artifacts, such as printed textiles, lace, hand-knit sweaters, and painted eggs. There are attractive crafts stores throughout the Czech Republic. Karlovy Vary is blessed with a variety of unique items to buy, including the strange pipelike drinking mugs used in the spas; roses; vases left to petrify in the mineral-laden water; and *Oblaten*, crispy wafers sometimes covered with chocolate. Here you'll also find *Becherovka*, a tasty herbal aperitif that makes a nice gift to take home.

Sports and Outdoor Activities

Bicycling Czechs are avid cyclists. The flatter areas of southern Bohemia and Moravia are ideal for biking. Outside of the larger towns, quieter roads stretch out for miles. The hillier terrain of northern Bohemia makes it popular with mountain-biking enthusiasts. Not many places rent bikes, though. Inquire at Čedok or at your hotel for rental information.

Boating and Sailing The country's main boating area is the enormous series of dams and reservoirs along the Vltava south of Prague. The most popular lake is Slapy, where it is possible to rent small paddleboats as well as to relax and swim on a hot day. If you have your own kayak, you can test your skills on one of the excellent rivers near Český Krumlov.

Camping There are hundreds of camping sites for tents and trailers throughout the Czech Republic, but most are open only in summer (May to mid-September). You can get a map of all the sites, with addresses, opening times, and facilities, from Čedok. Camping outside of official sites is prohibited. Some camping grounds also offer bungalows. Campsites are divided into categories A and B according to facilities, but both have hot water and toilets.

Fishing Many lakes and rivers are suitable for fishing, but you'll need both a fishing license—valid for a year—and a fishing permit—valid for a day, week, month, or year—for the particular body of water you plan to fish in. Both are available from Čedok offices. You'll have to bring your own tackle with you or buy it locally.

Golf There are very few golf courses in the Czech Republic. The best known and possibly most attractive 18-hole course is at the elegant Hotel Golf in Mariánské Lázně. You will also find smaller courses in Prague and Karlovy Vary. Ask at one of the larger hotels for details.

Hiking The Czech Republic is a hiker's paradise, with 40,000 kilometers (25,000 miles) of well-kept, marked, and signposted trails both in the mountainous regions and leading through beautiful countryside from town to town. You'll find the colored markings denoting trails on trees, fences, walls, rocks, and elsewhere. The colors correspond to the path-marking on the large-scale *Soubor turistickych* maps. The main paths are marked in red, others in blue and green; the least important trails are marked in yellow. The best areas for ambitious mountain walkers are the Beskydy Mountain range in northern Moravia and the Krkonoše range (Giant Mountains) in Northern Bohemia. The rolling Šumava hills of southern Bohemia are excellent for less ambitious walkers.

Skiing The two main skiing areas in the Czech Republic are the Krkonoše range in northern Bohemia and the Šumava hills of southern Bohemia (lifts at both operate from January through March). In the former, you'll find a number of organizations renting skis—although supplies may be limited. Both places are also good for cross-country skiing.

Tennis The larger hotels in resort areas can usually arrange for tennis courts if they don't have them in-house. In larger towns, ask at the Čedok office or in hotels for the address of public tennis courts.

Dining

The quality of restaurant cuisine in the Czech Republic remains uneven. Many excellent private restaurants have sprung up in Prague in recent years, but in the countryside the food is often monotonous and of low quality. The traditional dishes—roast pork or duck with dumplings, or broiled meat with sauce—can be light and tasty when well prepared. Frequently, however, they're just tossed onto your plate with little forethought or care. The problem stems from the years of communist rule, when private restaurants were shut down and replaced by state-run establishments with standardized menus and recipes. Often in smaller towns, the hotel restaurant, sadly, is still the only dining option available.

Restaurants generally fall into three categories. A *pivnice*, or beer hall, usually offers a simple menu of goulash or pork with dumplings at very low prices. The drawback is that the food is often poorly prepared, while the surroundings can be noisy and crowded (expect to share a table). More attractive (and more expensive) are the *vinárna* (wine cellars) and normal *restaurace* (restaurants), which serve a full range of dishes and are usually open only during mealtimes. Wine cellars, some occupying Romanesque basements, can be a real treat, and you should certainly seek them out. A fourth dining option, the *lahůdky* (snack bar or deli), is the quickest and cheapest option. At snack bars, typically, you order from a counter and eat standing up. Street stands sell a variety of traditional, if heavy, alternatives, including *párek* (hot dogs), *smažený sýr* (fried cheese), and *bramborák* (potato pancakes).

The increase in the number of visitors to the country has placed a strain on restaurants. To avoid disappointment, always try to book a table in advance, especially in Prague. You may stand a better chance if your hotel reserves a table than if you call yourself. If you don't have a reservation, try showing up just before mealtime (11:30 for lunch, 5:30 for dinner).

Most places do not serve foreign wines, so wine lists are usually limited to reasonably good Moravian wines. The best varieties come from Mikulov and Znojmo in Moravia and are as follows:

White: Müller Thurgau is green when young but yellows with maturity. The wine's fine muscat bouquet and light flavor go well with fish and veal. **Neuburské,** yellow-green in color and with a dry, smoky bouquet, is delicious with roasts. **Rulandské bílé,** a semidry white also known by its French name, burgundy, has a flowery bouquet and full-bodied flavor. It's a good complement to poultry and veal. The dry, smooth flavor of **Ryzlink Rýnský** is best enjoyed with cold entrées and fish. **Veltlínské zelené,** distinguished by its beautiful light-green color, also goes well with cold entrées.

Red: Frankovka, fiery red and slightly acidic, is well suited to game and grilled meats. **Rulandské cervené,** cherry-red in color and flavor, is an excellent dry companion to poultry, game, and grilled meats. **Vavřinecké,** a dark, semisweet red, stands up well to red meats.

Mealtimes Lunch, usually eaten between noon and 2, is the main meal for Czechs and offers the best deal for tourists. Many restaurants put out a special luncheon menu (*denní lístek*), usually printed only in Czech, with more appetizing selections at better prices. If you don't see it, ask your waiter. Dinner is usually served from 5 until 9 or 10, but don't wait too long to eat. First of all, most Czechs eat only a light meal or a cold plate of meat and cheese in the evening. Secondly, restaurant cooks frequently knock off early on slow nights, and the later you arrive, the more likely it is that the kitchen will be closed. In general, dinner menus do not differ substantially from lunch offerings, except that the prices are higher.

Ratings Czechs don't normally go in for three-course meals, and the following prices apply only if you are having a first course, main course, and dessert (excluding wine and tip).

Category	Prague*	Other Areas*
$$$$	over $25	over $20
$$$	$15–$25	$10–$20
$$	$7–$15	$5–$10
$	under $7	under $5

per person, including appetizer, main course, and dessert but excluding wine and tip

Lodging

The number of hotels and pensions has increased dramatically throughout the Czech Republic, in step with the influx of tourists. Finding a suitable room should pose no problem, although it is highly recommended that you book ahead during the peak tourist season (July and August, and the Christmas and Easter holidays). Hotel prices, in general, remain high. This is especially true in Prague and in the spa towns of western Bohemia. Better value often can be found at private pensions and with individual homeowners offering rooms to let. In the outlying towns, the best strategy is to inquire at the local tourist information office or simply fan out around the town and look for room-for-rent signs on houses (usually in German: *ZIMMER FREI, PRIVAT ZIMMER*).

Outside of Prague and the major tourist centers, hotels tend to fall into two categories: the old-fashioned hotel on the main square, with rooms above a restaurant, no private bathrooms, and a price lower than you can imagine; or the modern, impersonal, and often ugly high rise with all the basic facilities and a reasonable price. Nevertheless, you'll rarely find a room that is not clean, and some hotels (of both varieties) can be very pleasant indeed. Hostels are understood to mean dormitory rooms and are probably best avoided. In the mountainous areas you can often find little *chata* (chalets), where pleasant surroundings compensate for a lack of basic amenities. *Autokempink* (campsites) generally have a few bungalows.

The Czech Republic's official hotel classification, based on letters (Deluxe, A*, B*, B, C), is gradually being changed to the international star system, though it will be some time before the old system is completely replaced. These ratings correspond closely to our categories as follows: Deluxe or five-star ($$$$); A* or four-star ($$$); B* or three-star ($$); and B or two-star ($). We've included C hotels, some with cold water only, in our listings where accommodations are scarce. Often you can book rooms—both at hotels and in private homes—through Čedok. Otherwise, try calling or writing the hotel directly.

Ratings The prices quoted below are for double rooms during high season, generally not including breakfast. At certain periods, such as Easter or during festivals, prices can jump 15%–25%; as a rule, always ask the price before taking a room.

Category	Prague*	Other Areas*
$$$$	over $200	over $100
$$$	$100–$200	$50–$100
$$	$50–$100	$15–$50
$	under $50	under $15

All prices are for a standard double room during peak season.

Prague

"We are living in the Left Bank of the '90s," wrote Alan Levy, the editor in chief of the *Prague Post*, for the newspaper's debut edition in 1991. With those few words, Levy gave rise to one of the sweetest myths to grace the postrevolutionary period in Eastern Europe. Prague isn't really the modern equivalent of 1920s Paris, but the characterization isn't wholly inaccurate either. Like all other good myths, whether grounded in fact or fantasy, the belief that something special is happening here has achieved some measure of truth through sheer repetition and force of will. By hook or by crook, Prague has become, well, quite Bohemian in its own way.

In the five years since Prague's students took to the streets to help bring down the 40-year-old communist regime, the city has enjoyed an unparalleled cultural renaissance. Much of the energy has come from planeloads of idealistic young Americans, but the enthusiasm has been shared in near-equal measure by their Czech counterparts and by the many newcomers who have arrived from all over the world. Amid Prague's cobblestone streets and gold-tipped spires, new galleries, cafés, and clubs teem with bright-eyed "expatriates" and perplexed locals who must wonder how their city came to be Eastern Europe's new Left Bank. New shops and, perhaps most noticeably, scads of new restaurants have recently opened up, expanding the city's culinary reach far beyond the traditional roast pork and dumplings. Many have something to learn in the way of presentation and service, but Praguers still marvel at a variety that was unthinkable only a few years ago.

The arts and theater are also thriving in the "new" Prague. Young playwrights, some writing in English, regularly stage their own works. Weekly poetry readings are standing-room-only. The city's dozen or so rock clubs are jammed nightly; bands play everything from metal and psychedelic to garage and grunge.

All of this frenetic activity plays well against a stunning backdrop of towering churches and centuries-old bridges and alleyways. Prague achieved much of its present glory during the 14th century, during the long reign of Charles IV, king of Bohemia and Moravia, and Holy Roman Emperor. It was Charles who established a university in the city and laid out the New Town (Nové Město), charting Prague's growth.

During the 15th century, the city's development was hampered by the Hussite Wars, a series of crusades launched by the Holy Roman Empire to subdue the fiercely independent Czech noblemen. The Czechs were eventually defeated in 1620 at the Battle of White Mountain (Bílá Hora) near Prague and were ruled by the Habsburg family for the next 300 years. Under the Habsburgs, Prague became a German-speaking city and an important administrative center, but it was forced to play second fiddle to the monarchy's capital of Vienna. Much of the Lesser Town (Malá Strana), across the river, was built up at this time, becoming home to Austrian nobility and its Baroque tastes.

Prague regained its status as a national capital in 1918, with the creation of the modern Czechoslovak state, and quickly asserted itself in the interwar period as a vital cultural center. Although the city escaped World War II essentially intact, it and the rest of Czechoslovakia fell under the political and cultural domination of the Soviet Union until the 1989 popular uprisings that ended the 40-year reign of the country's pro-Soviet government. The election of dissident playwright Václav Havel to the post of national president in June 1990 set the stage for the city's renaissance, which has since proceeded at a dizzying, quite Bohemian rate.

Important Addresses and Numbers

Tourist Information Čedok, the ubiquitous state-run travel agency, is the first stop for general tourist information and city maps. Čedok will also exchange money, arrange guided tours, and book passage on airlines, buses, and trains. You can pay for Čedok services, including booking rail tickets, with any major credit card. Note limited weekend hours. *Main office: Na příkopě 18, tel. 02/2419–7111, fax 02/232–1656. Open weekdays 8:30–5, Sat. 8:30–12:30.*

The **Prague Information Service** (PIS, Staroměstské nám. 22, tel. 02/224311, fax 02/226067) is generally less helpful than Čedok but offers city maps and general tourist information. It can also exchange money and help in obtaining tickets for cultural events.

The friendly, English-speaking staff at **AVE**, located in the main train station (Hlavní nádraží, tel. 02/2422-3226, fax 02/2422-3463), will gladly sell you a map of Prague (cost: 10 Kč.) and answer basic questions. The organization also offers an excellent room-finding service and will change money. The office is open daily 6 AM-11 PM.

Prague Suites, located at Melantrichova 8 (tel. 02/2423-0467, fax 02/2422-9363), can assist in finding luxury accommodations in private apartments; it can also help secure concert tickets and provide general tourist information.

To find out what's on for the month and to get the latest tips for shopping, dining, and entertainment, consult one or both of Prague's two English-language newspapers, *The Prague Post* (weekly, 30 Kč.) and *Prognosis* (biweekly, 25 Kč.). Both have comprehensive entertainment listings and can be purchased at the AHC and most downtown newsstands. The monthly *Prague Guide*, available at newsstands and tourist offices for 25 Kč., provides a good overview of major cultural events and has comprehensive listings of restaurants, hotels, and organizations offering traveler assistance.

Embassies **U.S. Embassy.** Tržiště 15, Malá Strana, tel. 02/2451-0847.
British Embassy. Thunovská ul. 14, Malá Strana, tel. 02/2451-0439.
Canadian Embassy. Mickiewiczova ul. 6, Hradčany, tel. 02/2431-1108.

Emergencies **Police** (tel. 158). **Ambulance** (tel. 155). **Medical emergencies** tel. (02/5292-2146 or 02/5292-2191 on weekends). **Dentists** (tel. 02/2422-7663 for 24-hour emergency service).

English-Language Bookstores Part bookstore and part café, **The Globe** (Janovského 14, Prague 7, close to Vltavska metro station) carries a diverse and reasonably priced selection of used and new paperbacks. **Bohemian Ventures** (Nám. Jana Palacha, open weekdays 9-6, Sat. 9-12) at the Charles University Philosophical Faculty near Staroměstská metro station stocks mostly Penguin-published titles. Street vendors on Wenceslas Square and Na příkopě carry leading foreign newspapers and periodicals. For hiking maps and auto atlases, try **Melantrich** (Na příkopě 3, Nové Město).

Late-Night Pharmacy The pharmacy at Na příkopě 7 (tel. 02/220081), just a few steps down from Wenceslas Square, is open 24 hours.

Travel Agencies **Thomas Cook** (Václavské nám. 47, tel. 02/2422-9537, fax 02/265695) and **American Express** (Václavské nám. 56, tel. 02/2422-7786, fax 02/2422-7708) can make travel arrangements, exchange money, and issue and redeem traveler's checks. American Express maintains an automatic-teller machine for use by card members. Both agencies are open weekdays 9-6; American Express is also open Saturday 9-12.

Čedok (*see* Tourist Information, *above*) is a good source for international train and bus tickets and one of the few places in town where it is possible to use a credit card for purchasing train tickets.

Two agencies, **České Dráhy** (Na Příkopě 31, tel. 02/2422-4572) and **Wolff** (Na příkopě 22, tel. 02/2422-9957, fax 02/2422-8849), are good sources for discounted international air and bus tickets. Both are open weekdays 9-6 and Saturday 9-noon.

Arriving and Departing by Plane

Airports and Airlines

Ruzyně Airport is situated 20 kilometers (12 miles) northwest of the downtown area. The airport is small but uncongested and easily negotiated.

ČSA (the Czech national carrier) offers direct flights all over the world from Ruzyně. Major airlines with offices in Prague include **Air France** (tel. 02/2422–7164), **Alitalia** (tel. 02/2481–0079), **Austrian Airlines** (tel. 02/231–3378), **British Airways** (tel. 02/232–9020), **ČSA** (tel. 02/2421–0132), **Delta** (tel. 02/2481–2110), **KLM** (tel. 02/2422–8678), **Lufthansa** (tel. 02/2481–1007), **SAS** (tel. 02/2421–4749), and **Swissair** (tel. 02/2481–2111).

Between the Airport and Downtown

A special ČSA shuttle bus stops at all major hotels. The bus departs two to three times an hour between 7:40 AM and 9:30 PM from the bus stop directly outside the main entrance. You can buy your ticket (cost: 60 Kč.) on the bus. Regular municipal bus service (Bus 119) connects the airport and the **Dejvická** metro stop; the fare is 6 Kč. From Dejvická you can take a subway to the city center, but you must buy an additional ticket (6 Kč.). To reach Wenceslas Square, get off at the Můstek station.

Taxis offer the easiest and most convenient way of getting downtown. The trip is a straight shot down the Evropská Boulevard and takes approximately 20 minutes. The road is not usually busy, but you anticipate an additional 20 minutes during rush hour (7–9 AM and 4–7 PM). The ride costs about 300 Kč.

Arriving and Departing By Car, Train, and Bus

By Car

Prague is well served by major roads and highways from anywhere in the country. On arriving in the city, simply follow the signs to *centrum* (city center). During the day traffic can be heavy, especially on the approach to Wenceslas Square. Pay particular attention to the trams, which enjoy the right of way in every situation. Note that the immediate center of Prague, including Wenceslas Square itself, is closed to private vehicles.

By Train

International trains arrive at and depart from either the main station, **Hlavní nádraží,** about 500 yards east of Wencelas Square; or the suburban **Nádraží Holešovice,** situated about 2 kilometers (1½ miles) north of the city center. This is an unending source of confusion—always make certain you know which station your train is using. For train times, consult timetables in stations or get in line at the information office upstairs at the main station (tel. 02/2421–7654; open weekdays 6 AM–7 PM). The Čedok office at Na příkopě 18 (tel. 02/2419–7111) also provides train information and issues tickets.

Wenceslas Square is a convenient five-minute walk from the main station, or you can take the subway (line C) one stop to Muzeum. A taxi ride from the main station to the center will cost about 50 Kč. To reach the city center from Nádraží Holešovice, take the subway (line C) four stops to Muzeum.

By Bus

The Czech national bus line, **ČSAD,** operates its dense network from the sprawling main bus station on Na Florenci (metro stop: Florenc, lines B or C). For information about routes and schedules call 02/2421–1060, or consult timetables posted at the station. If the ticket windows are closed, you can usually buy a ticket from the driver.

Getting Around

To see Prague properly, there is no alternative to walking, especially since much of the city center is off limits to automobiles. And the walking couldn't be more pleasant—most of it along the beautiful bridges and cobblestone streets of the city's historic core. Before venturing out, however, be sure you have a good map.

By Subway Prague's subway system, the metro, is clean and reliable. Trains run every day from 5 AM to midnight. *Jizdenky* (tickets) cost 6 Kč. apiece and can be bought at hotels, tobacconists, or at vending machines at station entrances. Have some small coins handy for the machines. Validate the tickets yourself at machines before descending the escalators; each ticket is good for 60 minutes of uninterrupted travel. Special daily and extended passes, valid for all buses, trams, and subways, can be purchased at newsstands, train stations, and Čedok offices. A one-day pass costs 50 Kč., a two-day pass 85 Kč., a three-day pass 110 Kč., and a five-day pass 170 Kč. Trains are patrolled frequently; the fine for riding without a valid ticket is 200 Kč.

By Bus and Tram Prague's extensive bus and streetcar network allows for fast, efficient travel throughout the city. Tickets are the same as those used for the metro (cost: 6 Kč.), although you validate them at machines inside the bus or streetcar. Bus and tram tickets are valid only for a particular ride; if you change to a different tram or bus, or get on the metro, you must validate a new ticket. Signal to stop the bus by pushing the button by the doors. Tram doors open automatically at all scheduled stops. Special "night trams" run every night from around midnight to 5 AM and connect the city center with outlying areas.

By Taxi Dishonest taxi drivers are the shame of the nation. Luckily visitors do not need to rely on taxis for trips within the city center (it's usually easier to walk or take the subway). Typical scams include drivers doctoring the meter or simply failing to turn the meter on and then demanding an exorbitant sum at the end of the ride. In an honest cab, the meter will start at 10 Kč. and increase by 12 Kč. per kilometer (½-mile) or 1 Kč. per minute at rest. Most rides within town should cost no more than 80 Kč.–100 Kč. To minimize the chances of getting ripped off, avoid taxi stands in Wenceslas Square and other heavily touristed areas. The best alternative is to phone for a taxi in advance. Some reputable firms are **AAA Taxi** (tel. 02/342410), **BM Taxi** (tel. 02/256144), and **Sedop** (tel. 02/725110). Many firms have English-speaking operators.

Guided Tours

Čedok's (tel. 02/231–8949) three-hour "Historical Prague" tour (450 Kč.), offered year-round, is a combination bus-walking venture that covers all of the major sights. It departs daily at 10 AM from the Čedok office at Bilkova ulice 21 (near the InterContinental Hotel). Between May and September, "Panoramic Prague" (290 Kč.), an abbreviated version of the above tour, departs daily except Sunday at 11 AM and 4 PM from the Čedok office at Na příkopě 18. On Monday and Thursday Čedok also offers "Old Prague on Foot," a slower-paced, four-hour walking tour that departs at 9 AM from Na příkopě 18. The price is 290 Kč.

Many private firms now offer combination bus-walking tours of the city that typically last two or three hours and cost 300 Kč.–400 Kč. For more information, address inquiries to any of the dozen operators with

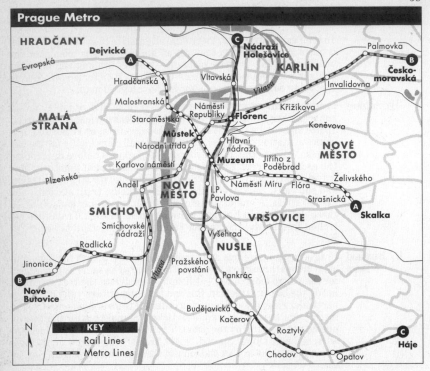

Prague Metro

booths on Staroměstské nám (near the Jan Hus monument) or Náměstí Republiky (near the Obecní Dům).

Personal Guides You can contact the Čedok office at Bilkova 6 (tel. 02/231–8949) to arrange a personalized walking tour. Times and itineraries are negotiable; prices start at around 350 Kč. per hour.

Highlights for First-Time Visitors

Charles Bridge (*see* Tour 3)
Old Town Square (*see* Tour 1)
Prague Castle (*see* Tour 5)
St. Nicholas Church in Malá Strana (*see* Tour 3)
Týn Church (*see* Tour 1)

Exploring Prague

The spine of the city is the river Vltava (also known as the Moldau), which runs through the city from south to north with a single sharp curve to the east. Prague originally comprised five independent towns, represented today by its main historical districts: **Hradčany** (Castle Area), **Malá Strana** (Lesser Town), **Staré Město** (Old Town), **Nové Město** (New Town), and **Josefov** (the Jewish Quarter).

Hradčany, the seat of Czech royalty for hundreds of years, has as its center the **Pražský Hrad** (Prague Castle), which overlooks the city from its hilltop west of the Vltava. Steps lead down from Hradčany to Malá Strana, an area dense with ornate mansions built by 17th- and 18th-century nobility.

Karlův Most (Charles Bridge) connects Malá Strana with Staré Město. Just a few blocks east of the bridge is the focal point of the Old Town, **Staroměstské náměstí** (Old Town Square). StaréMěsto is bounded by the curving Vltava and three large commercial avenues: **Revoluční** to the east, **Na příkopě** to the southeast, and **Národní třída** to the south.

Beyond lies the Nové Město; several blocks south is **Karlovo náměstí,** the city's largest square. Roughly 1 kilometer (½ mile) farther south is **Vyšehrad,** an ancient castle site high above the river.

On a promontory to the east of Wenceslas Square stretches **Vinohrady,** once the favored neighborhood of well-to-do Czechs; below Vinohrady lie the crumbling neighborhoods of **Žižkov** to the north and **Nusle** to the south. On the west banks of the Vltava south and east of Hradčany lie many older residential neighborhoods and enormous parks. About 3 kilometers (2 miles) from the center in every direction, communist-era housing projects begin their unappealing sprawl.

Tour 1: The Old Town

Numbers in the margin correspond to points of interest on the Prague (Tours 1–4) map.

❶ **Václavské náměstí** (Wenceslas Square), convenient to hotels and transportation, is an appropriate place to begin a tour of the Old Town (Staré Město). A long, gently sloping boulevard rather than a square in the usual sense, Václavské náměstí is bordered at the top (the southern end) by the Czech National Museum and at the bottom by the pedestrian shopping areas of **Národní třída** and **Na příkopě.** Visitors may recognize this spot from their television sets, for it was here that some 500,000 students and citizens gathered in the heady days of November 1989 to protest the policies of the former communist regime. The government capitulated after a week of demonstrations, without a shot fired or the loss of a single life, bringing to power the first democratic government in 40 years (under playwright-president Václav Havel). Today this peaceful transfer of power is proudly referred to as the "Velvet" or "Gentle" Revolution (*něžná revolucia*).

It was only fitting that the 1989 revolution should take place on Wenceslas Square. Throughout much of Czech history, the square has served as the focal point for popular discontent. In 1848 citizens protested Habsburg rule at the **Statue of St. Wenceslas** in front of the National Museum. In 1939 residents gathered to oppose Hitler's takeover of Bohemia and Moravia. It was here also, in 1969, that the student Jan Palach set himself on fire to protest the bloody invasion of his country by the Soviet Union and other Warsaw Pact countries in August of the previous year. The invasion ended the "Prague Spring," a cultural and political movement emphasizing free expression that was supported by Alexander Dubček, the popular leader at the time. Although Dubček never intended to dismantle communist authority completely, his political and economic reforms proved too daring for fellow comrades in the rest of Eastern Europe. In the months following the invasion, conservatives loyal to the Soviet Union were installed in all influential positions. The subsequent two decades ushered in a period of cultural stagnation. Thousands of residents left the country or went underground; many more resigned themselves to lives of minimal expectations and small pleasures.

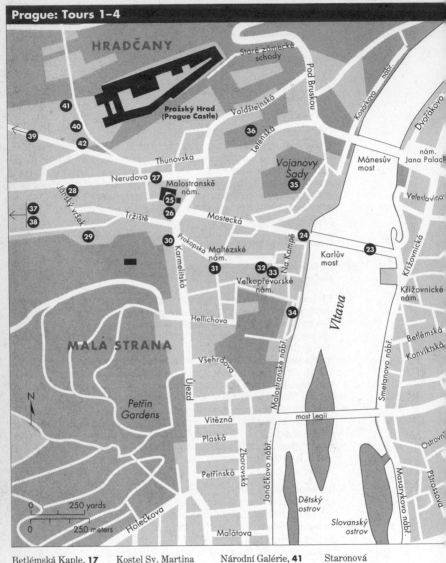

Map labels: HRADČANY, Staré zámecké schody, Pad Bruskou, Kozárkovo nábř., Dvořákovo, Pražský Hrad (Prague Castle), Valdštejnská, Letenská, Máneseův most, nám. Jana Palac, Thunovská, Vojanovy Sady, Velelavino, Nerudova, Malostranské nám., Mostecká, Jánský vršek, Tržiště, Prokopská, Maltézské nám., Karmelitská, Na Kampě, Karlův most, Karlův most, Křižovnická, Křižovnické nám., Velkopřevorské nám., Hellichova, Betlémská, Konviktská, MALÁ STRANA, Všehrdova, Vltava, Újezd, Smetanovo nábř., Petřín Gardens, Malostranské nábř., most Legii, Vítězná, Plaská, Zborovská, Ostrovn, Petřínská, Janáčkovo nábř., Masarykovo nábř., Pštrossova, Dětský ostrov, Slovanský ostrov, Holečkova, Malátova, 0 250 yards, 0 250 meters, N

Betlémská Kaple, **17**

Bretfeld Palác, **28**

Chrám Sv. Mikuláše, **26**

Clam-Gallas Palota, **15**

Hotel Europa, **4**

Hradčanské Náměstí, **40**

Jan Hus Monument, **11**

Kampa Island, **34**

Karlův Most (Charles Bridge), **23**

Kostel Sv. Jiljí, **16**

Kostel Sv. Martina ve Zdi, **18**

Kostel Sv. Mikuláše, **13**

Lennon Peace Wall, **33**

Loreto Church, **39**

Maislova Synagóga, **22**

Malá Strana Bridge Towers, **24**

Malé Náměstí, **14**

Malostranské Náměstí, **25**

Maltézské Náměstí, **31**

Náměstí Republiky, **7**

Národní Galérie, **41**

Národní Muzeum, **3**

Nerudova Ulice, **27**

Pohořelec, **37**

Schönbornský Palác, **29**

Schwarzenberg Palota, **42**

Sixt House, **8**

Staroměstská Radnice, **12**

Staroměstské Náměstí (Old Town Square), **9**

Staronová Synagóga, **20**

Starý Židovský Hřbitov, **21**

Statue of St. Wenceslas, **2**

Stavovské Divadlo, **5**

Strahovský Klášter, **38**

Týn Church, **10**

Václavské Náměstí (Wenceslas Square), **1**

Velkopřevorské Náměstí, **32**

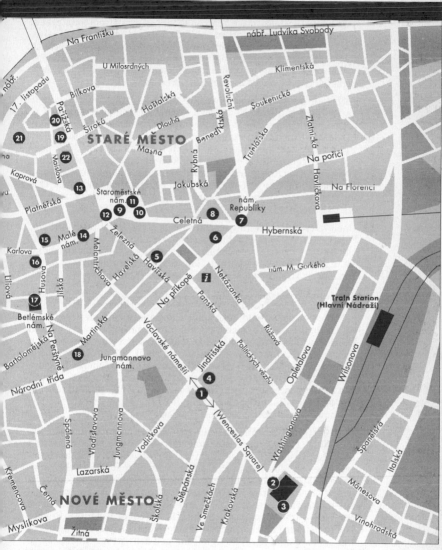

Vojanovy Sady, **35**
Vrtbovský Palác, **30**
Vysoká Synagóga, **19**
Zahrada
Valdštejnského
Paláca, **36**
Živnostenská Banka, **6**

Today Wenceslas Square comprises Prague's liveliest street scene. Don't miss the dense maze of arcades tucked away from the street in buildings that line both sides. You'll find an odd assortment of cafés, discos, ice cream parlors, and movie houses, all seemingly unfazed by the passage of time. At night the square changes character somewhat as dance music pours out from the crowded discos and leather-jacketed cronies crowd around the taxi stands.

Although Wenceslas Square was first laid out by Charles IV in 1348 as the center of the New Town (Nové Město), few buildings of architectural merit line the square today. Even the imposing structure of the **Národní Muzeum** (Czech National Museum), designed by Prague architect Josef Schulz and built between 1885 and 1890, does not really come into its own until it is bathed in nighttime lighting. During the day, the grandiose edifice seems an inappropriate venue for a musty collection of stones and bones, minerals, and coins. This museum is only for dedicated fans of the genre! *Václavské nám. 68, tel. 02/2423–0485. Admission: 20 Kč. Open Wed.–Mon. 9–5.*

❹ One eye-catching building on the square is the **Hotel Europa** at No. 25, a riot of Art Nouveau that recalls the glamorous world of turn-of-the-century Prague. Don't miss the elegant stained glass and mosaics of the café and restaurant. The terrace, serving drinks in the summer, is an excellent spot for people-watching.

To begin the approach to the Old Town proper, walk past the tall, Art Deco, Koruna complex (once an enormous fast-food joint, now an office complex) and turn onto the handsome pedestrian zone called **Na příkopě**. The name means "at the moat," harking back to the time when the street was indeed a moat separating the Old Town on the left from the New Town on the right. Today Na příkopě is prime shopping territory, its smaller boutiques considered far more elegant than the motley collection of stores on Wenceslas Square. But don't expect much real elegance here: After 40 years of communist orthodoxy in the fashion world, it will be many years before the boutiques really can match Western European standards.

Turn left onto Havířská ulice and follow this small alley to the glittering green-and-cream splendor of the newly renovated **Stavovské Divadlo** (Estates Theater). Built in the 1780s in the classical style and reopened in 1991 after years of renovation, the handsome theater was for many years a beacon of Czech-language culture in a city long dominated by German. It is probably best known as the site of the world premiere of Mozart's opera *Don Giovanni* in October 1787, with the composer himself in the conducting role. Prague audiences were quick to acknowledge Mozart's genius. The opera was an instant hit here, though it flopped nearly everywhere else in Europe. Mozart wrote most of the opera's second act in Prague at the Villa Bertramka, where he was a frequent guest (*see* Off the Beaten Track, *below*).

Return to Na příkopě, turn left, and continue to the end of the street. On weekdays between 8 AM and 5 PM, it's well worth taking a peek at the stunning interior of the **Živnostenská banka** (Merchants' Bank) at No. 20. The style, a tasteful example of 19th-century exuberance, reflected the city's growing prosperity at the time. Ignore the guards and walk up the decorated stairs to the beautiful main banking room (note, however, that taking photos is forbidden).

❼ Na příkopě ends abruptly at the **Náměstí Republiky** (Republic Square), an important New Town transportation hub (with a metro stop) but a square that has never really come together as a vital public space, perhaps because of its jarring architectural eclecticism.

Taken one by one, each building is interesting in its own right, but the ensemble is less than the sum of the parts. The severe Depression-era facade of the **Česka Národní banka** (Czech National Bank, Na příkopě 30) makes the building look more like a fortress than the nation's central bank.

Close by stands the stately **Prašná brána** (Powder Tower), its festive Gothic spires looming above the square. Construction of the tower, one of the city's 13 original gates, was begun by King Vladislav II of Jagiello in 1475. At the time, the kings of Bohemia maintained their royal residence next door (on the site of the current Obecní dům, the Municipal House), and the tower was intended to be the grandest gate of all. But Vladislav was Polish and thus heartily disliked by the rebellious Czech citizens of Prague. Nine years after he assumed power, fearing for his life, he moved the royal court across the river to Prague Castle. Work on the tower was abandoned and the half-finished structure was used to store gunpowder—hence its odd name—until the end of the 17th century. The oldest part of the tower is the base; the golden spires were not added until the end of the last century. The climb to the top affords a striking view of the Old Town and Prague Castle in the distance. *Nám. Republiky. Admission: 20 Kč. adults, 10 Kč. students. Open Apr.–Oct., daily 9–6.*

Adjacent to the dignified Powder Tower, the **Obecní dům** (Municipal House) looks decidedly decadent. The style, mature Art Nouveau, recalls the lengths the Czech middle classes went to at the turn of the century to imitate Paris, then the epitome of style and glamour. Much of the interior bears the work of the Art Nouveau master Alfons Mucha and other leading Czech artists. Mucha decorated the main Hall of the Lord Mayor upstairs. His magical frescoes depicting Czech history are considered a masterpiece of the genre. Throughout the year some of the city's best concerts are held in its beautiful Smetana Hall, on the second floor.

Time Out The **Obecni Dům café**, usually packed with tourists, serves good coffee and cake in a resplendent setting. Ignore the slow service and enjoy the view. If you prefer a subtler elegance, head around the corner to the café at **Hotel Paříž** (U Obecního domu 1), a Jugendstil jewel tucked away on a quiet street.

Walk through the arch at the base of the Powder Tower and down the formal **Celetná ulice,** the first leg of the so-called Royal Way, in years past the traditional coronation route of the Czech kings. Monarchs favored this route primarily for its stunning entry into **Staroměstské náměstí** (Old Town Square) and because the houses along Celetná were among the city's finest, providing a suitable backdrop to the coronation procession. (Most of the facades indicate that the buildings are from the 17th or 18th century, but appearances are deceiving: Many of the houses in fact have foundations dating from the 12th century or earlier.) The pink **Sixt House** at Celetná 2 sports one of the street's most handsome, if restrained, Baroque facades. The house itself dates from the 12th century—its Romanesque vaults are still visible in the wine restaurant in the basement.

9 **Staroměstské náměstí** (Old Town Square), at the end of Celetná, is dazzling (the scaffolding that obscured many of its finest buildings during recent renovations is finally down). Long the heart of the Old Town, the square grew to its present proportions when the city's original marketplace was moved away from the river in the 12th century. Its shape and appearance have changed little over the years. During the day the square takes on a festive atmosphere as musi-

cians vie for the favor of onlookers, hefty young men in medieval out-
fits mint coins, and artists display their renditions of Prague street
scenes. It's worth coming back to the square at night, as well, when
the unlit shadowy towers of the Týn Church (to your right as you enter the square) rise forebodingly over the glowing Baroque facades.
The crowds thin out, and the ghosts of the square's stormy past return.

During the 15th century the square was the focal point of conflict
between Czech Hussites and German Catholics. In 1422 the radical
Hussite preacher Jan Želivský was executed here for his part in
storming the New Town's town hall. Three Catholic consuls and
seven German citizens were thrown out of the window in the ensuing
fray—the first of Prague's many famous "defenestrations." Within
a few years, the Hussites had taken over the town, expelled the Germans, and set up their own administration.

⑩ The center of their activity was the double-spired **Týn Church**
(Kostel Panny Marie před Týnem), which rises over the square from
behind a row of patrician houses. Construction of its twin jet-black
spires, which still jar the eye, was begun by King Jiří of Poděbrad in
1461 during the heyday of the Hussites. Jiří had a gilded chalice, the
symbol of the Hussites, proudly displayed on the front gable between the two towers. Following the defeat of the Hussites by the
Catholic Habsburgs, the chalice was removed and eventually replaced by a Madonna. As a final blow, the chalice was melted down
and made into the Madonna's glimmering halo (you still can see it by
walking into the center of the square and looking up between the
spires). The entrance to Týn Church is through the arcades, under
the house at No. 604. *Celetná 5. Admission: 20 Kč. Open weekdays
9–6, Sat. 9–noon, Sun. 1–6.*

Although the exterior of Týn Church is one of the best examples of
Prague Gothic (in part the work of Peter Parler, architect of the
Charles Bridge and St. Vitus Cathedral), much of the interior, including the tall nave, was rebuilt in the Baroque style in the 17th
century. Some Gothic pieces remain, however: Look to the left of the
main altar for a beautifully preserved set of early Gothic carvings.
The main altar itself was painted by Karel Škréta, a luminary of the
Czech Baroque. Before leaving the church, look for the grave marker (tucked away to the right of the main altar) of the great Danish
astronomer Tycho de Brahe, who came to Prague as "Imperial
Mathematicus" in 1599 under Rudolf II. As a scientist, Tycho had a
place in history that is assured: Johannes Kepler (another resident
of the Prague court) used Tycho's observations to formulate his laws
of planetary motion. But it is myth that has endeared Tycho to the
hearts of Prague residents: The robust Dane, who was apparently
fond of duels, lost part of his nose in one (take a closer look at the
marker). He quickly had a wax nose fashioned for everyday use but
preferred to parade around on holidays and festive occasions sporting a bright silver one.

To the immediate left of Týn Church is **U Zvonů** (No. 13), a Baroque
structure that has been stripped down to its original Gothic elements. It occasionally hosts concerts and art exhibitions. The exhibitions change frequently, and it's worth stopping by to see what's
on.

A short walk away stands the dazzling pink-and-ocher **Palác
Kinských** (Kinský Palace), built in 1765 and considered one of
Prague's finest late-Baroque structures. With its exaggerated pink
overlay and numerous statues, the facade looks extreme when con-

trasted with the more staid Baroque elements of other nearby buildings. The palace once housed a German school (where Franz Kafka
was a student for nine misery-laden years) and presently contains
the National Gallery's graphics collection. The main exhibition room
is on the second floor; exhibits change every few months and are usu
ally worth seeing. It was from this building that communist leader
Klement Gottwald, flanked by his comrade Clementis, first addressed the crowds after seizing power in February 1948—an event
recounted in the first chapter of Milan Kundera's novel *The Book of
Laughter and Forgetting. Staroměstské nám. 12. Admission: 10 Kč.
adults, 5 Kč. children and students. Open Tues.–Sun. 10–6.*

⓫ At this end of the square, you can't help noticing the expressive **Jan
Hus monument.** Few memorials have elicited as much controversy as
this one, which was dedicated in July 1915, exactly 500 years after
Hus was burned at the stake in Konstanz, Germany. Some maintain
that the monument's Secessionist style (the inscription seems to
come right from turn-of-the-century Vienna) clashes with the Gothic and Baroque of the square. Others dispute the romantic depiction
of Hus, who appears here in flowing garb as tall and bearded. The
real Hus, historians maintain, was short and had a baby face. Still,
no one can take issue with the influence of this fiery preacher, whose
ability to transform doctrinal disputes, both literally and metaphor-
ically, into the language of the common man made him into a religious and national symbol for the Czechs.

⓬ Opposite the Týn Church is the Gothic **Staroměstská radnice** (Old
Town Hall), which gives the square its sense of importance. As you
walk toward the building from the Hus monument, look for the 27
white crosses on the ground just in front of the Town Hall. These
mark the spot where 27 Bohemian noblemen were killed by the
Habsburgs in 1621 during the dark days following the defeat of the
Czechs at the Battle of White Mountain. The grotesque spectacle,
designed to quash any further national or religious opposition, took
some five hours to complete, as the men were put to the sword or
hanged, one by one.

The Town Hall has served as the center of administration for the Old
Town since 1338, when King Johann of Luxembourg first granted
the city council the right to a permanent location. Walk around the
structure to the left and you'll see that it's actually a series of houses
jutting into the square; they were purchased over the years and suc-
cessively added to the complex. The most interesting is the **U
Minuty,** the corner building to the left of the clock tower, with its
16th-century Renaissance sgraffiti of biblical and classical motifs.

The impressive 200-foot **Town Hall tower** was first built in the 14th
century and given its current late-Gothic appearance around 1500
by the master Matyáš Rejsek. For a rare view of the Old Town and its
maze of crooked streets and alleyways, climb to the top of the tower.
The climb is not strenuous, but steep stairs at the top unfortunately
prevent the disabled from enjoying the view. Enter through the
door to the left of the tower.

As the hour approaches, join the crowds milling below the tower's
15th-century **Astronomical Clock** for a brief but spooky spectacle
taken straight from the Middle Ages. Just before the hour, look to
the upper part of the clock, where a skeleton begins by tolling a
death knell and turning an hour-glass upside down. The 12 apostles
parade momentarily, and then a cockerel flaps its wings and crows,
piercing the air as the hour finally strikes, solemnly. To the right of
the skeleton, the dreaded Turk nods his head, seemingly hinting at

another invasion like those of the 16th and 17th centuries. Immediately after the hour, guided tours in English and German (German only during winter) of the Town Hall depart inside from the main desk. However, the only notables inside are the fine Renaissance ceilings and Gothic Council Room. *Staroměstské nám. Admission to hall: 20 Kč. adults, 10 Kč. children and students; admission to tower: 10 Kč. adults, 5 Kč. children and students. Hall open daily 9–6; tower open daily 10–6.*

Time Out Staroměstské náměstí is a convenient spot for refreshments. **Tchibo,** at No. 6, has tasty sandwiches and excellent coffee, and an outdoor terrace in season.

Walk north along the edge of the small park beside the Town Hall to ⑬ reach the Baroque **Kostel svatého Mikuláše** (Church of St. Nicholas), not to be confused with the Lesser Town's St. Nicholas Church, on the other side of the river (*see* Tour 3, *below*). Though both churches were designed in the 18th century by Prague's own master of the late Baroque, Kilian Ignaz Dientzenhofer, this St. Nicholas is probably less successful than its namesake across town in capturing the style's lyric exuberance. Still, Dientzenhofer utilized the limited space to create a structure that neither dominates nor retreats from the imposing square. The interior is compact, with a beautiful but small chandelier and an enormous black organ that seems to overwhelm the rear of the church. The church often hosts afternoon concerts.

Franz Kafka's birthplace is just to the left of St. Nicholas on U radnice. A small plaque can be found on the side of the house. For years this memorial to Kafka's birth (July 3, 1883) was the only public acknowledgment of the writer's stature in world literature, reflecting the traditionally ambiguous attitude of the Czech government to his work. The Communists were always too uncomfortable with Kafka's themes of bureaucracy and alienation to sing his praises too loudly, if at all. As a German and a Jew, moreover, Kafka could easily be dismissed as standing outside of the mainstream of Czech literature. Following the 1989 revolution, however, Kafka's popularity soared, and his works are now widely available in Czech. A fascinating little museum has been set up in the house of his birth. *U radnice 5. Admission: 20 Kč. Open daily 10–7.*

⑭ Continue southwest from Old Town Square until you come to **Malé náměstí** (Small Square), a nearly perfect ensemble of facades dating from the Middle Ages. Note the Renaissance iron fountain dating from 1560 in the center of the square. The sgraffito on the house at No. 3 is not as old as it looks (1890), but here and there you can find authentic Gothic portals and Renaissance sgraffiti that betray the square's true age.

Look for tiny **Karlova ulice,** which begins in the southwest corner of Malé náměstí, and take another quick right to stay on it (watch the signs—this medieval street seems designed to confound the visitor). The character of Karlova ulice has changed in recent years to meet the growing number of tourists. Galleries and gift shops now occupy almost every storefront. But the cobblestones, narrow alleys, and crumbling gables still make it easy to imagine what life was like 400 years ago.

Turn left at the T-intersection where Karlova seems to end in front of the Středočeská Galérie and continue left down the quieter Husova třída (if you want to go on directly to Tour 3, veer to the right for the Charles Bridge and the other side of the river). Fans of unbri-

dled Baroque—the kind more common to Vienna than to Prague—
may want to pause first and inspect the exotic **Clam–Gallas palota**
(Clam-Gallas Palace) at Husova 20. You'll recognize it easily: Look
for the Titans in the doorway holding up what must be a very heavy
Baroque facade. The palace dates from 1713 and is the work of Johann Bernhard Fischer von Erlach, the famed Viennese virtuoso of
the day. Enter the building (push past the guard as if you know what
you're doing) for a glimpse of the finely carved staircase, the work of
the master himself, and of the Italian frescoes featuring Apollo that
surround it. The Gallas family was prominent during the 18th century but has long since died out. The building now houses the municipal archives and is rarely open to visitors.

Return to the T-intersection and continue down Husova. For a
glimpse of a less successful Baroque reconstruction, take a close
look at the **Kostel svatého Jiljí** (Church of St. Giles), across from No.
7, another important outpost of Czech Protestantism in the 16th
century. The exterior is powerful Gothic, including the buttresses
and a characteristic portal; the interior, surprisingly, is Baroque,
dating from the 17th century.

Continue walking along Husova třída to Na Perštýně, and turn right
at tiny Betlémská ulice. The alley opens up onto a quiet square of the
same name (Betlémské náměstí) and upon the most revered of all
Hussite churches in Prague, the **Betlémská kaple** (Bethlehem Chapel). The church's elegant simplicity is in stark contrast to the divert-
ing Gothic and Baroque of the rest of the city. The original structure
dates from the end of the 14th century, and Hus himself was a regular preacher here from 1402 until his death in 1415. After the Thirty
Years' War the church fell into the hands of the Jesuits and was finally demolished in 1786. Excavations carried out after World War I uncovered the original portal and three windows, and the entire
church was reconstructed during the 1950s. Although little remains
of the first church, some remnants of Hus's teachings can still be
read on the inside walls. *Betlémské nám. 5. Admission free. Open
Apr.–Sept., daily 9–6; Oct.–Mar., daily 9–5.*

Return to Na Perštýně and continue walking to the right. As you
near the back of the buildings of the busy **Národní třída** (National
Boulevard), turn left at Martinská ulice. At the end of the street, the
forlorn but majestic church **Kostel svatého Martina ve zdi** (St. Mar-
tin-in-the-Wall) stands like a postwar ruin. It's difficult to believe
that this forgotten church, with a NO PARKING sign blocking its main
portal, once played a major role in the development of Protestant practices. Still, it was here in 1414 that Holy Communion was first given to
the Bohemian laity with both bread and the wine, in defiance of the
Catholic custom of the time, which dictated that only bread was to be
offered to the masses, with wine reserved for the priests and clergy.
From then on, the chalice came to symbolize the Hussite movement.

Walk around the church to the left and through a little archway of
apartments onto the bustling Národní třída. To the left, a five-minute
walk away, lies Wenceslas Square and the starting point of the tour.

Time Out Turn right instead of left onto Národní třída and head to the newly
renovated **Café Slavia** (Národní třída 1, open daily 9–11), long considered one of Prague's most "literary" cafés. Enjoy the fine view of
Prague Castle while sipping a coffee.

Tour 2: The Jewish Ghetto

Leave Staroměstské Náměsti (Old Town Square) via the handsome Pařížská and head north in the direction of the river and the Hotel Inter-Continental to reach **Josefov,** the Jewish ghetto. The buildings and houses along the Pařížská date from the end of the 19th century, and their elegant facades reflect the prosperity of the Czech middle classes at the time. Here and there you can spot the influence of the Viennese Jugendstil, with its emphasis on mosaics, geometric forms, and gold inlay. The look is fresh against the busier 19th-century revival facades of most of the other structures.

The festive atmosphere, however, changes suddenly as you enter the area of the ghetto. The buildings are lower here, and older; the mood is hushed. Sadly, little of the old ghetto remains. The Jews had survived centuries of discrimination, but two unrelated events of modern times have left the ghetto little more than a collection of museums. Around 1900, city officials decided for hygienic purposes to raze the ghetto and pave over its crooked streets. Only the synagogues, the town hall, and a few other buildings survived this early attempt at urban renewal. The second event was the Holocaust. Under Nazi occupation, a staggering percentage of Prague's Jews were deported or murdered in concentration camps. And of the 35,000 Jews living in the ghetto before World War II, only about 1,200 returned to resettle the neighborhood after the war.

The treasures and artifacts of the ghetto are now the property of the **Státní židovské muzeum** (State Jewish Museum), a complex comprising the Old Jewish Cemetery and the collections of the remaining individual synagogues. The holdings are vast, thanks, ironically, to Adolf Hitler, who had planned to open a museum here documenting the life and practices of what he had hoped would be an "extinct" people. The cemetery and most of the synagogues are open to the public. Each synagogue specializes in certain artifacts,

⑲ and you can buy tickets for all the buildings at the **Vysoká synagóga** (High Synagogue), which features rich Torah mantles and silver. *Červená ulice (enter at No. 101). Tel. 02/231–0681. Admission: 20 Kč. adults, 10 Kč. students. Open Sun.–Fri. 10–12:30 and 1–6 (until 5 in winter).*

Adjacent to the High Synagogue, at Maislova 18, is the **Židovská radnice** (Jewish Town Hall), now home to the Jewish Community Center. The hall was the creation of Mordecai Maisel, an influential Jewish leader at the end of the 16th century. It was restored in the 18th century and given its clock and bell tower at that time. A second clock, with Hebrew numbers, turns to the left. The building also houses Prague's only kosher restaurant, Shalom.

⑳ The **Staronová synagóga** (Old-New Synagogue) across the street at Červená 2 is the oldest standing synagogue in Europe. Dating from the middle of the 13th century, it is also one of the most important works of early Gothic in Prague. The odd name recalls the legend that the synagogue was built on the site of an ancient Jewish temple and that stones from the temple were used to build the present structure. The synagogue has not only survived fires and the razing of the ghetto at the end of the last century but also emerged from the Nazi occupation intact and is still in active use. The oldest part of the synagogue is the entrance, with its vault supported by two pillars. The grille at the center of the hall dates from the 15th century. Note that men are required to cover their heads inside, and that during services men and women sit apart.

Continue along Červená ulice, which becomes the little street U staré ho hřbitova (At the Old Cemetery) beyond Maislova ulice. At the bend in the road lies the Jewish ghetto's most astonishing sight, the Starý židovský hřbitov (Old Jewish Cemetery). From the 14th century to 1787, all Jews living in Prague found their final resting place in this tiny, melancholy space not far from the busy city. Some 12,000 graves in all are piled atop one another in 12 layers. Walk the paths amid the gravestones. The relief symbols represent the name or profession of the deceased. The oldest marked grave belongs to the poet Avigdor Kara, who died in 1439. The best-known marker is probably that of Jehuda ben Bezalel, the famed Rabbi Loew, who is credited with having created the mythical Golem in 1573. Even today, small scraps of paper bearing wishes are stuffed into the cracks of the rabbi's tomb in the hope that he will grant them. Loew's grave lies just a few steps from the entrance, near the western wall of the cemetery.

Just to the right of the cemetery entrance is the **Obřadní síň** (Ceremony Hall), which houses a moving exhibition of drawings made by children held at the Nazi concentration camp at Terezín (Theresienstadt), in northern Bohemia. During the early years of the war the Nazis used the camp for propaganda purposes to demonstrate their "humanity" toward the Jews, and prisoners were given relative freedom to lead "normal" lives. Transports to death camps in Poland began in earnest in the final months of the war, however, and many thousands of Terezín prisoners, including many of these children, eventually perished. *U starého hřbitov. Admission to cemetery and Ceremony Hall: 20 Kč. adults, 10 Kč. children and students. Cemetery and hall open Sun.–Fri. 9–5 (until 4:30 in winter).*

Further testimony to the appalling crimes perpetrated against the Jews during World War II can be seen in the **Pinkasova synagóga** (Pinkas Synagogue), a handsome Gothic structure whose foundation dates from the 11th century. The names of 77,297 Bohemian and Moravian Jews murdered by the Nazis were inscribed in rows on the walls inside. Many of the names, sadly, were destroyed by water damage over the years. Enter the synagogue from Široká street on the other side of the cemetery. *Admission: 20 Kč. adults, 10 Kč. students. Open Sun.–Fri. 10–12:30 and 1–6 (until 5 in winter).*

Time Out U Rudolfa (Maislova 5) specializes in grilled meats, prepared before your eyes. Time your visit for off hours, however; the tiny restaurant fills up quickly. If there's no room, U Golema (Maislova 8) offers a strange mixture of Jewish, but not kosher, delicacies, including tasty Elixir Soup.

Return to Maislova ulice via U starého hřbitova, and turn right in the direction of the Old Town once again, crossing Široká ulice. Look in at the **Maislova synagóga** (Maisel Synagogue), which houses an enormous collection of silver articles of worship confiscated by the Nazis from synagogues throughout Central Europe. Here you'll find the State Jewish Museum's finest collection of Torah wrappers and mantles, silver pointers, breastplates and spice boxes, candle holders (the eight-branched Hanukkiah and the seven-branched menorah), and Levite washing sets. *Maislova 10. Admission: 20 Kč. adults, 10 Kč. students. Open Sun.–Fri. 10–12:30 and 1–6 (until 5 in winter).*

Tour 3: Charles Bridge and Malá Strana

Prague's **Malá Strana** (the so-called Lesser Quarter, or Little Town) is not for the methodical tourist. Its charm lies in the tiny lanes, the sudden blasts of bombastic architecture, and the soul-stirring views that emerge for a second before disappearing behind the sloping roofs. The area is at its best in the evening, when the softer light hides the crumbling facades and brings you into a world of glimmering beauty.

㉓ Begin the tour on the Old Town side of **Karlův most** (the Charles Bridge), which you can reach by foot in about 10 minutes from the Old Town Square. The view from the foot of the bridge is nothing short of breathtaking, encompassing the towers and domes of Malá Strana and the soaring spires of the St. Vitus Cathedral to the northwest. This heavenly vision, one of the most beautiful in Europe, changes subtly in perspective as you walk across the bridge, attended by the host of Baroque saints that decorates the bridge's peaceful Gothic stones. At night its drama is spellbinding: St. Vitus Cathedral lit in a ghostly green, the castle in monumental yellow, and the Church of St. Nicholas in a voluptuous pink, all viewed through the menacing silhouettes of the bowed statues and the Gothic towers (if you do nothing else in Prague, you must visit the Charles Bridge at night). During the day the pedestrian bridge buzzes with activity. Street musicians vie with artisans hawking jewelry, paintings, and glass for the hearts and wallets of the passing multitude. At night the crowds thin out a little, the musicians multiply, and the bridge becomes a long block party—nearly everyone brings a bottle.

When the Přemyslide princes set up residence in Prague during the 10th century, there was a ford across the Vltava at this point, a vital link along one of Europe's major trading routes. After several wooden bridges and the first stone bridge had washed away in floods, Charles IV appointed a 27-year-old German, Peter Parler, architect of St. Vitus Cathedral, to build a new structure in 1357. After 1620, following the defeat of Czech Protestants by Catholic Habsburgs at the Battle of White Mountain, the bridge and its adornment became caught up in the Catholic–Hussite (Protestant) conflict. The many Baroque statues, built by Catholics and which began to appear in the late 17th century, eventually came to symbolize the totality of the Austrian (hence Catholic) triumph. The Czech writer Milan Kundera sees the statues from this perspective: "The thousands of saints looking out from all sides, threatening you, following you, hypnotizing you, are the raging hordes of occupiers who invaded Bohemia three hundred and fifty years ago to tear the people's faith and language from their hearts."

The religious conflict is less obvious nowadays, leaving only the artistic tension between Baroque and Gothic that gives the bridge its allure. The **Old Town Bridge Tower** was where Paler began his bridge-building. The carved facades he designed for the sides of the bridge were destroyed by Swedish soldiers in 1648, at the end of the Thirty Years' War. The sculptures facing the square, however, are still intact; they depict the old gout-ridden Charles IV with his son, who later became Wenceslas IV. The climb of 138 steps is well worth the effort for the views it affords of the Old Town and, across the river, of Mala Strana and Prague Castle. *Admission: 20 Kč. adults, 10 Kč. children and students. Open Apr.–Oct., daily 9–6.*

It's worth pausing to take a closer look at some of the statues as you walk toward Malá Strana. The third on the right, a brass crucifix with Hebrew lettering in gold, was mounted on the location of a wooden cross that was destroyed in the battle with the Swedes (the golden lettering was reputedly financed by a Jew accused of defiling the cross). The eighth statue on the right, St. John of Nepomuk, is the oldest of all; it was designed by Johann Brokoff in 1683. On the left-hand side, sticking out from the bridge between the ninth and tenth statues (the latter has a wonderfully expressive vanquished Satan), stands a Roland statue. This knightly figure, bearing the coat of arms of the Old Town, was once a reminder that this part of the bridge belonged to the Old Town before Prague became a unified city in 1784. The square below is the Kampa Island, separated from the Lesser Town by an arm of the Vltava known as Čertovka (Devil's Stream) (*see below*).

In the eyes of most art historians, the most valuable statue is the twelfth, on the left. Mathias Braun's statue of St. Luitgarde depicts the blind saint kissing Christ's wounds. The most compelling grouping, however, is the second from the end on the left, a work of Ferdinand Maximilien Brokov from 1714. Here the saints are incidental; the main attraction is the Turk, his face expressing extreme boredom while guarding Christians imprisoned in the cage at his side. When the statue was erected, just 29 years after the second Turkish invasion of Vienna, it scandalized the Prague public, who smeared the statue with mud.

㉔ By now you are almost at the end of the bridge. In front of you is the striking conjunction of the two **Malá Strana Bridge Towers,** one Gothic, the other Romanesque. Together they frame the Baroque flamboyance of the St. Nicholas Church in the distance. At night this is an absolutely wondrous sight. The lower, Romanesque tower formed a part of the earlier wooden and stone bridges, its present appearance stemming from a renovation in 1591. The Gothic tower, **Mostecká věž,** was added to the bridge a few decades after its completion. If you didn't climb the tower on the Old Town side of the bridge, it's worth scrambling up the wooden stairs inside this tower for the views over the roofs of the Malá Strana and of the Old Town across the river. *Mostecká ul. Admission: 20 Kč. adults, 10 Kč. children and students. Open Apr.–Oct., daily 9–6.*

㉕ Walk under the gateway of the towers into the little uphill street called **Mostecká ulice.** You have now entered the **Malá Strana** (Lesser Quarter), established in 1257 and for years home to the merchants and craftsmen who served the royal court. Follow Mostecká ulice up to the rectangular **Malostranské náměstí** (Lesser Quarter Square), now the district's traffic hub rather than its heart. The arcaded houses on the left, dating from the 16th and 17th centuries, exhibit a mix of Baroque and Renaissance elements. The beautiful blue building at No. 10, on the far side of the square, houses one of Prague's best restaurants, U Mecenáše (*see* Dining, *below*).

㉖ On the left side of the square stands **Chrám svatého Mikuláše** (St. Nicholas Church). With its dynamic curves, this church is one of the purest and most ambitious examples of High Baroque. The celebrated architect Christoph Dientzenhofer began the Jesuit church in 1704 on the site of one of the more active Hussite churches of 15th-century Prague. Work on the building was taken over by his son Kilian Ignaz Dientzenhofer, who built the dome and presbytery; Anselmo Lurago completed the whole in 1755 by adding the bell tower. The juxtaposition of the broad, full-bodied dome with the slender bell tower is one of the many striking architectural contrasts that mark the Prague skyline. Inside, the vast pink-and-green space is impossible to take in with a single glance; every corner bristles with movement, guiding the eye first to the dramatic statues, then to the hectic frescoes, and on to the shining faux-marble pillars. Many of the statues are the work of Ignaz Platzer; they constitute his last blaze of success. When the centralizing and secularizing reforms of Joseph II toward the end of the 18th century brought an end to the flamboyant Baroque era, Platzer's workshop was forced to declare bankruptcy. *Malostranské nám. Admission: 20 Kč. adults, 10 Kč. children and students. Open daily 9–4 (until 5 or 6 in summer).*

㉗ From Malostranské náměsti, turn left onto **Nerudova ulice,** named for the 19th-century Czech journalist and poet Jan Neruda (after whom Chilean poet Pablo Neruda renamed himself). This steep little street used to be the last leg of the Royal Way, walked by the king before his coronation, and it is still the best way to get to Prague Castle (*see* Tour 5, *below*). Until Joseph II's administrative reforms in the late 18th century, house numbering was unknown in Prague. Each house bore a name, depicted on the facade, and these are particularly prominent on Nerudova ulice. House No. 6, **U červeného orla** (At the Red Eagle), proudly displays a faded painting of a red eagle. Number 12 is known as **U tří housliček** (At the Three Violins). In the early 18th century, three generations of the Edlinger violin-making family lived here. Joseph II's scheme numbered each house according to its position in Prague's separate "towns" (here, Malá Strana) rather than according to its sequence on the street. The red plates record these original house numbers; the blue ones are the numbers used in addresses today.

Time Out Nerudova ulice is filled with little restaurants and snack bars and offers something for everyone. **U zeleného čaje** at No. 19 is a fragrant little tea room, offering fruit and herbal teas as well as light salads and sweets. **U Kocoura** at No. 2 is a traditional pub that hasn't caved in to touristic niceties.

Two palaces break the unity of the burghers' houses on Nerudova ulice. Both were designed by the adventurous Baroque architect Giovanni Santini, one of the Italian builders most in demand by wealthy nobles of the early 18th century. The **Morzin Palace,** on the left at No. 5, is now the Romanian embassy. The fascinating facade, with an allegory of night and day, was created in 1713 and is the work of F. M. Brokov of Charles Bridge statue fame. Across the street at No. 20 is the **Thun-Hohenstein Palace,** now the Italian Embassy. The gateway with two enormous eagles (the emblem of the Kolovrat family, who owned the building at the time) is the work of the other great Charles Bridge statue builder, Mathias Braun. Santini himself lived at No. 14, the so-called **Valkoun House.**

㉘ While you're at this end of the street, it's worth taking a quick look at the Rococo **Bretfeld palác** (Bretfeld Palace), No. 33, on the corner of Nerudova ulice and Janský vršek. The relief of St. Nicholas on the facade is the work of Ignaz Platzer, but the building is valued more for its historical associations than for its architecture: This is where Mozart, his lyricist partner Lorenzo da Ponte, and the aging but still infamous philanderer and music lover Casanova stayed at the time of the world premiere of *Don Giovanni* in 1787. The Malá Strana recently gained a new connection with Mozart when its streets were used to represent 18th-century Vienna in the filming of Miloš Forman's *Amadeus.*

Go back down a few houses until you come to the archway at No. 13, more or less opposite the Santini **Kostel Panny Marie ustavičné pomoci u Kajetánů** (Church of Our Lady of Perpetual Help at the

Theatines). The archway, marked *Restaurace*, hides one of the many winding passageways that give the Malá Strana its enchantingly ghostly character at night. Follow the dog-leg curve downhill, past two restaurants, vine-covered walls, and some broken-down houses. The alleyway really comes into its own only in the dark, the dim lighting hiding the grime and highlighting the mystery.

You emerge from the passageway at the top of **Tržiště ulice**, opposite the **Schönbornský palác** (Schönborn Palace). Franz Kafka had an apartment in this building from March through August 1917, after moving out from Zlatá ulička (Golden Lane) (*see* Tour 5). The U.S. Embassy now occupies this prime location. If you look through the gates, you can see the beautiful formal gardens rising up to the Petřin hill; they are unfortunately not open to the public.

Follow Tržiště downhill until you come to the main road, **Karmelitská ulice**. Here on your right is No. 25, an unobtrusive door hiding the entranceway to the intimate **Vrtbovský palác** (Vrtba Palace and Gardens). Walk through the courtyard between the two Renaissance houses, the one to the left built in 1575, the one to the right in 1591. The owner of the latter house was one of the 27 Bohemian nobles executed by the Habsburgs in 1621 (*see* Tour 1). The house was given as confiscated property to Count Sezima of Vrtba, who bought the neighboring property and turned the buildings into a late-Renaissance palace. The *Vrtbovská zahrada* (Vrtba Gardens) boasts one of the best views over the Malá Strana rooftops and is a fascinating oasis from the tourist beat. Unfortunately, the gardens are perpetually closed for renovation, even though there is no sign of work in progress. The powerful stone figure of Atlas that caps the entranceway dates from 1720 and is the work of Mathias Braun. *Karmelitská ul. 25.*

Continue walking along Karmelitská until you reach the comfortably ramshackle **Kostel Panny Marie vítězné** (Church of Our Lady of Victories), the unlikely home of one of Prague's best-known religious artifacts, the Pražské Jezuliatko (Infant Jesus of Prague). Originally brought to Prague from Spain in the 16th century, this tiny porcelain doll (now bathed in neon lighting straight out of Las Vegas) is renowned worldwide for showering miracles on anyone willing to kneel before it and pray. Nuns from a nearby convent arrive at dawn each day to change the infant's clothes; pieces of the doll's extensive wardrobe have been sent by believers from around the world. *Karmelitská 9a. Admission free.*

Cross over Karmelitská and walk down tiny **Prokopská ulice**, opposite the Vrtba Palace. On the left is the former Baroque **Church of St. Procopius**, now oddly converted into an apartment block. At the end of the lane you'll emerge onto the peaceful **Maltézské náměstí** (Maltese Square), named for the Knights of Malta. In the middle of the square is a sculpture depicting John the Baptist. This work, by Ferdinand Brokov, was erected in 1715 to commemorate the end of a plague. The relief on the far side shows Salome engrossed in her dance of the seven veils while John is being decapitated. There are two intricately decorated palaces on this square, to the right the Rococo Turba Palace, now the Japanese Embassy, and at the bottom, the Nostitz Palace, the Dutch Embassy.

Follow Lázeňská street to the **Velkopřevorské náměstí** (Grand Priory Square). The palace fronting the square is considered one of the finest Baroque buildings in the Malá Strana, though it is now part of the Maltese Embassy and no longer open to the public. Opposite the palace is the flamboyant orange-and-white stucco facade of the Buquoy Palace, built in 1719 by Giovanni Santini and the present home of the French Embassy. From the street you can glimpse an enormous twinkling chandelier through the window, but this is about all you'll get to see of the elegant interior.

Across from this pompous display of Baroque finery stands the **Lennon Peace Wall,** a peculiar monument to the passive rebellion of Czech youth against the strictures of the former communist regime. Under the Communists, Western rock music was officially discouraged, and students adopted the former Beatle as a symbol of resistance. Paintings of John Lennon and lyrics from his songs in Czech and English began to appear on the wall sometime in the 1980s. Even today, long after the Communists have departed, new graffiti still turns up regularly. It's not clear how long the police or the owners of the wall will continue to tolerate the massive amounts of writing (which has started to spread to other walls around the neighborhood), but the volume of writing suggests that the Lennon myth continues to endure.

At the lower end of the square, a tiny bridge takes you across the Čertovka tributary to **Kampa Island.** The name Čertovka translates as Devil's Stream and reputedly refers to a cranky old lady who once lived on Maltese Square (given the river's present filthy state, however, the name is ironically appropriate). A right turn around the corner brings you to the foot of **Kampa Gardens,** whose unusually well-kept lawns are one of the few places in Prague where sitting on the grass is openly tolerated. If it's a warm day, spread out a blanket and bask for a while in the sunshine. The row of benches that line the river to the left is also a popular spot from which to contemplate the city. At night this stretch along the river is especially romantic.

Make your way north toward the Charles Bridge by following either Na Kampě or the network of small streets running parallel to the river. Walk underneath the Charles Bridge and onto the street named U lužického semináře. This area is known as the Venice of Prague. The house at No. 1 is the inn U tří Pštrosů (The Three Ostriches), one of Prague's oldest and most charming hotels. The original building stems from the 16th century, when one of the early owners was a supplier of ostrich feathers to the royal court. The top floors and curlicue gables were early Baroque additions from the 17th century. The inn was the site of the first coffeehouse in Prague, opened by the Armenian Deodat Damajian in 1714.

Time Out At the corner of Na Kampě, right next to the arches of the Charles Bridge, the small stand-up café **Bistro Bruncvík** (No. 7) serves hot wine and coffee in winter and cold drinks in summer. Its slices of pizza also are satisfying.

Continue along this Old World street, past a small square, until you reach a gate that marks the entrance to **Vojanovy sady,** once the gardens of the Monastery of the Discalced Carmelites, later taken over by the Order of the English Virgins and now part of the Ministry of Finance (entrance on Letenská). With its weeping willows, fruit trees, and benches, the park is another peaceful haven in summer. Exhibitions of modern sculptures are often held here, contrasting sharply with the two Baroque chapels and the graceful Ignaz Platzer statue of John of Nepomuk standing on a fish at the entrance. The park is surrounded by the high walls of the old monastery and new Ministry of Finance buildings, with only an occasional glimpse of a tower or spire to remind you that you're in Prague. *Open daily 8–5 (until 7 in summer).*

Continue north along U lužického semináře, bearing left along the main road briefly until the intersection with **Letenská ulice,** which veers off to the left. If you've had enough sightseeing, you can easily return to the Old Town via the metro from here (Malostranská station).

🖲 Otherwise, even though it is open only during summer, the **Zahrada Valdštejnského paláca** (Wallenstein Gardens) merit a short visit. Albrecht von Wallenstein, onetime owner of the house and gardens, began a meteoric military career in 1624 when the Austrian emperor Ferdinand II retained him to save the empire from the Swedes and Protestants during the Thirty Years' War. Wallenstein, wealthy by marriage, offered to raise 20,000 men at his own cost and lead them personally. Ferdinand II accepted and showered Wallenstein with confiscated land and titles. Wallenstein's first acquisition was this enormous area, where in 1623, having knocked down 23 houses, a brick factory, and three gardens, he began to build his magnificent palace (*Valdštejnský palác,* now government buildings closed to the public), with its idiosyncratic high-walled gardens. Walking around the formal paths, you'll come across numerous statues, an unusual fountain with a woman spouting water from her breasts, and a lava-stone grotto along the wall. *Off Letenská ul. Admission free. Open May 1–Sept. 30, daily 9–7.*

From here one option is to walk straight back down Letenská ulice to the Malostranská metro station. A more attractive route would take you up Letenská (past the U svatého Tomáše pub, where you can get wonderful dark beer), right on Tomášská ulice into Valdštejnské náměstí and down the exquisitely Baroque Valdštejnská ulice, ending up back at the Malostranské station, near the intersection with Pod Brouskou.

Tour 4: The Castle District

To the west of Prague Castle is the residential **Hradčany** (Castle District), the town that during the early 14th century emerged out of a collection of monasteries and churches. The concentration of history packed into one small area makes Prague Castle and the Castle District challenging objects for visitors not versed in the ups and downs of Bohemian kings, religious uprisings, wars, and oppression. The picturesque area surrounding Prague Castle, with its breathtaking vistas of the Old Town and Malá Strana, is ideal for just wandering; but the castle itself, with its convoluted history and architecture, is difficult to appreciate fully without investing a little more time, which is why we cover the castle on a separate tour (*see* Tour 5, *below*).

Our tour of the Castle District begins on Nerudova ulice, which runs east–west a few hundred yards south of Prague Castle. At the western foot of the street, look for a flight of stone steps guarded by two saintly statues. The stairs lead up to Loretánská ulice, affording panoramic views of St. Nicholas Church and Malá Strana. At the top of the steps, turn left and walk a couple hundred yards until you
🖲 come to a dusty elongated square named **Pohořelec** (Scene of Fire), the site of tragic fires in 1420, 1541, and 1741.

Time Out Busy Pohořelec Square is a good place to grab a quick bite before tackling the castle. **Sate Grill** at No. 3 (open daily 11–8) offers a very passable Czech interpretation of Indonesian cooking in a stand-up, fast-food setting. At No. 11, **Caffe Calafuria** is an agreeable spot for coffee and a pastry.

Go through the inconspicuous gateway at No. 8 and up the steps, and **38** you'll find yourself in the courtyard of the **Strahovský klášter** (Strahov Monastery). Founded by the Premonstratensian order in 1140, the monastery remained in their hands until 1952, when the Communists abolished all religious orders and turned the entire complex into the **Památník národního písemnictví** (Museum of National Literature). The major building of interest is the **Strahov Library,** with its collection of early Czech manuscripts, the 10th-century Strahov New Testament, and the collected works of famed Danish astronomer Tycho de Brahe. Also of note is the late-18th-century **Philosophical Hall.** Engulfing its ceilings is a startling sky-blue fresco completed by the Austrian painter Franz Anton Maulbertsch in just six months. The fresco depicts an unusual cast of characters, including Socrates' nagging wife Xanthippe, Greek astronomer Thales with his trusty telescope, and a collection of Greek philosophers mingling with Descartes, Diderot, and Voltaire. *Strahovské nádvoří 132. Admission: 20 Kč. adults, 10 Kč. children and students. Open daily 9–noon and 1–5.*

Retrace your steps to Loretánské náměstí, which is flanked by the **39** feminine curves of the Baroque **Loreto Church.** The church's seductive lines were a conscious move on the part of Counter-Reformation Jesuits in the 17th century who wanted to build up the cult of Mary and attract the largely Protestant Bohemians back to the church. According to legend, angels had carried Mary's house in Nazareth and dropped it in a patch of laurel trees in Ancona, Italy; known as *Loreto* (from the Latin for laurel), it immediately became a center of pilgrimage. The Prague Loreto was one of many re-creations of this scene across Europe, and it worked: Pilgrims came in droves. The graceful facade, with its voluptuous tower, was built in 1720 by Kilian Ignaz Dientzenhofer, the architect of the two St. Nicholas churches in Prague. Most spectacular of all is a small exhibition upstairs displaying the religious treasures presented to Mary in thanks for various services, including a monstrance studded with 6,500 diamonds. *Loretánské nám. 7, tel. 02/536–228. Admission: 30 Kč. adults, 5 Kč. children and students. Open Tues.–Sun. 9–12:15 and 1–4:30.*

Across the road, the 29 half-pillars of the **Černínský palác** (Chernin Palace) now mask the Czech Ministry of Foreign Affairs. During World War II this ungainly palace was the seat of the occupying German government. At the bottom of Loretánské náměstí, a little lane trails to the left into the area known as **Nový Svět**; the name means "new world," though the district is as Old World as they come. Turn right onto the street Nový Svět. This picturesque winding little alley, with facades from the 17th and 18th centuries, once housed Prague's poorest residents; now many of the homes are used as artists' studios. The last house on the street, No. 1, was the home of the Danish-born astronomer Tycho de Brahe. Living so close to the Loreto, so the story goes, Tycho was constantly disturbed during his nightly stargazing by the church bells. He ended up complaining to his patron, Emperor Rudolf II, who instructed the Capuchin monks to finish their services before the first star appeared in the sky.

Continue around the corner, where you get a tantalizing view of the cathedral through the trees. Walk past the Austrian Embassy to Kanovnická ulice, a winding street lined with the dignified but melancholy **Kostel svatého Jana Nepomuckého** (Church of St. John Nepomuk). At the top of the street, on the left, the rounded, Renaissance, corner house **Martinický palác** (Martinic Palace) catches the eye with its detailed sgraffito drawings.

40 Martinic Palace opens onto **Hradčanské náměstí** (Hradčany Square). With its fabulous mixture of Baroque and Renaissance housing, topped by the castle itself, the square featured prominently (ironically, disguised as Vienna) in the film *Amadeus*, directed by the exiled Czech director Miloš Forman. The house at No. 7 was the set for Mozart's residence, where the composer was haunted by the masked figure he thought was his father. Forman used the flamboyant Rococo **Arcibiskupský palác** (Archbishop's Palace), at the top of the square on the left, as the Viennese archbishop's palace. The plush interior, shown off in the film, is open to the public only on Maudy Thursday.

41 To the left of the Archbishop's Palace is an alleyway leading down to the **Národní galérie** (National Gallery), housed in the 18th-century Šternberský palác (Sternberg Palace). You'll need at least an hour to view the palace's impressive art collection—one collection in Prague you should not miss. On the first floor there's an exhibition of icons and other religious art from the 3rd through the 14th centuries. Up a second flight of steps is an entire room full of Cranachs and an assortment of paintings from Holbein, Dürer, Brueghel, Van Dyck, Canaletto, and Rubens, not to mention works by modern masters like Picasso, Matisse, Chagall, and Kokoschka. *Hradčanské nám. 15, tel. 02/352441 or 02/534457. Admission: 40 Kč. adults, 10 Kč. children and students. Open Tues.–Sun. 10–6.*

42 Across the square, the handsome sgraffito sweep of **Schwarzenberg palota** (Schwarzenberg Palace) beckons; this is the building you saw from the back side at the beginning of the tour. The palace was built for the Lobkowitz family between 1545 and 1563; today it houses the **Vojenské muzeum** (Military Museum), one of the largest of its kind in Europe. Of more general interest are the jousting tournaments held in the courtyard in summer. *Hradčanské nám. 2. Admission: 20 Kč. adults, 10 Kč. children and students. Open May 1–Sept. 30, Tues.–Sun. 9–4:30.*

Tour 5: Prague Castle

Numbers in the margin correspond to points of interest on the Tour 5: Prague Castle (Pražský hrad) map.

Despite its monolithic presence, **Pražský Hrad** (Prague Castle) is a collection of buildings dating from the 10th to the 20th century, all linked by internal courtyards. The most important structures are St. Vitus Cathedral, clearly visible soaring above the castle walls, and the Royal Palace, the official residence of kings and presidents and still the center of political power in the Czech Republic.

The main entrance to Prague Castle from Hradčanské náměstí is a little disappointing. Going through the wrought-iron gate, guarded at ground level by pristine Czech soldiers and from above by the ferocious *Battling Titans* (a copy of Ignaz Platzer's original 18th century statues), you'll enter the **První nádvoří** (First Courtyard), built **43** on the site of old moats and gates that once separated the castle from the surrounding buildings and thus protect the vulnerable western flank. This courtyard is one of the more recent additions to the castle, commissioned by the Habsburg empress Maria Theresa and designed by her court architect Nicolò Pacassi during the 1760s. Today

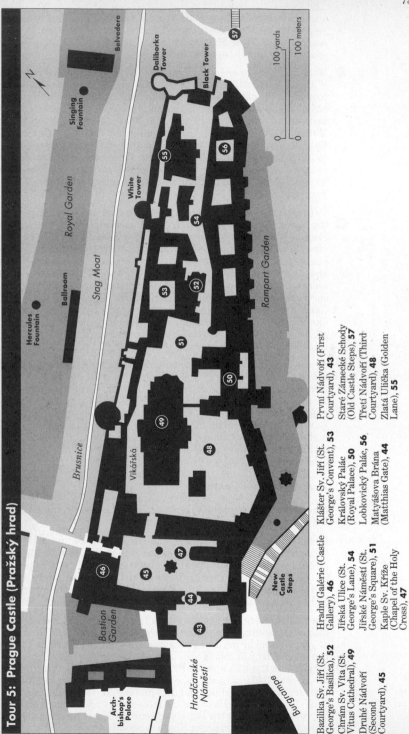

Tour 5: Prague Castle (Pražský hrad)

Belvedere

Daliborka Tower

Black Tower

57

56

Singing Fountain

Royal Garden

55

White Tower

Ballroom

Stag Moat

54

Hercules Fountain

53

52

Brusnice

51

Rampart Garden

50

Vikářská

49

48

47

46

45

44

43

New Castle Steps

Bastion Garden

Arch-bishop's Palace

Hradčanské Náměstí

Burggrampe

0   100 yards

0   100 meters

N

Bazilika Sv. Jiří (St. George's Basilica), **52**

Chrám Sv. Víta (St. Vitus Cathedral), **49**

Druhé Nádvoří (Second Courtyard), **45**

Hradní Galérie (Castle Gallery), **46**

Jiřská Ulice (St. George's Lane), **54**

Jiřské Náměstí (St. George's Square), **51**

Kaple Sv. Kříže (Chapel of the Holy Cross), **47**

Klášter Sv. Jiří (St. George's Convent), **53**

Královský Palác (Royal Palace), **50**

Lobkovický Palác, **56**

Matyášova Brána (Matthias Gate), **44**

První Nádvoří (First Courtyard), **43**

Staré Zámecké Schody (Old Castle Steps), **57**

Třetí Nádvoří (Third Courtyard), **48**

Zlatá Ulička (Golden Lane), **55**

it forms part of the presidential office complex. Pacassi's reconstruction was intended to unify the eclectic collection of buildings that made up the castle. From a distance, the effect is monumental. As you move farther into the castle, large parts appear to be relatively new, while in reality they cover splendid Gothic and Romanesque interiors.

44 It is worth looking closely at **Matyášova brána** (Matthias Gate) before going through to the next courtyard. Built in 1614, the stone gate once stood alone in front of the moats and bridges that surrounded the castle. Under the Habsburgs, the gate survived by being grafted as a relief onto the palace building. As you go through the gate, notice the ceremonial white-marble entrance halls on either side. These lead up to President Václav Havel's reception rooms, which are not open to the public.

45 The **Druhé nádvoří** (Second Courtyard) was the major victim of Pacassi's attempts at imparting classical grandeur to the castle. Except for the view of the spires of St. Vitus Cathedral towering above the palace, there's little for the eye to feast upon here. Built during the late-16th and early 17th centuries, this courtyard was part of an even earlier reconstruction program commissioned by Rudolf II, under whom Prague enjoyed a period of unparalleled cultural development. Once the Prague court was established, the emperor gathered around him some of the worlds's best craftsmen, artists, and scientists, including the brilliant astronomers Johannes Kepler and Tycho de Brahe.

Rudolf also amassed a large collection of art, surveying instruments, and coins. The bulk of the collection was looted by the Swedes and Habsburgs during the Thirty Years' War or auctioned off during the 18th century, but a small part of the collection was rediscovered in unused castle rooms during the 1960s and is now on **46** display in the **Hradní galérie** (Castle Gallery), on the left side of the Second Courtyard. Apart from works by such world-famous artists as Titian, Rubens, and Tintoretto, look for the rarer works of Rudolf's court painters Hans von Aachen and Bartolomeo Spranger, and of the Bohemian Baroque painters Jan Kupecký and Petr Brandl. The passageway at the gallery entrance is the northern entrance to the castle and leads out over a luxurious ravine known as the **Jeleni příkop** (Stag Moat). *Admission: 10 Kč. adults, 5 Kč. children and students. Open Tues.–Sun. 10–6 (until 5:30 in winter).*

The Second Courtyard also houses the religious reliquary of Charles **47** IV inside the **Kaple svatého Kříže** (Chapel of the Holy Cross). Displays include Gothic silver busts of the major Bohemian patron saints and a collection of bones and vestments that supposedly belonged to various saints. *Admission: 10 Kč. adults, 5 Kč. children and students. Open Tues.–Sun. 9–4 (until 5 in summer).*

48 Through the passageway on the far wall you'll come to the **Třetí nádvoří** (Third Courtyard). As you enter, the graceful soaring tow- **49** ers of **Chrám svatého Víta** (St. Vitus Cathedral) command your attention and admiration. The Gothic cathedral, among the most beautiful in Europe, has a long and complicated history, beginning during the 10th century and continuing to its completion in 1929. If you want to hear more about the ins and outs, English-speaking guided tours of the cathedral and the Royal Palace (*see below*) can be arranged at the Information Office around the left side of the cathedral, past the Vikářka restaurant.

Once you enter the cathedral, pause to take in the vast but delicate beauty of the Gothic interior, glowing in the colorful light that filters through the startlingly brilliant stained-glass windows. This back half, including the western facade and the two towers you can see from outside, was not completed until 1929, following the initiative of the Union for the Completion of the Cathedral set up in the last days of the 19th century. Don't let the neo-Gothic delusion keep you from examining this new section. The six stained-glass windows to your left and right and the large rose window behind are modern masterpieces. Take a good look at the third window up on the left. The familiar Art Nouveau flamboyance, depicting the blessing of the 9th-century St. Cyril and St. Methodius (missionaries to the Slavs and creators of the Cyrillic alphabet), is the work of the Czech father of the style, Alfons Mucha. He achieved the subtle coloring by painting rather than staining the glass.

If you walk a little farther, just past the entrance to your right, you will find the exquisitely ornate **Chapel of St. Wenceslas.** This square chapel, with a 14th-century tomb holding the saint's remains, is the ancient heart of the cathedral. Wenceslas (the "good king" of Christmas-carol fame) was a determined Christian in an era of widespread paganism. In 925, as prince of Bohemia, he founded a rotunda church dedicated to St. Vitus on this site. But the prince's brother, Boleslav, was impatient to take power and ambushed Wenceslas four years later near a church north of Prague. Wenceslas was originally buried in that church, but his grave produced so many miracles that he rapidly became a symbol of piety for the common people, something that greatly irritated the new Prince Boleslav. In 931 Boleslav was finally forced to honor his brother by reburying the body in the St. Vitus Rotunda. Shortly after that, Wenceslas was canonized.

The cathedral's rotunda was replaced by a Romanesque basilica during the late 11th century. Work was begun on the existing building in 1344 on the initiative of the man who was later to become Charles IV. For the first few years the chief architect was the Frenchman Mathias d'Arras, but after his death, in 1352, the work was continued by the 22-year-old German architect Peter Parler, who went on to build the Charles Bridge and many other Prague treasures.

The small door in the back of the chapel leads to the **Crown Chamber,** the repository of the Bohemian crown jewels. It remains locked with seven keys held by seven different people and is definitely not open to the public.

A little beyond the Wenceslas Chapel on the same side, a small cash desk marks the entrance to the **underground crypt** (admission: 5 Kč.), interesting primarily for the information it provides about the cathedral's history. As you descend the stairs, on the right you'll see parts of the old Romanesque basilica. A little farther, in a niche to the left, are parts of the foundations of the rotunda. Moving around into the second room, you'll find a rather eclectic group of royal remains ensconced in new sarcophagi dating from the 1930s. In the center is Charles IV, who died in 1378. Rudolf II, patron of Renaissance Prague, is entombed at the rear. To his right is Maria Amalia, the only child of Maria Theresa to reside in Prague. Ascending the wooden steps back into the cathedral, you'll come to the white marble **Royal Mausoleum,** atop which lie stone statues of the first two Habsburg kings to rule in Bohemia, Ferdinand I and Maximilian II.

The cathedral's **Royal Oratory** was used by the kings and their families when attending mass. Built in 1493, the work is a perfect example of the late-Gothic, laced on the outside with a stone network of gnarled branches very similar in pattern to the ceiling vaulting in the Royal Palace (*see below*). The oratory is connected to the palace by an elevated covered walkway, which you can see from outside.

From here you can't fail to catch sight of the ornate silver **sarcophagus of St. John of Nepomuk,** designed by the famous Viennese architect Fischer von Erlach. According to legend, when Nepomuk's body was exhumed in 1721 to be reinterred, the tongue was found to be still intact and pumping with blood. These strange tales sadly served a highly political purpose. The Catholic church and the Habsburgs were seeking a new folk hero to replace the protestant Jan Hus, whom they despised. The late Father Nepomuk was sainted and reburied a few years later with great ceremony in the 3,700-pound silver tomb, replete with angels and cherubim; the tongue was enshrined in its own reliquary.

The chapels around the back of the cathedral, the work of the original architect, Mathias d'Arras, are unfortunately closed to the public. Opposite the wooden relief, depicting the looting of the cathedral by Protestants in 1619, is the **Wallenstein Chapel.** Since the last century, it has housed the Gothic tombstones of its two architects, Mathias d'Arras and Peter Parler, who died in 1352 and 1399, respectively. If you look up to the balcony you can just make out the busts of these two men, designed by Parler's workshop. The other busts around the triforium depict various Czech kings.

The Hussite wars in the 15th century put an end to the first phase of the cathedral's construction. During the short era of illusory peace before the Thirty Years' War, lack of money laid to rest any idea of finishing the building, and the cathedral was closed by a wall built across from the Wenceslas Chapel. Not until the 20th century was the western side of the cathedral, with its two towers, completed according to Parler's original plans. *St. Vitus Cathedral. Admission free. Open May–Sept., Tues.–Sun. 9–5; Oct.–Apr., Tues.–Sun. 9–4.*

The contrast between the cool, dark interior of the cathedral and the brightly colored Pacassi facades of the Third Courtyard is startling. The clean lines of the courtyard are Plečnik's work from the 1930s, but the modern look is a deception. Plečnik's paving was intended to cover an underground world of wooden houses, streets, and walls dating from the 9th through 12th century that was rediscovered when the cathedral was completed. Since these are not open to the public, we are left with the modern structure (supplemented recently by an exchange office). Plečnik did add a few eclectic features to catch the eye: a granite obelisk to commemorate the fallen of the First World War, a black marble pedestal for the Gothic statue of St. George (the original is in the museum), and the peculiar golden ball topping the eagle fountain that unobtrusively marks the entrance to the **Královský palác** (Royal Palace). There are two main points of interest inside the externally nondescript palace. The first is the **Vladislavský sál** (Vladislav Hall), the largest secular Gothic interior space in Central Europe. The enormous hall was completed in 1493 by Benedict Ried, who was to late-Bohemian Gothic what Peter Parler was to the earlier version. The room imparts a sense of space and light, softened by the sensuous lines of the vaulted ceilings and brought to a dignified close by the simple oblong form of the early Renaissance windows, a style that was just beginning to make inroads in Central Europe. In its heyday, the hall was the site of jousting tournaments, festive markets, banquets, and coronations. In more recent times, it has been used to inaugurate presidents, from the Communist Klement Gottwald in 1948 to Václav Havel in 1990.

From the front of the hall, turn right into the rooms of the **Česká kancelář** (Bohemian Chancellery). This wing was built by the same Benedict Ried only 10 years after the hall was completed, but it shows a much stronger Renaissance influence. Pass through the Renaissance portal into the last chamber of the Chancellery. This room was the site of the Second Prague Defenestration in 1618, an event that marked the beginning of the Bohemian rebellion and, ultimately, of the Thirty Years' War. This peculiarly Bohemian method of expressing protest (throwing someone out of a window) had first been used in 1419 in the New Town Hall, an event that led to the Hussite wars. Two hundred years later the same conflict was reexpressed in terms of Habsburg-backed Catholics versus Bohemian Protestants. Rudolf II had reached an uneasy agreement with the Bohemian nobles, allowing them religious freedom in exchange for financial support. But his successor, Ferdinand II, was a rabid opponent of Protestantism and disregarded Rudolf's tolerant "Letter of Majesty." Enraged, the Protestant nobles stormed the castle and Chancellery and threw two Catholic officials and their secretary, for good measure, out of the window. Legend has it that they landed on a mound of horse dung and escaped unharmed, an event that the Jesuits interpreted as a miracle. The square window in question is on the left as you enter the room.

The exit to the **Palace Courtyard** is halfway down the Vladislav Hall on the left. Before leaving, you might want to peek into some of the other rooms. At the back of the hall, a staircase leads up to a gallery of the **All Saints' Chapel.** Little remains of Peter Parler's original work, but the church contains some fine works of art. The large room to the left of the staircase is the **Stará sněmovna** (Council Chamber), where the Bohemian nobles met with the king in a kind of prototype parliament. Portraits of the Habsburg rulers line the walls. As you leave the palace, be sure to notice the gradually descending steps. This is the **Riders' Staircase** to the left of the Council Chamber; this was the entranceway for knights who came for the jousting tournaments. *Royal Palace, tel. 02/2101. Admission: 10 Kč. adults, 5 Kč. children and students. Open Tues.–Sun. 9–5 (until 4 in winter).*

⑤ The exit from the Royal Palace will bring you out onto **Jiřské náměstí**
⑤ (St. George's Square); at its east end stands the Romanesque
Bazilika svatého Jiří (St. George's Basilica). This church was originally built during the 10th century by Prince Vratislav I, the father of Prince (and St.) Wenceslas. It was dedicated to St. George (of dragon fame), who, it was believed, would be more agreeable to the still largely pagan people. The outside was remodeled during early Baroque times, although the striking rusty-red color is in keeping with the look of the original, 10th-century structure. The interior, however, following substantial renovation, looks more or less as it did in the 12th century and is the best-preserved Romanesque relic in the country. The effect is at once barnlike and peaceful, the warm golden yellow of the stone walls and the small triplet arched windows exuding a sense of enduring harmony. The house-shaped, painted tomb at the front of the church holds the remains of the founder, Vratislav I. Up the steps, in a chapel to the right, is the tomb Parler designed for St. Ludmila, the grandmother of St. Wenceslas. *Tel. 02/2101. Admission: 10 Kč. adults, 5 Kč. children and students. Open Tues.–Sun. 9–5 (until 4 in winter).*

⑤ Next to the basilica on the square is the former **Klášter svatého Jiří** (St. George's Convent), which now houses the Old Bohemian Art Collection of the **Czech National Gallery.** The museum runs through the history of Czech art from the early Middle Ages, with exhibits that include religious statues, icons, and triptychs, as well as the rather more secular themes of the Mannerist school and the voluptuous work of the court painters of Rudolf II. *Tel. 02/535240 or 02/ 535246. Admission: 40 Kč. adults, 10 Kč. children and students. Open Tues.–Sun. 9–5:30.*

54
55 Walk down **Jiřská ulice** (St. George's Lane) until you come to a street leading to the left. At the top is **Zlatá ulička** (Golden Lane), an enchanting collection of tiny, ancient, brightly colored houses with long, sloping roofs, crouching under the fortification wall and looking remarkably like a Disney set for *Snow White and the Seven Dwarfs*. Legend has it that these were the lodgings of the international group of alchemists whom Rudolf II brought to the court to produce gold. The truth is a little less romantic: The houses were built during the 16th century for the castle guards, who supplemented their income by practicing various crafts outside the jurisdiction of the powerful guilds. By the early 20th century, Golden Lane had become the home of poor artists and writers. Franz Kafka, who lived at No. 22 in 1916 and 1917, described the house on first sight as "so small, so dirty, impossible to live in and lacking everything necessary." But he soon came to love the place. As he wrote to his fiancée: "Life here is something special . . . to close out the world not just by shutting the door to a room or apartment but to the whole house, to step out into the snow of the silent lane." The lane now houses tiny stores selling books, music, and crafts.

56 Return to Jiřská ulice and continue on down to **Lobkovický palác** (Lobkovitz Palace). From the beginning of the 17th century until the 1940s, this building was the residence of the powerful Catholic Lobkovitz family. It was to this house that the two defenestrated officials escaped after landing on the dung hill in 1618. During the 1970s the building was restored to its early Baroque appearance and now houses the permanent exhibition "Monuments of the Czech National Past." If you want to get a chronological understanding of Czech history from the beginnings of the Great Moravian Empire in the 9th century to the Czech national uprising in 1848, this is your chance. Copies of the crown jewels are on display here; but it is the rich collection of illuminated Bibles, old musical instruments, coins, weapons, royal decrees, paintings, and statues that makes the museum well worth visiting. Detailed information on the exhibits is available in English. *Admission: 10 Kč. adults, 5 Kč. children and students. Open Tues.–Sun. 9–5 (until 4 in winter).*

Turn right out of the Lobkovitz Palace and leave the castle grounds through the east gate. Take a look over the bastion on your right for one last great view of the city. From here, descend the romantic,
57 vine-draped **Staré zámecké schody** (Old Castle Steps), which come out just above the Malostranská metro station. A direct subway line runs from here to Wenceslas Square (Můstek station).

What to See and Do with Children

Prague's small but delightful **Zoologická zahrada** (zoo) is located north of the city in Troja, under the shadow of the Troja Castle. Take the metro line C to Nádraží Holešovice and change to Bus 112. *Admission: 30 Kč. adults, 10 Kč. children. Open May, daily 7–6; June–Sept., daily 7–7; Oct.–Apr., daily 7–3.*

An hour or two of **rowing on the Vltava** is a great way to spend a sunny afternoon in Prague. Boats are available for rent in season (May–September) on the island across from the embankment near the Národní Divadlo (National Theater) for 40 Kč. an hour.

One of the unique delights of Prague for children and adults alike is **feeding the swans** along the banks of the Vltava River, and one spot in Malá Strana is especially popular. Walk to the right from the exit of the Malostranská metro stop and walk up the street called U lužického semináře. The riverbank is accessible to your left just before you get to the Vojanovy park on the right. The atmosphere here is festive, especially on weekends, and the views over the city are breathtaking.

There are no fewer than three **puppet theaters** in Prague, all of which perform primarily for young children. Ask at Čedok or your hotel for details of performances.

Off the Beaten Track

Kafka's Grave. Kafka's modest tombstone in the New Jewish Cemetery (Židovské hřbitovy), situated beyond Vinohrady in a rather depressing part of Prague, seems grossly inadequate to Kafka's stature but oddly in proportion to his own modest ambitions. The cemetery is usually open for visitors; guards sometimes inexplicably seal off the grounds, but you can still glimpse the grave through the gate's iron bars. Take the metro to Želivského, turn right at the main cemetery gate, and follow the wall for about 100 yards. Dr. Franz Kafka's thin, white tombstone lies at the front of section 21.

Kostel Najsvětějšího Srdca Pana (Church of the Most Sacred Heart). If you've had your fill of Romanesque, Gothic, and Baroque, take the metro to Vinohrady (Jiřího z Poděbrad station) for a look at this amazing Art Deco cathedral. Designed in 1927 by Slovenian architect Jože Plečnik, the same architect commissioned to update the Prague Castle, the church more resembles a luxury ocean liner than a place of worship. The effect was conscious; during the 1920s and '30s, the avant garde carefully imitated mammoth objects of modern technology. Plečnik used many modern elements on the inside: Notice the hanging speakers, seemingly designed to bring the word of God directly to the ears of each worshiper. You may be able to find someone at the back entrance of the church who will let you walk up the long ramp into the fascinating glass clock tower.

Letenské sady (Letna Gardens). Come to this large, shady park for an unforgettable view from on high of Prague's bridges. From the enormous cement pedestal at the center of the park, the largest statue of Stalin in Eastern Europe once beckoned to citizens on the Old Town Square far below. The statue was ripped down during the 1960s, when Stalinism was finally discredited. Now the ideology-weary city fathers don't quite know what to do with the space. The room below the base is occasionally used as a venue for rock music. The walks and grass that stretch out behind the pedestal are perfect for relaxing on a warm afternoon. On sunny Sundays expatriates often meet up here to play ultimate Frisbee. To get to Letna, cross the Svatopluka Čecha Bridge, opposite the Hotel Inter-Continental, and climb the stairs.

Petřín. For a superb view of the city—from a mostly undiscovered, tourist-free perch—take the small funicular up through the hills of the Malá Strana to Prague's own miniature version of the Eiffel Tower. To reach the funicular, cross the Leglí Bridge near the Národní Divadlo (National Theater), and walk straight ahead to the Petřín Park. You can use normal public transport tickets for the funicular. Although the tower is closed to visitors, the area with the broken-down hall of mirrors and seemingly abandoned church is beautifully peaceful and well worth an afternoon's wandering. For the descent, meander on foot down through the stations of the cross on the pathways leading back to the Malá Strana. If you branch off to the left in the direction of the Strahov Monastery, you'll get one of the best views of Prague, with the castle out to the left, embracing the roofs of the Malá Strana and the Old Town far below.

Villa Bertramka. Mozart fans won't want to pass up a visit to this villa, where the great composer lived when in Prague. The small, well-organized museum is packed with memorabilia, including the program from that exciting night in 1787 when *Don Giovanni* had its world premiere in Prague. Also on hand is one of the master's pianos. Take the metro line B to the Anděl station, walk down Plzeňská ulice a few hundred yards, and take a left at Mozartova ulice. *Mozartova ul. 169, Smíchov, tel. 02/543893. Admission: 20 Kč. adults, 10 Kč. children. Open daily 10–5.*

Shopping

Despite the relative shortage of quality clothes—Prague has a long way to go before it can match the shopping meccas of Paris and Rome—the capital is a great place to pick up gifts and souvenirs. Bohemian crystal and porcelain deservedly enjoy a worldwide reputation for quality, and plenty of shops offer excellent bargains. The local market for antiques and artworks is still relatively undeveloped. In addition, the dozens of antiquarian bookshops can yield some excellent finds, particularly in German and Czech books and graphics. Another bargain is recorded music: LP and even CD prices are about half of what you would pay in the West.

Shopping Districts The major shopping areas are **Národní třída,** running past Můstek to Na příkopě, and the area around **Staroměstské náměstí** (Old Town Square). **Pařížská ulice, Karlova ulice** (on the way to the Charles Bridge), and the area just south of **Josefov** (the Jewish Quarter) are also good places to try boutiques and antiques shops. In the Malá Strana, try **Nerudova ulice,** the street that runs up to the Castle Hill district.

Department Stores These are generally poorly stocked, but a stroll through one may yield some interesting finds and bargains. The best are **Kotva** (Nám. Republiky 8), **Kmart** (Národní třída 26), **Bílá Labut'** (Na poříčí 23), and **Krone** (Václavské nám. 21).

Street Markets For fruits and vegetables, the best street market in central Prague is on **Havelská ulice** in the Old Town. But arrive early in the day if you want something a bit more exotic than tomatoes and cucumbers. The best market for nonfood items is the flea market in **Holešovice,** north of the city center, although there isn't really much of interest here outside of cheap tobacco and electronics products. Take metro line C to the Vltavská station, and then ride any tram heading east (running to the left as you exit the metro station). Exit at the first stop, and follow the crowds.

Specialty Stores **Antiques** *Starožitnosti* (antiques shops) are everywhere in Prague, but you'll need a sharp eye to distinguish truly valuable pieces from merely interesting ones. Many dealers carry old glassware and vases. Antique jewelry, many pieces featuring garnets, is also popular. Remember to retain your receipts as proof of legitimate purchases, otherwise you may have difficulty bringing antiques out of the country. Comparison shop at stores along Karlova ulice in the Old Town. Also check in and around the streets of the Jewish Ghetto for shops specializing in Jewish antiques and artifacts. **Art Program**

(Nerudova ul. 28) in the Malá Strana has an especially beautiful collection of Art Deco jewelry and glassware.

Books and Prints It's hard to imagine a more beautiful bookstore than **U Karlova Mostu** (Karlova ul. 2, Staré Město, tel. 02/2422–9205), with its impressive selection of old maps and prints, rare books, and even current copies of the *New York Review of Books*. One shop that comes close is **Antikvariát Karel Křenek** (Celetná 31, tel. 02/231–4734), near the Powder Tower in the Old Town. It stocks prints and graphics from the 1920s and '30s, in addition to a small collection of English books. The **Melantrich** (Na příkopě 3, tel. 02/267166) is a small but excellent source for high-quality art and graphics books. The store also stocks a full set of maps to most Czech cities, auto atlases, and English-language magazines and newspapers.

Crystal and Porcelain **Moser** (Na příkopě 12, tel. 02/2421–1293), the flagship store for the world-famous Karlovy Vary glassmaker, is the first address for stylish, high-quality lead crystal and china. Even if you're not in the market to buy, stop by the store simply to browse through the elegant wood-paneled salesrooms on the second floor. The staff will gladly pack goods for traveling. **Bohemia** (Pařížska 2, tel. 02/2481–1023) carries a wide selection of porcelain from Karlovy Vary. If you still can not find anything, have no fear: There is a crystal shop on just about every street in central Prague.

Food Specialty food stores have been slow to catch on in Prague. **Fruits de France** (Jindřišská ul., Nové Město) stocks fresh fruits and vegetables imported directly from France at Western prices. The bakeries at the **Krone** and **Kotva** department stores (*see above*) sell surprisingly delicious breads and pastries. Both stores also have large, well-stocked basement grocery stores.

Fun Things for Children Children enjoy the beautiful watercolor and colored-chalk sets available in nearly every stationery store at rock-bottom prices. The Czechs are also master illustrators, and the books they've made for young "pre-readers" are some of the world's loveliest. The best store to browse in is **Albatros** (Na perštýně 1, tel. 02/2422–3227), on the corner with Národní třída. Many stores also offer unique wooden toys, sure to delight any young child. For these, look in at **Obchod Vším Možným** (Nerudova 45, tel. 02/536941). For older children and teens, it's worth considering a Czech or Eastern European watch, telescope, or set of binoculars. The quality/price ratio is unbeatable.

Jewelry The **Granát** shop at Dlouhá 30 in the Old Town has a comprehensive selection of garnet jewelry, plus contemporary and traditional pieces set in gold and silver. Several shops specializing in gold jewelry line Wenceslas Square.

Musical Instruments **Dům hudebních nástrojů** (Jungmannova nám. 17, tel. 02/2422–2500) carries a complete range of quality musical instruments at reasonable prices. **Melodia** (Karmelitská 20, Malá Strana) carries a complete range of Czech-made accordions and other instruments.

Sports Equipment Try the large **Dům Sportu** (Jungmannova ul. 28) for reasonably priced tennis rackets, ice skates, sleds, skis, or whatever else you need but forgot to bring. **Adidas** has an outlet at Na Příkopě 15. Department stores (*see above*) also sometimes carry middle-quality sports equipment.

Participant Sports and Fitness

Fitness Clubs The best fitness clubs in town are at the **Forum Hotel** (Kongresova ul. 1, tel. 02/6119–1111; Vyšehrad metro station) and at the **Atrium**

Hotel (Pobřežní 1, tel. 02/2484–1111; Florenc metro station). Both are open to nonresidents, but call first to inquire about rates and to make an appointment.

Golf You can golf year-round at Prague's only course, located outside the city at the **Stop Motel** (Plzeňská ul. 215, tel. 02/523251). Take a taxi to the motel, or Tram 7 to the end of the line.

Jogging The best place for jogging is the **Letenské sady**, the large park across the river from the Hotel Inter-Continental. Cross the Svatopluka Čecha Bridge, climb the stairs, and turn to the right for a good, long run far away from the car fumes. The **Riegrový Sady**, a small park in Vinohrady behind the main train station, is also nice, but it is small and a bit out of the way.

Swimming The best public swimming pool in Prague is at the **Podolí Swimming Stadium** in Podolí, easily reached from the city center via Streetcar 3 or 17. The indoor pool is 50 meters long, and the complex also includes two open-air pools, a sauna, and a steam bath. The pool at the **Atrium Hotel** is smaller, but the location is more convenient (*see* Fitness Clubs, *above*).

Tennis Public courts are located at the **Spartakiade Stadium** in Břevnov. Take Tram 8 to the end from the Hradčanská metro stop, and change to Bus 143, 149, or 217. The **Atrium Hotel** (*see* Fitness Clubs, *above*) has two indoor courts available for public use.

Spectator Sports

Prague plays host to a wide variety of spectator sports, including world-class ice hockey, handball, tennis, and swimming. Most events, however, are held at irregular intervals. The best place to find out what's going on (and where) is the weekly sports page of *The Prague Post*, or you can inquire at your hotel.

Soccer National and international matches are played regularly at the Letna Stadium in Holešovice, behind the Letenské Sady (*see* Jogging, *above*). To reach the stadium, take Tram 1, 25, or 26 to the Sparta stop.

Dining

Dining possibilities in Prague have increased greatly in the past year as hundreds of new places have opened to cope with the increased tourist demand. Quality and price can vary widely, though. Be wary of tourist traps; cross-check prices of foreign-language menus with Czech versions. Also ask if there is a *denní lístek* (daily menu). These menus, usually written only in Czech, generally list cheaper and often fresher selections. Note that many places provide daily menus only for the midday meal.

The crush of visitors has placed tremendous strain on the more popular restaurants. The upshot is that reservations are nearly always required; this is especially true during peak tourist periods. If you don't have reservations, try arriving a little before standard meal times: 11:30 AM for lunch, or 5:30 PM for dinner.

A cheaper and quicker alternative to the sit-down establishments listed below would be to take a light meal at one of the city's growing number of street stands and fast-food places. Look for stands offering *Parky* (hot dogs) or *Smažený syr* (fried cheese). McDonald's, with several locations in the city, heads the list of Western imports. For more exotic fare, try a gyro (made from pork) at the stand on the

Staromětské náměstí or the very good vegetarian fare at **Country Life** (Melantrichova ul. 15, no tel. closed Saturday). The German coffeemaker Tchibo has teamed up with a local bakery and now offers tasty sandwiches and excellent coffee at convenient locations on the Staromětské náměstí and at the top of Wenceslas Square.

Highly recommended restaurants in each price category are indicated by a star ★.

$$$$ **Parnas.** This is the first choice for visiting dignitaries and businesspeople blessed with expense accounts. Creative, freshly prepared cuisine, more nouvelle than Bohemian, is served in an opulent 1920s setting. Window seats afford stunning views of Prague Castle. Parnas has a small, mostly Czech vintage wine list and a fine selection of appetizers and desserts (the chocolate mousse is a must). *Smetanovo nábřeží 2, Nové Město, tel. 02/2422–7614. Reservations advised. Jacket and tie required. AE, DC, MC, V.*

★ **U Mecenáše.** A fetching Renaissance inn from the 17th century, with dark, high-backed benches in the front room and cozy, elegant sofas and chairs in back, this is the place to splurge: From the aperitifs to the steaks and the cognac (swirled lovingly in oversize glasses), the presentation is seamless. *Malostranské nám. 10, Malá Strana, tel. 02/533881. Reservations advised. Jacket and tie required. AE, DC, MC, V.*

U Zlaté Hrušky. At this bustling bistro perched on one of Prague's prettiest cobblestone streets, slide into one of the cozy dark-wood booths and let the cheerful staff advise on wines and specials. Duck and carp are house favorites. After dinner, stroll to the castle for an unforgettable panorama. *Nový Svět 3, Hradčany, tel. 02/531133. Reservations required. Jacket and tie required. AE, DC, MC, V.*

★ **V Zátiší.** White walls and casual grace accentuate the subtle flavors of smoked salmon, plaice, beef Wellington, and other non-Czech specialties. Order the house *Rulandské červené*, a fruity Moravian red wine that meets the exacting standards of the food. In behavior unusual for the city, the benign waiters fairly fall over each other to serve diners. *Liliová 1, Betlémské nám., Staré Město, tel. 02/2422–8977. Reservations advised. Dress: casual but neat. AE, DC, MC, V.*

$$$ **Cerberus.** Traditional Czech cooking is raised to an uncommonly high level at this New Town restaurant. The Bohemian staples of pork, duck, rabbit, and game are prepared and presented (by an attentive staff) as haute cuisine. Despite the modern decor, the ambience is warm and intimate. *Soukenická 19, Nové Město, tel. 02/231–0985. Reservations advised. Dress: casual but neat. AE, MC, V.*

Fakhreldine. This elegant Lebanese restaurant, crowded with diplomats who know where to find the real thing, has an excellent range of Middle Eastern appetizers and main courses. For a moderately priced meal, try several appetizers—hummus and garlic yogurt, perhaps—instead of a main course. *Klimentská 48, Prague 1, tel. 02/232–7970. Reservations advised. Dress: casual but neat. AE, DC, MC, V.*

★ **Lobkovická.** This dignified *vinárna* (wine hall) set inside a 17th-century town palace serves some of Prague's most imaginative dishes. Chicken breast with crabmeat and curry sauce is an excellent main dish and typical of the kitchen's innovative approach to sauces and spice. Deep-red carpeting sets the perfect mood for enjoying bottles of Moravian wine brought from the musty depths of the restaurant's wine cellar. *Vlašská 17, Malá Strana, tel. 02/530185. Reservations advised. Jacket and tie required. AE, DC, MC, V.*

$$ Bella Napoli. Come here for real Italian food at a price/quality ratio
★ that's hard to beat in Prague. Ignore the faux-Italian interior and
the alabaster Venus de Milos astride shopping-mall fountains and
head straight for the 65-Kč. antipasto bar, which will distract you
with fresh olives, eggplant, squid, and mozzarella. For your main
course, go with any of a dozen superb pasta dishes or splurge with
shrimp or chicken parmigiana. The Italian-American chef hails from
Brooklyn and knows his stuff. *V jámě 8, Nové Město, tel. 02/2422–
7315. Reservations advised. Dress: casual. No credit cards.*

Myslivna. The name means "hunting lodge," and the cooks at this
far-flung neighborhood eatery certainly know their way around
venison, quail, and boar. Attentive staff can advise on wines: Try
Vavřinecké, a hearty red that holds its own with any beast. The
stuffed quail and the leg of venison with walnuts both get high
marks. A cab from the city center to Myslivna should cost under 200
Kč. *Jagellonska 21, Prague 3, tel. 02/6270209. Reservations ad-
vised. Dress: casual but neat. AE, V.*

★ **Penguin's.** The emphasis at this popular eatery is on classic Czech
and international dishes, served in an elegant mauve-and-matte-
black setting. Try any of the steaks or the chicken breast with pota-
toes. The penguin in the name refers to the Pittsburgh variety, of
hockey fame—the owner's favorite team. *Zborovská 5, Prague 5,
tel. 02/545660. Reservations advised. Dress: casual but neat. No
credit cards.*

Pezinok. Slovak cooking is hard to find in Prague, and this cozy wine
restaurant is still the best in town. Heavy furnishings and subdued
lighting add an oddly formal touch. Order à la carte (the set menus
are overpriced) and choose from homemade sausages or *halušky*,
boiled noodles served with a tangy sheep's cheese. The restaurant's
full-bodied wines come from the Slovak town for which the restau-
rant was named. *Purkyňova 4, Nové Město, tel. 02/291996. Reserva-
tions advised. Dress: casual but neat. AE, DC, MC, V.*

$ Demínka. This spacious 19th-century café offers some respite from
★ Prague's throngs of tourists. It's a perfect place to have coffee and
write a letter. Try the cheap and tasty *Smažený sýr* (fried cheese) or
the hearty goulash soup. A small sandwich or schnitzel at Demínka
makes a fine afternoon snack. *Škrétova 1, Prague 2, tel. 02/228595.
Reservations not necessary. Dress: casual but neat. No credit
cards.*

Na Zvonařce. This bright beer hall supplements traditional Czech
dishes—mostly pork, beer, and pork—with some innovative Czech
and international choices, all at unbeatably cheap prices. Notewor-
thy entrées include juicy fried chicken and English roast beef; fruit
dumplings for dessert are a rare treat. The service may be slow, but
that simply allows time to commune with a tankard of ale on the out-
side terrace during the summer. *Šafaříkova 1, Prague 2, tel. 02/
691–1311. Reservations advised. No credit cards.*

Profit. The unfortunate name masks a clean, spacious pub that
serves such excellent Czech standbys as goulash and pork with
dumplings and sauerkraut at astonishingly reasonable prices. The
central location could hardly be better. *Betlémské nám. 8, Staré
Město, tel. 02/2422–2776. Reservations not necessary. No credit
cards.*

★ **U Koleje.** This popular, laid-back pub is suitable for the entire fami-
ly. Besides offering excellent beers, U Koleje serves satisfying pork
and beef dishes. During peak hours you may have to share a table.
*Slavíkova 24, Prague 2, tel. 02/6274163. Reservations advised. No
credit cards.*

Prague Dining and Lodging

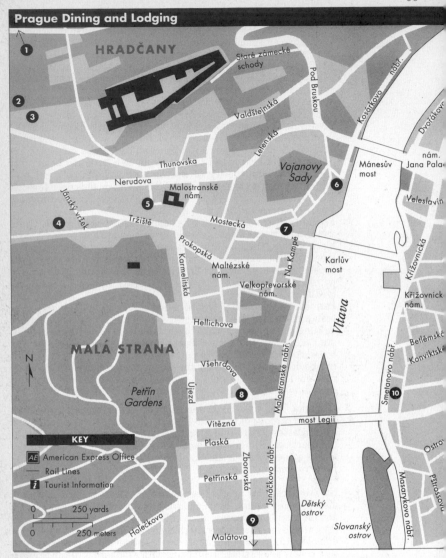

HRADČANY

Staré zámecké schody

Pod Bruskou

Valdštejnská

Kosárkovo nábř.

Dvořákovo

Letenská

Thunovska

Nerudova

Vojanovy Sady

Mánesův most

nám. Jana Pala

Jánský vršek

Malostranské nám.

Tržiště

Mostecká

Na Kampě

Veleslavín

Prokopská

Maltézské nám.

Karmelitská

Karlův most

Křižovnická

Velkopřevorské nám.

Křižovnick nám.

Hellichova

Vltava

MALÁ STRANA

Betlémsk

Konvíkisk

Všehrdova

Malostranské nábř.

Petřín Gardens

Újezd

Smetanovo nábř.

Vítězná

most Legii

Plaská

Ostro

KEY

AE American Express Office

Rail Lines

i Tourist Information

Zborovská

Petřínská

Janáčkovo nábř.

Masarykovo nábř.

Pstrossov

0   250 yards

0   250 meters

Holečkova

Malátova

Dětský ostrov

Slovanský ostrov

Dining
Bella Napoli, **27**
Cerberus, **15**
Demínka, **29**
Fakhreldine, **16**
Lobkovická, **4**
Myslivna, **32**
Na Zvonařce, **30**

Parnas, **10**
Penguin's, **9**
Pezinok, **25**
Profit, **11**
U Koleje, **31**
U Mecenáše, **5**
U Zlaté Hrušky, **2**
V Krakovské, **28**
V Zátiši, **12**

Lodging
Apollo, **13**
Axa, **19**
City Hotel Moráň, **26**
Diplomat, **1**
Grand Hotel Bohemia, **21**
Harmony, **18**
Hybernia, **23**
Kampa, **8**

Meteor Plaza, **22**
Opera, **17**
Palace, **24**
Paříž, **20**
Pension Louda, **14**
Pension U Raka, **3**
U Páva, **6**
U Tří Pštrosů, **7**

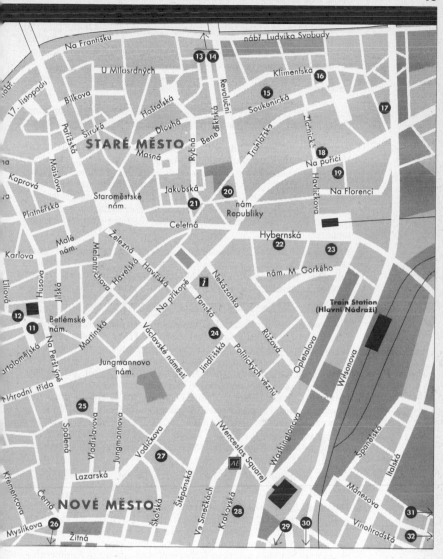

STARÉ MĚSTO

NOVÉ MĚSTO

Train Station
(Hlavní Nádraží)

V Krakovské. At this clean, proper pub that is close to the major tourist sights, the food is traditional and hearty; this is the place to try Bohemian duck, washed down with a dark beer from Domažlice in western Bohemia. *Krakovská 20, Nové Město, tel. 02/261537. Reservations advised. No credit cards.*

Lodging

Visitors are frequently disappointed by the city's lodging options. Hotel owners were quick to raise prices after 1989, when tourists first began flocking to Prague, but they have been much, much slower in raising their facilities to Western standards. In most of the Very Expensive and Expensive hotels, you can expect to find a restaurant and an exchange bureau on or near the premises. Bills are paid in Czech crowns, though some hotels still insist that you pay in hard (that is, Western) currency; be certain to inquire *before* making a reservation. During the summer season reservations are absolutely imperative; the remainder of the year they are sincerely recommended.

A cheaper and often more interesting alternative to Prague's generally mediocre hotels are private rooms and apartments. Prague is full of travel agencies offering such accommodations; the only drawback is that you may have to sacrifice a little privacy. The best room-finding service is probably **AVE** (tel. 02/2422–3226, fax 02/2422–3463), with offices in the main train station (Hlavní nádraží) and at Holešovice station (Nádraží Holešovice). Both offices are open daily from 7 AM to 10:30 PM. Prices start at around $15 per person per night. Insist on a room in the city center, however, or you may find yourself in a dreary, far-flung suburb. Other helpful room-finding agencies include **Hello Ltd.** (Senovazné nám. 3, Nové Město, tel. 02/224283), **City of Prague Accommodation Service** (Haštalské nám., Staré Město, tel. 02/231–0202, fax 02/231–4076; open daily 8–8, until 10 in summer), and **Prague Suites Accommodation Service** (Melantrichova 8, Staré Město, tel. 02/2422–9961). If all else fails, just take a walk through the Old Town: The number of places advertising "Accommodation" (often written in German as *Unterkunft* is astounding.

Highly recommended lodgings in each price category are indicated by a star ★.

$$$$ **Diplomat.** This sprawling complex opened in 1990 and is still re-
★ garded as the best business hotel in town. Even though it's in the suburbs, the Diplomat is convenient to the airport and, via the metro, to the city center. The modern rooms may not exude much character, but they are tastefully furnished and quite comfortable. The hotel staff are competent and many are bilingual. Guests have access to a pool, sauna, and fitness center. *Evropská 15, Prague 6, tel. 02/331–4111, fax 02/331–4215. 387 rooms with bath. Facilities: restaurant, bar, nightclub, pool, fitness center, sauna, conference room. AE, DC, MC, V.*

Grand Hotel Bohemia. This beautifully refurbished Art Nouveau town palace is just a stone's throw from the Old Town Square. The new Austrian owners opted for a muted, modern decor in the rooms but left the sumptuous public areas just as they were. Each room is outfitted with fax and answering machine. *Králodvorska 4, Staré Město, tel. 02/232–341), fax 02/232–9545. 78 rooms with bath. Facilities: restaurant, café. AE, DC, MC, V.*

Palace. For the well-heeled, this is Prague's most coveted address— an art-nouveau town palace perched on a busy corner only a block from the very central Wenceslas Square. Renovated in 1989, the hotel's spacious, well-appointed rooms, each with a private white marble bathroom, are fitted in velvety pinks and greens cribbed straight from an Alfons Mucha print. Two rooms are set aside for disabled travelers. The ground-floor buffet boasts the city's finest salad bar. *Panská 12, Nové Město, tel. 02/2409–3111, fax 02/2422–1240. 125 rooms with bath. Facilities: 2 restaurants, café, bar, snack bar, satellite TV, minibars. AE, DC, MC, V.*

Paříž. The smallish rooms hardly justify the high price, yet the hotel's unique Art Nouveau facade and its excellent location near the Old Town's Powder Tower keep the occupancy rate near 99%. Ask for a room away from the deceptively peaceful street. *U Obecního domu 1, Staré Město, tel. 02/2422–2151, fax 02/2422–5475. 86 rooms with bath. Facilities: restaurant, café. AE, DC, MC, V.*

★ **Pension U Raka.** This private guest house offers the peace and coziness of an alpine lodge, plus a quiet location on the ancient, winding streets of Nový Svět, just behind the Loretan Church and a 10-minute walk from Prague Castle. The dark wood building has only five rooms, but if you can get a reservation (try at least a month in advance), you will gain a wonderful base for exploring Prague. *Černínská ul. 10/93, tel. 02/351453, fax 02/353074. 5 rooms. No credit cards.*

$$$ **City Hotel Morán.** This 19th-century town house was tastefully renovated in 1992; now the lobby and public areas are bright and inviting, made over in an updated Jugendstil style. The modern if slightly bland rooms are a cut above the Prague standard for convenience and cleanliness; ask for one on the sixth floor for a good view of Prague Castle. A hearty Sunday brunch is served in the ground-floor restaurant. *Na Moráni 15, Prague 2, tel. 02/2491–5208, fax 02/297533. 53 rooms, most with bath. Facilities: restaurant, bar. AE, DC, MC, V.*

Meteor Plaza. This popular Old Town hotel, operated by the Best Western chain, combines the best of New World convenience and Old World charm (Empress Maria Theresa's son, Joseph, stayed here when he was passing through in the 18th century). The setting is ideal: a newly renovated, Baroque building that is only five minutes by foot from downtown. There is a good, if touristy, in-house wine cellar. *Hybernska 6, Nové Město, tel. 02/2422–0664, fax 02/2421–3005. 86 rooms with bath. Facilities: restaurant, business center, terrace. AE, DC, MC, V.*

★ **U Páva.** This newly renovated, neoclassical inn, set on a quiet gas-lit street in Malá Strana, offers upstairs suites that afford an unforgettable view of Prague Castle. Best of all, the U Páva is small and intimate—the perfect escape for those who've had their fill of cement high-rise resorts. The staff is courteous and helpful, while the reception and public areas are elegant and discreet. *U lužického semináře 106, Malá Strana, tel. 02/2451–0922, fax 02/533379. 11 rooms with bath. Facilities: restaurant, wine bar. AE, DC, MC, V.*

U Tří Pštrosů. The location could not be better—a romantic corner in the Malá Strana only a stone's throw from the river and the Charles Bridge. The airy rooms, dating back 300 years, still have their original oak-beamed ceilings and antique furniture; many also have views over the river. An excellent in-house restaurant serves traditional Czech dishes to guests and non-guests alike. *Dražického nám. 12, Malá Strana, tel. 02/2451–0779, fax 02/2451–0783. 18 rooms with bath. Facilities: restaurant. AE, DC, MC, V.*

$$ **Axa.** Funky and functional, this modernist high rise, built in 1932, was a mainstay of the budget-hotel crowd until a recent reconstruction forced substantial price hikes. The rooms, now with color tele-

vision sets and modern plumbing, are certainly improved; however, the lobby and public areas look decidedly tacky, with plastic flowers and glaring lights. *Na poříčí 40, tel. 02/2481–2580, fax 02/232–2172. 133 rooms, most with bath. Facilities: restaurant, bar, nightclub. No credit cards.*

Harmony. This is one of the newly renovated, formerly state-owned standbys. The stern 1930s facade clashes with the bright, "nouveau riche" 1990s interior, but cheerful receptionists and big, clean rooms compensate for the aesthetic flaws. Ask for a room away from the bustle of one of Prague's busiest streets. *Na poříčí 31, tel. 02/ 232–0720, fax 02/231–0009. 60 rooms with bath. Facilities: restaurant, snack bar. AE, DC, MC, V.*

★ **Kampa.** This early Baroque armory turned hotel is tucked away on a leafy corner just south of Malá Strana. The rooms are clean, if sparse, though the bucolic setting makes up for any discomforts. Note the late-Gothic vaulting in the massive dining room. *Všehrdova 16, Prague 1, tel. 02/2451–0409, fax 02/2451–0377. 85 rooms with bath. Facilities: restaurant, café. AE, DC, MC, V.*

Opera. Once the hospice of choice for divas performing at the nearby State Theater, the Opera greatly declined under the Communists. New owners, however, are working hard to restore the hotel's former luster. Until then, the clean (but smallish) rooms, friendly staff, and fin-de-siècle charm are still reason enough to recommend it. *Těšnov 13, tel. 02/231–5609, fax 02/231–1477. 66 rooms with bath. Facilities: restaurant, snack bar. AE, DC, MC, V.*

$ **Apollo.** This is a standard, no-frills, square-box hotel where clean rooms come at a fair price. Its primary flaw is its location, roughly 20 minutes by metro or bus from the city center. *Kubišova 23, tel. 02/6641–0628, fax 02/6641–4570. Metro Holešovice, then tram No. 5 or 17 to Hercovka. 32 rooms with bath or shower. No credit cards.*

Hybernia. The dull appearance of this train-station flophouse hardly suggests that it is actually a respectably clean, secure hotel. The rooms are of the two-bed-and-a-table variety but are perfectly adequate for short stays. The location, next to Masarykovo train station and a short walk from the main station, is excellent for the money. *Hybernska 24, tel. 02/2421–0440, fax 02/222204. 70 rooms, some with bath. Facilities: restaurant, bar, lounge. No credit cards.*

★ **Pension Louda.** The friendly owners of this family-run guest house, set in a suburb roughly 20 minutes by tram from the city center, go out of their way to make you feel welcome. The large, spotless rooms are an unbelievable bargain, and the hilltop location offers a stunning view of greater Prague. *Kubišova 10, Prague 8; tel. 02/843302. Take Tram 5 or 17 (Hercovka station) from metro Holešovice. 9 rooms. No credit cards.*

The Arts and Nightlife

The Arts   Prague's cultural flair is legendary, though performances are usually booked far in advance by all sorts of Praguers. The concierge at your hotel may be able to reserve tickets for you. Otherwise, for the cheapest tickets, go directly to the theater box office a few days in advance or immediately before a performance. **Bohemia Ticket International** (Na příkopě 16, tel. 02/2421–5031, and Wenceslas Square 25, tel. 02/2422–7253) sells tickets for major cultural events at semi-inflated prices. Tickets can also be purchased at **American Express** (*see* Important Addresses and Numbers, *above*).

For details of cultural events, look to the English-language newspapers *The Prague Post* and *Prognosis*, or to the monthly English-language *Prague Guide*, available at hotels and tourist offices.

Film If a film was made in the United States or Britain, the chances are good that it will be shown with Czech subtitles rather than dubbed. (Film titles, however, are usually translated into Czech, so your only clue to the movie's country of origin may be the poster used in advertisements.) Popular cinemas include **Blaník** (Václavské nám. 56, tel. 02/2421–6698), **Hvězda** (Václavské nám. 38, tel. 02/264545), **Paříž** (Václavské nám. 22), **Sevastopol** (Na příkopě 31, tel. 02/264328), and **Svetozor** (Vodičkova ul. 39, tel. 02/263616). Prague's English-language newspapers carry film reviews and full timetables.

Music Classical concerts are held all over the city throughout the year. The best venues are the resplendent Art Nouveau **Obecní dům** (Smetana Hall, Nám. Republiky 5, tel. 02/232–5858), home of the Prague Symphony Orchestra, and **Dvořák Hall** (in the Rudolfinum, nám. Jana Palacha), home of the Czech Philharmonic. Performances also are held regularly in the **National Gallery** in Prague Castle, in the **gardens** below the castle (where the music comes with a view), and at the **National Museum** on Wenceslas Square. Concerts at the **Villa Bertramka** (Mozartova 169, Smíchov, tel. 02/543893) emphasize the music of Mozart and his contemporaries (*see* Off the Beaten Track, *above*).

Fans of organ music will be delighted by the number of recitals held in Prague's historic halls and churches. Popular programs are offered at **St. Vitus Cathedral** in Hradčany, **U Křížovniků** near the Charles Bridge, the **Church of St. Nicholas** in Malá Strana, and **St. James's Church** on Malá Štupartská in the Old Town, where the organ plays amid a complement of Baroque statuary.

Opera and The Czech Republic has a strong operatic tradition, and perfor-
Ballet mances at the **Národní divadlo** (National Theater, Národní třída 2, tel. 02/2491–2673) and the **Statní Opera Praha** (State Opera House, Wilsonova 4, tel. 02/2422–7693), at the top of Wenceslas Square, can be excellent. Operas are usually sung in Czech, and the repertoire is heavy on the national composers Janaček, Dvořák, and Smetana. The historic **Stavovské divadlo** (Estates' Theater, Ovocný tř. 6, Staré Město, tel. 02/2421–5001), where *Don Giovanni* debuted during the 18th century, plays host to a mix of operas and dramatic works. The National and State theaters also occasionally have ballets.

Theater Most dramatic works are performed in Czech. For those who find the Czech language a vast mystery, try the excellent **Black Theater** mime group, based at Václav Havel's old theater, the **Divadlo na zábradlí** (Theater on the Balustrade, Anenské nám. 5, Staré Město, tel. 02/2422–1933). Performances usually begin at 7 or 7:30. Several English-language theater groups operate sporadically in Prague during the tourist season; pick up a copy of *The Prague Post* or *Prognosis* for complete listings.

Nightlife Bars or lounges are not traditional Prague fixtures; social life, of the
Pubs, Bars, drinking variety, usually takes place in pubs (*pivnici*), which are
and Lounges liberally sprinkled throughout the city's neighborhoods. Tourists are welcome to join in the evening ritual of sitting around large tables and talking, smoking, and drinking beer in enormous quantities. Before venturing in, however, it's best to familiarize yourself with a few points of pub etiquette: First, always ask before sitting down if a chair is free. To order a beer (*pivo*), do not wave the waiter down or shout across the room; he will usually assume you want beer and bring it over to you without asking. He will also bring subsequent rounds to the table without asking. To refuse, just shake your head or say no thanks. At the end of the evening, usually around 10:30 or 11:00, the waiter will come to tally the bill. Some of the most

popular pubs in the city center include **U Medvídků** (Na Perštýně 7), **U Vejvodů** (Jilská 4), and **U Zlatého Tygra** (Husova ul. 17). All can get impossibly crowded.

An alternative to Prague's pubs are the few American-style bars that have sprung up during the past year. **Jo's Bar** (Malostranské nám. 7), one of the best and a haven for younger expats, serves bottled beer, mixed drinks, and good Mexican food. **The James Joyce Pub** (Liliova 10) is authentically Irish, with Guinness on tap and excellent food. The major hotels also run their own bars and nightclubs. The **Piano Bar** (Hotel Palace, Panská ul. 12) is the most pleasant of the lot; jacket and tie are suggested.

Cabaret A multimedia extravaganza with actors, mime, and film is performed at **Laterna Magika** (Národní třída 4, Nové Město, tel. 02/2491-4129). Tickets range from 50 Kč. to 400 Kč. and sell out fast; the box office is open Monday 10–noon and 2–6 and Tuesday–Saturday 2–6. Noted Czech mime Boris Hybner performs nightly at 8 PM at the **Gag Studio** in the New Town (Národní 25, Nové Město, tel. 02/265436). "Bohemian Fantasy," which performs May through October every Monday, Wednesday, Friday, and Saturday evening at the **Lucerna Palace** (Štěpánská ul. 61, tel. 02/235-0909), is a glitzy, Las Vegas–style send-up of Bohemian history. Tickets cost $30 and can be purchased at the Lucerna box office. For adult stage entertainment (with some nudity) try the **Lucerna Bar** (Štěpánská ul. 61, Nové Město, tel. 02/235-0888) or **Varieté Praga** (Vodičkova ul. 30, Nové Město, tel. 02/235-0861).

Discos Dance clubs come and go with predictable regularity. The current favorite is **Radost FX** (Bělehradská 120, Prague 2, tel. 02/251210), featuring imported DJs playing the latest dance music and technopop from London. The café on the ground floor is open all night and serves wholesome vegetarian food. Two popular discos for dancing the night away with fellow tourists include **Lavká** (Lavká 1, Staré Město, near the Charles Bridge) and the **Classic Club** (Pařížsá 4, Staré Město, tel. 02/2319473). The former features open-air dancing by the bridge on summer nights. Wenceslas Square is also packed with discos; the best strategy for finding the right place is simply to stroll the square and size up the crowds and the music.

Jazz Clubs Jazz gained notoriety as a subtle form of protest under the Communists, and the city still has some great jazz clubs, featuring everything from swing to blues and modern. **Reduta** (Národní 20, tel. 02/2491-2246) features a full program of local and international musicians. **Agharta** (Krakovská 5, tel. 02/2421-2914) offers a variety of jazz acts in an intimate café/nightclub atmosphere. Music starts around 8 PM, but come earlier to get a seat. Check posters around town or any of the English-language newspapers for current listings.

Rock Clubs Prague's rock scene is thriving. Hard-rock enthusiasts should check out the **Rock Café** (Národní 20, tel. 02/2491-4416) or **Strahov 007** (near Strahov Stadium; take Bus 218 two stops from Anděl metro station). The trendiest underground spots are **Borát** (Újezd 18, Malá Strana, tel. 02/538362), one of Václav Havel's former hangouts; and **RC Bunkr** (Lodecká 2, Nové Město). The **Malostranska Beseda** (Malostranské nám. 21, tel. 02/539024) and the **Belmondo Revival Club** (Bubenská 1, Prague 7, tel. 02/791-4854) are dependable bets for sometimes bizarre, but always good, musical acts from around the country.

Bohemia

The turbulent history of the Czechs has indelibly marked the gentle rolling landscape of Bohemia. With Prague at its heart, and Germany and the former Austrian empire on its mountainous borders, the kingdom of Bohemia was for centuries buffeted by religious and national conflicts, invasions, and wars. But its position also meant that Bohemia benefited from the cultural wealth and diversity of Central Europe. The result is a glorious array of castles, walled cities, and spa towns, boasting a past that would be difficult to match in any other provincial area of Central Europe.

Southern Bohemia is particularly famous for its involvement in the Hussite religious wars of the 15th century, which revolved around the town of Tábor. But the area also has more than its fair share of well-preserved and stunning walled towns, built up through the ages by generations of the noble families of the day, who left behind layers of Gothic, Renaissance, and Baroque architecture (particularly notable in Český Krumlov). Farther north and an easy drive east of Prague is the old silver-mining town of Kutná Hora, once a rival to Prague for the royal residency.

Western Bohemia was, until World War II, the playground of Central Europe's rich and famous. Its three well-known spas, Karlovy Vary, Mariánské Lázně, and Františkový Lázně (better known by their German names: Karlsbad, Marienbad, and Franzensbad, respectively) were the annual haunts of everybody who was anybody—Johann Wolfgang von Goethe, Ludwig van Beethoven, Karl Marx, and England's King Edward VII, to name but a few. Although strictly "proletarianized" throughout the communist era, the spas still exude a nostalgic aura of a more elegant past and, unlike most of Bohemia, offer a basic tourist infrastructure that makes dining and lodging a pleasure.

Northern Bohemia is a paradox: While much of it was despoiled during the past 40 years by rampant industrialization, here and there you can still find areas of great natural beauty. Rolling hills, perfect for walking, guard the country's northern frontiers with Germany and Poland. Hikers and campers head for the Giant Mountains (Krkonoše) on the Polish border; this range is not so giant, actually, though it is very pretty. As you move toward the west, the interest is more historical, in an area where the influence of Germany was felt in less pleasant ways than in the spas. Most drastically affected was Terezín, better known as the infamous concentration camp Theresienstadt, where the Nazis converted the redbrick fortress town into a Jewish ghetto and prison camp during World War II.

Important Addresses and Numbers

Tourist Information Most major towns have a local or private information office, usually located in the central square and identified by a capital "I" on the facade. These offices are often good sources for maps and historical information and can usually help visitors book hotel and private accommodations. Most are open during normal business hours, with limited hours on Saturday (until noon), and are closed on Sunday and holidays.

Emergencies Police (tel. 158). Ambulance (tel. 155).

Late-Night Pharmacies Pharmacies take turns staying open late or on Sunday; for the latest information, consult the list posted on the front door of each pharmacy. For after-hours service, ring the bell; you will be served through a little hatch door.

Arriving and Departing by Plane

The only real option is to fly to Prague, from which it is quite easy to travel to any city in Bohemia by car, train, or bus.

Arriving and Departing by Car, Train, and Bus

Major trains from Munich and Nürnberg stop at Cheb and some of the spa towns. It is also an easy drive across the border from Bavaria on the E48 to Cheb, and from there to any of the spas. Several trains a day run from Vienna to Prague; most travel via Třeboň and Tábor in southern Bohemia, although some make the trip by way of Brno (through Moravia). To drive from Vienna, take the E49 from Gmünd. There is also a daily bus from Vienna to Karlovy Vary via Prague.

Getting Around

By Car Car travel affords the greatest ease and flexibility in this region. The major road from Prague south to Tábor and České Budějovice, though often crowded, is in relatively good shape. Exercise caution on smaller roads, many of which are poorly marked and maintained (and always have a good map or auto atlas handy). Most of the towns are very small and, depending on public transportation, may require you to schedule some overnight stays. Driving through Bohemia, motorists are rewarded with a particularly picturesque drive along the Labe (Elbe) River on the way to Střekov.

By Train Good, if slow, train service links all of the major towns west of Prague. The best stretches are from Františkovy Lázně to Plzeň and from Plzeň to Prague. The Prague–Karlovy Vary run takes longer than it should but has a romantic charm all its own. Note that most trains heading west to Germany (direction Nürnberg) stop at Mariánské Lázně. Most trains leave from Prague's Hlavní nádraží (main station), but be sure to check on the station if in doubt.

Benešov (Konopiště), Tábor, and Třeboň all lie along the major southern line in the direction of Vienna, and train service to these cities from Prague is frequent and comfortable. Good connections also exist from Prague to České Budějovice. For other destinations, you may have to combine the train and bus. Train connections in the north are spotty at best. Regular service connects Prague with Mělník and Ústí nad Labem, but to reach the other towns you'll have to resort to the bus.

By Bus All the major sights are reachable from Prague using ČSAD's dense bus network. Service between the towns, however, is far less frequent and will require some forethought. For information, consult schedules at local bus stations. The small letters or numbers beside the times indicate whether the bus runs on weekdays, holidays, and so on.

Guided Tours

Čedok (tel. 02/2419–7111) offers several specialized tours covering the sights listed in the tours below. Tour "G-O" combines a trip to Lidice in northern Bohemia with a visit to the spa town of Karlovy Vary. The trip takes a full day and departs three times weekly. Other tours include visits to České Budějovice, Hluboka Castle, Český Krumlov, Třeboň, Kutná Hora, and Český Sternberk. Čedok also offers a full-day excursion to the oldest glassworks in Central Europe, south of Prague. Prague departure points include the Čedok offices at Na Příkopě 18 and Bílkova ul. 6.

Several private companies also offer trips to Lidice and Terezín (Theresienstadt) in northern Bohemia. For the latter, try **Wittmann Tours** (tel. 02/439–6293). Bus tours leave from Pařížska 28 every Sunday at 11 AM, returning at 6 PM (450 Kč. adults, 350 Kč. for students and children).

Highlights for First-Time Visitors

Český Krumlov (*see* Tour 1)
Karlovy Vary (*see* Tour 2)
Konopiště Castle (*see* Tour 1)
Lidice Museum (*see* Tour 3)
Mariánské Lázně (*see* Tour 2)
Mělník Castle (*see* Tour 3)
Rosenberg Castle (*see* Tour 1)
St. Barbara's Cathedral in Kutná Hora (*see* Tour 1)
Tábor (*see* Tour 1)
Terezín (*see* Tour 3)

Exploring Bohemia

Tour 1: Southern Bohemia

❶

Numbers in the margin correspond to points of interest on the Bohemia map.

At one time Prague's chief rival in Bohemia for wealth and beauty, **Kutná Hora** lies about 70 kilometers (44 miles) east of the capital. To get there from Prague, follow the signs along Route 333 through the city's dusty eastern suburbs and little resort towns, such as Říčany, on the outskirts. The approach to Kutná Hora looks much as it has for centuries. The town's long economic decline spared it the postwar construction that has blighted the outskirts of so many other Czech cities.

Though it is undeniably beautiful, with an intact collection of Gothic and Baroque ruins, Kutná Hora can leave one feeling a bit melancholy. The town owes its illustrious past to silver, discovered here during the 12th century. For some 400 years the mines were worked with consummate efficiency, the wealth going to support grand projects throughout Bohemia. Charles IV used the silver to finance his transformation of Prague from a market town into the worthy capital of the Holy Roman Empire during the 14th century. As the silver began to run out during the 16th and 17th centuries, however, Kutná Hora's importance faded. What remains is the paradox you see today: poor inhabitants dwarfed by the splendors of the Middle Ages.

Forget the town center for a moment and walk to the **Chrám svatej Barbory** (St. Barbara's Cathedral), a 10-minute stroll from the main Palackého náměstí along Barborská ulice The approach to the cathedral, overlooking the river, is magnificent. Statues line the road, and the Baroque houses vie for your attention. In the distance, the netted vaulting of the cathedral resembles a large, magnificent tent more than a religious center; the effect gives the cathedral a cheerier look than the dignified Gothic towers of Prague. St. Barbara's is undoubtedly Kutná Hora's masterpiece. Built in the 14th and 15th centuries, it drew on the talents of the Peter Parler workshop as well

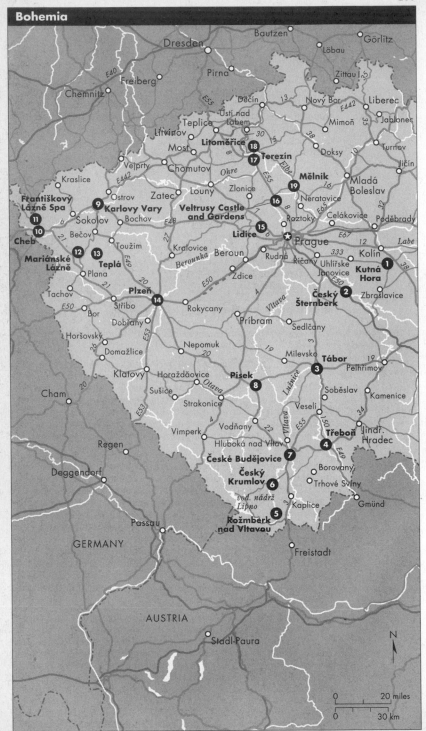

Bohemia

Dresden

Bautzen

Görlitz

Löbau

Pirna

Freiberg

E40

Chemnitz

Děčín

13

Nový Bor

Liberec

Zittau

E442

35

Jablonec

Ústí nad Labem

Teplice

Mimoň

Litvínov

30

15

38

Doksy

Turnov

Jičín

Most

Litoměřice

18

Terezín

17

Velprty

Chomutov

Ohře

Elbe

E55

Mělník

Mladá Boleslav

Kraslice

E442

Zatec

Louny

Zlonice

19

16

Neratovice

32

Poděbrady

Františkovy Lázně Spa

Ostrov

Karlovy Vary

9

Bochov

E48

Veltrusy Castle and Gardens

7

Celákovice

11

Sokolov

6

Roztoky

10

Bečov

Cheb

27

Kralovice

Lidice

15

6

Prague

Labe

12

Kolín

21

Toužim

Beroun

Berounka

Rudná

Říčany

333

1

Mariánské Lázně

12

13

Teplá

E49

20

Zdice

Uhlířské Janovice

Kutná Hora

E50

Plana

21

Plzeň

14

Rokycany

4

Vltava

E50

Tachov

Stříbro

Český Šternberk

2

Zbraslavice

Bor

Dobřany

Příbram

Sedlčany

Horšovský

26

Nepomuk

20

Milevsko

3

19

Domažlice

Klatovy

Horažďovice

Pisek

8

Lužnice

Tábor

3

Pelhřimov

19

Cham

20

Sušice

Otava

Strakonice

Soběslav

Kamenice

Regen

Vimperk

Vodňany

22

Vltava

E55

Veselí

34

Deggendorf

E53

4

Hluboká nad Vltav

Třeboň

4

150

Jindř. Hradec

České Budějovice

7

Borovany

E49

Český Krumlov

6

Trhové Sviny

Passau

vod. nádrž Lipno

Kaplice

Gmünd

GERMANY

Rožmberk nad Vltavou

5

Freistadt

AUSTRIA

N

Stadl-Paura

0   20 miles

0   30 km

as on other Gothic luminaries, such as Matthias Rejsek and Benedikt Ried.

St. Barbara is the patron saint of miners, and silver-mining themes dominate the interior. Gothic frescoes depict angels carrying shields with mining symbols. The town's other major occupation, coin production, can be seen in frescoes in the **Mintner's Chapel.** A statue of a miner, donning the characteristic smock and dating from 1700, stands proudly in the nave. But the main attraction of the interior is the vaulting itself, attributed to Ried (also responsible for the fabulous vaulting in Prague Castle's Vladislav Hall), which carries the eye effortlessly upward. *Barborská ul. Admission: 20 Kč. Open Apr.–Oct., daily 10–4; irregular hours at other times of the year.*

The romantic view over the town from the cathedral area, marked by the 260-foot tower of the St. James Church, is impressive, and few modern buildings intrude. As you descend into town, the **Hradek** (Little Castle), on your right along Barborská ulice, was once part of the town's fortifications and now houses a museum of mining and coin production. *Barborská ul. Admission: 20 Kč. adults, 10 Kč. children. Open Apr.–Oct., daily 8–noon and 1–5.*

Time Out The **Café U Hradků** is a pleasant place to stop for refreshments or a light home-cooked meal. Lamps and furnishings from the 1920s add a period touch. *Barborská ul. 33, tel. 0327/4277. Open Tues.–Sun. 10–7. No credit cards.*

More interesting, however, is the old mint itself, the **Vlašský dvůr** (Italian Court), which you'll find easily by following the signs through town. Coins were first minted here in 1300, struck by Italian artisans brought in from Florence—hence the mint's odd name. It was here that the famed Prague groschen, one of the most widely circulated coins of the Middle Ages, was minted until 1726, and here, too, that the Bohemian kings stayed on their frequent visits. Something of the court's former wealth can be glimpsed in the formal Gothic interiors of the chapel and tower rooms. A **coin museum,** open in spring and summer, allows you to see the small silvery groschen being struck and gives you a chance to buy replicas. Small wooden triptychs can be purchased in the chapel. *Havličkovo nám. Admission: 10 Kč. adults, 5 Kč. children. Open Apr.–Oct., daily 8–4.*

If the door to the **Chrám svatého Jakuba** (St. James Church) next door is open, peek inside. Originally a Gothic church dating from the early 1400s, the structure was almost entirely transformed into Baroque during the 17th and 18th centuries. The characteristic onion dome on the tower was added in 1737. The paintings on the wall include works of the best Baroque Czech masters; the *Pietà* is by the 17th-century painter Karel Škréta. Pause to admire the simple Gothic beauty of the 12-sided **kamenná kašna** (stone fountain) at the Rejskovo náměstí, just off Husova ulice. This unique work, some 500 years old, is supposedly the creation of Rejsek, one of the architects of St. Barbara's.

Before leaving the city, stop in the nearby suburb of Sedlec for a bone-chilling sight: namely, a chapel decorated with the bones of some 40,000 people. The All Saints' Cemetery Chapel, or "Bone Church," at the site of the former Sedlec Monastery, came into being in the 14th century, when development forced the clearing of a nearby graveyard. Monks of the Cistercian order came up with the bright idea of using the bones for decoration; the most recent creations date from the end of the last century. *Admission: 20 Kč., 10 Kč. children. Open daily 9–noon and 2–4.*

Leave Kutná Hora via Route 337; at Uhlířské Janovice switch to Route 125 and then, a little farther, to Route 111, which leads through gentle hills and pleasant countryside to the castle at **Český Šternberk.** At night this 13th-century castle, last renovated in the 17th century, looks positively evil, occupying a forested knoll over the Sázava River. By daylight, the structure is less haunting but still impressive. Although the castle became the property of the Czechoslovak state following the Second World War, Count Šternberk (the former owner) was permitted to occupy it until his death in 1966 as a reward for not cowering to the occupying German forces. In season, you can tour some of the rooms fitted out with period furniture (mostly Rococo); little of the early Gothic has survived the many renovations. *Admission: 20 Kč. adults, 10 Kč. children. Open May–Aug., Tues.–Sun. 8–5; Apr. and Oct., Sat. and Sun. 9–4; Sept., Tues.–Sun. 9–5.*

Given its remote location, Český Šternberk is ill-equipped for a meal or an overnight stay. Instead, continue on to the superior facilities of **Konopiště** (via the industrial town of Benešov) some 24 kilometers (15 miles) away. Konopiště is best known for its 14th-century castle, which served six centuries later as the residence of the former heir to the Austrian crown, Franz Ferdinand d'Este. Scorned by the Austrian nobility for having married a commoner, Franz Ferdinand wanted an impressive summer residence to win back the envy of his peers, and he spared no expense in restoring the castle to its original Gothic form, filling its 82 rooms with outlandish paintings, statues, and curiosities. Franz Ferdinand's dream came to a fateful end in 1914 when he was assassinated at Sarajevo, an event that precipitated World War I. The Austrian defeat in the war ultimately led to the fall of the Habsburgs. Ironically, the destiny of the Austrian empire had been sealed at the castle a month before the assassination, when Austrian kaiser Franz Joseph I met with Germany's kaiser Wilhelm II and agreed to join forces with him in the event of war.

Time Out The little cabin restaurant **Stodola** (tel. 0301/22732), next to the Konopiště Motel (*see* Lodging, *below*) serves excellent grilled meats, chicken, and fish in a traditional setting. The live folk music in the evenings is romantic rather than obtrusive; the wines and service are excellent.

To visit the castle, start from the Konopiště Motel, located about a kilometer (½ mile) off Route 3, and walk straight for about 2 kilometers (1 mile) along the trail through the woods. Before long, the rounded, neo-Gothic towers appear through the trees, and you reach the formal garden with its almost mystical circle of classical statues. Built by the wealthy Beneschau family, the castle dates from around 1300 and for centuries served as a bastion of the nobility in their struggle for power with the king. In what must have been a great affront to royal authority, at the end of the 14th century, Catholic nobles actually captured the weak King Wenceslas (Václav) IV in Prague and held him prisoner in the smaller of the two rounded towers. To this day the tower is known affectionately as the Václavka. Several of the rooms, reflecting the archduke's extravagant taste and lifestyle, are open to the public during the summer months. A valuable collection of weapons from the 16th to 18th century can be seen in the Weapons Hall on the third floor. Less easy to miss are the hundreds of stuffed animals, rather macabre monuments to the archduke's obsession with hunting. *Admission: 20 Kč. adults, 10 Kč. children. Open Apr.–Oct., daily 9–4.*

❸ The next stop, **Tábor,** is an easy 40 kilometers (25 miles) down Route 3. It's hard to believe this dusty Czech town was built to receive Christ on his return to Earth in the Second Coming. But that's what the Hussites intended when they flocked here by the thousands in 1420 to construct a society modeled on the communities of the early Christians. Tábor's fascinating history is unique among Czech towns. It started out not as a mercantile or administrative center but as a combination utopia and fortress.

Following the execution of Jan Hus, a vociferous religious reformer who railed against the Catholic church and nobility, reform priests drawing on the support of poor workers and peasants took to the hills of southern Bohemia. These hilltop congregations soon grew into permanent settlements, wholly outside the feudal order. The most important settlement, located on the Lužnice River, became known in 1420 as Tábor. Tábor quickly evolved into the symbolic and spiritual center of the Hussites (now called Taborites) and, together with Prague, served as the bulwark of the reform movement.

The early 1420s in Tábor were heady days for religious reformers. Private property was denounced, and the many poor who made the pilgrimage to Tábor were required to leave their possessions at the town gates. Some sects rejected the doctrine of transubstantiation (the belief that the Eucharist becomes the body and blood of Christ), making Holy Communion into a bawdy, secular feast of bread and wine. Still other reformers considered themselves superior to Christ—who by dying had shown himself to be merely mortal. Few, however, felt obliged to work for a living, and the Taborites had to rely increasingly on raids on neighboring villages for survival.

War fever in Tábor at the time ran high, and the town became one of the focal points of the ensuing Hussite wars (1419–34), which pitted reformers against an array of foreign crusaders, Catholics, and noblemen. Under the brilliant military leadership of Jan Žižka, the Taborites enjoyed early successes, but the forces of the established church proved too mighty in the end. Žižka was killed in 1424, and the Hussite uprising ended at the rout of Lipany 10 years later. But even after the fall, many of the town's citizens resisted recatholicization. Fittingly, following the Battle of White Mountain in 1620 (the final defeat for the Czech Protestants), Tábor was the last city to succumb to the conquering Habsburgs.

Begin a walking tour of the town at the **Žižkovo náměstí** (Žižka Square), named for the gifted Hussite military leader. A large bronze statue of Žižka from the 19th century dominates the square, serving as a reminder of the town's fiery past. The stone tables in front of the Gothic Town Hall and the house at No. 6 date from the 15th century and were used by the Hussites to give daily Communion to the faithful. Follow the tiny streets around the square, which seemingly lead nowhere. They curve around, branch off, and then stop; few lead back to the main square. The confusing street plan was purposely laid during the 15th century to thwart incoming invasions.

The **Museum of the Hussite Movement,** just behind the Town Hall, documents the history of the reformers. Note the elaborate network of tunnels carved by the Hussites below the Old Town for protection in case of attack. *Křivkova ul. 31. Admission: 20 Kč. adults, 10 Kč. children. Open Apr.–Oct., daily 9–4.*

Leave the square along **Pražská ulice,** a main route to the newer part of town, and note the beautiful Renaissance facades from the 16th century. Turn right at Divadelní and head to the Lužnice River to see the remaining walls and fortifications of the 15th century, irrefutable evidence of the town's vital function as a stronghold. The **Kotnov hrad** (Kotnov Castle), rising above the river in the distance to the right, dates from the 13th century and was part of the earliest fortifications. The large pond to the northeast of Tábor was created as a reservoir in 1492; since it was used for baptism, the fervent Taborites named the lake Jordan.

From Tábor head due south for 26 kilometers (16 miles) along Route 3 to Veselí nad Lužnicí; and then drive 22 kilometers (14 miles) along ❹ picturesque Route 150 through a plethora of ponds to **Třeboň,** another jewel of a town with a far different historical heritage than Tábor's. Třeboň was settled during the 13th century by the Wittkowitzes (later called the Rosenbergs), once Bohemia's noblest family. From 1316 to the end of the 16th century, the dynasty dominated southern Bohemia. Their wealth was based on silver and real estate. Their official residence was 40 kilometers (25 miles) to the southwest, in Český Krumlov, but Třeboň was an important second residence and repository of the family archives.

Thanks to the Rosenberg family, this unlikely landlocked town has become the center of the Czech Republic's fishing industry. During the 15th and 16th centuries, the Rosenbergs peppered the countryside with 6,000 enormous ponds, partly to drain the land and partly to breed fish. Carp breeding is still big business, and if you are in the area in the late autumn you may be lucky enough to witness the great carp harvests, when tens of thousands of the glittering fish are netted. The largest pond, bearing the Rosenberg name, lies just north of Třeboň. The **Rybnik Svět** (Svět Pond) is closest to town along the southern edge. Join the locals on a warm afternoon for a stroll along its banks and enjoy the mild breezes.

Begin a walking tour of Třeboň from the park outside the town walls, with the Svět Pond at your back. From here, the simple sgraffito Renaissance exterior of the castle, with its deep turrets, is highly impressive. The intact town walls, built during the 16th century, are among the best in the Czech Republic. Continue along the park, turning left at the first of the three gates into town. An 18th-century brewery, still producing outstanding beer, is off to the right. Beer enjoys nearly as long a tradition here as in Plzeň or České Budějovice, having been brewed since 1379 as the redbrick tower proudly boasts. Continue straight ahead to arrive at the main square, with its familiar collection of arcaded Renaissance and Baroque houses. Look for the **Bílý Koníček** (Little White Horse), the best-preserved Renaissance house on the square, dating from 1544. The large rectangular gable on the roof is composed of numerous tiny towers.

The entrance to **Třeboň hrad** (Třeboň Castle) lies at the southwest corner of the square. From here it looks plain and sober with its stark white walls, but the rooms (open to the public) are sumptuous re-creations of 16th-century life. The castle also houses a permanent exhibition of pond building. After passing out of the hands of the Rosenbergs, the castle eventually became the property of the Schwarzenberg family, who built their family tomb in a grand park across the other side of Svět Pond. It is now a monumental neo-Gothic destination for Sunday-afternoon picnickers. *Třeboň Castle. Admission: 20 Kč. adults, 10 Kč. children. Open Apr.–Oct., Tues.–Sun. 10–3:30.*

In the **Augustine monastery**, adjacent to the castle, stop to take a look at the famous **Altar of the Masters of Wittingau**, dating from the late 14th century. The altar was removed from the St. Giles Church (Chrám svatého Jiljí) on Husova třída in 1781. The paintings themselves, the most famous example of Bohemian Gothic art, are now in the National Gallery in Prague.

Time Out Before leaving Třeboň, sample some of the excellent local beer at the **Bílý Koníček** (tel. 0333/2818), now a modest hotel and restaurant on the square. You can also get a variety of nonalcoholic beverages as well as good local dishes at reasonable prices.

Drive south out of Třeboň along Route 155 in the direction of Borovany. From here you can continue straight to busy Route 3, which takes you down to Kaplice. A more scenic but time-consuming drive takes you down Route 157 via Trhové Sviny. The heavily forested countryside, regardless of the road you choose, is among the most unspoiled in Bohemia. Don't be surprised to see deer grazing, unfazed by passing cars. Once you reach Route 3, proceed in the direction of Linz, turning off to the right just before the border crossing with Austria. Follow the signs in the direction of Vyšší Brod and turn right at the sign to Rožmberk nad Vltavou.

❺ The little village of **Rožmberk nad Vltavou**, just a few kilometers from the former Iron Curtain, has been forgotten in the postwar years. The atmosphere is akin to that of a ghost town, especially at night with the darkened **Rosenberg hrad** (Rosenberg Castle) keeping lonely vigil atop the hill overlooking the Vltava River. A barely visible German sign, WIRTSCHAFT ZUM GOLDENEN BÄREN, on the battered facade of a beer hall across the bridge, adds to the feeling of abandonment, as if nothing has happened here in decades. Take a moment to enjoy the silence and walk up the hill to the castle. The slender tower, the Jakobínka, dates from the 13th century, when the Rosenberg family built the original structure. Most of the exterior, however, is neo-Gothic from the last century. During the summer you can tour some of the rooms, admiring the weapons and Bohemian paintings. From the castle gates, the Romanesque-Gothic church below, standing beside the lone figure of St. Christopher on the bridge, looks especially solemn. *Admission: 20 Kč. adults, 10 Kč. children. Open Apr.–Oct., daily 9–noon and 1–5.*

Continue north along the pretty Vltava River for about 20 kilome-
❻ ters (13 miles) to **Český Krumlov**, the official residence of the Rosenbergs for some 300 years. Český Krumlov is an eye-opener: None of the surrounding towns or villages, with their open squares and mixtures of old and new buildings, will prepare you for the beauty of the Old Town. Here the Vltava works its wonders as nowhere else but in Prague itself, swirling in a nearly complete circle around the town. Across the river stands the proud castle of the Rosenbergs, rivaling any in the country in size and splendor.

For the moment, Český Krumlov's beauty is still intact. The dilapidated buildings that lend the town its unique atmosphere remain untouched by developers. This, of course, has a negative side. In peak months, when visitors from Austria and Germany pack the streets, the few existing facilities for visitors are woefully overburdened. But overlook any minor inconveniences, and enjoy a rare, unspoiled trip through time. (Český Krumlov is also a good place for an overnight stay. The town has lots of private rooms and two older hotels, both rich in atmosphere, that provide a perfect complement to the town's splendors.)

Begin a tour of the Old Town from the main **Svornosti náměstí**. If you've booked a room at the Hotel Krumlov on the square, you can drive up the narrow Latrán and park in the square. Otherwise, park outside the town gates and walk. The square itself is disappointing; the arcades hide the richness of the buildings' architecture. The **Town Hall** at No. 1, built in 1580, is memorable for its Renaissance friezes and Gothic arcades. Tiny alleys fan out from the square in all directions. The **Horní ulice** begins just opposite the Hotel Krumlov. A quick visit to the **Městské Muzeum** (Museum of the City) on this street is a good way to familiarize yourself with the rise and fall of the Rosenberg dynasty. *Horní ul. 152. Admission: 20 Kč. adults, 10 Kč. children. Open Tues.–Fri. 10–noon and 12:30–6.*

Just opposite the museum at No. 154 are the Renaissance facades, complete with lively sgraffiti, of the former **Jesuit School**—now newly renovated as the luxurious Růže Hotel. Český Krumlov owes its abundance of Renaissance detailing to its location on the main trading routes to Italy and Bavaria—a perfect site for absorbing incoming fashions. The tower of the nearby late-Gothic **St. Vitus Church,** built in the late 1400s, rises from its position on the Kostelní ulice to offset the larger, older tower of the castle across the river. The view over the Old Town and castle is at its most spectacular from here.

To get to **Krumlov hrad** (Krumlov Castle), make your way from St. Vitus to the main street, the **Radniční,** via either **Masná** or **Kostelní ulice,** both of which form a big ring around the square. Cross the peaceful Vltava and enter at one of two gates along the Latrán. The oldest and most striking part of the castle is the round 12th-century tower, renovated like the rest of the building in the 16th century to look something like a minaret, with its delicately arcaded Renaissance balcony. The tower is part of the old border fortifications, guarding the Bohemian frontiers from Austrian incursion.

As you enter the castle area, look into the old moats, where two playful brown bears now reside—unlikely to be of much help in protecting the castle from attack. In season, the castle rooms are open to the public. The Hall of Masks is the most impressive interior, with its richly detailed 18th-century frescoes. After proceeding through a series of courtyards, you'll come to a wonderfully romantic elevated passageway, with spectacular views of the huddled houses of the Old Town. The Austrian Expressionist painter Egon Schiele made Český Krumlov his home in the early years of this century and often painted this particular view over the river. He entitled his now famous Krumlov series *The Dead Town*. From the river down below, the elevated passageway is revealed in all its Renaissance glory as part of a network of tall arches, looking like a particularly elaborate Roman viaduct. Up on top runs a narrow three-storied residential block (still inhabited), dressed in gray-and-white Renaissance stripes. At the end of the passageway you'll come to the luxuriously appointed castle gardens (open only in summer). In the middle is an open-air theater, one of Bohemia's first such theaters and remarkable for its still-intact gold stage. Performances are held here in July and August. *Český Krumlov Castle. Admission: 30 Kč. adults, 20 Kč. children. Open May–Aug., Tues.–Sun. 8–noon and 1–5; Apr. and Oct., Tues.–Sun. 9–noon and 1–4; Sept., Tues.–Sun. 9–noon and 1–5.*

⑦ From Český Krumlov, follow Route 159 and then Route 3 up to **České Budějovice,** an easy drive of some 22 kilometers (14 miles). After the glories of Český Krumlov, any other town would be a letdown—and České Budějovice, known as *Budweis* under the

Habsburgs and famous primarily for its beer, is no exception. The major attraction of what is basically an industrial town is the enormously proportioned main square, lined with arcaded houses and worth an hour or two of wandering. To get a good view over the city, it's well worth climbing the 360 steps up to the Renaissance gallery of the Černá Věž (Black Tower) at the northeast corner of the square next to the St. Nicholas Cathedral. *Admission: 10 Kč. Open Tues.– Sun. 9–5.*

From České Budějovice, follow the signs to **Hluboká nad Vltavou** about 9 kilometers (6 miles) north, to one of the Czech Republic's most curious castles. Although the structure dates from the 13th century, what you see is pure 19th-century excess, perpetrated by the wealthy Schwarzenberg family as proof of their good taste. If you think you've seen it somewhere before, you're probably thinking of Windsor Castle near London, on which it was carefully modeled. Take a tour of the inside; 41 of the 140 rooms are open to the public. The rather pompous interior reflects the "no holds barred" tastes of the time, but many individual pieces are interesting in their own right. The wooden Renaissance ceiling in the large dining room was removed by the Schwarzenbergs from the castle at Český Krumlov and brought here during the 19th century. Also look for the beautiful late-Baroque bookshelves of the library, holding some 12,000 books. If your interest in Czech painting wasn't satisfied in Prague, have a look at the **Aleš Art Gallery** in the Riding Hall, featuring the works of southern Bohemian painters from the Middle Ages to the present. The collection is the second largest in Bohemia. *Admission to castle and gallery: 10 Kč. adults, 5 Kč. children. Open Apr.–Oct., daily 9–noon and 1–4 (until 5 PM May–Aug.).*

In summer the castle grounds make a nice place for a stroll or a picnic. If you're in the mood for a more strenuous walk, follow the yellow trail signs 2 kilometers (1¼ miles) to the **Ohrada hunting lodge,** which houses a museum of hunting and fishing and also has a small zoo for children. *Open Apr.–Oct., daily 9–noon and 1–4; May– Aug., daily 1–5.*

❽ From Hluboká nad Vltavou, drive back in the direction of České Budějovice along Route 105, following the signs at the junction with Route 20 to Vodňany and eventually **Písek.** The 50 kilometers (31 miles) to Písek can be covered comfortably in about an hour. If it weren't for Písek's 700-year-old **Gothic bridge,** peopled with Baroque statues, you could easily bypass the town and continue on to Prague. After the splendors of Český Krumlov or even Třeboň, Písek's main square is admittedly plain, despite its many handsome Renaissance and Baroque houses.

The bridge, a five-minute walk from the main square along Karlovo ulice, was commissioned in 1254 by Přemysl Otakar II, who sought a secure crossing over the difficult Otava River for his salt shipments from nearby Prachatice. Originally one of the five major Hussite strongholds, Písek stood at the center of one of the most important trade routes to the west, linking Prague to Passau and the rest of Bavaria as early as the 9th century. The saintly Baroque statues were not added until the 18th century.

Return to the town square and look for the 240-foot tower of the early Gothic **Mariánský chrám** (Church of Mary). Construction was started at about the time the bridge was built. The tower was completed in 1487 and got its Baroque dome during the mid-18th century. On the inside, look for the *Madonna from Písek*, a 14th-century

Gothic altar painting. On a middle pillar is a rare series of early Gothic wall paintings dating from the end of the 13th century.

You can return to Prague from here via Route 20, turning north on Route 4 for the duration. If you've got room for still another castle, take a short detour at Route 121, about 10 kilometers (6 miles) north on Route 4, and head for **Zvíkov.** The castle, at the confluence of the Otava and Vltava rivers, is impressive for its authenticity. Unlike many other castles in Bohemia, Zvíkov survived the 18th and 19th centuries unrenovated and still looks just as it did 500 years ago. The side trip also brings you to the dams and man-made lakes of the Vltava, a major swimming and recreation area that stretches all the way back to Prague.

Tour 2: Western Bohemia ❾ From Prague, it's an easy two-hour drive due west on Route 6 to **Karlovy Vary,** better known outside the Czech Republic by its German name, Karlsbad. The most famous Bohemian spa, it is named for Emperor Charles (Karl) IV, who allegedly happened upon the springs in 1358 during a hunting expedition. As the story goes, the emperor's hound—chasing a harried stag—fell into a boiling spring and was scalded. Charles had the water tested and, familiar with spas in Italy, ordered baths to be established in the village of Vary. The spa reached its heyday in the 19th century, when royalty came here from all over Europe for treatment. The long list of those who "took the cure" includes Goethe (no fewer than 13 times, according to a plaque on one house in the Old Town), Schiller, Beethoven, and Chopin. Even Karl Marx, when he wasn't decrying wealth and privilege, spent time at the resort and wrote some of *Das Kapital* here between 1874 and 1876.

The shabby streets of modern Karlovy Vary, though, are vivid reminders that those glory days are long over. Aside from a few superficial changes, the Communists made little new investment in the town for 40 years; many of the buildings are literally crumbling behind their beautiful facades. Today officials face the daunting tasks of financing the town's reconstruction and carving out a new role for Karlovy Vary, in an era when few people can afford to set aside weeks or months at a time for a leisurely cure. To raise some quick cash, many sanatoriums have turned to offering short-term accommodations to foreign visitors (at rather expensive rates). It's even possible at some spas to receive "treatment," including carbon-dioxide baths, massage, and the ever-popular gas injections. For most visitors, though, it's enough simply to stroll the streets and parks and allow the eyes to feast awhile on the splendors of the past.

Whether you're arriving by bus, train, or car, your first view of the town on the approach from Prague will be of the ugly new section on the banks of the Ohře River. Don't despair: Continue along the main road—following the signs to the Grandhotel Pupp—until you reach the lovely main street of the older spa area, situated gently astride the banks of the little Teplá River. The walk from the New Town to the spa area is about 20 minutes; take a taxi if you're carrying a heavy load. The **Old Town** is still largely intact. Tall 19th-century houses, boasting decorative and often eccentric facades, line the spa's proud, if dilapidated, streets. Throughout you'll see colonnades full of the healthy and not-so-healthy sipping the spa's hot sulfuric water from odd pipe-shaped drinking cups. At night the streets fill with steam escaping from cracks in the earth, giving the town a slightly macabre feel.

Karlovy Vary's jarringly modern **Yuri Gagarin Colonnade,** home of the **Vřídlo,** is the town's hottest and most dramatic spring. The Vřídl o is indeed unique, shooting its scalding water to a height of some 40 feet. Walk inside the arcade to watch the hundreds of patients here take the famed Karlsbad drinking cure. You'll recognize them promenading somnambulistically up and down, eyes glazed, clutching a drinking glass filled periodically at one of the five "sources." The waters are said to be especially effective against diseases of the digestive and urinary tract. They're also good for the gout-ridden (which probably explains the spa's former popularity with royals!). If you want to join the crowds and take a sip, you can buy your own cup with a spout at vendors located within the colonnade.

Leave the colonnade and walk in the direction of the New Town, past the wooden **Market Colonnade,** currently undergoing reconstruction. Continue down the winding street until you reach the **Main Colonnade.** This neo-Renaissance pillared hall, built in 1871–81, offers four springs bearing the romantic names of Rusalka, Libussa, Prince Wenceslas, and Millpond. If you continue down the valley, you'll soon arrive at the very elegant **Park Colonnade,** a white, wrought-iron construction built in 1882 by the Viennese architectural duo of Fellner and Helmer, who sprinkled the Austro-Hungarian empire with many such edifices during the late 19th century and who also designed the town's theater (1886), a Market Colonnade (1883), and one of the old bathhouses (1895), now a casino (*see* Nightlife, *below*).

The 20th century emerges at its most disturbing a little farther along the valley across the river, in the form of the huge bunkerlike **Thermal Hotel,** built in the late 1960s. Although the building is a monstrosity, the view of Karlovy Vary from the rooftop pool is nothing short of spectacular. Even if you don't feel like a swim, it's worth taking the winding road up to the baths for the view. You can't miss the very imposing **Imperial Sanatorium** in the distance, a perfect example of turn-of-the-century architecture, with its white facade and red-tower roof. The Imperial was once the haunt of Europe's wealthiest financiers. Under the Communists, though, the sanatorium was used to house visiting Soviet dignitaries—a gesture of "friendship" from the Czech government. The Imperial has recently reopened as a private hotel, but it will be many years before it can again assume its former role.

Return to the Main Colonnade by crossing over the little Gogol Bridge near the Hotel Otova. Here you'll see steps leading behind the colonnade, through a park, and finally emerging onto the steep road **Zámecký vrch.** Walk uphill until you come to the redbrick **Victorian Church,** once used by the local English community. A few blocks farther along Petra Velikeho Street, you'll come to a splendiforous Russian Orthodox church, once visited by Czar Peter the Great. Return to the English church and take a sharp right uphill on the redbrick road. Then turn left onto a footpath through the woods, following the signs to **Jeleni Skok** (Stag's Leap). After a while you'll see steps leading up to a bronze statue of a deer towering over the cliffs, the symbol of Karlovy Vary. From here a winding path leads up to a little red **gazebo** (Altán Jeleni Skok), opening onto a fabulous panorama of the town.

Time Out Reward yourself for making the climb with a light meal at the nearby restaurant **Jeleni Skok.** You may have to pay an entrance fee if there is a live band (but you'll also get the opportunity to polka). If you don't want to walk up, you can drive from the church.

Take the steps down to the Marianská and enter the grounds of the **Grandhotel Pupp,** the former favorite of the Central European nobility and longtime rival of the Imperial. The Pupp's reputation was tarnished somewhat during the years of communist rule (the hotel was renamed the Moskva-Pupp), but the hotel's former grandeur is still in evidence. Even if you're not staying here, be sure to stroll around the impressive facilities and have a drink in the elegant cocktail bar.

Diagonally across from the Grandhotel Pupp, behind a little park, is the pompous Fellner and Helmer **Imperial Spa,** now known as **Lázně I** and housing the local casino. As you walk back into town along the river, you'll pass a variety of interesting stores, including the Moser glass store and the Elefant, one of the last of a dying breed of sophisticated coffeehouses in the Czech Republic. Across the river is the Fellner and Helmer theater. Continue on to the right of the Vřídlo, where we began the tour, and walk up the steps to the white **Kostel svatej Mauří Magdaleny** (Church of Mary Magdelene). Designed by Kilian Dientzenhofer (architect of the two St. Nicholas churches in Prague), this church is the best of the few Baroque buildings still standing in Karlovy Vary.

⑩ Known for centuries by its German name of Eger, the old town of **Cheb** lies on the border with Germany, an easy 42-kilometer (26-mile) drive from Karlovy Vary along Route 6. The town has been a fixture of Bohemia since 1322 (when the king purchased the area from German merchants), but as you walk around the beautiful medieval square, it's difficult not to think you're in Germany. The tall merchants' houses surrounding the square, with their long, red-tiled sloping roofs dotted with windows like droopy eyelids, are more Germanic in style than anything else in Bohemia. You'll also hear a lot of German on the streets—but more from the many German visitors than from the town's residents.

Germany took full possession of the town in 1938 under terms of the notorious Munich Pact. But following World War II, virtually the entire German population was expelled, and the Czech name of Cheb was officially adopted. A more notorious German connection has emerged in the years following the 1989 revolution. Cheb has quickly become the unofficial center of prostitution for visiting Germans. Don't be startled to see young women, provocatively dressed, lining the highways and bus stops on the roads into town. Prostitution of this sort is illegal, and the police have been known to crack down periodically on the women and their customers.

Begin a tour of the town in the bustling central square, the **Náměstí Krále Jiřího z Poděbrad,** once a large market area but now more a promenade for visiting Germans. The statue in the middle, similar to the Roland statues you see throughout Bohemia and attesting to the town's royal privileges, represents the town hero, Wastel of Eger. Look carefully at his right foot, and you'll see a small man holding a sword and a head—this denotes that the town had its own judge and executioner.

Walk downhill from the square to see two rickety groups of timbered medieval buildings, 11 houses in all, divided by a narrow alley. The houses, forming the area known as the **Špalíček,** date from the 13th century and were home to many Jewish merchants. **Židovská ulice** (Jews' Street), running uphill to the left of the Špalíček, served as the actual center of the ghetto. Note the small alley running off to the left of Židovská. This calm street, seemingly inappropriately named **ulička Zavražděných** (Murderers' Lane), was the scene of an outrageous act of violence in 1350. Pressures had been building for some time between Jews and Christians. Incited by an anti-Semitic bishop, the townspeople finally chased the Jews into the street, closed off both ends, and massacred them. Only the name attests to the slaughter.

Time Out Cheb's main square abounds with cafés and little restaurants, all offering a fairly uniform menu of schnitzels and sauerbraten aimed at the visiting Germans. The **Kaverna Špalíček**, nestled in the Špalíček buildings, is one of the better choices and has the added advantage of a unique architectural setting.

History buffs, particularly those interested in the Habsburgs, will want to visit the **Chebský muzeum** (Cheb Museum) in the Pachelbel House, situated behind the Špalíček on the main square. It was in this house that the great general of the Thirty Years' War, Albrecht von Wallenstein (Valdštejn), was murdered in 1634 on the orders of his own emperor, the Habsburg Ferdinand II. According to legend, Wallenstein was on his way to the Saxon border to enlist support to fight the Swedes when his own officers barged into his room and stabbed him through the heart with a stave. The stark bedroom with its four-poster bed and dark-red velvet curtains has been left as it was in his memory. The museum is also interesting in its own right: It has a section on the history of Cheb and a collection of minerals (including one discovered by Goethe). *Špalíček. Admission: 15 Kč. adults, 10 Kč. children. Open Tues.–Sun. 8–noon and 1–4.*

During the early 1820s, Goethe often stayed in the **Gabler House**, on the corner of the square at the museum. He shared a passionate interest in excavation work with the town executioner, and they both worked on the excavation of the nearby extinct volcano Komorní Hůrka. In 1791 Germany's second most famous playwright, Friedrich Schiller, lived at No. 2, at the top of the square next to the "new" town hall, where he planned his famous *Wallenstein* trilogy.

If you follow the little street on the right side of the square at the Gabler House, you will quickly reach the plain but imposing **Kostel svatého Mikuláše** (St. Nicholas Church). Construction began in 1230, when the church belonged to the Order of the Teutonic Knights. You can still see Romanesque windows under the tower; renovations throughout the centuries added an impressive Gothic portal and a Baroque interior. Just inside the Gothic entrance is a wonderfully faded plaque commemorating the diamond jubilee of Habsburg emperor Franz Josef in 1908.

From here walk down the little alley on to the Kammená and turn left onto the Křižovnická. Follow the Hradní road up to the **Chebský hrad** (Cheb Castle), situated on a cliff overlooking the Elbe River. The castle was built in the late 12th century for Holy Roman Emperor Frederick Barbarossa. The square black tower was built with blocks of lava taken from the nearby Komorní Hůrka volcano; the redbrick walls were added during the 15th century. Inside the castle grounds is the carefully restored double-decker chapel, built during the 12th century. The rather dark ground floor, still in Romanesque style, was used by commoners. The bright ornate top floor, with pointed Gothic windows, was reserved for the emperor and his family and has a wooden bridge leading to the royal palace. *Hradní ul. Admission: 15 Kč. adults, 10 Kč. children. Open Apr.–Oct., daily 9–4 (until 6 in summer).*

⓫ From Cheb it's a short drive to **Františkovy Lázně Spa**, only 6 kilometers (4 miles) away. If you're interested in seeing the **Komorní**

Hůrka volcano, take the first left off Route 21 from Cheb, or follow the red-marked footpath 3½ kilometers (2¼ miles) from Františkovy Lázně. The extinct volcano is now a tree-covered hill, but excavations on one side have laid bare the rock, and one tunnel is still open. Goethe instigated and took part in the excavations, and you can still barely make out a relief of the poet carved into the rock face.

Františkovy Lázně, or Franzensbad, the smallest of the three main Bohemian spas, isn't really in the same league as the other two (Karlovy Vary and Mariánské Lázně). Built on a more modest scale at the start of the 19th century, the town's ubiquitous Kaiser-yellow buildings weathered the communist occupation especially badly. Come here not so much to walk the once lovely gardens or to admire the faded elegance of the gently monumental Empire-style architecture but to bear witness to the effects of 40 years of wanton neglect. There is no town to speak of, just **Národní ulice,** the main street, which leads down into the spa park. The waters, whose healing properties were already known in the 16th century, are used primarily for curing infertility—hence the large number of young women wandering the grounds.

The most interesting sight in town may be the small **Spa Museum,** situated just off Národní ulice. There is a wonderful collection of spa antiques, including copper bathtubs and a turn-of-the-century exercise bike called a Velotrab. The guest books (*Kurbuch*) provide an insight into the cosmopolitan world of pre–World War I Central Europe. The book for 1812 contains the entry "Ludwig van Beethoven, composer from Vienna." *Ul. Doktora Pohoreckého 8. Admission: 15 Kč. adults, 10 Kč. children. Open weekends 9–noon and 2–5.*

Exploration of the spa itself should start on Národní ulice. Wander down through the street to the main spring, **Františkuv pramen,** under a little gazebo, filled with brass pipes. The colonnade to the left was decorated with a bust of Lenin that was replaced in 1990 by a memorial to the American liberation of the town in April 1945. Walk along the path to the left until you come to the **Lázeňská poliklinika,** where you can arrange for a day's spa treatment for around 350 Kč. The park surrounding the town is good for aimless wandering, interrupted by empty pedestals for discarded statues of historical figures no longer considered worthy of memorial.

Time Out Františkovy Lázně is blessed with some good restaurants. For a cut above the average fare, try lunch or dinner in the restaurant of the **Hotel Slovan** (tel. 0166/942841).

⓬ **Mariánské Lázně,** about 40 minutes' drive from Františkový Lázně (via Cheb), best fulfills visitors' expectations of what a spa resort should be. It's far larger and better maintained than Františkovy Lázně and is greener and quieter than Karlovy Vary. This was the spa favored by Britain's Edward VII; Goethe and Chopin, among other luminaries, also repaired here frequently. Mark Twain, on a visit to the spa in 1892, labeled the town a "health factory" and couldn't get over how new everything looked. Indeed, at that time everything was new. The sanatoriums, all built in the middle of the last century in a harmonious neoclassical style, fan out impressively around an oblong, finely groomed park. Cure takers and curiosity seekers alike parade through the two stately colonnades, both placed near the top of the park. Buy a spouted drinking cup (available at the colonnades) and join the rest of the sippers taking the drinking cure. Be forewarned, though: The waters from the

Rudolph, Ambrose, and Caroline springs, though harmless, all have a noticeable diuretic effect. For this reason they're used extensively in treating disorders of the kidney and bladder. Several spa hotels offer more extensive treatment, including baths and massage, to visitors. Prices are usually reckoned in U.S. dollars or German marks. For more information, inquire at the main spa offices at Masarykova 22 (tel. 0165/2170, fax 0165/2982).

A stay in Mariánské Lázně, however, can be healthful even without special treatment. Special walking trails, of all levels of difficulty, surround the resort in all directions. The best advice is simply to put on comfortable shoes, buy a hiking map, and head out. One of the country's few golf courses lies 3 or 4 kilometers (5 or 6 miles) from town to the east. Hotels can also help to arrange special activities, such as tennis and horseback riding. For the less intrepid, a simple stroll around the gardens, with a few deep breaths of the town's famous air, is enough to restore a healthy sense of perspective.

13 It is worth making the 15-kilometer (10-mile) detour to the little town of **Teplá** and its 800-year-old monastery, which once played an important role in Christianizing pagan Central Europe. If you don't have a car, a special bus departs daily in season from Mariánské Lázně (inquire at the information office in front of the Hotel Excelsior). The sprawling monastery, founded by the Premonstratensian order of France in 1193 (the same order that established Prague's Strahov monastery), once controlled the farms and forests in these parts for miles around. The order even owned the spa facilities at Mariánské Lázně and until 1942 used the proceeds from the spas to cover operating expenses. The complex you see before you today, however, betrays none of this earlier prosperity. Over the centuries, the monastery was plundered dozens of times during wars and upheavals, but history reserved its severest blow for the night of April 13, 1950, when security forces employed by the Communists raided the grounds and imprisoned the brothers. The monastery's property was given over to the Czech army, and for the next 28 years the buildings were used as barracks to house soldiers. In 1991 the government returned the monastery buildings and immediate grounds (but not the original land holdings) to the order, and the brothers began the arduous task of picking up the pieces—physically and spiritually.

The most important building on the grounds from an architectural point of view is the Romanesque **basilica** (1197), with its unique triple nave. The rest of the monastery complex was originally Romanesque, but it was rebuilt in 1720 by Baroque architect K. I. Dientzenhofer. There are several wall and ceiling paintings of interest here, as well as some good sculpture. The most valuable collection is in the **Nová knihovna** (New Library), where you will find illuminated hymnals and rare Czech and foreign manuscripts, including a German translation of the New Testament that predates Luther's by some 100 years. Tours of the church and library are given daily in German at 1 PM (English notes are available). The monastery also offers short-term accommodations to visitors (inquire directly at the monastery offices on the grounds). *Klášter. Admission: 20 Kč. Open daily 9–noon and 1–4.*

14 The sprawling industrial city of **Plzeň** is hardly a tourist mecca, but it's worth stopping off for an hour or two on the way back to Prague. Two sights here are of particular interest to beer fanatics. The first is the **Pilsner-Urquell brewery**, located to the east of the city near the railway station. Group tours of the 19th-century redbrick building are offered daily at 12:30 PM, during which you can taste the valuable brew, exported around the world. The beer was created in 1842 using the excellent Plzeň water, a special malt fermented on the premises, and hops grown in the region around Žatec. *U Prazdroje, tel. 019/ 2164. Admission: 60 Kč.*

Time Out You can continue drinking and find some traditional, cheap grub at the large **Na Stilce** beer hall just inside the brewery gates. The pub is open daily from 10 AM to 11 PM.

The second stop on the beer tour is the **Pivovarské muzeum** (Brewery Museum), located in a late-Gothic malthouse one block northeast of the main square. *Veleslavinova ul. 6. Admission: 10 Kč. adults, 5 Kč. children. Open Tues.–Sun. 10–6.*

The city's architectural attractions center on the main square, **náměstí Republiky,** dominated by the enormous Gothic **Chrám svatého Bartoloměja** (Church of St. Bartholemew). Both the square and the church towers hold size records, the former being the largest in Bohemia and the latter, at 102 meters (335 feet), the highest in the Czech Republic. The church was begun in 1297 and completed almost 200 years later. Around the square, mixed in with its good selection of stores, are a variety of other architectural jewels, including the town hall, adorned with sgraffiti and built in the Renaissance style by Italian architects during the town's heyday in the 16th century.

Tour 3: Northern Bohemia Nowhere else in the Czech Republic have modern history and postwar industrialization conspired to alter the landscape as severely as in northern Bohemia. The hilly land to the north of Prague, along the Labe (Elbe) River, has always been regarded as border country with Germany, and you needn't drive too far to reach the Sudetenland, the German-speaking border area that was ceded to Hitler by the British and French in 1938. Indeed, the landscape here is riddled with the tragic remains of the Nazi occupation of the Czech lands from 1939 to 1945.

Leave Prague on Route 7 (the road to Ruzyně Airport), and head in the direction of Slaný. After about 18 kilometers (11 miles), turn off at the **Lidice** exit and follow the country road for 3 kilometers (1¾ miles) straight through the little town to the **Lidice museum and monument,** where you'll find a large parking lot. In front of you is the museum area. The empty field to the right, with a large cross at the bottom, is where the town of Lidice stood until 1942, when it was viciously razed by the Nazis in retribution for the assassination of a German leader.

The Lidice story really begins with the notorious Munich Pact of 1938, according to which the leaders of Great Britain and France permitted Hitler to occupy the largely German-speaking border regions of Czechoslovakia (the so-called Sudetenland). Less than a year later, in March 1939, Hitler used his forward position to occupy the whole of Bohemia and Moravia, making the area into a protectorate of the German Reich. To guard his new possessions, Hitler appointed ruthless Nazi Reinhard Heydrich as Reichsprotektor. Heydrich immediately implemented a campaign of terror against Jews and intellectuals while currying favor with average Czechs by raising rations and wages. As a result, the Czech army-in-exile, based in Great Britain, soon began planning Heydrich's assassination. In the spring of 1942 a small band of parachutists was flown in to carry out the task.

The assassination attempt took place just north of Prague on May 27, 1942, and Heydrich died of injuries on June 4. Hitler immediately ordered that the little mining town of Lidice, west of Prague, be "removed from the face of the earth," since it was alleged (although later found untrue) that some of the assassins had been sheltered by villagers there. On the night of June 9, a Gestapo unit entered Lidice, shot the entire adult male population (199 men), and sent the 196 women to the Ravensbruck concentration camp. The 103 children in the village were sent either to Germany to be "Aryanized" or to death camps. On June 10, the entire village was razed. The assassins and their accomplices were found a week later in the Orthodox Church of Sts. Cyril and Methodius in Prague's New Town, where they committed suicide after a shoot-out with Nazi militia.

The monument to these events is a sober place. The arcades are graphic in their depiction of the deportation and slaughter of the inhabitants. The museum itself is dedicated to those killed, with photographs of each person and a short description of his or her fate. You'll also find reproductions of the German documents ordering the village's destruction, including the Gestapo's chillingly bureaucratic reports on how the massacre was carried out and the peculiar problems encountered in Aryanizing the deported children. The exhibits highlighting the international response (a suburb of Chicago was even renamed for the town) are heartwarming. An absorbing 18-minute film in Czech (worthwhile even for non-Czech speakers) tells the Lidice story. *Ul. 10. června 1942. Admission: 20 Kč. adults, 10 Kč. children and students. Open daily 9–5.*

Lidice was rebuilt after the war on the initiative of a group of miners from Birmingham, England, who called their committee "Lidice Must Live." Between new Lidice and the museum is a rose garden with some 3,000 bushes sent from all over the world. The wooden cross in the field to the right of the museum, starkly decorated with barbed wire, marks the place in old Lidice where the men were executed. Small remains of brick walls are visible here, left over from the Gestapo's dynamite and bulldozer exercise. Still, Lidice is a sad town and not a place to linger.

Leaving Lidice, turn back onto Route 7 in the direction of Prague and take the exit at Tuchoměřice (second exit after Lidice), driving in the direction of Kralupy nad Vltavou. The winding lane takes you through rolling countryside to Route 240, which will bring you, after another 11 kilometers (7 miles), to Kralupy, an industrial town better left unexplored. Drive through town, cross the Vltava River, **16** and take a right turn after a kilometer to **Veltrusy Castle and Gardens.** The Baroque splendor of Veltrusy Castle, vividly contrasting with Kralupy's ordinariness, is hidden in a carefully laid out English park full of old and rare trees and scattered with 18th-century architectural follies. The castle itself has been turned into a museum showcasing the cosmopolitan lifestyle of the imperial aristocracy, displaying Japanese and Chinese porcelain, English chandeliers, and 16th-century tapestries from Brussels. *Admission: 20 Kč. adults, 10 Kč. children and students. Open May–Oct., Tues.–Sun. 10–5.*

From Veltrusy Castle you can walk the 2½ kilometers (1⅛ miles) by marked paths to **Nelahozeves,** the birthplace in 1841 of Antonín Dvořák, the Czech Republic's greatest composer. By car, the route is rather more circuitous: Turn right out of Veltrusy onto the highway and over the river, then make a sharp left back along the river to Nelahozeves. Dvořák's pretty corner house on the main road (No. 12), with its tidy windows and arches, has a small memorial museum. In Dvořák's time, the house was an inn run by his parents, and it was here that he learned to play the violin. *Admission free. Open Tues.–Thurs., Sat., and Sun. 9–noon and 2–5.*

For those not enamored of the spirit of Dvořák's youth, the main attraction in town is the brooding Renaissance **castle,** with its black-and-white sgraffito, once the residence of the powerful Lobkowitz family. The castle now houses an excellent collection of modern art. *Admission: 20 Kč. adults, 10 Kč. children and students. Open May–Oct., Tues.–Sun. 10–5.*

Drive back to Route 8 and continue north 36 kilometers (22 miles) to ⑰ the old garrison town of **Terezín,** which gained notoriety under the Nazis as the nefarious Nazi concentration camp **Theresienstadt.** Theresienstadt is difficult to grasp at first. The Czechs have put up few signs to tell you what to see; the town's buildings, parks, and buses resemble those of any of a hundred other unremarkable places, built originally by the Austrians and now inhabited by Czechs. You could easily pass through it and never learn any of the town's dark secrets.

Part of the problem is that **Malá Pevnost** (Small Fortress), the actual prison and death camp, is located 2 kilometers (1¼ miles) south of Terezín. Visitors to the strange redbrick complex see the prison more or less as it was when the Nazis left it in 1945. Above the entrance to the main courtyard stands the cynical motto ARBEIT MACHT FREI (roughly, "Work Liberates"). Take a walk around the various rooms, still housing a sad collection of rusty bedframes, sinks, and shower units. At the far end of the fortress, opposite the main entrance, is the special wing built by the Nazis when space became tight. The windowless cells are horrific; try going into one and closing the door—and then imagine being crammed in with 14 other people. In the center of the fortress is a museum and a room where films are shown. *Admission: 50 Kč. adults, 25 Kč. children and students. Open May–Sept., daily 8–6:30; Oct.–Apr., daily 8–4:30.*

During World War II, Terezín served as a detention center for thousands of Jews and was used by the Nazis as an elaborate prop in a nefarious propaganda ploy. The large barracks buildings around town, once used during the 18th and 19th centuries to house Austrian soldiers, became living quarters for thousands of interred Jews. But in 1942, to placate international public opinion, the Nazis cynically decided to transform the town into a showcase camp—to prove to the world their "benevolent" intentions toward the Jews. To give the place the image of a spa town, the streets were given new names such as Lake Street, Bath Street, and Park Street. Numerous elderly Jews from Germany were taken in by the deception and paid large sums of money to come to the new "retirement village." Just before the International Red Cross inspected the town in early 1944, Nazi authorities began a beautification campaign and painted the buildings, set up stores, laid out a park with benches in front of the Town Hall, and arranged for concerts and sports. The map just off the main square shows the town's street plan as the locations of various buildings between 1941 and 1945. The Jews here were able, with great difficulty, to establish a cultural life of their own under the limited "self-government" that was set up in the camp. The inmates created a library and a theater, and lectures and musical performances were given on a regular basis.

Once it was clear that the war was lost, however, the Nazis dropped any pretense and quickly stepped up transport of Jews to the Auschwitz death camp in Poland. Transports were not new to the ghetto;

to keep the population at around 30,000, a train was sent off every few months or so "to the east" to make room for incoming groups. In the fall of 1944, these transports were increased to one every few days. In all, some 87,000 Jews were murdered in this way, and another 35,000 died from starvation or disease. The town's horrific story is told in words and pictures at the **Ghetto Museum**, located just off the central park in town. *Admission: 50 Kč. adults, 25 Kč. children and students. Open May–Sept., daily 8–6:30; Oct.–Apr., daily 8–4:30.*

For all its history, Terezín is no place for an extended stay. Locals have chosen not to highlight the town's role during the Nazi era, and hence little provision has been made for visitors. Instead, continue ⑱ the several kilometers along Route 15 to **Litoměřice**. Although it, too, lacks much in the way of modern facilities, Litoměřice is cheerier and its history dates from the far less harrowing 13th, 14th, and 15th centuries.

Given the decrepit state of the houses and streets, it's hard to believe that in the 13th century Litoměřice was considered one of Bohemia's leading towns and a rival to Prague. Bypassed by the railroad and left to drift, the town has remained largely untouched by modern development. Even today, although the food industry has established several factories in the surrounding area, much of central Litoměřice is like a living museum.

The best way to get a feel for Litoměřice is to start at the excellent **Městske Muzeum** (City Museum) on the corner of the main square and Dlouhá ulice in the building of the Old Town Hall. The entrance is under the Renaissance arcades. Unfortunately, the exhibits are described in Czech (with written commentary in German available from the ticket seller); but even without understanding the words, you'll find this museum fascinating. Despite its position near the old border with Germany, Litoměřice was a Czech and Hussite stronghold, and one of the museum's treasures is the brightly colored, illuminated Bible depicting Hus's burning at the stake in Constance. Note also the golden chalice nearby, the old symbol of the Hussites. Farther on you come to an exquisite Renaissance pulpit and altar decorated with painted stone reliefs. On the second floor the most interesting exhibit is from the Nazi era, when Litoměřice became a part of Sudeten Germany and a border town of the German Reich, providing soldiers for nearby Theresienstadt. Although most of the Communist party's exhibits have been removed, this section still boasts a number of posters proclaiming the victory of the working class, unwittingly marking the slide from one totalitarian state to another. *Mirové nám. Admission: 10 Kč. adults, 5 Kč. children and students. Open Tues.–Sun. 10–noon and 1–4.*

After leaving the museum, stroll along the busy but decaying central square, which sports a range of architectural styles from Renaissance arcades to Baroque gables and a Gothic bell tower. The town's trademark, though, is the chalice-shaped tower at No. 7, the **Chalice House,** built in the 1580s for an Utraquist patrician. The Utraquists were moderate Hussites who believed that laymen should receive wine as well as bread in the sacrament of Holy Communion. On the left-hand corner of the Old Town Hall is a replica of a small and unusual Roland statue (the original is in the museum) on a high stone pedestal. These statues, found throughout Bohemia, signify that the town is a "royal free town" and due all of the usual privileges of such a distinction. This particular statue is unique in that, instead of showing the usual handsome knight, it depicts a hairy caveman wielding a club. Even in the 15th century, it seems, Czechs had a sense of humor.

Time Out   For an ice cream, a fruit drink, or a cup of coffee, try the little stand-up **Atropic Cafe** next to the museum on the main square. Good beer and passable Czech food are served up daily in clean surroundings at the **Pivnice Kalich** (Lidická 9), a block from the main square.

The Baroque facade and interior of the **All Saints' Church,** to the right of the Town Hall, and **St. Jacob's Church,** farther down Dlouhá ulice, are the work of the 18th-century Italian master-builder Octavian Broggio. His most beautiful work, though, is the small **Kostel svatého Václava** (St. Wenceslas Chapel), squeezed into an unwieldy square to the north of town on the cathedral hill and now a Russian Orthodox church. **Dom svatého Štěpána** (St. Stephen's Cathedral), farther up the hill, is monumental but uninspired. Its one real treasure is a Lucas Cranach painting of St. Antonius—but unfortunately the cathedral door is often locked. There are also a number of paintings by the famed 17th-century Bohemian artist Karel Škréta.

Follow the Elbe River in the direction of the industrial town of Ústí nad Labem. The best route for views is Route 30 (accessed via Route 8 near Terezín): It passes through a long, unspoiled winding valley, packed in by surrounding hills, and has something of the look of a 16th-century landscape painting. As you near Ústí, your eyes are suddenly assaulted by the towering mass of **Střekov hrad** (Střekov Castle), perched precariously on huge cliffs, rising abruptly above the right bank. The fortress was built in 1319 by King Johann of Luxembourg to control the rebellious nobles of northern Bohemia. During the 16th century it became the residence of Wenceslas of Lobkowitz, who rebuilt the castle in the Renaissance style. The lonely ruins have served to inspire many German artists and poets, including Richard Wagner, who came here on a moonlit night in the summer of 1842. But if you arrive on a dark night, about the only classic that comes to mind is Mary Shelley's *Frankenstein*. Drive up to the castle by taking the first turnoff into Ústí and immediately turning left onto the bridge over the Elbe. Across the bridge, turn right and follow the signs.

❶⁹ From Střekov, continue on Route 261 through the picturesque hills of the Elbe banks back through Litoměřice and on to **Mělník,** 50 kilometers (31 miles) south. Park on the small streets just off the pretty but hard-to-find main square. Mělník is a lively town, known best perhaps as the source of the special "Ludmila" wine, the country's only decent wine not produced in southern Moravia. The town's **zámek,** a smallish castle a few blocks from the main square, majestically guards the confluence of the Elbe River with two arms of the Vltava. The view here is stunning, and the sunny hillsides are covered with vineyards. As the locals tell it, Emperor Charles IV was responsible for bringing wine production to the area. Having a good eye for favorable growing conditions, he encouraged vintners from Burgundy to come here and plant their vines.

The courtyard's three dominant architectural styles, reflecting alterations to the castle over the years, fairly jump out at you. On the north side, note the typical arcaded Renaissance balconies, decorated with sgraffiti; to the west, a Gothic tract is still easy to make out. The southern wing is clearly Baroque (although also decorated with arcades). Inside the castle at the back, you'll find a vinárna with mediocre food but excellent views overlooking the rivers. On the other side is a museum devoted to wine making and folk crafts.

Museum admission: 20 Kč. adults, 10 Kč. children. Open May–Oct., Tues.–Sun. 10–5.

To return to Prague, about 30 kilometers (20 miles) from Mělník, follow Route 9 south.

What to See and Do with Children

Children will be fascinated by Český Krumlov; its Old World streets and castle, complete with brown bears, make for a fairy-tale atmosphere. Karlovy Vary's warm open-air pool (on top of the Thermal Hotel) offers the unique experience of swimming comfortably even in the coolest weather. Terezín (Theresienstadt) makes a valuable educational outing for older children.

Off the Beaten Track

If you're not planning to go to the Tatras in Slovakia but nevertheless want a few days in the mountains, head for the Krkonoše range—the so-called Giant Mountains—near the Polish frontier. Here you'll find the most spectacular scenery in Bohemia, although it oversteps linguistic convention to call these rolling hills "giant" (the highest point is 1,602 meters, or 5,256 feet). Not only is the scenery beautiful, but the local architecture is refreshingly rural after all the towns and cities; the steep-roofed timber houses, painted in warm colors, look just right pitched against sunlit pinewoods or snowy pastures.

The principal resorts of the area are Janské Lázně (another spa), Pec pod Sněžkou, and Špindlerův Mlýn, this last being the most sophisticated in its accommodations and facilities. It is attractively placed astride the rippling Labe (Elbe) River, here in its formative stages. To get out and experience the mountains, a good trip is to take a bus from Špindlerův Mlýn via Janské Lázně to Pec pod Sněžkou—a deceptively long journey by road of around 50 kilometers (31 miles). From there, embark on a two-stage chair lift to the top of Sněžka (the area's highest peak), and then walk along a ridge overlooking the Polish countryside, eventually dropping into deep, silent pinewoods and returning to Špindlerův Mlýn. If you walk over the mountain instead of driving around it, the return trip is just 11 kilometers (7 miles)—a comfortable walk of about three to four hours. The path actually takes you into Poland at one point; you won't need a visa, but take your passport along just in case.

The source of the Labe also springs from the heights near the Polish border. From the town of Harrachov, walkers can reach it by a marked trail. The distance is about 10 kilometers (6 miles). From Špindlerův Mlýn, a beautiful but sometimes steep trail follows the Labe Valley up to the source near Labská Bouda. Allow about three hours for this walk, and take good shoes and a map.

To get to the Krkonoše area from Prague, take the D11 freeway to Poděbrady and then go through Jičín, Nová Paka, and Vrchlabí, finally reaching Špindlerův Mlýn. Excellent bus connections link Prague with the towns of Špindlerův Mlýn, Vrchlabí, and Pec pod Sněžkou.

Shopping

Bohemia is justly world-famous for the quality of its lead crystal, porcelain, and garnets. Stores offering a stunning array of these items, at excellent prices, can be found in practically any town frequented by tourists. In western Bohemia, Karlovy Vary is best known to glass enthusiasts as home of the **Moser** glass company, one of the world's leading producers of crystal and decorative glassware. In addition to running the flagship store at Na Příkopě 12 in Prague, the company operates an outlet in Karlovy Vary on Stará Louka, next to the Cafe Elefant. A number of outlets for lesser-known, although also high-quality makers of glass and porcelain can also be found along Stará Louka. For excellent buys on porcelain, try the **Pirkenhammer** outlet below the Hotel Atlantic (Tržiště 23). A cheaper but nonetheless unique gift from Karlovy Vary would be a bottle of the ubiquitous bittersweet (and potent) Becherovka, a liqueur produced by the town's own Jan Becher distillery. Always appreciated as gifts are the unique pipe-shaped ceramic drinking cups used to take the drinking cure at spas. Find them at the colonnades in Karlovy Vary and Mariánské Lázně. You can also buy boxes of tasty Oplatky wafers, sometimes covered with chocolate, at shops in all of the spa towns.

The garnet center of the country is in **Turnov,** northern Bohemia. The main producer there, **Granát Turnov,** maintains two outlets in town (at 5 Května ul. 27 and Palackého ul. 188) and one shop in České Budějovice (at Stejskala ul. 9). Bohemian garnets are noted for their hardness and color: deep, deep red. The stone is traditionally set in both silver and gold, with the better pieces reserved for the latter.

Sports and Outdoor Activities

Hiking The **Krkonoše** range near the Polish border is prime hiking and wandering territory. Before setting off, buy the excellent *Soubor Turistických* map No. 15 of the area, available in larger bookstores (try the Melantrich bookstore at Na příkopě 3 in Prague). Wear sturdy shoes, and be prepared for virtually any kind of weather. The Krkonoše range gets some type of precipitation about 200 days out of the year on average.

Skiing All three of the principal resorts in the Krkonoše are good ski bases, with lifts and runs nearby. An excellent cross-country course begins in **Horní Misecky,** and an 8-kilometer (5-mile) course runs through the Labe valley. Ask at the Čedok office in Vrchlabí about ski rentals; otherwise you may have to buy your own equipment at local sporting-goods shops.

Swimming You can swim in most of the larger carp ponds around **Třeboň.** The Svět pond is particularly appealing because of its little sandy beaches, although these are generally crowded in summer.

Dining and Lodging

The major towns of western and southern Bohemia offer some of the best accommodations in the Czech Republic. In northern Bohemia, however, only the Krkonoše (Giant Mountain) region has good hotels. In the area around Terezín and Litoměřice, tourist amenities are practically nonexistent; if you do choose to stay overnight, you'll generally be able to find a room in a primitive inn or a rather unwelcoming modern hotel. Towns with private rooms available are noted below.

In many parts of Bohemia the only real options for dining are the restaurants and cafés at the larger hotels and resorts.

Highly recommended restaurants and lodgings in a particular price category are indicated by a star ★.

České **Gomel.** This modern high rise, a 15-minute walk from the main
Budějovice square along the road to Prague, is probably best suited to business
Dining and travelers. The rooms are plain, but the hotel does offer a reasonable
Lodging range of facilities, including an English-speaking staff. *Pražská tř.
14, tel. 038/27949. 180 rooms with bath or shower. Facilities. 3 restaurants, café, nightclub, conference hall, parking. Breakfast not
included. AE, DC, MC, V. $$$*

Zvon. Old-fashioned, well-kept, and comfortable, the Zvon has an
ideal location, on the main town square. Don't be put off by the indif-
ferent staff and unpromising public areas—the rooms are bright,
and the period bathrooms have large bathtubs. The price is high,
however, for the level of facilities. *Nám. Přemysla Otakara II 28,
tel. 038/353 6168. 50 rooms, most with bath. Facilities: restaurant.
Breakfast not included. No credit cards. $$*

Český Český Krumlov is crammed with pensions and private rooms for let,
Krumlov many priced around $15 per person per night. The best place to look
is along the tiny Parkán ulice, which parallels the river just off the
main street. A safe bet is the house at Parkán No. 107, blessed with
several nice rooms and friendly management (tel. 0337/4396).

Dining and **Krumlov.** At this attractive older hotel located directly on the main
Lodging square, the ambience is decidedly homey: Wooden staircases and a
rambling floor plan add to the effect. The older rooms with bath tend
to be larger and nicer. The service is friendly but not overly efficient. *Svornosti nám. 14, tel. 0337/2255, fax 0337/3498. 36 rooms, 13
with bath. Facilities: restaurant. Breakfast included. AE, DC, MC,
V. $$$*

★ **Růže.** This Renaissance monastery has been renovated and trans-
formed into an excellent luxury hotel, only a five-minute walk from
the main square. The rooms are spacious and clean—some also have
drop-dead views of the town below, so ask to see several before
choosing. The restaurant, too, is top-rate; the elegant dining room is
formal without being oppressive, and the menu draws from tradi-
tional Czech and international cuisines. *Horní ul. 153, tel. 0337/
2245, fax 0337/3881. 110 rooms with bath. Facilities: restaurant,
café, snack bar. Breakfast not included. AE, DC, MC, V. $$$*

★ **Na louži.** Wood floors and exposed-beam ceilings lend a traditional
touch to this warm, inviting, family-run pub, which also has rooms
to let upstairs. The atmosphere is cozy and the service attentive.
The quality extends to the food, which is as close to homemade as
you'll find. This is a rare treat among the inns of Bohemia. *Kájovská
66, tel. 0337/5495, fax 0337/3253. 5 rooms with bath. Facilities: restaurant. Breakfast included. V. $*

Cheb (Eger) **Eva.** Of the many new private restaurants opened on and around the
Dining main square, the Eva is certainly one of the best. A decent array of
mostly Czech and German dishes is served in a stylish, contemporary setting that is carefully maintained by a troop of attentive waiters. *Jateční 4, tel. 0166/22498. Reservations advised. Dress: casual.
No credit cards. $$*

Lodging Cheb's hotels have failed to keep pace with the times; none offer
Western standards of cleanliness and all are overpriced. For a short
stay, a room in a private home (pension) is a better bet. Owners of an
older home at Valdstejnova 21 offer two clean and comfortable rooms
(tel. 0166/33088). Several houses along Přemysla Otakara street
north of the city have rooms available. Try the house at No. 7 (tel.
0166/22270).

Hradní Dvůr. This somewhat seedy, older hotel is due for a renova-
tion; until then, the plain rooms are kept acceptably clean even if the

facilities appear neglected. The hotel's prime asset is location, on a side street that runs parallel to the main square. *Dlouhá ul. 12, tel. 0166/22006. 21 rooms, some with bath. Breakfast not included. No credit cards. $$*

Hvězda. This turn-of-the-century hotel was last renovated in the 1970s, which partly accounts for its present disheveled look. The location at the top of the main square is excellent, but the dilapidated facilities do not justify the prices. *Nám. Krále Jiřího, tel. 0166/ 22549, fax 0166/22546. 38 rooms, most with bath. Facilities: restaurant. Breakfast included. No credit cards. $$*

Františkovy Lázně
Dining and Lodging

Centrum. Recent renovations have left the rooms clean and well-appointed if a bit sterile. Still, it is by far the best-run hotel in town and only a short walk from the main park and central spas. *Anglická 41, tel. 0166/943156, fax 0166/942843. 30 rooms with bath. Facilities: restaurant, wine bar, TV in rooms. Breakfast included. No credit cards. $$$*

★ **Slovan.** This is a quaint and gracious establishment, the perfect complement to this relaxed little town. The eccentricity of the original turn-of-the-century design survived a thorough renovation during the 1970s; the airy rooms are clean and comfortable, and some come with a balcony overlooking the main street. The main-floor restaurant serves above-average Czech dishes; consider a meal here even if you're staying elsewhere. *Národní 5, tel. 0166/942841. 25 rooms, most with bath. Facilities: restaurant, café, wine bar. Breakfast included. No credit cards. $$$*

Bajkal. This is an offbeat, older hotel with acceptably clean rooms and a friendly staff. It is located on the far side of the park from the main spas, roughly a 10-minute walk from the city center. The travel agency in the same building also books private accommodations. *Americká ul. 84/4, tel. and fax 0166/942501. 25 rooms, most with bath. Facilities: restaurant, parking. Breakfast not included. No credit cards. $$*

Karlovy Vary
Dining

Embassy. This cozy wine restaurant, conveniently located near the Grandhotel Pupp, serves an innovative range of pastas, seafoods, and meats: Tagliatelle with salmon in cream sauce makes an excellent main course. Highlights of the varied dessert menu include plum dumplings with vanilla sauce. *Nová Louka 21, tel. 017/23049. Reservations advised. Dress: casual but neat. AE, DC, MC, V. $$$*

★ **Karel IV.** Its location atop an old castle not far from the main colonnade affords diners the best view in town. Good renditions of traditional Czech standbys—mostly pork and beef entrées—are served in small, reclusive dining areas that are particularly intimate after sunset. *Zámecký vrch 2, tel. 017/27255. Reservations advised. Dress: casual but neat. AE, DC, MC, V. $$*

Vegetarian. This is a tiny meat-free oasis not far from the Hotel Thermal in the new town. Look for an impressive array of vegetarian standards and nontraditional variations of Czech dishes. *I.P. Pavlova 25, tel. 017/29021. Reservations not necessary. Dress: casual but neat. No credit cards. $*

Lodging
★ **Dvořák.** Consider a splurge here if you're longing for Western standards of service and convenience. Opened in late 1990, this Austrian-owned hotel occupies three renovated town houses a five-minute walk from the main spas. The staff is helpful and the rooms are spotlessly clean. If possible, request a room with a bay-window view of the town. *Nová Louka 11, tel. 017/24145, fax 017/22814. 76 rooms with bath. Facilities: restaurant, café, pool, massage, sauna, fitness room, beauty parlor, satellite TV, parking. Breakfast included. AE, DC, MC, V. $$$$*

★ **Grandhotel Pupp.** This enormous 300-year-old hotel, perched on the edge of the spa district, is one of Central Europe's most famous resorts. Standards and service slipped under the Communists (when the hotel was known as the Moskva-Pupp), but the present management is working hard to atone for the decades of neglect. Ask for a room furnished in 19th-century period style. The food in the ground-floor restaurant is only passable, but the elegant setting makes the hotel worth a visit. *Mírové nám. 2, tel. 017/209111, fax 017/24032. 350 rooms with bath. Facilities: 2 restaurants, lounge, satellite TV, sauna, fitness room. Breakfast included. AE, DC, MC, V. $$$$*

Atlantic. The Atlantic is a haven for eccentrics who can appreciate the fanciful Art Nouveau exterior (especially the comical porcelain figurines lining the roof) and for those who don't mind the lack of modern amenities and so-so service. Ask for a room with a balcony or with a view overlooking the town and colonnade. *Tržiště 23, tel. 017/25251, fax 017/29086. 38 rooms, some with bath or shower. Breakfast not included. AE, DC, MC, V. $$$*

Central. True to its name, this hotel is right in the middle of the old spa district immediately across from the theater. The service is good and the lobby and public areas pleasant, but the smallish rooms are merely adequate (ask for one overlooking the town). *Divadelní nám. 17, tel. 017/25251, fax 017/29086. 61 rooms with bath. Facilities: restaurant, disco, parking. Breakfast included. AE, DC, MC, V. $$$*

Elwa. Recent renovations successfully integrated modern comforts into this older, elegant spa resort located midway between the old and new towns. Modern features include clean, comfortable rooms (most with television) and an on-site fitness center. *Zahradní 29, tel. 017/28472, fax 017/28473. 17 rooms with bath. Facilities: restaurant, bar, beauty parlor, fitness center. Breakfast included. AE, DC, MC, V. $$$*

Konopiště
Dining and Lodging

Konopiště Motel. It has long been a favorite with diplomats in Prague, who come for the fresh air and horseback riding. The motel is located about 2 kilometers (1 mile) from Konopiště Castle, on a small road about a kilometer from the main Prague–Tábor highway (Route 3). The rooms are small but well appointed (ask for one away from the main road). The castle and gardens are an easy 20-minute walk away through the woods; a campground is nearby. *Jarkovicé, tel. 0301/22732, fax 0301/22053. 40 rooms with bath. Facilities: 2 restaurants, minigolf, horseback riding, satellite television, parking. Breakfast included. AE, DC, MC, V. $$$*

Kutná Hora
Lodging

Medínek. This is one of the few hotels in town with modern conveniences, so book in advance or risk being squeezed out by German and Austrian tour groups. The location, on the main square, puts you at an easy stroll from the sights, and the ground-floor restaurant offers decent Czech cooking in an atmosphere more pleasant than that found in the local beer halls. Yet, as with many of the hotels built during the 1960s and '70s, the modern architecture blights the surrounding square. *Palackého nám., tel. 0327/2741, fax 0327/2743. 90 rooms, some with bath. Facilities: restaurant, café. Breakfast not included. No credit cards. $$$*

U Hrnčíře. This is a picturesque little inn situated next to a potter's shop near the town center. The quaintness doesn't make up for the very standard, plain rooms, but the friendly staff gives the hotel a decidedly homey feel. The restaurant in the back garden features a beautiful view overlooking the valley. *Barborska 24, tel. 0327/2113. 6 rooms with bath. Facilities: restaurant, terrace. Breakfast not included. No credit cards. $$*

Litoměřice **Čínská Restaurace.** At this oasis of well-prepared, spicy Chinese
Dining food in an otherwise bleak culinary setting, excellent dumpling and
★ cold chicken appetizers give way to succulent renditions of Chinese
classics. Try Chicken Kung-Pao, prepared spicy-hot with peanuts,
or the steamed duck in honey sauce. For dessert the fried apple in
honey is deservedly popular. *Mírové nám., in the former Rak hotel,
tel. 041980/3008. No credit cards. $$*

Lodging At press time the Rak, the town's only hotel, was preparing to re-
open in late 1994, following a one-year renovation. Until then, other
accommodations are not readily available.

Mariánské **Filip.** This bustling wine bar is where locals come to find relief from
Lázně the sometimes large tourist hoard. A tasty selection of traditional
Dining Czech dishes—mainly pork, grilled meats, and steaks—is served by
a friendly and efficient staff. *Poštovní 96, tel. 0165/2639. Reserva-
tions not necessary. Dress: casual but neat. No credit cards. $$*
★ **Koliba.** This combination hunting lodge and wine tavern, set in the
woods roughly 20 minutes by foot from the spas, is an excellent alternative to the hotel restaurants in town. Grilled meats and shish
kebabs, plus tankards of Moravian wine (try the cherry-red
Rulandské Červené), are served up with traditional gusto.
*Dusíkova, on the road to Karlovy Vary, tel. 0165/5169. Reservations
advised. Dress: casual but neat. No credit cards. $$*
Classic. This small, trendy café on the main drag serves fine sand-
wiches and light meals throughout the day. Unusual for this part of
the world, it also offers a full breakfast menu until 11 AM. *Hlavní tř.
131/50, tel. 0165/2807. No reservations. Dress: casual but neat. No
credit cards. $*

Lodging The best place to look for private lodgings is along Paleckého ulice,
south of the main spa area. Private accommodations can also be
found in the neighboring villages of Zádub and Závišín, and along
roads in the woods to the east of Mariánské Lázně.

Hotel Golf. Book in advance to secure a room at this stately villa sit-
uated 3½ kilometers (2 miles) out of town on the road to Karlovy
Vary. A major renovation in the 1980s left the large, open rooms
with a cheery, modern look. The restaurant on the main floor is ex-
cellent, but the big draw is the 18-hole golf course on the premises,
one of the few in the Czech Republic. *Zádub 55, Mariánské Lázně
35301, tel. 0165/2651 or 0165/2652, fax 0165/2655. 25 rooms with
bath. Facilities: restaurant, satellite TV, golf, tennis, swimming
pool. Breakfast included. AE, DC, MC, V. $$$$*
★ **Bohemia.** This renovated spa resort is definitely worth the splurge;
beautiful crystal chandeliers in the main hall set the stage for a com-
fortable and elegant stay. The rooms are well appointed and com-
pletely equipped, though you may want to be really decadent and
request one of the enormous suites overlooking the park. The effi-
cient staff can arrange spa treatments and horseback riding. *Hlavní
tř. 100, tel. 0165/3251, fax 0165/2943. 100 rooms with bath. Facili-
ties: restaurant; TV and phones in rooms; fitness center; swim-
ming; horseback riding. Breakfast included. AE, DC, MC, V. $$$*
Excelsior. This lovely older hotel is on the main street and is conve-
nient to the spas and colonnade. The renovated rooms are clean and
comfortable, and the staff is friendly and helpful. The food in the adjoining restaurant is only average, but the romantic setting provides adequate compensation. *Hlavní tř. 121, tel. 0165/2705, fax
0165/5346. 53 rooms with bath. Facilities: restaurant, café, parking.
Breakfast included. AE, DC, MC, V. $$$*
Corso. This compact 19th-century hotel, due for a renovation, has
the distinction of being the cheapest hotel along the main drag. The

rooms and corridors are large and clean; the staff at the reception is helpful. You can dance in the wine bar during the evenings or enjoy above-average Bohemian cuisine in the quiet, elegant restaurant. *Hlavní tř. 61, tel. 0165/3091, fax 0165/3093. 28 rooms, 17 with bath. Facilities: restaurant, bar. Breakfast not included. No credit cards. $$*

Kavkaz. You'll either love or hate the heavy-handed 19th-century Empire style of this former spa hotel, located just behind the Main Colonnade area. The rooms are airy and large, and the public areas are still suitably elegant for entertaining past guests such as King Edward VII of England and the illustrious Goethe. Ask for one of the 10 recently renovated rooms. *Goethovo nám. 9, tel. 0165/3141. Facilities: restaurant. Breakfast not included. No credit cards. $$*

Mělník **Ludmila.** Though the hotel looks slightly ragged and is situated 4 ki-
Dining and lometers (2½ miles) outside of town, the Ludmila's English-speak-
Lodging ing staff keeps the plain but cozy rooms impeccably clean, and the restaurant is better than many you will find in Mělník itself. *Pražská ul., tel. 0206/2578. 73 rooms with shower or bath. Facilities: restaurant, parking, souvenir shop. Breakfast not included. No credit cards. $$*

Písek **Otava.** Originally a music school, this pleasant midsize hotel, located
Lodging a short walk from the city center, was built at the end of the last century; adorning the facade are 11 period frescoes depicting the history of the Czech nation. The gracious restaurant, with characteristic high ceilings and murals, provides a relaxing setting for an evening meal. The rooms, though less grand, are adequate for a short stay. *Komenského 58, tel. 0362/2861. 36 rooms with bath. Facilities: restaurant, café. Breakfast included. No credit cards. $$*

Plzeň **Central.** This angular 1960s structure (named the Ural until 1990) is
Dining and recommendable for its sunny rooms, friendly staff, and great loca-
Lodging tion, right on the main square. Indeed, even such worthies as Czar Alexander of Russia stayed here in the days when the hotel was a charming inn known as the Golden Eagle. *Nám. Republiky 33, tel. 019/226757, fax 019/226064. 84 rooms with shower. Facilities: restaurant, wine bar, café, parking. Breakfast not included. AE, DC, MC, V. $$$*

Continental. Situated just five minutes by foot from the main square, the fin-de-siècle Continental remains the best hotel in Pzleň, a relative compliment considering that the hotel is slightly run-down and the rooms, though large, are exceedingly plain. The restaurant, however, serves dependably satisfying traditional Czech dishes. *Zbojnická ul. 5, tel. 019/36477, telex 0154380. 53 rooms, half with bath or shower. Facilities: restaurant, café, parking. Breakfast included. AE, DC, MC, V. $$$*

Slovan. Though the gracious white facade, sweeping stairways, and large, elegant rooms attest to the Slovan's former grandeur, poor management of late has allowed a marked seediness to creep in. The restaurant still occupies the once beautiful ballroom, but the experience is spoiled by mediocre food and the rock-music accompaniment. The Slovan's best asset may be its location, a short walk from the main square. *Smetanový Sady 1, tel. 019/227256, fax 019/227012. 113 rooms, half with bath. Facilities: restaurant, café. Breakfast included. AE, DC, MC, V. $$*

Špindlerův **Montana.** This "modern" 1970s hotel is ill-suited to the rustic set-
Mlýn ting, and the rooms are more spartan than luxurious; but the service
Dining and is attentive, and the staff can offer good advice for planning walks
Lodging around this popular resort town. *54351 Špindlerův Mlýn, tel. 0438/*

93551, fax 0438/93556. 70 rooms with bath. Facilities: restaurant, café, bar, TV in rooms. Breakfast included. AE, DC, MC, V. $$$

★ **Savoy.** This Tudor-style chalet, more than 100 years old but thoroughly renovated in the early 1980s, is rich in alpine atmosphere and very comfortable—its cozy reception area is more typical of a family inn than a large hotel. The rooms, although on the smallish side and sparsely furnished, are immaculately clean. The restaurant serves fine traditional Czech dishes in a comfortably polished setting. *54351 Špindlerův Mlýn, tel. 0438/93521, fax 0438/93641. 50 rooms, most with bath or shower. Facilities: restaurant, bar. Breakfast included. AE, DC, MC, V. $$*

Nechanicky. At this private, older hotel located near the bridge in the center of town, the new management is working hard to improve the hotel's somewhat tarnished appearance. And despite some obvious disadvantages (bathrooms are communal and in the hallway), the rooms are bright, clean, and well proportioned; front-facing rooms enjoy an excellent view overlooking the town. *54351 Špindlerův Mlýn, tel. 0438/93263, fax 0438/93315. 12 rooms without bath. Facilities: restaurant. Breakfast not included. No credit cards. $*

Tábor
Lodging

The house at No. 189 Hradební 16 (tel. 0361/22109), just behind the square, has two large rooms to let for about $15 per person per night, including breakfast; one room even has a sauna. Otherwise, the private tourist office on Náměstí Františka Križíka will help book private accommodations (tel. 0361/23401; open daily 10–noon and 1–6).

Bohemia. Privatization has transformed this sleepy train-station hotel (known formerly as the Slavia) into a pleasant alternative to the stark Palcát. The young staff is cheerful, and the corridors and rooms (many with TV) are bright and clean. The restaurant on the main floor (open nightly until 10:30) is better than many other restaurants in town. *Husovo nám. 591, tel. 0361/22827, fax 0361/63341. 33 rooms, 22 with bath. Facilities: restaurant. Breakfast not included. No credit cards. $$*

Palcát. Located a 10-minute walk from the Old Town square, the slightly run-down Palcát is quite a contrast. The architecture is overwhelmingly drab, but the rooms, though plain, are bright and comfortable; those on the upper floors have a dazzling view of the Old Town. Still, you're probably better off at the Bohemia. *9 Května tř., tel. 0361/22901, fax 0361/22905. 68 rooms with shower. Facilities: restaurant, café, bar, conference hall, parking. Breakfast not included. MC, V. $$*

Třeboň
Dining and
Lodging

Zlatá Hvězda. The sparse but comfortable rooms in this newly remodeled town house on the main square offer good value for the money. The helpful staff can arrange tours and suggest sightseeing activities. The house restaurant is also excellent. *Masarykovo nám. 107, tel. 0333/3365, fax 0333/2604. 30 rooms with bath. Facilities: restaurant, bar. Breakfast included. AE, DC, MC, V. $$*

Bílý Koníček. This cheaper but very acceptable alternative to the Zlatá Hvězda occupies one of the most striking Renaissance buildings on the main square. The rooms fail to measure up to the splendid facade but are suitably clean. The ground-floor restaurant is a good place to have lunch. *Masarykovo nám. 27, tel. 0333/2818. 25 rooms with bath. Facilities: restaurant. Breakfast included. No credit cards. $*

The Arts and Nightlife

The Arts **Mariánske Lázně** sponsors a music festival each June, with numerous concerts featuring Czech and international composers and orchestras. The town's annual Chopin festival each autumn brings in fans of the Polish composer's work from around the world. Karlovy Vary and Františkový Lázně also offer concerts throughout the year. When in Karlovy Vary, pick up a copy of *KAM*, the town's monthly cultural magazine (available at major hotels). **Karlovy Vary** is also the site of a major international film festival, held yearly in the fall. An outdoor Renaissance theater in the castle gardens in **Český Krumlov** is a popular venue for plays and concerts throughout the summer.

Nightlife Nightlife in the towns and villages of Bohemia revolves around the *pivnice* (beer hall). If you want to see a piece of the real Czech Republic and can take the thick smoke, this is the place to go. The beer, of course, is excellent.

Drinking and dancing until dawn are understandably not part of the daily regimen of serious convalescent centers, especially when patients have to be in bed at 10 PM sharp. Still, the major spas of western Bohemia do offer some lively evening entertainment—if only for the more robust relatives of those receiving treatment. Both **Karlovy Vary** and **Mariánské Lázně** have casinos that stay open until the wee hours of the morning. In Mariánské Lázně, the **Casino Marienbad** is situated at Anglická 336 (open daily 6 AM–2 AM, tel. 0165/2056). In Karlovy Vary, go to the **Lázně I** (open daily 6 AM–2 AM, tel. 017/23100), situated near the Grandhotel Pupp.

For late-night drinks in Mariánské Lázně, try the **Hotel Golf** (*see* Lodging, *above*), which has a good nightclub with dancing in season. In Karlovy Vary, the action centers on the two nightclubs of the **Grandhotel Pupp.** The "little dance hall" is open daily 8 PM–1 AM. The second club is open Wednesday through Sunday 7 PM–3 AM. **Club Propaganda** (Jaltska 7) is Karlovy Vary's best venue for live rock and new music.

Moravia

Lacking the turbulent history of Bohemia to the west or the stark natural beauty of Slovakia farther east, Moravia, the easternmost province of the Czech Republic, is frequently overlooked as a travel destination. Still, though Moravia's cities do not match Prague for beauty, nor its gentle mountains compare with Slovakia's strikingly rugged Tatras, Moravia's colorful villages and rolling hills certainly do merit a few days of exploration. After you've seen the admittedly superior sights of Bohemia and Slovakia, come here for the good wine, the folk music, the friendly faces, and the languid pace.

What makes Moravia interesting is precisely that it's neither Bohemia nor Slovakia but rather a little of both. Culturally, Moravia is closer to Bohemia. The two were bound together as one kingdom for some 1,000 years, following the fall of the Great Moravian Empire (Moravia's last stab at Slavonic statehood) at the end of the 10th century. All of the cultural and historical movements that swept through Bohemia, including the religious turbulence and long period of Austrian Habsburg rule, were felt strongly here as well.

But, oddly, in many ways Moravia resembles Slovakia more than its cousin to the west. The colors come alive here in a way that is seldom seen in Bohemia: The subdued earthen pinks and yellows in towns such as Telč and Mikulov suddenly erupt into the fiery reds, greens, and purples of the traditional folk costumes farther to the east. Folk music, all but gone in Bohemia, is still very much alive in Moravia. You'll hear it, ranging from foot stomping to tear jerking, sung with pride by young and old alike.

Important Addresses and Numbers

Tourist Information Most major towns have a local or private information office, usually located in the central square and identified by a capital "I" on the facade. These offices are often good sources for maps and historical information and can usually help book hotel and private accommodations. Most are open during normal business hours, with limited hours on Saturday (until noon) and closed on Sunday and holidays.

Brno also has a helpful **Cultural and Information Center** (Radnická ul. 8, tel. 05/4221–1090), where you can get information on just about everything.

Emergencies Police (tel. 158). **Ambulance** (tel. 155).

Pharmacy Brno: The pharmacy at Kobližná ulice 7 is open 24 hours.

Arriving and Departing by Plane

ČSA, the national carrier of the Czech Republic, has regular flights to Brno from Prague and Bratislava. The distances between the cities are short, however, and it's ultimately cheaper and quicker to drive or take a bus. During the two large Brno trade fairs, in April and September, foreign carriers also connect the city with Frankfurt and Vienna. These flights are usually crowded with businessmen, so you'll have to book well in advance. For more information on flights, contact ČSA offices in Prague or Brno (tel. 05/4221–0739).

Arriving and Departing by Car, Train, and Bus

By Car Occupying the middle of the country, Moravia is within easy driving distance of Prague, Bratislava, and eastern Slovakia. Jihlava, the starting point for the tour below, is 124 kilometers (78 miles) southeast of Prague along the excellent D1 freeway. Brno, the capital, is 196 kilometers (122 miles) from Prague and 121 kilometers (75 miles) from Bratislava. Moravia is also easily reached by car from Austria. Major border crossings exist at Háté (below Znojmo) and Mikulov. Olomouc lies on the major east–west highway, convenient for returning to Prague or continuing farther east to the Tatras, eastern Slovakia, and Poland.

By Train Several trains daily make the three-hour run from Prague to Brno. Most use Prague's **Hlavní nádraží** (main station), but some depart from and arrive at the suburban station **Holešovice nádraží** (Holešovice station), or at **Masarykovo nádraží** (Masaryk station), on Hybernská ulice in the city center. Trains leaving Prague for Budapest and Bucharest (and some Vienna-bound trains) also frequently stop in Brno (check timetables to be sure).

By Bus Bus connections from Prague to Jihlava and Brno are excellent and inexpensive, and, in lieu of a car, the best way to get to Moravia. Moravian destinations are also well served from Bratislava and other points in Slovakia. Buses also run daily between Vienna and Brno, leaving Vienna's Wien-Mitte station at 7:30 AM, and leaving Brno for the return to Vienna at 5:30 PM. Round-trip tickets cost about AS340 ($27).

Getting Around

By Car Having your own car is the best way to tour Moravia; the roads are generally good, and there is little traffic. Avoid driving at night and in bad weather when possible, as many of the smaller roads are poorly marked.

By Train Train service in Moravia is thin, linking only the major towns. Moreover, sorting out the schedules and buying tickets can be a hassle. In any event, you'll inevitably have to resort to the bus to reach the smaller, out-of-the-way places on the tour below.

By Bus As in the rest of the Czech Republic, the national bus network, ČSAD, operates a dense network of lines in Moravia; with a little advance planning, you'll be able to reach all of the destinations on the tour. The prices are also reasonable. The only drawback is time, as the buses can sometimes be very, very slow. Watch for the little symbols on the timetables, which tell you if the bus runs on weekends and holidays. The Brno bus station is located behind the train station. To find it, simply go to the train station and follow the signs to ČSAD.

Highlights for First-Time Visitors

Brno (*see* Tour 2)
Main square in Telč (*see* Tour 1)
Moravian Caves (*see* Tour 3)
Olomouc (*see* Tour 3)
Vranov Castle (*see* Tour 1)

Exploring Moravia

Numbers in the margin correspond to points of interest on the Moravia map.

The first tour outlined below begins in the west of the province, along the highlands that define the "border" with Bohemia. Here, towns such as Jihlava and Telč are virtually indistinguishable from their Bohemian counterparts. The handsome squares, with their long arcades, bear witness to the prosperity enjoyed by this part of Europe several hundred years ago. The tour then heads south along the frontier with Austria—until recently a heavily fortified expanse of the Iron Curtain. Life is just starting to return to normal in these parts, as the towns and people on both sides of the border seek to reestablish ties going back centuries. One of their common traditions is wine making; and Znojmo, Mikulov, and Valtice are to the Czech Republic what the small towns of the *Weinviertel* on the other side of the border are to Austria.

Tour 2 covers **Brno** (pronounced *burrno*), Moravia's cultural and geographic center. Brno grew rich in the 19th century as the industrial heartland of the Austrian empire and doesn't look or feel like any other Czech or Slovak city. In the early years of this century, the city became home to the best young architects working in the cubist and constructivist styles. And experimentation wasn't restricted to architecture. Leoš Janáček, an important composer of the early modern period, also lived and worked in Brno. The modern tradition continues even today, and the city is considered to have the best theater and performing arts in the country.

Tour 3 covers the area just north of Brno, where you'll find the **Moravian Karst**, a beautiful wilderness area with an extensive network of caves, caverns, and underground rivers. Many caves are open to the public, and some tours even incorporate underground boat rides. Farther to the north lies Moravia's "second capital," **Olomouc**, an industrial but still charming city, with a long history as a center of learning. Paradoxically, despite its location far from the Austrian border, Olomouc remained a bastion of support for the Habsburgs and the empire at a time when cries for independence could be heard throughout Bohemia and Moravia. In 1848, when revolts everywhere threatened to bring the monarchy down, the Habsburg family fled here for safety. Franz Joseph, who went on to personify the stodgy permanence of the empire, was even crowned here as Austrian emperor that same year.

The green foothills of the **Beskydy range** begin just east of Olomouc, perfect for a day or two of walking in the mountains. Farther to the east you'll find the spectacular peaks of the Tatras, and the tour is a good jumping-off point for exploring eastern Slovakia or southern Poland. Similarly, if you're coming from Slovakia, you could easily begin in Olomouc and conduct the tour in reverse order.

Tour 1: Southern Moravia ❶ On the Moravian side of the rolling highlands that mark the border between Bohemia and Moravia, and just off the main highway from Prague to Brno, lies the old mining town of **Jihlava,** a good place to begin an exploration of Moravia. If the silver mines here had held out just a few more years, the townspeople claim, Jihlava could have become a great European city—and a household name to foreign visitors. Indeed, during the 13th century, the town's enormous **main square** was one of the largest in Europe, rivaled in size only by those in Cologne and Kraków. But history can be cruel: The mines went bust during the 17th century, and the square today bears witness only to the town's once oversize ambitions.

The **Kostel svatého Ignáce** (St. Ignace Church) in the northwest corner of the square is relatively young for Jihlava, built at the end of the 17th century, but look inside to see a rare Gothic crucifix, created during the 13th century for the early Bohemian king Přemysl Otakar II. The town's most striking structure is the Gothic **Kostel svatého Jakuba** (St. James Church) to the east of the main square, down the Farní ulice. The church's exterior, with its uneven towers, is Gothic; the interior is Baroque; and the font is a masterpiece of the Renaissance style, dating from 1599. Note also the Baroque **Chapel of the Holy Virgin,** sandwiched between two late-Gothic chapels, with its oversize 14th-century pietà. Two other Gothic churches worth a look are the **Kostelsvatého Kříža** (Church of the Holy Cross), north of the main square, and the **Minoritský kostel** (Minorite Church), to the west of the square. Just next to the latter is the last remaining of the original five medieval town gates.

❷ The little town of Telč, about 30 kilometers (19 miles) to the south via Route 406, has an even more impressive main square than Jihlava. But what strikes the eye most here is not its size but the unified style of the buildings. On the lowest levels are beautifully vaulted Gothic halls, just above are Renaissance floors and facades, and all of it is crowned with rich Baroque gables. The square is so perfect that you feel more as if you've entered a film set than a living town. The town allegedly owes its architectural unity to Zacharias of Neuhaus, for whom the main square is now named. During the 16th century, so the story goes, the wealthy Zacharias had the castle—originally a small fort overlooking the Bohemian border with Hungary—rebuilt in the Renaissance style. But the contrast between the new castle and the town's rather ordinary buildings was so great that Zacharias had the square rebuilt to match the castle's splendor. Luckily for

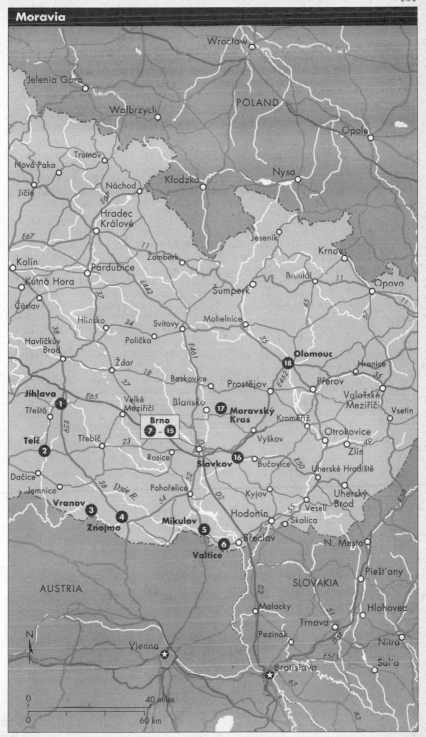

Moravia

architecture fans, the Neuhaus dynasty died out shortly thereafter, and succeeding nobles had little interest in refashioning the town according to the vogue of the day.

It's best to approach the main square on foot. If you've come by car, park outside the main walls on the side south of town and walk through the **Big Gate,** part of the original fortifications dating back to the 13th century. The tiny Palackého ulice takes you past the 160-foot Romanesque tower of the **Kostel svatého Ducha** (Church of the Holy Ghost) on your right. This is the oldest standing structure in Telč, dating from the first quarter of the 13th century. As you walk up Palackého ulice, the **square** unfolds nobly in front of you, with the castle at the top and beautiful houses, bathed in pastel reds and golds, gracing both sides. If you're a fan of Renaissance reliefs, note the black-and-white sgraffito corner house at No. 15, which dates from the middle of the 16th century. The house at No. 61, across from the Černý Orel hotel, is also noteworthy for its fine detail.

At the northern end of the square, the **Town Castle** forms a complex with the former **Jesuit college** and the **St. James Church.** The castle, originally Gothic, was built during the 14th century, when Telč first gained importance as a border town with the old Hungarian kingdom. It was given its current Renaissance appearance by Italian masters between 1553 and 1568. In season, you can tour the castle and admire the rich Renaissance interiors, equally as impressive as the Italian palaces on which the castle was modeled. Given the reputation of nobles for lively banquets lasting for hours, the sgraffito relief in the dining room depicting gluttony (in addition to the six other deadly sins) seems odd indeed. Other interesting rooms with sgraffiti include the Treasury, the Armory, and the Blue and Gold chambers.

Time Out The restaurant of the **Černý Orel** hotel on the main square is a good place to have coffee or a meal; the hotel itself is a fine place to spend the night. If you're looking for sweets, you can get good homemade cakes at a little private café, **Cukrárna u Matěje,** at Na baště 2.

Leave Telč and continue farther south into the heart of Moravian wine country. Follow the signs first to the picturesque little town of **Dačice,** then along Route 408 through **Jemnice,** and finally to the chain of recreation areas along the man-made lakes of the **Dyje** (Thaya) River. Turn right at Šumná and follow the signs to the little town of Vranov, nestled snugly between hill and river. In all, the trip from Telč is about 55 kilometers (34 miles).

❸ As a swimming and boating center for southern Moravia, **Vranov** would be a good place to stop in its own right. But what makes the town truly noteworthy is the enormous and colorful **Vranov Castle,** rising 200 feet from a rocky promontory. For nearly 1,000 years, this was the border between Bohemia and Austria and therefore worthy of a fortress of these dimensions. You'll either love or hate this proud mongrel of a building, as its multicolored Gothic, Renaissance, and Baroque elements vie for your attention. In the foreground, the solemn Renaissance tower rises over some Gothic fortifications. The structure is shored up on its left by a golden Baroque church, with a beautiful pink-and-white Baroque dome to the back. Each unit is spectacular, but the overall effect of so many styles mixed together is jarring.

Take your eyes off the castle's motley exterior and tour its mostly Baroque (and more harmonious) interior. The most impressive room is certainly the 43-foot-high elliptical **Hall of Ancestors,** the work of the Viennese master Johann Bernhard Fischer von Erlach (builder of the Clam-Gallas Palace in Prague and the Hofburg in Vienna). The frescoes, added by the Salzburg painter Johann Michael Rottmayr, depict scenes from Greek mythology. Look inside the **Castle Church** as well. The rotunda, altar, and organ were designed by Fischer von Erlach at the end of the 17th century.

➍ The old border town of **Znojmo** is an easy 20-kilometer (12-mile) drive to the east of Vranov. Follow Route 408 and turn right on the busier Route 38. Znojmo enjoys a long history as an important frontier town between Austria and Bohemia and is the cultural center of southern Moravia. The Přemyslide prince Břetislav I had already built a fortress here during the 11th century, and in 1226 Znojmo became the first Moravian town (ahead of Brno) to receive town rights from the king. But, alas, modern Znojmo, with its many factories and high rises, isn't really a place for lingering. Plan on spending no more than a few hours walking through the Old Town, admiring the views over the Dyje River, and visiting the remaining fortifications and churches that stand between the New Town and the river.

Znojmo's tumbledown **main square,** now usually filled with peddlers selling everything from butter to cheap souvenirs, isn't what it used to be when it was crowned by Moravia's most beautiful **town hall.** Unfortunately, the 14th-century building was destroyed in 1945, just before the end of the war, and all that remains of the original structure is the 250-foot Gothic tower you see at the top of the square—looking admittedly forlorn astride the modern department store that now occupies the space.

For a cheerier sight, follow the lovely Zelinářská ulice, which trails from behind the Town Hall Tower to the southwest in the direction of the old town and river. The Gothic **Kostel svatého Mikuláše** (St. Nicholas Church), on the tiny old town square (Staré Město), dates from 1338, but its neo-Gothic tower was not added until the last century, when the original had to be pulled down. If you can get into the church (it's often locked), look for the impressive Sacraments House, which was built around 1500 in the late-Gothic style.

Just behind St. Nicholas stands the curious, two-layered **Kostel svatého Václava** (St. Wenceslas Church), built at the end of the 15th century. The upper level of this tiny white church is dedicated to St. Anne, the lower level to St. Martin. Farther to the west, along the medieval ramparts that separate the town from the river, stands the original 11th-century **Rotunda svatej Kateřiny** (St. Catherine's Rotunda), still in remarkably good condition. Step inside to see a rare cycle of restored frescoes from 1134 depicting various members of the early Přemyslide dynasty.

The **Jihomoravské Muzeum** (South Moravian Museum), just across the way in the former town castle, houses an extensive collection of artifacts from the area, dating from the Stone Age to the present. However, unless you're a big fan of museums, there's little point in making a special visit to this one; and unless you can read Czech, you'll have difficulty making sense of the collection. *Přemyslovců ul., no tel. Admission: 10 Kč. adults, 5 Kč. children. Open Tues.– Sun. 9–5.*

Znojmo's other claims to fame have endeared the town to the hearts (and palates) of Czechs everywhere. The first is the Znojmo gherkin, first cultivated during the 16th century. You'll find this tasty accompaniment to meals at restaurants all over the country. Just look for the *Znojmo* prefix—as in *Znojemský guláš,* a tasty stew spiced with pickles. Znojmo's other treat is wine. As the center of the Moravian wine industry, this is an excellent place to pick up a few bottles of your favorite grape at any grocery or beverage store. But don't expect to learn much about a wine from its label: Oddly, you'll search in vain for the vintage or even the name of the vineyard on labels, and about the only information you can gather is the name of the grape and the city in which the wine was bottled. The best towns to look for, in addition to Znojmo, are Mikulov and Valtice (*see below*). Some of the best varieties of grapes are Rulandské and Vavřinecké (for red) and Ryslink and Müller Thurgau (for white).

⑤ Leave Znojmo by heading northeast on Route 54 in the direction of Pohořelice. Make a right turn when you see signs to **Mikulov,** eventually arriving in town along Route 52 after a semicircuitous drive of 54 kilometers (34 miles). Mikulov is known today chiefly as the border crossing on the Vienna–Brno road. If you want to leave the Czech Republic for a day to stock up on Western supplies, this is the place to do it. The nearest Austrian town, Poysdorf, is just 7 kilometers (4½ miles) away.

In many ways, Mikulov is the quintessential Moravian town. The soft pastel pinks and yellows of its buildings look almost mystical in the afternoon sunshine against the greens of the surrounding hills. But aside from the busy wine industry, not much goes on here. The main sight is the striking **castle,** which dominates the tiny main square and surrounding area. The castle started out as the Gothic residence of the noble Liechtenstein family in the 13th century and was given its current Baroque appearance some 400 years later. The most famous resident was Napoleon, who stayed here in 1805 while negotiating peace terms with the Austrians after winning the battle of Austerlitz (Slavkov, near Brno). Sixty-one years later, Bismarck used the castle to sign a peace treaty with Austria. The castle's darkest days came at the end of World War II, when retreating Nazi SS units set the town on fire. In season, take a walk from the main square up around the side of the castle into the **museum** of wine making. The most remarkable exhibit is a wine cask made in 1643 with a capacity of more than 22,000 gallons. This was used for collecting the vintner's obligatory tithe. *Admission: 20 Kč. adults, 10 Kč. children. Open May–Oct., Tues.–Sun. 9–4.*

If you happen to arrive at grape-harvesting time in October, head for one of the many private *sklípeks* (wine cellars), built into the hills surrounding the town. The tradition in these parts is simply to knock on the door; more often than not, you'll be invited in by the owner to taste a recent vintage.

⑥ The small town of **Valtice,** just 9 kilometers (6 miles) to the east of Mikulov along Route 414, would be wholly nondescript except for the fascinating **castle,** just off the main street, built by the Liechtenstein family in the 19th century. Next to the town's dusty streets, with their dilapidated postwar storefronts, the castle looks positively grand, a glorious if slightly overexuberant holdover from a long-lost era. But the best news of all is that you can also spend the night there if you like. Unusual for the country, the left wing of the castle has been converted into the Hubertus hotel (*see* Lodging, *below*). The rooms aren't luxurious, but the setting is inspiring (especially if the standard high-rise hotels are getting you down). The castle boasts some 365 windows, painted ceilings, and much ornate woodwork. A small museum on the ground floor demonstrates how the town and castle have changed over the years, according to aristocratic and political whim. Even if you're just passing through, enjoy a drink on the terrace behind the hotel, an ideal spot in which to relax on a warm afternoon. The Valtice winery is situated behind and to the right of the castle, but it is not open to the public. *Castle admission: 10 Kč. adults, 5 Kč. children. Open Tues.–Sun. 9–11:30 and 1–4.*

Time Out The little mountain town Pavlov, a short drive or bus ride from Mikulov or Valtice, has several wine cellars built into the hills and makes for a good refreshment stop. At **U Venuše** (Česká 27, dinner only), be sure to sample some of the owner's wine, which comes from his private *sklípek* across the lake in Strachotín. After dinner, stroll around the village, perched romantically overlooking a man-made lake.

Between Valtice and another aristocratic pile at **Lednice,** 7 kilometers (4 miles) to the northwest, the Liechtenstein family peppered the countryside with neoclassical temples and follies throughout the 19th century as a display of their wealth and taste. An abandoned summer palace lies just to the north of Valtice, not far from the tiny town of **Hlohovec.** In winter you can walk or skate across the adjoining Hlohovec Pond to the golden yellow building; otherwise follow the tiny lane to Hlohovec, just off Route 422 outside Valtice. Emblazoned across the front of the palace is the German slogan ZWISCHEN ÖSTERREICH UND MÄHREN (Between Austria and Moravia), another reminder of the proximity of the border and the long history that these areas share.

The extravagantly neo-Gothic castle at **Lednice,** though obviously in disrepair, affords stunning views of the surrounding grounds and ponds. Be sure to tour the sumptuous interior; particularly resplendent with the afternoon sunshine streaming through the windows are the blue-and-green silk wallcoverings embossed with the Moravian eagle in the formal dining room and bay-windowed drawing room. The grounds, now a pleasant park open to the public, even boast a 200-foot minaret and a massive greenhouse filled with exotic flora. *Zámek. Admission: 20 Kč. adults, 10 Kč. children. Open May–Sept. daily 9–4; Oct., weekends 9–4.*

From Lednice, follow the Dyje River to the northwest through the villages of Bulhary and Milovice and on to the tiny town of **Dolní Věstonice,** perched alongside another giant artificial lake. Although the town has little going for it today, some 20,000 to 30,000 years ago the area was home to a thriving prehistoric settlement, judging from ivory and graves found here by archaeologists in 1950. Some of the world's earliest ceramics were also discovered, among them a curvaceous figurine of ash and clay that has become known as the Venus of Věstonice. The original is kept in Brno, but you can see replicas, real mammoth bones, and much else of archaeological interest at the excellent **museum** in the center of town along the main road. *Admission: 20 Kč. adults, 10 Kč. children. Open May–Sept., Tues.–Sun. 8–noon and 1–4; Apr. and Oct., weekends 8–noon and 1–4.*

For walking enthusiasts, the **Pavlovské vrchy** (Pavlov Hills), where the settlement was found, offers a challenging climb. Start out by ascending the **Děvín Peak** (1,800 feet), located just south of Dolní Věstonice. A series of paths then follows the ridges the 10 kilometers (6 miles) to Mikulov.

Tour 2: Brno *Numbers in the margin correspond to points of interest on the Brno map.*

From Dolní Věstonice, follow Route 420 about 10 kilometers (6 miles) to the D2 freeway. From here it is a quick 23 kilometers (14

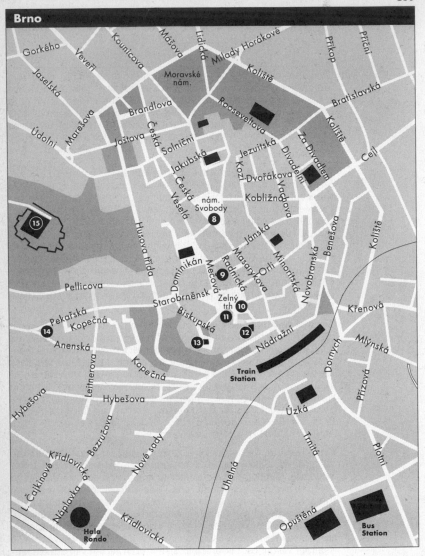

Brno

Dietrichstein
Palace, **11**

Dóm na Petrove, **13**

Kostel Náležení
Svatého Kříže, **12**

Monastery of
Staré Brno, **14**

Náměstí Svobody, **8**

Špilberk Hrad, **15**

Stará Radnice, **9**

Zelný Trh, **10**

7 miles) to **Brno,** whose 19th-century buildings show signs of a prosperity that is rare for Czech towns. Beginning with a textile industry imported from Germany, Holland, and Belgium, Brno became the industrial heartland of the Austrian empire during the 18th and 19th centuries—hence its "Manchester of Moravia" sobriquet. You'll search in vain for an extensive Old Town; you'll also find few of the traditional arcaded storefronts that typify other historical Czech towns. What you will see instead are fine examples of Empire and neoclassical styles, their formal, geometric facades more in keeping with the conservative tastes of the 19th-century middle class.

8 Begin the walking tour, which should take two or three hours at a leisurely pace, at the triangular **Náměstí Svobody** (Freedom Square), in the heart of the commercial district. The square itself is architecturally undistinguished, but here and along the adjoining streets you'll find the city's best stores and shopping opportunities.

Walk up the main **Masarykova ulice** toward the train station, and make a right through the little arcade at No. 6. to see the animated **9** Gothic portal of the **Stará radnice** (Old Town Hall), the oldest secular building in Brno. The door is the work of Anton Pilgram, architect of Vienna's St. Stephen's Cathedral, and was completed in 1510; the building itself is about 200 years older. Look above the door to see a badly bent pinnacle that looks as if it wilted in the afternoon sun. This isn't the work of vandals but was apparently done by Pilgram himself out of revenge against the town. According to legend, Pilgram had been promised an excellent commission for his portal, but when he finished, the mayor and city councillors reneged on their offer. So angry was Pilgram at the duplicity that he purposely bent the pinnacle and left it poised, fittingly, over the statue of justice.

Just inside the door are the remains of two other famous Brno legends, the **Brno Dragon** and the **wagon wheel.** The dragon—a female alligator to be anatomically correct—apparently turned up at the town walls one day in the 17th century and began eating the children and livestock. A young gatekeeper came up with the novel idea of filling a sack with limestone and placing it inside a freshly slaughtered goat. The dragon devoured the goat, swallowing the limestone as well, and went to quench its thirst at a nearby river. The water mixed with the limestone, bursting the dragon's stomach (the scars on the dragon's stomach are still clearly visible). The story of the wagon wheel, on the other hand, concerns a bet placed some 400 years ago that a young wheelwright, Jiří Birk, couldn't chop down a tree, fashion the wood into a wheel, and roll it from his home at Lednice (33 miles away) to the town walls of Brno—all between sun-up and sundown. The wheel stands as a lasting tribute to his achievement (the townspeople, however, became convinced that Jiří had enlisted the help of the devil to win the bet, so they stopped frequenting his workshop; poor Jiří died penniless).

No longer the seat of the town government, the Old Town Hall holds exhibitions and performances of various kinds. To find out what's on, look for a sign on the door of the exhibition room. The view from the top of the tower is one of the best in Brno, but the climb (five flights) is strenuous. What catches the eye is not so much any single building—although the cathedral does look spectacular—but the combination of old and new that defines modern Brno. In the distance, next to the crooked roofs and Baroque onion domes, a power plant looks startlingly out of place. *Radnická ul. 8. Admission: 10 Kč. adults, 5 Kč. children. Open Tues.–Sun. 9–5.*

Leave the tower by Pilgram's portal and turn right into the old
⑩ Zelný trh (Cabbage Market), the only place where Brno begins to
look like a typical Czech town. You'll recognize the market immediately, not just for the many stands from which farmers still sell vegetables but also for the unique **Parnassus** fountain that adorns its
center. This Baroque pile of rocks (you either love it or hate it)
couldn't be more out of place amid the formal elegance of most of the
buildings on the square. But when Johann Bernhard Fischer von
Erlach created the fountain during the late 17th century, it was important for a striving town like Brno to display its understanding of
the classics and of ancient Greece. Thus, Hercules slays a three-
headed dragon, while Amphitrite on top awaits the arrival of her
lover—all incongruously surrounded by farmers hawking turnips
and onions.

On the far side of the market, dominating the square, stands the se-
⑪ vere Renaissance Dietrichstein Palace at No. 8. The building was
once home to Cardinal Count Franz von Dietrichstein, who led the
Catholic Counter-Reformation in Moravia following the Battle of
White Mountain in 1620. Today the palace houses the **Moravské
muzeum** (Moravian Museum), with its mundane exhibits of local
birds and other wildlife. The museum is undergoing extensive renovation, and some of the more interesting exhibits (such as the ancient Venus of Věstonice) may not be open to the public. To enter the
museum, walk through the little gate to the left of the Dietrichstein
Palace and then through the lovely Renaissance garden. Note the arcades, the work of 16th-century Italian craftsmen. *Zelný trh 6. Admission: 10 Kč. adults, 5 Kč. students. Open Tues.–Sun. 9–5.*

⑫ From the garden, walk down the stairs to the Baroque **Kostel
Náležení svatého Kříže** (Church of the Holy Cross), formerly part of
the Capuchin monastery. If you've ever wondered what a mummy
looks like without its bandages, then enter the door to the
monastery's *hrobka* (crypt). In the basement are the mummified remains of some 200 nobles and monks from the late 17th and 18th centuries, ingeniously preserved by a natural system of air circulating
through vents and chimneys. The best-known mummy is Colonel
František Trenck, commander of the brutal Pandour regiment of
the Austrian army, who spent several years in the dungeons of the
Špilberk Castle before finding his final rest here in 1749. Even in
death the hapless colonel has not found peace—someone made off
with his head several years ago. One note of caution about the crypt:
The graphic displays may frighten small children, so ask at the admission desk for the small brochure (10 Kč.) with pictures that pre-
view what's to follow. *Kapucínské nám. Admission: 10 Kč. adults, 5
Kč. children. Open Tues.–Sat. 9–11:45 and 2–4:30, Sun. 11–11:45
and 2–4:30.*

⑬ Towering above the church and market is the **Dóm na Petrove** (Cathedral of Sts. Peter and Paul), Brno's main church and a fixture of
the skyline. The best way to get to the cathedral is to return to the
Cabbage Market (via the little street off the Kapucínské náměstí),
make a left at the market, and walk up the narrow Petrská ulice,
which begins just to the right of the Dietrichstein Palace. The normally picturesque Petrská is currently undergoing massive reconstruction; if the road is blocked, just follow your instincts up and
around to the cathedral. Sadly, Sts. Peter and Paul is one church
that probably looks better from a distance. The interior, a blend of
Baroque and Gothic, is light and tasteful but hardly overwhelming.
Still, the slim neo-Gothic twin spires, added in this century to give
the cathedral more of its original Gothic dignity, are a nice touch.

Don't be surprised if you hear the noon bells ringing from the cathedral at 11 o'clock. The practice dates from the Thirty Years' War, when Swedish troops were massing for an attack outside the town walls. Brno's resistance had been fierce, and the Swedish commander decreed that he would give up the fight if the town could not be taken by noon the following day. The bell ringer caught wind of the decision and the next morning, just as the Swedes were preparing a final assault, rang the noon bells—an hour early. The ruse worked and the Swedes decamped. Ever since, the midday bells have been rung an hour early as a show of gratitude.

Before leaving the cathedral area, stroll around the park and grounds. The view of the town from here is pretty and the mood is restful. Continue the tour by walking down the continuation of the Petrská ulice to Biskupská ulice (still more construction). Turn left at the Starobrněnská ulice and cross the busy Husova třída onto Pekařská ulice, which planners are hoping to transform into a lively area of boutiques and shops someday. At the end of the street is the ⑭ **Mendelovo náměstí** (Mendel Square) and the **Monastery of Staré Brno,** home during the 19th century to Gregor Mendel, the shy monk who became the father of modern genetic research. The uninspiring location seems to confirm the adage that genius can flourish anywhere. If you recall from high school science, it was Mendel's experiments with crossing pea and bean plants and his working out dominant and recessive traits that led to the first formulations of the laws of heredity. A small statue to his memory can be found in the garden behind the monastery.

Continue the tour along the busy and somewhat downtrodden Úvoz ulice in the direction of Špilberk castle. Take the first right and climb the stairs to the calmer residential street of Pellicova. If there's a unique beauty to Brno, it's in neighborhoods such as this one, with their attractive houses, each sporting a different architectural style. Many houses incorporate cubist and geometric elements of the early modern period (1920s and '30s).

⑮ Begin the ascent to **Špilberk hrad** (Špilberk Castle), the fortress-cum-torture chamber that, while long out of business as a prison, still broods over the town from behind its menacing walls. There is no direct path to the castle; just follow your instincts (or a detailed map) upward, and you'll get there. Before you're too far along on the 160-foot climb, however, it's only fair to warn you that the castle is closed for renovation and that no café or restaurant awaits to reward your effort. But push on anyway: You can still get a good look at the castle from the outside, and the views over the city are magnificent. From the top, look over to the west at the gleaming Art Deco pavilions of the Brno **Výstaviště** (Exhibition Grounds) in the distance. The buildings were completed in 1928, in time to hold the first cultural exhibition to celebrate the 10th anniversary of the Czech state. The grounds are now the site of annual trade fairs.

Špilberk's advantageous location was no secret to the early kings, who moved here during the 13th century from the neighboring Petrov hill. During the Thirty Years' War, Italian builders converted the old castle into a virtually impregnable Baroque fortress. Indeed, it successfully withstood the onslaught of the Swedes and fell only to Napoleon in 1805. But the castle is best known for its gruesome history as a prison and torture chamber for the Austro-Hungarian monarchy and, later, for the Nazis in World War II. After 1995, the public will again be able to tour this Moravian Alcatraz.

Walk down the opposite side of the hill to the east in the direction of the center of town. Sooner or later you'll come to the busy Husova třída again. Cross the street, continue walking straight, and you'll eventually run into the busy pedestrian zone of the Česká. Turn to the right along the Česká, and in a couple of minutes you're back at Náměstí Svobody.

Time Out After a long walk and a good climb, what could be better than one of the best beers you'll ever have? The **Stopkova Pivnice** at Česka 5 will set you up with a big one or a small one (or even a soft drink) in clean, comfortable surroundings. If you're hungry, try the house goulash, a tangy mixture of sausage, beef, rice, egg, and dumpling. If you want something more substantial, head for the restaurant on the second floor.

Before leaving Brno, fans of modern architecture will want to see the austere **Villa Tugendhat,** designed by Ludwig Mies van der Rohe and completed in 1930. The white villa, built in the Bauhaus style, counts among the most important works of the modern period. The emphasis here is on function and the use of geometric forms, but you be the judge as to whether the house fits the neighborhood. Badly damaged during the war, it now houses guests of the city of Brno and is closed to the public. The best way to get there is to take a taxi, or walk 20 minutes northeast of the city center to the area known as Černá Pole.

Numbers in the margin correspond to points of interest on the Moravia map.

Tour 3: Northern Moravia ⑯ Just 20 kilometers (12 miles) east of Brno lies the site of one of the great battlefields of European history, **Slavkov,** better known as **Austerlitz,** where the armies of Napoleon met and defeated the combined forces of Austrian emperor Franz II and Czar Alexander I in 1805. If you happen to have a copy of *War and Peace* handy, you will find no better account of it anywhere. Scattered about the rolling agricultural landscapes are a museum, a garden, and the memorial chapel of the impressive **Cairn of Peace.** In the town of Slavkov itself, the Baroque château houses more memorabilia about the battle; it's well worth visiting. From Brno, follow the D1 freeway to the east and turn onto Route 50, following the signs to Slavkov.

⑰ If it's scenic tourism you want, however, take a short trip north from Brno up the Svitava Valley and into the **Moravský Kras** (Moravian Karst), an area of limestone formations, underground stalactite caves, rivers, and tunnels. The most interesting part is near **Blansko** and includes the **Kateřinská** jeskyně (Catherine Cave), **Punkevní jeskyně** (Punkva Cave), and the celebrated **Macocha Abyss,** the deepest drop (more than 400 feet) of the karst. Several caves can be visited: Try the 90-minute Punkva tour, which includes a visit to the Macocha Abyss and a boat trip along an underground river. From Brno, follow Route 43 north in the direction of Svitavy. Turn off at Route 379 to Blansko and follow Route 380 to the Punkevní jeskyně, about 30 kilometers (19 miles) in all. *Admission: 20 Kč. adults, 10 Kč. students. Open Apr.–Sept., daily 8–3:15 (last tour 2:45 on weekends); Oct.–Mar., daily 7:30–1:45 (until 2:45 on Sun.).*

⑱ To reach **Olomouc** from Brno, drive north on the E462, following the signs all the way. With light traffic, you can cover the 77 kilometers (48 miles) in about an hour. Olomouc is a paradox—so far from Austria yet so supportive of the empire. The Habsburgs always felt at home here, even when they were being violently opposed by Czech nationalists and Protestants throughout Bohemia and much of Moravia. During the revolutions of 1848, when the middle class from all over the Austrian empire seemed ready to boot the Habsburgs out of their palace, the royal family fled to Olomouc, where they knew they could count on the population for support. The 18-year-old Franz Joseph was even crowned emperor here in 1848 because the situation in Vienna was still too turbulent.

Despite being overshadowed by Brno, Olomouc, with its proud square and prim 19th-century buildings, still retains something of a provincial imperial capital, not unlike similarly sized cities in Austria. The focal point here is the triangular **Horní náměstí** (Upper Square), marked at its center by the bright and almost flippantly colored Renaissance **radnice** (town hall) with its 220-foot tower. The tower was begun during the late 14th century and given its current appearance in 1443; the astronomical clock on the outside was built in 1422, but its inner mechanisms and modern mosaic decorations date from immediately after World War II. Be sure to look inside at the beautiful Renaissance stairway. There's also a large Gothic banquet room in the main building, with scenes from the city's history, and a late-Gothic chapel.

The eccentric **Trinity Column** in the northwest corner of the square, at more than 100 feet, is the largest of its kind in the Czech Republic and houses a tiny chapel. Four Baroque fountains, depicting Hercules (1687), Caesar (1724), Neptune (1695), and Jupiter (1707), dot the main square and the adjacent **Dolní náměstí** (Lower Square) to the south, as if to reassure us that this Moravian town was well versed in the humanities.

Just north of the Horní náměstí, along the small Jana Opletala ulice, stands the **Chrám svatého Mořice** (Church of St. Maurice), the town's best Gothic building. Construction began in 1412, but a fire some 40 years later badly damaged the structure, and its current appearance dates from the middle of the 16th century. The Baroque organ inside, the largest in the Czech Republic, is said to contain some 2,311 pipes.

The most interesting sights in Olomouc are not in the Old Town but about 400 yards to the east in the vicinity of the **Dóm svatého Václava** (Cathedral of St. Wenceslas). If you're approaching from the Horní náměstí, follow the tiny Ostružnícká ulice, turn right onto the busy Denisova ulice, and keep walking straight (beyond yet another Baroque fountain at the náměstí Republiky) until you reach Dómská ulice. As it stands today, the original Gothic cathedral is just another example of the overbearing neo-Gothic enthusiasm of the late 19th century. To the left of the church, however, is the entrance to the **Kostel svatej Anny** (St. Anne's Chapel), now a museum, where you can see early 16th-century wall paintings decorating the Gothic cloisters and, upstairs, a wonderful series of two- and three-arched Romanesque windows. This part of the building was used as a schoolroom some 700 years ago, and you can still make out drawings of animals engraved on the walls by early young vandals. You can get an oddly phrased English pamphlet to help you around the building. *Dómská ul. Admission: 20 Kč. adults, 10 Kč. children. Open Tues.–Sun. 9–12:30 and 1–5.*

The **deacon's house** opposite the cathedral, now part of the Palácký University, has two unusual claims to fame. Here in 1767, the young musical prodigy Wolfgang Amadeus Mozart, age 11, spent six weeks recovering from a mild attack of chicken pox. The 16-year-old King

Wenceslas III suffered a much worse fate here in 1306, when he was murdered, putting an end to the Přemyslide dynasty.

What to See and Do with Children

Small children will no doubt be amused by the enormous **alligator** hanging from the ceiling in the Old Town Hall in Brno and by some of the stories associated with how it got there (*see* Tour 2). If you're traveling with older children, head out to the **Moravian Karst** (*see* Tour 3) and take a tour of the caves. Some tours include an exciting boat ride on an underground river. The archaeological museum at **Dolní Věstonice** (*see* Tour 1) has mammoth bones and remains from Stone Age settlements to keep junior scientists occupied for a while. The park at the **Lednice** castle (*see* Tour 1) has plenty of ground for playing on, wandering around, throwing a Frisbee, or kicking a ball. In winter, the frozen ponds here and in the surrounding area are great for ice skating (but you'll have to buy skates, as rentals are impossible to find).

Off the Beaten Track

Fans of dream interpretation and psychoanalysis shouldn't leave Moravia without stopping at the little town of **Příbor,** the birthplace of Sigmund Freud. To find it, drive east out of Olomouc along Route 35, following the signs first to Lipník, then Hranice, Nový Jičín, and finally Příbor—about 50 kilometers (31 miles) in all. Park at the Náměstí Sigmunda Freuda Sigmund Freud Square. The seemingly obvious name for the main square is actually new; the former communist regime was not in favor of Freudians. The comfortable, middle-class house, marked with a plaque where the doctor was born in 1856, is a short walk away along Freudova ulice. At present, the house is still residential, so you can't go inside. *Freudova ul. 117.*

Admirers of Art Nouveau meister Alfons Mucha may want to make a short detour to the southern Moravian town of **Moravský Krumlov,** not far from the main highway linking Mikulov and Brno. The town museum is the unlikely home of one of Mucha's most celebrated works, his 20-canvas "Slav Epic." This enormous work, which tells the story of the emergence of the Slav nation, was not well received when it was completed in 1928; painters at the time were more interested in imitating modern movements and considered Mucha's representational art to be old-fashioned. Interest in Mucha's lyrical style has grown in recent years, however, and the museum annually attracts some 15,000 visitors.

Shopping

Moravia produces very attractive folk pottery, painted with bright red, orange, and yellow flower patterns. You can find these products in stores and hotel gift shops throughout the region. For more modern art objects, including paintings, stop by **Dílo** (Kobližná 4, tel. 05/4221–4930) in Brno. **Merkuria** (down the street at Kobližná 10) stocks a beautiful selection of crystal and porcelain from Karlovy Vary. You can buy English paperbacks in Brno at the **Zahraniční literatura** shop (nám. Svobody 18). The secret of Moravian wine is only now beginning to extend beyond the country's borders. A vintage bottle from one of the smaller but still excellent vineyards in Bzenec, Velké Pavlovice, or Hodonín would be appreciated by any wine connoisseur.

Sports and Outdoor Activities

For mountain walking or cross-country skiing (if you're not going on to the High Tatras), try the gentle peaks of the **Beskydy Mountains,** about 25 kilometers (16 miles) south of Příbor; follow Route 58 south in the direction of Rožnov. Stay the night at one of the modest but comfortable mountain chalets in the area. You'll find a good one, the **Chata Solan,** along the road between Rožnov and Velké Karlovice (*see* Lodging, *below*). Another place to try is **Tanečnice** (south of Frenštát). But be sure to take along a good map before venturing along the tiny mountain roads. Also, some roads may be closed during the winter.

Dining and Lodging

Don't expect gastronomic delights in Moravia. The food—especially outside of Brno—is reasonably priced, but the choices are usually limited to roast pork, sauerkraut, and dumplings, or fried pork and french fries. Moravia's hotels are only now beginning to recover from 40 years of state ownership, and excellent hotels are few and far between. In many larger towns, private rooms are preferred. In mountainous areas inquire locally about the possibility of staying in a *chata* (cabin). These are abundant and often a pleasant alternative to the faceless modern hotels. Many lack modern amenities, though, so be prepared to rough it.

It's best to avoid Brno at trade-fair time (April and September), when hotel and restaurant facilities are strained. If the hotels are booked, Brno's Čedok (Divaldení 3, tel. 05/4221–0942) offices will help you find accommodations.

Highly recommended restaurants and lodgings in a particular price category are indicated by a star ★.

Brno **Baroko vinárna.** This 17th-century wine cellar housed in a Minorite
Dining monastery offers excellent cooking in a fun, if touristy, setting. Try the roast beef Slavkov, named for the site of Napoleon's triumph not far from Brno. Mystery of Magdalene is a potato pancake stuffed with pork, liver, mushrooms, and presumably anything else the cook could get his hands on. *Orlí 17, tel. 05/4221–1344. No credit cards. Dinner only. $$*
La Braseria. Delicious pastas and pizzas (a welcome alternative to the heavy local fare) are served here in a casual, unhurried setting. Take a taxi or walk the 15 minutes from the center. *Pekařská 80, tel. 05/4321–4528. No credit cards. $$*
Modrá Hvězda. Liberal opening hours and a convenient location just to the west of náměstí Svobody make this cheery restaurant a good choice for a quick lunch or off-hours snack. *Šilingrovo nám. 7, tel. 05/4221–5292. No credit cards. $$*
Klub Restaurant Pod Petrovem. This typical Moravian inn, just behind the Zelný třída, serves authentic country cuisine at reasonable prices. Try the delicate Moravian goulash or the hard-to-find poppyseed dumplings, which nicely round off the usually heavy Czech cuisine. *Petrská 2, tel. 05/4221–1376. No credit cards. $*
Špalíček. This raucous pivnice is for serious beer drinkers only. Nevertheless, it serves hearty, simple beef and pork dishes, and on warm summer evenings the terrace overlooking the Cabbage Market is the best place in town to linger over a drink. *12 Zelný trh. No credit cards. $*

Lodging **Grand.** Though not really grand, this hotel, built in 1870 and thoroughly remodeled in 1988, is certainly comfortable and the best in

Brno. High standards are maintained through the hotel's association with an Austrian chain. The reception and public areas are clean and modern; service is attentive; and the rooms, though small, are well appointed. Ask for a room at the back, overlooking the town, as the hotel is situated on a busy street opposite the railroad station. *Benešova 18–20, tel. 05/4232–1287, fax 05/4221–0345. Facilities: 3 restaurants, minibar, satellite TV, casino, nightclub. Breakfast included. AE, MC, V. $$$$*

Holiday Inn. Opened in 1993, this modern but handsome representative of the American chain has become the hotel of choice for business travelers in town for a trade fair. It has all you'd expect for the price, including a well-trained, multilingual staff, clean and well-appointed rooms, and a full range of business services. The location, at the exhibition grounds about a mile from the city center, is inconvenient for those who don't have a car. *Křížkovského 20, tel. 05/4312–2111, fax 05/4115–9081. 205 rooms with bath. Facilities: restaurant, café, sauna, conference rooms. Breakfast included. AE, DC, MC, V. $$$$*

Slavia. The century-old Slavia, located just off the main Česká ulice, was thoroughly renovated in 1987, giving the public areas an efficient, up-to-date look and leaving the rooms plain but clean. The café, with adjacent terrace, is a good place to enjoy a cool drink on a warm afternoon. *Solniční 15–17, tel. 05/4221–5080, fax 05/4221–1769. 81 rooms with shower or bath. Facilities: restaurant, café, minibars, parking. Breakfast included. AE, DC, MC, V. $$$*

★ **Pegas.** This little inn, recently remodeled, is an excellent choice given its reasonable price and central location. The renovation left little in the way of character in its wake; nevertheless, the plain rooms are snug and clean, and the staff is helpful and friendly. Even if you don't stay here, be sure to have a meal at the house pub-microbrewery, the city's best. *Jakubská 4, tel. 05/4221–0104, fax 05/4221–1232. 15 rooms with bath. Facilities: restaurant. Breakfast included. AE, DC, MC, V. $$*

Jihlava
Dining and Lodging

Zlatá Hvězda. Centrally located on the main square, this reconstructed old hotel in a beautiful Renaissance house is comfortable and surprisingly elegant. You're a short walk from Jihlava's restaurants and shops, though the on-site café and wine bar are among the best in town. *Nám. Míru 32, tel. 066/29421, fax 066/29422. 18 rooms. Facilities: restaurant, wine bar, café. Breakfast included. No credit cards. $$*

Mikulov
Lodging

Rohatý Krokodýl. This is a prim, newly renovated hotel on a quaint street in the Old Town. The standards and facilities are the best in Mikulov, particularly the ground-floor restaurant, which serves a typical but delicately prepared selection of traditional Czech dishes. *Husova 8, tel. 0625/2692, fax 0625/3695. 15 rooms with bath. Facilities: restaurant, terrace. Breakfast included. No credit cards. $$$*

Olomouc
Dining and Lodging

Flora. Don't expect luxury at this 1960s cookie-cutter high rise, located about a 15-minute walk from the town square. To its credit, the staff is attentive (English is spoken), and the pleasant if anonymous rooms are certainly adequate for a short stay. *Krapkova ul. 34, tel. 068/412062, fax 068/412221. 175 rooms, most with bath or shower. Facilities: restaurant, parking. Breakfast not included. AE, DC, MC, V. $$$*

Národní Dům. Built in 1885 and located a block from the main square, this is a better choice than the Flora for evoking a little of Olomouc's 19th-century history. The handsome building recalls the era's industriousness, as does the large, gracious café on the main floor. Standards have slipped in the intervening years, though, and signs of decline are evident. *Ul. 8. května 21, tel. 068/522–4806, fax 068/522–4808. 63 rooms, most with bath or shower. Facilities: restaurant, café, snack bar. Breakfast not included. No credit cards. $$*

Telč
Dining and Lodging
★

Černý Orel. Here you'll get a very rare treat: an older, refined hotel that combines modern amenities in a traditional setting. The public areas are functional but elegant, and the inviting rooms are well balanced and comfortably furnished. The hotel, with its Baroque facade, is a perfect foil to the handsome main square outside; ask for a room overlooking it. Even if you don't stay here, take a meal at the hotel restaurant, the best in town. *Nám. Zachariase z Hradce 7, tel. and fax 066/962220. 30 rooms, most with bath. Facilities: restaurant. Breakfast not included. AE, DC, MC, V. $$*

Telč. This is a slightly upscale alternative to the Černý Orel, even though the bright, polished appearance of the reception area doesn't quite carry over to the functional but pleasant rooms. Some rooms open up onto a pleasant courtyard. The location, in a corner of the main square, is ideal. *Na Můstku 37, tel. 066/962109, fax 066/962979. 10 rooms with bath. Facilities: restaurant. Breakfast included. No credit cards. $$*

Valtice
Dining and Lodging
★

Hubertus. This comfortable hotel, tucked away in one wing of a neo-Renaissance palace, is not hard to find. Just look for the only palace in town; the hotel is on the left-hand side. Though the rooms are neither palatial nor furnished in period style, they are nevertheless generously proportioned and comfortable. The restaurant, with garden terrace, serves reasonable Moravian cooking and good wine. Book ahead in summer, as the hotel is popular with Austrians who like to slip across the border for an impromptu holiday. *Zámek, tel. 0627/94537, fax 0627/94538. 40 rooms with bath. Facilities: restaurant, wine bar. Breakfast not included. No credit cards. $$*

Velké Karlovice
Dining and Lodging

Chata Solan. This tiny lodge is perched amid the hills and trees of the Beskydy range. Follow the road from Rožnov in the direction of Velké Karlovice for about 10 kilometers (6 miles); the lodge is the small wooden building on the left. Don't expect many amenities (you may have to share a room), but the standards of comfort and cleanliness are very high. A good breakfast is served in the rustic restaurant on the first floor. *Velké Karlovice, tel. 0657/94365. 5 rooms share a bath. No credit cards. $*

Znojmo
Dining and Lodging

Dukla. There are no surprises at this fairly modernized hotel set on the road to Vienna about 7 kilometers (4 miles) south of town. The staff is competent, and the corridors and small rooms are dreary but clean. The restaurant serves good Czech dishes in a relaxed atmosphere. *Antonína Zápotockého 5, tel. 0624/76320, fax 0624/76322. 110 rooms with bath or shower. Facilities: restaurant, parking. Breakfast not included. AE, DC, MC, V. $$*

Pension Inka. Rather than stay in a hotel, you might consider staying in this tiny, family-run pension not far from the center of town. The facilities are modest, but the rooms are bright and well kept. The kitchen is available for the use of guests. *Jarošova ul. 27, tel. 0624/4059. 3 rooms without bath. Breakfast not included. No credit cards. $$*

The Arts and Nightlife

The Arts

Brno is renowned throughout the Czech Republic for its theater and performing arts. The two main locales for cultural events are the **Mahen theater** (for drama) and the modern **Janáček theater** (for opera and ballet). Both are located just to the northwest of the center of town, just off Rooseveltova ul. Don't miss an opportunity to attend a concert here. Check the schedule at the theater or pick up a copy of *KAM*, Brno's monthly bulletin of cultural events. Buy tickets directly at the theater box office 30 minutes before showtime.

Nightlife   Nightlife in **Brno** revolves around the local pivnice or vinárna. Several good places can be found along **Česká ulice**. If it's a warm evening, head for the **Spaliček** pivnice (12 Zelný trh), invariably packed but with a great terrace overlooking the central Cabbage Market.

More sophisticated entertainment can be found at the **casinos** at the **Grand** and **International** hotels (Husova 16, tel. 05/4212–2111); the tables usually stay open until 3 or 4 AM. Both hotels also have bars that serve drinks until the wee hours of the morning.

3 Slovakia

by Mark Baker

Mark Baker is a freelance journalist and travel writer living in Prague.

Despite more than 70 years of common statehood with the Czechs (which ended in 1993), Slovakia *(Slovensko)* differs from the Czech Republic in a great many aspects. Its mountains are higher and more rugged, its veneer less sophisticated, its people more carefree. Observers of the two regions like to link the Czech Republic geographically and culturally with the orderly Germans, while they put Slovakia with the Ukraine and Russia firmly in the east. This is a simplification, yet it contains more than a little bit of truth.

Although they speak a language closely related to Czech, the Slovaks managed to maintain a strong sense of national identity throughout the period of common statehood. Indeed, the two Slavic groups developed quite separately: Though united in the 9th century as part of the Great Moravian Empire, the Slovaks were conquered a century later by the Magyars and remained under Hungarian or Habsburg rule until 1918. Following the Tartar invasions in the 13th century, many Saxons were invited to resettle the land and develop the economy, including the rich mineral resources. In the 15th and 16th centuries, Romanian shepherds migrated from Wallachia through the Carpathians into Slovakia, and the merging of these varied groups with the resident Slavs bequeathed to the region a rich folk culture and some unique forms of architecture, especially in the east.

In the end, it was this very different history that split the Slovaks from the Czechs, ending the most successful experiment in nation-building to follow World War I.

For many Slovaks, the 1989 revolution provided for the first time an opportunity not only to bring down the Communists, but also to establish a fully independent state—thus ending what many Slovaks' saw as a millennium of subjugation by Hungary and the Hapsburgs, Nazi Germany, Prague's communist regimes, and ultimately the Czechs. Although few Slovaks harbored any real resentment toward the Czechs, Slovak politicians were quick to recognize and exploit the deep, inchoate longing for independence. Slovak nationalist parties won more than 50% of the vote in the crucial 1992 Czechoslovak elections, and once the results were in, the end came quickly: On January 1, 1993, Slovakia became the youngest country in Europe.

The outside world witnessed the demise of the Czechoslovak federation in 1993 with some sadness; the split seemed just another piece of evidence to confirm that tribalism and nationalism continue to play the deciding role in European affairs. Yet there is something hopeful to be seen in the fact that the separation took place peacefully. Despite lingering differences on dividing the federation's assets, no Czechs or Slovaks have yet died in nationalistic squabbles. For the visitor, the changes may in fact be positive. The Slovaks have been long overshadowed by their cousins to the west; now they have the unfettered opportunity to tell their story to the world.

Most visitors to Slovakia head first for the great peaks of the High Tatras, which rise magnificently from the foothills of northern Slovakia. The tourist infrastructure here is very good, catering especially to hikers and skiers. Visitors who come to admire the peaks, however, often overlook the exquisite medieval towns of Spiš in the plains and valleys below the High Tatras and the beautiful 18th-century country churches farther east. (Removed from main centers, these areas are short on tourist amenities, so if creature comforts are important to you, stick to the High Tatras.)

Bratislava, the capital of Slovakia, is at first a disappointment to many visitors. The last 40 years of communism left a clear mark on

Slovakia

the city, hiding its ancient beauty with hulking, and now dilapidated, futurist structures. Yet despite its gloomy appearance, Bratislava tries hard to project the cosmopolitanism of a European
capital, bolstered by the fact that it is filled with good restaurants
and wine bars, opera and art.

Before You Go

Government Tourist Offices

Čedok, the official travel bureau for both the Czech Republic and
Slovakia, is a travel agent rather than a tourist information office.
As such, it will supply you with hotel and tour information, and book
air, rail, and bus tickets, but do not expect much in the way of general information.

In the United States: 10 E. 40th St., New York, NY 10016, tel. 212/
689–9720. **In the United Kingdom:** 17–18 Old Bond St., London W1X
4RB, tel. 0171/629–6058.

Tour Groups

U.S. Tour Operators Although there are no U.S.-based operators that specialize in tours
to Slovakia and Bratislava, **General Tours** (245 5th Ave., New York,
NY 10016, tel. 212/685–1800 or 800/221–2216) arranges excursions
through Slovakia in conjunction with some of its East European
packages. For information about other operators that include Slovakia on their East European itineraries, *see* Before You Go in Chapter 1.

U.K. Tour Operators **Čedok Tours and Holidays** (17–18 Old Bond St., London W1X 4RB,
tel. 0171/629–6058) offers packages to Prague and the Czech Repub-
lic, with optional sightseeing excursions to Slovakia. Čedok also has
packages to Bratislava's music festival.

Danube Travel Ltd. (6 Conduit St.1, London W1R 9TG, tel. 0171/
493–0263) offers a variety of packages that include a few nights' stay
in Bratislava.

When to Go

Slovakia, with its four full seasons, is beautiful throughout the year.
The High Tatras come into their own in winter (January–March),
when skiers by the thousand descend on the major resorts. A smaller summer season in the mountains attracts mostly walkers and hikers looking to escape the heat and noise of the cities. Because of the
snow, many of the hiking trails, especially those that cross the
peaks, are open only between June and October.

Bratislava is best visited in the temperate months of spring and autumn. July and August, though not especially crowded, can be un-
bearably hot. In winter, when many tourist attractions are closed,
expect lots of rain and snow in the capital. Note that, year-round,
temperatures are much cooler in mountainous areas. Even in summer, expect to wear a sweater or jacket in the High Tatras.

Festivals and Seasonal Events

For the moment, Slovakia's only major festival is the **Bratislava Music Festival,** which attracts national and international musicians to
venues throughout the capital in late October.

Many towns and villages host annual folklore festivals, usually on a weekend in late summer or early fall. These frequently take place in the town center and are accompanied by lots of singing, dancing, and drinking. Information is hard to come by, which makes planning difficult. Čedok promises to compile and publish a list of regional Slovakian festivals sometime in 1995; keep an eye out for it.

What to Pack

As is the case throughout Eastern Europe, many consumer items are still in short supply in Slovakia. Be certain to pack any special medications, as well as any special toiletries or hygienic materials you may require (i.e., soaps, shampoos, contact-lens solution, nonaspirin pain relievers). You will need an electrical adapter for small appliances; the voltage is 220, with 50 cycles. If you plan to hike in the mountains, a sturdy pair of shoes or boots is a must.

Slovak Currency

The unit of currency in Slovakia is the crown (Sk.), which is divided into 100 halers. There are (little used) coins of 10, 20, and 50 halers; coins of 1, 2, 5, 10, and 20 Sk., and notes of 20, 50, 100, 500, and 1,000 Sk. The 100-Sk. notes are by far the most useful. The 1,000-Sk. note is not always accepted for small purchases, because the proprietor may not have enough change. Also note: Czech money is no longer accepted as legal tender in Slovakia. If you're headed for the Czech Republic, exchange your Slovakian crowns for Czech crowns before crossing the border.

Try to avoid exchanging money at hotels or private exchange booths. They routinely take commissions of 8%–10%. The best places to exchange are banks, where the commissions average 1%–3%. Although the Slovak crown is more or less convertible, you will still encounter difficulty in exchanging your money when you leave. To facilitate this process, keep your original exchange receipts so no one will think you bought your crowns on the black market. It is technically illegal to buy crowns abroad and bring them into Slovakia (or to take them out when you leave), although this is not strictly controlled. At press time (summer 1994) the official exchange rate was around 29 Sk. to the U.S. dollar and 45 Sk. to the pound sterling. There is no longer a special exchange rate for tourists.

What It Will Cost

Slovakia is a bargain by Western standards, particularly in the outlying areas and off the beaten track. The exception is the price of accommodations in Bratislava, where hotel rates often meet or exceed both the U.S. and Western European average. Accommodations outside of the capital, with the exception of the High Tatras resorts, are significantly lower. Tourists can now legally pay for hotel rooms in Slovakian crowns, although some hotels still insist on payment in "hard" (i.e., Western) currency.

Sample Costs   A cup of coffee, 15 Sk.; museum entrance, 10 Sk.–20 Sk.; a good theater seat, up to 100 Sk.; a cinema seat, 25 Sk.–30 Sk.; a half liter (pint) of beer, 15 Sk.; a 1-mile taxi ride, 60 Sk.; a bottle of Slovak wine in a good restaurant, 100 Sk.–150 Sk.; a glass (2 deciliters, or 7 ounces) of wine, 25 Sk.

Passports and Visas

American and British citizens do not need a visa to enter Slovakia. A
valid passport is sufficient for stays of up to 30 days. Questions
should be directed to the Slovakian Embassy (3900 Linnean Ave.
NW, Washington, DC, tel. 202/363–6315). Canadian citizens must
obtain a visa (C$50) before entering the country; for applications
and information contact the Slovakian Embassy (50 Rideau Terrace,
Ottawa, Ontario K1M 2A1, tel. 613/749–4442).

Customs and Duties

You may import duty-free into Slovakia 250 cigarettes or the equivalent in tobacco, one liter of spirits, two liters of wine, and ½ liter of
perfume. You are also permitted to import duty-free up to 1,000 Sk.
worth of gifts and souvenirs.

As with the Czech Republic, if you take into Slovakia any valuables
or foreign-made equipment from home, such as cameras, it's wise to
carry the original receipts with you or register the items with U.S.
Customs before you leave (Form 4457). Otherwise you could end up
paying duty upon your return.

Language

Slovak, a western-Slavic language closely related to both Czech and
Polish, is the official language of Slovakia. Czech and Slovak are mu-
tually comprehensible; if you speak Czech, you'll have little problem
in Slovakia. Learning English is popular among young people, but
German is still the most useful language for tourists. Don't be surprised if you get a response in German to a question asked in English.

Staying Healthy

Slovakia poses no great health risks for the short-term visitor. As is
the case throughout Eastern Europe, vegetarians and those on special diets will have trouble adjusting to Slovakia's pork- and beef-
based cuisine. Fresh fruits and vegetables are bountiful during
summer and fall but become scarce during winter.

Car Rentals

There are no special requirements for renting a car in Slovakia, but
be sure to shop around, as prices can differ greatly. **Budget** and
Hertz offer Western makes for as much as $500 per week. Smaller
local companies, on the other hand, can rent local cars for as low as
$130 per week. The following agencies are located in Bratislava:

Auto Danubius, Trnavská 31, tel. 07/213096
Budget, Vysoká 32, tel. 07/330709
Hertz, Bratislava airport, tel. 07/291482; Hotel Forum, tel. 07/
348155
Recar, Stefanikova 1, tel. 07/333420

Rail Passes

The **European East Pass** is good for unlimited first-class travel on
the national railroads of Austria, the Czech Republic, Slovakia,
Hungary, and Poland. The pass allows 5 days of travel within a 15-
day period ($169) or 10 days of travel within a 30-day period ($275).

Apply through your travel agent or through **Rail Europe** (226–230 Westchester Ave., White Plains, NY 10604, tel. 914/682–2999 or 800/848–7245).

The **EurailPass** and **Eurail Youthpass** are not valid for travel within Slovakia. The **InterRail Pass**, available to European citizens only through local student or budget travel offices, is valid for unlimited train travel in Slovakia and the other countries covered in this book. For more information, *see* Before You Go in Chapter 1, Essential Information.

Student and Youth Travel

ČKM is the center for student and youth discounts; it will also help book accommodations in hostels and cheaper hotels (Hviezdoslavovo nám. 19, Bratislava, tel. 07/331607). For general information about student identity cards, work-abroad programs, and youth hostels, *see* Before You Go in Chapter 1.

Further Reading

Slovak writers have long been overshadowed in the West by their Bohemian counterparts, hence little of Slovakia's literature is available to the English reader. Given the 74-year political union of Czechs and Slovaks, however, many Czech authors (*see* Before You Go in Chapter 2), including Milan Kundera, Josef Skvorecký, and Václav Havel, addressed themes of relevance to Slovakia. In addition, many of the general books on Eastern Europe listed in Chapter 1 contain chapters and background information on Slovakia.

Arriving and Departing

From North America by Plane

Airports and Airlines
At press time few international airlines provided direct service to Bratislava, hence the best airports for traveling to Slovakia remain Prague's Ruzyně Airport and Vienna's Schwechat Airport. ČSA, the Czech and Slovak national carrier (in U.S. tel. 718/656–8439), offers regular service to Prague from New York's JFK Airport, Chicago, Los Angeles, and Montreal. Many of these flights have direct connections from Prague to Bratislava ($60–$75 each way); the trip takes about an hour. ČSA also offers regular air service between Prague and the High Tatras (Poprad) and Košice. Vienna's Schwechat Airport lies a mere 50 kilometers (30 miles) to the west of Bratislava. Four buses a day stop at Schwechat en route to Bratislava; the journey takes just over an hour. Numerous trains and buses also run daily between Vienna and Bratislava.

Flying Time
From New York, a flight to Bratislava (with a stopover in Prague) takes 11–12 hours. From Montreal it is 8½ hours; from Los Angeles, 17 hours.

From the United Kingdom by Plane, Bus, Car, and Train

By Plane
British Airways (in U.K., tel. 0171/897–4000) has daily nonstop service to Prague from London; ČSA (in U.K., tel. 0171/255–1898) flies five times a week nonstop from London. The flight takes about three hours. Numerous airlines offer service between London and Vienna.

By Bus There is no direct bus service from the United Kingdom to Slovakia; the closest you can get is Vienna. **International Express** (Coach Travel Center, 13 Lower Regent St., London SW1Y 4LR, tel. 0171/ 439–9368) operates daily in summer.

By Car Hoek van Holland and Ostend are the most convenient ferry ports for Bratislava. From either, drive to Cologne (Köln) and then through Dresden or Frankfurt to reach Bratislava.

By Train There are no direct trains from London. You can take a direct train from Paris via Frankfurt to Vienna (and connect to another train or bus), or from Berlin via Dresden and Prague (en route to Budapest). Vienna is a good starting point for Bratislava. There are several trains that make the 70-minute run daily from Vienna's Südbahnhof.

Staying in Slovakia

Getting Around

By Plane Despite the splintering of the Czechoslovak federation, ČSA (Czechoslovak Airlines) maintains a remarkably good internal air service within Slovakia, linking Bratislava with Poprad (Tatras), Piešt'any, and Košice. The flights, by jet or turboprop aircraft, are relatively cheap and frequent. Reservations can be made through Čedok offices abroad or ČSA in Bratislava (tel. 07/311205).

By Train Trains vary in speed, but it's not really worth taking anything less than an "express" train, marked in red on the timetable. Tickets are relatively cheap; first class is considerably more spacious and comfortable and well worth the 50% increase over the price of standard tickets. If you don't specify "express" when you buy your ticket, you may have to pay a supplement on the train. If you haven't bought a ticket in advance at the station, it's easy to buy one on the train for a small extra charge. On timetables, departures appear on a yellow background; arrivals are on white. It is possible to book *couchettes* (sleepers) on most overnight trains, but don't expect much in the way of comfort. The European East Pass and InterRail Pass are valid for all rail travel within Slovakia (*see* Rail Passes, *above*).

By Bus ČSAD (Bratislava, tel. 07/63213), the national bus carrier for the Czech Republic and Slovakia, maintains a comprehensive network in both countries. Buses are usually much quicker than the normal trains and more frequent than express trains, though prices are comparable with train fares. Buy your tickets from the ticket window at the bus station or directly from the driver on the bus. Long-distance buses can be full, so you might want to book a seat in advance; any Čedok office will help you do this. The only drawback to traveling by bus is figuring out the timetables. They are easy to read, but beware of the small letters denoting exceptions to the time given.

By Car Slovakia has few multilane highways, but the secondary road network is in reasonably good shape, and traffic is usually light. Roads are poorly marked, however, so an essential purchase is the *Auto Atlas ČSFR* or the larger-scale *Velký Autoatlas Československá* (which also shows locations of lead-free gas pumps). Both are multilingual, inexpensive, and available at bookstores throughout Slovakia and the Czech Republic.

Slovakia follows the usual Continental rules of the road. A right turn on red is permitted only when indicated by a green arrow. Signposts with yellow diamonds indicate a main road where drivers have the right of way. The speed limit is 110 kph (70 mph) on four-lane highways; 90 kph (55 mph) on open roads; and 60 kph (40 mph) in built-up areas. The fine for speeding is roughly 300 Sk., payable on the spot. Seat belts are compulsory, and drinking before driving is prohibited.

To report an accident, call the emergency number (tel. 155). In case of an auto breakdown, in Bratislava contact the 24-hour towing service (tel. 07/249404). The *Auto Atlas ČSFR* has a list of emergency road-repair numbers in various towns.

Telephones

Local Calls A local call costs 1 Sk., and coin-operated telephones take either 1-Sk. coins exclusively or any combination of 1-, 2-, and 5-Sk. coins. To make a call, lift the receiver and listen for the dial tone (a series of long buzzes), then dial the number. Public phones are often out of order, however; try asking in a hotel if you're stuck.

International Calls Dial tel. 00–420–00101 (AT&T) or tel. 00–420–00112 (MCI) to reach an English-speaking operator who can effortlessly connect your direct, collect, or credit-card call to the United States. Otherwise, you can make a more time-consuming and expensive international call from Bratislava's main post office (Námestie SNP 36), or, for an even larger fee, at major hotels throughout the country.

Mail

Postal Rates Postcards to the United States cost 6 Sk.; letters, 11 Sk. Postcards to Great Britain cost 4 Sk.; a letter, 6 Sk. Prices are due for an increase in 1995, so check with your hotel for current rates. You can buy stamps at post offices, hotels, and many shops that sell postcards.

Receiving Mail If you don't know where you'll be staying, you can have mail held *poste restante* (general delivery) at post offices in major towns, but the letters should be marked *Pošta 1* to designate a city's main post office. You will be asked for identification when you collect mail. The poste restante window in Bratislava is at Námestie SNP 35.

Tipping

To reward good service in a restaurant, round up the bill to the nearest multiple of 10 (if the bill comes to 86 Sk., for example, give the waiter 90 Sk.). A tip of 10% is considered appropriate on group tabs. If you have difficulty communicating the amount to the waiter, just leave the money on the table. Tip porters who bring bags to your rooms 20 Sk. For room service, a 20-Sk. tip is sufficient. In taxis, round up the bill by 10%. Give tour guides and helpful concierges 20 Sk.–30 Sk.

Opening and Closing Times

Banks Bank hours vary, but most are open weekdays 8–3:30, with a one-hour lunch break.

Museums Museums are usually open daily 9–5 except Monday and sometimes Tuesday. Some tourist sights, including many castles, are open only May through October.

Stores Stores are generally open weekdays 9–6. Some grocery stores open at 6 AM, and some department stores often stay open until 7 PM. On

Saturday, most shops close at noon. Nearly all stores are closed on Sunday.

National Holidays

January 1; Easter Monday; May 1 (Labor Day); July 5 (Sts. Cyril and Methodius); August 29 (anniversary of the Slovak National Uprising); September 1 (Constitution Day); and December 24, 25, and 26.

Shopping

The best buys in Slovakia are folk-art products sold at stands along the roads and in **Slovart** stores in most major towns. Among the most interesting finds are batik-painted Easter eggs, cornhusk figures, delicate woven table mats, hand-knitted sweaters, and folk pottery. The local brands of firewater—*slivovice* (plum brandy) and *borovička* (a spirit made from juniper berries)—also make for excellent buys.

Sports and Outdoor Activities

Bicycling Slovaks are avid cyclists, and the flatter areas to the south and east of Bratislava and along the Danube are ideal for biking. Outside large towns, quieter roads stretch out for many kilometers. A special bike trail links Bratislava and Vienna, paralleling the Danube for much of its 40-kilometer (25-mile) length. Not many places rent bikes, however; inquire at Čedok or at your hotel for rental information.

Boating and Slovaks with boats head to the man-made lakes of Zemplínska
Sailing Širava (east of Košice near the Ukrainian border) or Orava (northwest of the Tatras near the Polish border). River rafting has been hampered in recent years by dry weather, which has also reduced river levels. However, raft rides are still given in summer at Červený Kláštor, north of Kežmarok (*see* Eastern Slovakia, *below*).

Camping There are hundreds of camping sites for tents and trailers throughout Slovakia, but most are open only in summer (May to mid-September). You can get a map of all the sites, with addresses, opening times, and facilities, from Čedok; auto atlases also identify campsites. Camping outside of official sites is prohibited. Some camping grounds also offer bungalows. Campsites are divided into categories A and B according to facilities, but both have hot water and toilets.

Fishing There are hundreds of lakes and rivers suitable for fishing in Slovakia, but because rental equipment is scarce, you should bring your own tackle or be prepared to buy it locally. To legally cast a line you must have a fishing license (valid for one year) plus a fishing permit (valid for a day, week, month, or year for the particular body of water you plan to fish on). Both are available from Čedok offices.

Hiking Slovakia is a hiker's paradise, with more than 20,000 kilometers (15,000 miles) of well-kept, marked, and signposted trails in both the mountainous regions and the rural countryside. You'll find the colored markings denoting trails on trees, fences, walls, rocks, and elsewhere. The colors correspond to the path-marking on the large-scale *Soubor turistickych* maps available at many bookshops and tobacconists. The main paths are marked in red, others in blue and green; the least important trails are marked in yellow. The best areas for ambitious mountain walkers are the Small Carpathians (near

Bratislava), the Fatra range in western Slovakia, and the High Tatras to the north.

Skiing The two main skiing areas in Slovakia are the Low Tatras (Nízke Tatry) and the High Tatras (Vysoké Tatry). The latter offers more reliable conditions (good snow throughout winter) and superior facilities. Lifts in both regions generally operate from January through March, though cross-country skiing is a popular alternative. In both areas you will find a number of organizations that rent limited equipment.

Tennis Large hotels and resorts can sometimes arrange for tennis courts if they don't have them in-house. In large towns, ask at the Čedok office or in hotels for the address of the nearest public tennis courts.

Dining

Slovak food is an amalgam of its neighbors' cuisines. As in Bohemia and Moravia, the emphasis is on meat, particularly pork and beef. But you will seldom find the Czechs' traditional (and often bland) roast pork and dumplings on the menu. The Slovaks, betraying their long link to Hungary, prefer to spice things up a bit, usually with paprika and red peppers. Roast potatoes or french fries are often served in place of dumplings, although occasionally you'll find a side dish of tasty *halušky* (noodles similar to Italian gnocchi or German spaetzle) on the menu. No primer on Slovak eating would be complete without mention of *bryndzové halušky*, the country's unofficial national dish, a tasty and filling mix of halušky, sheep's cheese, and a little bacon fat for flavor (it seldom makes it onto the menu at elegant restaurants, so look for it instead at roadside restaurants and snack bars). For dessert, the emphasis comes from upriver, in Vienna: pancakes, fruit dumplings (if you're lucky), poppy-seed dumplings, and strudel.

Eating out is still not a popular pastime among Slovaks, particularly since prices have risen markedly in the past few years. As a result, you will find relatively few restaurants about; and those that do exist generally cater to foreigners. Restaurants known as *vináreň* specialize in serving wines, although you can order beer virtually anywhere. The Slovaks, however, do not have an equivalent to the Czech *pivnice* (beer hall).

Slovaks pride themselves on their wines, and to an extent they have a point. Do not expect much subtlety, though, for the typical offering is hearty, sometimes heavy, but always very drinkable wines that complement the region's filling and spicy food. This is especially true of the reds. The most popular is *Frankovka*, which is fiery and slightly acidic. *Vavrinecké*, a relatively new arrival, is dark and semisweet and stands up well to red meats. Slovakia's few white wines are similar in character to the Moravian wines and, on the whole, are unexceptional.

Mealtimes Lunch, usually eaten between noon and 2, is the main meal for Slovaks and offers the best deal for tourists. Many restaurants put out a special luncheon menu, with more appetizing selections at better prices. Dinner is usually served from 5 until 9 or 10, but don't wait too long to eat. Cooks frequently knock off early on slow nights. The dinner menu does not differ substantially from lunch offerings, except that the prices are higher.

Ratings	Category	Cost*
	$$$$	over $20
	$$$	$15–$20
	$$	$7–$15
	$	under $7

per person for a three-course meal, excluding wine and tip

Highly recommended restaurants are indicated by a star ★.

Lodging

Slovakia's hotel industry has been slow to react to the political and economic changes that have taken place since 1989. Few new hotels have been built, and many of the older establishments are still majority-owned by the state. As a result, there has been little appreciable increase in quality outside of the major tourist centers: The facilities in the Tatras remain good, and Bratislava added a new hotel in 1993, but elsewhere things have been fairly quiet.

In general, hotels can be divided into two categories: edifices built in the 1960s or '70s that offer modern amenities but not much character; and older, more central establishments that are heavy on personality but may lack basic conveniences. Hostels are understood to mean cheap dormitory rooms and are probably best avoided. In the mountainous areas, you can often find little *chata* (chalets), where pleasant surroundings compensate for a lack of basic amenities. *Autokempink* (campsites) generally have a few bungalows available for visitors.

Slovakia's official hotel classification, based on letters (Deluxe, A*, B*, B, C), is gradually being changed over to the international star system, although it will be some time before the old system is completely replaced. These ratings correspond closely to our categories as follows: Deluxe or five-star ($$$$); A* or four-star ($$$); B* or three-star ($$); and B or two-star ($). We've included C hotels, some with cold water only, in our listings where accommodations are scarce. Nevertheless, prices in the upper ranges are difficult to predict, since hotels are free to set their own prices. As a rule, always ask the price before taking a room.

Ratings The prices quoted below are for double rooms, generally not including breakfast. Prices at the lower end of the scale apply to low season. At certain periods, such as Easter or during festivals, there may be an increase of 15%–25%.

Category	Cost*
$$$$	over $100
$$$	$50–$100
$$	$15–$50
$	under $15

All prices are for a standard double room, including tax and service.

Bratislava

Many visitors are initially disappointed when they see Europe's newest capital city, Bratislava. Expecting a Slovak version of Prague or Vienna, they discover instead a busy industrial city that seems to embody the Communists' blind faith in modernity rather than the stormy history of this once Hungarian and now Slovak capital. The problem, of course, is that Bratislava has more than its fair share of high-rise housing projects, faded supermodern structures, and less-than-inspiring monuments to carefully chosen acts of heroism. Even the handsome castle on the hill and the winding streets of the Old Town look decidedly secondary in their crumbling beauty.

The jumble of modern Bratislava, however, masks a long and regal history that rivals Prague's in importance and complexity. Settled by a variety of Celts and Romans, the city became part of the Great Moravian Empire around the year 900 under Prince Břetislav. After a short period under the Bohemian Přemysl princes, Bratislava was brought into the Hungarian kingdom by Stephan I at the end of the 10th century and given royal privileges in 1217. Following the Tatar invasion in 1241, the Hungarian kings brought in German colonists to repopulate the town. The Hungarians called the town Pozsony; the German settlers referred to it as Pressburg; and the original Slovaks called it Bratislava after Prince Břetislav.

When Pest and Buda were occupied by the Turks, in 1526 and 1541, respectively, the Hungarian kings moved their seat to Bratislava, which remained the Hungarian capital until 1784, and the coronation center until 1835. At this time, with a population of almost 27,000, it was the largest Hungarian city. Only in 1919, when Bratislava became part of the first Czechoslovak Republic, did the city regain its Slovak identity. In 1939, with Germany's assistance, Bratislava infamously exerted its yearnings for independence by becoming the capital of the puppet Slovak state, under the fascist leader Jozef Tiso. In 1945 it became the provincial capital of Slovakia, still straining under the powerful hand of Prague (Slovakia's German and Hungarian minorities were either expelled or repressed). In the run-up to the 1989 revolution, Bratislava was the site of numerous anticommunist demonstrations; many of these were carried out by supporters of the Catholic Church, long repressed by the regime then in power. Following the "Velvet Revolution" in 1989, Bratislava gained importance as the capital of the Slovak Republic within the new Czech and Slovak federal state, but rivalries with Prague persisted. It was only following the breakup of Czechoslovakia on January 1, 1993, that the city once again became a capital in its own right. But don't come to Bratislava expecting to beauty of Prague or the bustle of Budapest. Instead, plan to spend a day or two leisurely sightseeing before setting off for Slovakia's superior natural splendors.

Important Addresses and Numbers

Tourist Information Bratislava's tourist information service, **Bratislavská Informačná Služba (BIS)** (Panská 18, tel. 07/333715), is a good source for maps and basic information; it can also assist in booking private accommodations. The office is open weekdays 8–4:30 (until 6 in summer) and Saturday 8–1. The city's large Čedok office (Jesenského 5, tel. 07/52624; open weekdays 9–6, Sat. 9–noon) can help with finding hotel and private accommodations and will provide information on Bratislava and surrounding areas.

Embassies U.S. Embassy, Hviezdoslavovo 4, tel. 07/330861. British Embassy, Grösslingova 35, tel. 07/364420.

Emergencies Police (tel. 158). Ambulance (tel. 155).

English-Language Bookstores Several Slovak bookstores stock English-language titles. Try Big Ben Bookshop at Michalská 1 (tel. 07/333632). Another possibility is the beautiful secondhand bookstore Antikvariat Steiner (Venturská ul. 20, tel. 07/52834). The newsstand at Laurinská 2 is a good source for English-language newspapers and periodicals. The well-stocked reading room of the U.S. Embassy (*see above*) is open to the general public (Tues.–Fri. 9–2, Mon. noon–5). Bring a passport.

Late-Night Pharmacies The pharmacy at Špitálska 3, near the Old Town, maintains 24-hour service; other pharmacies hold late hours on a rotating basis.

Travel Agencies At press time, neither American Express nor Thomas Cook had offices in the Slovak capital, although this is likely to change. Čedok (*see above*) can provide basic travel agency services, such as changing traveler's checks and booking bus and train tickets to outside destinations. Tatratur (Františkánske nám. 7, tel. 07/335012) is another dependable local travel agency that can help arrange sightseeing tours throughout Slovakia.

Arriving and Departing by Plane

Although few international airlines provide direct service to Bratislava, ČSA (tel. 07/311205), the Czech and Slovak national carrier, offers frequent and convenient connections to Bratislava via Prague. Another possibility is to fly into Vienna's Schwechat Airport, about 50 kilometers (30 miles) to the west of Bratislava, and finish the hour-long journey by bus or train.

Arriving and Departing by Car, Train, Bus, and Boat

By Car There are good freeways from Prague to Bratislava via Brno (D1 and D2); the 325-kilometer (203-mile) journey takes about 3½ hours. From Vienna, take the A4 and then Route 8 to Bratislava, just across the border. Depending on the traffic at the border, the 60-kilometer (37-mile) journey should take about 1½ hours.

By Train Reasonably efficient train service regularly connects Prague and Bratislava. Trains leave from Prague's Hlavní nádraží (main station) or from Holešovice station, and the journey takes five hours. From Vienna, four trains daily make the one-hour trek to Bratislava. Bratislava's train station, Hlavná Stanica, is situated about 2 kilometers (1 mile) from the city center; to travel downtown from the station, take Streetcar 1 or 13 to Poštová ulica; or jump in a taxi.

By Bus There are numerous buses from Prague to Bratislava; the five-hour journey costs less than 250 Sk. From Vienna, there are four buses a day from Autobusbahnhof Wien Mitte. The journey takes 1½–2 hours and costs about AS150. Bratislava's main bus terminal, Autobus Stanica, is roughly 2 kilometers (1 mile) from the city center; to get downtown, take Trolley (*trolej*) 217 to Mierové námestie or Bus 107 to the castle (*hrad*); or flag down a taxi.

By Boat Hydrofoils travel the Danube between Vienna and Bratislava from April to December. Boats depart in the morning from Bratislava, on the eastern bank of the Danube just down from the Devin Hotel, and return from Vienna in the evening. Tickets cost $40–$70 per person and should be booked in person at the dock.

Getting Around

Bratislava is compact, and most sights can be covered easily on foot. Taxis are cheap and easy to hail; at night, they are the best option for returning home from wine cellars and clubs.

By Bus and Tram Buses and trams in Bratislava run frequently and connect the city center with outlying sights. Tickets cost 5 Sk. and are available from large hotels, news agents, and tobacconists. Validate the tickets on board the bus or tram (watch how the locals do it). The fine for riding without a ticket is 200 Sk., payable on the spot.

By Taxi Meters start at 10 Sk. and jump 10 Sk. per kilometer (½ mile). The number of dishonest cabbies, sadly, is on the rise, to avoid being ripped off, watch to see that the driver engages the meter. If the meter is broken, negotiate a price with the driver before even getting in the cab. Taxis are hailable on the street, or call 07/311311.

Guided Tours

The best tours of Bratislava are offered by **BIS** (*see* Tourist Information, *above*), although during the off-season tours are conducted only in German and only on weekends. Tours typically last two hours and cost 270 Sk. per person. Čedok (*see* Tourist Information, *above*) also offers tours of the capital from May through September. You can sometimes combine these with an afternoon excursion through the Small Carpathian Mountains, including dinner at the Zochová chata.

Highlights for First-Time Visitors

Bratislava Castle
Červený Kameň (*see* Excursions from Bratislava)
Kapitulská ulica
Old Town Hall

Exploring Bratislava

Numbers in the margin correspond to points of interest on the Bratislava map.

❶ Begin your tour of the city at the modern **Námestie SNP** square; SNP is the abbreviation for *Slovenské Národné Povstanie* (Slovak National Uprising), an addendum typically affixed to street names, squares, bridges, and posters throughout Slovakia. (The uprising was actually a protracted anti-Nazi resistance movement, involving partisan fighting, which began in the central part of the country in the final years of World War II.) In the middle of the square, formerly known as Stalinovo námestie (Stalin Square), are three larger-than-life statues: a dour partisan with two strong, sad women in peasant clothing. This was formerly the center for demonstrations in support of Slovak independence, and even now you will occasionally see the Slovak flag (red, blue, and white with a double cross) flying from the partisan's gun.

From here walk up toward **Hurbanovo námestie.** The golden-yellow
❷ Baroque **Kostol svätej Trojice** (Church of the Holy Trinity) is worth visiting—if the doors are open, which they often are not—for the almost three-dimensional, space-expanding frescoes on the ceiling, the work of Antonio Galli Bibiena in the early 18th century.

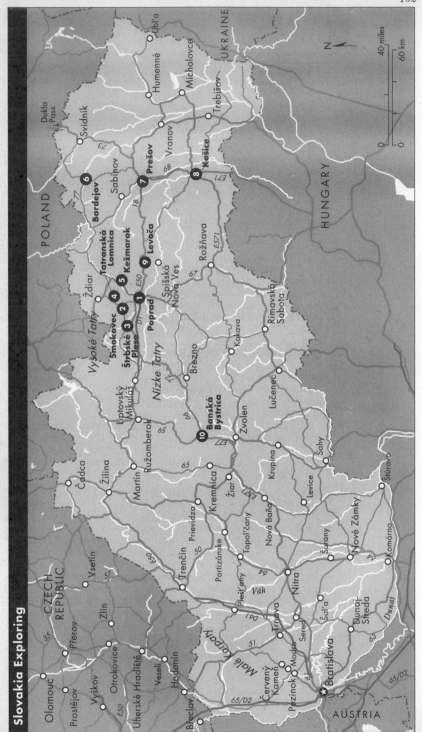

Slovakia Exploring

Dóm Sv. Martina, **7**
Františkánsky Kostol, **13**
Hrad, **9**
Jezuitské Kolégium, **6**
Jezuitský Kostol, **15**
Klariský Kostol, **5**
Kostol Kapucínov, **12**
Kostol Sv. Trojice, **2**
Michalská Brána, **3**
Mirbachov Palác, **14**
Most SNP, **8**
Múzeum Umeleckých Remesiel/ Múzeum Bratislavských Historických Hodín, **10**
Námestie SNP, **1**
Palác Uhorskej Kráľovskej Komory, **4**
Primaciálny Palác, **17**
Reduta, **19**
Slovenská Národná Galéria, **20**
Slovenské Národné Divadlo, **18**
Stará Radnica, **16**
Židovská Ulica, **11**

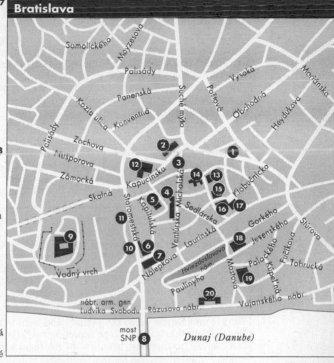

Bratislava

3 Across the road, unobtrusively located between a shoe store and a bookshop, is the enchanting entrance to the **Old Town**. A small bridge, decorated with wrought-iron railings and statues of St. John of Nepomuk and St. Michael, takes you over the old moat, now blossoming with trees and fountains, into the intricate barbican, a set of gates and houses that composed Bratislava's medieval fortifications. After going through the first archway, you'll come to the narrow **Michalská ulica**; in front of you is the **Michalská brána** (Michael's Gate), the last remaining of the city's three original gates. The bottom part of the tower, built in the 14th century, retains its original Gothic design; the octagonal section was added in the early 16th century; and the flamboyant copper onion tower, topped with a statue of St. Michael, is an addition from the 18th century.

On your left, before going through the tower, you'll find the **Farmaceutické múzeum** (Pharmaceutical Museum). Housed in the barbican wall, on the site of the former Pharmacy of the Red Crab, this small museum is worth visiting if only to see the beautifully carved wooden shelves and imaginative pharmaceutical receptacles. Next to the museum, a small arched gateway topped with the symbol of a crab leads down through an apartment building to the moatside garden, which affords good views of the looming fortifications. *Michalská ul. 26. Admission: 10 Sk. adults, 5 Sk. children and students. Open Tues.–Sun. 10–4:30.*

Through the Michalská brána, in a door to the left, is the entrance to the **Múzeum zbraní a mestského opevnenia** (Museum of Weapons and Fortifications), built into the tower. The museum itself is not really worth a lot of time, but the *veža* (tower) affords a good view over the city. *Michalská veža, Michalská ul. 24. Admission: 5 Sk. adults, 2 Sk. children. Open Wed.–Mon. 10–5.*

Continue down Michalská ulica. Many of the more interesting buildings along the street are undergoing renovation, but notice the eerie blue **Kaplnka svätej Kataríny** (Chapel of St. Catherine) at No. 6 on the left, built in 1311 but now graced with a sober classical facade. Opposite, at No. 7, is the Renaissance **Segnerova kúria** (Segner House), built for a wealthy merchant in 1648.

❹ A little farther down on the right is the **Palác Uhorskej kráľovskej komory** (Hungarian Royal Chamber), a Baroque palace that housed the Hungarian nobles' parliament from 1802 until 1848; it is now used as the University Library. Go through the arched passageway at the back of the building and you'll emerge in a tiny square dominated by the **Church and Convent of the Poor Clares** (Kostol Klarisiek); the convent is now the Slovak Pedagogical Library.

❺ The 14th-century **Klariský kostol** (church), stretched along Farská ulica ahead of you, is simple but inspiring, with a wonderfully peaceful early Gothic interior. Unfortunately, the church is now a concert hall—and usually locked, but you may be able to get in for a concert or during rehearsals. The small High Gothic steeple was added in an unusually secondary position at the back of the church during the 15th century; as a mendicant order, the Poor Clares were forbidden to build a steeple onto the church, so they sidestepped the rules and built it on a side wall.

Follow Farská ulica up to the corner, and turn left on **Kapitulská ulica** (noticing the ground stone depicting two kissing lizards). This street could be the most beautiful in Bratislava, but its array of Gothic, Renaissance, and Baroque buildings is in such disrepair that the effect is almost lost. Renovation has now begun, and you can see on No. 15 that the remains of a wall painting have been uncovered from a stone facade. At the bottom of the street on the right is the ❻ late-Renaissance **Jezuitské kolégium** (Jesuit College), a theological seminary since 1936; every few minutes, young men in black rush out of the door, cross the road, and disappear into the luxurious garden of the former Provost's Palace.

❼ Ahead of you is the side wall of the **Dóm svätého Martina** (St. Martin's Cathedral). Construction of this massive Gothic church, with its 280-foot steeple twinkling beneath a layer of golden trim, began in the 14th century. The cathedral was finally consecrated in 1452, and between the 16th and 19th centuries it hosted the coronation of 17 Hungarian royals. Numerous additions made over the centuries were unfortunately removed in the 19th century, when the church was re-Gothicized; nowadays the three equal-size naves give an impression of space and light, but the uplifting glory found in Bohemia's Gothic cathedrals is definitely missing. The peace is further disturbed by the noise of traffic zooming by on an elevated freeway built across the front entrance during the 1970s that nearly reduces the church to an irrelevant religious relic.

❽ As you leave the church and walk around to the front, the freeway leading to the futuristic spaceship bridge, **Most SNP**, is the first thing you will see. The road was built at the cost of destroying a row of old houses and a synagogue in the former Jewish quarter, outside of the city walls. The only good thing to be said for the road is that its construction led to the discovery of remains of the city's original walls, which have been partially restored and now line the freeway on the right. Follow the steps under the passageway and up the other side in the direction of the castle.

Time Out Walk across the pedestrian lane on the **Most SNP** bridge to have a drink at the café—reached via speedy glass-faced elevators for a minimal charge—perched on top of the pylons. One of Prague's English-language newspapers, *Prognosis*, has dubbed the café's retro-Socialist interior "*Starship Enterprise*-gone-cocktail lounge." However you may feel about the architecture, it's not a bad place for a reasonable snack and an excellent view of the city.

9 Continue up the steps, through a Gothic arched gateway built in 1480, until you reach the **hrad** (castle) area. From the top there are views over the Danube to the endless apartment blocks on the Petržalka side of the river. On a good day you can see over to Austria to the right.

Bratislava's castle has been continually rebuilt since its establishment in the 9th century. The Hungarian kings expanded it into a large royal residence, and the Habsburgs further developed its fortifications, turning it into a very successful defense against the Turks. Its current design, square with four corner towers, stems from the 17th century, although the existing castle had to be completely rebuilt after a disastrous fire in 1811. In the castle you'll find the **Slovenské národné múzeum** (Slovak National Museum), with exhibits that cover glass making, medieval warfare, and coin making. The layout is a little confusing, so unless you're an expert in one of these fields, you probably won't find this museum very meaningful. *Hrad, Zámocká ul. Admission: 40 Sk. adults, 10 Sk. children and students. Open Tues.–Sun. 10–5.*

10 Leave the castle by the same route, but instead of climbing the last stairs by the Arkadia restaurant, continue down the Old World Beblavého ulica. At the bottom of the street, on the right, is the **Múzeum umeleckých remesiel** (Museum of Artistic Handicrafts, Beblavého ul. 1); in front, in the tall and thin Rococo **Dom U dobrého pastiera** (House at the Good Shepherd), look for the **Múzeum bratislavských historických hodín** (Museum of Clocks, Židovská ul. 1). Neither museum is a must, but both are housed in attractive buildings, particularly the latter. *Admission to each museum: 10 Sk. adults, 5 Sk. children. Open Wed.–Mon. 10–5.*

Time Out Snuggle up to a mug of beer or a glass of wine at **Judy's Gallery Bar** (Beblavého ul. 4) and contemplate the offbeat local art hanging from the walls.

11 Go around the House at the Good Shepherd and continue along **Židovská ulica,** marred by the freeway and dominated by a rash of buildings under construction. (The street name, Jews' Street, marks this area as the former Jewish ghetto.) Continue on Židovská until you come to a thin concrete bridge that connects with the reconstructed city walls across the freeway. Standing in the middle of this bridge, looking toward the river, you'll get one of the best views of the incongruous and contradictory jumble of buildings that make up Bratislava. Directly to the south is the Most SNP bridge, surrounded by housing blocks; to the east (left) are the city walls, leading into St. Martin's Cathedral; to the west (right), the little Rococo house backed by construction and the towers of the castle.

12 If you turn left and walk along the city walls, you will come, after negotiating a series of steps, to the main road, **Kapucínska ulica.** Across the road on the left is the small, golden yellow **Kostol kapucínov** (Capuchin Chapel), in front of which is a pillar of Mary, commemorating the plague. The Baroque chapel, dating from 1717,

is of little artistic interest, but its peaceful interior is always filled
with worshipers—something not often seen in Slovakia.

Across the road are steps leading down into the Old Town. Turn left
at the bottom to access little Baštová ulica. Go through the arch at
the end and you'll find yourself back at Michael's Gate. Continue
straight along Zámočnícka ulica, which turns right heading in the direction of **Františkánske námestie.** To the left is the oldest preserved
⑬ building in Bratislava, the **Františkánsky kostol** (Franciscan
Church), consecrated in 1297 and funded by the Hungarian king
László IV to celebrate his victory over the Bohemian king Přemysl
Otakar II at the Battle of the Marchfeld, near Vienna. Only its presbytery is still in early Gothic style, the rest having been destroyed in
an earthquake during the 17th century and rebuilt in a mixture of
Baroque and Gothic.

Just around the corner, built onto the church, is another quite differ-
ent and much more stunning Gothic building, the 14th-century
Chapel of St. John the Evangelist, the burial chapel for Mayor Jakub.
Art historians believe that Peter Parler, architect of Prague's
Charles Bridge and St. Vitus Cathedral, may have worked on this
Gothic gem.

Across from the Franciscan church is the beautifully detailed Roco-
⑭ co **Mirbachov palác** (Mirbach Palace), built in 1770 for a brewery
owner. Nowadays the palace houses the **Municipal Gallery,** which
contains a reasonable collection of European art from the 18th and
19th centuries. *Františkánske nám. Admission: 10 Sk. adults, 5
Sk. children and students. Open Tues.–Sun. 10–7.*

Go through the Františkánske námestie, with its statues of little-
known Slovak World War II heroes, onto the adjoining square,
Hlavné námestie. This square is lined with old houses and palaces,
representing the spectrum of architectural styles from Gothic (No.
2), through Baroque (No. 4) and Rococo (No. 7), to a wonderfully
decorative example of Art Nouveau at No. 10. To your immediate
⑮ left as you come into the square is the richly decorated **Jezuitský
kostol** (Jesuit Church), originally built by Protestants who in 1636
were granted an imperial concession to build a place of worship on
the strict condition that it have no tower. The Jesuits took over the
towerless church in 1672 and, to compensate for its external simplicity, went wild with Baroque detailing on the inside.

Next to the Jesuit church is the colorful agglomeration of old bits
⑯ and pieces that make up the **Stará radnica** (Old Town Hall). The
building as it stands today developed gradually over the 13th and
14th centuries out of a number of burgher's houses. The imaginative
roofing stems from the end of the 15th century, and the wall paintings from the 16th century. The strangely out-of-place Baroque onion tower was a revision of the original tower. Walk through the
arched passageway, still with its early Gothic ribbing, into a wonderfully cheery Renaissance courtyard with romantic arcades and
gables. During the summer concerts are held here. Toward the back
of the courtyard, you'll find the entrance to the **Mestské múzeum**
(City Museum), which documents Bratislava's varied past.
*Primaciálne nám. Admission: 10 Sk. adults, 5 Sk. children and
students. Open Tues.–Sun. 10–5.*

Leaving the back entrance of the Old Town Hall, you'll come to the
Primaciálne námestie (Primates' Square), dominated by the glo-
⑰ rious pale-pink **Primaciálny palác** (Primates' Palace). If the building
is open, make your way to the dazzling Hall of Mirrors with its six
English tapestries depicting the legend of the lovers Hero and Lean-

der. In this room Napoleon and the Habsburg emperor Franz I signed the Bratislava Peace of 1805, following Napoleon's victory at the Battle of Austerlitz. In the revolutionary year of 1848, when the citizens of the Habsburg lands revolted against the imperial dominance of Vienna, the rebel Hungarians had their headquarters in the palace; ironically, following the failed uprising, the Habsburg general Hainau signed the rebels' death sentences in the very same room.

Walk down Uršulínska ulica and turn right at the bottom onto Laurinská ulica. If you continue to the left down Rybárska brána, you will emerge into the more modern part of the Old Town, with business and hotels stretched out along the rectangular **Hviezdoslavovo námestie** (Hviezdoslav Square). To your right is the
⑱ **Slovenské národné divadlo** (Slovak National Theater), Bratislava's excellent opera house. The theater was built in the 1880s by the famous Central European architectural duo of Hermann Helmer and Ferdinand Fellner. If you get a feeling of déjà vu looking at the voluptuous neo-Baroque curves, it's not surprising: The two men built opera houses in Vienna, Prague, and Karlovy Vary, to name but a few.

Across the square, on the corner of Mostová ulica and Palackého
⑲ ulica, is Bratislava's second musical center, the **Reduta,** home of the Slovak Philharmonic Orchestra. Also built in neo-Baroque style but dating from 1914, the Reduta is richly decorated. If you can't make it to a concert, try to sneak a peek inside. You can get tickets for concerts or the opera at the ticket offices directly before the performance; for advance reservations inquire at BIS (*see* Tourist Information, *above*).

Continue down Mostová ulica to the banks of the Danube. To the
⑳ right is the **Slovenská národná galéria** (Slovak National Gallery), a conspicuously modern restoration of an old 18th century barracks. However you feel about the strange additions to the old building, the museum itself has an interesting collection of Slovak Gothic, Baroque, and contemporary art, along with a small number of European masters. *Rázusovo nábrežie. Admission: 10 Sk. adults, 5 Sk. children and students. Open Tues.–Sun. 10–5.*

What to See and Do with Children

On a balmy summer's day you can take a pleasant 10-kilometer (6-mile) ride up the **Danube River** or a short ferry across to the **Petržalka gardens** on the far shore. The ferry operates between April and October and costs 10 Sk.; the ferry offices are on Fajnorovo nábrežie near the Slovak National Museum.

Off the Beaten Track

You can get a dose of communist Bratislava by walking up to the **Slavín Memorial.** This group of socialist-realist statues is a monument to the 6,000 who died during the Soviet liberation of Bratislava in 1945. Even if you're not interested in the sculpture, the monument gives fine views over Bratislava. Take a taxi for about 200 Sk.; or ride Bus 27, 48, 47, or 104 to Puškinová, where you can climb the long series of steps to the top.

Just west of the city is the ruined castle of **Devín,** beautifully located atop a hill overlooking both the Danube and the Morava rivers. Take Bus 29 from under the Most SNP bridge to Devín and follow the marked path up the hill to the castle.

Shopping

Bratislava is an excellent place to find Slovak arts and crafts of all types. **Folk Folk** has an excellent collection at its centrally located shop (Rybárska brána 2, tel. 07/334874). **Antikvariat Steiner** (Venturská ul. 20, tel. 07/52834) stocks beautiful old books, maps, and graphics and posters. For original pieces of art and pottery, try the **Gremium Café** (Gorkého 11, tel. 07/51818).

Dining

Prague may have its Slovak rival beat when it comes to architecture, but when it's time to eat, you can thank those lucky red stars you still see around town that you're in Bratislava. The long-shared history with Hungary gives Slovak cuisine an extra fire that Czech cooking admittedly lacks. Geographic proximity to Vienna, moreover, has lent something of grace and charm to the city's eateries. What it adds up to is that you'll seldom see pork and dumplings on the menu. Instead, prepare for a variety of shish kebabs, grilled meats, steaks, and pork dishes, all spiced to enliven the palette and served (if you're lucky) with those special noodles Slovaks call *halušky*. Wash it all down with a glass or two of red wine from nearby Modra or Pezinok.

A price-conscious alternative to restaurant dining is the city's many street stands. In addition to the ubiquitous hot dogs and hamburgers (no relation to their American namesakes), try some *langoš*—flat, deep-fried, and delicious pieces of dough, usually seasoned with garlic. Another budget option is Slovakia's unofficial national dish, *bryndzové halušky*, little noodles served with bacon and slightly sour sheep's cheese (don't knock it until you've tried it). One place certain to serve it is **Café Blankyt** (Obchodná 48, tel. 07/332248), which, despite the dingy surroundings, is quite respectable.

Highly recommended restaurants in each price category are indicated by a star ★.

$$$$ **Arkadia.** The elegant setting, at the threshold to the castle, sets the tone for a luxurious evening. There are several dining rooms to choose from, ranging from the intimate to the more boisterous, all decorated with period 19th-century furnishings. A standard repertoire of Slovak and international dishes, which include shish kebabs and steaks, is prepared to satisfaction. It is a 15-minute walk from the town center; take a taxi here and enjoy the mostly downhill walk back into town. *Zámocké schody, tel. 07/335650. Reservations advised. Jacket and tie required. AE, DC, MC, V.*

★ **Rybársky cech.** The name means Fisherman's Guild, and fish is the unchallenged specialty at this refined but comfortable eatery set on a quiet street by the Danube. Freshwater fish is served upstairs, with pricier saltwater varieties offered on the ground floor. *Žižkova 1, tel. 07/313049. Reservations advised. Dress: casual but neat. AE, DC, MC, V.*

$$$ **Kláštorná vináreň.** Located in the wine cellar of a former monastery,
★ this restaurant with its wine-barrel-shaped booths is pleasantly dark and intimate. The Hungarian-influenced spiciness of traditional Slovak cooking comes alive in such dishes as *Cíkos tókeň*, a fiery mixture of pork, onions, and peppers; or try the milder *Bravcové Ražnicí*, a tender pork shish kebab served with fried potatoes. *Františkanská ul., tel. 07/330430. Reservations advised. Dress: casual. No credit cards. Closed Sun.*

Veľkí Františkáni. This popular wine cellar has a menu and an atmosphere similar to that at Kláštorná. However, the Veľkí's expansive dining area nurtures a more raucous, giddy clientele. *Frantlškánske nám. 10, tel. 07/333073. Reservations advised. Dress: casual. No credit cards.*

$$ **Korzo.** Here you'll find delicious Slovak specialties—try a shish kebab or spicy grilled steak—served in a clean, cozy cellar setting. After dinner take a stroll along the Danube, right next door. The Korzo's ground-floor café is a great spot for people-watching or writing postcards. *Hviezdoslavovo nám. 11, tel. 07/334974. Reservations advised. Dress: casual. No credit cards.*

★ **Modra Hviezda.** The first of a new breed of small, privately owned wine cellars, this popular eatery eschews the international standards in favor of regional Slovak fare; try the sheep-cheese pie or the fiery goulash. *Beblavého 14, tel. 07/332747. Reservations advised. Dress: casual. No credit cards.*

Spaghetti and Co. This local representative of an American chain serves very good pizzas and pasta in a tourist-friendly, pleasant setting—a godsend if you're traveling with children. The adjacent "food court," right out of your local shopping mall, has booths selling Greek, Chinese, and health foods. *Gorkého l, tel. 07/332303. Reservations advised. Dress: casual. No credit cards.*

$ **Gremium.** This trendy restaurant caters to the coffee-and-cigarette crowd and to anyone in search of an uncomplicated light meal; choose from a small menu of pastries and sandwiches. Regulars consist of students and, because of the adjoining ceramics gallery, Bratislava's self-styled art crowd. *Gorkého 11, tel. 07/51818. No reservations. Dress: casual. No credit cards.*

Micháelska. This light and airy luncheon restaurant with an adjacent stand-up buffet is situated conveniently in the Old Town. Soup, *halušky* (boiled dumplings), and salad make a budget meal fit for a king. *Michálská 1, tel. 07/332389. No reservations. Dress: casual. No credit cards.*

★ **Stará Sladovňa.** To Bratislavans, this gargantuan beer hall is known lovingly, and fittingly, as *mamut* (mammoth). Locals come here for the Bohemian brews on tap, but it is also possible to get an inexpensive and filling meal. *Cintorínska 32, tel. 07/51101. No reservations. Dress: casual. No credit cards.*

Lodging

The lodging situation in Bratislava is poor and isn't likely to improve very quickly. The few decent hotels that do exist are very expensive; the cheaper hotels tend to be run-down and utterly depressing. The problem is compounded by the general lack of private rooms to rent, though Čedok (*see* Tourist Information, *above*) can assist you in locating whatever private accommodations are available.

Highly recommended lodgings in a particular price category are indicated by a star ★.

$$$$ **Danube.** Opened in 1992, this French-run hotel on the banks of the
★ Danube has quickly developed a reputation for superior facilities and service. The modern rooms are done in tasteful pastels; the gleaming public areas are everything you expect from an international hotel chain. *Rybné Nám. 1, tel. 07/340833, fax 07/314311. 280 rooms with bath. Facilities: 2 restaurants, nightclub, sauna, pool, solarium, health club, conference facilities. AE, DC, MC, V.*

Forum. Bratislava's most expensive hotel, built in 1989 right in the center of town, offers a complete array of services and facilities. It is a good choice for business trips; the staff is efficient and friendly, and the functional rooms are pleasantly, if innocuously, decorated. If creature comforts are an important factor, the Forum is for you. *Hodžovo nám. 2, tel. 07/348111, fax 07/314645. 219 rooms with bath. Facilities: 2 restaurants, 2 cafés, 2 bars, nightclub, casino, fitness center with pool and sauna, beauty salon. Breakfast not included. AE, DC, MC, V.*

$$$ **Devín.** This boxy 1950s hotel set on the banks of the Danube has managed to create an air of elegance in its reception area that doesn't translate into much else, despite its five-star status. The rooms are small and badly organized, and service is on the gruff side. Nevertheless, the hotel is clean and offers a good selection of services, with a variety of restaurants and cafés that serve dependably satisfying food. *Riečna ul. 4, 81102, tel. 07/330852, fax 07/330682. 98 rooms with bath. Facilities: 3 restaurants, café, 2 bars. Breakfast included. AE, DC, MC, V.*
Perugia. Finished in 1993, this stunning post-Modern jewel in a renovated building in the Old Town makes for an attractive luxury alternative to the big chain hotels. The light and airy architecture contrasts sharply with the dark, drab interiors of many of the city's buildings. The clean, colorful rooms are an eye-opener. *Zelená 5, tel. and fax 07/330719. 11 rooms with bath. Facilities: restaurant. Breakfast included. AE, DC, MC, V.*

$$ **Bratislava.** This bland but suitably clean cement-block hotel, situated in the suburb of Ružinov, has well-appointed rooms equipped with a television and private bathroom. It offers few facilities beyond a standard restaurant and lounge, though there is a large department store nearby where you can stock up on supplies. From the city center take Bus 34 or Tram 8. *Urxova ul. 9, tel. 07/239000, fax 07/236420. 344 rooms with bath. Facilities: restaurant, snack bar, lounge. Breakfast included. AE, DC, MC, V.*

★ **Zochová Chata.** If you have your own transportation, this attractive 1920s-style hunting chalet, located near Modra, 32 kilometers (20 miles) outside Bratislava, is a comfortable alternative to the latter's large luxury hotels. The rooms here are small but very comfortable, and the food served in the adjoining tavern a few doors down is top-rate. *90001 Modra-Piesok, tel. 070492/2956, fax 070492/2991. 10 rooms with bath. Facilities: restaurant, wine tavern. Breakfast not included. No credit cards.*

$ **Želing.** You can't beat this little pension for price and location, just a couple of blocks from the Old Town. The tiny rooms are clean, but the bathroom is down the hall. *Panenská 7, tel. 07/312982, fax 07/331207. 8 rooms, most without bath. Facilities: restaurant. Breakfast not included. No credit cards.*

The Arts and Nightlife

The Arts   Bratislava has a thriving arts scene. The celebrated **Slovak Philharmonic Orchestra** plays regularly throughout the year, and chamber-music concerts are held at irregular intervals in the stunning Gothic **Church of the Poor Clares.** In summer the Renaissance courtyard of the **Old Town Hall** is also used for concerts. Call BIS or Čedok for program details and tickets. Other good sources of information include the English-language *Prague Post* and *Prognosis*, two Prague-based newspapers with regular features on Bratislava's cultural life.

Concerts   The **Slovak Philharmonic Orchestra** plays a full program, featuring Czech and Slovak composers as well as European masters, at its home in the Reduta (Medená 3, tel. 07/333351). Buy tickets at the theater box office (open weekdays 1–5).

Film Most new releases are shown in their original language with Slovak subtitles. **Charlie Centrum** (Špitálska 4, tel. 07/363430) regularly shows American classics, in English, in a friendly, artsy environment.

Opera and The **Slovenské národné divadlo** (Slovak National Theater) at
Ballet Hviezdoslavovo námestie 1 (tel. 07/321146) is the place for high-quality opera and ballet in season. Buy tickets at the theater office on the corner of Jesenského and Komenského streets (open week-days noon–6) or at the theater 30 minutes before showtime.

Theater Traditional theater is usually performed in Slovak and is therefore incomprehensible to most visitors. For non-Slovak speakers, the **Stoka Theater** blends nontraditional theater with performance art in a provocative and entertaining way. For details contact the theater box office (Pribinova 1, tel. 07/68016).

Nightlife Bratislava doesn't offer much in the way of bars and lounges; after-
Bars and dinner drinking takes place mostly in wine cellars and beer halls.
Lounges For the former, try **Kláštorná vináreň** or **Vel'kí Františkáni** (*see* Din-ing, *above*), both located in vaulted, medieval cellars. For beer swill-ing, the best address in town is the mammoth **Stará Sladovňa** (*see* Dining, *above*).

Jazz Clubs Bratislava hosts an annual jazz festival in the fall, but the city lacks a good venue for regular jazz gigs. That said, **Mefisto Club** (Panenska 24, no tel.) occasionally features local jazz acts.

Rock Clubs Bratislava's live-music and club scene is expanding; new bands, run-ning the spectrum from folk and rock to rap, are constantly turning up. The venues are changing just as rapidly; check the *Prague Post* or *Prognosis* for the lowdown on the latest clubs. Dependable hot spots include **Rock Fabrik Danubius** (Komanárska ul. 3, no tel.), fea-turing loud and sweaty Czech and Slovak acts nightly; and the **U Club** (Pod Hradom ul., no tel.), where hard-core rock can be fun if you're into that sort of thing.

Excursions from Bratislava

The Wine Much of the country's best wine is produced within a 30-minute
Country drive of Bratislava, in a lovely mountainous region that offers a res-pite from the noise and grime of the capital. Two towns, Pezinok and Modra, vie for the distinction of being Slovakia's wine capital.

Pezinok, the larger of the two, is home to the Small Carpathian vine-yards, the country's largest wine producer. In this quaint, red-roofed town you can find enough to keep you busy for an entire day without ever stepping off its busy main street, **Stefanika ulica.** Take in the wine-making exhibits at the **Malokarpatksé muzeum** (Small Carpathian Museum, Stefanika ul., closed Monday), and then head next door to the outstanding bakery. Leave some room for lunch at the Zámocka wine cellar (open daily 11–11), situated in the town's castle at the end of the street. The castle also serves as a winery; around the side you'll find a sales counter offering a variety of locally produced wines.

Modra is a typical one-horse town, with some pretty folk architec-ture and a few comfortable wine gardens scattered about town. Combine a visit here with a night at the nearby Zochová Chata (*see* Lodging, *above*). A favorite hiking destination from the Zochová chalet is the Renaissance castle **Červený Kameň** (Red Rock). On the prettier yellow-marked trail, the walk takes upwards of 2½ hours; on the more plain blue-and-green trail, around 1½ hours. Although renovations to the castle are not expected to be finished until the end of 1995, visitors can still go to the most fascinating parts of the structure with a guide (who unfortunately is likely to speak only Slovak and German): the vast storage and wine cellars, with their movable floors and high, arched ceilings; and the bastions, completed with an intricate ventilation system and hidden pathways in the middle of the thick slate walls. *Castle admission: 10 Sk. adults, 5 Sk. children. Open daily 11–3 (closed Mon. Nov.–Apr.). Tours on the hour.*

Getting There Infrequent buses link Bratislava with Modra and Pezinok; most leave early in the morning, so contact ČSAD (Bratislava, tel. 07/ 63213), the national bus carrier, at least a day in advance. By car from Bratislava, take Route 502, 4 kilometers (2½ miles) past the village of Jur pri Bratislave and turn right down a smaller road in the direction of the villages Slovenský Grob and Viničné. At the latter, turn left onto Route 503 to reach Pezinok, a few kilometers beyond. Modra lies 4 kilometers (2½ miles) farther along the same road.

Trnava   **Trnava,** with its silhouette of spires and towers, is the oldest town in Slovakia, having received royal town rights in 1238. Trnava was the main seat of the Hungarian archbishop until 1821 and a principal Hungarian university center during the 17th and 18th centuries, until Marie Theresa shifted the scholarly crowd to Budapest. That Trnava's "golden age" coincided with the Baroque period is readily apparent in its architecture, beneath the neglected facades and pervasive industrial decay. Look for the enormous **University Church of John the Baptist,** designed by Italian Baroque architects, with fabulous carved-wood altars. The renowned 18th-century Viennese architect Franz Anton Hillebrandt was responsible for the central chapel of **St. Nicholas Cathedral,** which dominates the town with its large onion towers.

Getting There Bratislava and Trnava are connected by frequent bus and train service. By car, it's an easy 45-kilometer (28-mile) drive from Bratislava on the D61 highway.

The High Tatras

The *Vysoké Tatry* (High Tatras) alone would make a trip to Slovakia worthwhile. Although the range is relatively compact as mountains go (just 32 kilometers, or 20 miles, from end to end), its peaks seem wilder and more starkly beautiful than even those of Europe's other great range, the Alps. Some 20 Tatras peaks exceed 8,000 feet, the highest being **Gerlachovský Štít** at 8,710 feet. The 35 mountain lakes are remote and clear and, according to legend, can impart the ability to see through doors and walls to anyone who bathes in them, but take care before diving in: They are also very cold and sometimes eerily deep.

Man is a relative latecomer to the Tatras. The region's first town, Schmecks (today Starý Smokovec), was founded in the late-18th century, and regular visitors began coming here only after 1871 with the construction of a mountain railroad linking the resort to the bustling junction town of Poprad. In the late-19th and early 20th centuries, with the founding of Štrbské pleso and Tatranská Lomnica, the Tatras finally came into their own as an elegant playground for Europe's elite.

But the post–World War II communist era was hard on the Tatras. Almost overnight, the area became a mass resort for the mountain-starved, fenced-in peoples of the Eastern bloc, prompting much development and commercialization. But don't despair: The faded elegance of these mountain retreats and spa resorts remains intact, despite the sometimes heavy winter- and summertime crowds.

Important Addresses and Numbers

Tourist Information

The Čedok office in **Starý Smokovec** (tel. 0969/2417) is the best source for general information; it can change money, dispense hiking and driving maps, and assist in booking hotels (but not private rooms). For more in-depth information on hiking and skiing conditions, inquire next door at the **Mountain Rescue Service** (Horška služba, tel. 0969/2820). **Slovakoturist** (tel. 0969/2827), situated ½ kilometer east of Starý Smokovec in Horný Smokovec, can help arrange private accommodations, including stays in mountain cottages. In **Poprad** there is a Čedok office at Námestie Dukelských hrdinov 60 (tel. 092/23262).

Few books or pamphlets on the Tatras are available in English. One good overview of the area, including a list of services, hotels, and restaurants, is provided in the hard-to-find booklet *Everyman's Guide to the High Tatras*. Look for it at hotel gift shops.

Emergencies

Police (tel. 158). **Medical emergencies** (tel. 2444). **Car repair** (tel. 2704).

Late-Night Pharmacies

Pharmacies (*lekárna*) are located in all three major resorts and in the neighboring town of Ždiar (*see* Off the Beaten Track, *below*). The pharmacy in Nový Smokovec maintains late hours (tel. 0969/2577).

Arriving and Departing by Plane

ČSA, the Czech and Slovak national carrier, offers regular service to the Tatra city of Poprad from Prague and Bratislava. The flight from Prague takes a little over an hour. On arrival, take a taxi to your hotel or to the Poprad train station, from which you can catch an electric railroad to the Tatras resorts.

Arriving and Departing by Car, Train, and Bus

By Car

Poprad, the gateway to the Tatras, lies on the main east–west highway about 560 kilometers (350 miles) from Prague in the direction of Hradec Králové. The eight-hour drive from Prague is relatively comfortable and can be broken up easily with an overnight stay in Olomouc, in the Czech Republic province of Moravia. The road is well marked, with some four-lane stretches. The drive to Poprad from Bratislava is 328 kilometers (205 miles), with a four-lane stretch between Bratislava and Trenčín, and a well-marked, two-lane highway thereafter.

By Train

Regular rail service connects both Prague and Bratislava with Poprad, but book ahead, as the trains are often impossibly crowded, especially in August and during the skiing season. The journey from Prague to Poprad takes about 10 hours; several night trains depart from Prague's Hlavní nádraží (main station) and Holešovice station.

By Bus

Daily bus service connects Prague and Bratislava with Poprad, but on this run, trains tend to be quicker and more comfortable. From Prague the journey will take 10 hours or longer, depending on the route.

Getting Around

By Car Having a car is more of a hindrance than a help if you're just going to the High Tatras. Traveling the electric railway is much quicker than taking the winding roads that connect the resorts, and hotel parking fees can add up quickly. However, if you plan to tour the region's smaller towns and villages, or if you are continuing on to eastern Slovakia, a car will prove nearly indispensable.

By Train An efficient electric rail connects Poprad with the High Tatras resorts, and the resorts with one another. If you're going only to the Tatras, you won't need any other form of transportation.

By Bus ČSAD's bus network links all of the towns covered on the tour of Eastern Slovakia (*see below*); but budget a few extra days to compensate for connections and the sometimes infrequent service between smaller towns.

Guided Tours

From Poprad airport, **Slovair** offers a novel biplane flight over the Tatras region; contact the Čedok office in Poprad (tel. 092/23262). The Čedok office in Starý Smokovec (tel. 0969/2417) is also helpful in arranging tours of the Tatras and surrounding area.

Highlights for First-Time Visitors

Cable-car ride to Lomnický štít (*see* Walking Tour 1)
Magistrale trail (*see* Walking Tour 1)
Museum of the Tatras National Park (*see below*)

Exploring the High Tatras

Numbers in the margin correspond to points of interest on the Slovakia Exploring map.

Most of the tourist facilities in the High Tatras are concentrated in three towns: Štrbské pleso to the west, Smokovec in the middle, and Tatranská Lomnica to the east. All can be accessed by car or the electric railroad, though each is slightly different in terms of convenience and atmosphere.

The best way to see these beautiful mountains is on foot. Three of the best Tatras walks (three to five hours each) are outlined below, arranged according to difficulty (with the easiest and prettiest first), although a reasonably fit person of any age will have little trouble with any of the three. Yet even though the trails are well marked, it is very important to buy a walking map of the area—the detailed *Vysoké Tatry, Letná Turistická Mapa* is available for around 20 Sk. at newspaper kiosks. Another good source of information is the Mountain Rescue Service (*see* Tourist Information, *above*), next to Starý Smokovec's Čedok office. If you're planning to take any of the higher-level walks, be sure to wear proper shoes with good ankle support. Also use extreme caution in early spring, when melting snow can turn the trails into icy rivers. And don't forget drinking water, sunglasses, and sunscreen.

❶ **Poprad,** the gateway to the Tatras, is a good place to begin exploring the region. But don't expect a beautiful mountain village. Poprad fell victim to some of the most insensitive communist planning perpetrated in the country after the war, and as a result you'll see little more than row after row of apartment blocks, interspersed with factories and power plants. There's no need to linger here. Instead, drive or take the electric railroad to the superior sights and facilities of the more rugged resorts just over 30 kilometers (20 miles) to the north.

❷ The first town you'll reach by road or rail from Poprad is **Smokovec**, the undisputed center of the Slovak Tatras resorts and the major beneficiary of postwar development. Smokovec is divided into two principal areas, **Starý Smokovec** (Old Smokovec) and **Nový Smokovec** (New Smokovec), which are within a stone's throw of each other. Stay in Starý Smokovec if you want to be near grocery stores, bars, and the local Čedok office. The town is also a good starting point for many mountain excursions (from here, for example, a funicular can take you the 4,144 feet to Hrebienok and its many marked trails).

❸ **Štrbské pleso,** which lies 18 kilometers (11 miles) west of Smokovec, is the main center for active sports. As such, Štrbské pleso is best suited for skiers and those who thrive on crowds and commotion. The Tatras' best ski slopes are not far away, and the fine mountain lake is a perfect backdrop for a leisurely stroll. Štrbské pleso is also good for walkers, and many excellent trails are within easy reach. As for facilities, the town boasts not only the most modern hotels but also the most jarringly modern hotel architecture. This large resort also presides over the finest panoramas in the Tatras. For a breathtaking view over the valley and mountains, head for the lawn of the town's sanatorium.

❹ **Tatranská Lomnica,** on the eastern end of the electric rail line, offers a near-perfect combination of peace, convenience, and atmosphere. Spread out and relatively remote, the town is frequently overlooked by the masses of students and merrymakers, so it has been more successful in retaining a feel of "exclusivity" without being any more expensive than the other towns. Moreover, the lift behind the Grandhotel Praha brings some of the best walks in the Tatras to within 10 minutes or so of your hotel door.

If you want to brush up on the area's varied flora and fauna, visit Tatranská Lomnica's fascinating **Museum of the Tatras National Park (Tatranská Museum).** The museum is especially well suited to children, who will love the startlingly realistic stuffed animals on the first floor. Each animal is marked with a symbol: A red square denotes a common species, a blue triangle means the animal is native to the Tatras, and a yellow circle signals a rare or endangered species. The upper floor documents the life of local peasants, who still wear vibrantly colored traditional dress in many villages. *Tel. 0969/ 96795. Admission: 10 Sk. adults, 5 Sk. children. Open weekdays 8:30–1 and 2–5, Sat. and Sun. 9–noon.*

Walking Tour 1: Tatranská Lomnica to Starý Smokovec The **Magistrale,** a 24-kilometer (15-mile) walking trail that skirts the peaks just above the tree line, offers some of the best views for the least amount of exertion. A particularly stunning stretch of the route—which is marked by red signposts—begins in Tatranská Lomnica and ends 5 kilometers (3 miles) away in Starý Smokovec. Total walking time is three or four hours.

To start the walk, take the aerial gondola located behind the Grandhotel Praha in Tatranská Lomnica to Skalnaté pleso—a 10-minute proposition. From here you can access the trail immediately; or, if you are really adventurous, consider a 30-minute detour via cable car (25 Sk.) to the top of Lomnický Štít (8,635 feet), the second-highest peak in the range. Because of the harsh temperatures (be sure to dress warmly even in summer) you're permitted to linger at the top for only 30 minutes, after which you take the cable car back down.

Return to the cable-car station at Skalnaté pleso and follow the red markers of the Magistrale trail to the right (as you stand facing Tatranská Lomnica below). The first section of the trail cuts sharply across the face of the Lomnický Mountain just above the tree line. Note the little dwarf pines to the right and left of the trail. The trail then bends around to the right and again to the left through a series of small valleys, each view more outstanding than the last. Finally, you'll begin a small descent into the woods. Continue by following the signs to Hrebienok.

Time Out   Don't pass up the chance to have a snack and a hot or cold drink at the rustic **Bilková Chata,** situated in a little clearing just before you reach Hrebienok. This cozy cabin is a veritable oasis after the long walk.

From Hrebienok, take the funicular down to Starý Smokovec. The funicular runs at 45-minute intervals beginning at 6:30 AM and ending at 7:45 PM, but check the schedule posted at the Bilková Chata for any schedule changes. The funicular drops you off in the center of Starý Smokovec, just behind the Grand Hotel and convenient to shops and the electric rail.

Walking Tour 2: Starý Smokovec to Tery Chata   **Starý Smokovec** is the starting point for the second trek, which parallels a cascading waterfall for much of its three-hour length. From Starý Smokovec, walk out along the main road in the direction of **Tatranská Lomnica** for roughly 1 kilometer (½ mile). In **Tatranská Lesná,** follow the yellow-marked path that winds gently uphill through the pines and alongside a swift-running stream. In winter the walk is particularly lovely; the occasional burst of sunshine warms your cheeks and transforms the cold running water to a tropical blue-green.

Farther along there are red markers leading to the funicular at Hrebienok, which returns you to the relative comforts of Starý Smokovec. However, if you're in good physical shape and there is *plenty* of daylight left, consider extending your hike by four hours. (The extension is striking, but avoid it during winter, when you may find yourself neck-deep in snow). Just before the Bilková chata, turn right along the green path and then follow the blue, red, and then green trails in the direction of windswept **Tery chata,** a turn-of-the-century chalet perched amid five lonely alpine lakes. The scenery is a few notches above dazzling. Once you reach the chalet after two strenuous hours of hiking, backtrack to Bilková chata and follow the signs to the funicular at Hrebienok.

Walking Tour 3: Starý Smokovec to Sliezsky Dom   A more adventurous and rigorous five-hour walk starts in Starý Smokovec behind and to the west of the Grand Hotel. Begin by ascending to the tree line along the blue path. Thirty minutes of uphill hiking will take you to the Magistrale trail; follow the trail to the left, and after 20 minutes or so of moderately strenuous climbing, the trees thin out—leaving nothing but dwarf pines, the rocks, and the breathtaking peaks.

Sliezsky Dom, a 1960s cookie-cutter prefab (surely Slovakia's highest-elevation housing project), lies an hour down the trail. Forgive the building's architectural sins and head inside for a cup of tea and a bite to eat. The descent to Starý Smokovec along the green and then yellow trails is long and peaceful: Nothing breaks the silence save the snapping of twigs or, in winter, the crunch of snow underfoot.

What to See and Do with Children

If it's rainy or too cold for a stroll through the mountains, younger children will enjoy the stuffed animals and other exhibits at the **Museum of the Tatras National Park** in Tatranská Lomnica (*see* Exploring the High Tatras, *above*).

If there's snow on the ground and the children are too young to ski, you'll find a good sledding slope at **Hrebienok**, just above Starý Smokovec. To get there, take the funicular from behind the Grand Hotel. There is an even gentler slope at the Hotel Fis in **Štrbské pleso.** You can rent sleds from the Ski Service near the Grand Hotel in Starý Smokovec or purchase them for 200 Sk.–300 Sk. from local sporting-goods stores.

Off the Beaten Track

Ždiar, about 24 kilometers (15 miles) north of the Tatras range along the road to the Polish border, and its twin, **Javorina,** are noted for their unique folk architecture—mostly enchanting, vibrantly painted wood houses built in traditional peasant designs. The population of Ždiar is Polish in origin (the Polish border is less than 16 kilometers [10 miles] away), but the people have long considered themselves Slovak. To reach either village, leave Tatranská Lomnica heading east on Route 537 and turn left at Route 67.

Shopping

The Tatras resorts are short on shopping places. Still, you'll find good-quality, reasonably priced hiking and camping equipment at several sporting-goods stores. You can buy skis and equipment, plus a thousand other things, in the department store **Prior** at Štrbské pleso and at the **Mladost'** store in Starý Smokovec. The outlying towns around Ždiar are good sources for lace and other types of folk arts and crafts.

Sports and Outdoor Activities

Hiking and Climbing The Tatras are tailor-made for hikers of all levels; and since the entire area is a national park, the trails are well marked in different colors. Newspaper kiosks sell a reasonable and cheap walking map, which includes all the marked paths. For more detailed information on routes, mountain chalets, and weather conditions, contact the **Mountain Rescue Service** (Horská služba) in Starý Smokovec (tel. 0969/2820). This office can also provide guides for the more difficult routes for around 500 Sk. per day. Mountain climbers who do not want a guide have to be members of a climbing club (this also provides you with free mountain rescue). There are climbs of all levels of difficulty (although grade-1 climbs may be used only as starting points), the best being the west wall of **Lomnický Štít**, the north wall of the **Kežmarský Štít**, and the **Široká veža.**

Paragliding Local sports shops offer instruction and provide equipment for many newer sports, including paragliding and paraskiing. The rates, surprisingly, are very reasonable. For information, consult the sporting-goods store in Horný Smokovec (a 10-minute walk along the highway to the east of Starý Smokovec).

Skiing Moderately challenging slopes are found at the **Skalnaté pleso,** above Tatranská Lomnica; and around **Štrbské pleso.** Ždiar (*see* Off the Beaten Track, *above*), toward the Polish border, has a good ski area for beginners. The entire region is crisscrossed with paths ideal for cross-country skiing. You can buy a special ski map at newspaper kiosks. The season lasts from December through April, though the best months are traditionally January and February. Take your own equipment if you can, as not many places rent. However, one place that does rent a limited selection of equipment is the Ski Service in the **Švajčiarský Dom,** next to the Grand Hotel in Starý Smokovec (open 8–noon, 12:30–4). Arrive early to get the right-size skis; the equipment rents quickly when it snows. The **Sport Centrum** (tel. 0969/2953) in Horný Smokovec and the **Hotel Patria** in Štrbské pleso also rent skis. You can buy skis and equipment at low prices in the department store **Prior** at Štrbské pleso and at the **Mladost'** store in Starý Smokovec.

Swimming   Swimming is not permitted in the cold glacier lakes of the Tatras. Indoor pools can be found at the **Bellevue** and **Grand** hotels in Starý Smokovec and the **Hotel Patria** in Štrbské pleso.

Dining and Lodging

Despite the steady influx of visitors, finding a satisfying meal in the Tatras is about as tough as making the 1,000-foot climb from Starý Smokovec to Hrebienok. The best option is eating in one of the hotels; both the Grand Hotel in Starý Smokovec and the Grandhotel Praha in Tatranská Lomnica have decent restaurants that make up in style what they might lack in culinary excellence. An alternative to the restaurants are local grocery stores—try the one in Starý Smokovec—which stock basic sandwich fixings.

If you are looking to splurge on accommodations, you will find no better place than the Tatras. Several hotels—including the Grand and Bellevue in Smokovec and the Patria in Štrbské pleso—feature indoor swimming pools; and at the Grand you can combine a trip to the pool with a massage and a sauna. In older hotels, ask to see several rooms before selecting one, as room interiors can be quite quirky. Also note that prices fluctuate wildly between seasons. Prices are highest in January and February, when there is snow on the ground. Prices are lower during the off-season (late fall and early spring), and the mountains are just as beautiful.

Highly recommended restaurants and lodgings in a particular price category are indicated by a star ★.

Poprad   **Gerlach.** If the Europa (*see below*) is full, try this modern structure
Dining and   located a couple of blocks away from the station. Be forewarned: The
Lodging   Gerlach is as dreary as Poprad itself. The rooms are cheerier than the public areas, but the bathrooms are only just acceptable. If you're not satisfied with your room, ask to see an apartment (about double the standard room price). One is attractively, if incongruously, decorated with antique furniture. *Hviezdoslavova ul. 3, tel. 092/33759, fax 092/63663. 120 rooms, most with bath. Facilities: restaurant, café, hairdresser, parking. Breakfast not included. No credit cards. $$*
Europa. If you have to stay in Poprad, you could do far worse than this cozy little hotel just next to the train station. From the reception area to the modest, old-fashioned (but bathroomless!) rooms, the place exudes a faint elegance. In season, the bar and restaurant on the ground floor buzz with activity in the evenings. *Volkerová ul., tel. 092/32744. 73 rooms without bath. Facilities: restaurant, bar; no TV or telephone in rooms. Breakfast not included. AE, DC, MC, V. $*

Smokovec
Dining

Tatranská Kuria. This modest restaurant situated just down the street from Čedok and the train station is the only place for miles that offers genuine halušky with bryndza. Note the early 8 PM closing hours. *Starý Smokovec, tel. 0969/2806. No credit cards. $$*

Lodging

Bellevue. This modern hotel, just outside of Starý Smokovec along the road to Tatranská Lomnica, lacks the atmosphere of the Grand but nevertheless offers top services and clean, functional rooms. However, you will be a good 15-minute walk away from Starý Smokovec's grocers and bars. For skiers and sports enthusiasts, a sporting-goods rental shop is right next door. *Starý Smokovec, tel. 0969/2941, fax 0969/2719. 110 rooms with bath. Facilities: restaurant, pool. Breakfast included. AE, DC, MC, V. $$$*

★ **Grand Hotel.** Along with its sister hotel in Tatranská Lomnica, this hotel epitomizes Tatra luxury at its turn-of-the-century best. The hotel's golden Tudor facade rises majestically over the town of Starý Smokovec, with the peaks of the Tatras looming in the background. The location, at the commercial and sports center of the region, is a mixed blessing, however. In season, skiers and hikers crowd the reception area, and the hallways are filled with guests and visitors alike. The rooms themselves are quieter, and many come furnished in period style. *Starý Smokovec, tel. 0969/2154, fax 0969/2157. 83 rooms with bath. Facilities: restaurant, café, souvenir shop, pool, sauna. Breakfast included. AE, DC, MC, V. $$$*

Tatra. Centrally located in Starý Smokovec, the Tatra, known until recently as the Úderník, is a cheaper alternative to the Grand or Bellevue. Its informal atmosphere is popular with students and skiers who don't mind the noise and lack of amenities. The hallways and public areas are dark; the rooms functional and clean but uninviting. *Starý Smokovec, tel. 0969/2458. 37 rooms without bath. No credit cards. $$*

★ **Villa Dr. Szontagh.** Away from the action in Nový Smokovec, this be-steepled little chalet, formerly known as the Tokajík, offers mostly peace and quiet. The darkly furnished rooms and public areas are well maintained, and the courtly staff goes out of its way to please. The decent restaurant has an extensive wine cellar that's open only during summer and winter. *Nový Smokovec, tel. 0969/2061, fax 0969/2062. 11 rooms with bath. Facilities: restaurant, wine cellar. Breakfast not included. No credit cards. $$*

Štrbské Pleso
Dining and
Lodging

Panoráma. The architects of Štrbské pleso must have had a ball designing hotels. This one, built in the 1960s, resembles an upside-down staircase. The rooms are small and plain, with renovated bathrooms. What is special, though, is the truly panoramic view of the High and Low Tatras. Nevertheless, the public areas are unimpressive, and the hotel is too expensive for what it offers. *Štrbské pleso, across from bus and rail station, tel. 0969/92111, fax 0969/92810. 96 rooms with bath. Facilities: restaurant, bar, parking. Breakfast not included. AE, DC, MC, V. $$$*

★ **Patria.** This modern, slanting pyramid on the shores of a mountain lake has two obvious advantages: location and view. Ask for a room on a higher floor; those overlooking the lake have balconies, and the other side opens onto the mountains. The rooms are functional, bright, and clean. Sadly, the hotel managers have opted for darker interiors in the public areas and for facilities (except for the top-floor restaurant) that block out the marvelous view. Don't bother trying the Slovenka tavern on the side of the hotel—both the food and the atmosphere are abominable. *Štrbské pleso, tel. 0969/92591, fax 0969/92590. 150 rooms with bath. Facilities: 3 restaurants, café, souvenir shop, parking. Breakfast included. AE, DC, MC, V. $$$*

Fis. Located right next to the ski jump, within easy reach of several slopes, the Fis is for young, athletic types. It makes no pretense to elegance, preferring a busy jumble of track suits, families with young children, and teenagers on the make. The rooms, each with a balcony, are pleasant if a little institutional. The hotel also has bungalows for rent. *Štrbské pleso, tel. 0969/92221, fax 0969/92422. Facilities: 2 restaurants, sauna, pool, fitness center. No credit cards. $$*

Tatranská Lomnica
Dining

Zbojnická Koliba. This stylish cottage restaurant, situated near the Grandhotel Praha, serves up tasty shish kebab in a romantic setting, though the portions are snack-size. Stock up on the tasty bread and cheese appetizers. *Tatranská Lomnica, tel. 0969/967630. Reservations advised. Dress: casual. No credit cards. Closed Sun. $$*

Lodging
★

Grandhotel Praha. This large, multiturreted mansion, dating from the turn of the century and resting at the foothills of the Lomnický Štít Mountain, is one of the wonders of the Tatras. Although it is no longer filled with the rich and famous, the hotel has managed to retain an air of relaxed elegance. The staff is polite and attentive. The rooms are large and well appointed, some with period furniture—ask for a large corner room with a view of the mountains. Since the hotel is far from the action, the price remains reasonable for what's offered. Be sure to have a meal in the well-run restaurant, though arrive well before the 9 PM closing or you'll be hustled out the door. As an added compensation, the cable car to the peak is only a five-minute walk away. *Tatranská Lomnica, tel. 0969/967941, fax 0969/967891. Facilities: restaurant, bar, fitness center, sauna. AE, MC, V. $$$*

The Arts and Nightlife

Despite the crowds, nightlife in the Tatras is usually little more than a good meal and an evening stroll before bed. For discos, check out the **Patria** and **Panorama** hotels in **Štrbské pleso,** or the **Park Hotel** in **Nový Smokovec.** For a more sophisticated evening out, there's live dance music in the **Grandhotel Praha** nightclub, as well as a floor show (admission 30 Sk.).

Eastern Slovakia

To the east of the High Tatras lies an expanse of Slovakia that seldom appears on tourist itineraries. Here, the High Tatras Mountains become hills that gently stretch to the Ukrainian border, with few "musts" for visitors in between. For 1,000 years, eastern Slovakia was isolated from the West; much of the region was regarded simply as the hinterland of Greater Hungary. The great movements of European history—the Reformation and the Renaissance—made their impact here as elsewhere on the continent, but in an insulated and diluted form.

Isolation can have its advantages, however, and therein may lie the special charm of this area for the visitor. The Baroque and Renaissance facades that dominate the towns of Bohemia and Moravia make an appearance in eastern Slovakia as well, but early artisans working in the region often eschewed the stone and marble preferred by their western counterparts in favor of wood and other local materials. Look especially for the wooden altars in Levoča and other towns.

The relative isolation also fostered the development of an entire civilization in medieval times, the Spiš, with no counterpart in the Czech Republic or even elsewhere in Slovakia. The kingdom of the

Spiš eventually came to encompass 24 towns within Greater Hungary. The group had its own hierarchies and laws, which were quite different from those brought in by Magyar or Saxon settlers. Although the last Spiš town lost its independence 100 years ago, much of the group's architectural legacy remains—again, thankfully, to another by-product of isolation, namely economic stagnation. Spiš towns are predominantly Gothic beneath their graceful Renaissance overlays. Their steep shingled roofs, high timber-framed gables, and brick-arched doorways have survived in a remarkable state of preservation. Gothic churches with imposing Renaissance bell towers are other major features of the area, as are some quite stunning altar triptychs and exquisite wood carvings. Needless to say, Spiš towns are worth seeking out when you see them on a map; look for the prefix "Spišsky" preceding a town name.

Farther to the northeast, the influences of Byzantium are strongly felt, most noticeably in the form of the simple wooden churches that dominate the villages along the Slovak frontier with Poland and Ukraine. This area marks a border in Europe that has stood for a thousand years: the ancient line between Rome and Constantinople, between Western Christianity and the Byzantine Empire. Many of the churches here were built by members of the Uniat Church, Christians who acknowledge the supremacy of the Pope but retain their own organization and liturgy.

The busy industrial cities of Prešov and Košice, with their belching factories and rows of housing projects, quickly bring you back to the 20th century. Although these cities do bear signs of the region's historical complexity, come here instead for a taste of modern Slovakia, of a relatively poor country that is just beginning to shed a long legacy of foreign domination.

Important Addresses and Numbers

Tourist Information The Čedok offices in eastern Slovakia are the best—and often the only—places that provide basic assistance and information, but don't expect too much in the way of service. You've done very well if they exchange your currency and offer to book you a room at an uncle's or cousin's house. There are branch offices in the following towns: **Banská Bystrica** (Tř. SNP 4, tel. 088/242575), **Košice** (Rooseveltová ul. 1, tel. 095/23123), **Prešov** (Hlavná ul. 1, tel. 091/24042), and **Žilina** (Hodzová ul. 9, tel. 089/46532).

Emergencies Police (tel. 158). **Ambulance** (tel. 155).

Late-Night Pharmacies *Lekárna* (Pharmacies) take turns staying open late or on Sunday. Look for the list posted on the front door of each pharmacy. For after-hours service, ring the bell; you will be served through a little hatch door.

Arriving and Departing by Plane

The Tatras town of Poprad is well served by ČSA from Prague and Bratislava. ČSA also offers regular flights from Prague and Bratislava to Košice.

Arriving and Departing by Car, Train, and Bus

By Car Poprad, the starting point for the tour, lies on Slovakia's main east—west highway about 560 kilometers (350 miles) from Prague in the direction of Hradec Králové. The seven- to eight-hour drive from Prague can be broken up easily with an overnight in Olomouc. The drive from Bratislava to Poprad is 328 kilometers (205 miles), with a four-lane stretch from Bratislava to Trenčín and a well-marked two-lane highway thereafter.

By Train Trains regularly connect Poprad with Prague (10 hrs) and Bratislava (5 hrs), but book in advance to ensure a seat on these sometimes crowded routes. Several night trains make the run between Poprad and Prague's main station (Hlavní nádraží).

By Bus Daily bus service connects Prague and Bratislava with Poprad, but on this run, trains tend to be quicker and more comfortable. There's also daily bus service between Bratislava and Košice.

Getting Around

By Car A car is essential for reaching some of the smaller towns along the tour. Roads are of variable quality. Try to avoid driving at night, due to poor sign-posting. A good four-lane highway links Prešov with Košice.

By Train Regular trains link Poprad with Košice and some of the other larger towns, but you'll have to resort to the bus to reach smaller villages along the tour.

By Bus Most of the tour is reachable via ČSAD's extensive bus network. The only exceptions are some of the smaller towns in northeastern Slovakia. Most buses run only on weekdays; plan carefully or you may end up getting stuck in a small town that is ill-equipped for visitors.

Highlights for First-Time Visitors

St. Giles Church, Bardejov
Šaris Icon Museum, Bardejov
Spiš Castle, near Levoča
Wood Churches near the Dukla Pass

Exploring Eastern Slovakia

Numbers in the margin correspond to points of interest on the Slovakia Exploring map.

A kilometer and a half (1 mile) or so northeast of the High Tatras town of Poprad is the medieval hamlet of **Spišská Sobota,** now a suburb of Poprad but formerly one of the main centers of the historic Spiš empire. Sobota's lovely old square features a Romanesque church, rebuilt in Gothic style in the early 16th century, with an ornate altar carved by master Pavol of Levoča. The Renaissance belfry dates from the end of the 16th century. The square itself is a nearly perfect ensemble of Renaissance houses. But what impresses most of all is the setting, a 16th-century oasis amid the cultural desert of socialist realism.

The history of the Spiš is an interesting one. The territory of the kingdom, which spreads out to the east and south of the High Tatras, was originally settled by Slavonic, and later by German, immigrants who came here in medieval times to work the mines and defend the western kingdoms against an invasion from the East. No one really knows how the "Spiš" name originated. Some believe the word derives from the Latin word *saepes* ("fence"); others think the origin is Slovak for "collecting tithes." Some 24 towns in all eventually came to join the Spiš group, functioning as a minikingdom within the Hungarian kingdom. They enjoyed many privileges denied to other cities and could choose their own count to represent them before the Hungarian king.

As the mines thrived, Spiš power and influence reached their height. But the confederation also had its bad times. In 1412, the Holy Roman Emperor Sigismund, king of Hungary, decided to sell 13 of the towns to his brother-in-law, the king of Poland, in order to finance a war with Venice. The split lasted until 1769, when the towns were reunited with one another. In 1876, the last of the Spiš towns lost its privileges, and the German-speakers in the area were forced to learn Hungarian or emigrate—mainly to the United States. In 1919, when Slovakia became part of the new Czechoslovak state, the German-speakers were again allowed to establish German schools, but in 1945 almost all of them were forced to leave the country for real or suspected collaboration with the Nazis.

5 Return to Poprad and drive northeast via Route 67 to **Kežmarok**, the once great "second town" of the Spiš region. Kežmarok was founded by German settlers during the 12th century and for years waged an ultimately unsuccessful competition with Levoča to become the capital of this minikingdom. The main sights of Kežmarok today, however, have less to do with the Spiš tradition than with the town's later role within the greater Hungarian kingdom. The chief sight is the enormous Gothic-Renaissance **Tokolyho hrad** (Tököly Palace), situated east of the main square. It was from here in the late 17th century that Count Imre Tököly launched his unsuccessful uprising against the Habsburgs to form an independent Hungarian state in "Upper Hungary" (present-day Slovakia). The count initially enjoyed great success and soon united all of Upper Hungary, but he made the fateful decision of depending on the Ottoman Empire for support in his war. When the Turks were finally defeated by the Habsburgs in 1683 at the city walls of Vienna, the Habsburgs had the count condemned to death. Tököly escaped to Turkey, where he died in exile in 1705.

In the 19th century, the structure served as a barracks and was even used for a time as a textile factory. Today it houses a small museum of the town's history, with a cozy wine cellar in the basement. *Palace admission: 10 Sk. adults, 5 Sk. children. Open Tues.–Sun. 8–noon and 12:30–5.*

Walk from the Tököly Palace down Nová ulica to the **Kostol svätého kríža** (Church of the Holy Cross), a Gothic structure dating from the beginning of the 15th century, with impressive netted vaulting. The designs on the 16th-century bell tower, with its tin crown, are characteristic of the so-called Spiš Renaissance style. The large and handsome main square, befitting Kežmarok's history as a leader among the Spiš towns, is just a couple of minutes' walk from the church. *Nová ul. Admission free. Open weekdays 9–noon and 2–5.*

The other great sight in Kežmarok is the wooden **Protestant Church**, which stands just outside the former city walls a few blocks west of the main square. The church owes its existence to a congress held in 1681 in Sopron, Hungary, where it was decided that Protestants living on then-Hungarian lands could have their own churches only if the churches were located outside the town boundaries and were constructed completely of wood (without even iron nails or stone foundations). In 1717, Kežmarok's Protestants lovingly built this structure from red pine and yew, fashioning its gracious vaulting from clay. The church could accommodate some 1,000 worshipers. But the once idyllic setting has long since yielded to urban sprawl, and the church itself has been covered over in stone to protect the interior, so what you see today is something of a letdown. Still, next to the pompous pink-and-green Evangelical Church next door, built at the end of the last century in neo-Arabian Nights style, the church's elegant simplicity is still affecting. *Hlavné nám. Admission free. Open daily 8–noon and 1–5.*

❻ The journey to **Bardejov** takes you along the Poprad River valley, with the Tatras slowly disappearing behind, and then across another mountain range along the Polish border. Bardejov is a great surprise, tucked away in this remote corner of Slovakia yet boasting one of the nation's most enchanting squares. Indeed, Bardejov owes its splendors precisely to its location astride the ancient trade routes to Poland and Russia. It's hard to put your finger on exactly why the square is so captivating. Maybe it's the lack of arcades in front of the houses, which, while impressive, can sometimes overburden the squares of Bohemian and Moravian towns. It could also be the pointed roofs of the houses, which impart a lighter, almost comic effect.

The chief sight in town is certainly the **Kostol svätého Egídia** (St. Egidius [Giles] Church), situated on the northern edge of the square. The exterior of this Gothic structure, built in stages during the 15th century, is undeniably handsome, but take a walk inside for the real treasure. The main aisle is lined with 11 priceless Gothic side altars, all carved between 1460 and 1510 and perfectly preserved. Here you get pure Gothic, with no Renaissance or Baroque details to dampen the effect. A short commentary on the altars in several languages including German and French (but unfortunately no English) can be found on a pillar near the church entrance.

The most famous side altar is to the left of the main altar (look for the number 1 on the side). The intricate work of Stefan Tarner, it depicts the birth of Christ and dates from the 1480s. Other noteworthy altars include the figure of St. Barbara and the *Vir dolorum*, both on the right-hand side of the main altar. All of the altars, however, with their vivid detailing, reward close inspection. The rest of the church is also strikingly beautiful. The Gothic pulpit, just off the main aisle, is as old as the church itself. The early Baroque pews, with their sensuous curves, must have caused quite a sensation when they were added in about 1600.

Stroll around the square after leaving the church. The modest building in the center is the **Town Hall** (Radnice), sporting late-Gothic portals and Renaissance detailing. Next to the dark and imposing Gothic of the town halls in Bohemia and Moravia, this smaller, more playful structure is a breath of fresh air.

Make your way over to the pink **Šariš Icon Museum** on the southern side of the main square to view its collection of 16th-century icons and paintings, taken from the area's numerous Russian Orthodox churches. The museum affords a fascinating look at the religious motifs of the surrounding area from between the 16th and 19th centuries. Pick up the short but interesting commentary in English (5 Sk.) when you buy your ticket. Many of the icons feature the story of St. George slaying the dragon (for the key to the princess's chastity belt!). The legend of St. George, which probably originated in pre-Christian mythology, was often used to attract the peasants of the area to the more abstemious myths of Christianity. Take a close look at the icon of the Last Judgment on the second floor for what it reveals of this area's practices and fashions during the 16th century. The complex morality of the subject matter reflects quite sophisticated beliefs. Also on the second floor are models of the wood churches that dot the surrounding countryside and from which many of these icons and paintings were taken. *Nám. Osloboditel'ov 27. Admission: 10 Sk. adults, 5 Sk. children. Open Tues.–Sat. 8:30– 11:30 and 12:30–4:30.*

The **Rhody House,** just across the Rhodyho ulica from the museum, is Bardejov's best remaining example of Renaissance relief work. The house, essentially Gothic with the reliefs added in the 16th century, was one of the few structures in the city center that survived the great fire of 1878. Continue down the Rhodyho to Na Hradbach to see the **town walls,** built in the middle of the 14th century. Some eight of the 23 original bastions are still standing, mostly along the south and east walls.

Just 6½ kilometers (4 miles) to the north of Bardejov, off Route 77, lies the old spa town of **Bardejovské Kúpele.** Though it is no longer the favorite haunt of Hungarian counts, the spa is still a pleasant enough place to stroll around and take in the fresh air from the surrounding hills. Don't expect lots of beautiful architecture unless you're a fan of "postwar modern." The town was built up rapidly after the war to serve as a retreat for the proletariat, and little of its aristocratic heritage remains. Be sure to walk behind the space-age colonnade to view a lovely wooden Russian Orthodox church from the 18th century along with some older wooden houses that form an open-air museum. The church was brought here in 1932 as a specimen of the "primitive" age. Ironically, the 226-year-old structure is holding up markedly better than the 20-year-old buildings from the "advanced" culture surrounding it.

Leave the Bardejov area along Route 77, heading north and east in the direction of Svidník. This is really where *eastern* Slovakia, with its strong Byzantine influence, begins. The colors seem wilder here; the villages also look poorer, reflecting the area's physical—and cultural—insularity. Both the Orthodox and Uniat faiths are strong in these parts, echoing the work of Byzantine missionaries more than a millennium ago.

The area's great delight is doubtless the old wooden churches in their original village settings and still in use. The first church lies in the small village of **Jedlinka,** about 13 kilometers (8 miles) north of Bardejov along the road to Svidník. Most of the wooden churches, this one included, date from the 18th and 19th centuries and combine architectural elements from the Byzantine and Baroque styles. The three steeples, each dotted with a wooden Baroque onion, rise characteristically to the west. On the inside, the north, east, and south walls are painted with scenes from the Old and New Testaments, with the west wall reserved for icons (many of which hang in the icon museum in Bardejov). The churches are usually locked, and you'll need some luck to see the inside. If you happen across a villager, ask him or her (with appropriate key-turning gesticulations) to let you in. More often than not, someone will turn up with a key, and you'll have your own guided tour. If you see a collection plate inside, make a small donation—though there is no pressure to do so.

There are about a score of Uniat churches in the countryside north of Svidník, itself an uninteresting town destroyed during World War II and completely rebuilt during the 1960s. Some recommendations are churches in the villages of **Ladomirová, Hunkovce,** and **Nižný Komárnik.** Venture off the main road to see more churches at **Bodružal, Mirol'a, Príkra,** and **Šemetkovce**—but be sure to take along a good map.

World War II buffs will want to complete the drive north of Svidník to the **Dukelský Priesmyk** (Dukla Pass) on the Polish border. It was here in late 1944 that Soviet troops, along with detachments of Czech and Slovak resistance fighters, finally made their long-awaited advance to liberate Czechoslovakia from the Nazis. Most of the fighting took place between the town of Krajná Pol'ana and the border. Alongside the many war monuments, which are in odd juxtaposition to the tranquil loveliness of the wooden churches, you'll find bunkers, trenches, and watchtowers. The Germans mustered far more resistance than expected during the battle, and the number of dead on both sides grew to more than 100,000. Near the top of the pass, a great monument and cemetery commemorate the fallen Slovaks; their leader, General Ludvík Svoboda, went on to become president of the reborn Czechoslovak state.

7 Return to Svidník via the same road and continue on in the direction of **Prešov,** a lively town and the center of Ukrainian culture in Slovakia. Its other claim to fame is a little controversial now that the Communists have been ousted from power. It was here in 1919, from the black wrought-iron balcony at Hlavná ulica 73, that enthusiastic Communists first established their own Slovak Soviet Republic in 1919, just 17 months after the Bolshevik Revolution in Russia (this early attempt at communism lasted only three weeks, however). The balcony is still ceremoniously lit up at night, but the square's former name, Slovak Soviet Republic (SSR for short), was quickly changed back to Main Street in 1990.

8 In **Košice** you'll leave rural Slovakia behind. Traffic picks up, the smog settles in, and the high-rise apartment buildings of the suburbs suddenly seem to stretch out for miles. Košice is a sprawling, modern city, the second largest in Slovakia after Bratislava, and the capital of the province of East Slovakia. Situated along the main trade route between Hungary and Poland, the city was the second largest in the Hungarian empire (after Buda) during the Middle Ages. With the Turkish occupation of the Hungarian homeland in the 16th and 17th centuries, the town became a safe haven for the Hungarian nobility from which to oppose the Turks. Inevitably, however, it fell into economic decline as trade with Hungary came to a standstill. Relief did not come until 1861 with the advent of the railroad.

In this century the city has been shuttled between Hungary, Czechoslovakia, and now Slovakia. Sadly, Slovak efforts after World War II to eliminate Hungarian influence in Košice were remarkably successful. As you walk around, you'll be hard-pressed to find evidence that this was once a great Hungarian city—even with the Hungarian frontier just 20 kilometers (12 miles) away.

You won't see many Westerners strolling Košice's enormous medieval square, the **Hlavná ulica;** most of the tourists here are Hungarians on a day trip to shop and sightsee. The square is dominated on its southern flank by the huge tower of the Gothic **Dóm svätej Alžbety** (Cathedral of St. Elizabeth). Built throughout the 15th century and finally completed in 1508, the cathedral is the largest in Slovakia. First walk over to the north side of the cathedral (facing the square) to look at the famed "golden door." The reputed friend of the sick and aged, the Holy Elizabeth, after whom the cathedral is named, stands in the middle of the door. The reliefs above her depict her good works. Inside the church is one of Europe's largest Gothic altars, the 35-foot Altar of the Holy Elizabeth. The altar is a monumental piece of medieval wood carving attributed to the master

Erhard of Ulm. Although generally open to worshipers, the church is under renovation, and you may not be able to roam around at will.

Next door to the cathedral is the **Urbanová veža** (Urbans' Tower), a 14th-century bell tower remodeled in Renaissance style in 1612. But much of what you see today doesn't go back much farther than 1966, when the tower caught fire and had to be almost completely rebuilt, brick by brick. It now houses a permanent exhibition of bell making, but don't waste your time climbing to the top unless you're interested in forging and casting techniques. The view is disappointing and can't compensate for the eight floors of bell and iron exhibits you'll be subjected to on your way there. *Hlavná ul. Admission: 5 Sk. adults, 2 Sk. children. Open Tues.–Sat. 9–5, Sun. 9–1.*

On the other side of the cathedral is the even older **Kaplnka svätého Michala** (St. Michael's Chapel), which dates from around 1260. A relief on the portal shows the archangel Michael weighing the souls of the dead. Just across from the chapel, on the east side of the square, is the **Dom Košického vládneho programu** (House of the Košice Government Program), which played an important role in Czechoslovakia's history in the final days of World War II. It was from here that the "Košice Program" was proclaimed on April 5, 1945, announcing the reunion of the Czech lands and Slovakia into one national state.

The center of the square is dominated by the **Štátne Divadlo** (State Theater), a mishmash of neo-Renaissance and neo-Baroque elements, built at the end of the last century. This conscious imitation of architectural styles was all the rage in the Habsburg lands at the time; indeed, the building would be equally at home on Vienna's Ringstrasse. To the right of the State Theater, the impressive Rococo palace at Hlavná ulica 59, which once housed the city's wealthiest nobility, was the unlikely site of a Slovak Soviet Republic congress in 1919, just a week before the revolutionary movement was aborted. The relief on the house has nothing to do with communism but recalls the stay here of the Russian commander Mikhail Kutuzov, who in 1805 led the combined Russian-Austrian forces in battle against Napoleon at Austerlitz.

Time Out To feel as though you've really stepped into turn-of-the-century Vienna, have a cup of coffee or a cold drink within the elegant Jugendstil confines of the **Café Slavia** at Hlavná ulica 63.

A little farther up the square, take a right at **E. Adyho ulica** and continue to the end of the street to the town walls. During the 16th and 17th centuries, these bastions—which date from the 13th century—helped secure Košice as a safe haven for the Hungarian nobility; it was from here that they launched their attacks on the Turks occupying the Hungarian motherland.

The **Miklušova väznica** (Nicholas Prison), an old Gothic building used as a prison and torture chamber until 1909, now houses an excellent museum with exhibits on the history of Košice. *E. Adyho ul. (at Hrnčiarská ul.). Admission: 10 Sk. adults, 5 Sk. children. Open Tues.–Sat. 9–5, Sun. 9–1.*

An interesting day trip from Košice is to drive the 30 kilometers (20 miles) to the **Herl'any geyser.** Follow Route 50 east out of the city, making a right at Route 576 and following the signs. The geyser has an eruption interval of 32 to 36 hours. The display, with water shooting up nearly 130 feet, lasts for about 20 minutes. Check with the

Čedok office in Košice (Rooseveltová ul. 1, tel. 095/23123) for the expected eruption times.

Leave Košice via Route 547, following the signs in the direction of **Spišská Nová Ves.** The road quickly turns hilly, offering beautiful panoramas over several central Slovak ranges. Continue on Route 547 to **Spišské Podhradie,** turning left on Route 18 in the direction of ❾ **Levoča,** the center of the Spiš kingdom and the quintessential Spiš town.

You'll enter Levoča from Route 18 through the Košice Gate, emerging after a few hundred yards into the large and beautiful main square, surrounded by colorful Renaissance facades. Some are in appalling disrepair, and others are undergoing renovation, but this detracts little from the honest Old World feel. The main sights are in the middle of the square. The **Mestská radnica** (town hall), with its fine example of whitewashed Renaissance arcades, gables and clock tower, was built in 1551 after the great fire of 1550 destroyed the old Gothic building along with much of the town. The clock tower, which was added in 1656, now houses the excellent **Spiš Museum,** with exhibits of guild flags and a good collection of paintings and wood carvings. A ticket for the museum will also allow you to see the exquisite interior of St. Jacob's Church next door. *Hlavné nám. Admission: 10 Sk. adults, 5 Sk. children. Open Mon.–Sat. 10–5.*

The nearby **Kostol svätého Jakuba** (St. James Church) is a huge Gothic construction, originally begun in the early 14th century but not completed in its present form until a century later. The interior is a breathtaking concentration of Gothic religious art. It was here in the early 16th century that the greatest Spiš artist, Pavol of Levoča, created his most unforgettable pieces. The carved-wood high altar, said to be the world's largest and incorporating a truly magnificent carving of *The Last Supper* in limewood, is his most famous work. The 12 disciples are, in fact, portraits of Levoča merchants. Two of the Gothic side altars are also the work of master Pavol. The wall paintings on the left wall are fascinating in their detail and imagination; one depicts the seven deadly sins, each riding a different animal into hell.

Several houses on the square are worth a closer look. The house at No. 20 is the former residence of Pavol of Levoča. Farther up, at No. 7, is the golden sgraffiti-decorated **Thurzo House,** named for the powerful mining family. The wonderfully ornate gables are from the 17th century, though the sgraffiti was a 19th-century addition. At the top of the square is the **Small Committee House** (No. 60), the former administrative center of the Spiš region. Above the doorway in sgraffito style is the coat of arms of the Spiš towns. The monumental classicist building next door, the **Large Committee House,** was built during the early 19th century by Anton Povolný, also responsible for the Evangelical Church at the bottom of the square.

From Levoča, it's worth taking a short 16-kilometer (10 mile) detour east along Route 18 to the magnificent **Spišský hrad** (Spiš Castle), a former administrative center of the kingdom and now the largest castle in Slovakia (and one of the largest in Europe). Spiš overlords occupied this site starting in 1209; the castle soon proved its military value by surviving the onslaught of the Mongol hordes in the 13th century. The castle later came under the domination of the Hungarians. Now, however, it's firmly in Slovak hands and in season is open to the general public. The museum has a good collection of torture devices, and the castle affords a beautiful view of the surrounding hills and town. *Spišský hrad. Admission: 10 Sk. adults, 5 Sk. children. Open May—Oct., Tues.–Sun. 8–4.*

From Levoča, head south on Route 533 through Spišská Nová Ves, continuing along the twisting roads to the junction with Route 535. Turn right onto Route 535, following the signs to Mlynky and beyond, through the tiny villages and breathtaking countryside of the **Slovenský Raj** (*see* Off the Beaten Track, *below*), the national park whose name means "Slovak Paradise." When you finally reach Route 67, turn in the direction of Poprad until you cross Route 66 and see the signs for Banská Bystrica.

⑩ Next to the medieval grandeur of the Spiš towns, **Banská Bystrica's** provincial prosperity—with its prim white-and-yellow houses— looks admittedly bland. Even the hills and mountains that enfold the town are tame next to the splendors of eastern Slovakia proper. Still, the Lux Hotel (*see* Dining and Lodging, *below*) on the edge of town is a good place to pause on the return trip to Bratislava, and the town itself has enough interesting sights to justify a short stay.

Although it has been around since the 13th century, growing wealthy from the nearby copper mines, Banská Bystrica is known throughout Slovakia for its role in more recent history, namely as the center of the Slovak National Uprising during World War II. It was from here that the underground Slovak National Council called the uprising into existence on August 29, 1944. For some two months, thousands of Slovaks valiantly rose up against their Nazi oppressors, forcing the Germans to divert critically needed troops and equipment from the front lines. The Germans eventually quashed the uprising on October 27, but the costly operation is credited with accelerating the Allied victory.

You'll find reminders of the uprising (known in Slovak by its initials, SNP) just about everywhere. The mecca for fans is the **Múzeum Slovenského Národného Povstania** (Museum of the Slovak National Uprising), which stands in a large field just outside the center of town, between Horný ulica and ulica Dukelských Hrdinov. No matter where you stay in Banská Bystrica, you won't be able to miss the monument's massive concrete wings—surprisingly evocative of a captive people rising up to freedom. The effect is particularly striking at night. The museum itself isn't of much interest, however. The commentary is heavily biased toward a communist perspective, and as you look at the maps and photographs, you can't help feeling that you're getting half-truths. More telling, perhaps, is the absence of Slovak visitors; since the locals are no longer required to visit, the corridors are often empty. *Admission: 10 Sk. adults, 5 Sk. children. Open Tues.–Sun. 8–4.*

If you're partial to less-recent history, head for the main square, the **Námestie SNP,** with its cheery collection of Renaissance and Baroque houses. The most impressive is the **Thurzo house,** an amalgamation of two late-Gothic structures built in 1495 by the wealthy Thurzo family. The genuine Renaissance sgraffiti on the outside were added during the 16th century, when the family's wealth was at its height. Today the building houses the **City Museum,** which is more interesting for the chance to see inside the house than for its artifacts. *Nám. SNP. Admission: 10 Sk. adults, 5 Sk. children. Open weekdays 8–noon and 1–4, Sun. 9–noon and 1–4.*

Cross the main square in front of the 16th-century **Hodinová veža** (Clock Tower) and venture up the Jána Bakoša ulica to see the **Parish Church,** situated near the town walls. The church dates from 1255 and forms a unit with the other surviving structures of the former castle complex: the Gothic **Royal Palace** and the **Praetorium** (the former city hall). Inside the church, in **St. Barbara's Chapel,** you'll find a beautiful late-Gothic altar, another wooden masterpiece from Pavol of Levoča.

Off the Beaten Track

South of Levoča lies a wild and romantic area of cliffs and gorges, caves and waterfalls known as **Slovenský Raj** (Slovak Paradise). Once the refuge for Spiš villagers during the Tatar invasion of 1241–42 and now a national park, the area is perfect for adventurous hikers. The gorges are accessible by narrow but secure iron ladders. The main tourist centers are **Čingov** in the north and **Dedinky** in the south.

The sleepy border town of **Medzilaborce,** east of Svidník, is fast becoming the unlikely mecca for fans of pop-art guru Andy Warhol. It was here in 1991, near the birthplace of Warhol's parents, that the country's cultural authorities, in conjunction with the Andy Warhol Foundation for Visual Arts in New York, opened the **Warhol Family Museum of Modern Art.** In all, the museum holds 17 original Warhol silk screens, including two from the famous Campbell's Soup series, and portraits of Lenin and singer Billie Holiday. The Russian Orthodox church across the street from the museum lends a suitably surreal element to the setting. *Admission: 10 Sk. adults, 5 Sk. for children. Open daily 10–5.*

Sports and Outdoor Activities

Hiking and Walking Eastern Slovakia is a hiker's paradise. In addition to the offerings at **Slovenský Raj** (*see* Off the Beaten Track, *above*), trails fan out in all directions in the area known as Spišská Magura, to the north and east of Kežmarok.

Swimming Good outdoor swimming can be found in lakes in Slovenský Raj and in Michalovce, east of Košice.

Dining and Lodging

The dining revolution in evidence in the Czech Republic and the rest of Slovakia has been slow in coming to eastern Slovakia. You'll look in vain for truly innovative restaurants; the best bet, especially in smaller cities and towns, remains the hotel restaurant.

In eastern Slovakia the term "hotel" often refers to a less-than-cozy high rise, situated somewhere on the outskirts of town. Although they are typically overpriced for the level of comfort offered, they are often the only option available. Many towns will have some private rooms available; ask at Čedok for information.

Highly recommended restaurants and lodgings in a particular price category are indicated by a star ★.

Banská Bystrica
Dining and Lodging **Lux.** Located on the edge of town, the Lux is one of the few successful high-rise hotels in Slovakia, managing to combine modernity with some semblance of style. The rooms (especially on the upper floors facing town) have a magnificent view over the mountains, enlivened at night by the Museum of the Slovak National Uprising glowing in the foreground. The restaurant is elegant and serves a good range of Slovak specialties. A leisurely breakfast is served in the café. *Nové nám. 2, tel. 088/724141, fax 088/753853. 120 rooms*

with bath. Facilities: restaurant, café, bar, parking. Breakfast included. AE, DC, MC, V. $$

Národný dom. This plain, older hotel, just off the main square, is a cheaper alternative to the Lux. The staff is friendly and the rooms are clean, but the corridors have a stale air about them. *Národná ul., tel. 088/724331. 42 rooms, most with shower. Facilities: restaurant. Breakfast not included. No credit cards. $$*

Urpin. Similar to the neighboring Národný dom above, the Urpin offers clean rooms in an older, somewhat neglected hotel a block away from the city center. *Ul. Jána Cikkera 5, tel. 088/724556, fax 088/23731. 45 rooms, some with shower. Breakfast included. No credit cards. $$*

Lodging **Motel Uľanka.** Located 6 kilometers (4 miles) outside of town on the road to Ružomberok, this inexpensive motel is a good alternative for budget-minded travelers with a car. The surrounding mountain scenery is magnificent, but the rooms are only adequate, and the motel's strict rules are reminiscent of a youth hostel. *Uľanská cesta, tel. 088/53657. 50 rooms without bath. Breakfast not included. No credit cards. $*

Bardejov **Mineral.** Despite its location in a 19th-century spa town (the former
Dining and haunt of the Hungarian aristocracy), this aging 1970s structure is
Lodging fairly charmless. Yet as Bardejov lacks decent hotels, you may not have a real choice. The rooms, some with a nice view over the spa area, are acceptably clean, and the restaurant on the first floor serves a good breakfast. Follow Route 77 north about 5 kilometers (3 miles) out of town, turning at the sign to Bardejovské Kúpele. *Bardejovské Kúpele, tel. 0935/724122. 50 rooms with bath. Facilities: restaurant, nightclub. Breakfast not included. No credit cards. $*

Republika. This depressing socialist-realist structure is an acceptable alternative for travelers without a car and no easy access to the Mineral (*see above*). The hallways are cluttered with mismatched furniture; and the rooms, though clean, show a similar lack of forethought. The big advantage is location: A couple of steps and you're in Bardejov's beautiful medieval square. *Nám. Osloboditeľov, tel. 0935/2721, fax 0935/2657. 30 rooms, some with shower. Facilities: restaurant. Breakfast not included. No credit cards. $*

Kežmarok **Lipa.** This functional 1960s structure, located on a main road away
Dining and from the town square, remains the best choice in town. But don't ex-
Lodging pect more in atmosphere or services than a clean place to sleep. *Toporecova ul., tel. 0968/2037, fax 0968/2039. 78 rooms, most with bath or shower. Facilities: bar. Breakfast not included. No credit cards. $*

Košice **Slovan.** This unsightly high rise surprisingly does many things well.
Dining and The English-speaking staff is attentive, and the decor is contempo-
Lodging rary but tasteful. Choose a room on one of the upper floors for a beautiful view of Košice's main square, just a few minutes' walk from the hotel. *Hlavná ul. 1, tel. 095/622–7378, fax 095/622–8413. 212 rooms with bath. Facilities: restaurant, café, minibars, video-camera rental. Breakfast not included. AE, DC, MC, V. $$$*

Imperial. The gracious proportions of this older hotel, situated just off the main square, are marred somewhat by peeling wallpaper and other obvious signs of neglect. Nevertheless, as a cheaper alternative to the Slovan, it's fine for an overnight stay. The restaurant is bright and serves passable food. *Ul. Hrnčiarska 1, tel. 095/622–2146. 45 rooms, half with bath. Facilities: restaurant, café. Breakfast not included. No credit cards. $$*

Prešov
Dining and
Lodging

Dukla. Just down the main road from the center of town and right next to the theater, this hotel is a modern structure that works. The staff is friendly; the rooms, though nothing special, are comfortable and clean, with very immaculate bathrooms. Some rooms have a balcony. *Nám. Legionárov 2, 08001, tel. 091/22741–2, fax 091/32134. 89 rooms with bath. Facilities: restaurant, snack bar.* $$

Šariš. Though it is a little removed from the city center, the Šariš has facilities—including bike rentals—that you do not often find at a budget hotel. The staff is friendly and helpful, and the rooms, though small, are equipped with refrigerators. The bathrooms, however, are a bit on the old and worn side. *Sabinovská ul. 1, 08001, tel. 091/46351, fax 091/46551. 110 rooms. Facilities: restaurant, bar. No credit cards.* $

Žilina
Dining and
Lodging

Slovakia. This modern megastructure is made human by the friendly staff (English is spoken) and cheerful rooms. The location is excellent for a stopover: a five-minute walk from the town center but convenient to major roads. The restaurant serves good Slovak specialties at very reasonable prices. *Nám. L'udovita Stúra, 01000, tel. 089/46572, fax 089/47975. 140 rooms with bath. Facilities: restaurant, snack bar, sauna, pool. Breakfast included. AE, DC, MC, V.* $$

4 Hungary

By Alan Levy

Updated by
Julie Tomasz

Alan Levy,
American
author,
librettist, and
foreign
correspondent,
has covered
events in
Eastern
Europe for
more than 20
years; he is
currently the
editor in chief
of the Prague
Post. Julie
Tomasz lives
in Budapest
and is an
editor for the
Budapest
Sun.

Hungary sits at the crossroads of Central Europe, having retained its own identity by absorbing countless invasions and foreign occupations. Its industrious, resilient people have a history of brave but unfortunate uprisings: against the Turks in the 17th century, the Habsburgs in 1848, and the Soviet Union in 1956. Each has resulted in a period of readjustment, a return to politics as the art of the possible.

The 1960s and '70s saw matters improve politically and materially for the majority of Hungarians. Communist-party leader János Kádár remained relatively popular at home and abroad, allowing Hungary to expand and improve trade and relations with the West. The bubble began to burst during the 1980s, however, when the economy stagnated and inflation escalated. The peaceful transition to democracy began when young reformers in the party shunted aside the aging Kádár in 1988 and began speaking openly about multiparty democracy, a market economy, and a break from Moscow—daring ideas at the time.

Events quickly gathered pace, and by spring 1990, as the Iron Curtain fell, Hungarians went to the polls in the first free elections held in 40 years. A center-right government led by Prime Minister József Antal took office, sweeping away the Communists and their renamed successor party, the Socialists, who finished fourth.

Because Hungary is a small, agriculturally oriented country, visitors are often surprised by its grandeur and Old World charm, especially in the capital, Budapest, which bustles with life as never before. Hungarians like to complain about their economic problems, but they spare visitors bureaucratic hassles at the border and airport. Entry is easy and quick for Westerners, most of whom no longer need visas. Gone are the days when visitors were forced to make daily currency exchanges and register with local police on arrival.

Two rivers cross the country. The famous Duna (Danube) flows from the west through Budapest on its way to the southern frontier, and the smaller Tisza flows from the northeast across the Nagyalföld (Great Plain). What Hungary lacks in size it makes up for in beauty and charm. Western Hungary is dominated by the largest lake in Central Europe, Lake Balaton. Although some overdevelopment has blighted its splendor, its shores are still lined with Baroque villages, relaxing spas, magnificent vineyards, and shaded garden restaurants serving the catch of the day. In eastern Hungary, the Nagyalföld offers visitors a chance to explore the folklore and customs of the Magyars (the Hungarians' name for themselves and their language). It is an area of spicy food, strong wine, and the proud csikós (horsemen). The unspoiled towns of the provincial areas are rich in history and culture.

However, it is Budapest, a city of more than 2 million people, that draws travelers from all over the world. The hills of Buda rise from the brackish waters of the Danube, which bisects the city; on the flatlands of Pest is an imposing array of hotels, restaurants, and shopping areas. Throughout Hungary, comfortable accommodations can be found for comparatively modest prices, and there's an impressive network of inexpensive guest houses.

Hungarians are known for their hospitality and love talking to foreigners, although their strange language, which has no links to other European tongues, can be a problem. Today, however, everyone seems to be learning English, especially young people. Trying out a few words of German will delight the older generation. But what all Hungarians share is a deep love of music, and the calendar is star-

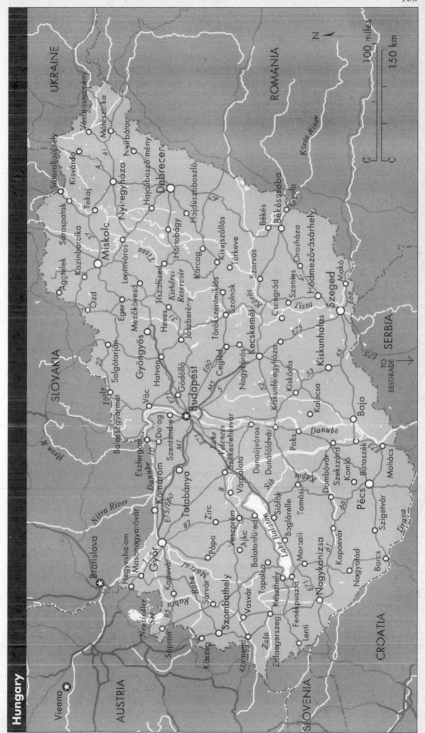

195

studded with it, from Budapest's famous opera to its annual spring music festival and the serenades of Gypsy violinists during evening meals.

Before You Go

Government Tourist Offices

In the U.S. **IBUSZ Hungarian Travel Company,** 1 Parker Pl., Fort Lee, NJ 07024, tel. 201/592–8585.

In Canada **Representative of the Hungarian Republic,** 7 Delaware Ave., Ottawa K2P 0Z2, Ontario, tel. 613/232–1549 or 613/232–1711.

In the U.K. **IBUSZ (Danube Travel, Ltd.),** 6 Conduit St., London W1R 9TG, tel. 0171/493–0263.

Tour Groups

U.S. Tour Operators **Caravan Tours** (401 N. Michigan Ave., Chicago, IL 60611, tel. 312/321–9800) covers Budapest, Vienna, Prague, Moscow, and Leningrad in 15 days.
Fugazy International Travel (770 Hwy. 1, North Brunswick, NJ 08902, tel. 800/828–4488) offers 10- to 14-day Budapest packages that include excursions throughout Hungary.
General Tours (245 5th Ave., New York, NY 10016, tel. 212/685–1800 or 800/221–2216) combines Budapest and Prague on a nine-day tour that features comprehensive city sightseeing as well as excursions to the Danube Bend in Hungary.
Love Holidays/Uniworld (Box 16000 Ventura Blvd., Encino, CA 91436, tel. 818/501–6868 or 800/733–7820) pairs Budapest with Vienna on a week-long tour.
Maupintour (Box 807, Lawrence, KS 66044, tel. 913/843–1211 or 800/255–4266) gives you a week to get acquainted with Budapest. Sightseeing includes full-day excursions through Eger and the Matra Mountains, the Danube Bend, and the districts of Buda and Pest.

Other operators that include Budapest on their Eastern European itineraries are **Delta Dream Vacations** (tel. 305/522–1440 or 800/338–2010), **Olson-Travelworld** (Box 10066, Manhattan Beach, CA 90226, tel. 310/546–8400 or 800/421–2255), **Trafalgar Tours** (21 E. 26th St., New York, NY 10010, tel. 212/689–8977 or 800/854–0103), and **TWA Getaway Vacations** (tel. 800/GETAWAY).

U.K. Tour Operators **Danube Travel Ltd.** (IBUSZ) (6 Conduit St., London W1R 9TG, tel. 0171/493–0263) offers packages to Budapest for three or more nights, with optional excursions from the city, and will make arrangements for the Budapest Spring Festival and the Hungarian Grand Prix.
Hamilton Travel Ltd. (6 Heddon St., London W1R 7LH, tel. 0171/439–3199) offers flight/accommodation packages for one or more nights to Budapest.
Sovereign Cities (Groundstar House, London Rd., Crawley, West Sussex RH10 2TB, tel. 0293/561–444) offers flight/hotel packages ranging from two to seven nights with a guided tour of the city and optional excursions.
Time Off Ltd. (Chester Close, Chester St., London SW1X 7BQ, tel. 0171/235–8070) offers packages to Budapest for two to seven nights with optional sightseeing excursions.

Travelscene Ltd. (Travelscene House, 11–15 St. Ann's Rd., Harrow, Middlesex HA1 1AS, tel. 0181/427–4445) offers three-, five-, and seven-night flight/hotel packages to Budapest with optional excursions.

When to Go

Many of Hungary's major fairs and festivals take place during the spring and fall. During July and August, Budapest can be hot and the resorts at Lake Balaton crowded, so spring (May) and the end of summer (September) are the ideal times to visit.

What to Pack

Clothing Although fashion was all but nonexistent in Hungary under communism, modern clothing styles have caught on quickly and today's urban Hungarians increasingly reflect the latest trends in Western dress. Don't worry about packing lots of formal clothing. A sport jacket for men, and a dress or pants for women, is appropriate for an evening out in Budapest. Everywhere else, you'll feel comfortable in casual corduroys or jeans.

Most of Budapest and the surrounding countryside is best seen on foot, so take a pair of sturdy walking shoes and be prepared to use them. If your plans include touring the hilly terrain along the Danube Bend or the northern shore of Lake Balaton, be sure the shoes have good traction and ankle support, as some of the trails can be quite challenging.

Miscellaneous Some items that you take for granted at home are either occasionally unavailable or of questionable quality in Hungary. If you're particular about using specific Western brands, it's probably best to take your own toiletries and personal hygiene products with you. Western cosmetics and toiletries are becoming increasingly available in large cities, but usually at significantly inflated prices. If you plan to play any sports, bear in mind that few places have equipment for rent. An alternative to bringing your own equipment would be to buy what you need locally and take it home with you. In general, sporting goods are relatively cheap and of good quality. You will need an electrical adapter for small appliances; the voltage is 220, with 50 cycles.

Hungarian Currency

The unit of currency is the forint (Ft.), divided into 100 fillérs (f.). There are bills of 50, 100, 500, 1,000, and 5,000 forints and coins of 10, 20, and 50 fillérs as well as 1, 2, 5, 10, 20, and the new but less common 50, 100, and 200 forints. A newly designed series of coins was introduced into the system in late 1993, precipitating mild confusion and general frustration with pay telephones and other coin-operated machines that still accept only the old coins. The tourist exchange rate was approximately 102 Ft. to the dollar and 151 Ft. to the pound sterling at press time (spring 1994). Note that official exchange rates are adjusted daily.

Hungary does not require you to exchange a certain sum of money for each day of your stay. Exchange money as you need it at banks, hotels, or travel offices—but not too much. Although in theory you can change back 50% (up to U.S. $100) of the original sum when you leave—provided you've kept the exchange receipts—it may prove difficult in practice.

Most credit cards are accepted, but don't rely on them in small towns or at less expensive accommodations and restaurants. Eurocheque holders can cash personal checks in all banks and in most hotels.

There is an illegal black market in currency, but you will not gain much and could actually lose a good deal by fraud or if you are caught by the police.

What It Will Cost

First-class hotel chains in Budapest charge standard international prices, but other quality hotels are still modest by Western standards. The introduction of the value-added tax (VAT) in 1988 has increased many of the prices in the service industry by up to 25%, and the annual inflation rate keeps creeping higher. Nevertheless, enjoyable vacations with all the trimmings still remain relatively inexpensive.

Sample Costs A cup of coffee, 30 Ft.–60 Ft.; a bottle of beer, 100 Ft.–120 Ft.; soft drinks, 40 Ft.–50 Ft.; a ham sandwich, 60 Ft.–100 Ft.; 1-mile taxi ride, 60 Ft.; museum admission, 30 Ft.–80 Ft.

Passports and Visas

U.S. Citizens A visa is not required to enter Hungary. A valid passport is sufficient for stays of up to 90 days. For additional information, contact the Hungarian Embassy, 3910 Shoemaker St. NW, Washington, DC 20008, tel. 202/362–6730.

If your passport is lost or stolen abroad, report it immediately to the nearest U.S. Embassy or consulate and to local police authorities. If you can provide the consular officer with the information contained in the passport, the office will probably be able to issue you a new passport. For this reason, it is a good idea to keep a copy of the data page of your passport in a separate place, or leave the passport number, date, and place of issuance with a relative or friend in the United States.

Canadian Citizens Canadian citizens need only a valid passport—visas are not required—to enter Hungary. To acquire a passport, send a completed application (available at any post office or passport office) to the Bureau of Passports, Suite 215, West Tower, Guy Favreau Complex, 200 René Levesque Boulevard West, Montreal, Quebec H2Z 1X4. Include C$25, two photographs, a guarantor, and proof of Canadian citizenship. Applications can be made in person at regional passport offices in many locations, including Edmonton, Halifax, Montreal, Toronto, Vancouver, and Winnipeg. Passports are valid for five years and are not renewable.

U.K. Citizens British citizens need a valid 10-year passport to enter Hungary (cost: £15 for a standard 32-page passport, £30 for a 94-page passport). Application forms are available from most travel agents and major post offices, and from the Passport Office (Clive House, 70 Petty France, London SW1H 9HD, tel. 0171/279–3434 for recorded information, or 0171/279–4000). A British Visitors Passport is not acceptable. A visa is no longer required.

Customs and Duties

If you are over 16 you may bring in 250 cigarettes or 50 cigars or 250 grams of tobacco; 2 liters of wine and 1 liter of spirits; 25 milliliters of perfume; and small gifts to a total value of 8,000 Ft. You may bring in any amount of foreign currency; however, technically you cannot bring in more than 1,000 Ft.

Official export rules state that travelers can take out objects—purchased or received as gifts—worth up to 3,000 Ft. Take care when leaving Hungary that you have the right documentation for exporting goods. Keep receipts of any items bought from Konsumtourist, Intertourist, or Képcsarnok Vállalat. A special permit is needed for the export of works of art, antiques, or objects of museum value. You are entitled to a VAT refund on new goods valued in excess of 25,000 Ft. For further information, inquire at the National Customs and Revenue Office at the Keleti station arrivals area (tel. 1/114–0203 or 1/114–0280). If you have trouble communicating, ask Tourinform (tel. 1/117–9800) for assistance.

Language

Hungarian (Magyar) tends to look and sound intimidating at first because it is not an Indo-European language. Generally, older people speak some German, and many younger people speak at least rudimentary English. It's a safe bet that anyone in the tourist trade will speak at least one of the two languages.

Car Rentals

There are no special requirements for renting a car in Hungary, but be sure to shop around, as prices can differ greatly. **Avis** and **Hertz** offer Western makes for as much as $400–$900 per week. Smaller local companies, on the other hand, can rent Hungarian cars for as low as $130 per week.

The following companies have offices at Budapest's Ferihegy Airport:

Avis, main office, tel. 1/118–4240; Terminal 1, tel. 1/157–6421; Terminal 2, tel. 1/157–7265; in the United States, 800/331–1212.
Budget, main office, tel. 1/156–6333; Terminal 1, tel. 1/157–9123; Terminal 2, tel. 1/157–8481; in the United States, 800/527–0700.
Europcar, main office, tel. 1/113–1492; Terminal 1, tel. 1/157–6680; Terminal 2, tel. 1/157–6610; in the United States, 800/227–7368.
Hertz/Fötaxi, main office, tel. 1/111–6116; Terminal 1, tel. 1/157–8618; Terminal 2, tel. 1/157–8606; in the United States, 800/654–3131.

Student and Youth Travel

The **International Student Identity Card** (ISIC) is accepted in Budapest and other large Hungarian cities, but not as widely as it is in Western countries. It will get you varying discounts on some museum admission, transportation fares, and tickets for sports and cultural events. You can obtain the card from CIEE in New York (*see* Student and Youth Travel in Chapter 1, Essential Information) for $16 or at any of the following **Express Youth and Travel Offices** in Budapest for about one-third the price (V, Zoltán utca 10; V, Szabadság tér 16; VII, Keleti train station; VIII, József kőrút 66; XI, Bartók Béla út 34; VII Semmelweis utca 4; VI, Andrássy út 35). Express offices have friendly, helpful staff who can provide information on all aspects of student and youth travel throughout the country. Note that most Express offices are open only on weekdays until 4 PM, sometimes until 3 PM on Friday; the exception is the branch at the Keleti train station, which is open daily from 8 AM to 7 PM.

Traveling with Children

Hotels The **Budapest Hilton** (tel. 1/175–1000) offers a "Family Plan," allowing children of all ages to stay free in their parents' room. Remarkably, there are no age limits: A 70-year-old parent with a 40-year-old
offspring can take advantage of the policy. In Budapest, the **Forum**
(tel. 1/117–8088) hotel allows one child under 14 to stay free in his or
her parents' room.

Baby-Sitting The **Children's Hotel** (XIX, Eotvos utca 11, tel. 1/157–4033) cares for
Services children aged 6 months to 6 years, 24 hours a day. The price is 150
Ft. for four hours and 600 Ft. for 24 hours, plus the cost of meals.
Only a passport is needed. English is not officially spoken, but some
staff members may happen to speak a little. Your best best is to in-
quire at the Tourinform bureau, look through the classified ads in
The Budapest Sun and *Budapest Week*, or ask at the hotel desk for
information about other options.

Hints for Disabled Travelers

In Budapest, information on special services and tours for the disabled is available from **Piknik Tours** (11, Pinceszer út 14–16, tel./fax
1/176–5101, 1/176–5555, or 1/176–5355; ask for Katarina Zákrány).
The advertised programs can be modified to suit the special requirements of different groups. Tours use buses that are accessible to
travelers in wheelchairs. If you send a fax in advance, Piknik Tours
can also arrange to meet your plane.

Arriving and Departing

From North America by Plane

Airports and Hungary's international airport, **Ferihegy Airport** in Budapest (the
Airlines nation's only commercial airport), is about 22 kilometers (14 miles)
southeast of the city. All **Malév Hungarian Airlines** and **Lufthansa**
flights operate from the newer, more streamlined **Terminal 2**, which
is 4 kilometers (2½ miles) farther from the city. Other airlines fly
into **Terminal 1.** For same-day flight information, call the airport authority (1/157–7155); the staff takes its time to answer calls and may
not be cordial. Malév and other national airlines fly nonstop from
most European capitals. In spring 1994, Malév and Delta merged
their direct service to and from the United States in order to offer
daily nonstop flights between Budapest and JFK International Airport in New York City.

British Airways, tel. 1/118–3299; at airport, tel. 1/157–6970; in the
United States, 800/247–9297.

Delta, tel. 1/266–1400; at airport, tel. 1/147–1972.

Lufthansa, tel. 1/266–4511; at airport, tel. 157–8017.

Malév, tel. 1/266–9033 or 1/266–7177; at airport, tel. 1/157–9123.

Flying Time From New York, a nonstop flight to Budapest takes 9–10 hours;
with a stopover, the journey will take at least 12–13 hours.

From the United Kingdom by Plane, Car, and Train

By Plane **British Airways** (tel. 0171/897–4000) and **Malév Hungarian Airlines**
(tel. 0171/439–0577) offer daily nonstop service to Budapest from
London (with connections to major British cities).

By Car The best ferry ports for Budapest are Hoek van Holland or Oostende, from which you drive to Köln (Cologne) and then through Munich to Vienna and on to Budapest.

By Train To travel from London to Budapest by train, make a reservation (required) on the *Oostende-Wien Express,* which provides convenient all-year service from Oostende. Connecting trains leave London's Victoria Station every day for Dover and Oostende (in summer you can leave Victoria Station at noon if you take the fast Jetfoil service). The train runs via Brussels and Köln to Vienna (West), which it reaches in good time to change to the *Wiener Walzer,* which makes the final leg of the trip to Budapest. (The *Wiener Walzer* connects Basel, Switzerland, with Budapest, running via Zürich, Salzburg, and Vienna; reservations are required.)

Staying in Hungary

Getting Around

By Plane There is no commercial domestic airline service in Hungary.

By Train Travel by train from Budapest to other large cities or to Lake Balaton is cheap and efficient. Remember to take *gyorsvonat* (express trains) and not *személyvonat* (locals), which are extremely slow. A *helyjegy* (seat reservation), which costs about 40 Ft. and is sold up to 60 days in advance, is advisable for all express trains, especially during weekend travel in summer. It is also worth paying a little extra for first-class tickets. The Hungarian Railroad Inter-City express—which links the country's major cities—is comfortable, clean, and almost always on time; the service costs only an extra 130 Ft.

Fares Only Hungarian citizens are entitled to standard student discounts on domestic rail travel; anyone over 60, however, including foreigners, can receive a 30% discount. InterRail cards are valid for those under 26, and the Rail Europe Senior Travel Pass entitles senior citizens to a 30% reduction on all trains. Snacks and drinks are available on all express trains, but the supply often runs out quickly, especially in summer, so pack a lunch just in case. For more information about rail travel, contact or visit **MAV Passenger Service** (Andrassy út 35, Budapest VI, tel. 1/122–7860 or 1/122–4052).

By Bus Long-distance buses link Budapest with most cities in Hungary as well as with much of Eastern and Western Europe. Services to the eastern part of the country leave from the Nepstadion station (tel. 1/252–4496). Buses to the west and south, to Austria and the former Yugoslavia, leave from the main Volán bus station at Erzsébet tér in downtown Pest (tel. 1/117–2966). Though inexpensive, these buses tend to be crowded, so reserve your seat. For the Danube Bend, buses leave from the bus terminal at **Árpád Bridge** (tel. 1/120–9229).

By Boat Hungary is well equipped with nautical transport, and Budapest is situated on a major international waterway, the Danube. Vienna is five hours away by hydrofoil or boat. For information about excursions or pleasure cruises, contact **MAHART Tours** (Belgrád rakpart, Budapest V, tel. 1/118–1704, 1/118–1586, or 1/118–1743); or the Hungarian travel bureau, **IBUSZ** (Károly körút 3/C, Budapest VII, tel. 1/121–1000 or 1/121–2932).

By Car To drive in Hungary, U.S. and Canadian visitors need an Interna-
Documentation tional driver's license, but domestic licenses are usually accepted anyway. U.K. visitors need a domestic driver's license.

| Road Conditions | There are three classes of roads: highways (designated by the letter M and a single digit); secondary roads (designated by a two-digit number); and minor roads (designated by a three-digit number). Highways and secondary roads are generally excellent; the condition of minor roads varies considerably. There are no toll charges on highways. |

Road
Conditions There are three classes of roads: highways (designated by the letter M and a single digit); secondary roads (designated by a two-digit number); and minor roads (designated by a three-digit number). Highways and secondary roads are generally excellent; the condition of minor roads varies considerably. There are no toll charges on highways.

Rules of the
Road Hungarians drive on the right and observe the usual Continental rules of the road. Unless otherwise noted, the speed limit in developed areas is 50 kph (30 mph), on main roads 90 kph (55 mph), and on highways 120 kph (75 mph). Seat belts are compulsory and drinking any amount of alcohol is strictly prohibited, with very severe penalties.

Gasoline Gas stations are not as plentiful in Hungary as in Western Europe, so fill up whenever possible and check tourist maps for the exact location of stations throughout the country. A gallon of *benzin* (gasoline) costs about $3.50. Unleaded gasoline, only slightly more expensive, is now available at most stations throughout the country. Interag Shell and Afor stations at busy traffic centers stay open all night; elsewhere, from 6 AM to 8 PM.

Breakdowns The **Hungarian Automobile Club** runs a 24-hour "Yellow Angels" breakdown service from Budapest XIV (Fráncia út 38/A, tel. 1/252–8000). There are repair stations in all major towns, with emergency telephones on the main highways.

By Bicycle A land of rolling hills and flat plains, Hungary is ideally suited to bicycling. The larger train stations around Lake Balaton have bicycles for rent at about 200 Ft. a day. For information about renting bicycles in Budapest, contact **Tourinform** (V, Šutő utca 2, tel. 1/117–9800). **IBUSZ Riding and Hobbies** department provides full service for a variety of guided bicycle tours (Ferenciek tere 10, tel. 1/118–2967).

Telephones

The Hungarian postal service is continuing to install refreshingly modern card-operated telephones all around Hungary. The cards, good for either 50 (250 Ft.) or 120 (600 Ft.) calls in Budapest (fewer when calling outside the city or abroad), save you from having to feed coins continually in the slot while you're making your call. If you plan to use pay phones fairly often, it's a good idea to purchase a telephone card to avoid the hassle of tracking down the increasingly outnumbered coin-operated phones. Cards are sold in post offices, by street vendors, at most newsstands and kiosks, and in IBUSZ offices. The card-operated telephone booth is gray and the receivers are blue.

Local Calls Coin-operated pay phones use 5-Ft. coins—the cost of a three-minute local call—and also accept 10- and 20-Ft. coins. At press time (spring 1994), pay phones had still not been converted to accept the new Hungarian coins. Most towns in Hungary can be called directly; dial 06, wait for the buzzing tone, then dial the local number.

International Calls Direct calls to foreign countries can be made from Budapest and all major provincial towns by dialing 00 and waiting for the international dialing tone; on pay phones, the initial charge is 20 Ft.

To place international collect or credit-card calls from Hungary using AT&T, dial 00–360–111; using MCI, 00–800–01411.

Operators International calls can be made through the operator by dialing 09; for operator-assisted calls within Hungary, dial 01. Dial 1/117–0170 for directory assistance; some operators speak English and, depending on their mood, may assist you in English. Be patient: The entire telephone system is slowly being updated.

Mail

Postal Rates An airmail postcard to the United States, the United Kingdom, and the rest of Western Europe costs 41 Ft.; postage for an airmail letter starts at 56 Ft. Postcards to the United Kingdom and the rest of Western Europe cost 35 Ft.; letters, from 50 Ft. Stamps can be bought at post offices.

In Budapest, the post offices at the Keleti (East) and Nyugati (West) train stations are open 24 hours.

Receiving A *poste restante* service is available in Budapest. The address is
Mail Magyar Posta, H-1052 Budapest, Petőfi Sándor utca 17–19.

Tipping

Four decades of socialism have not restrained the extended palm in Hungary—so when in doubt, tip. Coatroom and gas-pump attendants, hairdressers, waiters, and taxi drivers all expect tips. Although hotel bills include a service charge, you should also tip the elevator operator, chambermaid, and head porter; together, they should get 10% of the bill. At least an extra 10% should be added to a restaurant bill or taxi fare. If a Gypsy band plays exclusively for your table, you can leave 100 Ft. in a plate discreetly provided for that purpose.

Opening and Closing Times

Banks are generally open weekdays 8–1; many only until noon on Friday. **Museums** are generally open Tuesday through Sunday 10–6. Most department stores and gift shops are open weekdays 10–5 or 6, Saturday until 1. Grocery stores are generally open weekdays from 7 or 8 AM to 7 PM; "nonstops," or *éjjeli-nappali*, are open 24 hours.

National Holidays

January 1; March 15 (Anniversary of 1848 revolution); April 16 and 17 (Easter and Easter Monday); June 4 and 5 (Pentecost and Pentecost Monday); May 1 (Labor Day); August 20 (St. Stephen's and Constitution Day); October 23 (1956 Revolution Day); December 24–26.

Shopping

Among the most sought-after items in Hungary are peasant embroideries and the exquisite Herend and Zsolnay porcelain. Unfortunately, the prices on all makes of porcelain have risen considerably in the last few years. Hand-painted pottery and handmade lace are also attractive, as is the excellent cut glass. Dolls dressed in national costume are popular, and phonograph records are of good quality and inexpensive.

Sports and Outdoor Activities

Golf There is an 18-hole golf course in the small village of **Kisoroszi,** about 35 kilometers (22 miles) from Budapest. The clubhouse has a lounge, restaurant, and sports store, and equipment can be rented. You can make reservations through your hotel or through the **Hungarian Professional Golf Association** (tel. 1/117–6025 or 06/60–321–673).

Horseback Riding Traditionally a nation of horsemen, Hungary has more than 100 riding schools and stables. They range from small holdings with two or three horses to large establishments with 50 to 60 horses and comfortable guest houses. Among the many options available are one-day outings, 10-day tours covering up to 250 kilometers (155 miles), and even courses in carriage driving. Hungary is especially well suited to cross-country riders who have already acquired the basic skills. IBUSZ offices abroad will supply information and make reservations. In Budapest, Tourinform and IBUSZ's Riding and Hobbies recreational department (tel. 1/118–2967) can answer any queries.

Water Sports Lake Balaton and the Danube are the main centers. Yachts, rowboats, and sailboards can be rented at lake resorts, and sailing courses are organized for beginners. Sailing holidays on Lake Balaton can be arranged through **IBUSZ** (Budapest V, Petöfi tér 3, tel. 1/118–5707), **SIOTOUR** (Budapest VII, Klauzál tér 2–3, tel. 1/122–6080), and **Balatontourist** (Budapest VIII, Ulloi út 52/A, tel. 1/133–6982).

Budapest is dotted with swimming pools, many of which are attached to medicinal baths and mineral springs. Of the many pools in the country, the largest and finest is the Palatinus Lido on Margaret Island.

Dining

Throughout the lean postwar years, the Hungarian kitchen lost none of its spice and sparkle, particularly in restaurants favored by foreigners—for whom everything was and still is available. Consider sampling traditional dishes—goulash, paprika, cabbage, and pastries—at the breakfast buffets of the posh hotels, where leftovers are served up piping hot and still fresh. This will leave you free at lunch and dinner to explore Budapest's less familiar culinary treats, such as fiery fish soups; *fogas* (pike perch) from Lake Balaton; and goose liver, duck, and veal specialties. Portions are large, so don't expect to digest more than one main Hungarian meal a day. The desserts are lavish, and every inn seems to have its house *torta* (cake); though *rétes* (strudels), *Somlói galuska* (a steamed sponge cake soaked in chocolate sauce and whipped cream), and Gundel pancakes are ubiquitous. Unless you're taking a cure in a spa, don't expect to lose weight in Hungary.

Ratings	Category	Cost*
	$$$$	over $20
	$$$	$14–$20
	$$	$8–$14
	$	under $8

per person, for a three-course meal, excluding alcohol and tip

Wine **Tokay,** the best-known and most abundant white wine, can be too heavy, dark, and sweet for many tastes, even Hungarians (which is why red wine is often recommended with poultry, veal, and even fish dishes). However, **Tokaji Aszú,** the best of the breed, makes a good dessert wine. **Badacsony** white wines are lighter and livelier, though not particularly dry.

The gourmet, red table wine of Hungary, **Egri Bikavér** (Bull's Blood of Eger, usually with *el toro* himself on the label), is the best buy and the safest bet with all foods. Other good reds and the best rosés come from **Villanyi**; the most adventurous reds—with sometimes successful links to both Austrian and Californian wine making and grape growing—are from the **Sopron** area.

Before- and after-dinner drinks tend toward schnapps, most notably **Barack-pálinka,** an apricot brandy. A plum brandy called **Kosher szilva-pálinka,** bottled under rabbinical supervision, is very chic. Hard to find but worth the effort is **Blauer Engel** (the label that honors Marlene Dietrich), which looks like Windex but tastes like fairly dry champagne. **Unicum,** Hungary's national liqueur, is a dark, thick, vaguely minty, and quite potent drink that could be likened to Germany's Jägermeister. Its unique chubby green bottle makes it a good souvenir to take home.

Beer and Ale Major Hungarian beers are Köbányai, Dreher, Aranyhordó, Balaton, Világos, and Aszok. Czech, German, and Austrian beers are widely available on tap.

Lodging

Budapest is modestly equipped with hotels and hostels, but the increase in tourism since 1989 has put a strain on the city's often crowded lodgings. Advance reservations are strongly advised, especially at the lower-price hotels. Some hotels have large numbers of rooms reserved through booking agencies such as IBUSZ, but you can save yourself the commission if you book a room directly. If a hotel receptionist tells you no rooms are available, that means the rooms the hotel books itself are all occupied. Solo travelers are especially encouraged to make reservations to avoid an exhausting runaround; many hotels do not have single rooms, and the few that do should be reserved in advance.

In winter it's not difficult to find a hotel room, even at the last minute, and prices are usually reduced by 20%–30%. By far the cheapest and most accessible beds in the city are rooms (around 1,500 Ft. per person) in private homes. Although most tourist offices book private rooms, the supply is limited, so try to arrive in Budapest early in the morning.

There are no very expensive and few expensive hotels outside Budapest. The moderate hotels are generally comfortable and well run, although single rooms with bath are scarce. Establishments in the inexpensive category seldom have private baths, but plumbing is adequate almost everywhere. Reservations should be made well in advance, especially at the less expensive establishments, which are still in short supply.

Many of Hungary's old castles and mansions are being converted into hotels—some full-scale, others with just a few rooms for rent. Contact the IBUSZ Riding and Hobbies recreational department in Budapest (tel. 1/118–2967) for full details.

Rentals Apartments in Budapest and cottages at Lake Balaton can sometimes be rented on a short-term basis. A one-room Budapest apartment might cost 25,000 Ft. a week, while a luxury cottage for two on the Balaton costs about 35,000 Ft. a week. Rates and reservations can be obtained from IBUSZ offices in the United States and Great

Britain; in Budapest at the **IBUSZ** on Petőfi tér 3 (tel. 1/118–5707), which is open 24 hours a day; and at **Cooptourist** (tel. 1/175–2846, 1/175–2937, or 1/186–8240).

Guest Houses Also called pensions, these offer simple accommodations and rooms with four beds. They are well suited to younger people on a budget, and there are separate bathrooms for men and women on each floor. Some offer simple breakfast facilities. Arrangements can be made through local tourist offices or travel agents abroad.

In the provinces it is safe to accept rooms that you are offered directly, though reservations can also be made through any tourist office. *Szoba kiadó* (or the German *Zimmer frei*) means "room to rent." The rate per night for a double room in Budapest or at Lake Balaton is about 1,500 Ft., which includes the use of a bathroom but not breakfast.

Camping Most of the 140 campsites in Hungary are open from May through September. Since rates are no longer state-regulated, prices vary. An average rate is about 600 Ft. a day, usually with a small charge for hot water and electricity plus an accommodations fee of about 100 Ft. per person per night. Children frequently get a 50% reduction. Camping is forbidden except in appointed areas. Information and reservations can be obtained from travel agencies or through the **Hungarian Camping and Caravanning Club** (Budapest VIII, Üllői ú 6, tel. 1/133–6536), which publishes an informative brochure in English listing campsites and their facilities.).

Ratings

Category	Budapest*	Balaton*	Provinces*
$$$$	over $200	over $100	over $75
$$$	$130–$200	$80–$100	$55–$75
$$	$60–$130	$40–$80	$30–$55
$	under $60	under $40	under $30

All prices are for a standard double room with bath and breakfast during peak season.

For single rooms with bath, count on about 80% of the double-room rate. During the peak season (June through August), full board may be compulsory at the Lake Balaton hotels. During the off-season (in Budapest, September through March; at Lake Balaton, May and September), rates can be considerably lower than those given above. Note that most large hotels require payment in hard currency.

Budapest

Budapest, situated on both banks of the Danube, unites the colorful hills of Buda and the wide, businesslike boulevards of Pest. Though it was the site of a Roman outpost during the 1st century, the city was not actually created until 1873, when the towns of Óbuda, Pest, and Buda were joined. Since then, Budapest has been the cultural, political, intellectual, and commercial heart of Hungary; for the 20% of the nation's population who live in the capital, anywhere else is simply "the country."

Budapest has suffered many ravages in the course of its long history. It was totally destroyed by the Mongols in 1241, captured by the Turks in 1541, and nearly destroyed again by Soviet troops in 1945. But this bustling industrial and cultural center survived as the capital of the People's Republic of Hungary after the war—and then, as the 1980s drew to a close, it became one of the Eastern bloc's few thriving bastions of capitalism. Today, judging by the city's flourishing cafés and restaurants, markets and bars, the stagnation wrought by the Communists seems a thing of the very distant past.

Much of the charm of a visit to Budapest lies in unexpected glimpses into shadowy courtyards and in long vistas down sunlit cobbled streets. Although some 30,000 buildings were destroyed during World War II and in 1956, the past lingers on in the often crumbling architectural details of the antique structures that remain and in the memories and lifestyles of Budapest's citizens.

The principal sights of the city fall roughly into three areas, each of which can be comfortably covered on foot. The Budapest hills are best explored by public transportation. Note that street names have been changed during the past few years to purge all reminders of the communist regime. Underneath the new names, the old ones remain, canceled out by a big red slash. The overhaul was scheduled to be completed by now, but city governments have been known to miss deadlines before. If the street you're looking for seems to have disappeared, ask any local—though he or she may well be as bewildered as you are. Also note that a Roman-numeral prefix listed before an address refers to one of Budapest's 22 districts.

Important Addresses and Numbers

Tourist Information

Tourinform, the Hungarian National Tourist Information bureau (V, Sütő utca 2, tel. 1/117–9800), is open daily 8–8 and staffed by the most helpful multilingual people in Hungary. They can give you good advice and maps; book lodgings, sightseeing tours, or out-of-town trips; sell you theater tickets and guidebooks; or just listen to your problems and help you cope.

IBUSZ Hotel Service (V, Petőfi tér 3, tel. 1/118–5707) is open 24 hours. This office, and the many other IBUSZ offices scattered throughout the city, provides tourist information of all types. So, too, do the following private agencies: **American Express Travel Related Services** (V, Deák Ferenc utca 10, tel. 1/267–2024, 1/267–2022, or 1/266–8680, fax 1/267–2029); **Budapest Tourist** (V, Roosevelt tér 5, tel. 1/117–3555); and **Taverna Tourist Service** (V, Váci utca 20, tel. 1/118–1818).

Embassies

U.S. Embassy (V, Szabadság tér 12, tel. 1/112–6450, fax 1/132–8934). **U.K. Embassy** (V, Harmincad utca 6, tel. 1/266–2888, fax 1/266–0907). **Canadian Embassy** (XII, Budakeszi út 32, tel. 1/176–7711, fax 1/176–7689). **Australian Embassy** (VI, Délibáb utca 30, tel. 1/153–4233 or 1/153–4577).

Emergencies

Police (tel. 07).

Medical

Ambulance (tel. 04 or 1/112–3624); **S.O.S.** (VIII, Kerepesi út 15, tel. 1/118–8212 or 1/118–8288) is a 24-hour private ambulance service with English-speaking personnel. If you need a **doctor,** ask your hotel or embassy to recommend one or visit the **I.M.S.** (International Medical Services) clinic (XIII, Váci út 202, tel. 1/129–8423), a private clinic staffed by English-speaking doctors offering 24-hour emergency service. U.S. and Canadian visitors are advised to take out full medical insurance. U.K. visitors are covered for emergencies and essential treatment.

Belgyógyászati Klinika (General Clinic; VII, Korányi Sándor utca 2/a, tel. 1/133–0366) offers 24-hour medical service.

Dental **Stomatológiai Intézet** (Central Dental Institutes; VIII, Szentkirályi utca 40, tel. 1/133–0970) offers 24-hour dental service. Private English-speaking dental practices include those of **Dr. Pál Gerlóczy** (XII, Zugligeti út 60, tel. 1/176–3411 or 1/176–3049) and **Dr. Tibor Keptenger** (VII, Király utca 14, tel. 1/133–1716 or 1/114–1220). The latter's office is open 24 hours a day. Both dentists accept major credit cards.

Where to Change Money Every major hotel will change hard currency into Hungarian forints. You can also exchange money at all banks (most are open 9 AM–1 PM), nearly all travel agencies (including IBUSZ travel agency offices), and at official exchange offices at border entrances. In general, you will be able to find licensed exchange offices wherever there is heavy tourist traffic, but rates and commission charges do vary; your best bet is to change at a bank. For after-hours exchanging, the IBUSZ office at Petőfi tér 3 (tel. 1/118–5707) is always open and offers exchange services 24 hours a day. Also, the K&H Bank has several automatic teller machines, most of them downtown, at which you can exchange limited amounts of money 24 hours a day. Locations are at V, Sass utca 3; V, Kossuth tér 18; V, Károly körút 20; V, Andrássy út 49 (at Oktogon); II, Margit körút 43–45; and XIV, Örs Vezér tere 2.

English-Language Bookstores **Bestsellers** (V, Október 6 utca 11, tel. 1/112–1295) sells English-language books exclusively, packing thousands of volumes into its small store (open Mon.–Sat. 9–6). Other stores with selections of books in English include: **Libri International Bookshop** (V, Váci utca 32, tel. 1/118–2718); **Longman ELT** (VIII, Kölcsey utca 2, tel. 1/210–0170); **Atlantisz Book Island** (V, Piarista köz 1, no tel.); and **Interbright** (XII, Tartsay Vilmos út 11–13, tel. 1/156–5611).

English-Language Periodicals Several English-language weekly newspapers have sprouted up to placate Budapest's large expatriate community. *The Budapest Sun*, *Budapest Week*, the *Daily News*, and the *Budapest Business Journal* are sold at major newsstands, hotels, and tourist points.

English-Language Radio **Radio Bridge** on 102.1 FM broadcasts Voice of America news every hour on the hour. A colorful and informative program called "Budapest Day and Night," which features news, cultural programming, and taped National Public Radio (NPR) segments, also plays at 8 AM and 8 PM Monday through Friday.

Late-Night Pharmacies The state-run pharmacies close between 6 and 8 PM, but several pharmacies stay open at night and on the weekend, offering 24-hour service with a small surcharge for items that aren't officially stamped as urgent by a physician. Try the one at Teréz körút 41 in the sixth district, near the Nyugati train station; or the one at Rákóczi út 86 in the seventh district, near the Keleti train station. Other pharmacies take turns staying open late; addresses of the nearest ones that are open are usually posted in pharmacy doorways.

Lost and Found For items lost on the public transportation system, contact **BKV Talált Tárgyak Osztálya** (VII, Akácfa utca 18, tel. 1/122–6613), open weekdays 7:30–3 (Wed. until 7 PM; Fri. until 2 PM). For items lost on a Danube ship contact **MAHART** (V, Belgrád rakpart, tel. 1/118–1704); for items lost on a train, **Keleti Pályaudvar** (tel. 1/113–6835).

Arriving and Departing by Plane

Airport **Ferihegy Airport** (tel. 1/157–9123), Hungary's only commercial airport, is about 22 kilometers (14 miles) southeast of Budapest. All **Malév** flights (except Paris flights) operate from the new Terminal 2; other airlines use Terminal 1. For same-day flight information, call 1/157–7155.

Between the Airport and City Center	Many hotels offer their guests car or minibus transportation to and from Ferihegy, but all of them charge for the service. You should arrange for a pickup in advance.
By Taxi	Allow 40 minutes during nonpeak hours and at least an hour during rush hours (7 AM–9 AM from the airport, 4 PM–6 PM from the city). A taxi ride to the center of Budapest should cost no more than 1,000 Ft. with tip. Avoid taxi drivers who offer their services before you are out of the arrivals lounge.
By Bus	**LRI Airport Centrum** vans run every half hour from 6 AM to 10 PM to and from the Erzsébet tér bus station in downtown Budapest. It takes almost the same time as taxis but costs only 200 Ft. from either airport terminal.

LRI's **Airport Minibus Service** provides convenient door-to-door service between the airport and any address in the city. To get to the airport, call to arrange a pickup (tel. 1/157–8555 or 1/157–6283); to get to the city, make arrangements at LRI's airport desk. Service to or from either terminal costs 600 Ft. per person.

Arriving and Departing by Car, Train, Boat, and Bus

By Car	The main routes into Budapest are the M1 from Vienna (via Győr) and the M7 from Lake Balaton.
By Train	There are three main *pályaudvar* (train stations) in Budapest: **Keleti** (East), **Nyugati** (West), and **Déli** (South). Trains from Vienna usually operate from the Keleti station, while those to Balaton depart from the Déli.

The fastest train from Vienna is the *Lehár*, an early-morning EuroCity express (with a small surcharge that includes a seat reservation) that makes the 272-kilometer (170-mile) run in just under three hours. Later EuroCity expresses, the afternoon *Bartók* (coming from Munich) and the *Liszt* (coming from Frankfurt and German points north), take an hour longer. The cost is about 540 AS (first class), 430 AS (second class). Trains passing through Vienna to Budapest include the *Orient Express* (the slightly creaky original, not the luxurious charter special) from Paris and Stuttgart; and the *Wiener Walzer* from Basel and Zurich. Both have comfortable sleepers on their overnight runs. For information in Budapest, call 1/122–4052.

By Boat	From May to mid-September, two swift hydrofoils leave Vienna daily at 8 AM and 2:30 PM (once-a-day trips are scheduled in Apr., May, and mid-Sept.–mid-Oct.). After a 4- to 4½-hour journey downriver, with views of the Slovak capital, Bratislava, and of Hungary's largest church, the cathedral in Esztergom, the boats make a grand entrance into Budapest via its main artery, the Danube. The upriver journey takes an hour longer. For reservations and information in Budapest, call 1/118–1704. The cost is 750 AS ($62) one-way.
By Bus	Most buses to Budapest from the western region of Hungary, including those from Vienna, arrive at the Erzsebét tér station. Between April and October, four deluxe buses depart daily from Budapest at 7 AM, 9 AM, noon, and 5 PM; from Vienna, buses depart at 7 AM, 3 PM, 5 PM, and 7 PM. October through March, there is no 9 AM bus from Budapest and no 3 PM bus from Vienna. The journey takes just under four hours. For reservations and information in Vienna, call 43–1/50180; in Budapest, tel. 1/117–7777. The cost is 290 AS ($24) one-

way, 420 AS ($35) round-trip. For further bus information, call
Volánbusz (tel. 1/117–2318).

Getting Around

By Car   Budapest, like any Western city, is plagued by traffic jams during
the day, but motorists should have no problem later in the evening.
Parking, however, is a problem—prepare to learn new parking techniques such as curb balancing and sidewalk straddling.

By Public   Yellow tickets (30 Ft.) for the metro, tram, bus, and HÉV suburban
Transportation   railway can be bought at hotels, metro stations, newstands, and kiosks—they cannot be bought on board; they are canceled in the
time-clock machines on board or in station entrances. At press-time,
the Budapest transportation authority was threatening to raise the
cost of a single ticket by 5 forints. Tickets are valid for only one ride,
of any distance, and should be kept until the end of the journey, as
there are frequent checks by undercover inspectors; fines for traveling without a validated ticket are about 400 Ft. There is also a one-
day ticket (*Napijegy*) good for unlimited travel on all transportation
services within the city limits.

Metro   Service on Budapest's subways is cheap, fast, frequent, and comfortable; stations are easily located on maps and streets by the big
letter M (for metro) in a circle. Line 1 (yellow, marked Földalatti),
which starts downtown at Vörösmarty tér and follows Andrássy út
out past Gundel restaurant and the city park, is an antique tourist
attraction in itself, built in the 1890s for the Magyar Millennium; its
yellow trains with tank treads still work. Lines 2 and 3 were built 90
years later. Line 2 (red) runs from the eastern suburbs, past the
Keleti (East) station, through the Inner City area, and under the
Danube to the Déli (South) station. One of the stations, Moszkva tér,
is where the *Várbusz* (Castle Bus) can be boarded. Line 3 (blue) runs
from the southern suburbs to Deák tér, through the Inner City, and
northward to the Nyugati (West) station and the northern suburbs.
On lines 2 and 3, the yellow fare tickets are canceled in machines at
the station entrance; on line 1, tickets are canceled in the punch machines on the subway cars. All three metro lines meet at the Deák
tér station and run from 4:30 AM to 11 PM.

Streetcar   Streetcars and buses are abundant and convenient. Buses run from
and Bus   4:30 AM and trams from 5 AM. Most lines stop operating at 11 PM, but
there is all-night service on certain key lines. Consult the separate
night bus map posted in most metro stations for all-night routes.

By Taxi   Taxis are plentiful and a good value, but make sure they have a
working meter. Cabs can be hailed on the street or, more reliably,
ordered by phone. The standard initial charge is 30 Ft., with 40 Ft.
per kilometer (half-mile) and 12 Ft. for each minute of waiting time.
Some drivers try to charge outrageous prices, especially if they
sense that their passenger is a tourist. Your best bet is to avoid unmarked, "freelance" taxis and to stick with those affiliated with an
established company. The best rates are with **Fötaxi** (tel. 1/222–
2222), **6 X 6** (tel. 1/266–6666), **Citytaxi** (tel. 1/153–3633 or 1/211–
1111), **Volántaxi** (tel. 1/166–6666), and **Teletaxi** (tel. 1/155–5555).

By Boat   During summer a regular boat service links the north and south of
the city, stopping at points on both banks, including Margitsziget
(Margaret Island). From May to September boats leave from the
dock at Vigadó tér on 2-hour cruises between the Árpád and Petőfi
bridges. The trip, organized by **MAHART** (tel. 1/118–1704), runs
twice a day (at noon and 7 PM) and costs about 300 Ft.

Guided Tours

Orientation Three-hour bus tours of the city operate year-round and cost roughly 2,000 Ft. They take in parts of both Buda and Pest and are a good
introduction to further exploration on foot. Contact IBUSZ (*see* Important Addresses and Numbers, *above*) or **Gray Line Cityrama** (V,
Báthori utca 22, tel. 1/132–5344).

Special- IBUSZ, Cityrama, and Budapest Tourist organize a number of un-
Interest usual tours, featuring trips to the Buda Hills, goulash parties, and
Tours visits to such traditional sites as the National Gallery and Parlia-
ment. These companies will provide personal guides on request.
Also check at your hotel.

Boat Tours IBUSZ offers a one-hour tour on the Danube called "Budapest—The
Pearl of the Danube" that includes a stop at Margaret Island. While
on the island you can stroll under centuries-old chestnut trees or
purchase coffee and soft drinks on the terrace of Hotel Thermal.
*Buy tickets at the IBUSZ office at Petőfi tér 3, tel. 1/118–5707. De-
partures from the dock at Vigadó tér May–Sept., Thurs.–Sat. at 3
PM. Cost: 1,700 Ft.*

Gray Line Cityrama's "Budapest Potpourri" boat tour provides a
three-hour cruise through the city's grand sights, including a stop to
look inside the Parliament or the Opera House. *Tours meet at the Forum Hotel May–Sept., Tues.–Sun. at 2:30 PM. Cost: 2,200 Ft.*

Jewish-Heritage Between April and October, **Chosen Tours** (Károly krt. 3/c, tel. and
Tours fax 1/166–5165 or 1/165–9499) offers individual and group walks
through Budapest's historic Jewish quarter. Other tours cover Jewish heritage sights in both Buda and Pest. Most of the two- to three-
hour excursions are conducted in English and cost 1,000 Ft.–1,450
Ft. per person.

Personal The major travel agencies—**IBUSZ** and **Budapest Tourist**—will ar-
Guides range for guides. The weekly English-language newspapers, *The
Budapest Sun* and *Budapest Week,* sometimes carry advertisements
for guides.

Highlights for First-Time Visitors

Gellért Hill (*see* Tour 2)
Great Synagogue (*see* Tour 4)
Hungarian National Museum (*see* Tour 4)
Matthias Church (*see* Tour 1)
Museum of Fine Arts (*see* Tour 5)
Parliament (*see* Tour 4)
Royal Palace (*see* Tour 1)
Széchenyi Lánchíd (*see* Tour 1)
Szent István Bazilika (*see* Tour 4)
Váci utca (*see* Tour 4)

Tour 1: Castle Hill

*Numbers in the margin correspond to points of interest on the Tour
1: Castle Hill (Várhegy) map.*

Most of the major sights of Buda are on **Várhegy** (Castle Hill), a long,
narrow plateau banned to private cars (except for those of neighborhood residents and Hilton Hotel guests). If you're already on the
Buda side of the river you can take the Castle bus—*Várbusz*—from
the Moszkva tér Metro Station northwest of Castle Hill. If you're

starting out from Pest you can take a taxi or Bus 16 from Erzsébet tér.

Another, very scenic alternative if you're approaching from Pest is to cross the **Széchenyi Lánchíd** (Chain Bridge), the oldest of the Danube's eight bridges, on foot. Before the lánchíd was built, the river could be crossed only by ferry or by a pontoon bridge that had to be removed when ice blocks began floating downstream in winter. It was constructed at the initiative of the great Hungarian reformer and philanthropist Count István Széchenyi using an 1839 design by the French civil engineer William Tierney Clark, who had also designed London's Hammersmith Bridge. This classical, almost poetically graceful and symmetrical suspension bridge was finished by his Scottish namesake, Adam Clark, who also built the 383-yard tunnel under Castle Hill, thus connecting the Danube quay with the rest of Buda. After it was destroyed by the Nazis, the bridge was rebuilt in its original form (though slightly widened for traffic) and was reopened in 1949, on the centenary of its inauguration. At the Buda end of the bridge, you'll arrive at **Clark Ádám tér** (Adam Clark Square). From there you can ride up to Castle Hill on the sometimes crowded *Sikló* funicular rail. *Cost: 60 Ft. adults, 40 Ft. children. Runs daily 7:30 AM–10 PM.*

Either way, taxi, Sikló, and Várbusz will all deliver you to **Szent György tér** (St. George Square); Bus 16 will leave you at Dísz tér, one block to the north.

During a seven-week siege at the end of 1944, the entire Castle Hill district of palaces, mansions, and churches was turned into one vast ruin. The final German stand was in the **Királyi Palota** (Royal Palace), which was entirely gutted by fire; by the end of the siege its walls were reduced to rubble, and just a few scarred pillars and blackened statues protruded from the wreckage. The destruction was incalculable, yet it gave archaeologists and art historians an opportunity to discover the medieval buildings that once stood on the site of this Baroque and neo-Baroque palace. Fortunately, details of the edifices of the kings of the Árpád and Anjou dynasties, of the Holy Roman Emperor Sigismund, and of the great 15th-century king Mátthiás Corvinus had been preserved in some 80 medieval reports, travelogues, books, and itineraries that were subsequently used to reconstruct the complex.

The postwar rebuilding was slow and painstaking. In some places debris more than 20 feet deep had to be removed; the remains found on the medieval levels were restored to their original planes. Freed from mounds of rubble, the foundation walls and medieval castle walls were completed; and the ramparts surrounding the medieval royal residence were re-created as close to their original shape and size as possible. Out of this herculean labor emerged the Royal Palace of today, a vast museum complex and cultural center.

In front of the palace, facing the Danube by the entrance to Wing C, stands an equestrian **statue of Prince Eugene of Savoy,** a commander of the army that liberated Hungary from the Turks at the end of the 17th century. The hero's image has been prettified in bronze, for Eugene was a singularly ugly and unappreciated French nobleman, scorned by King Louis XIV for his ignoble appearance. The Habsburg emperor Leopold I, however, recognized the prince's military genius and enlisted him in 1683 to turn the tide of the Turkish siege of Vienna. Eugene also eventually humbled Louis XIV at the battle of Blenheim in 1704. From the terrace on which the statue stands there is a superb view across the river to Pest.

Budapesti Történeti Múzeum, **6**

Budavári Labirintus, **9**

Clark Ádám tér, **1**

Hadtörténeti Múzeum, **13**

Halászbástya, **11**

Ludwig Múzeum, **4**

Magyar Kereskedelmi és Vendéglátóipari Múzeum, **14**

Magyar Nemzeti Galéria, **5**

Mária Magdolna templom, **12**

Mátyás templom, **10**

Medieval Synagogue, **16**

Országos Levéltár, **17**

Országos Széchenyi Könyvtár, **7**

Statue of Prince Eugene of Savoy, **3**

Szent György tér, **2**

Várszínház, **8**

Zenetörténeti Múzeum, **15**

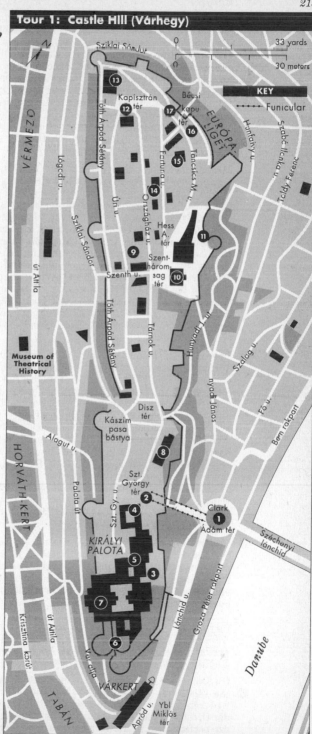

Tour 1: Castle Hill (Várhegy)

KEY

••••• Funicular

Until recently, the palace's northern wing (A) housed the Legujabbkori Történeti Múzeum (Museum of Recent History, formerly the Museum of the Hungarian Working Class Movement), but at press time plans were under way to close it by 1995 and transfer the entire collection to the National Museum's epic Hungarian history exhibit (*see* Tour 4, *below*). The **Ludwig Museum,** boasting a collection of more than 200 pieces of Hungarian and contemporary world art, including works by Picasso and Lichtenstein, has shared the northern wing with the Museum of Contemporary History since 1991 and was bidding to eventually spread into the building's vacated areas. *Buda Castle (Wing A), Dísz tér 17, tel. 1/175–7533. Open Tues.–Sun. 10–6. Admission: 80 Ft.*

The immense center block of the palace (made up of Wings B, C, and D) contains the **Magyar Nemzeti Galéria** (Hungarian National Gallery), which exhibits a wide range of Hungarian fine art, from medieval ecclesiastical paintings, stone carvings, and statues, through Gothic, Renaissance, and Baroque art, to works of the 19th and 20th centuries, which are richly represented. Especially notable are the works of the Romantic painter Mihály Munkácsy (1844–1900), the Impressionist Pál Szinyei Merse, and the neo-Surrealist Kosztka Csontváry. There is also a large collection of modern Hungarian sculpture. For an additional 25 Ft. groups of up to 25 can visit the **Crypt of the Habsburg Palatines** (the ruling royal deputies) below Wing C. *Dísz tér 17, Wings B, C, and D, tel. 1/175–7533. Admission: 40 Ft. adults; free on Sat. Tour with English-speaking guide, 800 Ft. Open mid-Mar.–mid-Nov., Tues.–Sun. 10–6, mid-Nov.–mid-Mar., Tues.–Sun. 10–4.*

The palace's Baroque southern wing (E) contains the **Budapesti Történeti Múzeum** (Budapest Historic Museum), with its permanent exhibitions "Gothic Statues of Buda's Royal Palace" and "The Medieval Royal Palace." Through historical documents, objects, and art they depict the medieval history of the Buda fortress and the capital as a whole. This is the best place to view remains of the medieval Royal Palace and other archaeological excavations. Some of the artifacts unearthed during excavations are in the vestibule in the basement; others are still situated among the remains of medieval structures. The splendidly restored **Reneszánsz Terem** (Renaissance Hall) is particularly impressive. Down in the cellars are the original vaults of the palace. *Szt. György tér 2, Buda Castle Palace, Wing E, tel. 1/175–7533. Admission: 40 Ft. adults; free on Wed. Open Jan.–Feb., Wed.–Mon. 10–4; Mar.–Oct., Wed.–Mon. 10–6, Nov.–Dec., Wed.–Mon. 10–5.*

The western wing (F) of the Royal Palace is home to the **Országos Széchenyi Könyvtár** (Széchenyi National Library), which houses more than 2 million volumes. Its archives include well-preserved medieval codices, manuscripts, and the correspondence of historic eminences. This is not a lending library, but the reading rooms are open to the public (though you must show a passport), and even the most valuable materials can be viewed on microfilm. Small, temporary exhibits on rare books and documents are usually on display. *Admission: 30 Ft. Reading rooms open Mon. 1–9, Tues.–Sat. 9–9; exhibits open Mon. 1–6, Tues.–Sat. 10–6. To arrange a tour with an English-speaking guide, call 1/175–7533, ext. 384.*

On Színház utca, a street connecting Szent György tér and Dísz tér, the **Várszínház** (Castle Theater) was once a Franciscan church but was transformed into a late-Baroque-style royal theater in 1787 under the supervision of courtier Farkas Kempelen. The first theatrical performance in Hungarian was held here in 1790. Heavily damaged during World War II, the theater was rebuilt and reopened in 1978. While the building retains its original facade, the interior was renovated with marble and concrete. It is now used as the studio theater of the National Theater, and there is usually a historical exhibition in its foyer. *Színház utca 1–3, tel. 1/175–8011.*

From Dísz tér, two interesting streets—**Tárnok utca** and **Úri utca**—funnel northward into **Hess András tér** (Hess András Square) and **Szentháromság tér** (Holy Trinity Square). Both streets and both squares are well worth exploring. Beginning near the **Batthyány Kastély** (Batthyány Palace) at Dísz tér 3, Tárnok utca's houses and usually open courtyards offer glimpses of how Hungarians have integrated contemporary life into Gothic, Renaissance, and Baroque settings; of particular interest are the houses at No. 16 (now the Arany Hordo restaurant) and, at No. 18, the 15th-century **Arany Sas Patika** (Golden Eagle Pharmacy Museum) with a naïf Madonna and child in an overhead niche. This tiny museum displays instruments, prescriptions, books, and other artifacts from 16th- and 17th-century pharmacies. *Tárnok utca 18, tel. 1/175–9772. Admission: 50 Ft.; free on Wed. Open Tues.–Sun. 10:30–5:30.*

Úri utca (one block to the west, parallel to Tárnok utca) has been less commercialized by boutiques and other shops; the longest and oldest street in the castle district, it is lined with many stately houses, all worth special attention for their delicately carved details. Both gateways of the Baroque palace at Nos. 48–50 are articulated by Gothic niches. The **Telefónia Museum** (Telephone Museum), at No. 49, is an endearing little museum entered through a peaceful, shady central courtyard shared with the local district police station. Although vintage telephone systems of museum value are still in use all over the country, both the oldest and most recent products of telecommunication—from the 1882 wooden box with hose attachment to the latest, slickest fax machines—can be observed and tested here. Opened in 1991 on the site of what was the Castle Hill district's telephone exchange from 1928 to 1985, the museum is dominated by the massive, original rotary exchange mechanism, which can be tested with help from the friendly staff of telephone enthusiasts. *Úri utca 49, tel. 1/115–4829. Admission: 30 Ft. Open Tues.–Sun. 10:30–6.*

At Úri utca 9, below a house dating to the beginning of the 18th century, is the **Budavári Labirintus** (Labyrinth of Buda Castle), used as a wine cellar and a source of water during the 16th and 17th centuries and as an air-raid shelter during World War II. Since 1984 it has housed a cave theater that presents a multimedia show, known as *Panoptikum*, that recounts early Hungarian history using marionettes and montages. Wednesday through Saturday, the Labyrinth Cafe has nightly live blues and jazz music (*see* The Arts and Nightlife, *below*). *Tel. 1/175–6858. Admission to Panoptikum show: 150 Ft. Open Tues.–Sun. 10–6.*

Szentháromság tér is named for its Baroque **Trinity Column**, erected in 1712–13 as a gesture of thanksgiving by survivors of a plague. The column stands in front of the Gothic **Mátyás templom** (Matthias Church), officially the Buda Church of Our Lady but better known by the name of the 15th-century's "Just King" of Hungary, who was married here twice. It is sometimes called the Coronation Church because the last two kings of Hungary were crowned here: the Habsburg emperor Franz Joseph in 1867 and his grandnephew Karl IV in 1916. Originally built for the city's German population during the mid-13th century, the church has endured many alterations and assaults. For almost 150 years it was the main mosque of the Turkish overlords—and the predominant impact of its festive pillars is decidedly Byzantine. Badly damaged during the recapture of Buda in 1686, it was completely rebuilt between 1873 and 1896 by Frigyes Schulek, who gave it an asymmetrical western front with one high and one low spire, and a fine rose window; the south porch is 14th-century. The paintings and sculptures are of great age and artistic value. Of particular interest in the **Szentháromság Kápolna** (Trinity Chapel) is an *encolpion*—an enameled casket, containing a miniature copy of the Gospel, to be worn on the chest; it belonged to the 12th-century king Béla III and his wife, Anne of Chatillon. Their burial crowns and a cross, scepter, and rings found in their excavated graves are also displayed here. The church's **treasury** contains Renaissance and Baroque chalices, monstrances, and vestments. High Mass is celebrated every Sunday at 10 AM with full orchestra and choir—and often with major soloists; get here early if you want a seat. During the summer there are usually organ recitals on Friday and Sunday at 8 PM. *Szentháromság tér 2, tel. 1/155–5657. Church and treasury open daily 9 AM–6 PM. Church admission free, except during concerts. Admission to treasury: 40 Ft. adults, 20 Ft. children.*

⑪ The church's wondrous porch overlooking the Danube and Pest is the neo-Romanesque **Halászbástya** (Fishermen's Bastion), a merry cluster of white stone towers and arches and columns above a modern bronze statue of St. Stephen, Hungary's first king. Medieval fishwives once peddled their wares here, but the site is now a mecca of souvenirs, crafts, and music. On a sunny summer morning you might hear a brass band in full uniform as well as a Hungarian zitherist sporting a white handlebar mustache and full folkloric garb, both competing for your ear.

Time Out Fishermen's Bastion is crowned by a round tower housing the elegant **Café-Restaurant Halászbástya,** which extends along the upper rampart. It is the perfect place from which to watch both the distant panorama and the bastion's passing parade. *Open daily noon–midnight.*

Behind Fishermen's Bastion, on **Hess András tér** (named after Hungary's first printer, who started work in 1473), are the remains of Castle Hill's oldest church, built by Dominican friars during the 13th century. Only its tower and one wall have survived, and in 1977 they were ingeniously incorporated in 1977 by Hungarian architect Béla Pintér into the remarkable **Hilton Hotel,** which successfully combines old and new forms while blending in with neighboring buildings.

Four parallel streets lead to the northern end of the Castle Hill district from the area around Szentháromság tér and Hess András tér. **Országház utca** (Parliament Street), which extends northward from the western end of Szentháromság tér, was the main thoroughfare of 18th-century Buda; it takes its name from the building at No. 28, which was the seat of Parliament from 1790 to 1807. Before it was appropriated for secular use, this building was the church and convent of the Order of St. Clare. Across the street at No. 17 is the **Régi Országház** (Old Parliament Restaurant), with its medieval wine cellar.

Both Országház utca and Úri utca end at **Kapisztrán tér,** named after St. John of Capistrano, an Italian friar, who, in 1456, recruited a crusading army to fight the Turks who were threatening Hungary. There's a statue of this honored Franciscan on the northwest corner of the square. On the south side of the square, all that remains of the

⑫ Gothic 12th-century **Mária Magdolna templom** (Church of St. Mary Magdalene) is its *torony* (tower), completed in 1496; the rest of the church was destroyed by air raids during World War II.

Across the square, at the northwestern corner, is the casern housing
⑬ the **Hadtörténeti Múzeum** (Museum of Military History). The exhibits, which include collections of uniforms and military regalia, trace the military history of Hungary from the original Magyar conquest in the 9th century, through the period of Ottoman rule, down to the middle of this century. *Tóth Árpád sétány 40, tel. 1/156–9522 or 1/ 156–9770. Admission: 20 Ft.; free on Sat. Open Mar. 1–Oct. 31, Tues.–Sat. 9–5, Sun. 10–6; Nov. 1–Feb. 28, Tues.–Sat. 10–4, Sun. 10 6.*

Fortuna utca, the smallest and most charming of the four streets, takes its name from the 18th-century Fortuna Inn that welcomed
⑭ guests at No. 4. The inn now houses the **Magyar Kereskedelmi és Vendéglátóipari Múzeum** (Hungarian Museum of Commerce and Catering). The Catering Museum, fragrant with a heavenly sweet vanilla aroma, contains an authentic pastry shop with genuine turn-of-the-century fixtures. The Commerce Museum, just across the courtyard, chronicles the history of Hungarian commerce from the late 19th century to 1947, when the new communist regime "liberated" the economy into socialism. The four-room exhibit includes everything from an antique chocolate and caramel candy vending machine to early shoe-polish advertisements. *Fortuna utca 4, tel. 1/ 175–6249. Admission: 30 Ft.; free on Fri. Open Mar. 15–Oct. 31, Tues.–Sun. 10–6; Nov. 1–Mar. 14, Tues.–Sun. 10–4.*

Táncsics Mihály utca, the last of these four streets, loops to the north off Hess András tér. It is named for a rebel writer imprisoned in the dungeons below the Baroque house (formerly the Royal Mint) at No. 9 and freed by the people on the Day of Revolution, March 15, 1848. Next door, at No. 7, where Beethoven stayed in 1800 when he
⑮ came to Buda to conduct his works, is the **Zenetörténeti Múzeum** (Museum of Music History), which displays rare manuscripts and old instruments downstairs in its permanent collection and temporary exhibits upstairs in a small, sunlit hall adorned with marble pillars. The museum also often hosts classical concerts on Monday evenings. *Táncsics Mihály utca 7, tel. 1/175–9011. Admission: 40 Ft. Open mid-Mar.–mid-Nov., Mon. 4–6 (until 9 during concerts), Wed.–Sun. 10–6; mid-Nov.–mid-Mar., Mon. 3–6 (until 9 during concerts), Wed.–Sun. 10–5.*

⑯ At Táncsics Mihály utca 26 is an excavated one-room **Medieval Synagogue** now used as a museum. On display are objects relating to the Jewish community, including religious inscriptions, frescoes, and tombstones dating to the 15th century. There are a number of Hebrew gravestones in the entranceway. *Táncsics Mihály utca 26, tel. 1/155–8764. Admission: 40 Ft. Open May–Oct., Tues.–Fri. 10–2, Sat., Sun., and holidays 10–6. Group tours can be arranged between Oct. and May.*

Fortuna utca and Táncsics Mihály utca empty onto **Bécsi kapu tér** (Vienna Gate Square), which has some fine Baroque and Rococo houses. It is dominated, however, by the enormous neo-Roman-
⑰ esque (1913–17) headquarters of the **Országos Levéltár** (Hungarian National Archives), which looks more like a cathedral, as befits a shrine to paperwork. The gate itself, opening toward Vienna—or, closer at hand, Moszkva tér—was rebuilt in 1936.

You can descend Castle Hill to Moszkva tér from here by foot or on the Várbusz, but those whose cobblestone-jostled feet haven't yet

protested can stroll back to Dísz tér on **Tóth Árpád sétány,** a romantic, tree-lined promenade along the Buda side of the hill. Beginning
at the Hadtörténeti Museum, the promenade takes you "behind the
scenes" along the back sides of the matte pastel Baroque houses you
saw on Úri utca, boasting regal, arched windows and wrought-iron
gate work. On a late-spring afternoon, the fragrance of the cherry
trees in full, vivid bloom may be enough to revive even the most
wearied feet and spirits.

Tour 2: Buda

*Numbers in the margin correspond to points of interest on the Buda-
pest (Tours 2–7) map.*

Tabán and There are many ways to descend from Castle Hill to the banks of the
Gellért Hill Danube; the easiest route leads south to the old quarter called the
Tabán (from the Turkish word for "armory"). A onetime suburb of
Buda, it was known at the end of the 17th century as Little Serbia
(*Rác*) because so many Serbian refugees settled here after fleeing
from the Turks. It later became a quaint and romantic district of
vineyards and small taverns. Though most of the small houses characteristic of this district have been demolished—mainly in the interest of easing traffic—a few picturesque buildings remain.

At Apród utca 1 is the house where Ignác Semmelweis, the great
Hungarian physician and discoverer of the cause of puerperal (child-
bed) fever, was born in 1818. His splendid Baroque house is now the
⑱ **Semmelweis Orvostörténeti Múzeum** (Seemelweis Museum of Medical History); exhibits trace the history of healing and include a number of articles and documents associated with his life. Semmelweis's
grave is in the garden. (The late Hungarian prime minister József
Antal was curator of this museum for several years before his election to Parliament after the Communists surrendered power.)
*Apród utca 1–3, tel.1/175–3533. Admission: 50 Ft.; free on Wed.
Open Tues.–Sun. 10:30–5:30.*

Around the corner, at No. 1 Szarvas tér, is the Louis XVI–style
Szarvas-ház (Stag House), named for the former Szarvas café, or,
more accurately, for its extant trade sign with an emblem of a stag
not quite at bay, which can be seen above the triangular arched en-
tryway. Today the structure houses the Arany Szarvas restaurant,
which is renowned for its excellent game dishes and preserves some
of the mood of the old Tabán.

Walk a few yards down Szarvas tér toward the Erzsébethíd
(Elizabeth Bridge), named for Empress Elizabeth (of whom the
Hungarians were particularly fond), the wife of Franz Joseph and a
beautiful but unhappy anorexic who was stabbed to death in 1898 by
an anarchist while boarding a boat on Lake Geneva. Built between
1897 and 1903, it was the longest single-span suspension bridge in
⑲ Europe at the time. This path will take you to the **Tabán plébánia-
templom** (Tabán Parish Church), built in 1736 on the site of a Turkish mosque and subsequently renovated and reconstructed several
times. Its present form—mustard-colored stone with a rotund,
green clock tower—could be described as "restrained Baroque."

Walk down Attila utca to Hegyalja út and go under the end of the
Elizabeth Bridge to the other side of Hegyalja. You are now at the
foot of the most beautiful natural formation on the Buda bank.
Gellért-hegy (Gellért Hill), 761 feet high, takes its name from St.
Gellért (Gerard) of Csanad, a Venetian bishop who came to Hungary
during the 11th century and was supposedly flung to his death from

the top of the hill by pagans. More misery awaits you as you ascend, but take solace from the cluster of hot springs at the foot of the hill.

⑳ On the riverbank are the **Rudas Fürdő** (Rudas Baths), fed by eight springs with a year-round temperature of 44°C (111°F). The finest part of the building is its original Turkish pool (*see* Sports and Fitness, *below*). *Döbrentei tér 9, tel. 1/156–1322.*

Near the ramp coming off the Elizabeth Bridge is another public bath, the **Rác Fürdő** (Rác Baths), built during the reign of King Zsigmond in the early 15th century and rebuilt by Miklós Ybl in the mid-19th century (*see* Sports and Fitness, *below*).

At the southern end of the park, at the foot of the Gellért Hill just past the green wrought-iron **Szabadsághíd** (Liberty Bridge), are

㉑ the beautiful Art Nouveau **Gellért Hotel and Thermal Baths** (*see* Lodging, *below*). Visiting this complex at this point in the tour would involve a detour, unless you want to take public transport up the hill; if so, you can take trams and buses a couple of stops beyond the Gellért Hotel to Móricz Zsigmond körtér and there board Bus 27 to the summit. If you have a car, the most direct way up to the top of the hill is via Hegyalja út (the road off the Elizabeth Bridge); turn left at the Citadella turnoff. On foot it's an easy 30-minute climb from Hegyalja út through pleasant parkland that's perfect for picnicking and sunbathing.

㉒ The **Citadella** fortress atop the hill was a much-hated sight for Hungarians. They called it the Gellért Bastille, for it was erected on the site of an earlier wooden observatory by the Austrian army as a lookout after the 1848–49 War of Independence. But no matter what its history may be, the views from here are breathtaking. Renovation as a tourist site during the 1960s improved its image with the addition of cafés, a beer garden, wine cellars, and a tourist hostel. In its inner wall is a small graphic exhibition (with some relics) of Budapest's 2,000-year history. *Admission free. Open 24 hours.*

Visible from many parts of the city, the 130-foot-high 1947 **Szabadság Szobor** (Liberation Memorial), which starts just below the southern edge of the fort and towers above it, honors the 1944–45 siege of Budapest and the Russian soldiers who fell in the battle. It is the work of noted Hungarian sculptor Zsigmond Kisfaludi-Stróbl, and from the distance it looks light, airy, and even liberating: A sturdy young girl, her hair and robe swirling in the wind, holds a palm branch high above her head. Until recently, she was further embellished with sculptures of giants slaying dragons, Red Army soldiers, and peasants rejoicing at the freedom that Soviet liberation promised (but failed) to bring to Hungary. Yet since 1992, her mood has lightened: In the Budapest city government's systematic purging of communist symbols, the Red Combat infantrymen who had flanked the Liberation statue for decades were hacked off and carted away. The soldier who had stood the highest and the one who was shaking hands with a grateful Hungarian worker are now on display among the other evicted statues in the new Szobor Park (Statue Park) in the city's 22nd district (*see* Off the Beaten Track, *below*).

North Buda Back down at Danube level, a northbound exploration of Buda could continue with the help of Bus 86, which covers the waterfront, or on foot, though distances are fairly great.

㉓ **Fő utca** (Main Street), a long, straight thoroughfare, starts at the Chain Bridge and is lined with late-18th-century houses. The first church you will encounter, the **Capuchin Church,** was converted from a Turkish mosque at the end of the 17th century. Damaged dur-

Batthyány tér, **26**

Bem József tér, **28**

Citadella, **22**

Corvin tér, **24**

Egyetem tér, **39**

Evangélikus Múzeum, **44**

Fő utca, **23**

Franciscan church, **38**

Gellert Hotel and Thermal Baths, **21**

Hősök tere, **50**

Iparművészeti Múzeum, **55**

Kálvin tér, **40**

Kapel Szent Roch, **53**

Király-fürdő, **27**

Korzó, **34**

Köztársaság tér, **54**

Liszt Ferenc Emlékmúzeum, **49**

Liszt Ferenc Zeneakadémia, **48**

Magyar Nemzeti Múzeum, **41**

Március 15 tér, **36**

Margit-sziget, **30**

Műcsarnok, **51**

Nagy Zsinagóga, **42**

Operaház, **47**

Országház, **31**

Postamúzeum, **46**

Roosevelt tér, **33**

Rózsadomb, **29**

Rudas Fürdő, **20**

Semmelweis Orvostörténeti Múzeum, **18**

Szabadság tér, **32**

Szent István Bazilika, **45**

Szépművészeti Múzeum, **52**

Szilágyi Dezső tér, **25**

Tabán plébánia-templom, **19**

Váci utca, **37**

Városház, **43**

Vigadó tér, **35**

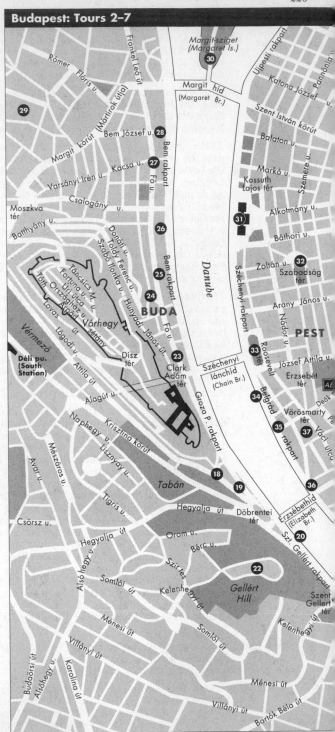

Budapest: Tours 2–7

Lehel
tér

Ferdinánd híd

Visegrádi u.

Váci út

Szinyei Merse u.

Balzac u.

Röppentyű u.

Dózsa György út

52

50

Hősök
tere

Városliget

Olof Palme sétány

51

Benczúr u.

Bajza u.

**Nyugati pu.
(West
Station)**

Nyugati
tér

Teréz körút

Podmaniczky utca

Szondi u.

Rózsa u.

Felső erdősor

Városligeti fasor

Rottenbiller utca

Damjanich u.

Dembinszky u.

Dózsa György út

Altási Dürer sor

Nagymező u.

Jókai u.

Teréz körút (Lenin körút)

Aradi u.

Andrássy út

Oktogon

49

Vörösmarty u.

48

István u.

Thököly u.

Verseny u.

Liszt Ferenc
tér

47

Lázár u.

Paulay Ede u.

Király u.

Erzsébet körút

Hársfa u.

**Keleti pu.
(East Station)**

Baross
tér

Kerepesi út

46

Deák
tér

Dob utca

Wesselényi utca

Klauzál u.

Rákóczi út

Fiumei út

Kerepesi
temető
(Cemetery)

44

i

Károly krt.

42

Dohány utca

Rákóczi út

53

József körút

Köztársaság
tér

Népszínház u.

54

43

Sándor u.

Kossuth L. u.

Puskin u.

Szentkirályi u.

Somogyi Béla u.

Bérkocsis u.

Luther u.

Teleki
László
tér

Ferenciek
tere

38

Múzeum krt.

Bródy Sándor u.

Déri Miksa u.

Mátyás
tér

Dankó u.

39

Váci utca

Veres Pálné u.

Molnár u.

41

Múzeum u.

Krúdy u.

József u.

N

Kálvin
tér

40

Üllői út

Baross utca

Baross utca

Lónyai u.

Ráday u.

Nap u.

Szigony u.

Diószeghy Sámuel u.

Szabadsághíd
(Liberty Br.)

Fővám tér

Vámház krt.

Közraktár u.

Práter u.

Tömő u.

55

Üllői út

Koranyi S. u.

Danube

Műegyetem rakpart

Mester u.

Thaly Kálmán u.

KEY

AE American Express Office

Rail Lines

i Tourist Information

Petőfihíd
(Petőfi Br.)

Borárós
tér

Márton u.

0   550 yards

0   500 meters

ing the revolution in 1849, it acquired its current Romantic-style exterior when it was rebuilt a few years later. Fő utca is punctuated by ㉔ **Corvin tér**, site of the turn-of-the-century **Folk Art Institute and** ㉕ **Buda Concert Hall** at No. 8 (tel. 1/201–5928); by **Szilágyi Dezső tér** ㉖ (Béla Bartok's house is at No. 4); and again by **Batthyány tér**, a lovely square open on its river side to afford a grand view of Parliament directly across the Danube. The M2 subway, the HÉV electric railway from Szentendre, and various suburban and local buses converge on the square. At No. 7 Batthyány tér is the beautiful Baroque twin-towered **Szent Anna-templom** (Church of St. Anne, 1740–62), its interior inspired by Italian art and its oval cupola adorned with frescoes and statuary.

Time Out The **Angelika** café (Batthyány tér 7, tel. 1/201–4847), housed in the Church of St. Anne's building, serves swirled meringues, chestnut-filled layer cakes, and a plethora of other heavenly pastries all baked on the premises from family recipes. You can sit inside on small velvet chairs at marble-topped tables or at one of the umbrella-shaded tables outdoors. It's open daily 10–10.

At Fő utca 84 is the royal gem of Turkish baths in Budapest, the ㉗ 16th-century **Király-fürdő** (King Baths), its cupola crowned by a golden moon and crescent. Diagonally across from the baths is the Greek **Szent Flórián-kapolna** (St. Florian Chapel), built in Rococo style between 1756 and 1760. It used to stand at the 18th-century elevation of old Buda but was later raised to the present street level. ㉘ Fő utca ends at **Bem József tér** (Joseph Bem Square), where you'll see a statue of the Polish general József Bem, who offered his services to the 1848 revolutionaries in Vienna and then Hungary. Reorganizing the rebel forces in Transylvania, he inflicted numerous defeats on the Habsburgs and was the war's most successful general. It was at this statue on October 23, 1956, that a great student demonstration in sympathy with Poles striving for liberal reforms exploded into the brave and tragic Hungarian uprising suppressed by the Red Army.

Just beyond Bem József tér, turn left on Fekete Sas utca, cross the busy Mártírok útja, and turn right on Mecset (Mosque) utca, a ro- ㉙ mantic little cobblestone street that climbs up **Rózsadomb** (Rose Hill) to the **Tomb of Gül Baba**, a 16th-century dervish and poet whose name means "father of roses" in Turkish. He fought in several wars waged by the Turks and fell during the siege of Buda in 1541. His tomb, built of carved stone blocks with four oval windows, remains a place of pilgrimages, for it is considered Europe's northernmost Muslim holy place and marks the spot where he was slain. Nearby is a good lookout for views of Buda and across the river to Pest. *Mecset utca 14, tel. 1/155–8764. Admission: 20 Ft. adults, 10 Ft. children. Open May–Sept., Tues.–Sun. 10–6; Oct., Tues.–Sun. 10–5. Group tours can be arranged between Nov. and May.*

Tour 3: Margaret Island

More than 2½ kilometers (1½ miles) long and covering nearly 80 ㉚ hectares (200 acres), **Margit-sziget** (Margaret Island) is ideal for strolling, jogging, sunbathing, or just delighting in the fragrances of its lawns and gardens. The island was first mentioned almost 2,000 years ago as the summer residence of the commander of the Roman garrison at nearby Aquincum. Later known as Rabbit Island (Insula Leporum), it was a royal hunting ground during the Árpád dynasty. King Imre, who reigned from 1196 to 1204, held court here, and several convents and monasteries were built during the Middle Ages. It takes its current name from St. Margaret, the pious daughter of King Béla IV, who, at the ripe age of 10, retired to a Dominican nunnery here. She died in 1271 at the age of 29.

Descending from the Árpád Bridge—the longest and widest of Budapest's eight bridges—at the northern end of the island, you will encounter a copy of the water-powered **Marosvásárhely Musical Fountain,** which plays songs and chimes. The original was designed more than 150 years ago by a Transylvanian named Péter Bodor. It stands near an artificial **rock garden** with Japanese dwarf trees and lily ponds. The stream coursing through it never freezes, for it comes from a natural hot spring whose healing properties have given rise to the Ramada Grand and Thermal hotels at this end of the island (*see* Lodging, *below*). Two spa hotels facing Margaret Island, the Aquincum on the Buda bank and the Hélia on the Pest side, have their waters piped in from springs on the island.

Through the center of the island runs the **Artists' Promenade,** lined with busts of Hungarian artists, writers, and musicians. It leads past the **Palatinus Baths** (toward the Buda side), built in 1921, which can attract tens of thousands of people on a summer day. Nearby are a tennis stadium, a youth athletic center, boathouses, sports grounds, and, most impressive of all, the **Nemzeti Sportuszoda** (National Sports Swimming Pool) designed by the architect Alfred Hájos (while still in his teens, Hájos won two gold medals in swimming at the first modern Olympic Games, held in Athens in 1896). A **rose garden** with several thousand kinds of flowers, the Casino Restaurant (dating to 1920), a fountain with illuminated waters that change color at night, and the Unification monument, honoring the merger of Buda, Pest, and Óbuda in 1873, mark the approach to the Margaret Bridge at the southern end of the island. Toward the end of 1944, the **Margithíd** (Margaret Bridge) was blown up by the retreating Nazis while it was crowded with rush-hour traffic. It was rebuilt in the same unusual shape—forming an obtuse angle in midstream, with a short leg leading down to the island. The original bridge was built during the 1840s by French engineer Ernest Gouin in collaboration with Gustave Eiffel. Bus 26 travels across the Margaret Bridge to and from Pest.

Tour 4: Downtown Pest

Start with the most visible, though not highly accessible, symbol of Budapest's left bank, the huge neo-Gothic **Országház** (House of Parliament). Mirrored in the Danube much the way Britain's Parliament is reflected by the Thames, it lies midway between the Margaret and Chain bridges and can be reached by the M2 subway (Kossuth tér station) and waterfront Tram 2. A fine example of fin-de-siècle, historicizing, eclectic architecture, it was designed by the Hungarian architect Imre Steindl and built by a thousand workers between 1885 and 1902. Both its exterior and interior reflect the taste of its time—grandiose yet delicate. The grace and dignity of its long facade and 24 slender towers, with spacious arcades and high windows balancing its vast central dome, lend this living landmark a refreshingly Baroque spatial effect. The outside is lined with 90 statues of great figures in Hungarian history; the corbels are ornamented by 242 allegorical statues. Inside are 691 rooms, 10 courtyards, and 29 staircases; some 40 kilograms (88 pounds) of gold were used for the staircases and halls. These halls are also a gallery of late-19th-century Hungarian art, with frescoes and canvases depicting Hungarian history, starting with Mihály Munkácsy's large painting of the Magyar Conquest of 896. Unfortunately, because Parliament is a workplace for legislators, the building is not open to individual visitors and must be toured in groups at certain hours on specific city tours organized by IBUSZ (tel. 1/118–5707) or Budapest Tourist (tel. 1/117–3555).

Dominated by the Parliament building, the surrounding district is the legislative, diplomatic, and administrative nexus of Budapest; most of the ministries are here, as are the National Bank and Courts of Justice. One of the buildings, an 1890s neoclassical temple opposite Parliament, formerly housed the Supreme Court and is proclaimed by such allegorical statuary as *Lawmaker and Master of Laws, Condemned and Acquitted,* and *Public Prosecutor and Defender.* It is now the **Néprajzi Múzeum** (Museum of Ethnography), whose vast, impressive permanent exhibition, "The Folk Culture of the Hungarian People," explains all aspects of peasant life from the end of the 18th century until World War I; explanatory texts are provided in both English and Hungarian. The central room of the building alone is worth the entrance fee: a majestic, cavernous hall with ornate marble staircases and pillars, and towering stained-glass windows. *Kossuth tér 12, tel. 1/112–4878 or 1/132–6340. Admission: 80 Ft. Open Tues.–Sun. 10–6. Occasional guided tours in English. Early and folk music concerts held frequently Oct.–July, Sun. 11 AM.*

③② Vecsey út, a slanting side street at the southeast corner of Kossuth tér, leads away from the Parliament building to **Szabadság tér** (Liberty Square), site of another solemn-looking neoclassical shrine, the **National Bank,** and the **Hungarian Television Headquarters,** a former stock exchange of Disneyland proportions, with what look like four temples and two castles on its roof. In the square's center remains one of the few monuments to the Russian "liberation" that was spared the recent cleansing of symbols of the past regime. The decision to retain this obelisk—because it represents liberation from the Nazis during World War II—caused outrage among many groups, prompting some to vow to haul it away themselves (though for the moment it remains). With the Stars and Stripes flying out in front, the **American Embassy** is at Szabadság tér 12.

③③ Rejoin Nádor utca, which leads south from Kossuth tér toward the heart of downtown (at Nádor utca 23, notice Franz Liszt's former apartment). At Vigyázó utca, turn right, toward the river, and enter **Roosevelt tér.** It is less closely connected with any U.S. president than with the progressive Hungarian statesman Count István Széchenyi, whom even his adversary, Kossuth, dubbed "the greatest Hungarian." The neo-Renaissance palace of the **Magyar Tudományos Akadémia** (Academy of Sciences) on your right was built between 1862 and 1864, after Széchenyi's suicide. It is a fitting memorial, for it was he who, back in 1825, donated a year's income from all his estates to establish the academy. Another Széchenyi project, the **Chain Bridge** (Széchenyi Lánchíd, *see* Tour 1), leads into the square, in which a statue of Széchenyi stands near one of another statesman, Ferenc Deák, whose negotiations led to the establishment of the dual monarchy after Kossuth's 1848–49 revolution failed. Both men lived on this square.

③④ The neighborhood to the south of Roosevelt tér has regained much of its past elegance—if not its architectural grandeur—with the erection of the Atrium Hyatt, Forum, and Budapest Marriott luxury hotels. Traversing all three and continuing well beyond them is the riverside **Korzó,** a pedestrian promenade lined with appealing outdoor cafés and restaurants from which one can enjoy postcard-perfect views of Gellért Hill and Castle Hill directly across the Danube.

Time Out Most inviting of the sidewalk respites along the Korzó is the pair of adjoining restaurants, **DuBarry** and **Ambassador**—also known as Schuk & Schuk because they are both owned by Hungarian hospitality magnate József Schuk. Desserts and a small menu of hot main dishes, half of which are already "out" by noon, change from day to day but are invariably first-rate; should you smell stuffed cabbage, search no further for your selection. Both are open Mon.–Sat. 9 AM–10 PM.

㉟ After passing Duna Corso's outdoor tables, turn left onto **Vigadó tér**, which takes its name from the **Vigadó Concert Hall** at No. 2. Designed in a striking Romantic style by Frigyes Feszl and inaugurated in 1865 with Franz Liszt conducting his own *St. Elizabeth Oratorio*, it is a curious mixture of Byzantine, Moorish, Romanesque, and Hungarian motifs, punctuated by dancing statues and sturdy pillars. Brahms, Debussy, and Casals are among the other immortals who have graced its stage. Mahler's *Symphony No. 1* and many works by Bartók were first performed here. Severely damaged in World War II, the Vigadó was rebuilt and reopened in 1980.

Continue along the Korzó past the bunkerlike former Inter-Continental Hotel, now the Budapest Marriott. Just before you reach a statue of the revolutionary poet Sándor Petőfi, find your way (usually through a side entrance) into the **Greek Orthodox Church** at Petőfi tér 2/b. Built at the end of the 18th century in late-Baroque style, it was remodeled a century later by Miklós Ybl, who designed the Opera House and many other landmarks that give today's Budapest its monumental appearance. The church retains some fine wood carvings and a dazzling array of icons by a late-18th-century Serbian master, Miklós Jankovich.

㊱ The Korzó ends at **Március 15 tér** (March 15 Square), which is bisected by the Elizabeth Bridge and flanked by two of Pest's more touristy restaurants, Mátyás Pince and Százéves. The ground is lower here, for you are walking around the remains of the **Contra Aquincum**, a 3rd-century Roman fortress and tower. Built on its walls at Március 15 tér 2 is the oldest ecclesiastical building in Pest, **Belvárosi plébánia templom** (Inner City Parish Church). It dates to the 12th century, and there is hardly any architectural style that cannot be found in some part or other, starting with a single Romanesque arch in its south tower. The single nave still has its original Gothic chancel and some 15th-century Gothic frescoes. Two side chapels contain beautifully carved Renaissance altarpieces and tabernacles of red marble from the early 16th century. During Budapest's years of Turkish occupation, the church served as a mosque—and this is remembered by a *mihrab*, a Muslim prayer niche. During the 18th century, the church was given two Baroque towers and its present façade. In 1808 it was enriched with a Rococo pulpit, and still later a superb winged triptych was added to the main altar. From 1867 to 1875, Franz Liszt lived only a few steps away from the church, in a town house where he held regular "musical Sundays" at which Richard and Cosima Wagner were frequent guests and participants. Liszt's own musical Sunday mornings often began in this church. An admirer of its acoustics and organ, he conducted many masses here, including the first Budapest performance of his Missa Choralis in 1872.

③⑦ Immediately north of Elizabeth Bridge is Budapest's best-known shopping street, **Váci utca,** a pedestrian precinct with electrified 19th-century lampposts, smart shops with chic window displays and credit-card emblems on ornate doorways. No bargain basement, Váci utca takes its special flavor from the mix of native clothiers, furriers, tailors, dress designers, shoe makers, folk artists, and others who offer alternatives to the global-boutique superstars. There are also bookstores—first- and secondhand in addition to foreign-language—and china and crystal shops, as well as gourmet food stores redolent of paprika. With rapid democratization, street commerce on Váci utca has shifted to a freer market: News vendors hawk today's Western press.

③⑧ Cross Kossuth Lajos utca at Ferenciek tere to reach the **Franciscan church** (1743). On the wall facing Kossuth Lajos utca is a bronze relief showing a scene from the devastating flood of 1838, which swept away many houses and people; the detail is so vivid that it almost makes you seasick. A faded arrow below the relief indicates the high-water mark of more almost four feet. Next to it is the **Fountain of Nereides,** a popular meeting place for students from the nearby Eötvös Loránd University that elaborates the square's nautical motif.

③⑨ Walk south on Ferenciek tere past the Franciscan church and the Eötvös Loránd University Library to **Egyetem tér** (University Square), which leads to the cool gray-and-green marble **Egyetemi Templom** (University Church), one of Hungary's best and most beautiful Baroque buildings. Built between 1725 and 1742, it boasts an especially splendid pulpit. Around the corner, on Szerb utca, is a **Serbian Orthodox Church** (1688) that is one of Budapest's oldest buildings. The lovely burnt-orange church sits in a shaded garden surrounded by thick stone walls of the same color detailed with large-tile mosaics and wrought-iron gates.

Szerb utca meets the nonpedestrian continuation of Váci utca near the Serbian church. If you follow Váci utca past the Liberty Bridge, crossing Vámház körút (Customshouse Boulevard, until recently named Tolbuhin after a World War II Soviet military commander), you will come to the waterfront's neo-Renaissance ex–Customs House. Built in 1871–74 by Miklós Ybl, it is now the **University of Economics** after a stint as Karl Marx University. In nearby Fővám tér (Customshouse Square, formerly Dimitrov) is the gigantic **Central Market Hall,** an interesting 19th-century iron-frame construction within which, even during the leanest years of communist shortages, the abundance of food came as a revelation to visitors from east and west. You may have to be content with an exterior view: The market was closed for repairs in 1994 and may not reopen for several years due to controversy as to who exactly is going to foot the bill.

④⓪ Return on Szerb utca to Egyetem tér, turning right on Kecskeméti utca and passing beneath the connecting bridge of the modern Hotel Korona; or else follow Vámház körút from the Market Hall. Either way, you will enter **Kálvin tér** (Calvin Square), which takes its name from the neoclassical **Protestant church** that tries to dominate this busy traffic hub; more glaringly noticeable, however, is the billboard of a giant pair of legs in red high-heeled pumps. On Kálvin tér once stood a main gate of Pest, the Kecskeméti Kapu, and a cattle market that was also a den of thieves. At the beginning of the 19th century, this was where Pest ended and the prairie began.

Time Out The Hotel Korona's popular café, **Korona Passage** (Kecskeméti utca
14, tel. 1/117–4111), has a *palacsinta* (crêpe) bar where you can
watch the cooks prepare giant Hungarian crêpes brimming with
such fillings as apple, chocolate, and *túró* (sweetened cottage
cheese). The café, open daily 10 to 10, serves soups and sandwiches
and has an impressive salad bar.

Pest is laid out in broad circular *körúts* (boulevards), and **Vámház
körút** is the first sector of the 2.7-kilometer (1.7-mile) **Inner Körút,**
which traces the Old Town wall from the Liberty Bridge to the
Nyugati (West) train station. Construction of the Inner Körút began
in 1872 and was completed in 1880. Changing names as it curves, after Kalvin tér it becomes Múzeum körút.

④ The **Magyar Nemzeti Múzeum** (Hungarian National Museum), built
between 1837 and 1847, is a fine example of 19th-century classi-
cism—simple, well proportioned, and surrounded by a large garden. In front of this building on March 15, 1848, Sándor Petőfi
recited his revolutionary poem, the "National Song" ("Nemzeti
dal"), and the "12 Points," a list of political demands by young Hungarians calling upon the people to rise against the Habsburgs. Celebrations of the national holiday commemorating the failed
revolution are held on these steps every year on March 15.

The museum's most sacred treasure, the **Szent Korona** (Holy
Crown), reposes with other royal relics in a domed Hall of Honor off
the main lobby. The crown sits like a golden soufflé above a Byzantine band of holy scenes in enamel and pearl and other gems. It
seems to date from the 12th century, so it could not be the crown that
Pope Sylvester II presented to St. Stephen in the year 1000, when
he was crowned the first king of Hungary. Nevertheless, it is known
as the Crown of St. Stephen and has been regarded—even by communist governments—as the legal symbol of Hungarian sovereignty and unbroken statehood for nearly a millennium. In 1945 the
fleeing Hungarian army handed over the crown and its accompanying regalia to the Americans rather than have them fall into Soviet
hands. In 1978 they were restored to Hungary.

Among the rarities in this often surprising treasure trove is an early
15th-century saddle adorned with small bone plates and showing
knights and horses and scenes of chivalry. There is also a completely
furnished Turkish tent; masterworks of cabinet making and wood
carving, including pews from churches in Nyírbátor and Transylvania; a piano that belonged to both Beethoven and Liszt; and, in the
treasury, masterpieces of goldsmithery, among them the 11th-cen-
tury Constantions Monomachos crown from Byzantium and the richly pictorial 16th-century chalice of Miklós Pálffy. Looking at it is like
reading the "Prince Valiant" comic strip in gold. The epic Hungarian
history exhibit was scheduled to be updated by 1995 with the addition of the post-1989 exhibits from the separate Museum of Contemporary History. The museum will be undergoing renovations for the
next few years and may close certain sections while they are being
worked on. *Múzeum körút 14–16, tel. 1/138–2122. Admission: 80
Ft. adults, 40 Ft. children. Open mid-Mar.–mid-Oct., Tues.–Sun.
10–6; mid-Oct.–mid-Mar., Tues.–Sun. 10–4:30.*

Continue along Múzeum körút past the major intersection where it
becomes Tanács körút. Farther along, at Dohány utca, stands the
④ **Nagy Zsinagóga** (Great Synagogue), Europe's largest, designed by
Ludwig Förs and built between 1844 and 1859 in a Byzantine-Moor-
ish style described as "consciously archaic Romantic-Eastern." Des-
ecrated by German and Hungarian Nazis, it is being reconstructed

with donations from all over the world, with particular help from the Emanuel Foundation, named for actor Tony Curtis's father, the late Emanuel Schwartz, who emigrated from Budapest to the Bronx. In the courtyard behind the synagogue, a weeping willow made of metal honors the victims of the Holocaust. Liszt and Saint-Saens are among the great musicians who have played its grand organ. *Dohány utca 2–8, tel. 1/142–1350. Admission free. Open Wed.–Fri. and Sun. 10–1, Mon. and Thurs. 2–6.*

Around the corner is the four-room **Zsidá Múzeum** (National Jewish Museum), with displays explaining the effect of the Holocaust on Hungarian and Transylvanian Jews. In late 1993, burglars ransacked the museum and got away with approximately 80% of its priceless collection. At press time (spring 1994), the museum was planning to reopen to display items that had been kept in storage and some that had been donated after the robbery. *Dohány utca 2, tel. 1/142–8949. Donation: 20 Ft. adults, 10 Ft. children. Open May–Oct., Tues.–Fri. and Sun. 10–1; Mon. and Thurs. 2–6.*

Karoly körút (Charles Boulevard) was called Tanács körút (Council Boulevard) until 1990 because of the monumental former City Council building, which used to be a hospital for wounded soldiers and then a resort for the elderly ("home" would be too cozy for so vast a hulk). It is now **Városház** (City Hall), overlooking the boulevard but entered through courtyards or side streets (Gerlóczy utca is the most accessible). Its 57-window facade, interrupted by five projections, fronts on Városház utca, which parallels the körút. The Tuscan columns at the main entrance and the allegorical statuary of Atlas, War, and Peace, are especially splendid. There was once a chapel in the center of the main facade, but now only its spire remains.

43

At **Deák tér,** where all three subway lines converge, is the neoclassical **Lutheran church.** The church's interior designer, János Krausz, flouted traditional church architecture of the time by placing a single large interior beneath the huge vaulted roof structure. The adjoining school, which the revolutionary poet Petőfi attended in 1833–34, is now the **Evangélikus Múzeum** (Lutheran Museum), which traces the role of Protestantism in Hungarian history and contains Martin Luther's original will. *Deák Ferenc tér 4, tel. 1/117–4173. Admission: 30 Ft. adults, 10 Ft. children. Open Tues.–Sun. 10–6.*

44

Funneling briefly off Deák tér toward Váci utca is Budapest's shortest street, **Sütő utca,** but its handful of addresses contains a key one for visitors. **Tourinform,** the Hungarian National Tourist Information Office at No. 2 (tel. 1/117–9800), is open every day of the year from 8 to 8 and is staffed by the most helpful multilingual people in Hungary.

Deák tér overlaps with **Erzsébet tér** (Elizabeth Square), which was Engels tér until 1990. Now more of a passenger marketplace, it is the site of Budapest's main bus terminal for international, long-distance, and airport services—and is particularly dense with exhaust fumes.

Walk north on Bajcsy-Zsilinszky út, past its intersection with Andrássy út and József Attila utca, and turn left onto Szent István tér. You will be facing the very Holy Roman front porch—its tympanum bustling with statuary—of the **Szent István Bazilika** (St. Stephen's Basilica), the city's largest church (it can hold 8,500). The church's dome and the dome of Parliament are by far the most visible in the Pest skyline, and this is no accident: With the Magyar Millennium of

45

1896 in mind, both domes were consciously planned to be 315 feet high.

The millennium was not yet in sight when architect József Hild began building the basilica in neoclassical style in 1851, two years after the revolution was suppressed. After Hild's death, in 1867, however, the project was taken over by Miklós Ybl, the architect who did the most to transform modern Pest into a monumental metropolis —in contrast to medieval Buda across the river. Wherever he could, Ybl shifted Hild's motifs toward the neo-Renaissance mode that Ybl favored. When the dome collapsed, partly damaging the walls, he made even more drastic changes with the millennium approaching. Ybl died in 1891, five years before the thousand-year celebration, and the basilica was completed in neo-Renaissance style by József Kauser—but not until 1905.

Below the cupola, the interior is surprisingly cool and restful, a rich collection of late-19th-century Hungarian art: mosaics, altarpieces, and statuary (what heady days the millennium must have meant for local talents!). There are 150 kinds of marble, all from Hungary except for the Carrara in the sanctuary's centerpiece: a white statue of King (St.) Stephen I, Hungary's first king and patron saint. Stephen's mummified right hand is preserved here as a relic. *V, Szent. István tér, tel. 1/117–2859. Open Mon.–Sat. 7 AM–7 PM, Sun. 1 PM–6 PM.*

Tour 5: Andrássy Út

Behind the basilica, back at the crossroad along Bajcsy-Zsilinszky út, begins Budapest's grandest avenue, **Andrássy út.** For too many years, this broad boulevard of music and mansions bore the tongue-twisting, mind-bending name of Népköztársaság (Avenue of the People's Republic) and, for a while before then, Stalin Avenue. In 1990, however, it reverted to its old name honoring Count Gyula Andrássy, a statesman who in 1867 became the first constitutional premier of Hungary. The boulevard that would eventually bear his name was begun in 1872, as Buda and Pest (and Óbuda) were about to be unified. Most of the mansions that line it were completed by 1884. It took another dozen years before the first **underground railway** on the Continent was completed for—you guessed it!—the Magyar Millennium in 1896. Though preceded by London's Underground (1863), Budapest's was the world's first electrified subway. Only slightly modernized, this "Little Metro" is still running a 3.7-kilometer (2.3-mile) stretch from Vörösmarty tér to the far end of the City Park. Using tiny yellow trains with tanklike treads, and stopping at antique stations marked FÖLDALATTI (Underground) on their wrought-iron entranceways, Line 1 is a tourist attraction in itself. Six of its 10 stations are along Andrássy út.

For this tour, however, you are urged to first walk the 2-kilometer (1¼ mile) length of Andrássy út from downtown to Hősök tere (Heroes' Square) and, after exploring the City Park beyond it, to take the Földalatti back to town. The first third of the avenue, from Bajcsy-Zsilinszky út to the eight-sided intersection called Oktogon, boasts a row of eclectic city palaces with balconies held up by stone giants. The best of them happens to be visitable, for in an apartment with frescoes by Károly Lotz (whose work adorned the basilica and the National Museum's grand staircase) and a fine marble fireplace is the **Postamúzeum** (Postal Museum), with an exhibition on the history of Hungarian mail, radio, and telecommunications. *Andrássy út 3, tel. 1/142–7938. Admission: 20 Ft.; free on Sun. Open Tues.–Sun. 10–6.*

At Andrássy út 22 stands Miklós Ybl's crowning achievement, the **Operaház** (Opera House), built between 1875 and 1884 in neo-Renaissance style. There are those who prefer its architecture to that of the Vienna State Opera, which it resembles on a smaller scale, and to the Paris Opera, which could swallow it up whole. Badly damaged during the siege of 1944–45, Budapest's Opera was restored to its original splendor for the 1984 centenary. Two buxom marble sphinxes guard the driveway; the main entrance is flanked by Alajos Strobl's "Romantic-Realist" limestone statues of Liszt and of another 19th-century Hungarian composer, Ferenc Erkel, the father of Hungarian opera. (His patriotic opera *Bánk bán* is still performed for national celebrations.) On the facade are smaller statues of composers and muses.

Inside, the spectacle begins even before the performance does. You glide up grand staircases and through wood-paneled corridors and gilded lime-green salons into a glittering jewel box of an auditorium. Its four tiers of boxes are held up by helmeted sphinxes beneath a frescoed ceiling that is also the work of Lotz. Lower down there are frescoes everywhere, with intertwined motifs of Apollo and Dionysus. In its early years, the Budapest Opera was conducted by Gustav Mahler (from 1888 to 1891) and, after World War II, by Otto Klemperer. The acoustics are good and the stage is deep. The singing and playing can vary from awful to great, and tickets are relatively cheap and easy to come by, at least by tourist standards. And descending from *La Bohème* into the Földalatti station beneath the Opera House has been described by travel writer Stephen Brook in *The Double Eagle* (1988) as stepping "out of one period piece and into another."

Fifty-minute tours of the Opera House are usually conducted daily at 3 and 4 PM; meet by the sphinx at the Dálszínház utca entrance. It's a good idea to call ahead to confirm that one is being given (tel. 1/131–2550, ext. 156). The cost is 300 Ft.

Across the street from the Opera House is the French Renaissance–style **Drechsler Kastély** (Drechsler Palace) at Andrássy út 25. An early work by Ödön Lechner, Hungary's master of Art Nouveau, it is now the home of the National Ballet School. Behind it, a playful Art Nouveau building at Paulay Ede utca 35 houses the Children's Theatre. This is Budapest's Broadway: One block past the Opera, Nagymező utca contains several theaters, cabarets, and nightclubs.

The culture trail continues at the next corner, **Liszt Ferenc tér**; at No. 8, two blocks to the right off Andrássy út, is the **Liszt Ferenc Zeneakadémia** (Franz Liszt Academy of Music), which, along with the Vigadó, visited earlier, is the city's main concert hall. Actually, the academy has two auditoriums: a green-and- gold-ornamented 1,200-seat main hall and a smaller hall for chamber music and solo concerts. Outside this exuberant Art Nouveau building, opened in 1907, Liszt reigns enthroned on the facade; the statue is by Strobl, who cast him standing up outside the Opera House. The academy has been operating as a highly revered teaching institute for almost 120 years; Liszt was its first chairman and Erkel its first director. The pianist Ernő (formerly Ernst) Dohnányi and composers Béla Bartók and Zoltán Kodály were teachers here.

Andrássy út alters when it crosses the Nagy körút (Outer Ring Road), at the Oktogon crossing. Four rows of trees and scores of flower beds make the thoroughfare look more like a garden promenade, but its cultural character lingers. No. 67 was the original location of the old Academy of Music; entered around the corner, it now

49 houses the **Liszt Ferenc Emlékmúzeum** (Franz Liszt Memorial Museum). *Vörösmarty utca 35, tel. 1/142-7320. Admission: 20 Ft.; free on Mon. Open weekdays 10–6, Sat. 10–5. Closed Sun. Chamber concerts Sept.–July, Sat. 11 AM.*

The templelike eclectic building at Andrássy 69 houses the **Magyar Állami Bábszínház** (National Puppet Theater), and at No. 71, the **Képzőművészeti Főiskola** (Academy of Fine Arts), in a neo-Renaissance version of a Tuscan palace decorated with sgraffiti. Three blocks farther is the **Kodály Körönd**, a handsome traffic circle with imposing statues of three Hungarian warriors—leavened by a fourth one of a poet—surrounded by plane and chestnut trees. The circle takes its name from the composer Zoltán Kodály, who lived just beyond it at Andrássy út 89.

The rest of Andrássy út is dominated by widely spaced mansions surrounded by private gardens. At No. 101 is the **National Association of Hungarian Journalists**; its espresso bar is open to the public Monday through Friday from 9 AM to 8 PM and on Saturday night from 6 PM on. Next door is the **Hopp Ferenc Kelet-Ázsiai Művészeti Múzeum** (Ferenc Hopp Museum of Eastern Asiatic Arts), housing a rich collection of exotica from the Indian subcontinent and Far Eastern ceramics. *Andrássy út 103, tel. 1/122-8476. Admission: 40 Ft.; free on Tues. Open Tues.–Sun. 10–6.*

50 Andrássy út ends in grandeur at **Hősök tere** (Heroes' Square), with Budapest's answer to Berlin's Brandenburg Gate. The **Millennial Monument** is a semicircular twin colonnade with statues of Hungary's kings and leaders between its pillars. Set back in its open center, a 118-foot stone column is crowned by a dynamic statue of the archangel Gabriel, his outstretched arms bearing the ancient emblems of Hungary. At its base ride seven bronze horsemen: the Magyar chieftains, led by Árpád, whose tribes conquered the land in 896. Most of the statues were sculpted by György Zala, whose rendition of Gabriel won him a Grand Prix in Paris in 1900. Before the column lies a simple marble slab, the **National War Memorial**, the nation's altar, at which every visiting foreign dignitary lays a ceremonial wreath. England's Queen Elizabeth upheld the tradition during her royal visit in May of 1992. In 1991 Pope John Paul II conducted a mass here. Just a few months earlier, half a million Hungarians had convened to recall the memory of Imre Nagy, the reform-minded communist prime minister who partially inspired the 1956 revolution.

Heroes' Square is flanked by two monumental art galleries, both built by Albert Schickedanz and Fülöp Herzog, who also collaborated on the Millennial Monument. On your right from Andrássy út **51** is the city's largest hall for special exhibitions, the **Műcsarnok** (Art Gallery), an 1895 temple of culture with a colorful tympanum. At press time it was wrapped in scaffolding and crawling with construction workers, but was scheduled to reopen in spring or summer of 1995 to once again bless Budapest with its exhibits of superb Hungarian modern art and contemporary foreign art as well as its rich series of films, theater, and concerts. During the renovation, the Műcsarnok's exhibits are on display at three other galleries in the city—the Ernst Museum, the Dorottya Gallery, and the Palme-ház (*see* Tour 6, *below*). *Hősök tere, tel. 1/122-7405. Projected hours and admission: Admission: 40 Ft. Open Tues.–Sun. 10–5:30.*

52 On your left is the **Szépművészeti Múzeum** (Museum of Fine Arts), begun in 1900 and opened in 1906. It houses Hungary's finest collection, rich in Flemish and Dutch Old Masters. With seven fine El

Grecos and five beautiful Goyas as well as paintings by Velázquez and Murillo, the collection of Spanish Old Masters is considered by many to be the best outside Spain. The Italian School is represented by Giorgione, Bellini, Correggio, Tintoretto, and Titian masterpieces and, above all, two superb Raphael paintings: his *Eszterházy Madonna* and immortal *Portrait of a Youth*, rescued after a world-famous art heist. Nineteenth-century French art includes works by Delacroix, Pissarro, Cézanne, Toulouse-Lautrec, Gauguin, Renoir, and Monet. There is also a display of more than 100,000 drawings (including five by Rembrandt and three studies by Leonardo), Egyptian and Greco-Roman exhibitions, late-Gothic winged altars from northern Hungary and Transylvania, and works by all the leading figures of Hungarian art up to the present. A new 20th-century collection was added to the museum's permanent exhibits in spring 1994, comprising a greatly varied but unified series of statues, paintings, and drawings by Chagall, Le Corbusier, and other artists of this century. *Dózsa György út 41, tel. 1/142–9759. Admission: 40 Ft. Open Tues.–Sun. 10–5:30. Occasional guided tours in English.*

Tour 6: Városliget (City Park)

Heroes' Square is the gateway to the **Városliget** (City Park): a square kilometer (almost half a square mile) of recreation, entertainment, beauty, and culture calculated to delight children and adults alike. A bridge behind the Millennial Monument leads across a boating basin that becomes an artificial ice-skating rink in winter; to the south of this lake stands a **statue of George Washington,** erected in 1906 with donations by Hungarian emigrants to the United States. Beside the lake stands **Vajdahunyad Kastély** (Vajdahunyad Castle), an art historian's Disneyland named for the Transylvanian home (today in Hunedoara, Romania) of János Hunyadi, a 15th-century Hungarian hero in the struggle against the Turks. This fantastic medley borrows from all of Hungary's historic and architectural past, starting with the Romanesque gateway of the cloister of Jak in western Hungary. A Gothic castle, Transylvanian turrets, Renaissance loggia, Baroque portico, and Byzantine decoration are all guarded by a spooky modern (1903) bronze statue of the anonymous medieval chronicler who was the first recorder of Hungarian history. Designed for the millennial celebration in 1896 but not completed until 1908, this hodgepodge houses the surprisingly interesting **Mezőgazdasági Múzeum** (Agricultural Museum) with intriguingly arranged sections on animal husbandry, forestry, horticulture, hunting, and fishing. *XIV, Vajdahunyad vár, Városliget, tel. 1/142–0573. Admission: 30 Ft.; free on Tues. Open Tues.–Sat. 10–5, Sun. 10–6. Occasional guided tours in English. Choral concerts, Sept.–June, Sun. 11 AM.*

Wandering counterclockwise through the City Park, you will first encounter the **Közlekedési Múzeum** (Transport Museum) with its collection of old vehicles. *Városliget körút 11, tel. 1/142–0565. Admission: 30 Ft. adults, children free; free Wed. Open Tues.–Fri. 10–4, Sat.–Sun. 10–6. Videos and occasional guided tours in English can be arranged ahead of time.*

Continuing counterclockwise you'll come next to **Petőfi Hall**, a leisure-time youth center and concert hall on the site of an old industrial exhibition. The vast **Széchenyi Fürdő** (Széchenyi Baths) are in a fine neo-Baroque building erected between 1909 and 1913; the complex was expanded in 1926 with the addition of open-air thermal pools where you can swim outdoors even in winter (*see* Sports and

Fitness, *below*). Other popular areas in the park include **Vidám Park**, an amusement-filled area; the **Fővárosi Nagycirkusz** (Municipal Grand Circus); and the **Budapesti Állatkert** (Budapest Zoo), a fairly depressing urban zoo brightened—for humans, anyway—by an elephant pavilion decorated with Zsolnay majolica and glazed ceramic animals (*see* What to See and Do with Children, *below*).

At this point you have come full circle through the City Park and back to Heroes' Square. From here, walk along Városligeti körút and make a left onto **Olof Palme sétány**. Here, set back in a poorly tended yard, is the often overlooked **Palme-ház** (Palme House), a little faded-brick mansion garnished with ornate, colorful stonework. Built during the mid-1890s for the millennial celebration, it is similar in style to the Műcsarnok on Heroes' Square. Until spring of 1992, the Palme-ház was a rest home for stonemasons but has since served as one of the temporary galleries for the Műcsarnok's displaced exhibits. Inside, the high-ceilinged, white-walled rooms with floor-to-ceiling windows opening out onto the lush green of City Park make an ideal display space for the art exhibits. At press time (spring 1994), Palme-ház directors were hoping to continue using the building as a gallery even after the Műcsarnok reopens. *Olof Palme sétány 1, tel. 1/122-7405 or 1/122-9041. Admission: 30 Ft. Open Tues.-Sun. 10-6.*

Tour 7: Eastern Pest and the Great Ring Road

Board the Földalatti at Heroes' Square, and ride it back to town. You can get off either at the next-to-last stop, Deák tér, or at the terminus, Vörösmarty tér. Try Deák tér if you want to visit the **Földalatti Múzeum** (Subway Museum). Situated in the Földalatti's 19th-century tunnel, the museum tells the story of the subway's construction. *Deák tér station, tel. 1/142-2130. Admission: 30 Ft. or a mass-transit ticket. Open Oct.-Mar., Tues.-Sun. 9-5; Apr.-Sept., Tues.-Sun. 10-6.*

From Deák tér, Deák utca leads to **Vörösmarty tér** at the northern end of the Váci utca shopping mall. Grouped around a white marble statue of the 19th-century poet and dramatist Mihály Vörösmarty are luxury shops, airline offices, and an elegant former pissoir. Now a lovely kiosk, it displays gold-painted historic scenes of the square's golden days, which may be returning since its 1984 restoration.

Time Out The best-known, tastiest, and most tasteful address on Vörösmarty Square belongs to the **Gerbeaud** pastry shop (Vörösmarty tér 7, tel. 1/118-1311; open daily 9-8), founded in 1858 by a French confectioner, Henri Kugler, and later taken over by the Swiss family Gerbeaud. Filling most of a square block, it offers at least 100 kinds of sweets at any time (as well as ice cream, sandwiches, coffee, and other drinks), served in a salon setting of green marble tables and Regency-style marble fireplaces or at tables outside in summer. A mildly hostile staff is an integral part of the Gerbeaud tradition.

Retrace your steps along Váci utca to Kossuth Lajos utca, but this time turn left instead of crossing Budapest's busiest shopping street. Try to look above and beyond the store windows to the architecture and activity along Kossuth Lajos utca and its continuation, Rákóczi út. As soon as you take a left onto Kossuth Lajos utca you'll see twin towers on either side of the heavily trafficked thoroughfare. They are the **Klotild** and **Matild buildings**, built in an interesting combination of Art Nouveau and eclectic styles, which house the headquarters of the IBUSZ travel agency, a casino, and a fashion boutique, among other tenants. At the corner of Petőfi Sándor utca, on the site of the former Inner City Savings Bank, are the **Paris Arcades,** a glass-roofed network of passages with boutiques and cafés. Built in 1914 in neo-Gothic and eclectic styles, they are among the most attractive and atmospheric meccas of Pest.

Continue down Kossuth Lajos utca to the Kis (Inner) körút at Astoria, which is where it becomes **Rákóczi út.** It is so named because it was on the 1906 route of the procession that brought back the remains of Prince Ferenc II Rákóczi of Transylvania, hero of an early 18th-century uprising against the Habsburgs, nearly two centuries after he died in defeat and exile in Turkey. At No. 21, the Moorish-style building of the **Uránia Cinema** also houses the College of Dramatic and Film Arts, which has its Studio Theater and other sections around the corner on Vas utca.

❺❸ At the corner of Rákóczi út and Gyulai Pál utca stands the charming yellow 18th-century **Kapel Szent Roch** (St. Roch Chapel), its impact rendered even more colorful by peasant women peddling lace and embroidery on its small square. The chapel is the oldest remnant of Pest's former outer district. It was built beside a hospice where doomed victims of the great plague of 1711 were sent to die as far away as possible from residential areas. The former St. Roch Hospital next door at No. 2 Gyulai Pál utca is now the **Semmelweis Hospital.** The section along Rákóczi út was built in 1841 on the site of the old hospice; the wing on Gyulai Pál utca dates to 1798.

❺❹ The rest of Rákóczi út is lined with hotels, shops, and department stores. A right turn onto Luther utca leads to **Köztársaság tér** (Square of the Republic) and the city's second opera house, the **Ferenc Erkel Theatre.** Budapest's largest, with 3,000 seats, it was built in 1910–11 and offers operas and concerts throughout the year. Composed of faceless concrete buildings, this square is not particularly alluring aesthetically but is significant in that it was where the Communist party of Budapest had its headquarters, and it was also the scene of heavy fighting in 1956.

Rákóczi út terminates at Baross Square and is crowned by the grandiose, imperial-looking **Keleti (East) Railway Station,** built in 1884 and considered Europe's most modern until well into this century. Its neo-Renaissance facade, which resembles a gateway, is flanked by statues of two British inventors and railway pioneers, James Watt and George Stephenson.

Doubling back on Rákóczi út to the major intersection at Blaha Lujza Square, you can now go either left or right on Pest's Great Ring Road, the **Nagy körút,** laid out at the end of the 19th century in a wide semicircle anchored to the Danube at both ends; an arm of the river was covered over to create this 114-foot-wide thoroughfare. The large apartment buildings on both sides also date from this era. Along with theaters, stores, and cafés, they form a boulevard unique in Europe for its "unified eclecticism," which blends a variety of historic styles into a harmonious whole. Its entire length of almost 4½ kilometers (2¾ miles) from Margaret Bridge to Petőfi Bridge is traversed by Trams 4 and 6, but strolling it in stretches is also a good way to experience the hustle and bustle of downtown Budapest.

As with its smaller counterpart, the Kis Körút (Little Boulevard), the **Great Ring Road** comprises streets of various names. The sector to your left (if you're facing Buda) is called József körút, and your exploration of it begins with the neo-Renaissance building of the Technology Institute, built in 1887–89.

At the corner of Üllői út, where the Great Ring Road becomes Ferenc körút, stands a templelike structure that is indeed a shrine to Hungarian Art Nouveau. It is the **Iparművészeti Múzeum** (Museum of Applied and Decorative Arts), and in front of it, drawing pen in hand, sits a statue of its creator, Ödön Lechner, Hungary's master of Art Nouveau. Opened in the millennial year of 1896, it was only the third museum of its kind in Europe. Its dome of tiles is crowned by a majolica lantern from the same source: the Zsolnay ceramicworks in Pecs. Inside its central hall are playfully swirling whitewashed double-decker Moorish-style galleries and arcades. The museum, which collects and studies objects of interior decoration and use, has five departments: furniture, textiles, goldsmithery, ceramics, and everyday objects. *Üllői út 33-37, tel. 1/ 217-5222. Admission: 40 Ft. adults, 20 Ft. children; free on Tues. Open Tues.-Sun. 10-6.*

If you had turned right back at Blaha Lujza Square, you would have been traveling along **Erzsébet körút** (Elizabeth Boulevard, formerly Lenin Boulevard). Right after Erzsébet becomes Teréz körút, you'll notice the **Terézvárosi Romai-Katolikus Templom** (Theresa Town Parish Church) with its classical altars and finely proportioned choir designed by Mihály Pollack. Beyond the busy Oktogon crossing with Andrássy út—boasting the biggest Burger King in the world—and the beautifully redone Hotel Béke Radisson, Teréz körút ends at the **Nyugati (West) Railway Station.** Its iron-laced glass hall is in complete contrast to—and much more modern than—the newer Keleti (East) station.

The final stretch of the Great Ring Road is **Szent István körút** (St. Stephen Boulevard), with the **Vígszínház** (Comedy Theater) at No. 14. Designed in neo-Baroque style by the Viennese imperial architectural team of Fellner and Helmer and built in 1895–86, it twinkles with just a tiny, playful anticipation of Art Nouveau and a happy ending to this marathon stroll through the sprawling heart of Pest.

Tour 8: Óbuda

Until its unification with Buda and Pest in 1872 to form the city of Budapest, **Óbuda** (the name means Old Buda) was a separate town that used to be the main settlement; now it is usually thought of as a suburb. Although the vast new apartment blocks of Budapest's biggest housing project are what first strike the eye, the historic core of Óbuda has been preserved in its entirety as an ancient monument.

Óbuda is easily reached by car, bus, or streetcar via the Árpád Bridge from Pest or by the HÉV suburban railway from Batthyány tér to Árpádhid. Behind the Thermal Hotel Aquincum is a serene Baroque gem built in the 18th century by the Zichy family (which owned all of Óbuda at the time): the **Óbuda Parish Church** (1744–49), which houses the tomb of Pál Zichy (1723) and many objects from the nearby Kiscelli Monastery.

From here, walk away from the river on Mókus utca, the tiny street at the southern end of the church, for a brief stroll among cobblestone streets lined with pastel-colored, mid-19th-century houses and antique lampposts. The popular Kehli restaurant (*see* Dining, *below*) is at Mókus utca 22. The cheery salmon-colored house at the center of the row on Dugovits Titusz tér was legendary Hungarian writer Gyula Krúdy's home and workplace from 1933 until his death.

Just northwest of Dugovits Titusz tér, the center of today's Óbuda, is **Flórián tér,** where Roman ruins were first discovered when the foundations of a house were dug in 1778. Two centuries later, careful excavations were carried out during the reconstruction of the square. Between 1981 and 1984, 48 rooms of Roman military baths known as **Thermae Maiores** were excavated, and some of them were formed into an open-air museum that can be viewed by those taking the pedestrian underpass to cross the square. Besides housing pools and steam chambers, the baths also had rooms for rest and recreation, a promenade, and a temple dedicated to the nymphs of healing. The open-air museum can be seen by groups if arrangements are made in advance; to arrange a visit, call 1/250–1650.

If you stroll southward toward the center of Buda along Pacsirtamező utca, at the busy junction where it meets Bécsi út you'll encounter a Roman **military amphitheater** that held some 16,000 people. It probably dates to the 2nd century. At 144 yards in diameter, this oval arena was one of Europe's largest. A block of dwellings called the Round House was later built by the Romans above the amphitheater; massive stone walls found in the Round House's cellar were actually parts of the amphitheater. Below the amphitheater are the cells where prisoners and lions were held while awaiting confrontation.

From here, climb eastward to the **Kiscelli Múzeum** on Remethegy (Hermit's Hill). This plain Baroque building was built between 1744 and 1760 as a Trinitarian monastery with funds donated by the Zichy family. Today it is a museum housing the interior of the old Golden Lion Pharmacy, 18th- and 19-century printing presses, temporary exhibitions of art and local history, and the fine-arts collection of the Budapest History Museum. It specializes in paintings, engravings, and sculptures related to the history of the city. Its 20th-century collection is small but valuable. *Kiscelli út 108, tel. 1/ 188–8560. Admission: 50 Ft. adults, 25 Ft. children. Open Nov.– Mar., Tues.–Sun. 10–4; Apr.–Oct., Tues.–Sun. 10–6.*

Follow Kiscelli út downhill to Flórián tér and continue toward the Danube; take a left at Hídfő utca or Szentélek tér to enter Óbuda's old main square, **Fő tér.** This area has been spruced up in recent years, and there are now several good restaurants and interesting museums in and around the Baroque **Zichy Kúria** (Zichy Mansion), which has become a neighborhood cultural center. Among the most popular offerings are the summer concerts in the courtyard and the evening jazz concerts.

One wing of the Zichy Mansion is taken up by the **Budai Helytörténeti Múzeum** (Óbuda Local History Museum); permanent exhibitions here include traditional rooms from typical homes in the district of Békásmegyer and a popular exhibit covering the history of toys from 1860 to 1960. *Zichy Mansion, Fő tér 1, tel. 1/250–1020. Admission: 40 Ft. Open Tues.–Fri. 2–6, Sat.–Sun. 10–6.*

Another wing of the Zichy Mansion houses the **Kassák Muzeum,** which honors the literary and artistic works of a pioneer of the Hungarian avant-garde, Lajos Kassák. *Zichy Mansion, Fő tér 1, tel. 1/ 168–7021. Admission: 20 Ft. Open Nov.–mid-Mar., Tues.–Sun. 10–5; mid-Mar.–Oct., Tues.–Sun. 10–6.*

What to See and Do with Children

Budapest has two zoos that provide excellent diversions for children (and adults) weary of museums and churches. At the **Budakeszi Vadaspark,** deer, wild sheep, wild boar, and birds (most indigenous to Hungary) can be seen in a lovely natural setting. *Take Bus 22 to* *the Kórnyi Hospital stop. Tel. 1/176-6783. Admission: 60 Ft. adults, 25 Ft. children. Open daily 8-dusk.*

The **Budapesti Állatkert** (Budapest Zoo) in Városliget (City Park) cares for a more exotic variety of animals, including hippos, a favorite of local youngsters. *XIV, Állatkerti körút 6-12, behind Heroes' Square, tel. 1/142-6303. Admission: 100 Ft. adults, 40 Ft. children. Open May-Sept., daily 9-5:30; Sept.-May, 9 AM-dusk.*

Next to the Budapest Zoo is **Vidám Park**, the city's main amusement park, open spring through fall. It has rides that cost 20 Ft.-50 Ft., game rooms, and a scenic railway. There are some rides for preschoolers. Next to the main park is a separate, smaller amusement park for toddlers. *Városliget, tel. 1/110-0990. Admission. Mar. Sept. 20 Ft.; free Oct.-Feb. Open Mar.-Sept., daily 10-8; Oct.-Feb., daily 10-late afternoon.*

The 12-kilometer (7-mile) **Pioneer Railway** (operated in communist days by the Young Pioneers) runs from Széchenyihegy to Hűvösvölgy. The sweeping views and fresh air make the trip well worthwhile for children and adults alike. Departures are from Széchenyihegy, which you can reach by taking the cogwheel railway from the station opposite Hotel Budapest (Szillágyi Erzsébet fasor 47). *Pioneer trains run mid-Jan.-late Mar. and late Sept.-Dec., Wed.-Sun. 8 AM-4 PM; rest of the year, Tues.-Sun. 8 AM-5 PM.*

Budapest's two puppet theaters—**Magyar Állami Bábszínház** (VI, Andrássy út 69, tel. 1/122-5051) and **Kolibri Színház** (VI, Jókai tér 10, tel. 1/153-4633)—produce colorful shows that both children and adults find enjoyable even if they don't understand Hungarian. Watch for showings of *Cinderella* (*Hamupipőke*) and *Snow White and the Seven Dwarfs* (*Hófehérke*), part of the theaters' regular repertoire.

Off the Beaten Track

A *libegő* (chair lift) will take you to the highest point in Budapest, the **Jánoshegy** (Janos Hill; 527 meters), where you can climb a lookout tower for the best view of the city. *Take Bus 158 from Moszkva tér to the last stop, Zugligeti út. Tel. 1/156-7975 or 1/176-3764. Admission: 60 Ft. one way, 100 Ft. round-trip. Open May 15-Sept. 15, daily 9-6; Sept. 16-May 14 (depending on weather), daily 9:30-4. Closed every other Mon.*

Far in the outskirts of Budapest, on Highway 70 in the 22nd district, is the new open-air museum where, since the political changes of 1989, dozens of communist statues and monuments have been put out to pasture. After many delays, **Szobor Park** (Statue Park) finally opened its gates to the public in the summer of 1993; presently on display you'll find statues of Béla Kunn and Tibor Szamueli—notorious Communists who seized power for three months in 1919—Marx, Lenin, and scores of other monuments glorifying Hungary's past regime. *Szabadkai út., tel. 1/227-7446. Admission: 99 Ft. adults, 19 Ft. children. Open Apr.-Oct., daily 10-6.*

Shopping

Shopping Districts The principal upscale shopping district in **Pest** is the **pedestrian zone** on and around **Váci utca** between the Elizabeth (Erzsébet) and Chain (Széchenyi Lánchíd) bridges. For fashion, try the boutiques in the **World Trade Center** passage at Váci utca 19-21. You'll find plenty of folk-art and souvenir shops, foreign-language bookshops, and record shops in and around Váci utca, but a visit to some of the smaller, more typically Hungarian shops on **Erzsébet** and **Teréz boulevards** and **Kossuth Lajos utca** may prove more interesting.

Department Stores **Skála Metro** (VI, Nyugati tér 1–2, tel. 1/112–3828), opposite the Nyugati (West) Railroad Station, is one of the largest and best-known department stores. Elsewhere downtown is **Divatcsarnok** (VI, Andrássy út 39, tel. 1/122–4000), with a good selection of clothes and an ornate hall decorated with frescoes by 19th-century Hungarian painter Károly Lotz. **S-Modell**, a Hungarian chain of boutiques located throughout the city, sells good-quality clothing at prices significantly less than those at its international counterparts. Most branches sell women's clothes (V, Váci utca 9; V, Szent István körút 10; VII, Andrássy út 15; XI, Bartók Béla utca 21); for men's fashions, visit the branch at József Attilla utca 12 (tel. 1/117–7288) in the fifth district. And for those willing to splurge on Western goods, there is a **Marks and Spencer** (V, Váci utca 10) store just past Vörösmarty tér. Farther down Váci utca is the **Made In World Center** (corner of Váci utca and Haris Köz), a tiny upscale, underground shopping arcade of trendy fashion boutiques, a music store, and gift shops.

Flea Markets For true bargains and often wild adventures, make a trip to one of the vast flea markets on the outskirts of the city. **Ecseri Piac,** a colorful, chaotic market flocked to for decades, is an arsenal of second-hand goods where you can find everything from frayed Russian army fatigues to Herend and Zsolnay porcelain vases to 150-year-old handmade silver chalices worthy of being in a museum. Goods are sold at permanent tables set up in rows, from trunks of cars parked on the perimeter, and by lone, shady characters clutching just one or two items. There's a good chance you'll witness a police sting while you're here, as many dealers are peddling their wares less than legally. As a foreigner, you may be overcharged, so prepare to haggle—it's part of the flea-market experience. Ecseri is open during the week, but you'll find the best selection on Saturday mornings. *Nagykőrösi út (take Bus 54 from Boráros tér). Open weekdays 8–4, Sat. 8–3.*

Specialty Stores **Antik Diszkont** (XIII, Róbert Károly körút 58, tel. 1/186–1835) sells
Antiques hundreds of items, some quite valuable and quite inexpensive. Other dealers include **Sallay** (V, Bank utca 6, tel. 1/112–8351), **Qualitás** (Néphadsereg utca 32, tel. 1/131–2292), **Antik** (VII, Wesselényi utca 34, tel. 1/141–0444), **Nagyházi Galéria** (XII, Járőr utca 33, tel. 1/176–0456), and **Polgar and Tarsa** (József körút 15). You'll find antiques of all forms and functions at the **Ecseri Piac** market (*see* Flea Markets, *above*).

Books You'll encounter **bookselling stands** throughout the streets and metro stations of the city, many of which sell English-language souvenir picture books at discount prices. **Váci utca** is lined with bookstores that sell glossy coffee-table books on Budapest and Hungary. **Universum** (V, Váci utca 31–33) has a particularly good selection.

Bookstores with English-language sections include **Libri International Bookshop** (V, Váci utca 32, tel. 1/118–2718), **Longman ELT** (VIII, Kölcsey utca 2, tel. 1/210–0170), **Atlantisz Book Island** (V, Piarista köz 1, no phone), and **Interbright** (XII, Tartsay Vilmos út 11–13, tel. 1/156–5611). **Bestsellers** (V, Október 6 utca, tel. 1/112–1295) sells English-language books exclusively.

China, Crystal, and Porcelain Hungary is famous for its **Herend** china (hand-painted in the village of Herend) and **Zsolnay** porcelain. Good selections can be found in the shops in the Forum and Hilton hotels. Also try Herend's own porcelain stores, **Herend Porcelán Márkabolt** (V, József Nádor tér 11, tel. 1/118–9200 or 1/117–2622) and **Herend Village Pottery** (II, bem rakpart 37). Hungarian and Czech **crystal** is also considerably less expensive here than in the United States. Try **Haas & Czjzek** (VI, Bajcsy-Zsilinszky út 23, tel. 1/111–4094), which has been in the business for more than 100 years. Crystal and porcelain dealers also sell their wares at the **Ecseri Piac** flea market (*see* Flea Markets, *above*), often at discount prices, but those looking for authentic Herend and Zsolnay should beware of imitations.

Folk Art Handmade articles, such as embroidered tablecloths and painted plates, are sold all over the city by Transylvanian women wearing traditional scarves and colorful skirts. You can usually find them standing along Váci utca, near the tram at Vigadó ter, and in the larger metró stations. All types of **folk art**—pottery, blouses, jewelry boxes, wood carvings, embroidery—can be purchased at one of the many branches of **Népművészet Háziipar,** also called Folkart Centrum, a large cooperative chain that handles the production and sale of folk art by many artisans. Prices are reasonable, and selection and quality good. A hint on how to check for authenticity: If the fourth to sixth digits of the serial number pasted onto the item are 900, the piece is handmade, usually by a well-known artisan. The main branch is on Váci utca (V, Váci utca 14, tel. 1/118–5840). Other, smaller branches include those at XI, Bartók Béla utca 50, tel. 1/166–4831; V, Kálvin tér 5, tel. 1/137–3785; and XIII, Szent István körút 26, tel. 1/131–0211). **Éva Dolls** (V, Kecskeméti utca 10, tel. 1/117–4305 has pricier but beautiful crafts.

Music Recordings of Hungarian folk music or of pieces played by Hungarian artists are increasingly available on compact discs, though cassettes and records are much cheaper and are sold throughout the city. **Universum** (V, Váci utca 31–33) is the biggest music store in town, with thousands of cassettes, CDs, and records of all varieties of music. **Hungaroton Hanglemez Szalon** (Vörösmarty tér 1, tel. 1/138–2810) has nearly as many items and is one of the few stores open on Sunday (until 2 PM), but only in July and August and during the Christmas season. At the **CD Bar** (VI, Székely Mihály utca 10, tel. 1/142–8380) you can relax with a beer or a cup of coffee from the bar and listen to any CDs in the store on one of the several stereos set up for browsing customers. Coffee and tea are on the house with any purchase.

Sports and Fitness

Golf Golf is still a new sport in Hungary, one that many Hungarians can't afford. The closest place to putt is 35 kilometers (22 miles) north of the city at the **Budapest Golfpark** in Kisoroszi. The park has an 18-hole, 72-par course and a driving range. Greens fees range from 2,500 Ft. to 3,000 Ft. Carts and equipment can be rented. The club also has two tennis courts. For more information, contact the **Hungarian Professional Golf Association** (V, Bécsi utca 5, tel. 1/117–6025 or 06/60–321–673).

Health and **Andi Stúdió** (V, Hold utca 29 and Bihari János utca, tel. 1/111–0740) *Fitness Clubs* is a trendy fitness club with two slightly cramped branches. For about 300 Ft. you can work out on the fitness machines for about an hour or take an aerobics class, held every hour. **Mirror Mozgásstúdió** (XII, Városmajor utca 36, tel. 1/135–2173), offers aerobics, bodybuilding machines, and some life-fitness equipment. A one-day pass costs 250 Ft. At **Club-Sziget** (XIII, Margitsziget, tel. 1/112–9472) on Margaret Island, you can work out in the weight room or take an aerobics class for about 250 Ft. each. Other options include **Astoria Fitness Center** (V, Károly körút 4, tel. 1/117–3603), **TSA Eurofit** (I, Pálya utca 9, tel. 1/156–9530), and **Sunbody Fitness Center** (IX, Ráday utca 16, tel. 1/217–9363). For good hotel facilities, try the **Kempinski** (V, Erzsébet tér 7–8, tel. 1/266–1000), **Forum** (V, Apáczai Csere János utca 12, tel. 1/117–8088), and **Atrium Hyatt** (V, Roosevelt tér 2, tel. 1/266–1234).

Horseback Riding Several stables in Budapest offer trail rides and lessons to equestrians of all levels. The average charge is 500 Ft.–600 Ft. per person, per hour for trail rides. Reservations are generally required in advance. Contact the **Budapest Horse Club** (VIII, Kerepesi út 7, tel. 1/133–1249), **Petneházi Club** (1029 Feketefej út 2, tel. 1/176–5937), or, farther afield (take the HÉV from Batthyány tér), **Alkov** (Pomáz, Mártírok útja 1–3, tel. 0626/325–560).

Jogging **Margaret Island** and, on the Pest waterfront, the **Korzó** (Corso) promenade are level and inviting; the hills of Buda are more challenging. The forests of the area in Buda called **Hűvösvölgy** are laced with meandering trails that are perfect for long, picturesque runs (or walks) above the pollution and bustle of Pest. Trails begin at the top of Törökvész út, off Bimbó út; take Bus 11 from Batthyány tér to the last stop. The **City Park,** near Heroes' Square, is another good, relatively flat place for a run or walk.

Spas and Thermal Baths Several thousand years ago, the first settlers of the area that is now Budapest chose their home because of its abundance of hot springs. Centuries later, the Romans and the Turks built baths and developed cultures based on medicinal bathing. One tourist brochure claims it is just barely a hyperbole to say that "it is enough to push a stick into the ground and up will come thermal water—and with a bit of luck, it will have a curative effect." Today Budapest has 14 working baths that attract ailing patients with medical prescriptions for specific water cures as well as "recreational" bathers—locals and tourists alike—wanting to soak in the relaxing waters, try some of the many massages and treatments, and experience the architectural beauty of the bath houses themselves.

For most, a visit to a bath involves soaking in several thermal pools of varying temperatures and curative contents—perhaps throwing in a game of aquatic chess—relaxing in a steam room or sauna, and getting a brisk, if not brutal, massage (average cost: 200 Ft. for a half-hour). Many bath facilities are single sex, and most people walk around nude or with miniature loincloths, provided at the door, with which one can only attempt to remain decent.

Gellért Thermal Baths (XI, Kellenhegyi út 4, tel. 1/166–6166) is in the oldest Hungarian spa hotel, with hot springs that have supplied curative baths for nearly 2,000 years. It is the most popular among tourists, with a wealth of treatments—including chamomile steam baths, salt-vapor inhalations, and hot mud packs—many of which require a doctor's prescription. Men and women have separate bathing facilities indoors; outside is a popular coed wave pool. *Open weekdays 6 AM–6 PM, Sat.–Sun., 6:30 AM–noon (no massage on Sun.). Admission to indoor baths and steam rooms: 150 Ft. per 1½ hours. Wave pool open May–early Sept., daily 6 AM–7 PM. Admission (indoors and pool): 400 Ft. per 3 hours.*

Király Baths (II, Fő utca 84, tel. 1/115–3000) was built during the 16th century by the Turkish pasha of Buda and boasts a stone cupola that arches over the steamy, dark pools indoors. It is open to men on Monday, Wednesday, and Friday; to women on Tuesday, Thursday, and Saturday. *Open weekdays 6:30 AM–6 PM, Sat. 6:30 AM–noon. Admission: 100 Ft.*

Lukács Baths (II, Frankel Leó utca 25–29, tel. 1/115–4280) was built during the 19th century but modeled on the Turkish originals and is fed with waters from a source dating from the Bronze Age and Roman times. Facilities are coed. *Baths open weekdays 6 AM–6 PM, Sat. 6 AM–3 PM, Sun 6 AM–noon. Admission: 120 Ft.*

Rác Baths (I, Hadnagy utca 8–10, tel. 1/156–1322) is a small bath facility tucked away at the foot of Gellért Hill near the Elizabeth Bridge. Its waters contain alkaline salts and other minerals. Women can bathe on Monday, Wednesday, and Friday; men on Tuesday, Thursday, and Saturday. *Open Mon.–Sat. 6:30 AM–6 PM. Admission: 120 Ft.*

Rudas Medicinal Baths (I, Döbrentei tér 9, tel. 1/156–1322) is open to men only and is possibly the most dramatically beautiful inside. A high, domed roof admits pinpricks of bluish green light into the dark, circular stone hall with majestic columns and arches. This facility's highly fluoridated waters have been known for 1,000 years. A less interesting outer swimming pool is open to both sexes. *Open weekdays 6 AM–6 PM, weekends 6 AM–noon. Admission: 120 Ft.*

Széchenyi Baths (XIV, Állatkerti körút 11, tel. 1/121–0310), dating from 1876, is in a beautiful neo-Baroque building in the middle of City Park and is one of the biggest spas in Europe. There are several thermal pools indoors as well as two outdoors, which remain open even in winter, when dense steam hangs thick over the hot water's surface—you can just barely make out the figures of elderly men, submerged shoulder-deep, crowded around waterproof chess boards. *Open weekdays 6 AM–7 PM, Sat.–Sun. 6 AM–noon (outdoor pool until 4 PM). Admission: 120 Ft.*

Newer, modern baths are open to the public at the **Ramada Grand Hotel** (XIII, Margitsziget, tel. 1/111–1000), the **Thermal Hotel Aquincum** (III, Árpád fejedelem útja 94, tel. 1/250–3360), and the **Thermal Hotel Helia** (XIII, Kárpát utca 62, tel. 1/270–3277). They lack the charm and aesthetic appeal of their older peers but provide the latest treatments in sparkling facilities.

Tennis and Squash **Thermal Hotel Helia** (XIII, Kárpát utca 62–64, tel. 1/270–3277) has two outdoor tennis courts available daily from 6 AM to 10 PM. Court fees are 700 Ft. per hour. **Pannon Sport and Recreation Center** (XI, Fehérvári út 204, tel. 1/186–9011, ext. 5549) has four clay courts available for 250 Ft.–300 Ft. per hour. Two have lighting for night games, but arrangements must be made, and fees paid, during the day. From mid-October to mid-April, the club erects a tent over two of the courts for winter playing; these courts cost 800 Ft.–900 Ft. per hour. On Margaret Island, **Club-Sziget** (XIII, Margitsziget, tel. 1/112–9472) charges 300 Ft. per hour to play on one of its eight clay courts (400 Ft. per hour if you don't reserve in advance).

City Squash Club (II, Marczibányi tér 13, tel. 1/212–3100) has four squash courts that are open until midnight and always packed. Fees are 500 Ft. per hour, per person during the day and 800 Ft. per hour, per person during squash "rush hour," between 5 and 10 PM. Racket and shoe rentals are also available at 100 Ft. and 50 Ft., respectively. **TSA Eurofit** (I, Pálya utca 9, tel. 1/156–9530) has two courts that are open daily from 7 AM to 11 PM. Rates run 400 Ft. per person, per half-hour, plus a court fee of 600 Ft. per half-hour. Rackets can be rented for 100 Ft. per hour. The **Budapest Marriott Hotel** (V, Apáczai Csere

János utca 4, tel. 1/266–7000) rents its only court for 500 Ft. per half-hour daily from 7 AM to 10 PM.

Dining

Eating out in Budapest can be a real treat and should provide you with some of the best value for the money of any European capital. Meats, rich sauces, and creamy desserts predominate, but the more health-conscious will also find salads, even out of season. There is a good selection of restaurants, from the grander establishments that echo the imperial past of the Habsburg era to the less expensive spots favored by locals. A large number of ethnic restaurants—Chinese, Mexican, Egyptian, Ethiopian—are also springing up throughout the city. In addition to restaurants (*vendéglő*), there are self-service restaurants (*önkiszolgáló étterem*), snack bars (*bisztró*, *büfé*, or *étel bár*), cafés (*eszpresszó*), bars (*drinkbár*), and pastry shops (*cukrászda*).

Highly recommended restaurants in each price category are indicated by a star ★.

$$$$ **Alabárdos.** As medieval as its name, which means "halberdier" (the
★ wielder of that ancient weapon, the halberd), this vaulted wooden room in a 400-year-old Gothic house across from the Matthias Church and Budapest Hilton is widely regarded as one of Hungary's best restaurants. It has only a handful of tables, set with exquisite Herend and Zsolnay porcelain, though in summer a courtyard garden doubles its capacity. The impeccable service, flowery decor, quiet music, and overriding discretion make this an excellent place for a serious business meal. Specialties are Hungarian meats and steaks with goose-liver trimmings. Start with *palócleves*, a sour-creamy soup of beef, potatoes, and green beans. The room's lights go out every time the flambéed mixed grill is delivered; if you don't like to be the center of attention, try the filet mignon in green-pepper sauce, also flambéed but without the pyrotechnics. The goose-liver-stuffed pork cutlets light their own fire, thanks to *lecsó*, a spicy mix of tomato, paprika, and onions. An extensive wine list offers the finest wines of Hungary's most famous vineyards, many unavailable anywhere else. *I, Országház utca 2, tel. 1/156–0851. Reservations required. Jacket and tie advised. AE, DC, MC, V. Closed Sun.*

★ **Gundel.** This is the shrine where Hungary's famous dessert, *Gundel palacsinta* (Gundel pancakes), was invented around the turn of the century by the restaurant's second owner, Károly Gundel. Filled with walnuts, lemon rind, raisins, and orange peel and coated with chocolate sauce, the crepes are flamed in rum at the table—and they never disappoint. The earlier courses are hardly a mere prelude, however. Appetizers, such as the wild rice and smoked quail-egg salad, are light and refined. The main dishes are delicious, particularly the duck roast with braised cabbage and the butter-fried lamb scaloppine served on cabbage pancakes. This austere place, redesigned by world-famous designers Adam Tihany, Emery Roth, and Milton Glaser with dark-wood paneling, navy-blue upholstered chairs and love seats, and tables set with Zsolnay porcelain and sterling silver, occupies a palatial mansion in the City Park, a 15-minute ride by subway or car from downtown Pest. England's Queen Elizabeth is among the many distinguished guests who have dined here. *XIV, Állatkerti körút 2, tel. 1/121–3550. Reservations advised. Jacket and tie advised. AE, DC, MC, V.*

Kisbuda Gyöngye. Considered one of the city's finest restaurants, this is the reincarnation of a venerable Budapest favorite at a new address in Óbuda. Antique furniture has been used throughout and the walls are creatively decorated with an eclectic but elegant patchwork of carved wooden cupboard doors and panels. A violinist sets a romantic mood, and in warm weather you can dine outdoors in the cozy back garden. Try the chicken Cumberland (grilled boneless breasts marinated in basil and spices) or the fresh trout smothered in a cream sauce nutted with mushrooms and capers. *III, Kenyeres utca 34, tel. 1/168–6402 or 1/168–9246. Reservations advised 2 days ahead. Dress: casual but neat. AE. Closed Sun. dinner.*

★ **Légrádi Testvérek.** This tiny, intimate restaurant on a narrow, curving street in the heart of Pest is one of the capital's most prestigious and luxurious offerings. Prompt, unobtrusive service is provided at candlelit, lace-covered tables set with Herend china and sterling silver cutlery. Hors d'oeuvres include smoked salmon, Russian caviar, and terrines of foie gras. Standard but beautifully presented entrées range from chateaubriand to wild boar. The game dishes are highly recommended. *V, Magyar utca 23, tel. 1/118–6804. Reservations advised. Jacket and tie advised. AE. Dinner only. Closed Sat.–Sun.*

Vadrózsa. The name means "wild rose," and there are always fresh ones on the table at this restaurant in an old villa perched on a hilltop in the exclusive Rózsadomb district of Buda. It's elegant to the last detail—even the service is white-glove—and the garden is delightful in summer. *II. Pentelei Molnár utca 15, tel. 1/135–1118. Reservations advised. Jackets and tie advised. AE, DC, MC, V. Dinner only. Closed Mon.*

$$$ **Arany Hordó.** True to its name (the Golden Barrel), this 14th-century building has a beer house on the ground floor. The cellar has a wine tavern, with candlelit tables tucked into nooks of the mazelike stone passageways, but the main attraction is the first-class, small restaurant on the second floor. The local specialty is *fogas*, a fish from Lake Balaton. There is Gypsy music in the evening. *I, Tárnok utca 14–16, tel. 1/156–6765. Reservations advised for restaurant. Dress: casual. AE, DC, MC, V.*

Aranymókus Kertvendéglő. This folksy Hungarian garden restaurant (the Golden Squirrel) high in the Buda Hills serves the kind of food that goes well with beer. There are no bones to pick with (or find in) the fiery carp soup, except that a cold drink must be standing by. Platters overflow with beef, veal, game, liver, and fish; the baked potatoes are huge. Fillet of fogas in crayfish and dill sauce tastes better than it looks, and the poppy-seed pancakes in coconut butter taste better than they sound—they'll send you waddling home happy. There's a good salad bar, too. Best of all is the atmosphere generated by the rustic wooden furniture and happy Hungarian diners. *XII, Istenhegyi út 25, tel. 1/155–6728. Reservations advised. Dress: casual. AE, DC, MC, V.*

Barokk. This small and intimate restaurant offers dishes adapted from 17th- and 18th-century recipes, creatively named with references to Pope Innocent XI and "the landed proprietor." A favorite is the thick tenderloin flavored with nuts, garlic, and honey and served with pancakes with grated apple. The 10 or so tables are set with gold-rimmed glasses and porcelain vases filled with fresh flowers. The warm atmosphere is enhanced by striking reproductions of Baroque furniture and piped-in Baroque music. Waiters, dressed in white, ruffled, Baroque-collared shirts, are friendly and quite expert in explaining the menu. *VI, Mozsár utca 12, tel. 1/131–8942. Reservations advised. Dress: casual but neat. AE.*

Fortuna. This appealing complex (restaurant, tavern, and nightclub), connecting three medieval houses across from the Hilton, is included mainly because Hungarians themselves like to be taken

Dining

Alabárdos, **15**
Arany Hordó, **17**
Aranymókus
Kertvendéglő, **19**
Bagolyvár, **44**
Barokk, **41**
Bohémtanya, **35**
Duna-Corso, **27**
Fészek, **39**
Fortuna, **16**
Gundel, **45**
Kehli, **4**
Kisbuda Gyöngye, **6**
Kispipa, **37**
Légrádi Testvérek, **31**
Marxim, **9**
Múzeum, **33**
Postakocsi, **1**
Remiz, **12**
Sipos Halászkert, **2**
Svejk, **40**
Tabáni Kakas, **20**
Vadrózsa, **10**
Vendégház Étterem, **3**

Lodging

Aquincum, **5**
Astoria, **34**
Atrium Hyatt, **25**
Buda Penta, **13**
Budapest Hilton, **14**
Budapest Marriott, **28**
Citadella, **23**
Flamenco, **22**
Forum, **26**
Gellért, **24**
Grand Hotel Corvinus
Kempinski, **30**
Grand Hotel
Hungaria, **38**
Helia, **8**
Ifjúság, **9**
Korona, **32**
Medosz, **42**
Nemzeti, **36**
Novotel, **21**
Panorama Hotels &
Bungalows, **18**
Radisson Béke, **43**
Ramada Grand
Hotel, **7**
Taverna, **29**

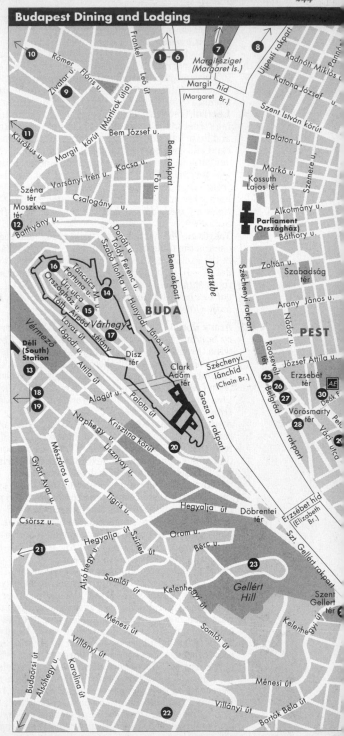

Budapest Dining and Lodging

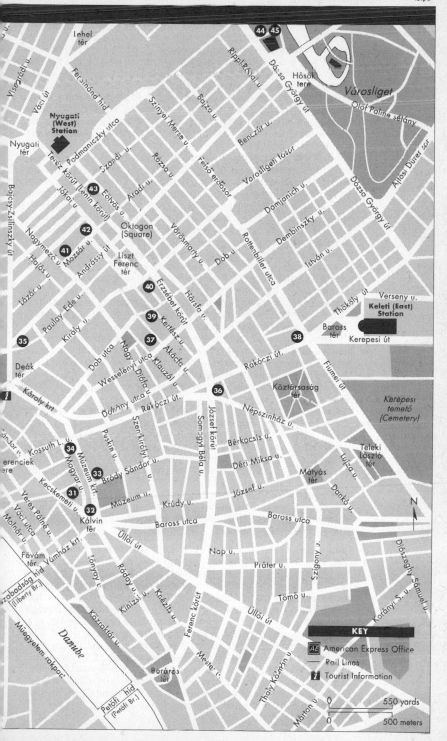

Lehel
tér

Visegrádi u.

Váci út

Ferdinánd híd

Szinyei Merse u.

Ripol-Rónai u.

Dósa György út

Hősök
tere

Városliget

Olof Palme sétány

Nyugati
(West)
Station

Nyugati
tér

Podmaniczky utca

Bajza u.

Benczúr u.

Aputsi Dürer sor

Bajcsy-Zsilinszky út

Teréz körút (Lenin körút)

Szondi u.

Rózsa u.

Felső erdősor

Városligeti fasor

Damjanich u.

Dózsa György út

43 Eötvös u.

Jókai u.

Aradi u.

Oktogon
(Square)

Vörösmarty u.

Dob u.

Dembinszky

Rottenbiller utca

István u.

42

41 Mozsár u.

Nagymező u.

Andrássy u.

Liszt
Ferenc
tér

Hajós u.

Lázár u.

Paulay Ede u.

40 Erzsébet körút

Hársfa u.

Thököly út

Verseny u.

Keleti (East)
Station

35

Deák
tér

Király u.

39 Kertész u.

Dob utca

Nagy Diófa u.

37 Akácfa u.

Wesselényi utca

Klauzál u.

38

Baross
tér

Kerepesi út

Károly krt.

Dohány utca

Rákóczi út.

36

Rákóczi út.

Köztársaság
tér

Fiumei út

Kerepesi
temető
(Cemetery)

Deák
tér

Sándor u.

Kossuth L. u.

34 Magyar u.

Puskin u.

Szentkirályi u.

József körút

Somogyi Béla u.

Népszínház u.

Bérkocsis u.

Teleki
László
tér

erenciek
ere

Kecskeméti u.

33 Múzeum krt.

Bródy Sándor u.

Déri Miksa u.

Luja u.

31 Veres Pálné u.

32 Kálvin
tér

Múzeum u.

Krúdy u.

József u.

Mátyás
tér

Dankó u.

Váci utca

Molnár u.

Üllői út

Baross utca

Baross utca

Diószeghy Sámuel u.

Fővám
tér

Lónyay u.

Nap u.

Szabadság híd
(Liberty Br.)

Vámház krt.

Ráday u.

Práter u.

Tömő u.

Üllői út

Szigony u.

Korányi S. u.

Koztaktár u.

Kinizsi u.

Knézits u.

Ferenc körút

Mester u.

Danube

Műegyetem rakpart

KEY

American Express Office

Rail Lines

Tourist Information

Petőfi híd
(Petőfi Br.)

Boráros
tér

Thaly Kálmán u.

Márton u.

0   550 yards

0   500 meters

N

here—although many Americans enjoy the atmosphere and food, too. The service can be slapdash and negligent. Nonetheless, Fortuna can be a good setting for a filling meal—either in the plush Rennaissance-style restaurant, decorated in pastels and rich shades of blue and gold; the rustic wooden tavern (as long as you get the waiters and musicians to leave you alone); or outside in the courtyard in summer. Downstairs is a champagne cellar, where you can have a bottle custom-dispensed and labeled. In the restaurant, if you have room for dessert, try the *Szent Györgyi palacsinta*, an unusual crepe made with nuts, eggs, meringue, and fruity sauce. *I, Hess András tér 4, tel. 1/175–6857. Reservations advised. Dress: casual but neat. AE, DC, MC, V.*

Kehli. Formerly known as Hídvendéglő (Bridge Inn), the Kehli is on a hard-to-find street near the Óbuda end of the Árpád Bridge, near the Hotel Aquincum (it's well worth the search, though). The inn is small, paneled, and sepia-toned, with an old wooden wagon out front and a garden (which in summer more than doubles the restaurant's capacity). Although this neighborhood tavern underwent an overhaul and a price hike, making it popular with the international tourist set, it still retains its warm, laid-back atmosphere. The food is appropriately hearty and heavy; just reading the menu could raise your cholesterol. Select from appetizers such as carp soup, bean soup with smoked pork knuckles, fried button mushrooms stuffed with brains, or hot bone marrow with garlic toast before moving on to fried goose livers with mashed potatoes or turkey breast stuffed with cheese and goose liver. *III, Mókus utca 22, tel. 1/188–6938. Reservations advised. Dress: casual. AE. Closed Sun.*

★ **Múzeum.** Fans swear that this elegant, candlelit salon with mirrors, mosaics, and swift-moving waiters features the best dining in Budapest. The salads are generous, the Hungarian wines excellent, and the chef dares to be creative. *VIII, Múzeum körút 12, tel. 1/138–4221. Reservations advised. Jacket and tie advised. AE. Closed Sun.*

Postakocsi. In this cavernous cellar under the main square of Óbuda stands the public stagecoach that set out on the first journey from here to Vienna in 1752. It serves as the bar of this large restaurant, which is decorated with saddles, horseshoes, and other equestrian doodads. The Hungarian menu includes such Transylvanian specialties as stuffed sirloin of beef. Goose liver is everywhere—inside mushrooms, in the dressings and secret stuffings of the steaks, fried with french fries, roasted with apples, and in the Hungarian goose-liver stew. Gypsy musicians wander from room to room, something of a mixed blessing. *III, Fő tér 2, tel. 1/188–9941. Reservations advised. Jacket and tie advised. AE, DC, MC, V.*

$$ **Duna-Corso.** One of Budapest's best-kept secrets is no longer so se-
★ cret. This stolid, family-oriented institution, which has stood on the riverfront square dominated by the Vigadó concert hall for nearly two decades, offers good, solid food at reasonable prices right in the center of Pest's luxury-hotel belt. Word of mouth, however, has spread Duna-Corso's fame, and now it's been discovered by foreign tourists. Menus are in Hungarian, German, and English. So far, neither price nor quality shows signs of changing for the worse. The bean and cabbage soup (laced with smoked pork), roast duck with sauerkraut, and all kinds of liver (beef, pork, chicken, goose) are as simple and hearty as ever, and the service is still pokey and friendly. This noisy, bustling spot is lively enough to forestall feelings of loneliness if you're by yourself. For views of the castle and Chain Bridge, a table on the vast outdoor terrace is the best seat in town. *V,*

Vigadó tér 3, tel. 1/118–6362. Reservations accepted. Dress: casual. No credit cards.

Kispipa. Under the same management as Fészek (*see below*), this tiny, well-known restaurant with arched, yellow-glass windows and piano bar features a similar, expansive menu of first-rate Hungarian cuisine. The kitchen has a loyal following of both locals and foreigners, and critics have named its venison ragout soup seasoned with tarragon the best in town. Prices are unexpectedly low, and reservations are essential. *VII, Akácfa utca 38, tel. 1/142 2587. Reservations required. Dress: casual but neat. No credit cards. Closed Sun.*

★ **Remiz.** Opened in 1993 by local restaurant pros, this airy, informal eatery quickly became one of the city's most popular restaurants. Named for the tram yard next door, Remiz offers home-style Hungarian and international cuisines specializing in fresh, flame-seared barbecue dishes. Service can be slow. In warm weather, the outdoor garden is delightful. *II Budakeszi út 5, tel. 1/176–1896. Reservations advised. Dress: casual. AE. Closed Mon.*

Sipos Halászkert. Károly Sipos founded Budapest's best-known fish restaurant, relocated and rebuilt here (after a fire) in 1983 with stones from an 11th-century church that once stood on this Óbuda site. It is now a folksy, touristy, meandering, farmhouse-and-garden complex of rooms with a red-and-black hurdy-gurdy in the entranceway that guests can crank and play. Each room is different— one hunter style, with red carpeting and animal skins; one pub style; one Victorian; one—a hallway—more like an afterthought. The inner garden with lampposts and cherry trees is perfect on a warm summer evening. The fish salad of carp, egg, and caviar will whet your appetite for an excellent and fiery fish soup. The fish stew in red wine with farmer cheese sauce is a superb main course. Waiters will recommend the right Badacsony white wines and Kecskemét red wines. *III, Fő tér 6, tel. 1/188–8745. Reservations advised. Dress: casual. AE, DC, MC, V.*

Svejk. This is the best of the several Czech–Slovak restaurants in town, named for Svejk, the antihero of Jaroslav Hašek's novel *The Good Soldier Schweik.* Situated in a bourgeois corner of downtown Pest (around the corner from Pizza Hut and Kentucky Fried Chicken), Svejk features Czech combinations of pork, dumplings, and sauerkraut, all rendered with a lighter and spicier Slovak touch and a slight Hungarian influence. A Slovak specialty, stuffed tenderloin Bratislava (breaded fillet filled with mushrooms, cheese, and ham), and Svejk cakes (fried potato gnocchi spiced with ham and sausage) should be washed down with fast-flowing Pilsner beer from the barrel. The jovial but subdued literary atmosphere (a long, masculine room in shades of brown, decorated with Jósef Lada's illustrations from the novel) and cordial but discreet service make Svejk a good locale for quiet, lingering evening meals. *VII, Király utca 59/b, tel. 1/122–3278. Reservations advised. Dress: casual. AE, V.*

Tabáni Kakas. Situated just below Castle Hill, this popular restaurant has a distinctly warm and friendly atmosphere and specializes in large helpings of poultry dishes, particularly goose. Try the catfish paprikás or the roast duck with steamed cabbage. A pianist plays and sings every evening except Monday. *I, Attila út 27, tel. 1/175–7165. Reservations advised. Dress: casual. AE, MC.*

Vendégház Étterem. Walking into this elegant restaurant in Óbuda is like entering the genteel living room of the wine merchant to whom the manor house belonged a century ago. Upstairs, the Round Room, decorated in turn-of-the-century sepia tones with a round table that seats 12–14, is excellent for large groups celebrating special occasions; some of Hungary's recent history was decided here. Downstairs is the Readberger beer cellar, an arcaded catacomb with adequate privacy for those who seek it, though there is Gypsy music some nights and, on Tuesday and Wednesday nights, fine jazz. Specialties include veal medallions Kalocsa style (in a sauce of paprika, egg, and tomato) and steak Vendégház (smothered in shellfish, mushrooms, and fruits). For dessert, try the pudding of apricots from Kecskemét, the fruit garden of Hungary's Great Plain. In summer you can sit in one of two gardens adorned with stuffed game and birds. *III, Hídfő utca 16, tel. 1/188–7399. Reservations advised. Dress: casual but neat. AE, DC, MC, V.*

$ **Bagolyvár.** When George Lang first opened this restaurant next door to his gastronomic palace, Gundel, in 1993, there was a buzz of disbelief among restaurant goers: How could such an attractive place serving such excellent food be so inexpensive? Two years later, the familial, informal yet elegant atmosphere remains and the kitchen continues to produce first-rate daily menus of home-style Hungarian specialties. The prices have steadily creeped up but still remain low, especially relative to the restaurant's overall high quality. Musicians entertain with cimbalom or accordion music nightly from 7 PM. In warm weather there is outdoor dining in a lovely back garden. *Állatkerti körút 2, tel. 1/121–3550, ext. 222. Reservations suggested. Dress: casual. AE, DC, MC, V.*

Bohémtanya. Locals have known and loved this place for years for its hearty, reliably tasty fare, huge portions, and relaxed atmosphere. The prices are equally appealing, and to help out newcomers the menu is arranged by price. The word is spreading, however, so be on the safe side and reserve a table. Comfortable, dark-wood booths and tables and friendly, witty waiters make you want to linger over your last, inexpensive beer. *VI, Paulay Ede utca 6, tel. 1/122–1453. Reservations advised. Dress: casual. No credit cards.*

★ **Fészek.** This elegant Hungarian restaurant in the heart of downtown Pest is difficult to find, tucked as it is inside the nearly 100-year-old Fészek Artist's Club. But the search is amply rewarded: a large, turn-of-the-century Classicist dining room with Seccessionist details boasts high ceilings hung with brass and glass chandeliers, and mustard-colored walls with ornate molding and dark-wood panels. In summer guests dine outdoors at candlelit tables set in a Venetian-style courtyard, originally monks' cloisters, with pillared archways, colorful majolica decorations, and blooming chestnut trees. The extensive, almost daunting menu features all the Hungarian classics, with such specialties as turkey stuffed with goose liver and a variety of game dishes. *VII, Dob utca 55 (corner of Kertész utca), tel. 1/122–6043. Reservations accepted. 50 Ft. Artist's Club cover charge. Dress: casual. AE. Garden dining May–late summer.*

Marxim. Just two years after the death of socialism in Hungary, this pizza and pasta restaurant opened up to mock the old regime—and milk it for all it's worth. From the flashing red star above the door outside to the clever puns on menu items, the theme of the place is "communist nostalgia." Classic black-and-white photos of decorated hard-liners and papier-mâché doves stuck in gnarled barbed-wire fences line the walls, and the flat, hard booths are painted a standard bland gray with touches of glorious red. But all this mock socialism has rubbed some the wrong way: At press time (spring 1994), the state charged that Marxim's owner was violating the 1993 ban in Hungary on the public display of totalitarian symbols. Young people cram into the booths, and rock music blares. Pizzas—with such names as "à la Anarchismo" and "à la Sztálinvárosese"—are good by Hungarian standards, and the skinny calzones are tasty. Allow some time to wait for a seat—and possibly your food—when it's

very busy. *II, Kisrókus utca 23, tel. 1/115–5036. No reservations.
Dress: casual. AE, DC, V. Closed Sun. lunch.*

Lodging

More of the major luxury and business-class hotel chains are represented in Budapest; however, all of them are Hungarian-run franchise operations with native touches that you won't find in any other Hilton or Ramada.

Addresses below are preceded by the district number (in Roman numerals) as well as the street address and Hungarian postal code. Districts V, VI, and VII are in downtown Pest; I is the main tourist district of Buda.

Highly recommended lodgings in a particular price category are indicated by a star ★.

\$\$\$\$ **Atrium Hyatt.** The spectacular 10-story interior—a mix of glass elevators, cascading water, a rain forest of tropical greenery, an open bar, and café—is surpassed only by the views across the Danube to the Royal Castle (rooms with a river view cost substantially more). Accommodations are modern but homey—you don't even feel as if you're in a hotel—and suites have Thonet bentwood rocking chairs. The breakfast buffet features a *muesli* table with grains, seeds, and cereals in addition to the more cholesterol-boosting spread. Well situated in the inner city near the Pest waterfront, the Hyatt and its facilities and amenities remain in the vanguard of the downtown hotels. *V, Roosevelt tér 2, H-1051, tel. 1/266–1234, fax 1/266–9101. 353 rooms, 27 suites. Facilities: 3 restaurants, 2 bars, casino, conference facilities, business center, beauty salon, indoor swimming pool, health club, sauna, solarium, ballroom, private underground parking on site, valet services, travel arrangements, IBUSZ agency, car hire, airport transfer service. Regency Clubs on 7th and 8th floors. AE, DC, V.*

★ **Budapest Hilton.** Built in 1977 around a 13th-century monastery, adjacent to the Matthias Coronation Church and overlooking the Danube from the choicest site on Castle Hill, this perfectly integrated architectural wonder is a thrilling place. Guests stay in ample Hilton-contemporary rooms with double-sink bathrooms. Every room has a remarkable view; Danube vistas cost more. Much of Budapest's international business seems to be conducted in the lobby bar. You can gamble in the casino on the top floor, and the ground-level Kalocsa and Dominican restaurants offer top-notch Continental and Hungarian cuisines. For swimming and sauna, there is free admission to the Thermal Hotel on Margaret Island, but it doesn't operate on weekends. Children, regardless of age, get free accommodation when sharing a room with their parents. Breakfast is not included in the room rate—a dubious distinction in Budapest; many guests are surprised, upon leaving an otherwise excellent morning feast, to be hit with a bill. *I, Hess András tér 1–3, H-1014, tel. 1/175–1000, fax 1/156–0285; in U.S. and Canada, tel. 800/445–8667. 323 rooms, 28 suites. Facilities: 3 restaurants, café, 2 bars; wine cellar, casino, hairdresser, cosmetic salon, conference rooms, ballroom, parking, gift shops, flower shop, boutiques, antiques shop, IBUSZ travel agency, business center. AE, DC, MC, V.*

Budapest Marriott. Opened December 31, 1969, as the Duna Inter-Continental, this was the first of Budapest's big chain hotels to open its doors—a square, boxy bunker guarding the Danube on the Pest side between the Elizabeth and Chain bridges, built to provide every room with a balcony and a river view. Today, fresh out of a \$13 million exhaustive overhaul by the Marriott chain, which bought it in 1993, this sophisticated yet friendly hotel has firmly placed itself at the top of its class. Attention to detail is evident from the moment you enter the lobby, from the impeccably presented buffet of color-fully glazed cakes and pastries to the feather-light ring of the front-desk bell. The decor is an elegant blend of contemporary and tradi-tional—marble floors, forest-green leather couches, dark-wood panels accented with brass lamps, and fresh flower arrangements in the lobby. Roomy beds, lushly patterned carpets, floral bedspreads, and etched glass create a serene ambience in the guest rooms. The layout takes full advantage of the hotel's prime Danube location, of-fering breathtaking views of Gellért Hill, the Chain and Elizabeth bridges, and Castle Hill from the lobby, ballroom, every guest room, and even the swimming pool. In summer you can bask in the sun on the front deck and watch the boats drift past on the Danube. *V, Apáczai Csere János utca 4, Box 100, H-1364, tel. 1/266–7000, fax 1/266–5000. 362 rooms, 20 suites. Facilities: 3 restaurants, bar, business center, conference room, ballroom, fitness center, squash court, tourist services desk, laundry and valet, gift shop, baby-sit-ting, garage, parking. AE, DC, MC, V.*

★ **Forum.** Much of this hotel's success has to do with the two-to-one ra-tio of staff to rooms. This is felt from the moment you enter the brightly lit lobby; whether you need a message hand-delivered across town or a button sewn, the staff is always ready—though never fawning. The rooms, 60% of which have Danube views, are done in shades of brown and cream, with welcoming upholstered fur-niture. A business center in the lobby provides computers, laser printers, fax machines, and the like to meet guests' business needs. In addition to providing the usual recreational amenities, the well-equipped Leisure Center offers state-of-the-art fitness and bodybuilding equipment, as well as pedicure services. The Viennese Coffeehouse prepares the best pastries in town. At press time (sum-mer 1994), plans were under way to renovate the lobby by 1995. In Budapest, at least, Forum is no longer the budget stepchild of the Inter-Continental chain. There is no charge for children under 14 staying in their parents' room; a single-room rate is charged if two children share a connecting room. *V, Apáczai Csere János utca 12–14, Box 231, H-1368, tel. 1/117–8088; in the U.S. and Canada, tel. 800/327–0200; fax 1/117–9808. 392 rooms, 16 suites. Facilities: 2 res-taurants, 2 cafés, bar, fitness center, business center, same-day va-let service, airport transfer, drugstore, travel desk, car rental, barbershop, beauty parlor, florist, theater reservations, doctor. AE, DC, MC, V.*

★ **Grand Hotel Corvinus Kempinski.** Opened in 1992, the Kempinski is the newest of Budapest's luxury hotels but has already become a fo-cal point of elite goings-on, such as hosting Sotheby's debut art auc-tion in Hungary. Unlike its peers, the Kempinski has no Danube views to offer, just a central location between a pedestrian arcade and a public park. Its dramatic modern design alternates surfaces of glass and polished stone arrayed in stylish geometries. The room de-cor is understated with an emphasis on functional touches, including three phones in every room; original Hungarian artwork and fresh-cut flowers help keep things from getting sterile. The Kempinski boasts all the usual facilities and amenities you would expect in a ho-tel of its caliber, although its indoor pool is rather undersize. Its flagship restaurant, Gourmet, offers a tempting prix fixe menu dai-ly. Be warned: Breakfast is not included in the room rates. *V, Erzsébet tér 7–8, H-1051, tel. 1/266–1000, in the U.S. and Canada, tel. 800/426–3135; fax 1/266–2000. 340 rooms, 28 suites. Facilities: 3 restaurants, 3 bars, business center, conference room, indoor swim-*

*ming pool, sauna, fitness center, private parking, valet services,
airport transfer, beauty salon, IBUSZ agency, boutiques, gift shop.
AE, DC, MC, V.*

$$$ Aquincum. This classy, glassy urban spa hotel opened in May 1991.
One of its three atriums lets the sun shine in on a long, sloping swim-
ming pool heated to 25°C (77°F), a thermal pool heated to 31°C
(88°F), a thermal healing pool heated to the fever pitch of 39°C
(102°F), and a whirlpool. The thermal waters are piped in from a
well on Margaret Island, which the Danube-view rooms overlook.
The waters are considered therapeutic for rheumatic and arthritic
problems, gout, circulatory disturbances, chronic bronchitis, recu-
peration from injuries, and even old age! Most of the patrons, how-
ever, are businesspeople and tourists who just want a place for
swimming before or after sightseeing. The hotel's location—on the
Buda side near the Árpád Bridge—seems a minus, but it's fairly
handy to public transport going everywhere in town (and right off
the HÉV suburban railway to Szentendre). It boasts a cordial, even
chummy, front desk staff, who greet guests by name, and extraordi-
narily solicitous room service. *III, Árpád fejedlem útja 94, H-1036,
tel. 1/250–3360 or 1/250–4177, fax 1/250–4672. 304 rooms with bath,
8 suites. No-smoking rooms and rooms for the disabled. Facilities:
restaurant, 2 bars, café, nightclub, sauna, fitness center, beauty sa-
lon, drugstore, gift shop, travel agency, car rental, minibars and
TVs in rooms, baby-sitting, parking. AE, DC, MC, V.*

Flamenco. Opened in 1989 next to a park with a lake behind Gellért
Hill, and convenient to downtown Pest via two nearby bridges, this
hotel is a welcome addition to the ranks of luxury hotels on the Buda
side of the river. Although it was originally conceived as a Spanish-
style hotel, somehow only the names of its restaurants and cafés—
La Bodega, Bolero, and Colombus Café—reflect the national char-
acter. The exterior is vanilla-slab, and the low-ceilinged lobby is
glitzy and spotlighted. Rooms are decorated in pleasant pastel
beiges and greens, with modern wooden furniture and minibars.
The Bolero restaurant serves international cuisine and features live
chamber music. The Flamenco is equipped with all the amenities for
work and play (including access to a nearby tennis center), and the
staff couldn't be nicer. When it is not booked solid with tour groups,
this can be one of the quietest, least bustling—in fact, almost resi-
dential—hotels in Budapest. *XI, Tas vezér utca 7, H-1113, tel. 1/
161–2250 or 1/166–9619, fax 1/165–8007. 330 rooms with bath, 14
suites. Facilities: wine bar, restaurant, café, sauna, swimming pool
with poolside bar, solarium, business center, travel agent, drug-
store, souvenir shop, garage, parking. AE, DC, MC, V.*

★ **Gellért.** The double-deck rotunda of this grand Hungarian hotel
leads you to expect a string orchestra, concealed behind massive
marble pillars, playing "The Emperor Waltz." Indeed, the Jugend-
stil (Art Nouveau) Gellért, built in 1918, was favored by Otto von
Habsburg, son of the last emperor, and by that other deposed mon-
arch, Richard Nixon. Rooms have early 20th-century furnishings,
including some Jugendstil pieces, along with views across the Dan-
ube (more expensive) or up Gellért Hill. Rooms and amenities are up
to date, and the coffee shop is among the city's best; but the pièce de
résistance is the monumental thermal baths, including an outdoor
pool with a wave machine. Admission to the spa is free to hotel
guests (medical treatments cost extra); corridors and an elevator
lead directly to the baths from the second, third, and fourth floors.
*XI, Gellért tér 1, H-1114, tel. 1/185–2200, fax 1/166–6631. 239 rooms
with bath, 15 suites. Facilities: restaurant, café, brasserie, business
center, baby-sitting, spa, thermal baths, parking. AE, DC, MC, V.*

Grand Hotel Hungaria. Budapest's largest hotel, rebuilt in 1985 on the site of the old Hotel Imperial, stands on a busy boulevard just across an impossible traffic circle from the handsome Keleti (East) station, where the *Orient Express* stops every day. Triple windows keep noise out of the large, fairly bland rooms, with their low beds, upholstered chairs, and orange-check rugs; the best views are from the upper floors, facing the railroad terminal and looking beyond over urban Pest. The hotel itself is well equipped and its staff efficient. *VII, Rákóczi út 90, H-1074, tel. 1/122–9050, fax 1/122–8029. 404 rooms with bath, 8 suites. Facilities: 2 restaurants, 3 bars, IBUSZ and Malév desk, gift shop, business center, photo service, garage. AE, DC, MC, V.*

★ **Helia.** Postcommunist Hungary's first privately built major hotel (financed with Hungarian, Finnish, and a little U.S. capital) opened in late 1990. The staff is friendly and helpful, and most of the comfortable rooms have Danube views. The reasonably priced Jupiter restaurant, open from morning to midnight, has an excellent cold buffet. Helia also boasts Budapest's most enjoyable hotel swimming complex—sun terrace, two hot thermal pools, a Jacuzzi, two saunas, two Turkish baths, a swimming pool, and a fitness center—all included in the room price. Located about 15 minutes by bus and 10 minutes by metro from downtown, the Helia is the perfect place to combine a little rest and relaxation with sightseeing. *XIII, Karpát utca 62–64, H-1133, tel. 1/270–3277, fax 1/270–2262; in the U.S. and Canada, tel. 800/223–5652. 262 rooms, 4 suites with sauna, 4 suites with bar. Facilities: 2 restaurants, café, fitness center, spa, tennis courts, beauty salon, business center. AE, DC, MC, V.*

Korona. Modern and functional, this Austrian-built hotel is on busy Kálvin tér in the center of the city, near the river and close to the National Museum and other sights. *V, Kecskeméti utca 14, tel. 1/117–4111, fax 1/118–3867. 433 rooms with bath. Facilities: pool, restaurant, bar, sauna, solarium, fitness club, massage, business center, parking garage.*

Novotel. This member of the French motor-inn chain is on the rim of a large park near the highways to Vienna and Lake Balaton. Connected to the Budapest Convention Center, it is favored by musicians as well as by convention delegates. Though the rooms are ordinary, with tiny bathrooms, soft mattresses, and a motel-generic decor, the amenities are more than ample, including closed-circuit TV news in English, French, and German; a complete business center; and, famous around town, the Bowling Brasserie, featuring "fried meats, draft beer," and a bowling alley. This is a more rewarding chain-hotel environment than at the Buda Penta. There is no charge for children under 16 staying in their parents' room. *XII, Alkotás út 63–67, Box 233, H-1444, tel. 1/186–9588, fax 1/166–5636; for reservations, tel. 1/166–9031; in the U.S., tel. 213/277–6915. 318 rooms with bath, 6 suites. Facilities: restaurant, 2 bars, swimming pool, bowling alley, hairdresser, drugstore, florist, clothing boutique, business center, parking. AE, DC, MC, V.*

★ **Radisson Béke.** In 1975 it was a family-oriented inn where a room cost less than $6 a night; a decade later the well-situated Béke (on a main boulevard near the Nyugati (West) Railroad Station underwent a lavish overhaul. Today it is a luxury hotel with a glittering turn-of-the-century facade, liveried doormen, a lobby lined with mosaics and statuary, and bellmen bowing before the grand marble staircase. Popular with Italians and Americans, this hotel has all the business amenities plus the efficient services of a helpful staff. Rooms resemble solidly modern living rooms. The breakfast buffet in the Shakespeare Room upstages a voluptuous *Twelfth Night* mural by offering the usual choices, all fresh and flavorful, plus creamy layer cakes and spicy stews that would make Sir Toby gluttonous. A lavish Sunday brunch, uncommon in Budapest, is also served. At night, feast on the spectacle at the Orfeum Casino. *VI, Teréz krt. 43, H-1067, tel. 1/132-3300, fax 1/153-3380. 238 rooms with bath, 8 suites. Facilities: 2 restaurants, café, 2 bars, casino, business center, conference rooms, swimming pool, sauna, solarium, hairdresser, gift shops, travel agency, parking. AE, DC, MC, V.*

The Ramada Grand Hotel. Built in 1873 and long in disrepair, this venerable hotel reopened in 1987 as perhaps the world's stateliest Ramada Inn, located on Margaret Island in the middle of the Danube. Room rates may have been raised, but the high ceilings haven't been lowered. Nor have the old-fashioned room trimmings—down comforters, ornate chandeliers, Old World furniture—been lost in the streamlining. Graham Greene always took the same suite that he had before World War II, and the U.S. Embassy likes to send visitors here. *XIII, Margitsziget, H-1138, tel. 1/111-1000, fax 1/153-3029; for hotel guests, tel. 1/132-1100; for reservations, tel. 1/131-7769; in the U.S., tel. 800/228-9898. 162 rooms with bath, 10 suites. Facilities: restaurant, ice cream shop, fitness center, spa. AE, DC, MC, V.*

$$ **Astoria.** At a busy intersection in downtown Pest stands a re-
★ vitalized turn-of-the-century hotel that remains an oasis of quiet and serenity in hectic surroundings. Staff members are always—albeit unobtrusively—on hand. Rooms are genteel, spacious, and comfortable, furnished rather like Grandma's sitting room, in slightly Victorian style with an occasional antique. Recent renovations have faithfully preserved the hotel's original decor and furnishings. Though the hotel lacks a business or fitness center, the Astoria's bar is a popular meeting place for businesspeople. *V, Kossuth Lajos utca 19-21, H-1053, tel. 1/117-3411, fax 1/118-6798. 130 rooms with bath or shower. Facilities: restaurant, bar, café, nightclub, IBUSZ desk, conference room. AE, DC, MC, V.*

Buda Penta. Situated by the South Railroad Station, and therefore convenient for jaunts to Vienna and most of Hungary, this is surely the least Hungarian-looking hotel in Buda—its flat gray exterior with orange details actually recalls Howard Johnson's; its Capri Pizzeria Pub (with good light and dark draft beer) and Krisztina Espresso café recall something of Coney Island. The bland modern rooms are small with low ceilings but comfortable. *I, Krisztina krt. 41-43, H-1013, tel. 1/156-6333; in the U.S. and Canada, tel. 800/225-3456; fax 1/155-6964. 391 rooms with bath. 5 suites. Facilities: restaurant, bar, café, sauna, swimming pool, business center. AE, DC, MC, V.*

Nemzeti. Another hotel that reflects the grand mood of the turn of the century, the lovely, pale-blue Nemzeti was completely restored in 1987. The high-ceilinged lobby and public areas—with pillars, arches, and wrought-iron railings—are elegant, but the guest rooms are small and unexceptional. It's located at bustling Blaha Lujza tér, in the center of Pest; to ensure a quiet night, ask for a room facing the inner courtyard. *VIII, József krt. 4, tel. 1/133-9160, fax 1/114-0019. 76 rooms. Facilities: restaurant, brasserie, drugstore, garage. AE, DC, MC, V.*

Panorama Hotels & Bungalows. Perched 1,017 feet above the Danube near the upper terminus of the cogwheel railway and surrounded by giant pine trees, the Panorama resembles a grand hunting lodge. Hotel rooms are modern and comfortable, decorated with cheerful pastel colors and prints. Rooms with views offer spectacular vistas over the hills of Buda and beyond to Pest. The charming bungalows, though a bit close together, are like miniature cabins in the woods, with pinewood floors and walls and a cozy sitting area; some also have kitchens. Unless you have vertigo, you will admire the view of the entire city from the terrace. The restaurant serves international cuisine and features live Gypsy music nightly. At press time (spring 1994), privatization negotiations were under way, making it likely that the Panorama would have a new owner by the publication of this edition. Contact Tourinform or any tourist office for the latest status. *XII, Rege utca 21, tel. 1/175–0522, fax 1/ 175–9727. 35 rooms with bath, 54 self-catering bungalows. Facilities: restaurant, bar terrace, pool, sauna, solarium. AE, DC, MC, V.*

Taverna. This 12-story, Austrian-built hotel is located in the heart of Pest's main shopping pedestrian zone, a few steps from the Danube and directly across Váci utca from International Trade Center 2; it was built around the same time (1985) and has a similar glass-needle style. The Taverna has an adequate range of facilities, including a popular bowling alley, and its cheerful, obliging staff makes Budapest less intimidating (and a good value) for the business traveler. *V, Váci utca 20, H-1052, tel. 1/138–4999, reservations 1/118–7500, fax 1/118–7188. 224 rooms with bath or shower. Facilities: 2 restaurants, café, 3 bars, fitness center, sauna, solarium, massage, bowling alley, garage. AE, DC, MC, V.*

$ **Citadella.** Comparatively basic, with four beds in some rooms and showers down the hall, the Citadella is nevertheless very popular for its price and stunning location—right inside the fortress. Half of the rooms compose a youth hostel, giving the hotel a young and lively communal atmosphere. None of the rooms have bathrooms, but half have showers. *XI, Gellérthegy, tel. 1/166–5794. 20 rooms, none with bath. No credit cards.*

Ifjúság. This concrete "youth" hotel is a boxy remnant of socialist architecture, but the location—a quiet, residential street at the top of a hill in Buda—is lovely and the rooms are modern and clean. Ask for a room with a view and a balcony, and you won't be sorry. *II, Zivatar utca 3, tel. 1/135–3331, fax 1/135–3989. 100 rooms with bath. Facilities: restaurant. AE, DC, MC, V.*

Medosz. One of Budapest's better small hotels, the Medosz offers a central Pest location near the Oktogon, a major transport hub. Its modern, Socialist Realism concrete appearance wins no points for architecture, but the surrounding buildings, including the nearby Opera House, more than compensate. Most rooms face a pleasant park in front, but if you prefer quiet, request one facing the rear. *VI, Jókai tér 9, H-1061, tel. 1/153–1700 or 1/153–1434, fax 1/132–4316. 63 rooms, 7 suites. Facilities: restaurant (for groups only). No credit cards.*

The Arts and Nightlife

The Arts Budapest's two major opera citadels, the **Magyar Állami Operaház** (Hungarian State Opera House) and the **Erkel Színház** (Erkel Theater), present an international repertoire of classical and modern works as well as such Hungarian favorites as Kodály's *Háry János*. The **Operetta Theater** features not just Lehár and Kalman but also Hungarian renditions of *My Fair Lady*, *Fiddler on the Roof*, and a *Singing in the Rain* that Broadway director Harold Prince calls the best stage production he's ever seen. Four musical theaters—**Arizona**, **Madách**, **Vígszínház**, and **Pesti**—offer such spectacles as *Cats* and *Les Misérables* in Hungarian. The **Merlin Theater** produces a series of plays in English every summer.

For the latest on arts events, consult the entertainment listings of the English-language newspapers. *The Budapest Sun*'s entertainment calendar maps out nine days and nights of all that's happening in Budapest's arts and culture world—from thrash bands in wild clubs to performances at the Opera House and traditional Hungarian folk-dancing lessons at local cultural houses. Another option is to stop in at the **National Philharmonic ticket office** at Vörösmarty tér 1 and browse through the scores of free programs and fliers and scan the walls coated with upcoming concert posters. Hotels and tourist offices will also provide you with a copy of the monthly publication *Programme*, which contains details of all cultural events.

Classical Music **Budai Vigadó** (Buda Concert Hall), I, Corvin tér 8, tel. 1/201–5928. **Budapest Kongresszusi Központ** (Budapest Convention Center), XII, Jagelló utca 1–3, tel. 1/161–2869. **Bartók Béla Emlékház** (Bartók Bélla Memorial House), II, Csalán út 29, tel. 1/176–2100. **Erkel Színház** (Erkel Theater; opera), VII, Köztársaság tér 30, tel. 1/133–0540. **Liszt Ferenc Zeneakadémia** (Franz Liszt Academy of Music), VI, Liszt Ferenc tér 8, tel. 1/141–4788. **Magyar Állami Operaház** (Hungarian State Opera House), VI, Andrassy út 22, tel. 1/153–0170. **Pesti Vigadó** (Pest Concert Hall), V, Vigadó tér 5, tel. 1/117–6222. **Régi Zeneakadémia** (Old Academy of Music), VI, Vörösmarty utca 35, tel. 1/122–9804.

English-Language Movies Many of the English-language movies that come to Budapest are subtitled in Hungarian rather than dubbed. There are more than 30 cinemas that regularly show films in English, and tickets are very inexpensive by Western standards (about 150 Ft.). Consult the movie matrix in *The Budapest Sun* for a weekly list of what's showing.

Folk Dancing Many of Budapest's district cultural centers regularly hold traditional folk-dancing evenings, often with general instruction at the beginning. In addition to offering good exercise, these sessions provide a less touristed way to taste Hungarian culture. Ask your hotel clerk to find out the latest programs at these more popular cultural centers.

Almássy Recreation Center, VII, Almássy tér 6, tel. 1/142–0387. **First District Cultural Center,** I, Bem Rakpart 6, tel. 1/201–0324. **Fővárosi Cultural House,** XI, Fehérvári út 47, tel. 1/181–1360. **Kosztolányi Cultural Center,** IX, Török Pál utca 3, tel. 1/118–0207. **Marczibányi tér Cultural Center,** II, Marczibányi tér 5/a, tel. 1/115–1208.

Galleries Budapest has dozens of art galleries showing and selling old works as well as the very latest. The following is just a sampling.

Csontváry Gallery (V, Vörösmarty tér 1, tel. 1/118–4594). Right in the center of town, this is a good place to view works by today's Hungarian painters. **Dovin Gallery** (V, Haris köz 1, 1st floor, tel. 1/118–3524 or 1/118–3574). This gallery specializes in Hungarian contemporary paintings. **Gallery 56** (V, Falk Miksa utca 7, tel. 1/269–2529). New York celebrity Yoko Ono opened this gallery in fall 1992 to show art by internationally famed artists, such as Keith Haring, as well as her own works. **Qualitas Gallery** (V, Bécsi utca 2, tel. 1/118–4438). Here you can view works by the most significant Hungarian painters of the 20th century.

Roczkov Gallery (VI, Andrássy út 1, tel. 1/268–0026). Contemporary paintings, installations, and sculptures are shown in this tiny gallery run by three young sisters.

Vigadó Gallery (V, Vigadó tér 2, tel. 1/118–7932). This gallery, located in the vast Pest Concert Hall (Pesti Vigadó), features traditional paintings by contemporary Hungarian artists.

Theater **Arany János Színház,** VI, Paulay Ede utca 35, tel. 1/141–5626.

Arizona, VI, Nagymező utca 22–24, tel. 1/112–4230.

József Attila Theater, VII, Váci utca 63, tel. 1/120–8239; ticket office, tel. 1/140–9428.

Madách Theater, VII, Erzsébet körút 31–33, tel. 1/122–0677; ticket office, tel. 1/122–2015.

Merlin Színház, V, Gerlóczy utca 4, tel. 1/117–9338.

Operetta Theater, VI, Nagymező utca 17, tel. 1/132–0535.

Pesti Theater, V, Váci utca 9, tel. 1/118–5255; ticket office, tel. 1/118–5547.

Várszínház (Castle Theater), I, Színház utca 1–3, tel. 1/175–8649.

Vígszínház (Comedy Theater), XIII, Szent István körút 14, tel. 1/111–1650; ticket office, 1/111–0430.

Ticket Offices Tickets can be bought at the venues themselves, but several ticket offices sell them without extra charge. Theater and opera tickets are sold at the **Central Theater Booking Office** (Pest: VI, Andrassy út 18, tel. 1/112–0000; Buda: II, Moszkva tér 3, tel. 1/135–9136). For concert tickets, go to the **National Philharmonic Ticket Office** (V, Vörösmarty tér 1, tel. 1/117–6222). Prices are dirt-cheap, so markups of even 30% shouldn't dent your wallet if you book through your hotel. Other outlets for tickets are **Music Mix Ticket Service** (V, Váci utca 33, tel. 1/138–2237 or 1/117–7736) and **Tourinform** (V, Sütő utca 2, tel. 1/117–9800).

Nightlife Budapest's nightlife is vibrant and diverse. For basic beer and wine drinking, *sörözős* (beer bars) and *borozős* (wine bars) abound, although the latter tend to serve the early-morning-spritzer-before-work types rather than nighttime revelers.

For quiet conversation there are *drink-bárs* in most hotels and all over town, but beware of the inflated prices and steep cover charges. Cafés are preferable for unescorted women.

Most night spots and clubs have bars, pool tables, and dance floors. As is the case in most other cities, the life of a club or disco in Budapest can be somewhat ephemeral. In one year, several different clubs may open and close at the same address. Those listed below are quite popular and seem to be here to stay. But for the very latest on the more transient "in"-spots, consult the nightlife sections of *The Budapest Sun* and *Budapest Week*.

A word of warning to the smoke-sensitive: Budapest is a city of smokers. No matter where you spend your night out, chances are you'll come home smelling of cigarette smoke.

Bars and Clubs **Cafe Pierrot,** an elegant piano bar in the Castle Hill district with rattan furniture and Pierrot-theme decor, has live piano music nightly beginning at 8 PM and an extensive cocktail menu. *I, Fortuna utca 14, tel. 1/175–6971.*

Corvinus Bar is the place to go for a peaceful, elegant evening out. Inside the Kempinski Hotel, the bar is decorated with polished woods and brass and features a wide, if pricey, selection of cocktails. Live jazz ensembles play frequently, and on Friday and Saturday night starting at 10 PM, the Corvinus becomes a disco with DJ dance music. *Kempinski Hotel: V, Erzsébet tér 7–8, tel. 1/266–1000.*

Fehér Gyűrű Söröző (White Ring Beer Bar) is a low-key, low-ceilinged pub with cozy wooden booths that is popular with locals. Beer and drinks are good and are reasonably priced, and the sandwiches are first-rate. *V, Balassi Bálint utca 27, tel. 1/112–1863.*

Fortuna, located in a historic medieval house on Castle Hill, is a popular disco with a large dose of "attitude," occasionally demanding mysterious membership cards from would-be patrons. On these occasions, dressing up a bit may increase your chances of getting in. *I, Hess András tér 4, tel. 1/175–2401.*

Fregatt, an English-Irish pub popular with travelers and young Hungarians, serves Guinness beer and frequently features live music. *V, Molnár utca 26, tel. 1/118–9997.*

The Jazz Cafe is a small basement club featuring good live jazz bands every night starting at 8 PM. *V, Balassi Bálint utca 25, tel. 1/132–4377.*

Labirintus Kávézó (Labyrinth Cafe), set in the tunnels of the historic Buda Castle labyrinth, is an elegant, cultured, and literally cool café of zigzagging nooks and stone walls brightened with live plants and flowers. Top local blues and jazz bands play Wednesday through Saturday nights. *I, Úri utca 9, tel. 1/153–0566. Open from 6 PM; closed Sun. and Mon.*

Mad Block is a popular disco in the ornate Baroque theater that once housed the Moulin Rouge nightclub. Live bands play Sunday through Thursday, and the disco on Friday and Saturday keeps revelers dancing into the wee hours. *VI, Nagymező utca 17, tel. 1/112–4492.*

Made Inn Music Club is a contemporary bar and disco in an elegant, old stone mansion near Heroes' Square. Televisions playing MTV are embedded in the floor, even in the men's bathroom. In summer you can sit at tables on the large patio that has its own bar and pool table. *VI, Andrássy út 112, tel. 1/111–3437.*

Merlin, located above the Merlin Theater, is Budapest's most famous jazz club. It's low on atmosphere but features the biggest names in Hungarian and international jazz. Patrons can order dinner and drinks from the full menu or just sit at the tables and listen. *Live music Fri.–Sun. only. V, Gerlóczy utca 4, tel. 1/117–5935.*

Morrison's Music Pub, just behind the Opera House, opened in spring 1993 to immediate success. A heavy green metal door leads down to this corridor-shaped, basement bar with wooden tables and a popular dance floor. *VI, Révay utca 25, tel. 1/269–4060.*

Piaf, named for the legendary French chanteuse, is a popular, classy club with a touch of pretentiousness, frequented by the local arts circle. The atmosphere, though densely smoky, is hard to beat, with red velvet chairs and low, candlelit tables in tiny, cozy brick rooms. *Open from 10 PM. VI, Nagymező utca 20, tel. 1/112–3823.*

Picasso Point is a hip bar with live background jazz and an artsy mix of international regulars. Decor plays on the Pablo theme, with several Picasso-figure-shaped tables and changing contemporary art exhibits on the walls. *VI, Hajós utca 31, tel. 1/132–4750.*

Tilos az Á attracts a hip, "alternative" crowd to drink, dance, and hang out amid walls painted with New York City–scape murals. Bands that span the spectrum—from traditional Gypsy ensembles to jazz-punk groups called Blurt—play in the brick, tunnel-shaped cellar. *VIII, Mikszáth Kálmán tér 2, tel. 1/118–0684.*

Casinos **Casino Orfeum.** In the Radisson Béke Hotel. VI, Teréz körút 43. Open daily 2 PM–4 AM.

Citadella Casino. On Gellért Hill. XI, Gellérthegyi sétány, tel. 1/166–7686 or 1/185–7883. Open daily 6 PM–5 AM.

Golden Gate Casino. VI, Teréz körút, tel. 1/122–0886. Open 24 hours a day.

Gresham Casino. In the Gresham Palace. V, Roosevelt tér 5, tel. 1/117–2407. Open daily 2 PM–4 AM.

Hilton Casino. In the Budapest Hilton Hotel. I, Hess András tér, tel. 1/175–1333. Open daily 5 PM–4 AM.

Imperial Casino. V, Szabadsajtó utca 5, tel. 1/118–2404. Open daily 4 PM–4 AM.

Las Vegas Casino. Sylvester Stallone is an owner. V, Roosevelt tér 2, tel. 1/117–6022. Open 24 hours a day.

Schönbrunn Casino Boat. V, Roosevelt tér–lower dock, tel. 1/138–2016. Open daily 4 PM–4 AM.

Várkert Casino. I, Miklós Ybl tér 9, tel. 1/202–4244. Open daily 2 PM–4 AM.

Vigadó Casino. In the Pest Concert Hall building. V, Vigadó utca 2, tel. 1/117–0869. Open daily 2 PM–4 AM.

The Danube Bend

About 40 kilometers (25 miles) north of Budapest, the Danube abandons its eastward course and turns abruptly south toward the capital, cutting through the Börzsöny and Visegrád hills. This area is called the Danube Bend and includes the Baroque town of Szentendre, the hilltop castle ruins and town of Visegrád, and the cathedral town of Esztergom. The attractive combination of hillside and river should dispel any notion that Hungary is one vast, boring plain.

The Danube Bend is the most scenically varied part of Hungary. There is a whole chain of riverside spas and beaches, bare volcanic mountains, and limestone hills. Here, in the heartland, are the traces of the country's history—the remains of the Roman Empire's frontiers, the battlefields of the Middle Ages, and the relics of the Hungarian Renaissance.

The west bank of the Danube is the more interesting side, with three charming and picturesque towns—Szentendre, Visegrád, and Esztergom—all of which richly repay a visit. The district can be covered by car in one day, the total round-trip being no more than 112 kilometers (70 miles), although this affords only a cursory look. Two days, with a night at either Visegrád or Esztergom (both of which have good hotels), would suffice for a more thorough and leisurely experience of this delightful part of Hungary.

On the Danube's eastern bank, Vác is the only larger town of any real interest. The Danube is not crossed by any bridges; but there are numerous ferries (between Visegrád and Nagymaros; Basaharc and Szob; Szentendre Island and Vác), making it possible to combine a visit to both sides of the Danube on the same excursion.

Work had started on a hydroelectric dam near Nagymaros, across from Visegrád, during the mid-1980s. The project was proposed by Austria and Czechoslovakia and reluctantly agreed to by Hungary, but protests from the Blues (Hungary's equivalent of Germany's Greens), coupled with rapid democratization, seem to have aborted the project and rescued a region of great natural beauty.

Important Addresses and Numbers

Tourist Information Esztergom: IBUSZ (Lőrinc utca 1, tel. 33/312–552, fax 33/311–643); Komtourist (Lőrinc utca 6, tel. 33/312–082).

Szentendre: IBUSZ (Bogdányi út 11, tel. 26/313–596, tel. and fax 26/310–333); Dunatours (Bogdányi út 1, on the quay, tel. 26/311–311).
Vác: IBUSZ (Széchenyi utca 4, tel. 27/317–011); Dunatours (Széchenyi utca 14, tel. 27/310–940); Tourinform (Dr. Csányi krt. 45, tel. 27/316–160).
Visegrád: FANNY Travel Agency (Fő út 44, tel. and fax 26/398–268).

Emergencies Police (tel. 07). Ambulance (tel. 04). Fire (tel. 05).

Late-Night Pharmacy In Szentendre, the pharmacy at Liget utca 5 (tel. 26/310–487) has late hours.

Travel Agency In Budapest, IBUSZ and the main office of Dunatours (Bajcsy Zsilinszky út 17, tel. 1/131–4533, fax 1/111–6827) can supply information about the Danube Bend.

Getting Around

If you have enough time, you can travel by boat from Budapest, a leisurely and pleasant journey, especially in summer and spring. Boats for Esztergom leave from the main Pest dock near Vigadó tér. On summer Sundays and public holidays a hydrofoil service brings Visegrád within an hour and Esztergom within two hours of Budapest. Timetables are on display at the dock (tel. 861/118–1223), in major hotels, and at most travel agencies in Budapest. Trains run frequently to Szentendre from Batthyány tér in Buda. By car via Szentendre–Visegrád–Esztergom follow Highway 11, which more or less hugs the Buda bank of the Danube.

To reach Vác from Budapest you can travel by boat (Vigadó tér dock), by bus (from Árpádhid), by train from the Nyugati (West) station, or by car via Highway 2.

Exploring the Danube Bend

Numbers in the margin correspond to points of interest on the Danube Bend map.

This tour moves northward along the west bank of the Danube, starting in Budapest in the district of Óbuda (for more information about Óbuda, *see* Tour 4 in Budapest, *above*). Szentendrei út, or Highway 11, is the main road leading to the Danube Bend; it begins at Flórian tér in Óbuda and leads first to the reconstructed remains

❶ of **Aquincum,** a Roman settlement dating from the 1st century AD and the capital of the Roman province of Pannonia. Before leaving the center of Óbuda, however, it's worth making a short detour to see the **Hercules Villa.** Just a few blocks west of Szentendrei út on Meggyfa utca, this fine 3rd-century Roman dwelling takes its name from the myth depicted on its beautiful mosaic floor. The ruin was unearthed between 1958 and 1967. *Meggyfa utca 19–21. tel. 1/250–1650. Admission: 30 Ft. Open May–Nov., Tues.–Sun. 10–6.*

Careful excavations at Aquincum have unearthed a varied selection of artifacts and mosaics, giving a tantalizing inkling of what life was like in the provinces of the Roman Empire. A gymnasium and a central heating system have been unearthed, along with the ruins of two baths and a shrine to Mithras, the Persian god of light, truth, and the sun.

The **Aquincum Museum** displays the dig's most notable finds: ceramics signed by the city's best-known potter, Ressatus of Aquincum; a red-marble sarcophagus showing a triton and flying Eros on one

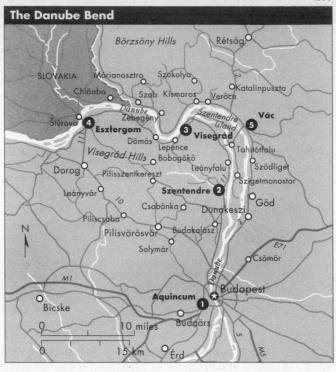

The Danube Bend

side and, on the other, Telesphorus, the angel of death, depicted as a hooded dwarf; and jewelry from a Roman lady's tomb. *Szentendrei út 139, tel. 1/250–1650. Admission: 40 Ft. Open May–Nov., Tues.–Sun. 10–6.*

Just beyond Aquincum is **Római Camping,** one of Budapest's two main campsites and one of the city's most enjoyable open-air bathing areas. *Szentendrei út 189, tel. 1/168–6260 or 1/188–7167, fax 1/250–0425. The bath is open May–Nov., the camping sites, including expensive bungalows and tent space, year-round.*

Rising above Óbuda and Aquincum are the thickly wooded **Buda Hegység** (Buda Hills), the city's "green lung" and biggest playground, full of hikers and picnickers in summer and skiers and sledders in winter. The area is easily accessible by public transport. A favorite way to make the ascent is to ride the cogwheel railway that starts opposite the Hotel Budapest and climbs to **Széchenyi Hill.** On Szilágyi Erzsébet fasor, the tree-lined boulevard leading to the Hotel Budapest, stands a new bronze statue of Raoul Wallenberg, the Swedish diplomat who saved some 100,000 Hungarian Jews during World War II and then disappeared in early 1945 near Debrecen while in the custody of the advancing Red Army.

② **Szentendre** (Saint Andrew), some 20 kilometers (12 miles) to the north, is the highlight of the Danube Bend: a romantic town with a lively, almost Mediterranean atmosphere and a flourishing artists' colony. Szentendre was first settled by Serbs and Greeks fleeing the advancing Turks in the 14th and 17th centuries. They built houses and churches in their own style—rich in reds and blues seldom seen elsewhere in Hungary. The local cuisine, too, has a tangible Mediterranean influence.

To savor Szentendre before you start sightseeing, stroll along the flower-lined **Danube Promenade** between the Boat Landing and Görög utca, ducking into any and every little cobblestone side street that appeals to you. Baroque houses with shingle roofs (often with an arched eye-of-God upstairs window) and shingle walls will enchant your eye and pique your curiosity.

Görög utca, or Greek Street, begins with a Greek restaurant, Görög Kancsó (The Grecian Urn), at No. 1 (*see* Dining, *below*) and ends inevitably at the so-called **Greek Church,** which is actually a Serbian Orthodox church that takes its name from the Greek inscription on a red marble gravestone set in its wall. This elegant edifice was built between 1752 and 1754 by a Rococo master, Andreas Mayerhoffer, on the site of a wooden church dating to the Great Serbian Migration (around 690). Its greatest glory—a symmetrical floor-to-ceiling panoply of stunning icons—was painted between 1802 and 1804 by Mihailo Zivkovic, a Serbian painter from Buda.

Though you enter on Görög utca, the Greek Church fronts **Fő tér** (Main Square), the centerpiece of which is an ornate **Memorial Cross** erected by Serbs in gratitude for the town's being spared a plague. The cross has a crucifixion painted on it and stands atop a triangular pillar adorned with a dozen icon paintings. During the overlapping Szentendre Spring, Szentendre Summer, and Szentendre Days (festivals of music, theater, and art, respectively, covering most of the warm-weather season from late March to early September), you are likely to witness a Cimarosa or Mozart opera performed in the square by an ensemble from Budapest with full chamber orchestra.

Every house on Fő (formerly Marx) tér is a designated landmark, and three of them are open to the public: the **Ferenczy Museum** at No. 6 with paintings of Szentendre landscapes and statues and tapestries by a distinguished family of artists; the **Kmetty Museum** at No. 21 with works of Hungarian cubist painters; and the **Szentendrei Képtár** (Municipal Gallery) at Nos. 2–5 with local contemporary art. *Admission to all 3 museums: 30 Ft. Open Apr.–Oct., Tues.–Sun. 10–6; Nov.–Mar., Tues.–Sun. 10–4.*

The roads uphill from Fő tér lead to a troop of stoic churches; particularly worthwhile is the one set atop **Vár-domb** (Castle Hill), the **Catholic Parish Church,** dating to the 13th century and the town's oldest surviving monument. After many reconstructions, its oldest visible part is a 15th-century sundial in the doorway, outside of which is an arts-and-crafts market and, on weekends in summer, all-day street entertainment.

On the adjoining hill, also reached from Fő tér, stands the imposing red **Serbian Orthodox Cathedral,** built in the 1740s with a much more lavish but far less beautiful iconostasis than is found in the Greek Church below it. In a restful park in the religious complex is the **Serbian Orthodox Museum** with icons, altars, robes, 16th-century prayer books, and a 17th-century cross with a bullet hole through it. The local Serbian minority holds its annual festival here each August 19. *Pátriárka utca 5, tel. 26/312–399. Admission: 30 Ft. adults, 15 Ft. children. Open Wed.–Sun. 10–4.*

Szentendre has even more museums than churches, with the farthest-flung being the **Szabadtéri Néprajzi Múzeum** (Open-air Ethnographic Museum). Located 5 kilometers (3 miles) to the northwest, it is reachable by bus from the Szentendre terminus of the HÉV suburban railway. The museum itself is a living recreation of 18th- and 19th-century village life—the sort of place where blacksmith shops and a horse-powered mill compete with wooden houses and folk handcrafts for your attention. *Szabadságforrás út, tel. 26/312–304. Admission: 60 Ft. adults, 30 Ft. children. Open Apr.–Oct., Tues.– Sun. 10–6.*

If you have time for only one museum in Szentendre, don't miss the **Margit Kovács Museum,** which displays the collected works of Budapest artist Margit Kovács, who died in 1977. She left behind a wealth of richly textured work that ranges from ceramics to life-size sculptures. Admission to the museum is limited to 15 persons at a time, so it is wise to line up early or at lunchtime, when the herds of tour groups are occupied elsewhere. *Vastagh György utca 1 (off Görög utca), tel. 26/310–244. Admission: 60 Ft. Open Tues.–Sun. 10–6. (in winter until 4).*

Continue north along the west bank of the Danube for 23 kilometers (14 miles)—past Leányfalu, a pleasant holiday resort with a tourist ❸ hotel and a campsite—to **Visegrád.** This was the seat of the Hungarian kings during the 14th century, when a fortress built here by the Angevin kings became the royal residence. If you have only a short time to visit Visegrád, spend it at the **Fellegvár (Citadel),** at the top of the hill overlooking the village. In the Middle Ages, the Citadel was where the Holy Crown and other royal regalia were kept, until they were stolen by a dishonorable maid of honor in 1440; 23 years later, King Matthias had to pay 80,000 Ft. to retrieve them from Austria. (Now the crown is safe in the Hungarian National Museum in Budapest, after the United States returned it from Fort Knox in 1978). From the Citadel there are excellent views of the Danube and the surrounding plains. *Admission: 30 Ft. Open Tues.–Sun. 9–6.*

A century later, King Matthias Corvinus had a separate palace built on the banks of the Danube. It was eventually razed by the Turks, and not until 1934 were the ruins finally excavated. Nowadays you can see the disheveled remnants of the palace, known as the **Mátyás Király Múzeum,** via the entrance on Fő utca. Especially worth seeing is the red marble well built by a 15th-century Italian architect and later decorated with the arms of King Matthias. It is situated in a ceremonial courtyard restored in accordance with designs found in ancient documents. Above the courtyard rise the palace's various halls; on the left you can still see a few fine original carvings, which give an idea of how magnificent the palace must once have been. The nearby lookout tower on Nagy Villám Hill offers spectacular views of the Danube Bend. Throughout August, the Mátyás Király Múzeum features a Renaissance festival called Castle Games, where performers sport costumes and play medieval music. *Fő utca 29, tel. 26/398–026. Admission: 30 Ft. adults, 10 Ft. children. Open Apr.– Nov., Tues.–Sun. 9–5; Nov.–Mar., Tues.–Sun. 8–4.*

❹ **Esztergom,** 21 kilometers (13 miles) upriver, stands on the site of a Roman fortress. St. Stephen, the first Christian king of Hungary, was crowned here in the year 1000. Esztergom's **Bazilika** (Cathedral), the largest in Hungary, stands on a hill overlooking the town; it is now the seat of the cardinal primate of Hungary. Its most interesting features are the **Bakócz chapel** (1506), named for a primate of Hungary who only narrowly missed becoming pope; and the sacristy, which contains a valuable collection of medieval ecclesiastical art. *Szent István tér. Admission free. Open June–Oct., daily 5:30–5; Nov.–May, daily 5:30–4.*

Below the cathedral lie the narrow streets of **Viziváros** (Watertown), lined with bright-painted Baroque buildings. Considered by many to be Hungary's finest art gallery, Watertown's **Keresztény Múzeum** (Museum of Christian Art), situated in the Primate's Palace, houses a large collection of early Hungarian and Italian paintings (the 14th- and 15th-century Italian collection is unusually large for a museum outside Italy). Unique holdings include the so-called *Coffin of Our Lord* from Garamszentbenedek, now in the Czech Republic; the wooden statues of the Apostles and of the Roman soldiers guarding the coffin are masterpieces of Hungarian Baroque sculpture. The building also houses the Primate's Archives, which contains 20,000 volumes, including several medieval codices. Permission to visit the archives must be obtained in advance. *Primate's Palace, Berényi ut 2, tel. 33/313–880. Admission: 40 Ft. adults, 20 Ft. children. Open Tues.–Sun. 10–5:30.*

To the south of the cathedral, on **Szent Tamás Hill,** is a small church dedicated to St. Thomas à Becket of Canterbury. From here you can look down on the town and see how the Danube temporarily splits, forming an island that locals use as a base for waterskiing and swimming, in spite of the pollution.

At Esztergom, the Danube marks the border between Hungary and Slovakia. The bridge that once joined these two countries was destroyed by the Nazis near the end of World War II, though parts of the span can still be seen. A ferry now shuttles passengers across the border; at press time, however, only passengers with Hungarian or Slovakian passports were permitted to use this crossing.

Though the Danube Bend's west bank contains the bulk of historical sights, the less traveled east bank has the excellent hiking trails of the Börzsöny Mountain range, which extends along the Danube from Vác to Zebegény before curving toward the Slovak border.

⑤ With its lovely promenade, its cathedral, and less delightful Triumphal Arch, the small city of **Vác,** on the Danube's east bank, is well worth a short visit if only to watch the sun slowly set from the promenade. (Another good vantage point is Vác's stunning Baroque bridge, complete with stone statues of sundry historical luminaries.)

Sunsets aside, Vác's 18th-century **cathedral** on Konstantin tér is the pride of the town. Built in 1763–77 by Archbishop Kristóf Migazzi to the designs of the Italian architect Isidor Carnevale, the structure is considered an outstanding example of Hungarian neoclassicism. The most interesting features are the murals by the Austrian Franz Anton Maulbertsch, both on the dome and behind the altar. Roses line the front entrance, and exquisite frescoes decorate the walls inside. To find it, head south down Köztársaság út from Március 15 tér—it's definitely hard to miss.

If you have time to kill, stop by the **Vak Bottyán Múzeum,** one block down from the cathedral. The collection is composed of some less than riveting artifacts from the Middle Ages and mementos from the 1848 War of Independence. *Múzeum utca 4. Admission: 10 Ft.*

In 1764, when Archbishop Migazzi heard that Queen Maria Theresa planned to visit his humble town, he hurriedly arranged the construction of a **Triumphal Arch.** The queen came and left, but the awkward arch remains, near a prison for Hungary's hardened criminals. *Köztársaság út.*

Vácrátóti Arborétum, 4 kilometers (2¼ miles) from Vác, is Hungary's biggest and best botanical garden, with over 12,000 plant species.

The arboretum's top priority is botanical research and collection under the auspices of the Hungarian Academy of Sciences, but visitors are welcome during spring and summer. *Open Mar.–Sept., Tues.– Sun. 8–6.*

Along the Danube north of Vác lies a string of pleasant summer resorts, nestling below the picturesque Börzsöny Hills and stretching as far as Szob, just east of the Slovakian border.

Shopping

Flooded with tourists in summer, **Szentendre** naturally has the requisite souvenir shops. Among the overpriced goods sold in every store are dolls dressed in traditional folk costumes, wooden trinkets, pottery, and colorful hand-embroidered tablecloths, doilies, and blouses. The best bargains are the hand-embroidered blankets and bags sold by dozens of elderly women in traditional folk attire, who stand for hours on the town's crowded streets. Visegrád Ágasház, a small shopping arcade near the king's palace, was designed by Imre Makovecz, Hungary's premier architect (Makovecz designed the Hungarian pavilion at the 1992 Seville World Fair). The arcade is built in raw wood. Small shops sell folk art and crafts, and a popular restaurant features Hungarian cuisine.

Sports and Outdoor Activities

Bicycling The waterfront and streets beyond **Szentendre**'s main square are perfect for a bike ride—very wide and relatively calm and quiet. Rentals are available from IBUSZ and Dunatours (*see* Tourist Information, *above*).

Boating and Water Sports Take advantage of **Szentendre**'s riverside location and head to the **Viking Motor Yacht Club** (Duna korzó 3, tel. 26/311–707), a short walk north along the Danube from the center of town. From May through October the yacht club has expensive rental rates for water-skis (7,000 Ft. an hour); jet-skis (7,200 Ft. an hour for two people; 6,000 Ft. for one person); canoes and kayaks (each 1,000 Ft. an hour); and motorboats (7,000 Ft. an hour). The rentals are available on the dock daily 9–8. The club's main office is located on a ship (which also houses a good restaurant).

Hiking A well-marked hiking trail (posted with red signs) leads from the edge of Visegrád to Pilisszentlászló: a wonderful journey among the oak and beech trees of the Visegrád Hills into the Pilis conservation region. Bears, bison, deer, and wild boar roam freely here; less menacing flora include fields of yellow blooming spring pheasant's eye and black pulsatilla.

Horseback Riding **Pomáz,** just 15 minutes away from Szentendre by HÉV, is known for its well-respected **riding school,** Pomázi Lovas–iskola. Reasonably experienced riders can enjoy one-hour excursions (400 Ft.) through a 3-acre range near Kőhegy and Meseliahegy (Stone and Fabulous Hill), at the foot of the Pilis Mountain range. Schiffer Sándor, the owner of the school, takes good care of his team of 10 Hungarian half-bloods and gives riding lessons for 300 Ft. per half-hour. Reservations are preferred; if you call the school after 4 PM you have a good chance of reaching someone who speaks English.

Swimming The Danube at Visegrád is out of bounds for swimmers; but there are excellent outdoor pools at **Lepence,** 3 kilometers (2 miles) southwest of Visegrád on Route 11. To use the local spa facilities and outdoor pool in **Esztergom,** inquire at the IBUSZ office.

Toboggan Winding through the trees near Visegrád is the **Wiegand Toboggan**
Slide **Run** (open Apr.–Sept., 10–5), one of the longest slides you've ever
seen. You ride on a small cart that is pulled uphill by trolley, then
you careen down the slope in a small trough that resembles a bobsled
run.

Dining and Lodging

Highly recommended establishments in a particular price category
are indicated by a star ★.

Esztergom **Kispipa.** Lively and popular with Hungarians, the Kispipa, not far
Dining from the town center, is especially memorable for its good choice of
wines. The food menu includes soups, stews, and traditional Hungarian dishes such as fried goose with heavy cream. *Kossuth Lajos*
utca 19, no tel. No reservations. Dress: casual. No credit cards. $$
Alabárdos. This restaurant, attached to the *panzió* (pension) of the
same name, is a real favorite among locals. A pianist plays during
dinner while customers eat by candlelight in carved-wood booths.
The Hungarian meatballs are particularly tasty. *Bajcsy-Zsilinszky*
utca 49, tel. 33/312–640. No reservations. Dress: casual. No credit
cards. Closed Mon. $
Halászcsárda. The specialty at this friendly, informal restaurant is
fish (the fish soup is especially good). The casual outdoor patio,
shielded by a straw roof, gives the place a backyard-barbecue feel.
After dinner explore the nearby island formed by the branching of
the Danube. *Szabad Május sétány 14, no tel. No reservations.*
Dress: casual. No credit cards. $

Lodging **Alabárdos Panzió.** Conveniently located downhill from the basilica,
this cozy, remodeled home provides an excellent view of Castle Hill
from upstairs. The rooms (doubles and quads) are large. If the care-
taker isn't in, you might find him working in the adjoining restau-
rant. *Bajcsy-Zsilinsky utca 49, tel. 33/312–640. 13 rooms with bath.*
Facilities: restaurant. No credit cards. $$
Hotel Esztergom. Located on Primás sziget (Primate's Island), a
popular park and recreation area just across the Kossuth Bridge
from the Parish Church, this is a stylish, comfortable and sports-or-
iented hotel. *Primás sziget, Nagy Duna Setány, tel. 33/312–355 or*
33/312–883. 34 rooms. Facilities: restaurant, roof terrace café,
sports center, boating, tennis. No credit cards. $$
Ria Panzioí. In this small, friendly guest house near the cathedral,
all rooms face a garden courtyard. *Batthányi utca 11, tel. 33/313–*
115. 4 rooms. No credit cards. $
Vadvirág. This small guest house on the outskirts of town offers sim-
ple accommodations, a restaurant, and tennis courts. *Bánomi*
üdülő, tel. 33/311–174. 28 rooms, some with bath. No credit cards.
Closed Oct.–Apr. $

Szentendre **Viking.** The restaurant of the Viking Motor Yacht Club is, appropri-
Dining ately, a boat moored on the Danube. The atmosphere is irresistible,
★ with a one-man band singing along with his synthesizer at night; on
some summer evenings there is a show of Gypsy music, songs, and
dances. The house specialty is fish prepared in a dozen ways; the
"Viking Secret" appetizer is cold fogas, herring, and cockle salad
with caviar and a stuffed egg. There is crayfish cream soup as well as
Danube fish soup. Interesting main dishes on the English-language
menu include squid in beer cake, paprika catfish, and crayfish ra-
gout in dill-cream sauce. A whole ox is open-air roasted each week-
end. There is also a salad bar. *Duna korzó 3, tel. 26/311–707.*

Reservations advised. Dress: casual. AE, DC, MC, V. Closed Nov.–Mar. $$$

★ **Aranysárkány.** On a hillside above the city (on the road up to the Serbian Orthodox Cathedral), the "Golden Dragon" lies in wait with seven large tables, which you share with strangers on a busy night. The delicious food is prepared before your eyes in a turbulent open kitchen where dishes break and exuberance is rampant. All the activity is justified by the cold cherry soup with white wine and whipped cream; or the hot Dragon Soup with quail eggs, meatballs, and vegetables. Try the grilled goose liver Orosházi style, wrapped in bacon and accompanied by a layered potato-and-cheese cake, broccoli, and a grilled tomato flying a basil-leaf flag. The apricot pudding and cheese dumplings are also recommended. *Alkotmány utca 1/a, tel. 26/311–670. Reservations advised. Dress: casual. AE. $$*

Görög Kancsó. The Grecian urn from which the inn takes its name is displayed and illuminated in a handsome interior room, but in summer most of the dining and socializing take place in the garden restaurant on the banks of the Danube. Greek specialties and Hungarian pork livers are given equal care and flavor; the help is young, charming, and very efficient. *Görög utca 1, tel. 26/315–528. Reservations advised. Dress: casual. AE. $$*

Korona. This revamped traditional-style restaurant is on the main square in an 18th-century Baroque house. The menu is based on fish and various Hungarian specialties. Try the *bableves* (bean soup). The view of local comings and goings from its sidewalk café is unmatched. *Fő tér 19, tel. 26/311–516. Reservations advised. Dress: casual. No credit cards. $$*

Rab Ráby. Fish soup and fresh grilled trout are the specialties in this popular restaurant with wood beams and equestrian decorations. *Péter Pál utca 1, tel. 26/310–819. Reservations advised in summer. Dress: casual. No credit cards. $$*

Régi Módi. This attractive upstairs restaurant is approached through a courtyard across from the Margit Kovács Múzeum. The bright decor, fine wines, and game specialties compensate for the slow service. *Futó utca 3, tel. 26/311–105. Reservations advised. Dress: casual. AE, DC, MC, V. $$*

Vidám Szerzetesek. The "Happy Monk" opened as a family restaurant in 1981, though in recent years it has become something of a tourist haunt; the menu, after all, is in 18 languages—including English, Arab, Chinese, Turkish, Serb, and Japanese. The food is typically Hungarian: heavy, hearty, and delicious. *Bogdányi út 5, tel. 26/310–544. Reservations advised. Dress: casual. No credit cards. Closed Mon. $*

Lodging **Duna Club Hotel.** This is Szentendre's most beautiful and luxurious
★ modern hotel, opened in 1992 and set on the banks of the Danube next to the Viking restaurant. The hotel surrounds a courtyard containing a swimming pool and a manicured grassy area, marvelous for sunbathing and relaxation. The staff is multilingual, and the service is excellent. *Duna korzó 5, tel. 26/312–491, fax 26/314–101. 29 rooms with bath. Facilities: restaurant, bar, air-conditioning, sauna, massage, Jacuzzi, solarium, fitness club, lighted tennis courts; parking. AE, DC, MC, V. $$$*

Coca-Cola Panzió. Removed just enough from busy motorway 11 to offer a reasonably sound night of sleep, this modern panzió offers all the comforts of home, plus a grassy lawn, a picnic table, and a barbecue pit. You can even call home on the international red phone in the lobby. It's a five-minute walk from the town center and directly opposite the bus stop. *Dunakanyar krt. 50, tel. 26/310–410, fax 26/ 310–339. 12 rooms with bath. AE. $$*

Fenyves. Atop a flight of stone steps, this run-down but striking villa is basically a bed-and-breakfast with luxurious trappings. *Ady Endre út 26, H-2000, tel. 26/311–882. 9 rooms with shared baths, 1 283apartment. Facilities: TV, refrigerator, bar, outdoor pool, playground, sun terrace, barbecue. No credit cards. $$*

★ **Hárgita Eldorádo Panzió.** Named for the Hargita Mountains in Transylvania, this remodeled panzió atop a grassy incline has all the makings of a Swiss chalet. Attic space has been converted into modernized rooms with television sets and sparkling tile showers. On a warm day you can eat breakfast on the outside patio. *Egressy út 22, tel. 26/311–928. 10 rooms with bath. Facilities: restaurant. AE. $$*

Átrium Panzió. Built in 1992, this lovely and quiet pension is opposite the famous Serbian Orthodox Museum, a short walk from the main square. The building is rustic, with raw-wood interiors and slanted alpine-style ceilings. The hosts are friendly and welcoming and will organize sightseeing tours. *Pátriarka utca 6, tel. 26/314–006, fax 26/313–998. 7 rooms with shower. Facilities: restaurant, bar. Breakfast included. No credit cards. $*

Bükkös Panzió. West of the main square and across the bridge over Bükkös brook, this is one of the most conveniently located hotels in the village. Just five minutes from the HÉV and bus stations, it books up well in advance during July and August, so plan ahead. *Bükkös part 16, tel. 26/312–021, fax 26/310–782. 16 rooms with bath. Facilities: restaurant, bar. No credit cards. $*

Danubius. On the highway near the Danube bank, north of town, this very ordinary hotel is considered the best in an area where most visitors are campers and motorists just passing through. The rooms are small and the bathrooms tiny, but the staff is obliging. *Ady Endre út 28, H-2000, tel. 26/312–489, fax 26/312–511. 48 rooms and 2 apartments, all with bath. Facilities: restaurant, tavern, bowling alley, barbecue. AE, DC, MC, V. $*

Papszigeti Camping. On Szentendre Island in the Danube, this campsite also offers a good range of housing for the nonmotorized, non-tent-bearing traveler. *Papsziget, H-2000 Szentendre, tel. 26/ 310–697. Camping places for 220 trailers and tents, 14 bungalows, and 5 rooms with bath; 20 motel rooms and 40-bed hostel. Facilities: restaurant, beach, water sports. Closed Oct.–Apr. $*

Visegrád
Dining
★

Gulás Csárda. This brand-new restaurant, decorated with antique folk art and memorabilia, has only four tables inside, but additional tables are added outside during the summer. The cuisine is typical home-style Hungarian, with a limited selection of top-rate traditional dishes (they don't microwave frozen food here). Try the fish soup served in a pot and kept warm on a small spirit burner. *Nagy Lajos király utca. No tel. Reservations advised. Dress: casual. No credit cards. $$*

Sirály Restaurant. Right across from the ferry station, the elegant "Seagull" restaurant is justifiably well regarded for its rolled fillet of deer; and its many vegetarian dishes, including fried soya-steak with vegetables. In summer, when cooking is often done on the terrace overlooking the Danube, expect barbecued meats and stews, soups, and gulyas served in old-fashioned pots. Music is provided by a Gypsy band on some evenings and by a traditional orchestra on others. *Rév út 7, tel. 26/398–376. Reservations advised. Dress: casual. No credit cards. $$*

Skandinávia. New Swedish owners have added Swedish cuisine, in addition to seafood and salads, to the Hungarian dishes (try the fried carp, a local specialty). The service is prompt and the prices cheap, and there is a pleasant outdoor patio. Be warned, however, that slightly higher summer prices are not marked on the winter menus; ask for prices before ordering. *Fő út 48, tel. 26/398–131. No reservations. Dress: casual. No credit cards. $$*

Fekete Holló. The popular "Black Raven" restaurant has an elegant yet comfortable atmosphere—a great place for a full meal or just a beer. Try the Hungarian beef stew with potatoes, but save room for the *palacsinta* (sweet pancakes with fruit or chocolate). *Rév út 12, tel. 26/398–158. No reservations. Dress: casual. No credit cards. Closed Mon. $*

Lodging **Silvanus.** Located on a hill and offering spectacular views, the Silvanus is recommended for motorists mostly because it is nowhere near a bus stop. There are linking hiking trails in the forest for the more active. *Fekete-hegy, tel. 26/398–311, fax 26/398–170. 74 rooms, most with bath; 4 suites. Facilities: restaurant, brasserie, terrace café. AE, DC, MC, V. $$*

ELTE Vendégház. Just north of the town center, this hotel has freshly painted walls, new carpeting, and shiny, clean bathrooms. The guest rooms are minimally furnished. *Fő út 117, tel. 26/398–165. 33 rooms with bath. Facilities: restaurant. Breakfast included. No credit cards. $*

Haus Honti. This intimate alpine-style pension, named after its owner, József Honti, is situated in a quiet residential area far away from the main highway but close to the Danube ferry, which shuttles passengers to Nagymaros. A stream running close to the house creates a rustic ambience. *Fő utca 66, tel. 26/398–120. 5 rooms with bath. No credit cards. $*

Lake Balaton

Lake Balaton, the largest lake in Central Europe, stretches 80 kilometers (50 miles) across Hungary. Yet Balaton—regarded as the most popular playground of this landlocked nation—is just 90 kilometers (56 miles) to the southwest of Budapest, so it is within easy reach of the capital by car, train, bus, and even bicycle.

On the lake's hilly northern shore, ideal for growing grapes, is **Balatonfüred,** Hungary's oldest and most famous spa town. The national park on the **Tihany Peninsula** is just to the south, and regular boat service links Tihany and Balatonfüred with Siófok on the southern shore. Although this shore is not as attractive as the northern one (it's flatter and more crowded with resorts, cottages, and trade-union rest houses), the southern shore does have shallower, warmer waters, which are ideal for swimming—just ask one of the thousands of portly Hungarian grandmothers splashing themselves on a hot summer day.

A circular tour taking in Veszprém, Balatonfüred, and Tihany could be managed in a single day. Two days, with a night in Tihany or Balatonfüred, would allow for detours to Herend and its porcelain factory or to the striking castle at Nagyvázsony.

Important Addresses and Numbers

Tourist Information Two separate agencies provide information about the Balaton region: **Balatontourist** covers the northern shore; **Siotour,** the southern shore.

Balaton tourist has offices in: **Balatonfüred** (Blaha Lujza utca 5, tel. 86/342–822 or 86/343–471); **Budapest** (Üllői út 52/a, tel. 1/133–6982, fax 1/133–9929); **Tihany** (Kossuth utca 20, tel. 86/348–519; **Veszprém** (Kossuth Lajos utca 21, tel. 88/426–874). In **Keszthely** call **Keszthely Tourist** (Kossuth Lajos utca 25, tel. 83/314–288).

Siotour has offices in **Balatonföldvár** (Széchenyi tér 9–11, tel. 84/340 099); **Budapest** (Kluuzál tér 2–3, tel. 1/112–6080, fax 1/142–1197); **Fonyód** (Vasutallomas, tel. 85/361–214 or 85/361–850); **Siófok** (Szabadság tér 6, tel. 84/310–900, fax 84/310–307); **Zamárdi** (Petőfi út 1, tel. and fax 84/331–072).

Emergencies Police (tel. 07). **Ambulance** (tel. 04). **Fire** (tel. 05).

Arriving and Departing

By Train There are daily express trains from Budapest's Deli (South) Station to Siófok and Balatonfüred. The two-hour trips cost less than $10 each way.

By Car Highway E71 connects Budapest with Lake Balaton's southern shore. The drive from Budapest to Siófok, for example, takes less than two hours, except on weekends, when traffic can be severe.

By Bus Buses headed for the Lake Balaton region depart from Budapest's Erzsebét tér station daily; contact **Volánbusz** (tel. 1/117–2318) for current schedules.

Getting Around

By Car Road 71 runs along the northern shore; M7 covers the southern shore. Traffic can be heavy during summer weekends, and driving around the lake can be slow.

By Train Trains from Budapest serve all the resorts on the northern shore; a separate line links resorts on the southern shore. An express train from Budapest takes just over two hours to reach Siófok or Balatonfüred. Be sure to book tickets well in advance.

By Bus Buses frequently link Lake Balaton's major resorts, but book ahead to avoid long waits. Buses leave from Erzsébet tér in Budapest and stay in most towns along Balaton's northern and southern shores. Reservations can be made through IBUSZ (*see* Guided Tours, *below*) or Volánbusz (tel. 1/117–2318).

By Boat The slowest but most scenic way to travel between Lake Balaton's major resorts is by ferry. Schedules for MAHART (tel. 1/117–2331), the national ferry company, are available from most of the tourist offices listed above.

Guided Tours

IBUSZ has several tours to Balaton from Budapest; inquire at the head office in Budapest (Petőfi tér 3, tel. 1/118–5707). Other tours more easily organized from hotels in the Balaton area include boat trips to vineyards, folk-music evenings, and overnight trips to local inns.

Highlights for First-Time Visitors

Badacsony (*see* Tour 1)
Festetics Palace, Keszthely (*see* Tour 1)
Fonyód beaches (*see* Tour 2)
Héviz (*see* Tour 1)
Tihany (*see* Tour 1)

Exploring Lake Balaton

Numbers in the margin correspond to points of interest on the Lake Balaton map.

Tour 1: **Balatonfüred,** the lake's oldest and most internationally noted **The Northern** health resort, has every amenity. Above its beaches and promenade, **Shore** the twisting streets of the **Old Town** climb hillsides thickly planted ❶ with vines. There is plenty of sunshine but also pleasant shade— ideal for a spa. Balatonfüred's 11 medicinal springs are said to have stimulating and beneficial effects on the heart and nerves. The climate and landscape also make this one of the best wine-growing districts in Hungary.

Great plane and poplar trees welcome you as you arrive at the busy boat landing, where you can also park your car and start your stroll by ascending to the center of town in **Gyógy tér** (Spa Square), where the bubbling waters from five volcanic springs rise beneath a slim, colonnaded pavilion. In the square's centerpiece, the neoclassical **Well House** of the Kossuth Spring, you can sample the water, which has a pleasant, surprisingly cool, refreshing taste despite the sulfurous aroma. All of the buildings on the square are pillared like Greek temples. At No. 3 is the **Horváth Ház** (Horváth House), where the Szentgyörgyi-Horváth family arranged the first ball in 1825 in honor of their daughter Anna. It was there that she fell in love with Erňo Kiss, who became a general in the 1848–49 War of Independence and died a hero.

The Anna Balls, the event in Lake Balaton that most approximates a debutante cotillion, are now held every July in another colonnaded building on the square, the **Trade Unions' Sanatorium** (1802). Under its arcades is the **Balaton Pantheon**: aesthetically interesting tablets and reliefs honoring Hungarian and foreign notables who either worked for Lake Balaton or spread the word about it. Among them is the Czech author of *The Good Soldier Schweik*, Jaroslav Hašek, who also wrote tales about Balaton. On the eastern side of the square is the **Cardiac Hospital**, where hundreds of patients from all over the world are treated. Here, too, Rabindranath Tagore, the Indian author and Nobel Prize winner, recovered from a heart attack in 1926. The tree that he planted to commemorate his stay still stands in a little grove at the bottom of steps leading from the square down to the lakeside. Tagore also wrote a poem for the planting, which is memorialized beneath the tree on a strikingly animated bust of Tagore:

When I am no longer on earth, my tree,
Let the ever-renewed leaves of thy spring
Murmur to the wayfarer:
The poet did love while he lived.

In the same grove are trees honoring visits by another Nobel laureate, the Italian poet Salvatore Quasimodo, in 1961; and Indian prime minister Indira Gandhi, in 1972. An adjoining grove honors Soviet cosmonauts and their Hungarian partner-in-space, Bertalan Farkas. The grove opens onto the **Tagore sétány** (Tagore Promenade), which runs on for nearly a kilometer (almost ½ mile) and is lined by trees, restaurants, and shops.

Back up at Gyógy tér, if you follow **Blaha Lujza utca,** you will pass such landmarks as the **Blaha Lujza Ház** (Lujza Blaha House), a neoclassical villa built in 1867 and, later, the summer home of this famous turn-of-the-century actress, humanist, and singer; a **pharmacy** (1782); and the **Kerek templom** (Round Church), consecrated in 1846. Behind the church is the summer house of Hungarian

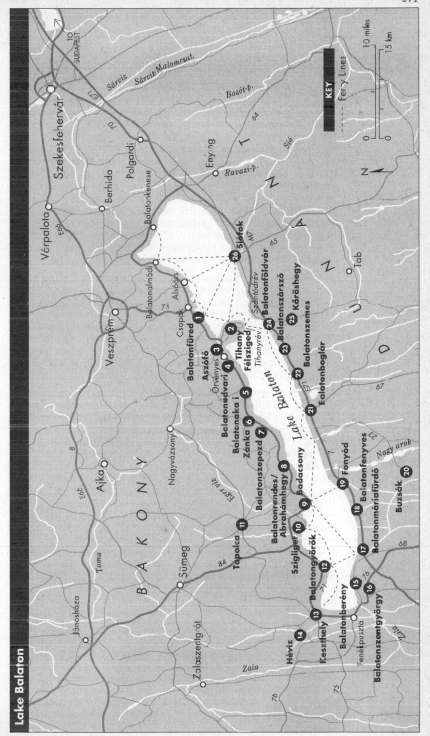

Lake Balaton

KEY
Ferry Lines

10 miles
15 km

TO BUDAPEST

Szekesfehervár

Sárviz

Sárviz-Malomcsat.

Bozót-p.

Enying

Ravazi-p.

Polgardi

Berhida

Balatonkenese

Siófok

Balatonföldvár

Tab

Vérpalota

Balatonalmádi

Alsóörs

Csopak

Szántódrév

Balatonszárszó

Kőröshegy

Veszprém

Balatonfüred

Aszófő

Örvényes

Tihany
Félsziged

Tihanyrév

Balatonszemes

Balatonszepezd

Balatonakali

Zánka

Badacsony

Lake Balaton

Balatonboglár

Nagyvázsony

Balatonrendes/
Ábrahámhegy

Fonyód

Balatonfenyves

Nagy árok

Ajka

Szigliget

Balatongyörök

Balatonmáriafürdő

Buzsák

Tapolca

Sümeg

Balatonberény

Keszthely

Hévíz

Jánosháza

Fenékpuszta

Balatonszentgyörgy

Zalaszentgrót

Zala

BAKONY

Toma

Eger víz

Eger

Nagyvázsony

author Mór Jókai, now a museum honoring his work. *Honvéd utca 1. Admission: 20 Ft. adults, 10 Ft. children. Open Feb.–Oct., Tues.–Sun. 10–6.*

Time Out   At Blaha Lujza utca 7 is the plush **Kedves Café,** built in 1795 and to-day Lake Balaton's most popular and famous pastry shop. It is fre-quented in summer by actors and writers, who give periodic readings on the premises; there is also a Sunday-morning puppet show for children. The Kedves also boasts a summer garden and a first-class restaurant.

②   Entered from the west of Balatonfüred (south off Highway 71) is the **Tihany Félsziget** (Tihany Peninsula), joined to the mainland by a nar-row neck and jutting 5 kilometers (3 miles) into the lake. Only 12 square kilometers (less than 5 square miles), the peninsula is not only a major tourist resort but perhaps the most historic part of the Balaton area. In 1952 the entire peninsula was declared a national park, and because of its geological rarities, it became Hungary's first nature-conservation zone. On it are more than 110 geyser cra-ters, remains of former hot springs reminiscent of those found in Iceland, Siberia, and Yellowstone Park in the United States.

As the peninsula broadens you will pass two lakes. The **Külső Tó** (Outer Lake), which dried up two centuries ago, has recently been refilled with water. The smooth **Belső Tó** (Inner Lake), 82 feet high-er than Lake Balaton, is more impressive. Around it are barren yel-lowish-white rocks and volcanic cones rising against the sky. Standing atop any hill in the area, you can see water in every di-rection. Though the hills surrounding the lake are known for their white wines, the peculiarities of this peninsula give rise to a notable Hungarian red, Tihany cabernet.

Between the Inner Lake and the eastern shore of the peninsula lies the village of **Tihany,** crowned by its **abbey** with foundations laid by King Andras I in 1055. The abbey's charter—containing some 100 Hungarian words in its Latin text, thus making it the oldest written source of the Hungarian language—is kept in Pannonhalma. Re-built in Baroque style between 1719 and 1784, the abbey church tow-ers above the village in feudal splendor. Its gilded-silver high altar, abbot's throne, pulpit, organ case, choir parapet, and swirling crowd of saintly and angelic faces are all the work (between 1753 and 1765) of Sebestyén Stuhlhoff. A joiner from Augsburg, Stulhoff lived and worked in the monastery as a lay brother for 25 years after the death of his Hungarian sweetheart. Local tradition says that he immortalized her features in the angel kneeling on the right-hand side of the altar to the Virgin Mary. The magnificent Baroque or-gan, adorned by stucco cherubs, can be heard on Tuesday and Wednesday evenings in summer. *Első András tér 1, tel. 86/348–405. Admission: 20 Ft. Open May–Oct., daily 10–5; Nov.–Apr., daily 10–3.*

In a Baroque house adjoining the abbey is the Tihany **Historical Mu-seum,** visited by more than 100,000 tourists annually. The best ex-hibits are in the basement lapidarium: relics from Roman colonization, including mosaic floors; a relief of David from the 2nd or 3rd century AD; and 1,200-year-old carved stones—all labeled in English as well as Hungarian. Three of the upstairs rooms were lived in for five days in 1921 by the last emperor of the dissolved Austro-Hungarian monarchy, Karl IV, in a futile foray to regain the throne of Hungary. Banished to Madeira, he died of pneumonia there a year later. The rooms are preserved with nostalgic relish for

Franz Joseph's doomed successor and his empress, Zita. *Batthyány ulca, tel. 86/348-650. Admission: 30 Ft. Open Apr.-Aug., Tues.- Sun. 10-5.*

Just outside the abbey complex, a pair of contemporary statues offer a startling contrast. Imre Varga's reverent 1972 statue of King Andras I is called *The Founder*; Amerigo Tot's strikingly modern 1970 abstraction is irreverently titled *His Majesty the Kilowatt.*

Time Out The café and pastry shop next to the abbey, the **Rege Cukrászda,** offers not only fresh and creamy desserts but also a panoramic view of Lake Balaton from its terrace.

Descend the stairs into the village. Along its main Pisky promenade you will find the **House of Folk Art,** a crafts store built in the local sloped-roof style with a charming arched porch. Next door is the **Open-air Museum of Ethnography,** an unlikely ensemble of old houses that includes a potter's shed (with a local artist-in-residence); a wine-growing exhibition; a display of agricultural implements; a farmhouse with exquisitely carved peasant furniture; and the former house of the Fishermen's Guild, with an ancient boat (used until 1934) parked inside. *Szabad tér 1. Admission: 30 Ft. adults, 15 Ft. children. Open May-Oct., Wed.-Mon. 10-6.*

Just north of the House of Folk Art, at the end of Piski István sétány, is **Visszhang domb** (Echo Hill), where as many as 16 syllables can be bounced off the abbey wall. Nowadays, with the inroads of traffic and construction, you'll have to settle for a two-second echo.

Time Out You can practice projecting from the terraces of the **Echo Restaurant,** an inn atop Echo Hill. Whet your whistle with anything from a cup of coffee to fogas (young pike perch), carp, and catfish specialties.

Footpaths crisscross the entire peninsula, allowing visitors to climb the small hills on its west side for splendid views of the area. If in midsummer you climb its highest hill, the **Csúcshegy** (761 feet), you will find the land below carpeted with purple lavender and the air filled with its fragrance (introduced from France into Hungary, lavender thrives on the lime-rich soil and strong sunshine of Tihany). The **State Lavender and Medicinal Herb Farm** at Csúcshegy (traversed by the red walking trail from the port of Tihany) supplies the Hungarian pharmaceutical and cosmetics industries.

Highway 71, the main street of Balatonfüred, is also the shore road around the north, east, and west rims of Lake Balaton. Follow it west 7 kilometers (4 miles) from Balatonfüred—past the turnoff for ❸ Tihany—to the charming village of **Aszófő,** which dates to Roman times.

Aszófő's restored ruin of a 13th-century **Romanesque church,** notable for the arched gable of its facade, was itself built upon the remains of a Roman building. The neoclassical **St. Ladislas Church** (1832-34) has a Baroque altar and an Empire-style pulpit. The town's vineyards are under landmark preservation because of the **Vörösmáli pincesor,** a row of barrel-vaulted wine cellars with Baroque decorations. Built during the 19th century, they stand behind buildings that house the winepresses. Aszófő also has a fine campground (*see* Dining and Lodging, *below*) and a big wooden mill wheel that, alas, no longer turns.

Swallow your disappointment, for **Örvényes,** only 2 kilometers (1¼ miles) farther, has the only working water mill in the Balaton region. Built during the 18th century, it still grinds grain into flour while serving as a museum as well. In the miller's room is a collection of folk art, wood carvings, pottery, furniture, and pipes. *Admission: 20 Ft. adults, 10 Ft. children. Open June–mid-Sept., daily 10–6.*

Near the mill, a statue of St. John of Nepomuk stands on a Baroque stone bridge built during the 18th century. On a hill near the mill and road are the ruins of a Romanesque church; only its chancel has survived. On the town's only street is the Baroque Church of St. Imre, built during the late 18th century.

❹ **Balatonudvari,** 1 kilometer (½ mile) to the west, is a pleasant beach resort with a 13th-century **Catholic church** (on a low hill near the highway) that has retained its Romanesque structure and apse, though the choir and tower were rebuilt in neoclassical style. A **Reformed church** (1790) has a gabled porch and late-Baroque characteristics. The cemetery at the eastern end of the village has been declared a national shrine for its heart-shape tombstones carved from white limestone at the turn of the 19th century. Balatonudvari's beach itself is at **Kiliántelep,** 2 kilometers (2 miles) to the west.

❺ The thriving beach resort of **Balatonakali,** 3 kilometers (2 miles) west of Kiliántelep, has ferry service and three large camping grounds. On the slopes of Fenye-hegy above the town are vineyards (muscatel is the local specialty) lined with thatched-roof, white-washed, stone-cellar winepress houses similar to those at Örvényes, if not as ornate. A 4-kilometer (2½-mile) excursion into the volcanic hills north of Balatonakali leads to the village of Dörgicse, with the ruins of three 12th- and 13th-century churches; a 10-minute walk takes you into the strange rock formations and caves of **Kő-völgy** (Stone Valley), beyond which are fine mountain views.

❻ Back on Highway 71, 5 kilometers (3 miles) west of Balatonakali is the popular beach resort of **Zánka.** Its shallow water is always wavy or rippling due to the nearby (and iron-rich) **Vérkút** (Blood Spring), which put Zánka on the map as a spa late in the 19th century. The town's **Reformed church** is of medieval origin, but it was rebuilt in 1786 and again a century later with various elements preserved—leaving a pulpit supported by Roman foundations and Romanesque columns.

Just west of Zánka, the landscape is disfigured by a monster-size (formerly Communist Pioneer) children's resort capable of housing 2,500 youngsters. It has its own railway station and a **Garden of Ruins** from a destroyed medieval village, the walls of which were built by the Romans. The village was discovered during an excavation during the 1960s.

❼ The centerpiece of **Balatonszepezd,** 3 kilometers (2 miles) west of Zánka, is a **Catholic church** that combines Romanesque and Gothic features with a minimum of mid-19th-century reconstruction.

Four kilometers (2½ miles) farther west is **Révfülöp,** where eight or more ferries cross the lake every day to Balatonboglar on the southern shore. The ruins of Révfülöp's 13th-century Romanesque church stand in striking contrast to the town's new railway station.

Three kilometers (2 miles) inland, to the northwest, is **Kővágóörs,** one of the prettiest villages of the Balaton, with a fine array of cottages in the local peasant style.

Beginning 3 kilometers (2 miles) after Révfülöp on Highway 71 are
⑧ the combined communities of **Balatonrendes** and **Ábrahámhegy,**
which form one of Lake Balaton's quieter resorts. Ábrahámhegy has
the northern shore's only sandy beach as well as a nudist beach. On
Balatonrendes's Fő utca (Main Street) is a Baroque 18th-century
Catholic church. Near the beach is the summer home of Endre
Bajcsy-Zsilinszky, a Communist killed by the Fascists prior to
World War II. It is now a **Memorial Museum** that may pique your curiosity after you've crossed a Bajcsy-Zsilinszky Street in virtually
every Hungarian town you visit.

⑨ All this, however, is a prelude to the **Badacsony,** a mysterious,
coffinlike basalt peak of the Balaton Highlands along the northern
shore. **Mount Badacsony** (1,437 feet high), its slopes rising from the
lake, is actually an extinct volcano flanked by smaller cone-shaped
hills. The masses of lava that coagulated here created bizarre and
beautiful rock formations. At the upper edge, salt columns tower
180–200 feet like organ pipes in a huge semicircle. In 1965 Hungarian conservationists won a major victory that ended the quarrying of
basalt from Mount Badacsony, which is now a protected nature-pre-
servation area.

The land below has been tilled painfully and lovingly for centuries.
There are vineyards everywhere and splendid wine in every inn and
tavern. In descending order of dryness, the best-loved Badacsony
white wines are *Rizlingszilváni, Kéknyelű* and *Szürkebarát.* Their
proud producers claim that "no vine will produce good wine unless it
can see its own reflection in the Balaton." They believe that it is not
enough for the sun simply to shine on a vine; the undersides of the
leaves also need light, which is reflected from the lake's mirrorlike
surface. Others claim that the wine draws its strength from the fire
of old volcanoes.

Badacsony is really an administrative name for the entire area and
includes not just the mountain but also five settlements at its foot.
Boats and trains deliver you to **Badacsony-Üdülőtelep** (Badacsony
Resort), where sightseeing could start with a visit to the **József
Egry Memorial Museum,** formerly the home and studio of an evoca-
tive painter of Balaton landscapes. *Egry sétány 52, tel. 87/331–140.
Admission: 20 Ft. adults, 10 Ft. children. Open May–Oct., Tues.–
Sun. 10–6.*

You can start up the mountain by car or by infrequent bus, or plod
uphill on foot along **Szegedy Róza út.** This steep street is paved with
basalt stones and is flanked by vineyards and villas; water from the
Kisfaludy Spring flows downhill along the side of the road. This is
the place to get acquainted with the writer Sándor Kisfaludy and his
beloved bride from Badacsony, Róza Szegedy, to whom he dedicated
his love poems. At the summit of her street is **Róza Szegedy Ház**
(Róza Szegedy House), a Baroque winepress house built in 1790 on a
grand scale—with thatched roof, gabled wall, six semicircular arcades, and an arched and pillared balcony running the length of the
four raftered upstairs rooms (it was here that the hometown girl met
the visiting bard from Budapest). The house is now a memorial museum to both of them, furnished much the way it was when he was
doing his best work immortalizing his two true loves, the Badacsony
and his wife. *Szegedy Róza út. Admission: 20 Ft. adults, 10 Ft. children. Open Mar.–Oct., Tues.–Sun. 10–5.*

Nearby are a **Bormúzeum** (Wine Museum) built of basalt and offering wine tastings, as well as the **Museum of the Badacsony State
Farm,** with an exhibition of utensils, documents, photos, and charts

illustrating 20 centuries of viticulture in the region. *Viktorlásház, Hegyalja út. Admission to both: 20 Ft. adults, 10 Ft. children. Open mid-May–mid-Oct., Tues.–Sun. 10–4.*

Time Out A short climb up from the museums is the **Kisfaludy-ház** restaurant, once a winepress house owned by the poet's family. Its wine cellar lies directly over the Kisfaludy Spring, which accompanied your upward hike, but the stellar attraction is a vast two-tiered terrace that affords a breathtaking panoramic view of virtually the entire lake. Stop for a snack or a drink on your way up and a meal on your way down; the grilled meats and *palacsinta* desserts are excellent, if expensive.

Serious summitry begins behind the Kisfaludy House at the **Rózsakő** (Rose Stone), a flat, smooth basalt slab with many carved inscriptions. Local legend has it that if a boy and a girl sit on it with their backs to Lake Balaton, they will marry within a year. From here, a trail marked in yellow leads upstairs to the foot of the columns that stretch to the top. Steep flights of stone steps take you through a narrow gap between rocks and basalt walls until you reach a tree-lined plateau. You are now at the 1,391-foot level. Follow the blue triangular markings along a path to the **Kisfaludy Lookout Tower.** When you have climbed its 46-foot height, you have scaled Mount Badacsony. Even with time out for rests and views, the ascent from the Rose Stone should take less than an hour.

If you rejoin the railroad or Highway 71 westbound after an adventure in the Badacsony, the village of **Szigliget,** formerly an island, is 11 kilometers (7 miles) away by the coast road and only 5 kilometers (3 miles) by train. Towering over the town is the ruin of the 13th-century **Óvár** (Old Castle), also known as "The Queen's Skirt" because it seems to spread out like a crinoline. A fortress so well protected that it was never taken by the Turks, it was demolished during the early 18th century by Habsburgs fearful of rebellions. Down in the village, the Romanesque remains of the **Avas templon** (Avas Church) from the Arpad dynasty still contain a 12th-century basalt tower with stone spire.

The **Eszterházy Summer Mansion** in the main square, Fő tér, was built during the 18th century and rebuilt in neoclassical style in the 19th. Lately a holiday retreat for writers, it has a 25-acre park with yews, willows, walnuts, pines, and more than 500 kinds of ornamental trees and shrubs. Szigliget also has a fine array of thatched-roof winepress houses.

From Szigliget or Badacsony, you can travel 11 kilometers (7 miles) north by bus or car to **Tapolca,** the chief city of the region. It has a fine square, **Batsányi tér,** built around an old mill pond. The mill itself now houses the **Hotel Gabriella** (*see* Dining and Lodging, *below*), which retains its original architectural style. In the square, too, is a **parish church** of medieval origin with a 15th-century Gothic chancel, though the church was enlarged and rebuilt in Baroque style during the 18th century. A statue of the Holy Trinity stands in front of it.

If you stay on the shore, continuing west 10 kilometers (6 miles) from Szigliget, you will reach **Balatongyörök,** a busy resort with three beaches; a **Roman spring**; and a pine-covered hillside, the **Szépkilátó** (Belvedere), planted by Prince Taszilo Festetics von Tolna for his English wife, the Duchess of Hamilton. **Vonyarcvashegy,** 4 kilometers (2½ miles) farther west, has a wine shop and restaurant, the Helikon Tavern, converted from one of Prince Taszilo's wine cellars. In the village cemetery is a small neoclassical Szentkereszt Kápolna (Holy Cross Chapel) with gabled facade and tower.

① You are now approaching **Keszthely,** the largest town on the northern shore. Founded in 1404, Keszthely today offers a rare combination of historic cultural center and restful summer resort. Its Gothic **parish church** (on Kossuth Lajos utca), built in 1386, was rebuilt and embellished several times (some 15th-century frescoes were recently revealed in the interior). The **Pethő Ház** (at Kossuth Lajos utca 22), a striking town house of medieval origin, was rebuilt in Baroque style with a handsome arcaded gallery above its courtyard. In 1830 the house became the birthplace of Karl Goldmark, who composed the opera *The Queen of Sheba*. Around the corner is the **Georgikon Farm Museum,** which shows the school's history and development. *Bercsényi Miklos utca 67. Admission: 30 Ft. Open Apr.–Oct., Tues.–Sat. 10–5, Sun. 10–6.*

Near the railroad station, housed in an imposing neo-Baroque building (1928), the **Balaton Museum** contains rich and varied exhibits of regional history, ethnography, folk art, and painting. *Múzeum utca 2, tel. 83/312–351. Admission: 20 Ft. adults, 10 Ft. children. Open Tues.–Sun. 10–6 (Nov.–Apr. until 5).*

The jewel of Keszthely is the magnificent **Festetics Vár** (Festetics Palace), one of the finest Baroque complexes in Hungary. Begun around 1745, it was the seat of the enlightened and philanthropic Festetics dynasty, which had acquired Keszthely six years earlier. The palace's distinctive churchlike tower and more than 100 rooms were added between 1883 and 1887, and the interior is exceedingly lush. The **Helikon Könyvtér** (Helikon Library) in the south wing contains some 52,000 volumes and precious codices and documents of Festetics family history, but it can also be admired for its carved-oak furniture and collection of etchings and paintings. Chamber and orchestral concerts are held in the **Mirror Gallery** ballroom or, in summer, in the courtyard. The palace opens onto a splendid park lined with rare plants and fine sculptures. *Kastély utca 1, tel. 83/314–194. Admission: 250 Ft. adults, 50 Ft. children; family ticket, 550 Ft. Open Apr.–June and Sept., Tues.–Sun. 10–6; July–Aug., Tues.–Sun. 9–7; Oct.–Mar., Tues.–Sun. 9–5.*

① Six kilometers (4 miles) inland is the spa of **Héviz,** with the largest natural curative thermal lake in Europe. Lake Héviz covers nearly 60,000 square yards with warm water that never grows cooler than 33°–35° C (91.4°–95° F) in summer and 30°–32° C (86°–89.6° F) in winter, thus allowing year-round bathing, particularly in the part of the lake that is covered by a roof and looks like a racetrack grandstand. The vast spa park houses hospitals, sanatoriums, hotels, and a casino.

Highway 71 turns south along the western rim of Lake Balaton at Keszthely. At **Fenékpuszta,** about 8 kilometers (5 miles) south of Keszthely, lie the ruins of the Roman settlement of **Valcum** and a three-naved early Christian **basilica** from the 4th century.

The largest river feeding Balaton, the Zala, enters the lake at its southwestern corner. On either side there is a vast swamp, formerly part of the lake. Known as **Kis-Balaton** (Little Balaton), almost 3,500 acres of marshland were put under nature preservation in 1949. In 1953 a bird-watching station was opened nearby, and ornithologists have found some 80 breeds nesting among the reeds, many of them rare for this region. The white egret is the most treasured species. The area can be visited only by special permission of the National Office of Environmental Conservation—Ornithological Institute (Országos Környezet-és Természetvédelmi Hivatal—Madártani Intézet), which has an office in Budapest (Költő utca 21, H-1121) and Veszprém (Tolbuhin utca 31, H-8201). The Kis-Balaton is entered near where Highway 71 ends its trip around the lake and yields to Highway 76 continuing south.

Tour 2: There are fewer sights along this side of the lake; instead what you'll
The Southern find is an almost unbroken chain of summer resorts. The water is
Shore shallow, and you can walk for almost 2 kilometers (1¼ miles) before it deepens. This makes it ideal for children and their parents, if not for serious swimmers. The water warms up to 25°C (77°F) in summer.

Highway 7 traverses this side of the water and takes over from
⑮ Highway 71—which circles the rest of the lake—near **Balatonberény,** a village settled during the Arpád dynasty. Bronze Age and Roman relics have been unearthed here. The Roman Catholic **parish church** at Kossuth Lajos utca 58 dates to the 14th and 15th centuries, and though it was rebuilt in Baroque style in 1733, it retains numerous Gothic features: pointed arches of the chancel, clergy seats, and a tabernacle. There is an excellent view of the Keszthely Hills across the lake. There is also a nudist campsite here; the identifying initials (FKK for Freie Körper-Kultur) are the same, but Hungarian nudists are much more reticent than their German and Austrian colleagues, who like to come out and wave at every passing boat.

It's worth making a 5-kilometer (3-mile) detour to the southwest to
⑯ the railway junction of **Balatonszentgyörgy** to see **Csillagvár** (Star Castle), built during the 1820s as a hunting lodge for László, the Festetics family's eccentric. Though it is not star-shaped inside, wedge-shaped projections on the ground floor give the outside this effect. Today it is a museum of 16th- and 17th-century life in the border fortresses of the Balaton and is worth exploring for its fine cut-stone stairs and deep well, from which drinking water is still drawn; refreshments are available in the adjoining former-stable. *Irtási dűlő, tel. 85/377-532. Admission: 30 Ft. adults, 10 Ft. children. Open Mar.–Apr. and Sept.–Oct., Tues.–Sun. 9–5; May–Aug., Tues.–Sun. 9–7.*

Downtown, almost 3 kilometers (2 miles) away, is another architecturally interesting museum, the beautifully furnished **Talpasház** (House on Soles), so named because its upright beams are encased in thick foundation boards. The house is filled not only with exquisite antique peasant furniture, textiles, and pottery but also with the work of contemporary local folk artists; some of their work is for sale on the premises. *Csillagvár utca 68. Admission: 30 Ft. adults, 10 Ft. children. Open mid-Apr.–May and Sept.–mid-Oct., Tues.–Sun. 9–12:30 and 1–5; mid-May.–Aug., Tues.–Sun. 9–7.*

⑰ Back on Highway 7, **Balatonmáriafürdő** is a quiet family resort established during the 1960s. Set among vineyards, it has an excellent beach stretching along 10 kilometers (6 miles) of lakeshore.

⑱ The next community, **Balatonfenyves,** stands near the **Nagyberek,** an old bay of Lake Balaton that clogged and dammed itself over the centuries into a 28,500-acre marshland. Since 1950, however, with pumping, canalization, and the planting of woodland strips, some three-quarters of the Nagyberek has been reclaimed and turned into arable land. The **Nagyberek State Farm,** established on the drained marshland, specializes in livestock and game. Every year it markets a half-million pheasants and wild ducks.

⑲ With seven beaches stretching 7 kilometers (almost 4½ miles) along the shore, **Fonyód** is second only to Siófok among the most-developed resorts on the southern shore of the lake. Vacationers from Pécs, 90 kilometers (56 miles) to the southeast, particularly favor Fonyód for their summer homes. An ancient settlement where late Stone Age and Bronze Age tools as well as Roman ruins have been excavated, Fonyód sits at the base of a twin-peaked hill rising directly from the shore. Atop one of the peaks, **Vár-hegy** (764 feet), stood an important fortress during Turkish times. Only its trenches and the foundation walls of a Romanesque church still stand; the peak is worth climbing for the views of its crowning ruin from the disheveled courtyard: You look across the lake almost directly at Badacsony and, off in the distance to the left, Keszthely.

⑳ An interesting excursion from Fonyód is the village of **Buzsák,** 16 kilometers (10 miles) to the south. Buzsák is famous for its colorful folk art, unique peasant needlework, and fine carving, mostly by shepherds. Today's products can be bought in local shops, but earlier masterworks are displayed in the **Regional House Museum,** housed in three venerable, well-decorated rustic buildings. Inquire about the village saint's festival, known as the *Buzsáki Búcsú*, held in August. *Tanács tér 7. Admission: 20 Ft. adults, 10 Ft. children. Open mid-May–end of May and Sept.–mid-Oct., Tues.–Sun. 9–5; June–Aug., Tues.–Sun. 9–7. On Mon. and mid-Oct.–mid-May, visits can be made by prior arrangement.*

㉑ Returning to Highway 7, travel 10 kilometers (6 miles) east from Fonyód to the communities of **Balatonboglár** and **Balatonlelle.** At the rate these resorts are mushrooming, they may soon merge into a minimegalopolis with Fonyód.

Balatonboglár, mentioned as a community as early as 1211, is, along with Fonyód, the only other place on the southern shore that has hills by the lake. Eruptions of basalt tuff (stratified volcanic detritus) created these hills: At 541 feet, Balatonboglár's highest, **Vár-hegy,** is 223 feet lower than Fonyód's peak of the same name. Near its summit are the double ramparts of early Iron Age defensive earthworks as well as the foundation walls of a Roman watchtower. There is a good view from the spherical **Xantus Lookout Tower.** Atop the smaller **Sándor-hegy,** the crater of the tuff volcano is still visible. On **Temető-domb** (Cemetery Hill), two gaudy chapels with a sculpture garden catch the eye: The **Red Chapel** was built in 1856 and the **Blue Chapel** in 1892, both in a multitude of styles. They are the scene of an annual summer art show. *Kápolna köz. Admission: 20 Ft. adults, 10 Ft. children. Open June–mid-Sept., Tues.–Sun. 9–8.*

There are many fine houses in the village; one neoclassical (1834) mansion is headquarters of a huge State Wine Farm and Research Station that supplies much of Hungary and Europe with Balaton wines. The village is separated from the beach resort by railroad tracks and Highway 7. Frequent ferries to Révfülöp offer quick transport to the northern shore.

Balatonlelle is a busy resort with some interesting modern architecture, such as the **Trade Unions' Holiday Home** on Köztársaság út. It also has a few elegant homes. In the garden of a villa at Szent István utca 38 is a 300-year-old willow tree; the oldest in Hungary, it is 23 feet in circumference. The annual meeting of wood-carving folk artists is held in the antebellum-like 1838 neoclassical **House of Culture** at Kossuth Lajos utca 2.

㉒ **Balatonszemes** is an older, established lakeside resort with a town history dating to the 14th century. Now a school, the former

Hunyady Mansion on Gárdonyi Géza utca was built in Baroque style in the second half of the 18th century, as was the former granary opposite it. The **parish church** at Fő utca 23 was built in Gothic style in the 15th century, and some of its ornamented windows and the buttressed walls of the chancel still survive. Its richly decorated pastorium is from 1517.

One of Balatonszemes's more unique attractions is **Bagolyvár** (Owl Castle), an eccentric stronghold with many turrets. It was built by an Italian architect at the beginning of this century on the site of an old Turkish fort known as Fool's Castle (Bolondvár). The two southern round bastions of the old Fool's Castle are incorporated in the relatively recent Owl Castle.

Balatonszemes also has a **Postamúzeum** (Postal Museum) in a Baroque building where, from 1789 until early in this century, post and stagecoach horses were stabled. Some of their old coaches are on display; the museum inside exhibits old postal equipment, uniforms, and stamps. In the summer season there is a special post office where mail is postmarked with an imprint representing a mail coach. *Bajcsy-Zsilinszky utca 46, tel. 84/345–160. Admission: 20 Ft. Open June–Oct., Tues.–Sun. 10–6.*

㉓ **Balatonszárszó,** 5 kilometers (3 miles) to the east, is where the Hungarian poet Attila József—one of the few Hungarian poets whose genius survives translation—committed suicide in 1937 by throwing himself under a train. The boardinghouse where he spent his last weeks is now the **Attila József Memorial Museum,** with extensive documentation of his life, death, and work. *József Attila utca 7. Admission: 30 Ft. adults, 10 Ft. children. Open Tues.–Sun. 10–6 (Nov.–Mar. until 2 PM).*

㉔ The second part of **Balatonföldvár**'s name means "earthwork," and, indeed, this charming village was built beside an old Celtic fortification that has largely been damaged and obscured by posh villas along Petőfi Sándor utca and József Attila utca. The destruction of the past can perhaps be justified, if not excused, by the result: Balatonföldvár is the southern shore's most beautifully laid-out resort. Its picture-book harbor is alive with sailboats in summer; on the shore, weeping willows droop to the water as if in homage. An alley of plane trees is crowned by a superb view of the hills of Tihany across the water. Forests of flowers and spacious, symmetrical promenades all contribute to the impression that the entire town is one big park, if not the Garden of Eden. South of the railroad station, on the other side of the tracks from the water, is **Fenyves** (Pinewood Park) with an open-air theater and a brook. Campgrounds are spacious, attractive, and even luxurious, and there are excellent beaches and a wide selection of hotels, pensions, motels, and restaurants.

㉕ Four kilometers (2½ miles) south of Balatonföldvár and accessible by bus as well as car is the village of **Kőröshegy,** with a single-nave 15th-century Gothic Catholic church. Restored in 1969, it retains many of its original features: fortresslike Franciscan design, walls decorated with peasant carvings, a Viennese altarpiece, and a delicate rose window above a robust Gothic portal. The church has excellent acoustics and is the scene of organ, choral, and chamber concerts in summer. The **Széchenyi** mansion, built in the French Baroque style of the late 18th century, is under landmark preservation, as is its former Dézsma Pince (Tithe Cellar). Here the serfs had to deliver a portion of their wine harvest as payment to the landowner. There was formerly a spring inside the cellar, and it covered the walls with stalactites and stalagmites.

Continue a few kilometers to **Szántódpuszta,** just opposite the Tihany Peninsula on the southern shore of Lake Balaton, where the narrow neck of water separates Szántód from the peninsula (a ferry takes passengers across). Szántódpuszta itself is a living museum and entertainment center; the group of buildings erected there during the 18th and 19th centuries and recently reconstructed feature several exhibits, including relics of local history, the works of fine and folk art, and a display of industrial history. Between May and September the museum hosts a variety of programs that include horse and dog shows, and folk-art displays and fairs. *Tel. 84/331–014 or 84/331–246. Admission: 100 Ft. Open May–Sept., daily 8:30–5; Mar.–Apr. and Oct.–Dec., Tues.–Fri. 8:30–2, Sat. and Sun. 8:30–11; Jan.–Feb., Tues.–Fri. 8:30–2.*

㉖ **Siófok** is the largest city on the southern shore and one of Hungary's major tourist and holiday centers. It has a resident population of some 23,000, but in the high season the number swells to more than 100,000. In 1863 a railway station was built for the city, paving the way for its "golden age" at the turn of the century, when a horse-racing course was built with stands to accommodate 1,500 spectators. During the closing stages of World War II the city sustained heavy damage; to boost tourism during the 1960s, the Pannonia Hotel Company built four of what many consider to be the ugliest hotels in the area. Modern attractions include the birthplace of composer Imre Kálmán (1882–1953), known as the Prince of Operetta. Inside his small house-cum-museum are his favorite piano, original scores, his smoking jacket, and lots of old pictures. *Kálmán Imre sétány 5, tel. 84/311–287. Admission: 30 Ft. Open Tues.–Sun. 9–5.*

Sports and Outdoor Activities

Bicycling Lake Balaton is one of the few places where you can rent bicycles in Hungary—should you tire of swimming, sailboarding, or sunbathing. Most rental shops are clustered along the beaches; also try the Füredi Camping Site (*see* Dining and Lodging, *below*).

Horseback Riding In **Balatonfüred** you can rent horses for 650 Ft. per hour at the **M & M Riding School** (Vazsónyi út 2). From the riding stables in **Felsőors,** 10 kilometers (6 miles) from Veszprem on the road to Csopak, you can hit the trail with a guide for 500 Ft. an hour; groups of six or more can travel in more style in a horse-drawn carriage.

Miniature Golf For those interested in less strenuous exercise, there is a miniature golf course at the Füredi Camping Site (*see* Dining and Lodging, *below*).

Sailing and Water Sports In **Balatonfüred,** visitors can rent sailboards and sailboats on the public beach. Since motorboats are forbidden on the lake, Balatonfüred's electric waterski towing machine, near the Füredi Camping Site (*see* Dining and Lodging, *below*), is the *only* way avid skiiers can get their feet wet in Lake Balaton.

Tennis Hotels in the Füred area will usually allow nonguests to use and reserve hotel tennis courts; the going rate is 300 Ft. per hour, per court.

Dining and Lodging

Lake Balaton is the major source of fish in Hungary, particularly for *süllő,* a kind of perch. Most restaurants offer it breaded, although some will grill it. Hungarians are also very fond of carp (*ponty*), pike (*csuka*), catfish (*harcsá*), and eel (*angolna*), which are usually stewed in a garlic-and-tomato sauce. Popular nonfish entrées include fried goose liver, turkey breast Kiev, *gulyásleves* (goulash), *gombás rostélyos* (stewed steak with mushrooms), and *töltöttpaprika* (stuffed paprika).

The Balaton area probably has more sleeping accommodations per square foot than any other part of Hungary, ranging from elegant hotels to comfortable private rooms and camping facilities.

Highly recommended establishments in a particular price category are indicated by a star ★.

Aszófő
Lodging

Diana Camping. In a sylvan setting where the songs of birds are nature's best entertainment, this is the most enchanting of Balaton's 46 campsites. Despite its capacity of 2,400 guests, Diana Camping is also one of the hardest to book because nearly 80% of its loyal campers (largely Austrian, German, and Dutch) return year after year. The longtime director, Aranka Minorits, is everybody's ultimate Earth Mother. Though 3 kilometers (2 miles) from the lake, this unspoiled 30-acre site is nicely situated near the turnoff from Balatonfüred to Tihany. *2 km (1¼ mi) north of Hwy. 71 from Aszófő, H-8241, tel. 86/345–013. Tent and trailer camping only. Facilities: shower and toilet areas, communal kitchen, grocery, restaurant, rustic wine tavern, lounge with TV, tennis courts, soccer field. No credit cards. $*

Badacsony
Dining
★

Szőlőskert. During the late 1980s, Janos Peter leased a decaying turn-of-the-century villa from a trade union that had been abusing it and, by guaranteeing two years of hot meals free, assembled a team of workers to remodel it without pay. With private banquet rooms, the house also serves as kitchen and wine cellar for an adjoining garden restaurant. Peter the Great's empire now straddles both sides of the road above it, continuing uphill through vineyards to a large but rustic indoor-outdoor terrace restaurant with wide-screen views of Balaton and Badacsony. It comes almost as icing on the pancake to add that the food and drink are first-rate—from the cold platters with deer salami in the villa garden to the rolled turkey breast filled with ham and mushrooms and topped with melted cheese. The Zöldszilváni (Green Sylvaner) wine should not be neglected. *Kossuth utca 16, tel. 87/331–248. Reservations advised. Dress: casual. No credit cards. Closed Nov.–Apr. $$*

Lodging

Club Tomaj. Located on the shore of Lake Balaton in the Badacsonytomaj neighborhood, this is the largest hotel in the area. It's just a step away from the hotel to the Club's private beach. *Badacsonytomaj, Balatoni ut. 14, tel. 87/331–040. 52 rooms. Facilities: restaurant, café, sauna, private beach. No credit cards. $$*

Balatonakali
Dining

Mandula Csárda. Named for its almond trees, this 19th-century vintner's house is now an elegantly rustic, totally romantic, thatched-roof roadside inn with a shady vineyard terrace where Gypsy musicians serenade you as you sip delicious Balaton and Badacsony wines. It also has a playground for children. The management is fond of—and good at—organizing such activities as Gypsy, outlaw, and goulash parties as well as horseback riding and carriage outings to interesting surroundings. *On Hwy. 71, halfway between Balatonudvari and Balatonakali, H-8243, tel. 86/344–511. Reservations advised. Dress: casual. No credit cards. Closed late Sept.–early May. $$*

Balatonfüred **Fekete Lovaghoz Középkori Étterem.** The building housing the
Dining "Black Knight Medieval Restaurant" is a registered landmark dating to 1484, the oldest in Balatonfüred. The restaurant itself,
opened in 1992, has long wooden tables that accommodate 85 diners—somewhat reminiscent of a monastery's dining room. Guests
are given only a handmade wooden spoon and a big bib; all the food—
supposedly served medieval style—thus becomes finger food. To
stimulate the medieval appetite there are waiters dressed in costume and prerecorded Renaissance music. *Bajcsy-Zsilinszky út 32,
tel. 86/348–345. Reservations advised. Reservations advised. Dress:
casual. AE, DC, MC, V. Open Easter–Oct. for dinner only. $$$*
Tölgyfa Csárda. On a hillside away from the beach, this restaurant
takes its arboreal name from a large oak tree nearby. It's currently
the most expensive restaurant in town, with a decor and menu wor-
thy of a first-class Budapest restaurant. It's got Gypsy music and a
nice view, and the staff works to keep customers happy. *Meleghegy
(walk north on Jókai Mór út and turn right on Mérleg út), tel. 86/
343–036. Reservations advised. Dress: casual but neat. AE. $$$*
Baricska Csárda. Perched on a hill overlooking wine and water—its
own vineyard and Lake Balaton—this rambling reed-thatched rustic inn, crawling with vines, comes alive at 6 PM and doesn't skip a
beat until well past midnight. Through its many wood-rafter rooms,
vaulted cellars, and terraces traipse tour groups that tend to stay until
closing. The food is hearty yet ambitious: spicy soups in kettles,
roasted trout and fogas, fish paprikash with gnocchi to soak up the
rich, creamy sauce, and desserts that mix pumpkin and poppyseed
with a flair known nowhere else. Try the *Baricska béles*, which lies
somewhere between soufflé and pudding. The inn has achieved European recognition by winning a gold medal from the International
Organization of Press for Tourism and Gastronomy (FIPREGA) and
a certificate pronouncing it a "Maison de Qualité." *Baricska dűlő,
off Hwy. 71 (Széchenyi út) behind Shell station, tel. and fax 86/343–
105. Reservations advised. Dress: casual. AE, V. Closed Nov. 11–
Mar. 14. $$*
Hordó Csárda. Although this venerable inn is overshadowed by its
noted next-door neighbor, the Baricska, it does have its own advan-
tages—namely Gypsy music; Transylvanian meat specialties and
fish soup and goulashes prepared in outdoor cauldrons; and wine
tastings in September accompanied by a folklore show. If you have
any room left after the hearty dinner, try the pumpkin and poppy-
seed strudels. *Baricska dűlő, off Hwy. 71, tel. 86/343–417. Reserva-
tions advised. Dress: casual. AE. Closed Nov.–Mar. $$*
Halászkert Étterem. Known as the Fisherman's Garden, this
beachfront restaurant features more than 30 fish dishes and is famous for its Balaton pike perch, which tastes best when grilled over
an open flame. Meals are served until 1 AM during the summer. In
between courses you can twirl on the restaurant's outdoor dance floor.
*Széchenyi 2, off Jókai Mór út, near dock, tel. 86/343–039. Reserva-
tions advised for dinner. Dress: casual but neat. AE, MC, V. $*

Lodging **Marina.** The spiffy 12-story beachfront skyscraper from the mid-
1980s has much less character than the refurbished and more pricey
Lido wing, which dates to 1970 and opens directly onto the water.
Lido guests can, of course, use the high-rise facilities, too, which include a large indoor swimming pool and a rooftop restaurant.
Thanks to a youthful staff that is friendly, helpful, and never impersonal or condescending, even the glitzy main lobby radiates warmth
and personality. *Széchenyi út 26, H-8230 Balatonfüred, tel. 86/343–
644, fax 86/343–052. 375 rooms and 29 apartments, all with bath.
Facilities: restaurant, beer tavern, bar, nightclub, boating, beach,*

indoor swimming pool, sauna, solarium, bowling alley. AE, DC, MC, V. Closed Oct.–May (indoor pool open year-round). $$–$$$

Annabella. Situated in the spa park overlooking the Tagore Promenade and Lake Balaton, this large, modern hotel offers excellent swimming and water-sports facilities. It is just around the corner from the town's main square. *Deák Ferenc utca 25, H-8230 Balatonfüred, tel. 86/342–222, fax 86/343–084. 390 rooms; all double rooms have bath. Facilities: restaurant, bar, pool. AE, DC, MC, V. Closed Oct.–Mar. $$*

Blaha Lujza. This sober summer house, built in a classic Roman style, was formerly owned by Hungarian actress Blaha Lujza. Nowadays it's a friendly, unassuming bed-and-breakfast within short walking distance of the lake. The facilities and simple rooms are neither too old nor new; rather, they're simply clean and functional. *Blaha Lujza utca 4, tel. and fax 86/342–603. 18 rooms with shower, 2 suites. Facilities: restaurant, coffee shop, terrace, billiards, parking. No credit cards. $$*

Füred. This 12-story lakefront hotel caters to small conventions and groups but is a pleasant place for individual guests, too. The hotel lies close to the lake and has a beach of its own. *Széchenyi út 20, H-8230 Balatonfüred, tel. 86/343–033, fax 86/343–034. 125 rooms with bath, 27 suites. Facilities: 2 restaurants, bar, coffee shop, tennis court, bowling alley, sailing, parking. AE, DC, MC, V. $$*

Margaréta. This attractive apartment hotel stands across the street from the lakefront Hotel Marina, and its guests are expected to use the Marina's facilities. It is smaller and more intimate than some of its neighbors, and its restaurant is popular locally. All apartments have kitchen, balcony, phone, TV, and radio. *Széchenyi út 29, H-8230 Balatonfüred, tel. 86/343–824, fax 86/343–824. 52 apartments with bath. Facilities: restaurant, bar, snack bar, parking, beach, fishing. AE, DC, MC, V. $$*

Füredi Camping Site. At water's edge next door to the Hotel Marina, there is nothing primitive about Hungary's biggest and best campsite. On 67 acres with facilities to accommodate 3,500 people (including tourists without tents or vehicles), it is a self-contained village with its own post office, beauty parlor, self-service laundry, and supermarket. *Széchenyi út 24, H-8230 Balatonfüred, tel. 86/342–822. Facilities: restaurant, cafés, snack bars, bathing, boating, waterskiing, water chute, tennis courts, bowling alley, minigolf, sauna, solarium, fishing. AE, MC, V. Closed Oct.–Apr. $*

Balatongyörök
Dining

Panoráma Csárda. This restaurant lives up to its name, providing a stunning panorama of the lake from its hillside location; even the hill it's built on is called Szépkilátó ("beautiful view"). Once you've chosen such dishes as Wiener schnitzel or pork with dumplings, you can hang out for quite a while, enjoying the view and writing postcards. The view makes the taxi or bus ride out here worthwhile. *Balatongyörök, Hwy. 71. Bus from Keszthely to Tapolca stops in front of restaurant. No reservations. Dress: casual. Wheelchair access. AE. Closed Nov.–Feb. $*

Balatonmária-fürdő
Lodging

Hotel Maria. This lakeshore hotel, in a three-story modern building reconstructed in 1986, has its own private beach and easy access to nearby tennis courts and other sports activities. *Rákóczi út 1, Box 37, H-8847, tel. 84/376–038 or 84/376–039. 94 rooms with bath. Facilities: bar, breakfast lounge, parking, hotel taxi. AE, DC, MC, V. Closed Oct.–Apr. $$*

Fonyód
Dining

Présház Csárda. Above the remains of Fonyód Castle, the driveway leading to a four-pillar veranda is so imposing that you may expect to be greeted by Scarlett O'Hara. But behind the noble facade of this "winepress-house inn" is a thatched-roof structure typical of the region and a wine cellar 24 yards long, all with cozy rustic furnishings. The Hungarian dishes and local wines are excellent. *Lenke utca 22. No reservations. Dress: casual. No credit cards. $$*

Héviz
Lodging

Aqua Thermal Hotel. This large, luxurious spa-hotel has its own thermal baths and physiotherapy unit (plus a full dental service!). It has a convenient city-center location, but the rooms are smaller than average and therefore not suited to families who intend to share a single room. *Kossuth Lajos utca 13–15, H-8380, tel. 83/340–947, fax 83/340–970, telex 35–247. 230 rooms with bath. Facilities: restaurant, bar, pool, sauna, solarium, hairdresser, medical services. AE, DC, MC, V. $$$*

Thermal Hotel Héviz. Very similar in its offerings to those of its neighbor the Aqua Thermal (*see above*), this large spa-hotel has the additional attraction of a casino. *Kossuth Lajos utca 9–11, H-8380, tel. 83/341–180, fax 83/340–660, telex 35–286. 203 rooms with bath. Facilities: restaurant, sauna, thermal baths, solarium, medical services. AE, DC, MC, V. $$$*

Keszthely
Dining

Gösser Söröző. This centrally located beer garden keeps long hours and plenty of beer on tap for its mostly Austrian clientele. The food is better than you might guess judging just from the touristy atmosphere. Aside from barroom snacks, the menu features Hungarian specialties, such as gulyásleves, gombás rostélyos, and töltött-paprika. Vegetarians can opt for the salad bar. In summer, live music starts at 6 PM. *Kossuth Lajos utca 35, just north of Fő tér, tel. 83/312–265. No reservations. Dress: casual. Wheelchair access. AE, DC, V. $*

Lodging

Helikon Castle. Usually reserved for small, secluded conferences, 19 guest rooms within Keszthely's grandest sight are occasionally available to individuals. *Kastély utca 1, H-8360, tel. 83/314–194. 19 rooms with bath. Facilities: conference room. No credit cards. $$$*

Helikon Hotel. This large and comfortable lakeside hotel is convenient and popular with groups. Guests can choose from numerous sports facilities, such as an indoor swimming pool, an indoor tennis court, bowling, a sauna, a solarium, sailing, surfing, rowing, fishing and, in winter, skating. The hotel also offers slimming treatments and beauty care. *Balaton part 5, H-8360, tel. 83/315–944, fax 83/315–403. 240 rooms with bath. Facilities: restaurant, bar, pool, fitness center. AE, DC, MC, V. $$$*

Amazon. Behind a beautiful facade in the style of late-18th-century French architecture is this simple tourist hostel in the center of town. *Kastély utca 11, H-8360, tel. 83/314–213. 16 rooms, 8 with bath. Facilities: restaurant, bar, nightclub. No credit cards. $$*

Siófok
Dining

Janus Étterem. This elegant restaurant, once an old villa, was renovated in 1992 under the guidance of Imre Makovecz, one of Hungary's preeminent architects (Makoveca also designed the church across the street). The green-and-white dining room is air-conditioned, a rarity in Hungary. The menu features excellent if not typical Hungarian specialties in addition to vegetarian dishes that use unique Swiss cookware to eliminate the need for oil. *Fő utca 93–95, tel. 84/312–546. Reservations advised. Dress: casual. AE, DC, MC, V. $$*

★ **Csárdás Étterem.** The oldest and one of the best restaurants in Siófok, Csárdás has consistently won awards for its hearty, never-bland Hungarian cuisine, service, and ambience. In summer you can sit on the terrace pondering your English-language menu. *Fő utca 105, tel. 84/310–642. Reservations advised in summer. Dress: casual. AE. Closed Nov.–Mar. 15. $*

Lodging **Janus.** Every room in this brand-new luxury hotel, opened in 1993, contains a minibar and a safe. The "relaxation center" downstairs features a swimming pool, sauna, and whirlpool. *Fő utca 93–95, tel. 84/312–546, fax 84/312–432. 17 rooms and 7 suites, all with bath. Facilities: restaurant, bar, fitness center. AE, DC, MC, V. $$*

Villa Juhász. At this private family-operated pension in the middle of Siófok, the rooms are comfortable, clean, and modern; each comes equipped with a bathroom, television, and minibar. In summer, the pension's restaurant is open 24 hours. *Zéchenyi út 14, tel. and fax 84/312–588. 10 rooms and 2 suites, all with bath. Facilities: restaurant. AE, DC, MC, V. $$*

Moló. This hotel, once a trade-union resort, is close to the Balaton shore, the town harbor, and a public swimming pool. Budget-minded visitors will appreciate the price: 800 Ft. per night, including breakfast. Bathrooms and showers are in the hallway. *Petőfi sétány 1, tel. 84/312–244. 102 rooms without bath. Facilities: restaurant. No credit cards. $*

Tapolca **Aspa Panzio.** The owners can organize a variety of outdoor treks—
Lodging from horseback riding to sailing—at this comfortable pension in the center of town. *Kossuth Lajos utca 19, H-8300, tel. 87/311–695. 9 rooms with bath. Facilities: restaurant, bar, tennis. No credit cards. $*

Hotel Gabriella. This is a small, charming hotel in a converted mill on the main square, which is also the main attraction of this road and rail junction. *Batsányi tér 7, H-8300, tel. 87/312–642. 14 rooms. Facilities: restaurant. No credit cards. $*

Tihany **Sport.** Beautifully situated near the Tihany boat landing, this first-
Dining class garden restaurant faces south to afford a panoramic view of Lake Balaton. Large bay windows allow similar views from inside the 1920s main house, where the back wall is richly painted by women folk artists from Kalocsa. Fish soup is a main-course specialty. There is disco dancing in the evening. *Fürdőtelep 34, tel. 86/348–251. Reservations advised. Dress: casual. AE, DC, MC, V. Closed Oct.–Easter. $$$*

Halásztánya. The relaxed atmosphere and Gypsy music in the evening contribute to the popularity of the Halásztánya, which specializes in fish. *Visszhang utca 11, no tel. No reservations. Dress: casual. AE. Closed Nov.–Mar. $$*

★ **HBH Kolostor söröző.** At the foot of the abbey steps, this beer restaurant and moderately priced pension hotel offers striking views of the church complex above, shimmeringly illuminated through the trees at night. There is an outdoor grill in the garden. Inside this spacious chalet, which seats 400, is a glass-enclosed, working brewery, and during the day you can watch men in blue smocks sipping seriously and puckering for quality control. It is all very thirst-provoking, as are the fish specialties, which include eel paprikash; trout with almonds; the Balaton's ubiquitous pike perch, fogas; and its young, *süllő*, served in fillets with tiny crayfish and dill sauce. *Kossuth utca 14, tel. 86/348–408. Reservations advised in summer. Dress: casual. AE, MC, V. Closed Jan.–Easter. $$*

Lodging **Club Tihany.** This 32-acre holiday village calls itself an "island of opportunities" for sports and recreation; essentially, it is a year-round resort complex of Club Med proportions at the tip of the Tihany Peninsula. The list of activities is staggering: bathing, boating, surfing, tennis, squash, badminton, ping-pong, bowling, biking, hiking, horseback riding, fishing, sauna, fitness, and gymnastics. Housing is provided in 161 luxury bungalows that offer a choice of architecture—suburban A-frame, modern atrium, or

Fortunately, when you travel on Rail Europe, there are some sights you'll miss.

No goofy hats. No big sunglasses. No plaid shirts with striped shorts. Instead, on Rail Europe, you'll experience Europe the way Europeans do. You'll enjoy scenic countryside no one else can show you. And meet unique and interesting people. In short, you'll explore Europe the way it was meant to be explored. When it comes to visiting 33 European countries, get real. Go Rail Europe. Because traveling any other way could end up showing you some pretty dreadful sights. To learn more, call your travel agent or 1-800-4-EURAIL. (1-800-438 7245)

≡ *Rail Europe*

Europe. To the trained eye.

All the Best Trips Start with Fodor's

COMPASS AMERICAN GUIDES
Titles in the series: Arizona, Canada, Chicago, Colorado, Hawai'i, Hollywood, Las Vegas, Maine, Manhattan, New Mexico, New Orleans, Oregon, San Francisco, South Carolina, South Dakota, Utah, Virginia, Wisconsin, Wyoming.

"A literary, historical, and near-sensory excursion."—*Denver Post*

"Tackles the 'why' of travel...as well as the nitty-gritty details."—*Travel Weekly*

FODOR'S BED & BREAKFASTS AND COUNTRY INN GUIDES
Titles in the series: California, Canada, England & Wales, Mid-Atlantic, New England, The Pacific Northwest, The South, The Upper Great Lakes Region.

"In addition to information on each establishment, the books add notes on things to see and do in the vicinity."
— *San Diego Union-Tribune*

THE BERKELEY GUIDES
Titles in the series: California, Central America, Eastern Europe, Europe, France, Germany, Great Britain & Ireland, Italy, London, Mexico, The Pacific Northwest & Alaska, Paris, San Francisco.

The best choice for budget travelers, from the Associated Students at the University of California at Berkeley.

"Berkeley's scribes put the funk back in travel." — *Time*

"Fresh, funny and funky as well as useful." — *The Boston Globe*

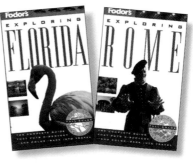

EXPLORING GUIDES
Titles in the series: Australia, Britain, California, Caribbean, Florida, France, Germany, Ireland, Italy, London, New York City, Paris, Rome, Singapore & Malaysia, Spain, Thailand.

"Authoritatively written and superbly presented, they make worthy reading before, during or after a trip."
— *The Philadelphia Inquirer*

"A handsome new series of guides, complete with lots of color photos, geared to the independent traveler."
— *The Boston Globe*

Visit your local bookstore, or call 24 hours a day 1-800-533-6478
Fodor's The name that means smart travel.

sloped-roof minifarmhouse, all with kitchen facilities; or you can stay in the bland main building, the Hotel Tihany, which has 330 rooms and a swimming pool in the lobby. Scattered around the premises are two restaurants, two beer halls, three bars, a wine restaurant festooned with antlers and other hunt trophies, and, in the center of the complex, the lovely Lavender Restaurant, with muted flower decor and beef specialties. *Rév utca 3, H-8237, tel. 86/348–088, fax 86/348 110. 330 rooms with bath; 161 bungalows. AE, DC, MC, V. $$$*

Veszprém **Club Skorpió.** Opened in 1992, this city-center restaurant is reminis-
Dining cent of an alpine hut. The house specialties are grilled meats, and the menu is in English, Italian, and German. Service is friendly and efficient. *Virág Benedek utca 1/b, tel. 88/420–319. Reservations advised. Dress: casual. No credit cards. $$*
Diana Étterem. The Diana is just a little southwest of the town center but worth the trip if you want to experience the old-fashioned charm of a small, provincial Hungarian restaurant. The decor could be called "cozy traditional" and the fish and game specialties are perennial favorites. *József Attila utca 22, tel. 88/421–061. Reservations advised. Dress: casual. No credit cards. $$*

Lodging **Kristály.** This quiet alpine-style lodge, favored by communist bigwigs until 1989, is surrounded by woods and set on a small hill overlooking Veszprém and its castle. The views are first-rate, while the furnishings and decor are elegant but not too flashy. The management can help arrange tours of Lake Balaton. *Jutasi út 18/3, 2 km from city center, tel. and fax 88/321–296. 7 rooms with bath, 2 suites. Facilities: bar, sauna. No credit cards. $$*
Veszprém. This modern and comfortable hotel in the center of town is convenient to most of the major sights. *Budapesti utca 6, tel. 88/324–677, fax 88/324–076. 72 rooms and 4 suites, most with bath. Facilities: restaurant. No credit cards. $*

Northern Hungary and the Great Plain

Northern Hungary stretches from the Danube Bend, north of Budapest, along the northeastern frontier with Slovakia as far west as Sátoraljaújhely. It is a clearly defined area, marked by several mountain ranges of no great height but of considerable scenic beauty. Most of the peaks reach 3,000 feet and are thickly wooded almost to their summit. Oak, beech, and ash are the main forest trees, with comparatively few patches of pine and fir. Naturalists, botanists, geologists, ethnographers, and folklorists find much of interest in the hills. Grottoes and caves abound, as well as thermal baths. In the state game reserves, herds of deer and wild boar roam freely, and eagles and the very rare red-footed falcon are not uncommon sights.

Hungary's Great Plain—the **Nagyalföld**—stretches south from Budapest to the borders of Croatia and Serbia and as far east as Ukraine and Romania. It covers an area of 51,800 square kilometers (20,000 square miles) and is what most people think of as the typical Hungarian landscape. Almost completely flat, it is the home of shepherds and their flocks and, above all, of splendid horses and the *csikós*, their riders. The plain has a wild, almost alien air; its sprawling villages consist mostly of one-story houses, though there are many large farms and up-to-date market gardens. The plain, which is divided into two almost equal parts by the Tisza River, also contains several of Hungary's most historic cities. However, even though the Great Plain preserves much from medieval times (largely because it was never occupied by the Turks), today it remains the least developed area of Hungary.

Historically, the valleys of northern Hungary have always been of considerable strategic importance, as they provided the only access to the Carpathian Mountains. **Eger,** renowned throughout Hungarian history as one of the guardians of these strategic routes, retains its splendor, with many ruins picturesquely dotting the surrounding hilltops. The **Mátra Mountains,** less than 90 kilometers (55 miles) from Budapest, provide opportunities for year-round recreation and are the center for winter sports. Last but not least, this is one of the great wine-growing districts of Hungary, with Gyöngyös and Eger contributing the "Magyar nectar" and Tokaj producing the "wine of kings."

Important Addresses and Numbers

Tourist Information
Debrecen: Hajdútourist County Tourist Office (Kálvin tér 2/a, tel. 52/315–588, fax 52/319–616).
Eger: Tourinform (Dobó tér 2, tel. 36/321–807).
Hajdúszoboszló: Hajdútourist (József Attila utca 2, tel. 52/362–214 or 52/362–966).
Hajdúszoboszló: Tourinform (Szilfákalja 2, tel. 52/361–612, fax 52/362–448).
Nyíregyháza: Nyirtourist County Tourist Office (Dózsa György út 3, tel. 42/311–544).
Szeged: Tourinform (Hugo Victor utca 1, tel. 62/311–711).
Szolnok: Tiszatour County Tourist Office (Ságvári körút 4, tel. 56/424–803).

Emergencies
Debrecen
Police (tel. 52/318–300). **Ambulance** (tel. 52/314–333). **Hospital** (University Clinic, Nagyerdei körút 98, tel. 52/311–600). Emergency medical service at night: for adults, Bethlen utca 5–7, tel. 52/316–222; for children, Bajcsy Zsilinszky utca 32, tel. 52/315–330.

Hajdúszoboszló
Police (tel. 07). **Ambulance** (tel. 04). **Hospital** (Central Clinic, Szilfákalja út 1–3, tel. 52/362–222).

Late-Night Pharmacies
Debrecen: Széchenyi utca 1, tel. 52/326–666; and Piac utca 33.
Hajdúszoboszló: Hősök tere 10, tel. 52/361–975; Szilfakkalja út 26, tel. 52/362–430.
Hortobágy: Kossuth Lajos utca 3, tel. 52/369–141.

Arriving and Departing by Plane, Car, Train, and Bus

By Plane There is no commercial air service to this part of Hungary. The closest major airport is in Budapest.

By Car Highway 3 is the main link between Budapest and northern Hungary.

By Train Service to the Great Plain from Budapest is quite good; daily service is available from the capital's Nyugati (West) and Keleti (East) stations. Express trains run between Budapest and Békéscsaba, Cegléd, Debrecen, Gyula, Hódmező-vásárhely, Kecskemét, Kisunhalas, Makó, Nyíregyháza, Szeged, and Szolnok. *Information: tel. 1/142–9150, 1/122–8056, or 1/122–8049.*

By Bus Volanbusz (tel. 1/118–7315) operates service from Budapest's Népstadion bus terminal and the terminal in Erzsébet tér to towns throughout the Great Plain.

Highlights for First-Time Visitors

Debrecen (*see* Tour 2)
Eger (*see* Tour 1)
Hortobágy (*see* Tour 2)
Tokaj (*see* Tour 1)

Exploring Northern Hungary and the Great Plain

Numbers in the margin correspond to points of interest on the Northern Hungary and the Great Plain map.

Tour 1: Northern Hungary ❶ Rising to the northeast of Budapest is the **Mátra**, Hungary's best-developed mountain vacation area. The city of **Gyöngyös**, famous for its excellent wines (don't pass up the chance to sample the *Debrői hárslevelű*, a magnificent white wine), lies at the base of this volcanic mountain group. Early in the 1960s huge lignite deposits were discovered, and the large-scale mines and power stations established since then have changed the character of the entire region. Among the chief sights of the town is the 14th-century church of **Szent Bertalan** (St. Bartholomew), on Fő tér. It is Hungary's largest Gothic church; unfortunately, it is often closed in an ongoing restoration (the best times for a visit, it seems, are in the morning and for Sunday services). Also worth visiting is the **Mátra Múzeum** (Mátra Museum), which exhibits folk art of the region. *Kossuth Lajos utca 40, tel. 37/311–447. Admission: 20 Ft. Open Tues.–Sun. 9–5.*

To the north of Gyöngyös lie many beautiful resorts, popular in summer for their invigorating mountain air and in winter for their ski trails. The best-known is **Mátrafüred**, at 1,300 feet, which can be reached by narrow-gauge railway from Gyöngyös. Just a few kilometers from Mátrafüred is **Kékestető**, the highest point in Hungary (1,014 meters).

❷ With vineyard surroundings and more than 175 of Hungary's historic monuments—a figure surpassed only by Budapest and Sopron—the picture-book Baroque city of **Eger** is ripe for exploration. Eger, which lies in a fertile valley between the Mátra Mountains and their eastern neighbor, the Bükk Range, bears witness to much history, heartbreak, and glory. It was settled quite early in the Hungarian conquest of the land; and it was one of five bishoprics created by King Stephen I when he Christianized the country almost a millennium ago.

Eger Vár (Eger Castle), now a haunting ruin, was built after the devastating Tartar invasion of 1241–42; when Béla IV returned from exile in Italy, he ordered the erection of mighty fortresses like those he had seen in the West. Within the castle walls, an imposing Romanesque cathedral was built and then, during the 15th century, rebuilt in Gothic style; today only its foundations remain. Inside the foundation area, a statue of Szent István (Saint Stephen), erected in 1900, looks out benignly over the city. Nearby are catacombs—which you sometimes can tour with an English-speaking guide, so be sure to ask for one—that were built in the second half of the 16th century by Italian engineers. Also on the castle grounds is the Gothic-style **Püspök Ház** (Bishop's House); in the basement is a numismatist museum where coins can be minted and certified (in English). The coins are of various exotic types, including Turkish. A prison museum near the main entrance is open from May to October. *Vár utca 1. Castle admission: 60 Ft. adults, 30 Ft. children. Bishop's House admission: 10 Ft. Open Tues.–Sun. 9–5 (Bishop's House until 3:30).*

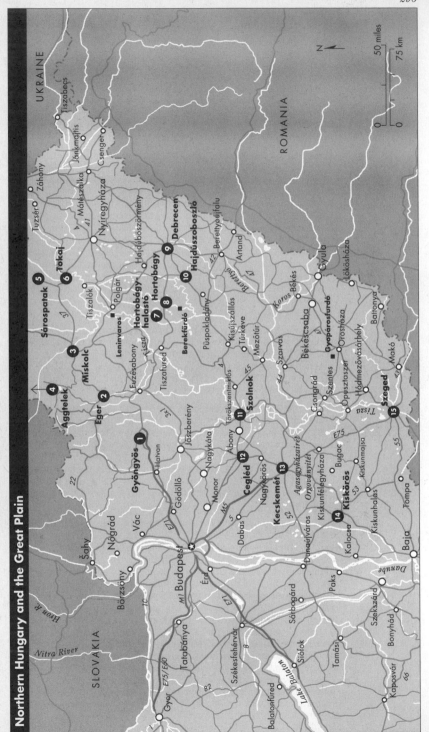

Northern Hungary and the Great Plain

In 1552 the city was attacked by the Turks, but the commander, István Dobó, and fewer than 2,000 men and women held out for 38 days against 80,000 Turkish soldiers and drove them away. One of Hungary's great legends tells of the women of Eger pouring hot pitch onto the heads of the Turks as they attempted to scale the castle walls (the event is depicted in a famous painting now in the National Gallery in Budapest). Near the foot of the castle, a restaurant memorializes the women's efforts in its name, Forró Szurok (Hot Pitch). Despite such heroism, however, Eger fell to the Turks in 1596 and became one of the most important northern outposts of Muslim power until its reconquest in 1687.

The grand neoclassical **Nagy Templom** (Basilica), the second-largest cathedral in Hungary, was built in the center of town early in the 19th century. It is approached by a stunning stairway flanked by statues of saints Stephen, László, Peter, and Paul—the work of the 19th-century Italian sculptor Marco Casagrande, who also carved 22 biblical reliefs inside and outside the building. *Eszterházy tér, tel. 36/316–592. Admission free.*

Opposite the cathedral is a former **Lyceum**, now the Eszterházy Teacher Training College. A square block of a Baroque building, the Lyceum boasts a handsome library with a fine trompe-l'oeil ceiling fresco that presents an intoxicating illusion of depth. High up in the structure's six-story observatory, built in 1776 and now a museum, are a horizontal sundial with a tiny gold cannon, which, when filled with gunpowder, used to explode at exactly high noon. Also notice the meridian line on the marble floor, along which the noonday sun, shining through a tiny aperture, makes a palm-size silvery spot. Climb higher to the grand finale: being shut in a darkened room with a man who manipulates three rods of a periscope—in operation since 1776—to project panoramic views of Eger onto a round table. Children squeal with delight as real people and cars hurry and scurry across the table like hyperactive Lego. *Eszterházy tér 2, tel. 36/310–466, ext. 71. Admission: 30 Ft. Library open Tues.–Fri. 9–1, Sat.–Sun. 9:30–noon. Museum open summer, Tues.–Sun. 9:30–1:30; winter, Tues.–Sun. 10–1. Show given Mar. 15–Dec. 20, Tues.–Sun. at frequent intervals between 9:30 AM and 12:30 PM; in winter, Sat. and Sun. only.*

Though the restored old buildings on **Zalár utca** are worth a stroll (you should peek into every courtyard you find open), Eger's most picturesque street is **Kossuth Lajos utca,** which is lined with Baroque and Rococo buildings. The **Provost's House,** at No. 4, is a small Rococo palace still considered one of Hungary's finest mansions despite abuse by the Red Army (soldiers ruined several frescoes by heating the building with oil). Those in the octagonal hall upstairs, as well as the hall's stuccowork, have been restored at great cost. The Provost's House now serves as European headquarters of the International Committee of Historic Towns (ICOMOS); on weekdays only, you can visit its tiny gallery of ceramics by Transylvanian-born Ilona Kiss Roóz. *Kossuth Lajos utca 4. Admission free. Open Tues.–Sat. 10–4.*

The wrought-iron balcony of the Provost's House is the work of German artist Henrik Fazola. During a brief stay in Eger (1758–61), Fazola graced many buildings with his work, but none so exquisitely as the multilevel, mirror-image twin gates to the **Megye Ház** (County Council Hall). Sent to Paris in 1889 for the international exposition, the gates won a gold medal 130 years after their creation. On the wall of the city hall, note the sign that indicates the level of floodwaters during the flooding of the Eger stream on August 31,

1878. In fact, if you stay alert, you will see similar signs throughout this area of the city. *Kossuth Lajos utca 9, tel. 36/310–011 or 36/313–011. Admission: 10 Ft. Open weekdays 8–4.*

As the house numbers rise along Kossuth Lajos utca, so does the street, leading up to what's left of Eger's castle. Near the first gate is a recently discovered 15th-century fresco of the coat of arms of Ippolito d'Este, later bishop of Esztergom. Another gate brings you into the castle, with its three deep wells (because the castle had its own water supply, a Turkish attempt to poison the inhabitants during the siege of 1552 was unsuccessful); remnants of a medieval Romanesque and Gothic cathedral; and a labyrinth of underground tunnels. By racing back and forth through the tunnels and appearing at various ends of the castle, the hundreds of defenders tricked the Turks into thinking there were thousands of them.

Downtown, **Dobó István tér** is marked by two intensely animated statues produced early in this century by a father-and-son team. *Dobó the Defender* is by Alajos Stróbl; the sculpture of a Magyar battling two Turks, by Stróbl's son, Zsigmond Kisfaludi-Stróbl. Their works flank a **Minorite church,** which, with its twin spires and finely carved pulpit, pews, and organ loft, is considered one of the best Baroque churches in Central Europe.

A bridge over the Eger stream—it's too small to be classified as a river—leads to an early 17th-century Turkish **minaret,** from the top of which Muslims were called to prayer; this is the northernmost surviving Turkish building in Europe. The minaret is 40 yards high and has 97 steps that lead to an observation platform. *Admission: 20 Ft. Open Tues.–Sun. 10–6.*

Eger's Rococo **Cistercian church,** closed for many years, has been reclaimed by the order and can be visited during mass on Saturday (7:15 AM) and throughout Sunday morning; its other opening hours are erratic. The church was built during the first half of the 18th century. Its main altar (1770) is dominated by a splendid statue of St. Francis Borgia kneeling beneath Christ on the cross; surrounding stuccowork depicts sacrifices by Abraham and Moses. *Széchényi utca 15. Admission free.*

Just beyond the other end of Széchényi utca, on a hilltop almost a kilometer away, is the light and lovely **Ráctemplom** (Serbian Orthodox Church), which contains more than 100 icon paintings on wood that look as if they were fashioned from gold and marble. From the graveyard you can enjoy a fine view of Eger. *Open Tues.–Sun. 10–noon and 2–4. If locked, look for the caretaker next door.*

Time Out Eger wine is renowned beyond Hungary. The best-known variety is *Egri Bikavér* (Bull's Blood of Eger), a full-bodied red wine. Other outstanding vintages are the *Medoc Noir,* a dark red dessert wine; *Leányka,* a delightful dry white; and the sweeter white *Muskotály.* The place to sample them is the **Szépasszony-völgy,** a vineyard area within Eger's city limits. Some 250 small wine cellars (some of them literally holes-in-the-wall and most of them now private) stand open and inviting in the warm weather, and a few are there in winter, too. Wines will be tapped from the barrel into your glass by the wine maker himself at the tiniest cost (5 Ft. or 10 Ft.) Try **Cellar No. 36,** a network of cellars situated 15 minutes by taxi from Eger and occupied by various wine makers. The large complex is owned by Sándor Csabai, a pioneer who privatized in 1982, three years ahead of most others. For a huge meal lubricated by wine tastings, try **Ködmön**

Csárda (tel. 36/313–172), an inexpensive cellar restaurant at the main entrance to the valley.

❸ East of the Bükk Mountains lies industrial **Miskolc,** the third-largest city (pop. 200,000) in Hungary. Though cluttered with factories and industrial plants (many of them now idle), Miskolc is surrounded by beautiful countryside, and the city itself contains some interesting Baroque buildings in addition to the medieval castle of **Diósgyőr.** South of the city is the spa-suburb of Miskolc-Tapolca, with the town's best hotels and an interesting assortment of caves, lakes, and thermal baths.

❹ One of the most extensive cave systems in Europe lies 55 kilometers (35 miles) north of Miskolc at **Aggtelek,** right on the Slovak border. The largest of the caves, the Baradla, is 24 kilometers (15 miles) long, with stalactite and stalagmite formations of extraordinary size: Some are more than 49 feet high. In one of the chambers of the cave is a 400-seat concert hall where classical music is performed in mid-August. Additional caves are being discovered and opened to the public. There are two entrances, one in Aggtelek and one in the village of Jósvafő. A full tour takes five hours, though one of the shorter tours will give you a good overall impression of this natural marvel.

❺ **Sárospatak,** some 80 kilometers (50 miles) northeast of Miskolc, is the region's cultural center. It is a picturesque old town, with many fine medieval houses. Its castle was begun during the 11th century and contains a museum of old furniture. Sárospatak's former **Calvinist College** (currently a state-run school) was founded in 1531 and for many years had close links with Britain. During the 18th century George II of England took a personal interest in the college, and for about 50 years education was conducted in both English and Hungarian.

❻ **Tokaj,** home of Hungary's famous Aszú wine, lies about 54 kilometers (33 miles) east of Miskolc. The surrounding countryside is beautiful, especially in October, when the grapes hang from the vines in thick clusters. The region's famed wine, *Tokay,* the "wine of kings and king of wines," is golden yellow with slightly brownish tints and an almost oily texture. Other countries—France, Germany, and Russia included—have tried without success to produce the wine from Tokaj grapes; the secret apparently lies in the combination of volcanic soil and climate. Tokaj's **Museum of Local History** displays objects connected with the history of the wines' production. *Petőfi út, tel. 41/311–073. Admission: 24 Ft. adults, 10 Ft. children. Open Tues.–Sun. 9–5.*

Tour 2: The Great Plain If you're approaching the Great Plain (Nagyalföld) from Eger, drive 15 kilometers (9 miles) south to Füzesabony; then join Highway 33, a two-lane road that travels eastward across the Great Plain to Debrecen. After crossing the Tisza River at Tiszafüred (where there are roadside restaurants and motels as well as camping facilities), you will soon find yourself driving in a hypnotically straight line through the dream landscape of the **Hortobágy,** a grassy *puszta,* or prairie. Covering more than 250,000 acres of grassy flatland, the Hortobágy became the first of Hungary's four national parks in 1973; its flora and fauna—its primeval breeds of longhorn cattle and *racka* sheep, prairie dogs, and *nóniusz* horses—are all under strict protection.

❼ The destination for dedicated bird-watchers is the **Hortobágy-halastó** (Great Fish Pond), where some 150 species are in residence. A nature walk around the 5,000-acre pond will take most of a day and requires advance permission from the National Park's headquarters. *Hortobágyi Nemzeti Park Igazgatóság, Sumen utca 2, H-4024 Debrecen, tel. 52/319–472 or 52/319–206, fax 52/310–645.*

The main visitor center for the prairie is the little village of
8 **Hortobágy,** 39 kilometers (24 miles) west of Debrecen. Traveling from the east, you'll reach this town immediately after you cross the Hortobágy River on Hungary's longest (548 feet) and most remarkable stone road span, which is supported by a curving nine-arched bridge. The road then leads to the **Nagycsárda** (Great Inn) of Hortobágy, a brown-and-white structure with a stork nest—and occasionally storks—on its chimney. The inn, built in 1699, has been a regional institution for most of the last three centuries. Though it now has only two guest rooms, its restaurant and service facilities have expanded vastly in recent years (*see* Dining and Lodging, *below*).

Back across the bridge from Hortobágy and barely a kilometer to the right off Highway 33 is the hamlet of **Máta,** where from around Easter to mid-November there is a daily two-hour "Rangeman's Show" at the Epona Riding Center. Groups of 20 can ride the prairie in covered wagons pulled by horses of the prize-winning *nóniusz* breed and driven by herders in blue shirts and skirts. You'll see herds of racka sheep with twisted horns, gray cattle, water buffalo, and wild boars, all tended by shepherds, cowherds, and swineherds dressed in distinctive costumes and aided by shaggy puli and Komondor sheepdogs. At various stops along the route of this perambulatory minirodeo, csikós herdsmen do stunts with the animals; the best involves five horses piloted by one man who stands straddling the last two. The safari returns to Máta, making a final stop at a café where you can gaze upon the scene while sipping apricot brandy, coffee, or mineral water. *Departures at 10 AM, 2 PM, and 4 PM (more frequently if demand warrants). Cost: riding shows and wagon tours, 850 Ft. per person; horseback riding, 600 Ft.–900 Ft. per person; riding lessons, 1,000 Ft. per hour.*

9 With a population approaching a quarter of a million, **Debrecen** is Hungary's second-largest city. Though it has considerably less clout than Budapest, Debrecen itself was twice the capital of Hungary, albeit only briefly. In 1849 Kossuth declared Hungarian independence from the Habsburgs; in 1944, the Red Army liberated Debrecen from the Nazis and made the city the provisional capital until Budapest was taken.

Debrecen has been inhabited since the Stone Age. It was already a sizable village by the end of the 12th century and, by the 14th, a privileged and important market town. It takes its name from a Slavonic term for "good earth," and indeed, much of the country's wheat, fruit, and vegetables as well as meat, pork, and poultry have been produced in this area for centuries.

For almost 500 years, Debrecen has been the stronghold of Hungarian Protestantism—its inhabitants have called it "the Calvinist Rome." In 1536 Calvinism began to replace Roman Catholicism in Debrecen, and two years later the **Reformed College** on what is now Kálvin tér (Calvin Square) was founded. Early in the 19th century, the college's medieval building was replaced by a pillared structure that offers a vivid lesson in Hungarian religious and political history: The facade's busts honor prominent students and educators as well as Calvin and Zwingli. Inside, the main staircase is lined with frescoes of student life and significant moments in the college's history (all painted during the 1930s in honor of the school's 400th anniversary). At the top of the stairs is the Oratory, which has twice been the setting for provisional parliaments. In 1849 Kossuth first proclaimed Hungarian sovereignty here, and the new National Assembly's Chamber of Deputies met here during the last stages of the doomed revolution. Again in 1944, the Provisional National Assembly met in this somber room of dark, carved wood and whitewashed walls. Kossuth's pulpit and pew are marked, and two rare surviving flags of his revolution hang on the front wall. Some relics from 1944 line the back wall.

Also worth seeing at the Reformed College are its library, which rotates exhibitions of illuminated manuscripts and rare Bibles; and two museums—one of the school's history (it includes a classroom), the other of religious art. *Kálvin tér 16, tel. 52/314–744. Admission: 25 Ft. Open Tues.–Sat. 9–5, Sun. 10–1.*

A **memorial garden** connects the Reformed College and the adjoining Great Church. Statues honor the local poet Mihály Csokonai Vitéz (1773–1805) and Prince István Bocskai of Transylvania. A column with a bronze ship commemorates 41 Hungarian Protestant pastors condemned for their faith to be galley slaves in 1675, and the Dutch admiral, Michael de Ruyter, who rescued them near Naples.

Because the Oratory was too small, Kossuth reread his Declaration of Independence by popular demand to a cheering public in 1849 in the twin-turreted **Nagytemplom** (Great Church), which has a capacity of 5,000 people. The church was built at the start of the 19th century in neoclassical style. As befits the austerity of Calvinism, the Great Church is devoid of decoration, but, with all the Baroque throughout Hungary, you may welcome the contrast. *Piac utca 4–6, tel. 52/327–017. Church admission: 12 Ft. Tower admission: 30 Ft. Open weekdays 9–12 and 2–4, Sat. 9–12, Sun. 11–4.*

Debrecen's main artery, **Piac utca** (Market Street), which has reverted to its old name after decades as Red Army Way, runs from the Great Church to the railroad station and passes several interesting sights. At the corner of Széchenyi utca, the **Small Reformed Church**—Debrecen's oldest surviving church, built in 1720—looks like a Rococo chess-piece castle. It is known to the locals as the "truncated church" because, early in this century, its onion dome was blown down in a gale.

On the other side of Piac utca, at No. 54, is the **Megyeház** (County Hall), built in 1911–12 in Transylvanian Art Nouveau, a darker and heavier version of the Paris, Munich, and Vienna versions. The ceramic sculptures and ornaments on the facade are of Zsolnay majolica. Inside, stairs and halls are illuminated by brass chandeliers that also spotlight the elegant symmetry and restraint of the decor. In the Council Hall upstairs, stained-glass windows by Károly Kernstock depict seven leaders of the tribes that conquered Hungary in 896. *Piat utca 54. Open weekdays 8–4.*

A 10-minute walk along Kossuth Lajos utca will take you to **Méliusz tér** and the **Vörös Templom** (Red Church), as remarkable a Calvinist church as you'll find anywhere in Europe. Outwardly an undistinguished redbrick house of worship built in 1886 and consecrated in 1888 with the usual unadorned interior, the church celebrated its 50th anniversary at the zenith of the applied-arts movement in Hungary. Its worshipers decided to mark the occasion with something festive: They commissioned artist Jenő Haranghy to paint the walls with biblical allegories using no human bodies or faces (just an occasional limb) but rather plenty of grapes, trees, and symbols. The result is a gaudy, splashy Sunday-school lesson covering the walls, ceilings, niches, and crannies. Giant frescoes represent, among other subjects, a stag in fresh water, the Martin Luther anthem "A Mighty Fortress Is Our God," and the 23rd Psalm (with a dozen sheep representing the 12 tribes of Israel and the 12 apostles). The Red Church is open only during religious services (10 AM on Sunday and religious holidays), but you might try asking at the deaconage on Kossuth Lajos utca for a private visit (tel. 52/325–736).

Debrecen has two notable museums. The **Déri Muzeum** in Déri tér, behind the Reformed Church, was founded during the 1920s to house the art and antiquities of a wealthy Hungarian silk manufacturer living in Vienna. Its two exhibition floors are devoted to local history, archaeology, and weapons, as well as to Egyptian, Greek, Roman, Etruscan, and Far Eastern art. On the top floor are Hungarian and foreign fine art from the 15th to the 20th century, including a striking *Ecce Homo* by Mihály Munkácsy. In front of the museum are recumbent statues symbolizing four branches of learning: the woman wearing a helmet and holding the head of a hammer is Archaeology; the young man with book in hand is Science; the young woman (with the face of the sculptor's daughter) holding a tiny sculpture of a man is Art; and the old man holding an animal's horn is Anthropology. Executed in 1930 by Ferenc Medgyessy, these sculptures won a Grand Prix at the international exposition in Paris seven years later. *Déri tér 1, tel. 52/317–561. Admission: 30 Ft. adults, 15 Ft. children. Open Tues.–Sun. 10–6.*

If you like what you see outside the Déri Museum, venture up Péterfia utca (the continuation of Piac utca) to No. 28. A restored 18th-century house, it has served variously as barracks, city jail, and tenement and has been transformed into the **Ferenc Medgyessy Memorial Museum.** Vibrant, confrontational, and comprehensive, the exhibit juxtaposes Medgyessy's works with photomontages showing where they originally stood or where copies of them now stand. *Péterfia utca 28, tel. 52/313–572. Admission: 25 Ft. adults, 10 Ft. children. Open Tues.–Sun. 10–6.*

Debrecen has only one trolley line (appropriately numbered 1), but it runs fast and frequently, in a nearly straight line from the railroad station along Piac utca and out to the **Nagyerdő** (Great Forest), a huge city park with a zoo, sports stadium, swimming pools, artificial rowing lake, a 20-acre thermal spa, cemetery, crematorium, amusement park, restaurants, open-air theater, and the **Lajos Kossuth University**—one of the few central European universities with a real campus. Every summer, from mid-July to mid-August, it is the setting for a world-renowned Hungarian-language program.

About 20 kilometers (13 miles) southwest of Debrecen (via Highway 4) is the spa of **Hajdúszoboszló,** not just a restorative center for those with rheumatic or digestive problems but also a popular destination for families and young people from Debrecen. This spa town could almost be classified as an amusement park, so numerous are its attractions: 14 outdoor pools (several steamy enough for winter bathing, others with artificial waves, water massage, and huge slides); five indoor pools; an open-air theater; a Turkish snack bar; a milk bar; cozy inns; and a man-made lake (popular with rowers). There is an admission charge to the spa recreational area.

If the weather is bad you might want to visit **Tőzsér Gyüjtemény,** a private collection of antiques, folk art, fine art, furniture, and religious objects. The collector-owner is Imre Tőzsér, a confectioner who began collecting objects in 1960; the collection is on the second floor; the old-fashioned confection, on the first. *Szilfákalja 51, tel. 52/364-320. Admission: 50 Ft. Open Tues.-Sun. 10-6.*

Bocskai Muzeum, the local historical museum, is housed in two different localities: one at Bocskai út 12 for local history and the other at Bocskai út 21 for folk art. At the second address look for the courtyard-exhibition of antique farm tools, carts, and carriages. *Admission: 20 Ft. each. Open Tues.-Sun. 9-1 and 2-6.*

⑪ Straddling the Tisza River 100 kilometers (63 miles) southwest of Hajdúszoboszló is the county seat of **Szolnok** at the geometric center of the Great Plain. As befits an important junction, the railway station is a fine example of modern architecture, as is the **Anniversary Monument** celebrating the city's founding nine centuries ago. The arcaded **Városház** (Council House) was built in neoclassical style and the **Franciscan church** in Baroque. Szolnok has supported a notable artists' colony for more than a century.

⑫ **Cegléd,** 25 kilometers (16 miles) to the west via Highways 4 and 40, has a market square that was the setting for two of the most inflammatory speeches in Hungarian history. In 1514 radical nobleman György Dózsa sparked an abortive peasant revolt here, and, in 1848, revolutionary Lajos Kossuth made the most stirring of his many calls to arms. The **Kossuth Museum** can fill you in on his life. *Múzeum utca 5, tel. 53/310-637. Admission: 20 Ft. adults, 10 Ft. children. Open Tues.-Sun. 10-6.*

At Cegléd you are only 72 kilometers (45 miles) and less than an hour from Budapest by train or car (via Highways 40 and 4). But if you have a day to spare veer south toward Hungary's "Garden of Eden," the nation's fruit basket. It starts not quite 20 kilometers (12 miles) south of Cegléd at **Nagykőrös,** a primary source of apples, pears, and sour cherries. In addition to visiting the town's bustling **marketplace,** take in the Gothic **Reformed Church,** the 16th-century **Reformed College,** the Baroque one-story **Council House,** and some unusual wooden grave markers in the **Reformed Cemetery.**

⑬ Another 15 kilometers (9 miles) southwest of Nagykőrös along Route 441 will take you to **Kecskemét,** the fruit center of the Great Plain. The Kecskemét area produces 25% of Hungary's fruit exports, 30% of its wine output, and, best known of all, *Barackpálinka,* a smooth yet tangy apricot brandy. Ask for home-brewed *hazi pálinka,* which is much better than the commercial brews.

The heart of the sprawling town is formed by two vast adjoining squares, Szabadság tér (Liberty Square) and Kossuth tér. Along Szabadság tér is a remarkable double **synagogue,** recently restored and housing some public collections. A fine, Hungarian-style Art Nouveau building called the **Cifrapalota** (Ornamental Palace) stands opposite; today it is the home of the local trade union council. Farther along Kossuth tér is the **Városház** (Town Hall), built in 1893-96 by Ödön Lechner in the Hungarian Art Nouveau style that he created. The oldest and most important building on Kossuth tér is the **Szent Miklós Templom** (Church of St. Nicholas) on the south side, built in Gothic style during the 15th century but rebuilt in Baroque style during the 18th century.

A little more than 20 kilometers (12 miles) southeast of Kecskemét on Highway 5 is the farm town of **Kiskunfélegyháza,** where Hungary's great poet of revolution, Sándor Petőfi (1823-49), spent his boyhood. If your interest in him is more than passing, then you ⑭ might want to detour from Kecskemét to his birthplace in **Kiskőrös,**

51 kilometers (32 miles) to the southwest along Route 54. On the other hand, you may want to go there on your way back north from Szeged, for it is not far off the road to Kalocsa. Either way, the tiny house—Petőfi's father was the village butcher—is now a **Memorial Museum**. *Petőfi tér 1. Open Tues.–Sun. 9–5.*

A lesser detour 14 kilometers (9 miles) southwest of Kiskunfélegyház will take you to the **Bugac puszta** (Bugac Prairie), the center of a large, sandy grassland area that has provided Hungarian poets and artists with inexhaustible material.

If you stay on Highway 5, approximately 60 kilometers (37 miles) southeast of Kiskunfélegyháza you'll come to **Szeged,** the largest city in southern Hungary and the nation's fifth largest. Szeged was almost completely rebuilt after a disastrous flood in 1879 and constructed on a concentric plan not unlike that of the Pest side of Budapest. There is an inner boulevard (still named after Lenin) and an outer ring, whose sections, named for Rome, Brussels, Paris, London, Moscow, and Vienna, recall the international help given in reconstructing the city. Avenues connect these two boulevards like the spokes of a wheel.

Szeged is famous for two things: its open-air festival, held each year in July or August; and its paprika, an important ingredient of Hungarian cuisine. Whether attached to fish soup or goulash, Szeged is synonymous with spicy all over Central Europe, just as Esterházy always means rich, whether applied to a meat sauce or a pastry. In late summer and early autumn, Szeged offers a rich array of rack after rack of red peppers drying in the open air.

The heart of the inner city is the large **Széchenyi tér,** lined with trees and surrounded by imposing buildings, among them the neo-Baroque **Városház** (Town Hall) and a large hotel, the Tisza, which has a fine concert hall. A few blocks away is Szeged's most striking building, the **Votive Church** (really a cathedral), a neo-Romanesque edifice built between 1912 and 1929 in fulfillment of a municipal promise made after the great flood. One of Hungary's largest churches, it seats 6,000 and has a splendid organ with 12,000 pipes. The church forms the backdrop to the open-air festival, held in Dóm tér (Cathedral Square). Outstanding performances of Hungary's great national drama, Imre Madách's *The Tragedy of Man*, are given each summer at the festival, as well as a rich variety of other theatrical pieces, operas, and concerts.

At Hajnoczi utca 12 is Szeged's **Régi Zsinagóga** (Old Synagogue), built in 1839 in neoclassical style. On its outside wall a marker written in Hungarian and Hebrew shows the height of the floodwaters in 1879. Nearby, at the corner of Gutenberg utca and Jósika utca, is the larger **Uj Zsinagóga** (New Synagogue), finished in 1905; it is Szeged's purest and finest representation of Art Nouveau. Its wood and stone carvings, wrought iron, and furnishings are all the work of local craftsmen. A memorial to Szeged's victims of Nazism is in the entrance hall. *Gutenberg utca 20, tel. 62/311–402. Admission: 20 Ft. Open Mon.–Thurs. 9–noon and 2–5, Fri. 9–noon and 2–3.*

About 100 kilometers (62 miles) northeast of Szeged, near the Romanian border, the town of **Gyula** has developed into a major spa resort. It also offers visitors a variety of neoclassical houses, as well as a medieval castle, which is the setting for summer theater.

Off the Beaten Track

Raoul Wallenberg, the Swedish diplomat who in 1944–45 saved many thousands of Jews in Budapest from extermination at the hands of the Nazis and Hungarian Arrow Cross fascists, was taken into Soviet custody in early 1945 on the outskirts of Debrecen. He had gone there to plead with Red Army marshal Rodion Malinovsky to liberate Pest ahead of Buda, because Jews were being massacred on the eastern bank of the Danube. Wallenberg disappeared into the gulag, and about a decade later a statue of the diplomat in Budapest, by the sculptor Pál Pátzay, vanished. It was replaced with a work by one of his pupils.

In just one of the many ironies surrounding the Wallenberg case, the torso from the original statue turned up in the 1960s—in Debrecen, of all places—at the gateway of a pharmaceuticals manufacturer in the Nagyerdő city park. But now instead of symbolizing Wallenberg wrestling with the tentacles of Nazism, the work was presented as a symbolic representation of man's struggle against the serpent of disease; it was also attributed to another sculptor. Only recently has the following inscription been added: "This Pál Pátzay work represents mankind defeating evil. It also commemorates the missing Swedish diplomat, Raoul Wallenberg. He rescued thousands of people threatened by the Nazi Arrow Cross killers in 1944." Statue and stone with inscription can be viewed outside the **Biogal** plant at Pallagi út 1–3.

Shopping

Shepherd's flasks, silver buckles, and many of the costumes and trappings of the Hortobágy Plain are the best buys in **Debrecen.** The best and, surprisingly, least expensive place to purchase these items is in the ornate lobby of the elegant **Arany Bika Hotel** (*see* Dining and Lodging, *below*). One of the best of these lobby stores is the father-and-daughter crafts shop of the Szoboszlai family (he is the craftsman; she, the multilingual vendor); they feature a wide selection of leather and metal goods as well as "whatever else happens to be fashionable in Budapest." The Szoboszlais also have a summer outlet in **Hortobágy**; for more information, ask at their hotel store or call their workshop in Debrecen (tel. 52/311–365).

For books in English and Hungarian as well as a good supply of maps, try **Csokonai** (Piac utca 45–47, Debrecen, tel. 52/314–984). The internationally well-regarded line of Hungarian natural cosmetics, Helia-D, is made in Debrecen and the manufacturer has a shop at Piac utca 20 (tel. 52/314–002). **Centrum Áruház,** a department store in a downtown shopping mall, is good for browsing (Piac utca 34, Debrecen, tel. 52/316–066).

Dining and Lodging

Highly recommended restaurants and lodgings in a particular price category are indicated by a star ★.

Debrecen
Dining
★

Csokonai. Across the street from the Oriental-appearing Csokonai theater is Csokonai restaurant, Debrecen's best (evidenced by the fact that most of the guests are local residents). It is a consistent winner of the gastronomic award *védnöki tábla,* a much-coveted honor. The restaurant has a reputation among gourmands for its shellfish, turtle soup, beer soup, roasted-at-the-table skewered meats, frogs' legs, paprika crab, cheese fondue, and many kinds of fish. The new owner renovated the restaurant in 1988; one of his innovations is to let guests cook their own meat *à la Willa-franca* (a hot old-fashioned iron that you press on the meat to cook it). *Kossuth utca 21, tel. 52/368–073. Reservations advised. Dress: casual. No credit cards. Open dinner only Sun. $$*

★ **Gambrinus.** In this venerable family restaurant where diners have been feeling at home for generations, the menus (including the one in English) end with this admonition: "Our honoured guests are allowed to ask for a half portion of our dishes." The portions are indeed generous, but the food is so good that you are more likely to wish for seconds than halves. There are seven turkey specialties—Óvár-style, with ham and cheese, is recommended—and five "aflame dish specialties," including the Gambrinus roast: two skewers of beef and pork coated with mushroom sauce flambéed (at tableside) and served with rice and roast potatoes. Chestnut pancakes with chocolate sauce are a favorite dessert. Two very skillful red-vested Gypsy musicians—a strolling violinist and a stationary zitherist—serenade diners with Liszt, Hortobágy shepherd songs, and selections from *Fiddler on the Roof*. *Gambrinus köz (an alley off Piac utca 28), tel. 52/326–692. Reservations advised. Dress: casual. AE, V. $*

Sörpince a Flaskához. When you walk into this completely unpretentious and very popular neighborhood pub (the name means Beer Cellar at the Flask), you may be surprised when you're presented with a nicely bound menu in four languages. The English section proclaims the virtues of "salty Hungarian pancake dishes," which include pancakes stuffed with fish and "Beer Cellar pork pancakes baked from salty batter." They taste even better than they read, and so do the pigs' feet, a house specialty; the sour-cream-based soups; and delicate desserts. *Miklós utca 2, tel. 52/314–582. Reservations advised. Dress: casual. AE, V. $*

Lodging **Arany Bika Hotel.** The "Golden Bull" is an Art Nouveau classic
★ erected in 1915 by a Renaissance man named Alfréd Hajós, who won two Olympic gold medals for swimming in Athens in 1896 and another gold medal for architecture in Paris in 1924. A new wing added to this downtown landmark in 1966 serves to enhance the light and spacious feeling of the original building, in which panels of stained glass illuminate a solidly, but not stolidly, elegant foundation. The guest rooms are not only attractive (the floor designs are particularly striking) but comfortable as well. If the young staff at the front desk can sometimes be a little distracted, the service and food provided beneath the murals of the wide-open *puszta* (plain) in the Hortobágy dining room are impeccable. Try the local specialty, *töltöttkáposzta* (stuffed cabbage). *Piac utca 11–15, tel. 52/416–777, fax 52/412–709. 247 rooms with bath. Facilities: 3 restaurants, casino, bar, nightclub, pool table, solarium, sauna. AE, DC, MC, V. $$$*

Hotel Cívis. Fronting on Debrecen's main square and backing onto a stylish shopping center of which it is a part, this new hotel was built in 1989 as an apartment house with studio apartments. But because the purchase prices were too high, no one moved in, which left only one option—make it a hotel. Since it was built for private use, every suite contains a well-equipped kitchen (every door also has a mail slot). Many of the rooms are quiet, except for those facing the main street. The decor—inside and out—is uniformly brown; on the walls of the lobby, halls, restaurants, and guest rooms (as if to reinforce the color scheme) are sepia-toned photos of Debrecen in earlier times. The breakfast buffet is ample and can be interesting, depending on what was served in the hotel's restaurant the night before.

Kávin tér 4, tel. 52/418-522 or 52/418-132. 60 rooms with bath, 4 suites. Facilities: restaurant, jazz bar. AE, DC, MC, V. $$

Eger **Fehér Szarvas.** The name of this sleekly paneled rustic cellar adjoin-
Dining ing the Park Hotel means White Stag, and game is the uncontested
specialty of the house: sliced fillet of stag in a mustard-cream sauce
with potato croquettes; venison fillet served in a pan sizzling with
chicken liver, sausage, and herb butter; leg of wild boar in a red-
wine sauce of mushrooms and bacon. The food is rich and often deli-
cately seasoned. The skulls and skins hanging from rafters and walls
make the inn look like Archduke Franz Ferdinand's trophy room.
Live music is sometimes featured in the evenings. *Klapka György
utca 8, tel. 36/411-129. Reservations advised. Dress: casual. Open
for dinner only. AE, MC, V. $$*

Talizmán. It is located in a rustic arched basement room a few doors
away from Eger's castle gate and is one of the most popular restaurants in the region (many people make the trip from Budapest just to
eat here). The menu, in English and German, features *legényfogó
leves* ("wedding soup," or, literally, "catcher of young men"). Made
with meat, vegetables, cream, and liver, this stew is one of the lures
that young Hungarian girls have used for centuries to attract potential husbands. A less poetic but equally exotic offering is the cabbage with goose legs. *Kossuth Lajos utca 19, tel. 36/420-883.
Reservations required. Dress: casual. No credit cards. $$*

Belvárosi. The name means City Center, and that's appropriate,
since the Belvárosi is right in the heart of downtown Eger, near
Dobó István Square. From breakfast at 9 AM to closing sometime af-
ter 10 PM, this large but cozy restaurant, partitioned into sections and
private rooms and furnished in peasant style, offers cordial service of
specialties that make use of regional wines; try the white-wine cream
soup or pork sirloin in red-wine sauce. The fish soup may have a little
wine in it, too, but it is subdued by the spices. *Bajcsy Zsilinszky út 8,
tel. 36/311-872. Reservations advised. Dress: casual. No credit
cards. $*

HBH Bajor Sörház. Although designed to look like a Bavarian beer
tavern, this place does not reek of hops or smoke. In fact, it is an ele-
gant family restaurant decorated with sepia photos of old Eger.
Specialties include a lemony oxtail soup, served family style in a sil-
ver tureen; and the Beer Drinker's Delight—a pork cutlet stuffed
with brains and baked in a pastry crust. Both sit well with the Mu-
nich Hofbrauhaus beer that gives the house its initials. More deli-
cate is the Hungarian tenderloin: beef in a ragout of chicken liver,
peas, and mushrooms served with potato croquettes. *Bajcsy
Zsilinszky út 19, tel. 36/316-312. Reservations advised. Dress: ca-
sual. AE. $*

Kazamata. This vast ancient wine tavern in the catacombs beneath
the cathedral has many layers of atmosphere but very ordinary food.
However, it's a great place to drop in for a drink. *Mártirok tér 3, tel.
36/311-538. No reservations. Dress: casual. No credit cards. $*

Lodging **Flora Hotel.** Eger is noted not just for its full-bodied wines but also
for its thermal waters; and the Flora, once a trade-union spa, specia-
lizes in treatment for rheumatic ailments. A comfortably overgrown
chalet located near the city's large open-air baths, it has its own in-
door therapeutic and recreational facilities, but you don't need a
doctor's prescription to enjoy your stay. *Fürdő utca 5, tel. 36/320-
211, fax 36/320-815. 196 rooms with bath. Facilities: restaurant,
bar, coffee shop, swimming pool, sauna, solarium, tennis court.
AE, DC, MC, V. $$*

★ **Hotel Park-Eger.** Two very different hotels share the same phone
number and a connecting passageway but have separate addresses

around the corner from each other and seem a century apart. The Park is an old-fashioned grand hotel, very genteel and with spacious rooms, though it usually closes from November through March. The Eger, built in 1982, is tastefully and imaginatively modern inside and fully equipped year-round. Guests are free to use the facilities of both hotels, so you can have your cake at the Eger's Dobós Confectionery and charge it to your room at the Park. Or you can dine at the adjoining (and loosely affiliated) Fehér Szarvas restaurant (*see above*) and charge it to the Eger. *Park: Klapka György utca 8. Eger: Szálloda utca 1–3, tel. 36/413–233, fax 36/413–213, telex 36/63–555. 202 rooms with bath. Facilities: 2 restaurants, 3 bars (1 with beer, bowling, and billiards), swimming pool, sauna, solarium, fitness center, tennis court. AE, DC, MC, V. $$*

Minaret. This quaint hotel stands opposite the 17th-century Turkish tower in an old quarter of town, where it blends in as though it's been here forever. The atmosphere is friendly and informal. *Nezics Károly utca 4, tel. 36/410–233, 36/410–473, or 36/410–020, fax 36/410–713. 38 rooms with shower. AE, DC, MC, V. $*

Unicornis. This central hotel at the foot of the castle has a pleasant atmosphere, a good-humored staff, and a lively downstairs café where young people shoot pool. The rooms are an all-around bargain and are clean, aside from tattered carpeting. The hotel is open year-round, but large groups tend to monopolize it in August and September. *Dr. Hibay Károly utca 2, tel. 36/312–886. 47 rooms, some with bath or shower. Facilities: restaurant, café, currency exchange. Breakfast included. $*

Hajdúszoboszló
Dining and Lodging

Arany Oroszlán Étterem. The "Golden Lion" restaurant was built in 1990 by a Hungarian German who returned home after the political transition. It is located in the city center close to the swimming pool and spa. The prices are reasonable and the portions are generous. Its major attraction is self-service meat grilled on volcano stone heated by a spirit stove (guests cook their own meals). The restaurant shares the building with an upstairs pension (three rooms with shower). *Bessenyei utca 14, tel. and fax 52/363–987. Reservations accepted. Dress: casual. No credit cards. $$*

Karikás Panzió. The rooms—bargain-priced at 2,000 Ft. for two— are unusually large and light by Hungarian hotel standards and quite clean. The attached restaurant of the same name serves traditional Hungarian cuisine in a clean, colonial-style setting (reservations advised). Try the excellent stuffed cabbage, or any of the fish, chicken, or game dishes. *Hőforrás utca 27, tel. and fax 52/362–251. 11 rooms with bath. Facilities: restaurant, TV and minibar in rooms, parking, laundry. AE, V. Restaurant and pension: $*

Lodging

Hotel Délibáb. The hotel's name means Miracle, but there is nothing miraculous about its lobby: an unsoothing jumble of modern reception desk, elegant restaurants, and noisy pinball machines rigged to undo any therapeutic "cure." Built in 1969 on a downtown corner of the spa and expanded in 1987, the Délibáb does offer quiet and comfortable rooms—much more relaxing than its entranceway. You may not find health food in the adjoining Szoboszló restaurant, but its local specialties, such as *betyárleves* (a meat soup) and *subaszelet* (a fried cutlet), are well prepared. *József Attila utca 4, tel. 52/361–788, fax 52/362–059. 252 rooms with bath. Facilities: 4 restaurants, coffeehouse, beer bar with bowling, fitness center, access to spa facilities, parking. AE, DC, MC, V. $$*

Muskátli Panzió. Built in 1991, this beautiful pension is close to the swimming pool–spa complex. Every room has a shower and television. *Daru-zug 5, tel. 52/361–027. 7 rooms with shower. Facilities: restaurant, terrace, parking. No credit cards. $$*

Róna Penzió. This charming family-run bed-and-breakfast puts its own garden at the disposal of guests and treats them like family. The two floors are delightfully furnished with folk art and vivid landscape paintings. Reserve well in advance, as this place tends to get booked up with German families. *Gábor Áron utca 123, H-4200, tel. 52/361-544. 6 double rooms with bath. Facilities: bar, parking. Breakfast included. AE. $*

Hortobágy
Dining
★

Hortobágyi Nagycsárda. This historic roadside inn could get by on fame and trappings alone—dried corn-and-paprika wreaths, flasks, saddles, and antlers hang from its rafters and walls—but its kitchen concentrates on food that rewards the wayfarer's palate. This is the place to order the regional specialty: *Hortobágyi húsospalacsinta* (Hortobágy pancakes), which are filled with beef and braised with a tomato-and-sour-cream sauce. The portions are small, so follow the pancakes with *bográcsgulyás*—goulash soup *puszta* style, with meat and dumplings and the spicier components of the kitchen cabinet simmering in a copper pot. Veal paprikash and solid beef and lamb *pörkölt* (thick stews with paprika and sour cream) are also recommended, as are the cheese-curd or apricot-jam dessert pancakes. All this comes with Gypsy music at night. *Petőfi tér 1, tel. 52/369-139. Reservations not required except during annual horse show and bridge fair. Dress: casual. AE. $$*

Transdanubia

Western Hungary, often referred to as Transdanubia (Dunántúl in Hungarian) is that part of the country south and west of the Danube, stretching to the Slovak and Austrian borders in the west and north and to Slovenia and Croatia in the south. It presents a highly picturesque landscape, including several ranges of hills and small mountains. Most of its surface is covered with farmland, vineyards, and orchards—all nurtured by a climate that is noticeably more humid than that of the rest of the country.

The Romans called the region Pannonia (for centuries it was a frontier province; today it is far richer in Roman ruins than the rest of Hungary). Centuries later, the 150-year Turkish occupation left its mark on the region, particularly in the south, where it's not uncommon to see a former mosque serving as a Christian church. As in much of the rest of Hungary, Austrian influence is clearly visible in the region's Baroque buildings, particularly in the magnificent Eszterházy Palace in Fertőd.

The varied terrain of Transdanubia offers much to explore, from the vineyards of Villány to the dense forest around Sopron, where a wide swath cut through the trees serves as a reminder of the recent past—when Transdanubia's western perimeter formed part of the now defunct Iron Curtain. These days, however, the area is blooming as Hungary's gateway to Western Europe; Vienna, after all, is rarely more than a few hours' drive away.

Important Addresses and Numbers

Tourist
Information

Kőszeg: Savaria Tourist (Várkör utca 69, tel. and fax 94/360-238). IBUSZ (varkör utca 3, tel. 94/360 376).
Pécs: Cooptourist (Irgalmasok útja 22, tel. 72/313-407, fax 72/324-255); Mecsek Tourist (Széchenyi tér 9, tel. 72/313-300, fax 72/312-044). IBUSZ (Széchenyi tér 8, tel. 72/312-169).
Sopron: Ciklámen Tourist (Ógabona tér 8, tel. 99/312-040); IBUSZ (Várkerület 41, tel. 99/312-455 or 99/313-281).

Szombathely: IBUSZ (Szell Kálmán utca 3, tel. 94/314–141, fax 94/325–189); Savaria Tourist (Mártirok tere 1, tel. 94/312–348, fax 94/311–314).

Getting Around

There are good rail connections from Budapest (South and East stations) and Vienna (South and West stations). Local trains and buses are adequate, but, of course, a car offers the greatest freedom.

Highlights for First-Time Visitors

Eszterházy Palace, Fertőd
Kőszeg
Sopron
Szombathely
Vasarely Museum, Pécs

Exploring Transdanubia

Numbers in the margin correspond to points of interest on the Transdanubia map.

Lying on the Austrian frontier, between Lake Fertő (in German, Neusiedlersee) and the Sopron Hills, **Sopron** is one of Hungary's most picturesque towns. Barely an hour away from Vienna by car, Sopron is a shopping center for many Austrians, who flock here for the day to buy goose liver, salami, apricot brandy, eyeglasses, and dentures—all considerably less expensive here than in Austria. The joke in Sopron is that every day at noon, "We play the Austrian national hymn so that the Austrians have to stand still for two minutes while we Hungarians shop."

There is much more to Sopron, however, than conspicuous consumption by foreigners. Behind the narrow storefronts along the City Ring, **Várkerület** (called Lenin Boulevard until 1989), and within the city walls (one set built by Romans, the other by medieval Magyars) lies a horseshoe-shaped inner city that is a wondrous eclectic mix of Gothic, Baroque, and Renaissance. Its faithful and inspired restoration won a 1975 Europe Prize Gold Medal for Protection of Monuments, and the work continues slowly but carefully.

Today's city of 60,000 was a small Celtic settlement more than 2,300 years ago. During Roman times, under the name of Scarabantia, it stood on the main European north–south trade route, the Amber Road; it also happened to be near the junction with the east–west route used by Byzantine merchants. In 896 the Magyars conquered the Carpathian basin and later named the city Suprun for a medieval Hungarian warrior. After the Habsburgs took over the territory during the Turkish wars of the 16th and 17th centuries, they renamed the city Ödenburg (Castle on the Ruins) and made it the capital of the rich and fertile Austrian Burgenland. Ferdinand III, later Holy Roman Emperor, was crowned king of Hungary here in 1625, and at a special session of the Hungarian Parliament in 1681, Prince Paul Esterházy was elected palatine (royalty's ruling deputy) of Hungary. And always, under any name or regime, Sopron was a fine and prosperous place in which to live.

Symbol of today's and yesterday's and surely tomorrow's Sopron—and entranceway to the Old City—is the 200-foot-high **Tűztoróny** (Fire Tower), with foundations dating to the days of the Árpád

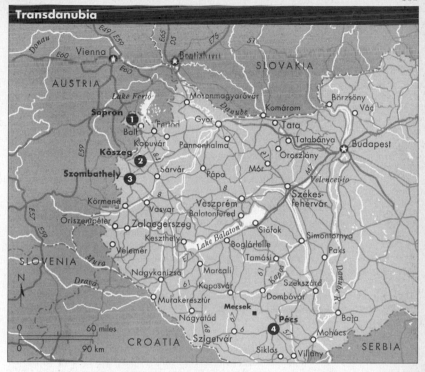

dynasty (9th–13th centuries) and perhaps further back, if Roman
archaeological finds in its cellar signify more than treasure.
Remarkable for its uniquely harmonious blend of architectural
styles, the tower has a Romanesque base rising to a circular balcony
of Renaissance loggias topped by an octagonal clock tower that is itself capped by a brass Baroque onion dome and belfry from more recent times. The upper portions were rebuilt in Baroque style after
most of the earlier Fire Tower was, appropriately, destroyed by the
Great Fire of 1676, started by students roasting chestnuts in a high
wind. Throughout the centuries the tower bell tolled the alarm for
fire or the death of a prominent citizen, and from the loggias live musicians trumpeted the approach of an enemy or serenaded the citi-
zenry. Both warning concerts were accompanied by flags (red for
fire, blue for enemy) pointing in the direction of danger. *Fő tér, tel.
99/311–463. Admission: 40 Ft. adults, 20 Ft. children. Open Tues.–
Sun. 10–6.*

Passing the late-19th-century **Városház** (City Hall), the street funnels into **Fő tér**, a charming main square of perfectly proportioned
Italianate architecture. Turn right and admire, at No. 8, Sopron's
finest Renaissance building: the turreted **Storno Ház** (Storno
House). Inside its two-story loggia, an upstairs museum houses a remarkable and surprising family collection of furniture, porcelain,
sculptures, and paintings. The Stornos were a rags-to-riches dynasty of chimney sweeps who, over several generations, bought or just
relieved grateful owners of unwanted treasures and evolved into a
family of painters and sculptors themselves. The dynasty died out in
Switzerland and Germany a few years ago, but its heirs and the Hungarian state have agreed that nothing will be removed from the

Storno House. On an exterior wall of the house hangs a plaque commemorating visits by King Matthias Corvinus (1482–83) and Franz
Liszt (1840 and 1881). *Fő tér 8, tel. 99/311–327. Admission: 50 Ft.
adults, 20 Ft. children. Open Apr.–Sept., Tues.–Sun. 10–6; Oct.–
Mar., Tues.–Sun. 10–6. Tape-recorded tours on cassette are available in several languages.*

The house next door at Fő tér 7, Baroque on the outside with some
Gothic patches exposed in the courtyard, is called the **General's
House** because the military governor of Sopron was quartered here
in 1681, but it is better known and loved locally as the former residence of Dr. Kristóf Lackner. An early 17th-century mayor and
goldsmith with degrees from the universities of Graz and Padua,
Lackner not only promoted the arts in Sopron but also opened its
Academy of Science to women. *Főtér 7, tel. 99/311–463. Admission:
40 Ft. Open Tues.–Sun. 10–6.*

At Fő tér 6, the fine Renaissance courtyard of the Fabricius House
leads to the **Rómaikori Kőtár** (Roman Archaeology Museum) in the
vaulted medieval, churchlike cellar, a perfect setting for the gigantic statues of Jupiter, Juno, and Minerva unearthed beneath the
square during the digging of foundations for City Hall a century
ago. On the second floor a separate museum (with identical hours
and admission prices) re-creates the living environment of 17th- and
18th-century apartments. *Fő tér 6, tel. 99/311–327. Admission: 40
Ft.adults, 20 Ft. children. Open Tues.–Sun. 10–6 (Oct.–Mar. until
4 PM).*

Across the square at No. 2, the 19th-century Angels' Drugstore is
now the **Angyal Patika Múzeum** (Angel Pharmacy Museum), with
old Viennese porcelain vessels and papers pertaining to Ignaz
Philipp Semmelweis (1815–65), the Hungarian physician who made
childbirth safer by pioneering antiseptics in Vienna. *Fő tér 2, tel. 99/
313–855. Admission: 40 Ft. Open Tues.–Sun. 9:30–noon and
12:30–2.*

The centerpiece of the square is a sparkling, spiraling three-tiered
Holy Trinity Column, aswirl with gilded angels—the earliest (1701)
and loveliest Baroque monument to a plague in all of Hungary. It
stands before and harmonizes handsomely with the early Gothic
(1280–1300) **Goat Church,** named, legend has it, for a medieval billy
goat that scratched up a treasure that enabled early-day Francis-
cans to build a church on the site. (The Benedictines took over in
1802.) More likely, however, the name comes from the figures of
goats carved into its crests: the coat of arms of the Gutsch family,
who financed the church. The Goat Church is built of limestone and
has a soaring, pointed 141-foot-high 14th-century steeple, three
naves, its original Gothic choir (betraying French influence), and,
after several rebuildings, a Hungarian Gothic-Baroque red-marble
pulpit, a Rococo main altar, Baroque altars by Croatian craftsmen,
and a painting of St. Stephen by one of the Stornos. *Templom utca.
Admission free. Open daily 9–5.*

Four streets fan out from Fő tér, and if you walk them you will see
most of the wonders that the Old City has to offer. Turn the corner of
Templom utca (Church Street), and at No. 1 you will find the Gothic
Chapter House of the Goat Church. Here, where monks meditated,
they could contemplate, on the curved pillars, the Seven Deadly Sins
in sculptures similar to those atop Notre Dame Cathedral in Paris.
Avarice is a monkey; Lewdness, a bear; Incredulity, a griffin; Incon-
stancy, a crab crawling backward; and Vanity, a woman with a mirror in hand. *Templom utca 1. Admission free (donations accepted).*

Across Templom utca at No. 2 is the former **Eszterházy Kastély** (Eszterházy Palace)— part medieval, part Baroque—now a mining museum with many musical memories buried within. Here, in 1773, the Eszterházys' music master, Franz Joseph Haydn, met Empress Maria Theresa. Two doors down, in the **Bezerédy Palace**, Franz Liszt gave a piano recital in 1840; during intermission, one young woman filched one of the maestro's white gloves, after which she cut it up into 29 pieces, which she then shared with the other ladies present.

Doubling back on **Új utca** (New Street)—which, despite its name, is Sopron's oldest—you will pass a charmingly restored red Gothic house at No. 16; appropriately, it is headquarters of the local monuments-preservation commission. New Street used to be named Jew Street, with good reason. No. 22 is a medieval **zsinagóga** (synagogue) complete with stone *mikva*, a ritual bath for women. This synagogue is now a religious **museum**, with a plaque honoring the 1,587 Jews of Sopron who were murdered by the Fascists; only 274 survived, and today there are scarcely enough Jews to muster a minyan (quorum of 10), let alone a congregation. *Új utca 22. Admission: 40 Ft. Open Wed.–Mon. 9–5.*

At No. 11 is another **synagogue**, this time from the late-13th century (it was discovered during restorations in the 1970s). Its interior can be glimpsed from the entranceway to a popular ice cream parlor that shares its courtyard.

At the other end of the inner city's fourth main artery, **Szent György utca** (St. George Street), the pastel-green **Cézár Ház** (Cézár House) boasts a popular wine cellar. Upstairs, in rooms where the Hungarian Parliament met in 1681, is a private **museum** created by the widow of József Soproni-Horváth (1891–1961), a remarkable artist who prefixed his hometown's name to his own so he wouldn't be just another of many Joe Croats. This Horváth nevertheless stands out in the world of art for the wonders he worked with watercolors. He used that fragile medium to bring large surfaces alive in a density usually associated with oil paintings, while depicting realistic scenes such as a girl grieving over her drowned sister's body. *Hatsokapu utca 2, tel. 99/312–326. Admission: 30 Ft. Open Tues.–Fri. 10–1, Sat.–Sun. 3–6.*

Along St. George Street, numerous dragons of religion and architecture coexist in sightly harmony. The **Erdődy Vár** (Erdődy Palace) at No. 16 is Sopron's richest Rococo building. Two doors down, at No. 12, is the house where the widow of Prince Johann Eggenberg held Protestant services during the harshest days of the Counter-Reformation and beyond. A stone pulpit in the Eggenberg House's courtyard bears the Hohenzollern coat of arms. But the street takes its name from St. George's, a 14th-century Catholic church so sensitively "Baroqued" some 300 years later that its interior is still as soft as whipped cream. *Open daily 9–5.*

If you leave the inner city by its lesser gate, **Hátsókapu** (literally, "back door"), near the Cézár House, or at the high-number end of Templom utca, you will reach **Széchenyi tér,** the heavily trafficked but still symmetrical and splendid main square of Sopron's downtown business district. On the south side of the square stands the fine Baroque **Dominican Church** (1719–25). This puts you near the Varkerület körút, the City Ring.

If you exit by the **Előkapu** (Outer Gate), your eye will be greeted by another superb Baroque specimen: **St. Mary's Column** (1745), with its finely sculpted biblical reliefs. Cross the bridge across the Ikva

River, and as you climb uphill toward the Hotel Sopron you will pass through the **Poncichter wine quarter.**

Less than an hour's drive and only 45 kilometers (28 miles) south of Sopron (and barely two hours from Vienna) is the border city of **②** **Kőszeg,** at an altitude of 886 feet Hungary's highest and also one of its most enchanting cities.

Park in the spacious main square, Fő tér, just outside the city's historic core, where very little has changed since the 18th century. Before you penetrate the city wall, however, peek into the **Jézus Szíve Plébánia Templom** (Sacred Heart Church), a creamy neo-Gothic concoction by Viennese architect Ludwig Schöne. Erected between 1892 and 1894 on the site of a onetime coffeehouse, it is reminiscent both of Vienna's St. Stephen's Cathedral (for its mosaic roof and spires) and, inside, of Venice's San Marco (for the candy-stripe pillars supporting its three naves). If, after inspecting the church, you stand outside admiring its facade from Chernel utca at the right rear, you will see a wholly different church with flying buttresses and wriggly little pinecone spires.

Chernal utca itself is a cobblestone street with several centuries of art history, styles, and colors harmonizing as happily as Haydn, who spent many of his creative years in Kőszeg as court composer to the Eszterházys. As you pass through a gap in the Old City wall and approach the bend of L-shaped Chernal utca, you will spot a muted orange tower in the near distance. It belongs to the fortified 13th-century **vár** (castle), where, in 1532, a few hundred Hungarian serf-soldiers beat back a Turkish army of nearly 200,000 and forced Sultan Suleiman I to abandon his attempt to conquer Vienna. To celebrate Christianity's narrow escape, the bells of Kőszeg's churches and castle toll every day at 11 AM, the hour the Turks turned tail. And the castle itself is named not for the nobility who have inhabited it over the years but for the Croatian captain, Miklós Jurisics, who commanded its defense. Also named for him is the inner city's main square, Jurisics tér, which you will reach by turning right at the end of Chernal utca.

Before you turn, however, you will be confronted by two splendid churches on the Rájnis József utca side of the square. The first, the **Szent Jakab templom** (St. James Church), is the treasure of the city. St. James dates back way beyond its 18th-century Baroque facade and even beyond its Gothic interior; in fact, St. James is the oldest church in Kőszeg. Inside are astonishingly well-preserved 15th-century wall paintings, one of the Virgin Mary with mantle (painted in fresco technique, on wet plaster) and one of a giant St. Christopher (painted *al secco,* on dry wall). The Baroque main altar, commissioned in 1693 by Prince Paul Eszterházy, boasts a Gothic wooden Madonna with child from the late-15th or early 16th century. *Open daily 9–5.*

Next to Saint James is the smaller **Szent Imre templom** (St. Emerich's Church). If you're wondering why two landmarks serving the same purpose were planted side by side, they symbolize Kőszeg's ethnic mix, formed over the centuries by Hungarian tribes moving west and by Germans expanding to the east. Not long after the Counter-Reformation, St. Imre's Church converted to Catholicism and replaced many of its Protestant trappings with Baroque furnishings, most notably a high altar flanked by gilded and vivid statues of St. Stephen inviting, and St. Ladislas defending, the Virgin Mary. The 1805 altar painting by Stephan Dorffmeister, Jr., shows St. Imre, who was a 7th-century bishop of Poitiers, in the garb of a Hungarian nobleman. *Open daily 9–5.*

Your trail of churches now funnels into **Jurisics tér** (like other fine squares in this part of Hungary, Jurisics Square is not square but triangular). On your right is a sprightly Gothic dowager of a **Városház** (City Hall), dressed for a midsummer ball with red and yel low stripes skirting the ground floor; the upper level is decorated with medallions of the Kőszeg, Hungarian, and Jurisics crests, painted in 1712. Inside the front door is a surprising courtyard with walls painted cool white and brown, reminiscent of a Hungarian *csárda* (inn). Without question, this is one of Hungary's most beautiful city halls. *Jurisics tér 8, tel. 94/360–046. Open weekdays 8 3.*

Jurisics Square converges upon the handsome **Hősi kapu** (Heroes' Gate), whose imposing tower's Renaissance-Gothic facade belies the fact that it was erected in 1932 to celebrate the 400th anniversary of the Turkish siege. This historic victory is commemorated in relief inside the portal, where another relief mourns Kőszeg's loss of life in World War I, a defeat that also cost the city two-thirds of its market for textiles and agriculture in the breakup of the Austro-Hungarian Empire. The observation tower affords fine views; within the tower you can climb through a small natural-history museum up to a loggia and survey the city's charms. *Jurisics tér 6, tel. 94/360–240. Admission: 30 Ft. Open Tues.–Sun. 10–5.*

The **Sgraffitóház** at No. 7 Jurisics tér dates to the Renaissance, when sgraffito was still a respectable art form. Beneath a loft for drying medicinal herbs, the **Apotéka az Arany Egyszarvúhoz** (Golden Unicorn Pharmacy) at No. 11 is now a pharmacy museum (Patika Múzeum) with enough antique furniture and paintings to stock a small museum of Austrian Baroque art. *Jurisics tér 11, tel. 94/36–0337. Admission: 30 Ft. Open Tues.–Sun. 10–6.*

Along Schneller utca, the grand square peters out into a Videothek and the shabby shell of Kőszeg's grandiose but beloved **Ballhouse**, where Franz Liszt gave a concert in 1846. Go through the city wall at this point, continue for a few steps along the **Várkör** (City Ring) that girdles the inner town, and turn left on **Rájnis József utca.** Here you are welcomed back into the old quarter by statues of saints Leonard and Donatus. The former carries a chain, for he is patron saint of prisoners and blacksmiths (as well as shepherds, animals, and sick people). The latter, the patron saint of wine, should hang his holy head a little. Kőszeg wine growers thrived until the turn of the 20th century, when a plague of lice called phylloxera wiped out their industry. Now Kőszeg "imports" its wine from nearby Sopron.

Rájnis utca is nevertheless lined with wine cellars and gardens, though its principal attraction is the **Jurisics Vár** (Jurisics Castle), which you enter by crossing two moats. In the first enclosure are a youth hostel, a bathhouse where the local brass band rehearses, and a modern (1963) statue of the heroic Captain Jurisics. One of the most interesting exhibits in the **Jurisics Miklós Vármúzeum** (city and castle museums) is the "Book of the Vine's Growth," a chronicle kept for more than a century and a half, starting in 1740, by a succession of town clerks whose duty was to trace the sizes and shapes of vine buds drawn in their true dimensions on April 24 of each year. *Rájnis József utca 9, tel. 94/360–240. Admission: 30 Ft. adults, 15 Ft. children. Open Tues.–Sun. 10–5.*

A city of 80,000 some 20 kilometers (13 miles) south of Kőszeg, **Szombathely** (pronounced *SOME-baht-hay*) was founded as Savaria by the Roman emperor Claudius in AD 43. It was an important settlement along the Amber Route from the Baltic to Rome. Some of that road can be seen in the **Járdányi Paulovits István Romkert** (Garden of Ruins), which also boasts the well-preserved remains of a 4th-century mosaic floor. *Alkotmány utca 1–3, tel. 94/313–369. Admission: 20 Ft. adults, 10 Ft. children. Open Apr.–Oct., Tues.–Sun. 10–6.*

In front of the garden is the city's **Katedrál** (Cathedral), a soaring Baroque masterpiece designed by the 18th-century Tyrolean architect Melchior Hefele, who also built the Bishop's Palace and girls' boarding school that flank it. *Rákóczi Ferenc utca 12. Admission to cathedral and palace: 30 Ft. Open Tues.–Sun. 9–4.*

Sala Terrena, the ground-floor museum in the Bishop's Palace, is an amusing attempt by Dorfmeister, Sr., to extend the impression of the Roman garden with frescoes of portals and ruins, gods and goddesses. *Berzsenyi Daniel tér. Admission: 20 Ft. Open Wed.–Fri. 9:30–4, Sat. 9:30–noon.*

In a Baroque house at the other end of splendid Berszenyi Daniel tér, the eccentric **Dr. Lajos Smidt Museum** displays the treasures of a surgeon who was an incorrigible collector of everything—from high straw shoes to Empire furniture, from form-letter military mail sent by combat infantrymen during World War I to concentration-camp currency from World War II. *Hollán utca 2, tel. 94/311–038. Admission: 30 Ft. Open Tues.–Sun. 10–5.*

Another grand square that isn't a square but rather a vast triangular funnel is the nearby **Köztársaság tér** (Republic Square), the business center of the city. Sealed off to traffic, it is crowned at one end by the 18th-century **St. Elizabeth Church.** In harmonious contrast at the other end is a silvery blue, turreted bank built in 1912 in Secessionist style (the Austro-Hungarian Art Nouveau) with inlaid jewels around its clock; it now houses the Centrum department store.

Time Out   At the corner of Köztársaság tér and Bajcsy Zsilinszky utca, **Café Claudia** bakes pastries worthy of Vienna's best Konditorei. They are served by waitresses in well-starched, turn-of-the-century uniforms; everything else here is cream and sugar, sweetness and light.

Off the south side of Köztársaság tér, where Rákóczi utca begins, is a curious conglomeration. On one side are the remnants (dating to the 2nd century AD) of a temple of Isis, shrine of a Roman cult that made animal sacrifices to the Egyptian goddess on this spot; these relics are separated from the modern **Municipal Art Gallery** by some old gravestones. Across the street the culture shock is even more severe: The acoustically modern **Béla Bartók Concert Hall** has been built into the back side of a huge redbrick, onion-dome, Byzantine-style former synagogue created in 1881 by Ludwig Schöne (the Viennese architect who gave Kőszeg its Heart of Jesus Parish Church). At the locked front end of the former synagogue, a monument honors the 4,228 Jews of Szombathely exterminated in the Holocaust.

④ The southwest's premier city, and the fifth largest in Hungary, **Pécs** (pronounced *paytch*) went through various incarnations in the course of its long history. The Franks called it Quinque Ecclesiae; the Slavs, Pet Cerkve; and the Habsburgs, Fünfkirchen; all three names meant "five churches." Today there are many more churches, plus two mosques, and a handsome synagogue. Pécs is also the seat of Europe's sixth-oldest university (1367). In any language, however, Pécs could just as well be renamed City of Many Museums, for on one square block alone there are seven. Three of them—the Zsolnay, Vasarely, and Csontváry—justify a two- or three-day stay in the sparkling, eclectic city in the Mecsek Hills, just 30 kilometers (19 miles) north of the Slovenian border.

At the foot of **Széchenyi tér,** the grand sloping monumental thoroughfare that is the pride of the city, stands the dainty **Zsolnay Fountain,** a petite, Art Nouveau, majolica temple guarded by ox-headed gargoyles that gush pure drinking water piped into Pécs via Roman aqueducts.

Széchenyi tér is crowned by a Turkish oddity that is a tourist's delight: a 16th-century **mosque.** Dating from the years of Turkish occupation (1543–1686), the mosque is now a Catholic church, which you might infer from the cross surmounting a gilded crescent atop the dome. Despite the fierce religious war raging on its walls—Christian statuary and frescoes beneath Turkish arcades and mihrab (prayer niches)—the **Gazi Khassim Pasha Belvárosi plébánia templom** (Gazi Khassim Pasha Inner City Parish Church) remains the largest and finest relic of Turkish architecture in Hungary. *Open mid-Apr.–mid-Oct., weekdays 10–4, Sunday 11:30–4; mid-Oct.–mid-Apr., weekdays 11–noon, Sun. noon–2.*

Go around the back of the mosque church and follow Szepesy Ignác utca up its one-block length to **Káptalan utca,** known as Museum Street. The **Zsolnay Muzeum** occupies the upper floor of the oldest surviving building in Pécs, dating from 1324 and built and rebuilt in Romanesque, Renaissance, and Baroque styles over its checkered history. A stroll through its rooms is a merry show-and-tell waltz through a revolution in pottery that started in 1851, when Miklós Zsolnay, a local merchant, bought the site of an old kiln and set up a stoneware factory for his son Ignác to run. Ignác's brother, Vilmos, a shopkeeper with an artistic bent, bought the factory from him in 1863, imported experts from Germany, and, with the help of a Pécs pharmacist for chemical experiments and his daughters for hand-painting, created the distinctive porcelain with which the name Zsolnay has since been associated.

Among the museums's exhibits are Vilmos's early efforts at Delft-blue handmade vases, cups, and saucers; his two-layer ceramics; examples of the gold-brocade rims that became a Zsolnay trademark; table settings for royal families; Madonnas and baptismal fonts; and landscapes and portraits made of china. There is a Zsolnay store in the center of Pécs at Jokai tér 2, where you can purchase a wide selection of ceramics. *Káptalan utca 2, tel. 72/324–822. Admission: 50 Ft. adults, children free. Open Tues.–Sun. 10–6.*

If you haven't had enough Zsolnay by now, join the groups of tourists (usually German or Hungarian) braving heavily trafficked Zsolnay Vilmos utca to visit the **Zsolnay Porcelain Factory,** where gleaming monumental towers and statuary of seemingly pollution-proof porcelain hold their own among giant smokestacks. *Zsolnay Vilmos utca 69. Tour information, tel. 72/313–643.*

On a hill behind the factory is the ultimate monument to the dynasty's founder, who died in 1900: the **Zsolnay Alapítvány** (Zsolnay Mausoleum), similar to Napoleon's Tomb in Paris, with the bones of Vilmos and his wife in a blue ceramic well and, over the doorway, a relief of Vilmos, with disciples wearing the faces of his wife, daughters, and son kneeling before him. *Zsolnay Vilmos utca 69, tel. 72/313–643. Open daily 10–4.*

Time Out If your eyes have glazed over after viewing so much porcelain, you can refresh yourself with a drink or an ice cream in the **garden café** at the high-numbered end of Káptalan utca.

At Káptalan utca 3 is the **Vasarely Múzeum** (Vasarely Museum). The pioneer of Op Art (who later settled in France) was born Győző Vásárhelyi in 1908 in this merry funhouse. You enter through a ground floor of visual tricks devised by his disciples: a loom that swirls, Deutschemarks that change color, a bizarre "media bazaar," and a TV without any vertical hold. As if that's not enough, at the end of the corridor you'll approach a hypnotic canvas of shifting cubes by Jean-Pierre Yvaral. Upstairs, the illusions grow profound: A zebra gallops by while chess pieces and blood cells seem to come at you. At one point it seems as if you are inside a prison looking out, and then suddenly you are outside looking in. Without a doubt, you leave the Vasarely with all your certainties overturned. *Káptalan utca 3, tel. 72/324-822. Admission: 50 Ft. Open Tues.-Sun. 10-6.*

Sharing the grounds of the Vasarely Museum is a **mining museum** devoted to the Hungarian mining industry. Inside, a labyrinth of tunnels realistically replicates an active mine; wooden support structures make space for an old mining cart attached to a short rail line, and old mining technology—tools and lamps and other paraphernalia—lies strewn about. *Káptalan utca 3. Admission: 30 Ft. Open Tues.-Sun. 10-5.*

On the same street stands the **Endre Nemes Múzeum,** with displays (accompanied by English texts) of the ceramics of Vilmos Zsolnay and his followers. Another section of the museum contains a street scene constructed entirely of white foam plastic by the sculptor Erzsébet Schaár. The people on the street are constructed of gypsum, simple in body structure but with finely drawn heads and faces (the heads of Marx and Sándor Petőfi, the famous Hungarian poet, also are visible). *Kápptalan utca 5. Admission: 50 Ft. Open Tues.-Sun. 10-6.*

The third major gallery in Pécs, the **Csontváry Múzeum,** is just around the corner; but if you've just left the Vasarely and you have the time, it's probably best to wait a day and bring a fresh eye to this next museum. Mihály Tivadar Csontváry Kosztka (1853-1919) was a pharmacist in the Tatra Mountains who, in his late twenties, sketched a scene of an ox cart outside his drugstore on a prescription pad. Told he had artistic talent, he worked and studied and saved money for 24 years to achieve enough financial and artistic independence to, as he put it, "catch up with, let alone surpass, the great masters." An early expressionist and forerunner of surrealism, Csontváry influenced Picasso; his work is to be found almost exclusively here in Pécs and in a room of the Hungarian National Gallery in Budapest.

The paintings in the five rooms of the museum in Pécs are arranged to show Csontváry's progression from soulful portraits to seemingly conventional landscapes executed with decidedly unconventional colors to his 1904 Temple of Zeus in Athens (about which Csontváry said, "This is the first painting in which the canvas can no longer be seen.") A few months later, with an even greater intensification of unexpected colors, *The Ruins of Baalbek* and *The Wailing Wall in Jerusalem* filled giant canvases. After a 1905 tryout in Budapest, Csontváry was ready for a 1907 exhibition in Paris, which turned out to be a huge critical success. Not long after finishing his last great epic painting, *Mary at the Well in Nazareth* (1908), megalomania gripped him. Though his canvases grew ever larger, Csontváry finished nothing that he started after 1909 except a patriotic drawing of Emperor Franz Joseph at the start of World War I in 1914.

After he died in Budapest in 1919, Csontváry's canvases were about to be reused as furniture covers when a collector from Pécs named Gedeon Gerlóczy rescued them with a ransom of 10,000 forints. The collection in Pécs is now valued at more than $10 million. *Janus Pannonius utca 11, tel. 72/310–544. Admission: 50 Ft. Open Apr.– Sept., Tues.–Sun. 10–6.*

From the Csontváry Museum, look across and take note of one of Europe's most magnificent cathedrals. It is the famous **Pécs Katedrál** (Pécs Cathedral) on nearby Dóm tér. At the beginning of the 19th century, Mihály Pollack directed the transformation of the exterior, changing it from Baroque to neoclassical; its interior remained Gothic. Near the end of the century, Bishop Nándor Dulánszky decided to restore the cathedral to its original Árpád period—the result is a four-spired monument that dominates the Pécs skyline.

In front of the cathedral is a small park, just beyond which is an early Christian **mausoleum.** Some of the subterranean crypts and chapels date to the 4th century, and the murals on the walls (Adam and Eve, Daniel in the lion's den, Christ's resurrection) are in remarkably good condition. In 1987, the mausoleum–museum won a World Biennial Prize for architecture. *Dóm tér, tel. 72/311–526. Admission: 50 Ft. Open Tues.–Sun. 10–5.*

Dining and Lodging

Highly recommended restaurants and lodgings in a particular price category are indicated by a star ★.

Kőszeg
Dining

Bécsikapu Söröző. One of the best family-run places in Transdanubia, this brasserie near the castle cooks a great deer-steak bourguignonne with potato dumplings. It's also one of the few places where an English menu doesn't mean inflated prices. *Rájnis József utca 5, tel. 94/360–297. Reservations advised. Dress: casual. No credit cards. $*

Lodging

Írottkő. Centrally located on the town's main square, this modern but not at all unsightly hotel harmonizes nicely with the fine ensemble of old houses above the storefronts. Inside is a four-story atrium so sleek that you wonder when the next monorail will pass through. At lobby level, there is a dental clinic heavily patronized by Austrians. Guest rooms are functional, but not so luxurious that you'd want to stay indoors when there's so much to see outside. The staff is friendly and multilingual. *Fő tér 4, H-9730, tel. 94/360–373. 52 rooms with bath or shower. Facilities: bar. No credit cards. $$*

Alpokalja Pánzió. Located near a stream at the western edge of town along the highway to Austria, this new pension is convenient for travelers with cars. *Szombathelyi ut 8, tel. 94/360–056, 13 rooms with shower. Facilities: restaurant. No credit cards. $*

Szálloda az Arany Strucchoz. This former Baroque inn was built in 1718 and is now one of the oldest hotels in Hungary. Much of the ground floor is given over to a smoky café with pinball machines and, fortunately, a separate entrance around the corner. Within the hotel portion are wide arches and spacious, comfortable rooms, including a corner room with 19th-century Biedermeier furnishings and a balcony looking out onto Kőszeg's main square. *Várkör 124, H-9730, tel. 94/360–323. 18 rooms with bath or shower. Facilities: breakfast. No credit cards. $*

Pécs **Iparos Kisvendéglő.** The very popular "Craftsman" restaurant has a
Dining wide selection of pork, turkey, chicken, veal, and game dishes, as
well as a small selection of fresh salads. *Rákóczi út 24–26, tel. 72/
333–400. Reservations advised. Dress: casual. AE, DC, MC, V. $$*
Szőlőskert Étterem. The name means Vineyard, and it is fittingly lo-
cated in a former vineyard on the outskirts of Pécs—with good
views of town from the outdoor terrace. In 1963 the winepressing
room was transformed into a restaurant; a 1986 renovation moder-
nized the facilities and enlarged the dining room. The cuisine and de-
cor are traditional Hungarian. It is open from 6 AM to serve guests
from the neighboring Hotel Hunyor. *Kisszókó utca 4, tel. 72/315–886.
Reservations advised on weekends. Dress: casual. AE. $*

Lodging **Hotel Hunyor.** Like the Szőlőskert restaurant above, the Hunyor
also occupies a former hillside vineyard; every room has a fine view
overlooking the city. The hotel itself was built in 1986 and is clean
and functional. *Jurisics Miklós utca 16, tel. 72/315–677, fax 72/315–
926. 51 rooms with bath, 3 suites. Facilities: restaurant, bar. AE,
DC, MC, V. $$*

★ **Palatinus.** Situated in the pedestrian-only center of Pécs, the
Palatinus maintains a good balance between old and new: The outside of the renovated building has fully preserved its traditional aspect, while the rooms are modern in most every respect (each is
equipped with a telephone, minibar, and color television with satellite hookup). The hotel's stunning ballroom, built in the Hungarian
Secessionist style, is well suited for parties, balls, and conferences;
in fact, the Hungarian composer Béla Bartók held a concert of his
own here in 1923. *Király utca 5, tel. 72/433–022, fax 72/432–261. 88
rooms with bath, 6 suites. Facilities: restaurant, brasserie, bowling,
terrace, sauna, massage, solarium. AE, DC, MC, V. $$*

Sopron **Barokk Étterem.** The "Baroque Restaurant" opened in 1992, sup-
Dining planting authentic baroque designs with pastel colors and modern
fixtures. Still, the entrance is through a lovely courtyard, and the
dining room has a soothing arched ceiling. Specialties of the house
include meat fondue, trout, and beef Wellington with goose-liver
stuffing. *Várkerület 25, tel. 99/312–227. Reservations advised.
Dress: casual. AE, MC. $$*

★ **Palatinus Étterem.** This is a popular, informal restaurant where
everything is prepared fresh daily—even the sauerkraut. The cordial chefs are often willing to cook up something not on the menu;
otherwise, stick with the traditional Hungarian offerings. English
menus are available. Lunch and dinner guests are entertained by a
pianist; breakfast guests simply get fine food. *Új utca 23, tel. 99/
311–395. Reservations advised. Dress: casual. AE, DC, MC, V. $$*

Lodging **Palatinus hotel.** Built in 1981 and privatized in 1993, the new owner
of the Palatinus recently completed a thorough renovation. The ho-
tel is situated in the city center within reach of every important
sight. The staff is friendly and multilingual. *Új utca 23, tel. 99/311–
395. 29 rooms with shower, 4 suites. Facilities: restaurant, bar. AE,
DC, MC, V. $$*

Szombathely **Kispityer Halászcsárda.** From huge kettles, this large, noisy inn on
Dining the south side of town dishes out the best and widest selection of fish
★ yet encountered in this land of lakes and rivers. Begin your meal
with the spicy, almost boneless fish soup unless you want its bonier
big brother, carp soup, the "Pride of the Hungarian Kitchen." Move
on to the Rába-style sheet fish served with sauerkraut and sour
cream; or to any of the two dozen other fish specialties, described
quite comically in English (translation may not be the chef's strong
point). In 1993, the restaurant won an International Hotel and

Gastronic Association "Golden Bull" award for food and service, one of the top awards available and given to only four other Hungarian restaurants in the last 20 years. Strolling musicians will play everything and anything for you at tableside, whether or not you want to hear it. *Rumi út 18, tel. 94/311-227. Reservations advised. Dress: casual. AE, MC, V. Closed Mon. $$*

Gyöngyös Étterem. This centrally located restaurant, a stone's throw from the Savaria hotel, is the cheapest sit-down place in town. The food on the multilingual menu is wholesome; *Eszterházy pecsenye* (Eszterházy-style pork loin) and *gombás rostélyos* (mushroom steak) are worth a try, if they're available. *Széll Kámán utca 8, tel. 94/312-665. Reservations advised. Dress: casual. No credit cards. Closed Mon. $*

★ **Pásztorcsárda.** This charming country inn on the road to Kőszeg boasts a simple, scrubbed interior adorned by a pitch-fork and by paintings of rustic scenes that might have taken place on this farmstead. The limited menu of home-cooked dishes includes game specialties, all prepared in a traditional manner with extraordinary finesse. A terrace is open in the summer. *Dolgozók útja 1. No reservations. Dress: casual. MC. $*

Lodging **Claudius.** Named for the Roman emperor who colonized Szombathely, this large lakeside hotel occupies a green setting about a 15-minute walk from downtown. Though its amenities are not quite luxurious, the balcony views from most rooms are rewarding and relaxing. Breakfast, cooked to order and included in the room rate, is served in an elegant dining room. Your hotel registration card grants you free admission to a large indoor public swimming complex next door: It includes a 164-foot pool and other basins heated with thermal water, as well as sauna and fitness rooms; only massage costs extra. Beware, however, of the dragonesses who run the checkroom where you show your credentials. *Bartók Béla krt. 39, H-9700, tel. 94/313-760, fax 94/313-545, telex 94/337-262. 98 rooms with bath, 6 suites. Facilities: restaurant, nightclub, parking. AE, DC, MC, V. $$*

★ **Savaria.** From the rear, its glittering winter garden–ballroom gives the impression of a theater; from the front terrace, its palatial café-restaurant—with cluster chandeliers and tapering mirrors, copper and marble, and a wooden balcony above the bar—suggest a five-star grand hotel. It is neither: just a two-star downtown hostelry that happens to be a severe Secessionist classic from the turn of the century, recently and perfectly renewed. The personnel is young and obliging. The very reasonable room rate includes breakfast in that glorious café. *Mártirok tér 4, H-9700, tel. 94/311-440, fax 94/324-532, telex 94/337-200. 93 rooms (30 with bath, 30 with shower, 33 with sink). Facilities: restaurant, coffeehouse, parking. AE, DC, MC, V. $$*

Liget. In 1989 the Liget, situated 2 kilometers (about a mile) from the city center in a lush green area close to the Claudius hotel, was completely renovated, leaving it a quiet, clean, not-quite-luxury but still comfortable hotel. Rates include admission to the nearby swimming pool. *Szent István part 15, tel. and fax 94/314-168. 37 rooms with shower, 1 suite. V. $*

5 Poland

By Emma Harris, with contributions from Witold Orzechowski

A longtime resident of Warsaw, Emma Harris is the director of the English Studies Institute at Warsaw University.

Poles are fond of quoting, with a wry grimace, the old Chinese vale-diction, "May you live in interesting times." The times are certainly interesting in 1990s Poland, the home of the Solidarity trade union movement that sent shock waves through the Soviet bloc in 1980, and the first of the Eastern European states to shake off communist rule. But as the grimace implies, being on the firing line of history — something that the Poles are well used to—can be an uncomfortable experience. You will be constantly reminded that the current return to free-market capitalism after 45 years of state socialism is an ex-periment on an unprecedented scale that brings inconveniences and surprises as well as benefits.

With 38 million inhabitants living in a territory of 315,000 square ki-lometers (121,000 square miles), Poland entered the 1990s sus-pended between the old world and the new, and the images can be confusing. You will see bright, new, privately owned shops with smiling assistants next to shabby state-sector outlets with the old "take it or leave it" attitudes. Glowing new billboards advertise goods that most Poles cannot afford. Policemen wearing the dark blue uniforms that symbolize a return to prewar traditions work alongside policemen in the old communist-militia gray. Buildings can change function overnight as they are handed back to their pre-war owners. Public services, such as transportation, can be cut off suddenly without warning, as local authorities discover that they have insufficient funds to keep the show on the road. Blatantly neon-lighted sex shops in city centers coexist awkwardly with the church-backed campaign to strengthen family life by banning abortion and divorce.

The official trappings of the communist state were quickly disman-tled after the Solidarity victory in the 1989 elections. The nation's name was changed back to the Republic of Poland (although you will notice that many documents still bear the old legend of the Polish People's Republic); the state emblem is now, as before the war, a crowned eagle. Statues of communist leaders have largely disap-peared from public places (a suggestion, made by one town planner, that as an economy measure only the heads should be removed and replaced by the heads of Polish artists or patriots, was not followed up); many street names have been changed, and Communist-party buildings have been turned into schools, universities, or banks. For some, it may be surprising that the symbols of the past 45 years could disappear so quickly.

Communism, of course, never sat easily with the Poles. It repre-sented yet another stage in their age-old struggle to retain their identity in the face of pressure from the lifestyles of neighbors to the west and east. Converted to Christianity and founded as a unified state during the 10th century on the great north European plain, which affords no easily demarcated or defended frontiers, Poland lay for a thousand years at the heart of Europe, precisely at the half-way point on a line drawn from the Atlantic coast of Spain to the Ural Mountains. This has never been an enviable position. During the Middle Ages, Poland fought against German advance, uniting with her eastern neighbors in 1410 to inflict a crushing defeat upon the Teutonic Knights in the Battle of Grunwald. In the Golden Age of Polish history during the 16th and 17th centuries—of which you will be reminded by splendid Renaissance buildings in many parts of the country—Poland pushed eastward against her Slavic neighbors, taking Kiev and dreaming of a kingdom that stretched from the Bal-tic to the Black Sea. It saw itself now as the bastion of Christendom against the hordes from the east, a role best symbolized when Polish

king John III Sobieski led the allied Christian forces to defeat the Turks at Vienna in 1683. This role is often referred to in the context of more recent Polish history.

By the end of the 18th century, powerful neighbors had united to obliterate Poland—with its outmoded tendency to practice democracy at the highest levels of state and elect foreigners to the throne—from the map of Europe; its territories were to remain divided among the Austrian, Prussian, and Russian empires until World War I. This period of partition, which has left marked traces upon the Polish psyche, is often used to explain patterns of character or public behavior—the Polish tendency to subvert all forms of organized authority, for example, or Polish devotion to the Roman Catholic church as a marker of national identity, a devotion that would later survive the disapproval of the communist state.

The period of partition has also left physical traces on the map of Poland, despite the tendency of the postwar years to impose uniformity. The formerly Prussian-ruled regions of western Poland, centered in Poznań, are still regarded as cleaner and better organized than the Russian-ruled central areas around the capital, Warsaw; the former Austrian zone in the south, particularly the city of Kraków, retains a reputation for stuffiness and dignified behavior on the Habsburg model. The architecture of the three regions also bears traces of distinct 19th-century imperial styles.

During the 20th century, after a brief period of revived independence in the interwar years, Poland fell victim to peculiarly vicious forms of the old struggle between east and west. It was first crushed by Hitler's *Drang nach Osten* (drive toward the east), which killed 6 million Polish citizens, including 3 million of the Jews who had played such a major role in the nation's history. In 1945 Poland's borders were shifted 322 kilometers (200 miles) farther west (via the annexation of German territory), and the country was placed behind the Iron Curtain in Stalin's postwar settlement. These mid-century experiences are embedded deep in the Polish soul. The 19th-century insurrectionary tradition was revived in resistance to the Nazi occupation and is still honored throughout Poland in the candles and flowers placed in front of memorials to its victims. These are now being joined by monuments to those who died fighting against Soviet power during the 1940s and '50s—including the victims of the Katyn massacre.

This is one aspect of a respect for national traditions that makes Poland—despite all its hardships and shortcomings—such a fascinating place for the visitor with an inquiring mind. Its historic cities—Kraków, Warsaw, Gdańsk—tell much of the tale of European history and culture. Its countryside offers unrivaled possibilities of escape from the 20th century. Paradoxically, communism—which after 1956 dropped attempts to collectivize agriculture and left the Polish peasant on his small, uneconomic plot—has preserved rural Poland in a romantic, preindustrial state. Despite appalling pollution, which has attracted public attention but is mercifully largely confined to the industrial southwest, cornflowers still bloom, storks hunt for frogs in marshland or perch atop untidy nests by cottage chimneys, and horse carts make their way lazily along field tracks.

And, despite a certain wary reserve in public behavior that can verge on rudeness in some contexts, the Poles will win you over wherever you go with their strong individualism—expressed in flair in dress and style—their well-developed sense of humor, and their capacity for enjoyment and conviviality.

Before You Go

Government Tourist Offices

In the U.S. Orbis Polish Travel Bureau, Inc., 342 Madison Ave., New York, NY 10173, tel. 212/867–5011.

In Canada Poland has no travel office in Canada; for information, contact the Polish Consulate in Toronto (2603 Lakeshore Blvd. W, Ontario MAV 1GS, tel. 416/252–5471).

In the U.K. Polorbis Travel Ltd., 82 Mortimer St., London, W1N 7DE, tel. 071/637–4971.

Tour Groups

Special-Interest Tours Orbis Special Interest Travel (ul. Stawki 2, 00–193 Warsaw, tel. 022/27–01–71) arranges customized tours built around particular themes, primarily for preorganized groups. Recent excursions have focused on music, opera houses, the castles and palaces of Poland, regional folklore and cuisine, Polish Judaica, beekeeping, farming, and gardening.

When to Go

Spring, though sometimes late, is usually mild and sunny and is a good time for intense, energetic sightseeing. Summers can be hot and humid, especially in southern Poland, but this is still the busiest tourist season. Hotels, especially those on the coast and in the mountain resorts, now charge higher seasonal rates in the summer (from May to September on the coast; in July and August in the mountains). There are also brief high-season rates for specific reasons, as, for example, in Poznań during the June trade fair. If you are interested in the arts, remember that theaters and concert halls close down completely in the summer for at least two months (July and August) and often do not get going with the new season's programs until October. The fabled Polish Golden Autumn, when landscapes are at their best, lasts until November and can be a good time for touring. The winter sports season is from December to March, when high-season rates are once again in effect in the mountains. In general, central heating is universal and efficient in Poland, but air-conditioning is a rarity. On major church holidays—Christmas, Easter, Corpus Christi—almost everything except your hotel will close down.

Festivals and Seasonal Events

May: Chamber music festival, Łańcut; Festival of contemporary drama, Wrocław; International Book Fair, Warsaw.

May–June: International Festival of Short Feature Films, Kraków.

June: International Trade Fair, Poznań; Polish Song Festival, Opole; Jan Kiepura Song Festival, Krynica; Midsummer ceremonies (June 23), which include throwing candlelit wreaths into the Vistula, Warsaw; Sunday morning open-air Chopin concerts at the Chopin memorial in Warsaw's Łazienki Park and at Żelazowa Wola (until October); Festival of Folk Dance and Music Ensembles, Kazimierz Dolny; Łowicz Fair.

July–August: Organ music festival, Gdańsk–Oliwa.

August: Dominican Fair and Festival (August 1–14), Gdańsk; International Festival of Highland Folklore, Zakopane; Country Music Festival, Mrągowo; International Song Festival, Sopot. International Chopin Festival, Duszniki Zdrój.

September: Wratislavia Cantans, oratoria and cantata music festival, Wrocław; "Warsaw Autumn" festival of contemporary music, Warsaw; Festival of Karol Szymanowski's music, Zakopane; Festival of Highland Folklore, Zakopane.

October: Jazz Jamboree, Warsaw.

November: All Saints' Day (November 1), when thousands of candles are placed on graves in cemeteries; International Theater Festival, *Spotkanie Teatralne*, Warsaw.

December: St. Nicholas Day (December 6), when children receive gifts and dress as mummers, particularly in the south; Christmas crèche competition, Kraków.

What to Pack

Clothing Poles, though relatively formal in their codes of dress, have no hard-and-fast rules and do not go to extremes: You are very unlikely to need an evening jacket or long evening dress. It would, however, be a good idea for men to have a tie and women a skirt for some evening occasions. Winter weather can be very cold indeed, so pack a hat as well as a warm coat.

Miscellaneous If you are attached to a particular brand of toiletries or cosmetics, it is best to bring a supply along; although many Western items are now on sale, the selection is random and unpredictable. Though toilet paper is now regularly on sale in Polish shops (for the first time since the war), it may not be supplied in public places, and you would be wise to carry some with you. Since Poland operates on a 220-volt electrical current, British equipment (240 volts) can be used without problems; but if you are coming from the United States, bring a converter, as they are hard to find in Poland.

Polish Currency

The monetary unit in Poland is the *złoty*, which, because of massive inflation during the late 1980s, appears exclusively in the form of bank notes—in denominations of 50, 100, 200, 500, 1,000, 2,000, 5,000, 10,000, 20,000, 50,000, 100,000, 500,000, 1 million, and 2 million. Coins are never seen now, and the *grosz*, a one-hundredth part of a złoty, is only a figure of speech. At press time (summer 1994), the exchange rate was zł 22,000 to the dollar and zł 32,500 to the pound sterling. Foreign currency can be exchanged for złoty at banks or at private bureaux de change *(Kantor Wymiany Walut)*, where the rate offered can be slightly higher than the bank rate and the service swifter. Currency-exchange controls are still officially in force, although they are now largely ignored. However, you are still required by law to declare all foreign currency when you enter Poland. Technically speaking, you also cannot export a larger sum of currency than you brought in, and you are legally forbidden to export złoty.

What It Will Cost

For a time, the economic reforms introduced in January 1990 seemed to be on the way to controlling inflation, which was lowered to two figures from an annual rate of nearly 1,000% in 1989. At press time, however, the annual rate was again approaching 100%. This has brought the złoty under pressure, and a sliding devaluation scale has been introduced. The złoty is still probably overvalued against Western currencies, although this does not always work to the tourist's disadvantage; it is a question of watching the rate day by day. The days when you could exchange $50 on the black market and feel like a millionaire have gone forever. Even though most goods and services are considerably cheaper than in the West, they are creeping up to recognizably European levels. On the other hand, the deregulation of hotel prices offers visitors a greater range of options in selecting appropriate accommodations. Though the top hotels have retained the złoty equivalent of the old fixed-dollar price, many others have dropped their charges; and in the provinces it is not a problem to find a decent hotel room for as little as $10. Overall, you can still get very good value for your money in Poland, and the farther you venture off the beaten track the cheaper your holiday becomes.

Taxes A value-added tax (VAT) is applied to hotel and restaurant services at a level ranging from 20% in the top categories to 7% in the lower. Hotel and restaurant taxes apply only in the Zakopane region, where the local authorities have imposed a 10% tax on all goods and services for nonresidents (locals produce their identity card, if necessary, in shops). There are no airport taxes.

Sample Costs A cup of coffee will cost about zł 10,000–zł 35,000; a bottle of beer, zł 10,000–zł 40,000; a soft drink, zł 5,000–zł 25,000; a 1½-kilometer (1-mile) taxi ride, zł 20,000; a 240-kilometer (150-mile) train trip (first-class single), zł 300,000.

Passports and Visas

U.S., British, French, and German citizens are no longer required to obtain visas for entry to Poland (a valid passport will suffice). Canadian citizens must pay C$40 or C$80 for a single- or double-entry visa. Apply at any Orbis office (*see* Government Tourist Offices, *above*), an affiliated travel agent, or at the Polish Consulate General in any country. Each visitor must complete three application forms and provide two passport-size photographs. Allow about two weeks for processing. Visas are issued for 90 days but can be extended in Poland, either through the local police headquarters or through Orbis.

Customs and Duties

You may bring into Poland duty-free: personal belongings, including musical instruments; a typewriter or word processor; a radio; up to two cameras and 24 rolls of film; up to 250 cigarettes or 50 cigars; and one half liter each of wine and spirits, together with goods that are not for your personal use up to the value of $200. Although customs checks have relaxed greatly since 1990, antique jewelry or books published before 1945 should be declared on arrival to avoid possible problems in taking them out of the country.

Language

Polish is a Slavic language that uses the Roman alphabet but has several additional characters and diacritics. Because it has a much higher incidence of consonant clusters than English, most English speakers find that it's a difficult language to decipher, much less pronounce (when you try to speak Polish, your mouth may feel as if it's full of wet cement, at least in the early stages). Bring a phrase book and a pocket dictionary with you (they're expensive and hard to find in Poland), and the people you're trying to communicate with will appreciate the effort.

Older Poles are more likely to know French or German—and, of course, Russian, which they will not admit to—than English. Educated people under 40 are likely to have learned some English; everyone, at least in the cities, is apparently attending classes. You will almost always find an English speaker in hotels—even in small, out-of-the-way places; but away from the cities you will rarely be able to use English in shops, post offices, or other everyday situations. Although it is now chic to give shops an English name, this does not necessarily mean that they will speak your language inside.

Car Rentals

A valid driver's license issued in the United States, Canada or Britain, or indeed in almost any other country will enable you to drive without a special permit. You do, however, need green-card insurance if you are driving your own car.

You can rent a car through **Orbis** (*see* Government Tourist Offices, *above*), which is affiliated with Hertz. Cars with both manual and automatic transmissions are available, starting at about $500 a week (including insurance and unlimited mileage). Car rentals are available in Warsaw, Gdańsk, Katowice, Łódź, Kraków, Poznań, Szczecin, and Wrocław.

At press time (summer 1994), gasoline cost about 60¢ a liter, gas stations were being opened, and some Western companies had moved into the market.

Rail Passes

At press time the Eurailpass was not accepted in Poland. The InterRail pass (*see* Rail Passes in Chapter 1, Essential Information), available exclusively to residents of the European Community, entitles travelers to unlimited, free second-class rail travel throughout Poland.

The **European East Pass** covers Poland, Czechoslovakia, Hungary, and Austria. Passes (first class only) cost $169 for 5 days' travel (spread over a 15-day period) and $275 for 10 days' travel (spread over a 30-day period). If Austria is not on your itinerary, this isn't much of a bargain. For more information, contact Orbis.

Student and Youth Travel

Almatur (Ul. Kopernika 23, Warwaw, tel. 022/23512), the Polish student-travel organization, can provide information on LOT airlines' volunteer work camps through CCIVS (Coordinating Committee of International Voluntary Service), study programs, and home stays through the Experiment in International Living. The group may also be able to help you find inexpensive accommodations, either in a youth hostel or a student hotel; but don't expect comprehensive budget-lodging information.

The **International Student Identity Card (ISIC)**, available at all Council Travel Agencies, will get you a 50% discount on entry fees to all museums, second-class train fares, and intercity bus fares. Apply to the **Council on International Educational Exchange (CIEE)** (205 E. 42nd St., New York, NY 10017, tel. 212/661–1414).

Further Reading

Heart of Europe, A Short History of Poland, by Norman Davies, gives a clear, readable account of modern Polish history. For the full spectrum of Poland's past, the same author's *God's Playground, A History of Poland* is the work to consult; it takes the reader from prehistory to Solidarity in two big volumes (better to read this *before* going). Neal Ascherson's *The Struggles for Poland* deals with the history and politics of modern Poland.

Denis Hills' *Return to Poland,* an idiosyncratic look at the country in the 1980s, from an author who first lived in Poland during the 1930s and had many adventures, is entertaining and revealing. Janine Wendel's *The Private Poland* recounts her three years living among Poles. The character of the Poles is perhaps best-captured in a historical trilogy, *With Fire and Sword,* by Nobel Prize–winning novelist Henry K. Sienkiewicz.

Frank Tuohy's *The Ice Saints* gives a vivid picture of life in Poland during the 1950s and early '60s. The author drew on his experiences as a teacher at the Jagiellonian University in Kraków during that period. *Mila 18,* by Leon Uris, offers a fictionalized account of the Warsaw Ghetto uprising. Jerzy Kosinski relates a child's wanderings in Poland and beyond during World War II in his painful, somewhat grosteque autobiographical novel, *The Painted Bird.*

Arriving and Departing

From North America by Plane

Airports and Airlines All flights from North America arrive at Terminal 1 of Warsaw's Okęcie Airport (Port Lotniczy), just southwest of the city. **LOT** Polish Airlines offers direct service from the United States. The flying time from New York is 7 hours, 40 minutes; from Chicago, 9 hours, 25 minutes; from Los Angeles, 12 hours, 30 minutes.

From the United Kingdom by Plane, Car, Ferry, Train, and Bus

By Plane **LOT** (tel. 02/630–50–07) and **British Airways** (tel. 02/628–94–31) operate flights from London's Heathrow Airport to Warsaw's Okęcie Airport. In the summer LOT also offers flights to Kraków and Gdańsk. Flying time is 2 hours, 30 minutes to Warsaw; 2 hours, 40 minutes to Kraków; and 2 hours, 20 minutes to Gdańsk.

Discount Fares Certain travel agents charter seats on scheduled British Airways and LOT flights and offer budget fares on an Apex basis if you are staying for less than a month. Contact **Fregata Travel** (100 Dean St., London, W1, tel. 0171/734–5101).

By Car and Ferry **Polske Linie Oceaniczne** (Polish Ocean Lines, Informacja Morskiego Biura Podróży, Chałubińskiego 8, tel. 022/30–29–63) no longer operates a regular ferry service from London to Świnoujście or Gdańsk, though PLO offers occasional crossings during high season; it will also book you (and your car) onto cargo boats. The port city of Świnoujście is convenient if you plan to tour Poland's north coast. For destinations in central and southern Poland, it's more sensible to take the ferry from Harwich to Hamburg and then drive across northern Germany.

By Train Direct trains to Warsaw run either from Victoria Station via Dover and Oostende or from Liverpool Street Station via Harwich and Hoek van Holland; their routes converge in Germany and enter Poland via Kunowice and Poznań. You can change at Poznań for Kraków and Gdańsk. Travel time direct to Warsaw is approximately 33 hours; to Kraków, approximately 37 hours; and to Gdańsk, 39 hours. In Poland, Orbis deals with the purchase of international rail tickets, as do all main city stations.

By Bus A number of new companies are operating bus services from Glasgow, Birmingham, Manchester, and London to Poznań, Warsaw, and Kraków. Most travel nonstop and take about 36 hours. What you lose in comfort you make up for in cost: The bus fare is roughly half the train fare. Contact **Fregata Travel** (100 Dean St., London, W1, tel. 0171/734–5101, or 117A Withington Rd., Manchester, tel. 061/226–7227).

Staying in Poland

Getting Around

By Plane **LOT Polish Airlines** recently cut back on its domestic services, and connections are now available for only five Polish cities: **Warsaw, Kraków, Gdańsk, Wrocław,** and **Rzeszów.** Most days there is at least one flight between Warsaw and each of the other cities; flying time in each case is about 40–50 minutes. Compared with rail travel, flying is expensive (two to three times the price of a first-class rail ticket), and most airports are some distance from the city center. However, for Wrocław and Rzeszów, rail connections with Warsaw are so poor (Wrocław–Warsaw, seven hours) that flying is a real time-saver. But if you are a nervous air traveler, you should know that LOT domestic flights largely use ancient and noisy Soviet-made Ilyushin aircraft.

By Train Polish trains run at three speeds: *ekspresowy* (express), *pośpieszny* (fast), and (the much cheaper) *osobowy* (slow). "Intercity" expresses have recently been introduced on major routes; these provide high-standard accommodations, and coffee and sandwiches are included in the price of the ticket. Only the first two categories can be guaranteed to have first-class accommodations, and it is only on express trains that you can reserve a seat (indeed, these are by reservation only, although the conductor usually comes up with something at the last moment). Couchettes and sleeping cars (three berths to a car in second class, two berths in first class) are available on long-distance routes (e.g., Warsaw–Zakopane or Warsaw–Wrocław). Though buffet cars are usually available on express trains, it is a good idea to take along some food on a long trip; the buffet is quite likely to be canceled at the last moment, and the food that it supplies can be unappetizing. Lines for tickets have sped up thanks to the introduction of computers at ticket windows. Tickets are issued for a given date, after which you get only two days' leeway to travel; thereafter they are invalid. Rail tickets are also available through Orbis.

By Bus **PKS,** the national bus company, offers long-distance service to most cities. Express buses, on which you can reserve seats, are somewhat more expensive than trains but often—except in the case of a few major intercity routes—get to their destination more quickly. For really out-of-the-way destinations, the bus is often the only means of transportation.

By Car Poland has no full-blown highways, although some major roads (e.g., Warsaw–Katowice) are now entirely two-lane. This is still the exception rather than the rule, however, and traffic conditions can be difficult on long-distance routes. Horse-drawn traffic still causes congestion even on major roads, and carts are particularly dangerous at night, when they often have inadequate lighting. Poles drive on the right, and there is an overall speed limit of 100 kph (62 mph). The speed limit in built-up areas is 60 kph (37 mph); the beginning and end of these are marked by a sign bearing the name of the town in a white rectangle. The price of gas is $8–$10 for 10 liters of high-octane. Filling stations appear about every 40 kilometers (25 miles) on major roads but can be difficult to find when you travel on side roads. They are usually open from 6 AM to 10 PM, although there are some 24-hour stations, usually in cities. For emergency road help, dial 981. The **Polish Motoring Association** (*PZMot*) provides free breakdown and repair services for members of affiliated organizations. Check details with Orbis. It is a good idea to carry spare parts, which can still be difficult to get for Western models. If you break down in a really remote area, you can usually find a local farmer who will help with a tractor tow and some mechanical skills. There are no motor-rail services in Poland.

By Ferry You can take ferries or hydrofoils between various points on the Baltic coast, two of the more popular routes being Szczecin to Świnoujście, near the German border on the coast; and Sopot to Hel, farther east near Gdańsk.

Telephones

Local Calls Public phones vary in type. Card phones are gradually being introduced in large cities. Phone cards cost zł 50,000 or 100,000 and are available from post offices. Other types of public phones take tokens (*żetony*), which can be purchased from post offices and some kiosks for zł 1,000. The most modern type of phone, gradually replacing older models, has a slot in the upper right-hand corner in which you place your token; when your call is connected, the token will be absorbed. A token buys you three minutes, after which you will be cut off without warning—but you can avoid this by feeding the slot with as many tokens as you like at the beginning of your call or during your conversation. Though many pay phones are out of order, you can use the phones in RUCH kiosks for the appropriate payment. Long-distance calls must be made from special pay phones, usually located in post offices. For these, you use special tokens (cost: zł 5,000, 10,000, or 20,000).

International Calls International calls are best made from post offices, where the counter clerk connects you and collects your payment; You'll avoid having to shovel large numbers of tokens into the pay phone, if you can't find the card-operated type. You can dial direct to almost all European countries and to the United States. For international collect and credit-card calls, dial an Englishspeaking operator at 0–0104–800222 (MCI). Or call 010–480–0111 (AT&T) from within Warsaw or 0–010–480–0111 (AT&T) from outside Warsaw.

Operators and Information **International operator:** dial 901 (international operators speak English).

Local inquiries: dial 913.

Long-distance inquiries: dial 912.

Mail

Postal Rates Airmail letters to the United States and Canada cost zł 8,000; postcards, zł 5,000. Airmail letters to the United Kingdom cost zł 6,500, postcards zł 4,000. Airmail Express costs an extra zł 15,000 flat charge and cuts the travel time in half.

Telegrams and Faxes You can send telegrams from any post office. The cost to the United States is about zł 24,000 per word, half that to points in Europe. Fax machines are available in most hotels and main post offices.

Receiving Mail The main post office in every town has *poste restante* (general delivery) facilities. Friends and family who send you mail should write "No. 1" (signifying the main post office) after the name of the city.

Tipping

Inflation has brought disorientation to Poland, but one thing for sure is that people expect higher tips in Warsaw than in the provinces. Service charges are added to bills in more expensive restaurants, but it is still customary to leave something, usually another 10%, for the waiter. Taxi drivers are not usually tipped, although you can round up to the nearest 5,000 złoty if you wish. A tip of zł 10,000 is in order for porters carrying bags or for room service, although in Very Expensive hotels you could raise this to zł 20,000. Concierges and tour guides should also get at least zł 20,000.

Opening and Closing Times

During the past few years, since the economic reforms, all the rules about opening hours have been broken, and there is much greater variation across the country and even within cities. On the whole, the farther you get from the capital and the bigger cities, the earlier shops will open and close: 11–7 is standard in Warsaw, 10–6 in provincial towns. On Saturday, shops are now usually open until 1 or 2 PM. Banks are generally open Monday to Friday 8–3 or 8–6. Museum hours, which have always been highly unpredictable, remain so. There is a very general rule that museums are closed Monday and the day after public holidays, but even this is far from universal. Apart from that, hours vary from day to day, so it's best to check each case separately.

Shopping

Although the range of choice in shops has been increasing, Poland is by no means a shopper's paradise, and many local products have disappeared entirely—thanks to the manufacturing slump that has followed the economic reforms. But Polish leather products are well designed, of high quality, and cheaper than their Western counterparts. The best region for leather is the south, Kraków for more sophisticated products, the mountains for folk equivalents. Amber and silver jewelry are on sale all over Poland, but it is on the Baltic coast that amber is found, and this is the best place to search for unusual pieces. Wood, woven, and embroidered folk arts and crafts are often intriguing to Western visitors and are to be found in Cepelia stores all over Poland; if possible, try to visit local folk artists' workshops. Glassware, including cut glass, is beautifully designed and relatively cheap. And, of course, anywhere in the country, you will find Polish vodka (*wódka*): **Polonez** or **Żytnia** are clear rye vodkas;

Żubrówka is pale green and flavored with bison grass from the Białowieska forest; *Jarzębiak* is flavored with rowan berries.

Sports and Outdoor Activities

Bicycling The flat areas of the north are perhaps best for biking, but there are many parts of the country where you can enjoy touring tracks and byroads. Renting bicycles is not easy but can be done. Contact the bicycle section of **PTTK** (Krakowskie Przedmieście 4–6, Warsaw, tel. 022/26–30–11). Tourist information offices in the provinces can also advise you.

Boating and Sailing The Masurian lake district (*Mazury*) is a paradise for these sports. Local tourist enterprises there rent boats; consult the tourist offices for details. The city of Giżycko is a good place to start.

Camping In theory, you are allowed to camp only at recognized sites, but there are plenty of these. Standards vary and many are now being privatized, making the situation a little uncertain. Local branches of PTTK are a good place to seek information.

Hiking There are endless possibilities for hiking in Poland. All national parks have well-marked trails that cover some of the most beautiful countryside. The most spectacular terrain is in the south, in the Tatra Mountains, Podhale region, and the wild and deserted Bieszczady region in the southeast (on the Slovak and Ukrainian borders). The national parks have the additional advantage of providing overnight accommodations at regular intervals in walkers' huts and hostels, which can, however, be fairly primitive. Elsewhere in the country, it is more difficult to guarantee that you'll find a bed at the right point on your route.

Skiing Southern Poland is the main region for winter sports, with skiing facilities both in the Tatras and the Podhale region and farther west in the Beskid Mountains. Here, Szczyrk has recently become a very popular center. The facilities in these resorts can be overcrowded, and you should not expect very sophisticated après-ski. For cross-country skiing, there is also good terrain in the northeast, for example around Mrągowo.

Water Sports The Mazury region provides the best opportunities for water sports, especially waterskiing. The main centers are Giżycko, Mrągowo, and Wilkasy.

Dining

The traditional, waiter-service restaurant is still the main feature of the dining scene in Poland, across all price ranges. It is usually assumed that you can take time to enjoy a leisurely meal, but if you are in a hurry there is more variety than ever. The old low-cost, self-service "milk bars" (*bar mleczny*) and cheap cafeterias are fast disappearing, replaced by pizza parlors and other fast-food outlets of a kind that will be familiar to Western visitors. Many cafés serve hot snacks alongside the traditional tea, coffee, and cakes. And if you are really pressed for time, you will nearly always be able to find a street stall (usually housed in a small white caravan) that serves *zapiekanki*: French bread toasted with cheese and mushrooms.

Even Poland's most ardent fans will admit that it does not have one of the world's great cuisines. And the place to taste really good Polish food is in private homes, not restaurants. Nonetheless, many privately owned restaurants have been trying to revive traditions of "old Polish cuisine," and standards all around are slowly improving.

Old Polish cuisine uses a great deal of butter and cream, as well as many honey-based sauces for sweet-and-sour dishes. If all this sounds rather rich, most restaurants in cities will also serve a more traditional menu, with sauceless grills and steaks. Soups are invariably excellent, often thick and nourishing, with lots of peas and beans. Clear beet soup, *barszcz*, is regarded as the most traditional, but soured barley soup, *żurek*, should be tried at least once. Pickled or soused herring is also a favorite Polish entrée, and usually very good. But the Polish chef's greatest love affair is with pork, in all its varieties, including suckling pig and wild boar. Traditional sausages, *kiełbasy*, usually dried and smoked, are delicious: *Myśliwska* (hunter's sausage) is regarded as the greatest delicacy. You should not miss another hunter's dish, *bigos*, which is made from soured and fresh cabbage, cooked (for several days or weeks) together with many different kinds of meat and sausage. There is not a major tradition in Poland of serving desserts to follow meals. *Kompot* (stewed fruit) is customarily served at an early stage in the meal, and you sip the juice rather than eat the fruit. Expensive restaurants in cities will offer cakes and pastries; otherwise you can go on to a café for coffee and one of Poland's excellent cakes, perhaps one of the great range of cheesecakes offered.

A somewhat random selection of French, German, and Eastern European wines can usually be found in restaurants; the last often represent the best value for the money, especially the Hungarian reds (such as *Egri Bikavér*, "Bull's Blood of Eger") or one of the Bulgarian *Sofia* varieties.

Although upscale city restaurants have adapted to Western mealtimes, and some offer lunch starting at noon, Poles traditionally eat their main meal of the day (*obiad*, dinner) between 3 and 5. Many restaurants therefore open at 1 and do not get into full swing until midafternoon. They also tend to close relatively early, and it may be difficult to order a meal after 9. A few restaurants offer fixed-price meals between about 1 and 5; these do not always represent a savings over à la carte prices.

Like so much else in today's Poland, official ratings of restaurants (from category *Lux* down through *S* and 1 to 4) have long been out of date and are currently in flux. Certainly the top categories (*L*, *S*, and 1) do not tell you a great deal, and many new restaurants remain uncategorized, regardless of their quality.

Although standards of hygiene are improving steadily, it can still be inadvisable to eat meat dishes in cheap restaurants in summer; hors d'oeuvres made with mayonnaise should be avoided. You are advised not to purchase ice cream from small provincial cake shops or wayside stands, as salmonella outbreaks are not uncommon.

Ratings Prices are for one person and include three courses and service but no drinks. Prices are given in U.S. dollars.

Category	Warsaw	Other Areas
$$$$	over $30	over $25
$$$	$20–$30	$15–$25
$$	$10–$20	$7–$15
$	under $10	under $7

Lodging

Lodging options in most parts of Poland are still fairly restricted. State control of lodging facilities was virtually absolute until 1990, and private investment has not yet had time to make a real mark in this sector. Cheap and comfortable bed-and-breakfast accommodations in private homes or pensions are widely available only in the mountains or on the coast, look for signs in windows with the words *pokoje gościnne* (guest rooms), or inquire at tourist-information offices in resorts. In cities, private bed and breakfast accommodations are to be used only as a last resort; they are often run by disreputable landladies who charge exorbitant prices.

Some privately owned hotels and wayside inns opened as long as a decade ago, and their number has increased rapidly since 1989. But often in the cities, your choice will be limited to hotels in, or just emerging from, the state sector. Only a small number of hotels—for example, the Marriott in Warsaw—are owned and managed by international chains; all other hotels bearing familiar names (Holiday Inn, Novotel) are run by Orbis, the state travel conglomerate, which is shortly to be privatized. Orbis hotels throughout the country offer a good international standard of accommodation, usually at international prices. Standards at municipally owned hotels vary enormously; have a good look at your room before checking in. **Gromada,** the peasant cooperative, runs excellent, inexpensive hotels. **PTTK,** the Polish Tourist Association, also has a network of relatively inexpensive hotels throughout Poland, but single and double rooms are limited in number and most of the accommodations are in dormitories.

Since 1990, when state controls on hotel prices were abandoned, prices have fluctuated greatly. If you check rooms and price lists carefully, you may find real bargains outside the major cities. Service charges are included in the room price, but value-added tax—introduced in July 1993—is usually quoted as an additional percentage, ranging from 20% in the case of top-category hotels, down to 7%. Breakfast is also usually included in the price quoted by hotels for overnight accommodation, but this is not universal and it is worth checking. Government star ratings (from five down to one) are outdated and refer to ownership category and size as much as to standards; they do, however, give an indication of price, which by no means always reflects the quality of the accommodations offered. Bathrooms may be fitted with either tubs or showers, and this is not necessarily reflected in the price. High-season prices on the coast (May to September) and in the southern mountain region (December to March and July through August) are up to 50% higher than off-season prices. Seasonal variations elsewhere in the country are less marked, apart from brief high-season rates for special occasions, as in Poznań during the trade fair.

Ratings The following chart is based on a rate for two people in a double room, with bath or shower and breakfast. Prices are given in U.S. dollars.

Category	Cost
$$$$	over $200
$$$	$100–$200

$$	$50–$100
$	under $50

Warsaw

Your first view of Warsaw is likely to produce an impression of monotony and gray concrete, broken suddenly by a curious wedding-cake edifice rising majestically in the center of the city: Stalin's 1950s gift of the Palace of Culture and Science. An American entrepreneur is currently attempting to purchase it, in order to cut off the elaborate pinnacle and crenellated outbuildings, and turn it into a skyscraper that will house a business center. And Varsovians, after decades of mocking this symbol of Russian imperialism, are shyly admitting to a certain sentimental attachment to it. It will probably still be there, to act as a useful orientation point to visitors, in 1995.

Central Warsaw's predominating bleakness is a heritage of the city's 20th-century history: 75% destroyed by Hitler's armies in 1944, it was rebuilt in the functional styles of the 1950s and '60s and then, as economic times grew harder, largely left to decay. The local topography does not help: Warsaw is entirely flat, apart from the drop down the Vistula embankment, which runs through the city north to south.

But as you explore, you will forget your initial reservations. Fragments of the old Warsaw that survived the war acquire a special poignancy in their isolation: odd rows of Art Nouveau tenements like those on the south side of the great square around the Palace of Culture and Science or on ulica Wilcza; the elegant aleje Ujazdowskie, now the diplomatic quarter, leading to the Belvedere Palace (the official residence of President Lech Wałęsa); and the Łazienki palace and park. The reconstructed areas of the city—the historic Old Town area, rebuilt brick by brick during the 1950s; the Royal Castle; the Ujazdowski Palace—are a moving tribute to the Poles' ability to survive and preserve their history and traditions.

Moreover, Warsaw is at last getting a face-lift, and the pace of change is so fast that even locals can't keep up. The butcher shop where customers have faithfully lined up for meat over the past 25 years closes down one evening and is replaced the next day by a smart white-tiled computer store. The local grocery turns overnight into a well-lit boutique selling imported fashions at prices that seem like a king's ransom. All this is brightening the face of the city; gleaming paint and tiles in strong primary colors, clean windows, and fierce strip lighting are all a novelty in Warsaw. While some may live to regret the disappearance of the local shoemaker or tailor—those picturesque survivors that communism froze in a time warp—the new arrivals undoubtedly create a more cheerful and vibrant image. Visitors in search of "Old World charm" may be disappointed, but they can console themselves with the thought that the range of facilities available in many areas—notably dining out—is markedly improved.

Like all other capital cities, Warsaw is often in a hurry, full of out-of-town visitors, pushy and unconcerned. It can seem rude and heartless. But relax, turn a corner, sit down at a café table, and observe the smiles, elegant manners, and animated conversation all around. Warsaw, like all other cities, is a place of contrasts that are worth exploring.

Important Addresses and Numbers

Tourist Information COIT (plac Zamkowy 1/13, tel. 02/635-18-81), on Castle Square on the edge of the Old Town, is open 9-6 weekdays, 11-6 weekends. Orbis has many offices in the city, but not all specialize in helping foreign visitors. Go to the ORBIS desk at any major hotel or one of the following offices: ulica Marszałkowska 142 (corner of ulica Królewska, tel. 022/27-36-73) or Krakowskie Przedmieście 13 (tel. 022/26-16-67).

Embassies All three embassies listed below are on or just off of aleje Jerozolimskie; the British Consulate is closer to the center of town.

U.S. Embassy, aleje Ujazdowskie 29-31, tel. 02/628-30-41.
Canadian Embassy, ulica Matejki 1-5, tel. 022/29-80-51.
British Embassy, aleja Róż 1, tel. 02/628-10-01.
British Consulate, ulica Emilii Plater 28, tel. 02/625-30-30.

Emergencies For **police,** dial 997. For an **ambulance,** dial 999. This will link you with the central emergency station on the corner of ulica Hoża and ulica Poznańska; hospitals do not have emergency rooms.

Doctors You can schedule same-day appointments at the following centrally located clincs: **Izis,** ulica Marszałkowska 55-73, tel. 022/29-34-25 (open weekdays 7 AM-8 PM, Sat. 8 AM-10 AM); **Prywatna Przychodnia Lekarzy Specjalistów,** ulica Marszałkowska 62, tel. 02/628-39-26 (open weekdays 8-8).

Dentists **Stołeczna Przychodnia Stomatoligiczna,** ulica Chmielna 18, tel. 022/27-95-28; **Primadent,** ulica A. Struga 1/2, tel. 022/22-99-18.

Where to Change Money The **Kantor Wymiany Walut** at ulica Marszałkowska 66, on the corner of ulica Wilcza, has swift, friendly service and usually offers slightly better rates than hotels and banks (open weekdays 11-7, Sat. 9-2). Two other options are **WIMPEX,** ulica Chmielna 26, tel. 022/26-06-66 (open weekdays 11-7) and **TEBOS,** at the Central Railway Station on aleje Jerozolimskie, at the foot of the staircase leading from the main hall to the access passage to platforms (open 24 hours a day; exercise caution, however—the central station is a haunt of pickpockets).

English-Language Bookstores **Prus** (Krakowskie Przedmieście 7, tel. 022/26-18-35) and **Batax** (Al. Jerozolimskie 61, tel. 022/25-41-46) have a reasonable selection of English-language books. Otherwise, try the secondhand bookstore **Logos** (aleje Ujazdowskie 16, tel. 02/621-38-67), which usually offers quite a wide range of fiction and nonfiction.

Late-Night Pharmacies The following pharmacies (*apteka*) are open 24 hours a day: ulica Zielna 45, tel. 022/20-92-32; ulica Leszno 38, tel. 022/32-13-92; and ulica Puławska 39, tel. 022/49-82-05. The **Swiss Pharmacy** (aleja Róż 2, tel. 02/628-94-71, open 10-6) carries a variety of Western medications.

Travel Agencies **Thomas Cook** (ul. Nowy Świat 64, tel. 022/26-47-29) is a centrally located travel agency. **American Express** is at ulica Krakowskie Przedmieście 11, (tel. 02/635-20-02).

Arriving and Departing by Plane

Airports and Airlines Warsaw's **Okęcie Airport** (tel. 02/650-46-28) is 7 kilometers (4 miles) south of the city center. Terminal 1 serves European and transatlantic flights, while Terminal 2 deals with domestic traffic. **LOT,** the Polish airline (Al. Jerozolimskie 65/79, tel. 02/630-50-07, for reservations tel. 952), takes the lion's share of flights to and from

Warsaw. Other airlines flying to Warsaw include **British Airways** (tel. 02/628–94–31; at Okęcie, tel. 022/46–05–72); **Air France** (tel. 02/628–12–81; at Okęcie, tel. 022/46–03–03); and **Lufthansa** (tel. 022/27–54–36; at Okęcie, tel. 022/46–25–27).

Between the Airport and Downtown The direct route to downtown, where almost all hotels are located, is along aleje Żwirki i Wigury and ulica Raszyńska. Traffic can be heavy here in peak afternoon rush hours (3–5), and taxis may divert along aleje Lotników or ulica Wawelska and aleje Niepodległości. City buses, which depart from Terminal 1 and take the direct route are cheap but can be very crowded by the time they reach the city center; Terminal 2 is less well served by city bus lines. Some hotels operate a minibus service from the airport.

By Bus Warsaw city transport Bus 175 leaves Okęcie every 10 minutes during peak hours and every 14 minutes at other times. It runs past almost all major downtown hotels and is reliable and cheap. Purchase tickets at the airport RUCH kiosks or from the automatic vending machine outside the arrivals hall for zł 6,000 and cancel one ticket per person and item of luggage; the ride downtown takes 20 to 30 minutes in off-peak periods. A bus marked "Airport–City" leaves Terminal 1 every 20 minutes, beginning on the hour, and stops at all the major hotels and Central Station. Tickets cost zł 25,000, and the trip takes 15 to 20 minutes.

By Taxi The Okęcie Airport authority recently licensed a special fleet of marked taxis that stand directly outside the exits from the terminals. You can prepurchase a voucher for your trip at an office inside the airport, directly beside the main exit; the charge is around zł. 250,000 for the trip into town, which takes 10 to 15 minutes in off-peak periods. You would be wise to ignore taxi touts and unmarked vehicles. The Marriott hotel operates its own fleet of marked taxis that shuttle guests between the airport and hotel. If none of these services are available, try calling the **Radio Taxi** service (tel. 919).

Arriving and Departing by Car, Train, and Bus

By Car Within the city, a car can be more of a problem than a convenience. Metro construction has closed many roads in the city center, creating major snarls. Parking, though largely unregulated, causes difficulties. There is a real threat of theft—of contents, parts, or the entire car—if you leave a Western model unattended, and it is not easy to get quick service or repairs. If you do bring your car, leave it overnight in a guarded car park.

By Train Warsaw's **Dworzec Centralny** (Central Station) (tel. 022/25–50–00; international rail information, 022/20–45–12; domestic rail information, 022/20–03–61) is, as the name implies, right in the heart of the city, at aleje Jerozolimskie 54, between the Marriott and Holiday Inn hotels. The station is very conveniently situated but has recently been plagued by teams of pickpockets and muggers who prey on passengers as they board or leave trains. Since Warszawa Centralna is only a transit station, you might therefore be wise to join or leave your train at its terminus station. For trains running to the south and west (Poznań, Kraków, Wrocław, Łódź), use the eastern station, **Warszawa Wschodnia** (ul. Kijowska, tel. 022/19–06–79); for trains running east, go to the western station, **Warszawa Zachodnia** (in the western district of Czyste, just north of aleje Jerozolimskie, tel. 022/36–59–34).

Local trains run from **Warszawa Śródmieście**, next to Dworzec Centralny on aleje Jerozolimskie (tel. 02/628–47–41) or from **Dworzec Wileński** (ul. Targowa, tel. 022/18–35–21).

Even though computers have been introduced at most of the mainline stations, purchasing tickets can still be a time-consuming business. You can prepurchase tickets up to a month in advance at most stations, and the Central Station offers a telephone order and home delivery service (tel. 022/25–60–33). Orbis offices also sell rail tickets.

By Bus Warsaw's main bus station, **Dworzec PKS** (just north of aleje Jerozolimskie in Czyste, next to the Warszawa Zachodnia railway station, tel. 022/23–63–94) serves most long-distance express routes and most tourist destinations west of the city (such as Chopin's birthplace, at Żelazowa Wola). Local services for points north of the city (such as the Puszcza Kampinoska) run from **Dworzec PKS Marymont** in the northern district of Żoliborz (corner of ul. Marymoncka and ul. Żeromskiego, tel. 022/34–74–44); buses headed east leave from **Dworzec PKS Stadion** (at the intersection of ul. Targowa, ul. Jana Zamoyskiego, and al. Zieleniecka, on the east bank of the Vistula, tel. 022/18–54–73). Tickets for all destinations can be purchased at the main bus station, which is often very crowded.

International bus services operated by private companies usually arrive and depart from the east side of the central railway station on aleje Jerozolimskie.

Getting Around

Although 1½ million people live in Warsaw, which stretches more than 32 kilometers (20 miles) in each direction, the sights of greatest interest to most tourists are concentrated primarily in two areas: Śródmieście, Warsaw's downtown, along ulica Marszałkowska; and Stare Miasto, the Old Town, just over 2 kilometers (1½ miles) away and centered on Rynek Starego Miasta. Both areas are best explored on foot; public transportation, though cheap and efficient, can be uncomfortably crowded. Taxis are readily available and are often the most convenient option for covering longer distances.

By Tram Trams are the fastest means of public transport since they are not affected by traffic hold-ups. Purchase tickets from RUCH kiosks for zł 6,000 and cancel one ticket in the machine on the tram for each ride. Trams run on a north–south and east–west grid system along most of the main city routes, pulling up automatically at all stops. Each tram has a diagram of the system.

By Bus A trip on a Warsaw city bus costs zł 4,000; you have to purchase tickets in advance at a RUCH kiosk and cancel one in the machine on the bus for each ride. Buses, which halt at all stops along their route, are numbered from 100 up. Express buses are numbered from E-1 upward: Buses numbered 500–599 stop at selected stops. Check carefully on the information board at the bus stop before boarding. Night buses (marked from 600 up) operate between 11 PM and 5 AM; the fare is zł 12,000, but for these buses you can either buy tickets directly from the driver or use two zł 6,000 tickets.

By Taxi Since drivers are not allowed by law to pick up fares when flagged down in the street, the best place to pick up a taxi is at a standard city cab rank (marked TAXI). Avoid taxi ranks outside hotels (apart from chartered hotel fleets), as you are likely to be charged far more than the going rate. The standard charge for 1½ kilometers (1 mile) is about zł 20,000, and many taxis now have meters showing the exact fare; otherwise they will have a sign on the meter showing that the fare indicated is to be multiplied by at least 500. It is not customary to tip taxi drivers.

The **Radio Taxi** service (dial 919) is reliable and efficient, but you will usually need a Polish speaker to place your order. There is no additional charge for ordering a cab by phone.

Opening and Closing Times

Although standard Polish opening hours still apply for most Warsaw institutions, a number of food stores are now open late at night, and most shops are open Saturday 9–2.

Guided Tours

Orbis is still the only reliably established agency that offers guided tours by bus, minibus, or limousine. Most tours start out from one of the major Orbis hotels and can be booked either there or at one of the Orbis offices listed above (*see* Important Addresses and Numbers, *above*).

Orientation Orbis's standard half-day tour covers the Old Town, Central Warsaw, and Łazienki Park. The all-day tour also takes in Wilanów.

Personal Guides Orbis can arrange to have a qualified guide, registered with the Polish Tourist Association (PTTK), give you a customized tour of the city. Rates start at $50 a day for individual tourists with their own means of transportation.

Highlights for First-Time Visitors

Muzeum Narodowe (National Museum, *see* Tour 2)
Rynek Starego Miasta (Old Town Square, *see* Tour 1)
Łazienki Palace and Park (*see* Tour 2)
Wilanów Palace and Park (*see* Tour 2)
Zamek Królewski (Royal Castle, *see* Tour 1)

Exploring Warsaw

The geographical core and political center of Poland since 1611, when King Zygmunt III moved the capital here from Kraków, Warsaw (Warszawa) will doubtless shock the first-time visitor with its bleak postwar architecture. When one learns, however, of the history of this city, dismay is sure to turn first to amazement and then to deep appreciation for the surviving one third of its inhabitants who so energetically rebuilt their city—literally from the ashes—starting in 1945. Warsaw was in the worst location possible during World War II, and perhaps nowhere else in Europe are there so many reminders of that time; plaques can be found all over describing the multiple massacres of Polish citizens by the Nazis. (The city's darkest hours came in April 1943, when the inhabitants of the Jewish ghetto rose up in arms against the Nazis and were viciously and brutally put down, and in the summer of 1944, when the Warsaw Uprising was suppressed.)

Amid the drabness of modern Warsaw you will find a few architectural attractions. Although most of the buildings in central Warsaw were built in an austere, quasi-Gothic Stalinist style, a large number of prewar buildings were carefully restored or, in many cases, completely reconstructed from old prints and paintings. A case in point is the beautiful **Rynek Starego Miasta** (Old Town Square). Closed to all traffic except horses and carriages, the cobblestone square is an impressive reproduction of the original market place. The streets that radiate from the square, with their handsome burcher's houses, churches, and palaces, have likewise been painstakingly rebuilt. The Royal Palace, which houses a museum, is the greatest of the rebuilt monuments. Just outside the palace is the Zygmunt Column, one of two symbols of Warsaw—the other being the mermaid statue on the banks of the Wisła River.

Apart from the embankment carved out by the Wisła, which runs through the city north to south, Warsaw is entirely flat. Most sights, attractions, and hotels lie to the west of the river. Major thoroughfares include **aleje Jerozolimskie,** which runs east–west, and **Nowy Świat,** which runs north–south through a main shopping district, passes the university, and ends at the entrance to the **Stare Miasto** (Old Town). Be careful about Nowy Świat: Its name changes six times between its starting point in Wilanów (where it's called aleja Wilanowska) and its terminus (where it's named Krakowskie Prezedmieście). To orient yourself, start at the central train station, the Marriott Hotel, or the Palace of Culture, all of which sit within a block of one another on aleje Jerozolimskie (the Marriott, a glass skyscraper, and the Palace of Culture, the enormous brick monstrosity that looks like a wedding cake, are the two most visible buildings in town). Walk west toward the river on aleje Jerozolimskie two blocks to Nowy Świat. Heading north, this street is a main shopping district; in about 20 minutes the street will terminate at **plac Zamkowy,** the plaza that marks the entrance to the Old Town. North of here is **Nowe Miasto** (New Town), a primarily residential area, and west lie **Muranów** and **Mirów,** former Jewish districts. **Praga,** a poorer quarter of workers and artisans that emerged from the war fairly intact, and the enormous **Zoological Park,** are situated east of the Wisła.

Tour 1: The Old Town *Numbers in the margin correspond to points of interest on the Warsaw map.*

The Old Town is, of course, not at all "old" but dates from the 1950s, when it was reconstructed from the total ruin sustained in World War II. But the loving attention paid to detail in the work of reconstruction and the weathering of the past 40 years mean that the atmosphere of the place survives. The Old Town is for those who enjoy museums, art, and historic architecture, away from the bustle of everyday city life. The Old Town is closed to traffic, and in its narrow streets you can relax and leave the 20th century behind for a while.

❶ Start your visit beside the **Zygmunt Column** on **plac Zamkowy** (Castle Square). A popular rendezvous, this column honors King Zygmunt III Wasa, king of Poland and Sweden, who in the early 17th century transferred the capital of the country from Kraków to Warsaw. Avoiding the skateboarders who have recently made the gently sloping square their province, walk over to the left-side entrance to Warsaw's **Zamek Królewski** (Royal Castle). The princes of Mazovia first built a residence on this spot overlooking the Vistula during the 14th century; its present Renaissance form dates from the reign of King Sigismund III, who needed a magnificent palace for his new capital. Reconstructed later than the Old Town, in the 1970s, it now gleams as it did in its earliest years, with gilt, marble, and wall paintings; it houses impressive art collections—including the famous views of Warsaw by Bernardo Bellotto (also known as Canaletto)—and period furniture. Tours with an English-speaking

Archikatedralna
Bazylika św. Jana, **9**

Barbakan, **4**

Femina Cinema, **36**

Former Headquarters
of the Polish
Communist Party, **25**

Galeria Zachęta, **17**

Gestapo
Headquarters, **30**

Grób Nieznanego
Żołnierza, **15**

Jewish Cemetery, **39**

Jewish Historical
Institute and
Museum, **35**

Kościół
Karmelitów, **12**

Kościół Najświętszej
Marii Panny, **6**

Kościół św.
Aleksandra, **27**

Kościół św. Anny, **10**

Kościół św. Krzyża, **22**

Kościół Wizytek, **21**

Muzeum
Etnograficzne, **18**

Muzeum
Narodowe, **26**

Ogród Saski, **16**

Pałac Belweder, **33**

Pałac Czapskich, **19**

Pałac
Kazanowskich, **11**

Pałac Krasińskich, **7**

Pałac
Łazienkowski, **32**

Pałac Ostrogskich, **23**

Pałac Potockich, **13**

Park
Łazienkowski, **31**

Park Ujazdowski, **29**

Plac Zamkowy, **1**

Pomnik Bohaterów
Getta, **37**

Pomnik Bohaterów
Warszawy
1939–1945, **8**

Radziwiłł Palace, **14**

Rynek Nowego
Miasta, **5**

Rynek Starego
Miasta, **2**

Sejm, **28**

Stara Prochownia, **3**

Statue of Nicholas
Copernicus, **24**

Umschlagplatz, **38**

Warsaw
University, **20**

Wilanów Palace, **34**

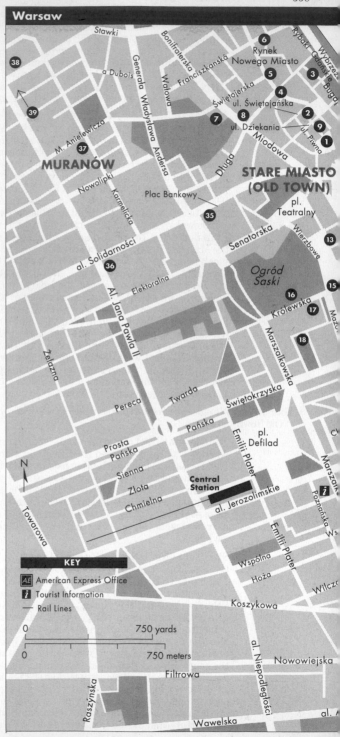

Warsaw

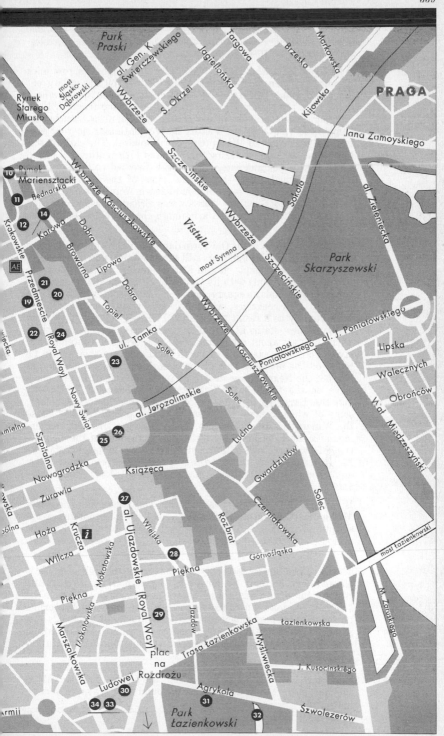

guide begin from the side entrance every hour or by previous appointment. *Pl. Zamkowy 4, tel. 02/635–39–95. Admission: zł 60,000 adults, zł 30,000 children. Tours start hourly from side entrance. Open Tues.–Sat. 10–2:30, Sun. 9–2:30.*

When you leave the castle, make your way along narrow ulica Kanonia and then ulica Jezuicka. Along the way you'll pass the great cracked **Zygmunt bell** in the middle of a quiet, cobbled square, where it fell from the cathedral tower during the bombardment of 1939. You might turn through one of the archways on ulica Jezuicka and admire the view over the Vistula before continuing on your way to the **Rynek Starego Miasta** (Old Town Square). The earliest settlers came to this spot during the 10th and 11th centuries. Legend has it that a peasant named Wars was directed to the site by a mermaid named Sawa—hence the name of the city in Polish, *Warszawa.* (Sawa has been immortalized in Warsaw's official emblem.) In the 14th century Warsaw was already a walled city, and in 1413 its citizens obtained a borough charter from the princes of Mazovia.

The present layout of the Old Town dates from this time, and traces of the original Gothic buildings still surround the Old Town Square. At No. 21, for example, is the **Klucznikowska mansion** (now the **Krokodyl** restaurant) with its Gothic brick portal and cellars. The appearance of today's square, however, largely dates from the late 16th and 17th centuries, when Warsaw's wealth and importance grew rapidly as a result of the 1569 Polish-Lithuanian union and Warsaw's new status as capital city. The great merchant families of the city set about rebuilding their properties in contemporary style. Four fine examples of these Renaissance mansions can be found on the northern side of the square: the **Talenti mansion** at No. 38, the **Negro House** at No. 36 (note the scuplture of a black slave on the facade), the **Szlichtyngowska mansion** at No. 34, and the **Baryczka mansion** at No. 32. These historical homes, some of which contain Renaissance ceiling paintings, now house the **Warsaw Historical Museum.** The museum offers daily screenings of a short documentary film made in 1945 about the destruction of Warsaw. *Rynek Starego Miasta 28–42, tel. 02/635–16–25. Admission: zł 20,000 adults, 10,000 children. Open Tues. and Thurs. noon–7; Wed., Fri., and Sat. 10–3:30; Sun. 10:30–4:30.*

If you are interested in Polish writers, you might visit the **Adam Mickiewicz Museum of Literature,** at No. 20, which contains manuscripts, mementos, and portraits, particularly from the Romantic period. *Tel. 022/31–40–61. Admission: zł 10,000. Open Tues.–Sat. 10–2:30.*

The Old Town Square is usually very busy, even though no traffic is allowed and there is no longer a formal market. Artists and craftspeople of all kinds still sell their wares out-of-doors here in the summer, but don't expect many bargains—the tourist is their prime target. Musical performances are often held here on weekends on a stage erected at the north end. Horse-drawn cabs await the visitor, who wants to pay zł 500,000 to be driven around the Old Town in traditional style.

Time Out **Hortex,** at Rynek Starego Miasta 3–9, has a large open-air café in summer; at the same address on the ground floor is a quick-service lunch bar.

From the northeast corner of the square, take Krzywe Koło (Crooked Wheel) Street to the reconstructed ramparts of the Old Town wall. From this corner, which is graced by a towering stone mermaid known as the *Warszawska Syrenka*, you can again look out over the Vistula and also over Warsaw's New Town (Nowe Miasto), stretching to the north beyond the city walls. As you look out over the town walls and down the Vistula embankment, you will see the Ⓙ **Stara Prochownia** (Old Powder Tower) on ulica Boleść, just past the intersection with ulica Bugaj; this has now been turned into an interesting theater, a popular venue for poetry readings, music, and drama.

Walk to the left along the top of the city wall to the pinnacled, Ⓞ redbrick **Barbakan**, the mid-16th-century stronghold that now houses a tiny private gallery at the top of a narrow staircase; less successful artists festoon the walls outside with their wares. Pass through the gateway and continue along ulica Freta. The Baroque **Kościół Dominkanów** (Dominican Church) at No. 8–10 was badly damaged in the aftermath of the 1943 uprising, when the adjoining monastery served as a field hospital for wounded insurrectionists. A few steps farther down ulice Freta is the house in which Marie Curie was born; a small museum inside—the **Muzeum Marii Skłodowskiej-Curie**—is dedicated to the great physicist, chemist, winner of two Nobel Prizes, and discoverer of radium. *Ul. Freta 16, tel. 022/31–80–92. Admission: zł 10,000 adults, zł 5,000 children. Open Tues.–Sat. 10–4:30; Sun. 10–2:30.*

Ⓢ One block farther down, ulica Freta opens up into the leafy **Rynek Nowego Miasta** (New Town Square), slightly more irregular and relaxed than its Old Town counterpart. Facing you on the far side is the cool white **Kościół Sakramentek** (Church of the Sisters of the Blessed Sacrament), built as a thanksgiving offering by King John Sobieski's queen, Marysieńka, after his victory against the Turks at Vienna in 1683.

If you cross over the square to ulica Kościelna, passing houses with curiously stark and formalized wall paintings, you will see the old-Ⓞ est church in the New Town, the **Kościół Najświętszej Marii Panny** (St. Mary's Church). Built as a parish church for the New Town by the princes of Mazovia in the early 15th century, St. Mary's was destroyed and rebuilt many times throughout its history. The Gothic bell tower dates from the early 16th century. *Przyrynek 2.*

Return through the square to ulica Freta, then take ulica Świętojerska to ulica Bonifraterska, which once formed the eastern boundary between "Aryan" and Jewish Warsaw. Facing you as you emerge from ulica Świętojerska is the Chinese Embassy, built on the site of a notorious brush factory at the entrance to Warsaw's Nazi-ordained Jewish ghetto. This was the scene of heroic fighting during the 1943 Ghetto Uprising, though it was later destroyed when the Germans systematically torched the city with flamethrowers.

Turn left, passing on your right the late-17th-century Baroque Ⓞ **Pałac Krasińskich** (Krasinski Palace), which now houses the historic prints collection of Poland's National Library. On the corner of ulica Długa you will see yet another reminder of World War II: the Ⓞ **Pomnik Bohaterów Warszawy 1939–1945** (Monument to the Heroes of the Warsaw Uprising), unveiled in 1989. Massive bronze figures raise defiant fists above the opening to sewers used by Polish resistance fighters to escape from the Nazis.

Return along ulica Długa to the Old Town Square and take ulica Świętojańska back to the Royal Castle. On your left, halfway down, you will see the **Archikatedralna Bazylika świętego Jana** (Cathedral Church of St. John), which gives the street its name. St. John's was built at the turn of the 14th century; coronations of the Polish kings took place here from the 16th to the 18th century. The crypts contain the tombs of the last two princes of Mazovia, those of the archbishops of Warsaw, and those of such famous Poles as the 19th-century, Nobel Prize–winning novelist Henryk Sienkiewicz, the author of *Quo Vadis?*

Time Out | **Zapiecek** (ul. Piwna 34–36) is a large, friendly café where you can also select from a short menu of hot dishes.

On the left-hand side of the entrance to the cathedral is the early 17th-century **Jesuit Church,** founded by King John Sobieski, the Victor of Vienna. Throughout the postwar years, a visit to this church at Eastertime was considered a must by Varsovians: Its Gethsemane decorations always contained a hidden political message (in 1985, for example, the risen Christ had the face of Father Jerzy Popiełuszko, the Warsaw priest who was murdered the previous year by members of the Polish security service).

Tour 2: The Royal Route This tour of historic Warsaw moves along the Royal Route that led from the Royal Castle to the summer palace at Wilanów. The first stage of the route is **Krakowskie Przedmieście,** a wide thoroughfare lined with fine churches and elegant mansions. On your left immediately south of plac Zamkowy is the **Kościół świętej Anny** (St. Anne's Church), built in 1454 by Anne, princess of Mazovia. It was rebuilt in high-Baroque style after destruction during the Swedish invasions in the 17th century; thanks to recent redecoration and regilding it once again glows in its original splendor. A plaque on the wall outside marks the spot where Pope John Paul II celebrated Mass in 1980, during his first visit to Poland after his election to the papacy.

A hundred yards farther, the steeply sloping, cobbled ulica Bednarska leads down to **Rynek Mariensztacki,** a quiet, leafy 18th-century square that is worth a detour. At Krakowskie Przedmieście 62, on the corner of ulica Bednarska, is the **Pałac Kazanowskich** (Kazanowski Palace). Built in the mid-17th century, it was given a neoclassical front elevation in the 19th century. The courtyard at the rear still contains massive late-Renaissance buttresses and is worth a visit because of its plaque commemorating Zagloba's fight with the monkeys from Sienkiewicz's historical novel *The Deluge.* In the small garden to your right as you pass ulica Bednarska stands a monument to the great Polish Romantic poet Adam Mickiewicz. It was here that Warsaw University students gathered in March 1968, after a performance of Mickiewicz's hitherto banned play *Forefathers' Eve,* and set in motion the events that led to the toppling of Poland's long-serving communist leader Władysław Gomułka.

Note on your left the late-17th-century Baroque **Kościół Karmelitów** (Church of the Discalced Carmelites), and on your right at Krakowskie Przedmieście 15, through a narrow wrought-iron gate, the charming semi-Rococo 18th-century **Pałac Potockich,** which now houses the Ministry of Arts.

At No. 46–48, on your left, is the **Radziwiłł Palace.** Built in the 17th century by the Radziwiłł family (into which Jackie Kennedy's sister later married), this palace at one time functioned as the administrative office of the czarist occupiers. In 1955 the Warsaw Pact was signed here, and now the palace serves as the headquarters for the Presidium of the Council of Ministers. In the forecourt is an equestrian statue of Prince Józef Poniatowski, a nephew of the last king of Poland, and one of Napoleon's marshals. He was wounded and drowned in the Elster River during the Battle of the Nations at Leipzig in 1813, following the disastrous retreat of Napoleon's Grande Armée from Russia.

Adjoining this complex, on the corner of ulica Karowa, is the newly renovated **Hotel Bristol,** a fin-de-siècle gem where Ignacy Paderewski, the great pianist and Polish patriot, made his headquarters upon his return to Poland after World War I to take up the office of prime minister. Across the street you will see the slightly less illustrious **Hotel Europejski,** completed in 1877.

Time Out The café of the **Europejski** still has palm trees and a grand piano despite the recently introduced yellow-plastic furniture. It serves sandwiches as well as the usual cakes and drinks.

Continue past the Europejski and turn right on ulica Królewska to reach plac Piłsudskiego. To your right is the **Opera House,** built in the 1820s and reconstructed after the war. In front of you is the
⑮ **Grób Nieznanego Żołnierza** (Tomb of the Unknown Soldier), a surviving fragment of the early 18th-century Saxon Palace, which used to stand here. Built as a memorial after World War I, the tomb contains the body of a Polish soldier brought from the eastern battlefields of the Polish-Soviet war of 1919–1920—a fact that was not much mentioned in the 45 years of communist rule after World War II. Ceremonial changes of the guard take place here at 10 AM on Sunday; many visitors may be faintly surprised to see that the Polish Army still uses the goose step on occasions of this kind.
⑯ Behind the tomb stretches the palace park, the **Ogród Saski** (Saxon Gardens), designed by French and Saxon landscape gardeners; visitors can still admire the 18th-century sculptures, man-made lake, and sundial.

⑰ Across ulica Królewska stands the **Galeria Zachęta** (Zachęta Gallery), built in the last years of the 19th century by the Society for the Encouragement of the Fine Arts. It was in this building that the first president of the post–World War I Polish Republic, Gabriel Narutowicz, was assassinated by a right-wing fanatic in 1922. It has no permanent collection but organizes thought-provoking special exhibitions (primarily modern art) in high, well-lit halls. *Pl. Małachowskiego 3, tel. 022/27–69–09. Admission varies. Open Tues.–Sun. 10–6.*

Behind the Zachęta Gallery stands the 18th-century **Kościół Ewangelicko-Augsburski** (Augsburg Evangelical Church), which is often used for concerts. If you turn right onto ulica Kredytowa, you will see in front of you at No. 1 the long yellow building of the
⑱ **Muzeum Etnograficzne** (Ethnographic Museum), which has a fascinating collection of Polish folk art, crafts, and costumes. *Ul. Kredytowa 1, tel. 022/27–76–41. Admission: zł 20,000 adults, zł 10,000 children. Open Tues., Thurs., and Fri. 9–4; Wed. 11–6; Sat., Sun., and holidays 10–5.*

Head back toward Krakowskie Przedmieście along ulica Traugutta.
⑲ On the corner, at Krakowskie Przedmieście 5, is the **Pałac Czapskich** (Czapski Palace), dating from the late 17th century but rebuilt in 1740 in Rococo style. Zygmunt Krasiński, the Polish Romantic poet, was born here in 1812, and Chopin once lived in the palace mews. It is

now the home of the Academy of Fine Arts. Opposite its main en-
㉒ trance are the high wrought-iron gates of the **Warsaw University,** at
Krakowskie Przedmieście 26–28.

Time Out Parnas (Krakowskie Przedmieście 4–6) is a freshly redecorated,
white-tiled café that offers Greek specialties in addition to the usual
café fare. It also has takeout.

Just to the north, at the edge of the park that skirts ulica Karowa, is
㉑ the late-Baroque **Kościół Wizytek** (Church of the Visitation Sisters),
in front of which stands a statue of Cardinal Stefan Wyszyński, primate of Poland from 1948 to 1981. Wyszyński was imprisoned during
the 1950s but lived to see a Polish pope and the birth of Solidarity;
the fresh flowers always lying at the foot of the statue are evidence
of the warmth with which he is remembered.

Continue south along Krakowskie Przedmieście. Just past the uni-
㉒ versity, on the right, is the **Kościół świętego Krzyża** (Holy Cross
Church), with a massive sculpted crucifix atop the steps. Inside,
immured in a pillar, is the heart of Poland's most famous composer, Fryderyk Chopin. You may wish at this point to make a detour into ulica Tamka to the headquarters of the **Chopin Society,** in
㉓ the 17th-century **Pałac Ostrogskich** (Ostrogski Palace), which towers impressively above the street. The best approach is via the
steps from ulica Tamka. In the 19th century the Warsaw Conservatory was housed here (its students included Paderewski); now a
setting for Chopin concerts, it has a small museum with mementos
of the composer. *Ul. Okólnik 1, tel. 022/27–54–71. Admission free.
Open Mon.–Wed., Fri., and Sat. 10–2; Thurs. noon–6. Closed holidays.*

Back on Krakowskie Przedmieście you will see a sedate seated
㉔ **statue of Nicholas Copernicus** holding a globe. This, like many other
notable Warsaw monuments, is the work of the 19th-century Danish
sculptor Bertel Thorvaldsen. Appropriately, it stands in front of the
headquarters of the Polish Academy of Sciences, in the early 19th-
century neoclassical **Staszic Palace.** South of this massive palace, the
Royal Route runs along ulica Nowy Świat (New World Street), now
lined with fashionable boutiques, jewelry shops, and art galleries.
(If you don't want to browse, take any bus south one stop to reach
the next sight).

Time Out Blikle (Nowy Świat 35), Warsaw's oldest cake shop, has now opened
a black-and-white tiled café that offers savory snacks as well as
Blikle's famous doughnuts.

At the far end of New World Street, at its intersection with aleje
㉕ Jerozolimskie, is the **former headquarters of the Polish Communist
party.** This despised, solid white symbol of oppression has been converted into a banking center and stock exchange. To the left and fac-
㉖ ing the party headquarters is the **Muzeum Narodowe** (National
Museum of Warsaw), which has an impressive collection of contemporary Polish and European paintings, Gothic icons, and works from
antiquity. The famous Canaletto paintings that were used to facilitate the rebuilding of Warsaw after the war are also on display here.
*Al. Jerozolimskie 3, tel. 02/621–10–31. Admission: zł 20,000, free
Wed. Open Wed., Fri., and Sat. 10–4; Thurs. noon–6; Sun. and holidays 10–5. Closed day after holidays.*

If you're more interested in the romance of the military, you might
want to visit the adjacent **Muzeum Wojska Polskiego** (Polish Army

Museum). Exhibits of weaponry, armor, and uniforms trace Polish military history for the past 10 centuries. Heavy armaments are displayed outside. *Al. Jerozolimskie 3, tel. 022/29–52–71. Admission: zł 10,000, free Wed. Open Wed. noon–6, Thurs.–Sat. 11–4, Sun. and holidays 10:30–5. Closed day after holidays.*

Back on the Royal Route, continue south along Nowy Świat to plac Trzech Krzyży (Three Crosses Square). One of the crosses in question is on the Kościół świętego Aleksandra (St. Alexander's Church), built in the early 19th century as a copy of the Roman Pantheon. On the left of the square is another building dating from roughly the same period: the Deaf and Blind Institute, established in 1817, and one of the first in Europe.

Beyond plac Trzech Krzyży you enter aleje Ujazdowskie, a fashionable avenue where the rich built residences during the late 19th century. Many now hold foreign embassies (this is the diplomatic quarter). At ulica Matejki, make a detour to the left to see the Polish Houses of Parliament, the Sejm. The round, white debating chamber was built during the 1920s, after the rebirth of an independent Polish state.

Time Out Ambasador (ul. Matejki 4) is a large, bright café decorated with brocade. It's at its best in the summer, when it offers seating on a tree-lined garden terrace.

Farther along the Royal Route, on the corner of ulica Piękna, you may wish to enter the Park Ujazdowski and weigh yourself at the 19th-century weighing booth just inside the gate. At plac Na Rozdrożu you'll leave the diplomatic quarter and enter Warsaw's "Whitehall." This part of the Royal Route is lined with government buildings, among them the office of the Council of Ministers. Turn right and head south on aleja Szucha. The first building on the right, now the Ministry of National Education, was Gestapo headquarters during World War II; a small museum commemorates the horrors that took place behind its peaceful facade. *Al. Szucha, tel. 022/29–49–19. Admission free. Open Tues.–Sat. 10–2.*

Just beyond plac Na Rozdrożu lie the Botanical Gardens, laid out in 1818, and, at the entrance, the neoclassical observatory, now part of the Warsaw University. Behind the observatory stretch the 180 acres of Park Łazienkowski (Łazienki Park), commissioned during the late 18th century by King Stanisław August Poniatowski. The focal point of the park is the neoclassical Pałac Łazienkowski (Palace on the Lake). This magnificent summer residence was so faithfully reconstructed after the war that there is still no electricity—be sure to visit when it's sunny, or you won't see anything inside. The palace holds some splendid 18th-century furniture as well as part of Stanisław August's art collection. *Tel. 02/621–82–12. Admission: zł 20,000 adults, zł 12,000 children. Open Tues.–Sun. 9:30–3.*

One of the most beloved sights in the park is the Chopin Memorial, a sculpture that shows the composer in a typical Romantic pose, with flowing hair under a streaming willow tree. The surrounding rose beds are lined with benches, and in the summer outdoor concerts of Chopin's piano music are held here every Sunday. The park's Museum of Hunting is also worth a visit; it contains a fascinating collection of stuffed birds and animals found in Poland. If you prefer live fauna, look out for the peacocks that wander through the park and the delicate red squirrels that in Poland answer to the name of "Basia," a diminutive of Barbara.

Leave the park by the gate in front of the Chopin memorial and continue south along aleje Ujazdowskie. On your left, beyond the main **㉝** park gates, is the **Pałac Belweder** (Belvedere Palace), the official residence of Poland's president. Built in the early 18th century, it was reconstructed in 1818 in neoclassical style by the then Russian governor of Congress Poland, the Grand Duke Constantine. Lech Wałęsa and his wife and eight children have now moved in. Farther down the hill on the right is another reminder of Poland's long and tangled relationship with Russia: the massive, Colonial-style **Soviet Embassy**—now the embassy of the Commonwealth of Independent States—which for 45 years after World War II channeled directives from Moscow to a more or less compliant Polish communist government.

At this point you may cross the intersection to the next bus stop and board Bus 122 for Wilanów, since the rest of the Royal Route, which until recently ran through open countryside, is now lined on both sides by high-rise housing developments. When you reach the bus terminus at Wilanów, you must cross the main road and turn right toward the palace drive. Before you is a Baroque gateway and false **㉞** moat, leading to the palace courtyard, and beyond it, **Wilanów Palace** itself, built from 1681 to 1696 by King John III Sobieski. After his death, the palace passed through various hands before being bought at the end of the 18th century by Stanisław Kostka Potocki, who was responsible for amassing a major collection of art and for the layout of the gardens, and who opened the first public museum here in 1805. Potocki's neo-Gothic tomb can be seen to the left of the driveway as you approach the palace. The palace interiors still hold much of the original furniture; there's also a striking display of 16th- to 18th-century Polish portraits on the first floor. English-speaking guides are available.

Outside, to the left of the main entrance, is a Romantic park with pagodas, summerhouses, and bridges overlooking a lake. Behind the palace is a formal Italian garden from which you can admire the magnificent gilded decoration on the palace walls and the large sundial. There's also a **gallery** of contemporary Polish art on the grounds, and stables to the right of the entrance now house a poster gallery. The latter is well worth visiting, for this is a branch of art in which Poland excels. *Ul. Wiertnicza 1, tel. 022/42–81–01. Admission to palace and gallery: zł 30,000 adults, zł 15,000 children. Admission to park and gallery only: zł 15,000. Open Wed.–Sun. 9:30–2:30.*

Tour 3: Jewish Warsaw   About 395,000 Jews lived in Warsaw in 1939, roughly one-third of the city's population. By the end of World War II they had disappeared, sent to their death in the gas chambers of Treblinka as part of Hitler's "final solution." The history of this city is closely interwoven with the history of its Jewish community, and although this tour of a ghost world is continually overshadowed by the specter of the Holocaust, it is one that many still wish to make.

Begin at plac Bankowy, which until recently was named for Felix Dzerzhinsky, commandant of the notorious Soviet secret police from 1917 to 1926. Dzerzhinsky was Polish, and when his statue was removed from the square in 1989, a huge crowd of onlookers gathered to cheer and jeer. Behind the glittering new office block on the southeast corner of the intersection—the site of what had been the largest temple in Warsaw, the Tłomackie synagogue—you will find **㉟** the **Jewish Historical Institute and Museum.** It displays a permanent collection of mementos and artifacts and periodically organizes special exhibitions. *Al. Solidarności 79, tel. 022/27–18–43. Admission free. Open weekdays 9–3.*

Time Out **Gessler's** (ul. Senatorska 37, tel. 022/27–06–63), a combination restaurant and café, is decorated with exotic statuary and climbing plants and has a large terrace opening onto the Ogród Saski.

On leaving the museum, walk west along aleja Solidarności. Before the war this was the heart of Warsaw's Jewish quarter, which was walled off by the Nazis in November 1940 to isolate the Jewish community from "Aryan" Warsaw. At No. 115 is the **Femina cinema**, one of the few buildings in this area that survived the war. It was here that the ghetto orchestra organized concerts in 1941 and 1942; many outstanding musicians found themselves behind the ghetto walls and continued to make music despite the odds.

From the corner of Solidarności and ulica Jana Pawła II, take a tram two stops north to ulica Mordechaja Anielewicza. Turn right and walk down two blocks to a green square, on the east side of which stands the **Pomnik Bohaterów Getta** (Monument to the Heroes of the Warsaw Ghetto). On April 19, 1943, the Jewish Fighting Organization began an uprising in a desperate attempt to resist the mass transports to Treblinka that had been taking place since the beginning of the year. Though doomed from the start despite their reckless bravery, the ghetto fighters managed to keep up resistance for a month. But by May 16, General Jürgen Stroop could report to his superior officer that "the former Jewish district in Warsaw had ceased to exist." The ghetto was a smoldering ruin, razed by Nazi flamethrowers. The monument marks the site of the house at **ulica Miła 18,** in which the command bunker of the uprising was situated and where its leader, Mordechai Anielewicz, was killed.

Walk north along ulica Karmelicka to ulica Stawki. At the corner of ulica Stawki and ulica Dzika was the **Umschlagplatz,** the rail terminus from which tens of thousands of the ghetto's inhabitants were shipped in cattle cars to the extermination camp of Treblinka, about 100 kilometers (60 miles) northeast of Warsaw. The low building to the left of the square was used to detain those who had to wait overnight for transport, and the beginning of the rail tracks survives on the right. At the entrance to the square is a symbolic gateway, erected in 1988 as a memorial on the 45th anniversary of the uprising.

Continue west along ulica Stawki to ulica Okopowa. Here you can either take a tram southward for two stops or walk until you reach a high brick wall on the right of the road. This is Warsaw's **Jewish Cemetery,** an island of continuity amid so much destruction. The cemetery survived the war, and although badly overgrown and neglected during the postwar period, it is now gradually being restored. Here you will find fine 19th-century headstones and much that testifies to the Jewish community's role in Polish history and culture. Ludwik Zamenhof, the creator of Esperanto, is buried here, as are Henryk Wohl, minister of the treasury in the national government during the 1864 uprising against Russian rule; Szymon Askenazy, the historian and diplomat; Hipolit Wawelberg, the cofounder of Warsaw Polytechnic; and poet Bolesław Leśmian.

Short Excursion from Warsaw

Kampinoski National Park Beginning just outside the city boundaries, this forested national park, Puszcza Kampinoska in Polish, stretches more than 230 square kilometers (89 square miles) to the west of the city. It contains a wide variety of wildlife, including elk, deer, and wild boars, as well as many species of birds; if you are lucky, you'll see a stork's nest perched atop a cottage. Walking routes through the forest are marked by colored bands on trees.

Getting There Take Bus 708 (fare: zł 12,000) from Dworzec PKS Marymont to the village of Truskaw, or get off at Laski or Izabelin en route. At all of these places marked paths begin at the bus stop, and a large map of the forest is displayed. The trip to Truskaw takes roughly half an hour.

What to See and Do with Children

Special **concerts of classical music** for children are held in the Filharmonia Narodowa (Philharmonic Hall) on Thursday and Sunday. They are very popular and have been run for years by Jadwiga Mackiewicz, who is herself almost a national institution. *Ul. Jasna 5, tel. 022/26–72–81. Admission: from zł 10,000. Concerts at 3 PM.*

Warsaw has several good puppet theaters. The two most popular are **"Lalka" Teatr Lalek** in the Palace of Culture and Science (entrance on north side, tel. 022/20–49–50) and **"Gulliver" Teatr Lalek** (ul. Różana 16, tel. 022/45–16–76).

There is a good **playground** for small children, with sand, swings, and slides, in the **Ujazdowski Park** on aleje Ujazdowskie (entrance on ul. Piękna).

Off the Beaten Track

The best view of Warsaw is from the **30th floor of the Palace of Culture and Science;** the old joke runs that this is because it is the only place in Warsaw from which the palace itself cannot be seen. You ride up by elevator (purchase tickets from the cash desk behind the coatroom at the east entrance), and on a clear day you can see for miles in all directions.

In October 1984, parish priest Jerzy Popiełuszko was brutally murdered by the Polish secret service because he spoke out against the regime. Once his murder was discovered, Father Popiełuszko's church, the **Kościół św. Stanisława Kostki,** became the site of frequent Solidarity demonstrations. You can visit the grave of this martyr on the grounds of this church in the district of Żoliborz, north of Nowe Miasto. Take Bus A or J to plac Komuny Paryskiej, then walk two blocks west along ulica Zygmunta Krasinskiego. *Ul. Stanisława Hozjusza 2.*

Warsaw's oldest cemetery, **Powązki,** dating from 1790, is well worth a visit if you are in the mood for a reflective stroll. Many well-known Polish names appear on the often elaborate headstones and tombs; there is a recent memorial to the victims of the Katyn massacre. Enter from ulica Powązkowska, which you can reach by taking Bus 170 from plac Bankowy.

The **Bazar Różyckiego** on the east side of the Vistula River is one of the largest open markets in Eastern Europe and a haven of free enterprise that survived 45 years of communist rule. Here you can find traders from all over the former Eastern bloc and farther afield, selling an amazing variety of goods, from computers to Russian vodka. Beware of pickpockets. *Ul. Targowa 55. Take tram 7 from al. Jerozolimskie.*

Shopping

At press time Warsaw's shopping scene was confusing. The old state-controlled, cooperative trading outlets are closing down one by one, and it's hard to tell which of the many new shops will survive.

Because economic reforms have also brought with them a manufacturing slump, locally produced items are often much harder to find than the ridiculously expensive imported items. Such Polish specialties as leather goods, amber and silver jewelry, or crystal and glass are in relatively short supply, although it's still possible to find bargains. If you are looking for Polish goods, it's often easiest to find them on street stalls, which still exist at certain points—for example along Nowy Świat and Chmielna, despite Warsaw city council's largely successful recent attempts to drive them into designated market areas.

Shopping hours have also been deregulated to a certain extent. Although many have kept to the old system of opening from 11 AM to 7 PM, an increasing number of privately owned shops are establishing new hours. RUCH kiosks, which sell bus and train tickets, newspapers, and cosmetics, are usually open from 7 AM to 7 PM (most of these outlets have also recently been privatized).

Shopping Districts
Warsaw's four main shopping streets are **ulica Marszałkowska** (from ulica Królewska to plac Zbawiciela), **aleje Jerozolimskie** (from the Central Station to plac Generala de Gaulle), **ulica Nowy Świat**, and **ulica Chmielna** (formerly ulica Rutkowskiego). Ulica Marszałkowska and aleje Jerozolimskie offer mainly larger stores, including, at press time, a small number of international chains. Nowy Świat and ulica Chmielna have smaller stores and more specialized boutiques.

Department Stores
Warsaw's old **Central Department Stores** (ul. Marszałkowska 104–122), divided into the **Wars, Sawa,** and **Junior** sections, have changed their image. The old empty halls, through which people hurried searching for a rare special delivery, are gone; instead, the stores have now rented out space to small private boutiques that sell mainly imported fashion items. A major refurbishment of these stores was under way at press time (summer 1994).

Warsaw's oldest department store, **Braci Jabłkowskich,** at the corner of ulica Krucza and ulica Chmielna, which has a monumental staircase and Art Nouveau stained-glass windows, is currently being expensively renovated. At press time the ground floor had already been reopened.

Street Markets
At the moment, street markets spring up overnight and disappear just as quickly. The market in the great square on the east side of the Palace of Culture and Science has been tamed by city authorities and forced into standardized wooden stalls, where you can find every imaginable Polish and imported product, from fox coats to stereo equipment. On the steps leading up to the palace, individual dealers sell goods imported from as far afield as China or Thailand. The largest Warsaw market, composed largely of private sellers hawking everything from antiques to blue jeans, is at the **Tysiąclecie Sports Stadium,** on the other side of the river at Rondo Waszyngtona.

Specialty **Stores** *Antiques*	**Desa** stores (ul. Marszałkowska 34–50 and ul. Nowy Świat 51) have a fine range of antique furniture, art, and china. Remember, however, that many antiques cannot be exported; they are marked in Desa stores with a pink label.
Art Galleries	The **Desa** galleries (ul. Nowy Świat 23 and ul. Koszykowa 60–62) offer an interesting selection of paintings and work in pottery and glass.
Folk Art and *Crafts*	**Cepelia** stores (pl. Konstytucji 5 and Rynek Starego Miasta 8–10) sell a variety of folk art, including traditional wooden household utensils, wood carvings, silver and amber jewelry, and tapestries.
Glass and *Crystal*	Two shops in downtown Warsaw specialize in glassware: at ulica Piękna 26–34 and Rynek Starego Miasta 11–13. Also try **Majolica** at ulica Puławska 12a.
Herbs	**Herbapol** stores (Krakowskie Przedmieście 1 and ul. Złota 3) stock herbs for every ailment or beauty need. Many customers come just for the herbal toothpaste or exotic herbal teas.
Honey	Beekeeping is a popular hobby among Poles, and **Pszczelarski** (ul. Piękna 45–45a) caters to enthusiasts as well as consumers attracted by the large selection of honey. Mead is also available, as are queen's jelly and granulated pollen dust (for health nuts).
Hunting and *Fishing* *Equipment*	All kinds of fishing tackle, waders, gun cases, and shooting sticks (collapsible triangular stools on a spiked base) are available at the **Sklep Myśliwski** (ul. Krucza 41–43).
Jewelry	**Orno** shops (ul. Nowy Świat 52 and ul. Marszałkowska 83) sell handcrafted silver and amber pieces; they will also do customized designs. **Dziupla** (Krakowskie Przedmieście 23) sells original leather jewelry.
Leather	The shops at ulica Nowy Świat 21 and aleje Jerozolimskie 29 both carry a range of bags, gloves, and jackets.
Vodka	The greatest of all Polish specialties, *wódka* is available in several varieties all over town. Try **Delikatesy Lux** (ul. Marszałkowska 85) or plain old **Delikatesy** (ul. Świętokrzyska 30).

Sports and Fitness

Participant **Sports** *Health Clubs*	The very expensive hotels in Warsaw all have good health-club facilities, but they don't admit nonmembers. The next best thing is the **Stegny Sports Center** (ul. Idzikowskiego 4, tel. 022/42–27–00), which has a sauna and exercise rooms.
Jogging	Along with dogs and bicycles, joggers are banned from Warsaw's largest and most beautiful park, the Łazienki (although an exception was made for George Bush). Indeed, Varsovians still find joggers faintly ridiculous. The best routes are the 9½-kilometer (6-mile) trail through parkland and over footbridges from the Ujazdowski Park to Mariensztat (parallel to the Royal Route); the Vistula embankment (the paved surface runs for about 12 kilometers [8 miles]); the Pilsudski Park, which has a circular route of about 4½ kilometers (3 miles); or the more restricted pathways of the Ogród Saski.
Swimming	Warsaw's indoor pools tend to be overcrowded, and some restrict admission to those with a season ticket; it's best to check first. Try **Inflancka** (ul. Inflancka 8, tel. 022/31–36–83), **Szczęśliwice** (ul. Bitwy Warszawskiej 1920 r. 15–17, tel. 022/22–42–96), **Wisła** (Wał Miedzeszyński 407, tel. 02/617–24–94). All charge zł 15,000–zł 25,000 per hour.

So, you're getting away from it all.

Just make sure you can get back.

AT&T Access Numbers
Dial the number of the country you're in to reach AT&T.

*AUSTRIA[†††]	022-903-011	*GREECE	00-800-1311	NORWAY	800-190-11
*BELGIUM	078-11-0010	*HUNGARY	00◇-800-01111	POLAND[†♦²]	0◇010-480-0111
BULGARIA	00-1800-0010	*ICELAND	999-001	PORTUGAL[†]	05017-1-288
CANADA	1-800-575-2222	IRELAND	1-800-550-000	ROMANIA	01-800-4288
CROATIA[†♦]	99-38-0011	ISRAEL	177-100-2727	*RUSSIA[†] (MOSCOW)	155-5042
*CYPRUS	080-90010	*ITALY	172-1011	SLOVAKIA	00-420-00101
CZECH REPUBLIC	00-420-00101	KENYA[†]	0800-10	S. AFRICA	0-800-99-0123
*DENMARK	8001-0010	*LIECHTENSTEIN	155-00-11	SPAIN•	900-99-00-11
*EGYPT[†] (CAIRO)	510-0200	LITHUANIA♦	8◇196	*SWEDEN	020-795-611
*FINLAND	9800-100-10	LUXEMBOURG	0-800-0111	*SWITZERLAND	155-00-11
FRANCE	19◇-0011	F.Y.R. MACEDONIA	99-800-4288	*TURKEY	00-800-12277
*GAMBIA	00111	*MALTA	0800-890-110	UKRAINE[†]	8◇100-11
GERMANY	0130-0010	*NETHERLANDS	06-022-9111	UK	0500-89-0011

Countries in bold face permit country-to-country calling in addition to calls to the U.S. **World Connect**[SM] prices consist of **USADirect**® rates plus an additional charge based on the country you are calling. Collect calling available to the U.S. only. *Public phones require deposit of coin or phone card. ◇Await second dial tone. †May not be available from every phone. †††Public phones require local coin payment through the call duration. ♦Not available from public phones. • Calling available to most European countries. ¹Dial "02" first, outside Cairo. ²Dial 010-480-0111 from major Warsaw hotels. ©1994 AT&T.

Here's a travel tip that will make it easy to call back to the States. Dial the access number for the country you're visiting and connect right to AT&T. It's the quick way to get English-speaking AT&T operators and can minimize hotel telephone surcharges.

If all the countries you're visiting aren't listed above, call **1 800 241-5555** for a free wallet card with all AT&T access numbers. Easy international calling from AT&T. **TrueWorld Connections.**

AT&T

American Express offers Travelers Cheques built for two.

Cheques *for Two*™ from American Express are the Travelers Cheques that allow either of you to use them because both of you have signed them. And only one of you needs to be present to purchase them.

Cheques *for Two* are accepted anywhere regular American Express Travelers Cheques are, which is just about everywhere. So stop by your bank, AAA* or any American Express Travel Service Office and ask for Cheques *for Two*.

Spectator Sports	You can reach Warsaw's racecourse by taking Tram 14 or 36 or one of the special buses marked *Wyścigi*, which run from the east side of
Horse Racing	the Palace of Culture and Science on Saturday in season (May–Oct.). Betting is on a tote system. *Ul. Puławska 266, tel. 022/43-14-41. Admission to stands: zł 50,000.*
Soccer	Warsaw's soccer team, *Legia,* plays at the field at ulica Łazienkowska 3. *Tel. 02/621-08-96. Admission: zł 20,000.*

Dining

Like everything else in Warsaw, the dining scene is changing rapidly. Some of the better-known state-controlled restaurants have gone swiftly downhill, and some have been privatized and gone uphill. Privately owned restaurants are opening every day, and many offer ethnic cuisine, such as Asian or Italian. Much of the new investment money has filtered down to the bottom end of the market, in small fast-food outlets, and it is here that the changes are most spectacular. Gone are the old and seedy bars, replaced by clean and brightly tiled pizza parlors. Prices have also risen spectacularly, and Warsaw is now much more expensive for eating out than are other Polish towns.

Wine lists, although still restricted by Western standards, are also much improved, and you can usually be sure of a choice of Western and Eastern European wines in more expensive restaurants.

Highly recommended restaurants in a particular price category are indicated by a star ★.

$$$$ **Belvedere.** You could not find a more romantic setting for dinner than this elegant restaurant recently opened in the New Orangery at Łazienki Park. The lamp-lit park spreads out beyond the windows, and candles glitter below the high ceilings within. Polish cuisine is a specialty, and many dishes are prepared with a variety of fresh mushrooms; try the mushroom soup. Also recommended is the roast boar, served with a fine assortment of vegetables. *Park Łazienki, enter from Agrykola or ul. Gargarina, tel. 022/41-48-06. Reservations advised. Jacket and tie advised. AE, DC, MC, V. Closed public holidays.*

★ **Canaletto.** Reproductions of Canaletto's most famous painting of 18th-century Warsaw hang on the walls of this cool and exclusive restaurant on the ground floor of the Victoria Hotel. The furnishings, like the personnel, are unobtrusive; the discreetly curtained windows overlook the Zachęta Gallery. By far the most sedate of the restaurants in this price category, this is a good place for a quiet dinner with conversation. The cuisine is internationalized Polish and Continental. The *bliny* (small pancakes) with caviar are an expensive but delicious way to start your meal. For a main course try one of the flambé specialties, perhaps the traditional *kabanosy* (thin pork sausages), smoked and dried. *Ul. Królewska 11, tel. 022/27-92-71. Reservations required. Jacket and tie advised. AE, DC, MC, V. Closed 4-7 and public holidays.*

Fukier. This long-established wine bar in the Old Town Square has now become a fascinating network of elaborately decorated dining rooms: There is a talking parrot in a cage, and candles on all available shelf space (sometimes dangerously close to clients' elbows). There are solid oak tables, discreetly attentive waiters, and in summer you can dine under the stars on a courtyard patio. The food is "light Old Polish": Steak, served on a grill, is a specialty and might be followed by one of a range of rich cream gâteaux. *Rynek Starego Miasta 27, tel. 022/31-10-13. Reservations required. Jacket and tie*

Dining
Ambasador, **19**
Bazyliszek, **4**
Belvedere, **30**
Canaletto, **9**
Dongnam, **16**
Flik, **26**
Fukier, **3**
Gdańska pod
Retmanem, **8**
Kamienne Schodki, **1**
Krokodyl, **2**
Mekong, **17**
Polonia, **13**
U Hopfera, **5**
Wilanów, **29**
Zajazd
Napoleoński, **22**

Lodging
Belfer, **20**
Bristol, **7**
Dom Chłopa, **10**
Europejski, **6**
Forum, **14**
Grand, **18**
Gromada, **24**
Holiday Inn, **11**
Jan III Sobieski, **23**
Marriott, **12**
Metropol, **15**
Novotel, **25**
Pensjonat Biała
Dalia, **28**
Solec, **21**
Uniwersytecki, **27**
Victoria
InterContinental, **9**
Zajazd
Napoleoński, **22**

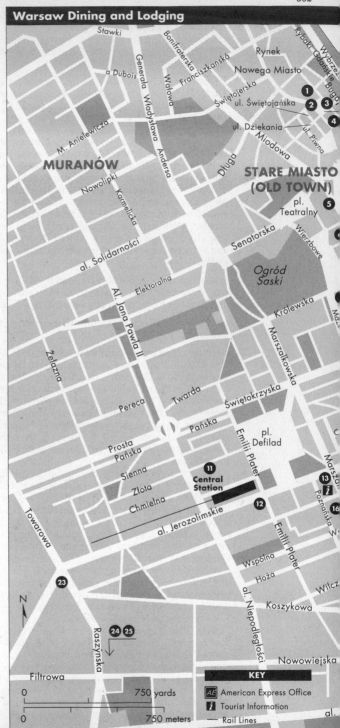

Warsaw Dining and Lodging

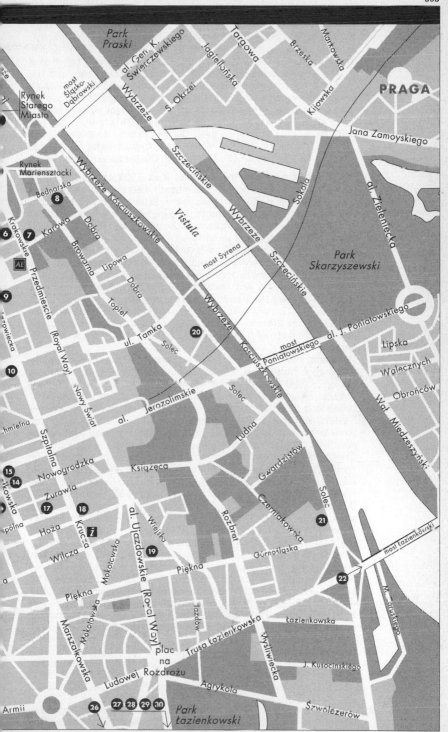

advised. AE, DC, MC, V. Open until last guest leaves; closed public holidays.

Krokodyl. You come here mainly for the setting, a bare-brick, candlelit cellar in one of the historic houses on the Old Town Square. This old fixture of the Warsaw dining scene was recently taken over by the Gessler brothers, sons of a prewar restaurateur, and the quality of the cooking has improved. Try the stewed veal, in a thick cream-base sauce with mushrooms, or the escalope of veal served with soft noodles. The service is smooth—efficient waiters in long white aprons constitute a novelty in Warsaw. This is one of the few restaurants that stay open until the wee hours—to 3 AM. *Rynek Starego Miasta 19–21, tel. 022/31–44–27. Reservations advised. Dress: casual but neat. AE, DC, MC, V. Closed public holidays.*

$$$ ★ **Bazyliszek.** Under new management since 1990, this second-floor restaurant in a 17th-century merchant's house on the Old Town Square gets top marks for atmosphere. Dine here under high ceilings of carved wood, if possible in the Knight's Room, where suits of armor and crossed swords decorate the walls. Waitresses in period dress, who can be relied on to speak English, glide between well-spaced tables. Bazyliszek is a favorite gathering place for special celebrations, and there will usually be a few toasts and songs. The mainstay of the menu is traditional Polish fare, with an emphasis on game dishes. Begin your meal with a platter of home-cured cold cuts, and then try the stewed hare in cream sauce, served with beets and noodles. There is a wide selection of desserts, and the wine list is good. *Rynek Starego Miasta 3–9, tel. 022/31–18–41. Reservations required. Jacket and tie advised. AE, DC, MC, V. Closed public holidays.*

Dongnam. Opened in 1991, this Vietnamese restaurant has rapidly won a good reputation. The cavernous first-floor dining room is a classic example of Socialist-Realist architecture on ulica Marszał kowska. It formerly housed a Romanian restaurant but has been subdivided by silk screens to create a more intimate atmosphere. Eastern lanterns and paper butterflies adorn the walls. Service tends to be slow; but the food, dished out in very large portions, is good (it's popular with Vietnamese families residing in Warsaw). The beef dishes are excellent: Try stewed beef with bean sprouts, or the beef with mushrooms. A fair range of wines is available as well. *Ul. Marszałkowska 45–49, tel. 02/621–32–34. Reservations advised. Dress: casual. No credit cards. Closed public holidays.*

Wilanów. Part of the Forum hotel group, this restaurant is housed in an old stable building opposite the Wilanów Palace, the summer residence of King John III Sobieski, 13 kilometers (8 miles) from the city center. The dimly lit main dining room on the ground floor, known as the Hunters' Hall, is decorated with stuffed trophies. The tables are set in wood-paneled half-booths of an odd kidney shape, which can make conversation rather difficult for small parties. The historic setting and period decor are not the restaurant's asset; the service is polite and efficient, with English-speaking waiters supervised by a maître d' of the old school. The chef has a fine reputation, and the restaurant offers a unique variety of Polish and Continental dishes. Among the former are *Wawelska* steak, larded with prunes and cooked in a bacon wrap, and the *Sobieski* pork cutlet in a sweetish, fruit-base sauce, served with rice and apples. A reasonable wine list is now available. *Ul. Wiertnicza 27, tel. 022/42–13–63. Reservations advised. Jacket and tie advised. AE, DC, MC, V. Closed Christmas Day, Easter.*

★ **Zajazd Napoleoński.** Thirteen kilometers (8 miles) from downtown, this ground-floor restaurant opens out onto the walled garden of an

18th-century inn with Napoleonic associations. We are not told whether the emperor enjoyed the cooking when he stayed here in 1812, but busts and portraits of the inn's most famous visitor are everywhere in the cool, arched dining rooms; overhead are bare oak beams. This would be an appropriate setting in which to sample some traditional Polish dishes like *barszcz* (borscht) with small dumplings, followed by roast suckling pig, which comes elaborately garnished and glazed. The restaurant is on the main bus route into downtown Warsaw, and taxis are on call. *Ul. Płowiecka 83, tel. 022/ 15–30–68. Reservations required. Jacket and tie advised. AE, DC, MC, V. Closed public holidays.*

$$ **Ambasador.** This brightly lit, white-and-gilt restaurant is on the ground floor of a 1960s apartment block on Warsaw's diplomatic mile, aleje Ujazdowskie, a stone's throw from the Polish Parliament (the *Sejm*). The spacious dining room is broken up by ranks of potted plants, and noise levels are muted; the restaurant is popular for lunch and provides a relaxed setting for conversation. The basically Polish cuisine has some international additions: the *kotlet królew-ski*—pork with a traditional potato stuffing—is recommended. This is also a good place to sample the Polish version of *shashlik*, made with pork loin. Special orders for wines or dishes are accepted with a few days' notice. *Ul. Matejki 4, tel. 022/25–99–61. Reservations advised. Dress: casual but neat. AE, DC, MC, V. Closed public holidays.*

Flik. Set on a corner overlooking the Morskie Oko Park, this restaurant in Mokotów, opened in 1992, has a geranium-lined white terrace that makes a fine setting for outdoor summer dining. Inside, the dining room is spacious, with well-spaced tables, light cane furniture, and lots of greenery. The fresh salmon starter is delicious and could be followed—for local flavor—by *zrazy* (rolled beef fillot stuffed with mushrooms). There is a self-service salad bar, and downstairs a small café and art gallery. *Ul. Puławska 43, tel. 022/49–44–06. Reservations advised. Jacket and tie advised. AE, DC, MC, V. Closed public holidays.*

★ **Kamienne Schodki.** This vaulted restaurant, on the ground floor of a 16th-century house on the corner of the Old Town Square, is famed for its roast duck served with apples, which was for a long time the only dish offered. Redecoration has brought back the big crystal mirrors to reflect the candlelit tables, and more items have been added to the menu. It would be a pity to miss the duck, but chicken or pork *à la polonaise* with garlic stuffing are also quite good. Save room for the light and creamy pastries. *Rynek Starego Miasta 26, tel. 022/31–08–22. Reservations advised. Jacket and tie advised. AE, DC, MC, V. Closed public holidays.*

Mekong. You'll always find a crowd at this small Vietnamese restaurant on a side street behind the Forum Hotel. Concessions to Asian decoration have been made in the rather dark dining room, but the management has not gone overboard with this. Compared with that of other restaurants in this price category, the space is rather cramped and tables are close together. Friendly service and delicious food have, however, made Mekong very popular. The duck stewed with peanuts is an interesting sweet-and-sour dish, and the pork in red-pepper sauce looks as good as it tastes. Only a limited selection of wines is available. *Ul. Wspólna 35, tel. 02/621–18–81. Reservations advised. Dress: casual. AE, V. Closed public holidays.*

Polonia. This restaurant in the Polonia Hotel has a splendidly preserved fin-de-siècle interior, with galleries (in which a small private dining room can be booked), original marble fireplaces, and brass chandeliers. The decor is in itself a major reason for paying a visit. The tables are well spaced in three split-level dining areas; in the evenings there is a small orchestra, and couples waltz on the parquet dance floor. The clientele is varied, while the service is polite if sometimes slow. The cuisine is mainly Polish: The *kotlet myśliwski* (hunter's pork cutlet with mushrooms) is recommended, as is the traditional mainstay *bigos* (cabbage cooked with sausages, various meats, prunes, and red wine). *Al. Jerozolimskie 45, tel. 02/628–72–41. Reservations advised. Jacket and tie advised. AE, DC, MC, V. Closed public holidays.*

$ **Gdańska pod Retmanem.** Wooden trestle tables and folk decorations form the backdrop for a solid, traditional meal in this large restaurant in Mariensztat. The dining room is split-level, and booths provide privacy for quiet conversation. The service is swift and friendly, but don't expect the waiters to speak English. The *polędwica po hetmańsku*—fillet of beef with mushrooms and cream—is recommended. *Ul. Bednarska 9, tel. 022/26–87–58. Reservations advised. Dress: casual but neat. AE, DC, MC, V.*

U Hopfera. This small and busy restaurant on the Royal Way has brightly checked tablecloths, fresh flowers, and a friendly and efficient staff. It specializes in Polish dishes, ranging from *schab ze śliwkami* (pork baked with plums) to homemade pierogi with beef stuffing. Open midday to 3 AM, it is probably the only inexpensive restaurant where you can find a meal late at night. *Ul. Krakowskie Przedmieście 53, tel. 02/635–73–52. Reservations advised. Dress: casual but neat. AE, DC, MC, V.*

Lodging

Warsaw's overall shortage of hotel beds is likely to continue well into the 1990s. The situation at the top end of the price range has been improving steadily since the opening of the Marriott Hotel and Holiday Inn (1989), and the Sobieski (1991) and the Bristol (1992). But lower down the price scale, options are very restricted. Bed-and-breakfast accommodation is difficult to find and is often as expensive as a hotel; try the **Romeo i Julia** bureau (ul. Emilii Plater 30, m.15, tel. 022/29–29–93) or the **Polonaise** bureau (ul. Świętojerska 4/10, tel. 02/635–07–65) for information. In summer there are generally more options: Student hostels rent out space, and chalets are available at campsites. Demand is high, so book well in advance.

Warsaw is a small city, and the location of your hotel is not of crucial importance as far as travel time to major sights or night spots. Many hotels are clustered in the downtown area near the intersection of ulica Marszałkowska and aleje Jerozolimskie. This is not an especially scenic area, with very little green space; nevertheless, the neighborhood doesn't turn into a "concrete desert" after business hours, since there are still a lot of residential property as well as restaurants and entertainment facilities. And despite a rising crime rate throughout Poland, it is still safe to stroll at night through downtown Warsaw; the greatest hazards are likely to be uneven pavements and inadequate lighting. You would, however, be well advised to avoid the Central Station at most hours of the day or night.

The hotels on plac Piłsudskiego (formerly plac Zwycięstwa), which is close to parks and within easy walking distance of the Old Town, offer more relaxing surroundings. Most of the suburban hotels have no particular scenic advantage, though they do provide immediate access to larger tracts of open space and fresh air.

Highly recommended lodgings in a particular price category are indicated by a star ★.

$$$$ **Bristol.** Built in 1901 by a consortium headed by Ignacy Paderewski,
★   the concert pianist who served as Poland's prime minister in 1919–
1920, the Bristol was always at the center of Warsaw's social life.
Distinguished guests have included General Charles de Gaulle and
Marlene Dietrich. Impressively situated on the Royal Way, next to
the Radziwiłł Palace, the Bristol survived World War II more or less
intact. Now, after a decade of extensive renovations—practically
everything except the original facade has been rebuilt—the Bristol
has finally reopened as a Trust House–Forte hotel. The Forte organization aims to revive the hotel's long tradition of luxury and elegance; according to the manager, "Warszawa is currently
witnessing the rebirth of a legend." *Krakowskie Przedmieście 42–
44, 00–325, tel. 02/625–25–25, fax 02/625–25–77. 163 rooms, 43
suites, all with bath. Facilities: 2 restaurants, 2 bars, café, sauna,
solarium, pool. Breakfast not included in rates. AE, DC, MC, V.*

Holiday Inn. Designed, and later franchised, by Holiday Inn, this
gleaming six-story complex opposite Warsaw's Central Station
avoids some of the standard chain-hotel impersonality. Softly carpeted and furnished throughout in shades of gray and blue, the public areas—including three restaurants, the Wiener Kaffeehaus, and
two small bars—are full of light provided by the tree-filled steel-
and-glass conservatory that fronts the building up to the third floor.
The generously proportioned guest rooms have projecting bay windows that overlook the very center of the city, but unfortunately
there's no air-conditioning on the residential floors, so the rooms can
become stuffy in hot weather. The young staff in this fairly new hotel
is friendly and helpful. *Ul. Złota 2, 00–120, tel. 022/20–03–41, fax
022/31–05–69. 338 rooms, 10 suites. Facilities: 3 restaurants, café, 2
bars. AE, DC, MC, V.*

Jan III Sobieski. This massive hotel is Austrian-owned and appropriately named for the Polish king who in 1683 saved Vienna from the
Turks. Since it opened in 1991, its bright pink, blue, and yellow illusionist facade has startled more than a few Varsovians. Inside, however, the decor is more conventional, and service is impeccable. The
rooms are reasonably sized and warmly furnished in soft rosewood
and flowered prints. *Pl. Zawiszy 1, 00–973, tel. 02/658–34–44, fax
02/659–8828. 436 rooms. Facilities: 2 restaurants, bar, café. Breakfast included. AE, DC, MC, V.*

★   **Marriott.** Opened in 1989 in the high-rise Lim Center opposite the
Central Station, the Marriott currently offers the city's most prestigious accommodations; it's the only hotel in Poland that's under direct American management. The staff is well trained and helpful;
everyone, from the maids up, speaks some English. The views from
every room—of central Warsaw and far beyond—are spectacular on
a clear day. The health facilities are the best in town. This is not the
place to stay, however, if you want local color: The Marriott specializes in chintzy international decor. The Lila Weneda restaurant on
the second floor runs a special Sunday brunch, complete with
Dixieland band. *Al. Jerozolimskie 65–79, 00–697, tel. 02/630–6306,
fax 022/21–12–90. 481 rooms, 24 suites. Facilities: 5 restaurants, 3
bars, nightclub, casino, health club, pool, business center, shops,
parking. Breakfast included. AE, DC, MC, V.*

Victoria InterContinental. Overlooking plac Piłsudskiego, the 16-
year-old Victoria was until 1989 Warsaw's only luxury hotel, hosting
innumerable official visitors and state delegations. The large and
comfortable furnished guest rooms are decorated in tones of brown
and gold, which continues the white-and-bronze theme of the exteri-

or. Health facilities include an attractive basement swimming pool and three exercise rooms, and the hotel is just across the street from the jogging (or walking) paths of the Saxon Gardens. A 10-minute walk from the Old Town, the hotel is in hearing distance of many of Warsaw's main sights and recreational opportunities; the Teatr Wielki, for example, is on the opposite side of the square. *Ul. Królewska 11, 00–065, tel. 022/27–92–71, fax 022/27–98–56. 328 rooms, 32 suites. Facilities: 3 restaurants, bar, nightclub, casino, health club, pool, shops, parking. Breakfast included. AE, DC, MC, V.*

$$$ Europejski. Although it retains traces of its earlier grandeur, this hotel is now clearly struggling to keep up its traditional standards of service. Built during the late 19th century, the Europejski was opened in 1962 after postwar reconstruction; the renovators managed to retain some original features, including two grand marble staircases. The rooms are very diverse in size and shape but are comfortably furnished, and almost all have views overlooking historic Warsaw—on one side the Royal Route, on the other plac Piłsudskiego. The nearby Saxon Gardens provides terrain suitable for morning jogging; there are no health-club facilities as such, though guests can sometimes obtain access to the facilities at the nearby Victoria Hotel, which is under the same management. *Krakowskie Przedmieście 13, 00–071, tel. 022/26–50–51, fax 022/26–11–11. 226 rooms, 13 suites. Facilities: restaurant, bar, nightclub, shops. No air-conditioning. Breakfast included. AE, DC, MC, V.*

Forum. This dun-colored, 30-story, Swedish-designed metal cube has been a fixture on the Warsaw skyline since 1974. Guest rooms are of average size, and those on the east side of the building offer good views—but don't choose the Forum if you want cheerful surroundings. Depressing tones of brown and green predominate, and the furnishings seem to have been chosen with an eye for function rather than comfort (many pieces are distinctly the worse for wear). The staff, used to dealing with rapid-turnover group tours, can be offhand. There are no health or exercise facilities, and the Forum is in the middle of a heavily built-up district. On the plus side, the hotel does have two restaurants and is within easy reach of the entertainment districts. *Ul. Nowogrodzka 24, 00–511, tel. 02/621–02–71, fax 022/25–81–57. 750 rooms, 13 suites. Facilities: 2 restaurants, bar, casino, parking. No air-conditioning. Breakfast included. AE, DC, MC, V.*

★ Zajazd Napoleoński. Napoléon is believed to have stayed here on his way to Moscow with the Grande Armée in 1812. Lovingly restored and opened as a small family-run hotel in 1984, the Napoleoński stresses the Empire theme throughout; most of the furnishings, for example, are period reproductions. Although the inn is on the main road out of Warsaw to the east, it stands in its own walled garden, and the thick stone structure keeps the sound of traffic at bay. The rooms are spacious, and the fixtures are of unusually high quality. Senator Edward Kennedy has stayed here, and the hotel is generally popular with foreign visitors, who find that the distance from downtown (13 kilometers, 8 miles) is more than compensated for by the unique atmosphere and high standards of personal service. *Ul. Płowiecka 83, 04–501, tel. 022/15–30–68, fax 022/15–22–16. 22 rooms, 3 suites, all with bath. Facilities: restaurant. No air-conditioning. AE, DC, MC, V.*

$$ Dom Chłopa. This five-story white hotel in the center of Warsaw was built during the late 1950s by the Gromada peasants' cooperative and originally had a horticultural and agricultural bookshop and plant-and-seed store on the ground floor. Times have changed: The store has given way to a TV store. The hotel still offers clean and reasonably priced accommodations; rooms are rather small and spartan, but the colors are cheerful, and the downtown location is excellent. *Pl. Powstańców Warszawy 2, 00–030, tel. 022/27–49–43, fax 022/26–14–54. 160 rooms with bath. Facilities: restaurant. No air-conditioning. No TV in rooms. AE, DC, MC, V.*

Grand. The Grand, an 11-story squat stone tower, was built during the mid-1950s, so don't be fooled by the ebullient name. Ongoing maintenance work has not kept pace with the structure's deterioration, and though the rooms are clean and adequately furnished, a note of seediness pervades the residential floors. Single rooms and bathrooms throughout are cramped; rooms fronting on ulica Krucza can be noisy. The hotel's main advantage is its excellent location in the heart of downtown Warsaw. *Ul. Krucza 28, tel. 022/29–40–51, fax 02/621–97–24. 370 rooms, 16 suites. Facilities: restaurant, bar, nightclub, sauna, pool. No air-conditioning. Breakfast included. AE, DC, MC, V.*

Metropol. This glass-front seven-story hotel, built in 1965 at Warsaw's main downtown intersection, was until recently regarded as very downscale. However, a major renovation carried out in 1989–1990 has vastly improved the standards of the accommodations, which are now better than in many expensive hotels. The furnishings are impressively solid and comfortable; bathrooms, though small, are attractively tiled and fitted. The single rooms (which form the majority) are large enough to contain a bed, armchairs, and desk without feeling crowded. Each, however, has a balcony overlooking busy ulica Marszałkowska, and traffic noise can be very intrusive when the windows are open. *Al. Jerozolimskie 45, 00–024, tel. 02/621–43–54, fax 02/628–66–22. 175 rooms, 16 suites, all with bath. Facilities: restaurant. No air-conditioning. No TV in rooms (sets can be rented from reception). AE, DC, MC, V.*

Novotel. This small, three-story hotel, built in 1976 around a paved and shrub-filled courtyard, is only five minutes from Okęcie Airport (fortunately, *not* under any flight paths). Its situation is almost rural: Surrounded by trees, the Novotel lies across the road from a major area of gardens and parkland. Though removed from the heart of the city, the Novotel is on the main bus routes; Bus 175 will take you downtown in 10–15 minutes. The atmosphere is friendly, and the rooms light, clean, and comfortable in a predictable, stripped-down style. There are no health or entertainment facilities, and the Novotel is to be recommended mainly if you like to retire from the hustle and bustle of the city center for a good night's sleep. *Ul. 1 Sierpnia 1, 02–134, tel. 022/46–40–51, fax 022/46–36–86. 150 rooms with bath. Facilities: restaurant, bar, parking. No air-conditioning. AE, DC, MC, V.*

Polonia. The Art Nouveau Polonia, completed in 1913, was the only Warsaw hotel to survive World War II intact. General Eisenhower stayed here in 1945, and the U.S. Embassy was housed here in the period immediately after the war. Much of the hotel's splendor was lost in a major renovation completed in 1974, when the rooms were standardized. The high-ceilinged rooms are, however, still reasonably spacious and comfortable; many of the doubles and suites still have stylish bay windows and balconies, and many of the bathrooms are large and well appointed. The restaurant (*see* Dining, *above*) is a marvelous set piece of fin-de-siècle elegance. Despite its lack of facilities and amenities, the Polonia has many regular Western guests. *Al. Jerozolimskie 45, tel. 022/28–51–06, fax 022/28–66–32. 206 rooms, 28 suites, all with bath. Facilities: restaurant. No air-conditioning. No TV in rooms (sets can be rented from reception). AE, DC, MC, V.*

Solec. The Swedish construction workers for whom this prefabricated three-story building served as a hostel in 1973 have long since departed. The flimsy clapboard exterior is slightly misleading, as the hotel is now comfortably if not luxuriously furnished. The bedrooms are a good size, and improvements are being made to the bathrooms. The service is good, and the atmosphere informal and friendly. Although it is near to the city center as the crow flies, the Solec really is a bit off the beaten track. Unless you order a taxi for the trip downtown, you face a brisk 20-minute walk through parkland up Warsaw's only hill (the Vistula escarpment). *Ul. Zagórna 1, tel. 022/25–92–41, fax 022/21–64–42. 147 rooms, 2 suites, all with bath. Facilities: restaurant, bar, parking. No air-conditioning. AE, DC, MC, V.*

$ **Belfer.** This hotel is conveniently situated in Powiśle, across the road from the Vistula River and only 10 minutes by foot (admittedly all uphill) from the Royal Route. Traffic noise can be a problem in summer in front-facing rooms, but courtyard-facing rooms are peaceful. The decor throughout is dull, with plenty of dark-wood paneling and chocolate-brown paint, though the rooms are spacious and comfortable, and everything is spotlessly clean. *Wybrzeże Kościuszkowskie 31/33, tel. and fax 02/625–26–00. 360 rooms, 56 singles and 10 doubles with bath. Facilities: restaurant, café. No air-conditioning. Breakfast included. No credit cards.*

Pensjonat Biała Dalia. This very small, privately owned pension in Konstancin Jeziorna, 24 kilometers (15 miles) from the center of Warsaw, stands in a beautifully kept garden and is elegantly furnished in blue and white. The rooms are fairly large, clean, and comfortable, with large, solid beds and heavy, upholstered armchairs; flower patterns predominate on the carpets and wallpaper. *Ul. Sobieskiego 24, Konstancin Jeziorna, 06–727, tel. 022/56–33–70. 5 rooms, 4 with bath. No air-conditioning. No TV or phone in rooms. Breakfast included. No credit cards.*

Uniwersytecki. This three-story Socialist Realist building on the edge of Łazienki Park was taken over from the Communist Central Committee in 1990 by the Warsaw University. It is used mainly for university guests, but remaining rooms are rented throughout the year. The spartanly decorated rooms are of good size, with high ceilings. It is probably the best-located hotel in the price range. *Ul. Belwederska 26/30, tel. 022/41–02–54. 90 rooms. Facilities: restaurant, bar. No TV in rooms. No air-conditioning. Breakfast included. No credit cards.*

Campsite **Gromada Campsite.** This large campsite on the edge of the Piłsudski Park is open May 1–October 30. It's only five minutes by bus from the center of town; despite the screen of trees that separates the chalets from the main road and bus routes, staying here can be noisy. The bathrooms are rudimentary—there is hot water—but they are very cramped. *Al. Żwirki i Wigury 3–5, tel. 022/25–43–91. 120 beds in 2-person chalets (bedding provided). Facilities: cafeteria. No credit cards.*

The Arts and Nightlife

The Arts Warsaw has much to offer those interested in the arts. Find out what's on from the recently revived *WiK,* the daily *Gazeta Wyborcza* or *Życie Warszawy,* or the English-language weekly *Warsaw Voice*— or go to Warsaw's only major ticket agency, *ZASP,* at aleje Jerozolimskie 25 (tel. 02/621–94–54), which has listings of most events for two weeks ahead. The tickets for most performances are still relatively inexpensive, but if you want to spend even less, remember that most theaters and concert halls sell general-admission entrance tickets—*wejściówki*—for only about zł 10,000 immediately before the performance. These do not entitle you to a seat, but you can usually find one that is not taken. Wejściówka are often available for performances for which all standard tickets have been sold.

Film Since 1989 it seems every cinema in Warsaw has been showing foreign films—mainly U.S. box-office hits—nonstop. These are generally shown in their original version with subtitles, allowing you to catch up on what you've missed back home. **Relax** (ul. Złota 8, tel. 022/27-77-62) is a popular large cinema in the center of town; it's full for almost all showings. **Skarpa** (ul. Kopernika 7-9, tel. 022/26-48-96), off ulica Nowy Świat, is large and modern and offers buffet facilities.

Don't count on seeing many Polish films while visiting Warsaw; only one cinema specializes in Polish features, **Iluzjon Filmoteki Narodowej** (ul. Żurawia 3/5/7, tel. 02/628-7431). That said, **Wars** (Rynek Starego Miasta 5-7, tel. 022/31-44-88), an older cinema on the New Town Square, occasionally forgets about box-office success and shows an old Polish classic.

Music The **Filharmonia Narodowa** (National Philharmonic, ul. Jasna 5, tel. 022/26-57-12) regularly offers an excellent season of concerts, with visits from world-renowned performers and orchestras as well as Polish musicians.

Studio Koncertowe Polskiego Radia (Polish Radio Concert Studio, ul. Woronicza 17, tel. 022/44-32-50), opened in 1992, has excellent acoustics and popular programs.

Towarzystwo im. Fryderyka Chopina (Chopin Society, ul. Okólnik 1, tel. 022/27-95-99) organizes recitals of Chopin's music and chamber concerts in the Pałac Ostrogskich.

Opera and **Teatr Wielki** (plac Teatralny, tel. 022/26-32-87), Warsaw's grand
Dance opera, stages spectacular productions of the classic international opera and ballet repertoire, as well as Polish operas and ballets. Stanisław Moniuszko's 1865 opera *Straszny Dwór* (*The Haunted Manor*), a lively piece with folk costumes and dancing, is a good starting point if you want to explore Polish music: the visual aspects will entertain you, even if the music is unfamiliar. English plot summaries are available at most performances.

Warszawska Opera Kameralna (Al. Solidarności 76, tel. 022/31-22-40), the Warsaw chamber opera, which recently moved to a beautifully restored 19th-century theater building in the Muranów district, has a very ambitious program and a growing reputation.

Operetka (ul. Nowogrodzka 49, tel. 02/628-0360) offers a range of musicals and light opera, including Polish versions of such old favorites as *My Fair Lady*. Try to get a seat in one of the boxes upstairs.

Theater **Teatr Powszechny** (ul. Zamoyskiego 20, tel. 022/18-25-16) on the east bank of the Vistula River has a good reputation for modern drama and performs many American and British plays in translation.

Teatr Studio (Pałac Kultury i Nauki [Palace of Culture and Science], east entrance, tel. 022/20-21-02) stages a great deal of experimental drama, which may be a good choice for those who don't understand Polish.

Teatr Współczesny (ul. Mokotowska 14, tel. 022/25-59-79) concentrates on Polish classics and those of other nations, though it also occasionally ventures into modern drama.

Teatr Żydowski (ul. Grzybowska 12–15, tel. 022/20–70–25), Warsaw's Jewish theater, performs in Yiddish, but most of its productions are colorful costume dramas in which the action speaks as loudly as the words. Translation—into Polish—is provided through headphones.

Nightlife Though Warsaw's range of options has widened recently, it is still—on the whole—a sedate city that goes to bed early. As throughout Central Europe, people tend to meet for a drink in the evenings in *kawiarnie* (cafés)—where you can linger for as long as you like over one cup of coffee or glass of brandy—rather than in bars (most cafés are open until 10 PM). There are a few Western-style bars in the big hotels, and a few "pubs" have opened. *Winiarnie* (wine bars) have a longer tradition but are often geared to serious drinking rather than conversation. Discos and rock clubs are usually part of a student club; jazz clubs have a much wider audience. Casinos, a new feature on the Warsaw scene, are mainly the haunt of foreign visitors and a tiny group of the new, rich business class of Poles.

Bars and Lounges The dimly lit and superficially sedate **Zielony Barek** on the ground floor of the Victoria InterContinental Hotel (ul. Królewska 11) used to be the nearest thing to an upscale bar that Warsaw had to offer until it was upstaged by the upholstered luxury of the ground-floor **Lounge Bar** of the Hotel Bristol (Krakowskie Przedmieście 42–44). The English-style **pub** in the lobby of the Marriott (al. Jerozolimskie 65–79) provides a relaxing background for a quiet drink. The **Irish Pub** (Midowa 3) has become intensely popular since its opening in 1992. Although pints of Guinness are expensive, there is a varied program of folk music until 3 AM most nights. **Harenda** (Krakowskie Przedmieście 4–6, entrance from ul. Obożna) is open all night and has a crowded outdoor terrace in summer.

Cabarets All the major hotels have nightclubs with floor shows. Try **Kamieniolomy** in the Europejski (Krakowskie Przedmieście 13), **Czarny Kot** in the Victoria InterContinental (ul. Królewska 11), or **Orpheus** in the Marriott (al. Jerozolimskie 65–79).

Casinos The **Casino Marriott** on the first floor of the hotel is Warsaw's plushest and most sedate casino; the clients are often Western businessmen and visitors or Polish jet-setters (al. Jerozolimskie 65–79, open 1 PM–3 AM). The **Victoria Casino** is popular with Middle Eastern visitors and Polish businesspeople (ul. Królewska 11, open 1 PM–3 AM).

Discos Weekend discos in the **Riviera–Remont** student club (ul. Waryńskiego 12, tel. 022/25–74–97) are reportedly the best in Warsaw. Others, for example **Hybrydy** (ul. Złota 7–9, tel. 022/27–37–63) or **Stodoła** (ul. Stefana Batorego 10, tel. 022/25–60–31), have earned a reputation for violence.

Jazz Clubs **Akwarium** (ul. Emilii Plater 49, tel. 022/20–50–72), the Polish Jazz Association's club, runs a regular evening program of modern jazz in crowded, smoky surroundings; top Polish players and foreign groups perform here. **Piwnica Wandy Warskiej** (ul. Wałowa 7, tel. 022/31–17–39), in the Old Town, is very popular; you'll need to book ahead. Hotels also often have jazz sessions, as do student clubs. A new and very popular jazz spot is **Jazz Club 77** (ul. Marszałkowska 77/79).

Wine Bars **Amfora** (ul. Złota 11, tel. 022/27–30–48), a small and crowded second-floor bar popular with students and young adults, usually offers a variety of good wines.

Kraków and the South

Kraków (Cracow), seat of Poland's oldest university and once the nation's capital (before finally relinquishing the honor to Warsaw in 1611), is one of the few Polish cities that escaped devastation during World War II; Hitler's armies were driven out before they had a chance to destroy it. Today Kraków's fine rampart, tower, facades, and churches, illustrating seven centuries of Polish architecture, make it a major attraction for visitors. Its location, about 270 kilometers (170 miles) south of Warsaw, also makes it a good base for hiking and skiing trips in the mountains of southern Poland.

Just to the south of Kraków, Poland's great plains give way to the gently folding foothills of the Carpathians, building to the High Tatra range on the Slovak border. The climate is more decidely Continental here, with harsh, snowbound winters but hot summers. The fine medieval architecture of many towns in this region, known as **Małopolska** (Little Poland), comes from a period when the area prospered as the meeting point of thriving trade routes. In the countryside, wood homesteads and strip farming tell another story, that of the hardships and poverty that the peasantry endured before the 20th century brought tourists to the mountains. During the 19th century, when this part of Poland was under Austrian rule as the province of western Galicia, hundreds of thousands of peasants escaped from grinding toil on poor soil to seek their fortune in the United States; it sometimes seems as if every family here has a cousin in America.

Although the tourist trade has brought increased prosperity, made visible in the spate of recent house-building, Małopolska remains intensely Catholic and conservative (it is no accident that Lech Wałęsa found his strongest support here during the 1990 presidential elections), and the traditional way of life in the countryside is relatively untouched. Folk crafts and customs are still very much alive, both in mountainous and foothill (*Podhale*) areas: you may see carved-wood beehives in mountain gardens or worshipers setting out for church on Sunday in white-felt embroidered trousers.

Important Addresses and Numbers

Tourist Information
In **Kraków**, contact **IT, Tourist Information Center** (ul. Pawia 8, tel. 012/22–04–71), **Orbis** (Hotel Cracovia, al. Marszałka Ferdinanda Focha 1, tel. 012/22–86–66), or **Gromada** (plac Szczepański 6, tel. 012/22–37–45). In **Częstochowa**, go to **IT** (al. Najświętszej Marii Panny 39–41, tel. 034/2467 55). In **Zakopane**, try **IT** (ul. Kościuszki 7, tel. 0165/140–00) or **Orbis** (Ul. Krupówki 22, tel. 0165/141–51).

Emergencies Police: dial 997. Ambulance: dial 999.

Late-Night Pharmacies
Individual chemists stay open for 24 hours on a rotating basis; and newspapers carry listings of when the various *apteki* are open. For information in Kraków, dial 012/22–05–11. In Zakopane, check at ulica Krupówki 7 (tel. 0165/146–39).

Arriving and Departing by Plane

Airports and Airlines
Kraków's **Balice Airport** (tel. 012/11–67–00), 11 kilometers (7 miles) west of the city, is the only airport serving the region. It is small, and in spring and fall problems with fog can cause long delays.

There are LOT flights most days to Balice Airport from Warsaw (flying time: 40 minutes) and, during the summer, weekly LOT flights from London. LOT's office in Kraków is at ulice Basztowa 15 (tel. 012/22–70–78; open 8–6).

Arriving and Departing by Car, Train, and Bus

By Car A car will not be of much use to you in Kraków, since most of the Old City is closed to traffic, and distances between major sights are short. A car will be invaluable, however, when you set out to explore the rest of the region. You can approach Kraków either by the E–77 highway (from Warsaw and north), or via the E–40 (from the area around Katowice). There is a high incidence of car thefts in most cities, so make sure your car is locked securely before you set out to explore. Use the parking facilities at your hotel or one of the attended municipal gargage car parks (try plac Szczepański or plac Św. Ducha).

By Train Nonstop express trains from Warsaw take only 2¾ hours and arrive at **Kraków Główny** station on the edge of the Old Town (plac Kolejowy, tel. 012/933); they run early in the morning and in the late afternoon. The onward trip to Zakopane takes another six hours because of the rugged nature of the terrain. Unless you take the overnight sleeper from Warsaw, which arrives in Zakopane at 6 AM, it's better to change to a bus in Kraków: The bus station is just across the square from Kraków Główny station.

By Bus Express bus service to Kraków runs regularly from most Polish cities. From the PKS bus station in Warsaw (al. Jerozolimskie), the journey takes three hours. Buses arrive at the main PKS station on plac Kolejowy (tel. 012/936), where you can change for buses to other destinations in the region. There are also through services from Warsaw to Zakopane (travel time: five hours).

Getting Around

By Car It is not strictly necessary to have a car to explore the southern region. Public transport will take you to even the most remote and inaccessible places. But it will take time and can be uncomfortably crowded. On the other hand, the narrow mountain roads can be trying for drivers. Although the Kraków–Zakopane highway has recently been much improved, some stretches are still single-lane, and horse-drawn carts can cause major delays.

By Train Trains move slowly in the hilly region south of Kraków, but most towns are accessible by train, and the routes can be very picturesque. In Zakopane you can get more information from the station on ulica Chramcówki (tel. 0165/145–04).

By Bus Almost all villages in the region, however isolated, can be reached by PKS bus. The buses themselves are unfailingly ancient, rickety, and overpacked with standees—reason enough to take an express service if it operates to your destination. An express bus—for which seats can be reserved in advance—runs from Kraków to Zakopane and back every two hours. In Zakopane information is available from the bus station on ulica Kościuszki (tel. 0165/144–53).

Guided Tours

Orbis (Hotel Cracovia, al. Marszałka Ferdinanda Focha 1, tel. 012/ 22–86–66) is still the main tour operator; all of its tours are either by bus, minibus, or limousine, at prices ranging from $15 for a half-day coach tour to $140 for a full-day tour in a chauffeur-driven car.

Orientation Orbis offers a standard half-day tour of **Kraków**, as well as junkets to **Pieskowa Skała** and **Ojców**. A day trip to the **Dunajec River gorge** (including a journey down the river by raft) is also available in the summer.

Special-Interest A one-day visit to the Nazi concentration camp at **Oświęcim** (Auschwitz) is offered throughout the year. Orbis also organizes day trips to the Pope's birthplace at **Wadowice**, to the Bernadine monastery at **Kalwaria Zebrzydowska**, and to the Pauline monastery at **Częstochowa**.

Exploring Kraków and the South

Numbers in the margin correspond to points of interest on the Kraków map.

Tour 1: Kraków Listed by UNESCO in 1978 as one of the 12 great historic cities of the world, Kraków should be a priority in the region if you are interested in art, architecture, or Polish history. Despite problems caused by pollution from nearby industrial Śląsk (Silesia), it is a uniquely preserved medieval city. A thriving market town in the 10th century, Kraków became Poland's capital in 1037. The original walls are gone, pulled down according to the fashion of the early 19th century, and replaced by a ring of parkland known as the **Planty**. Only one small section of the wall still stands, centered on the 15th-century **Barbakan**, one of the largest of its kind in Europe. It is now being renovated so that visitors will again be able to climb its turrets.

The surviving fragment of the city wall opposite the Barbakan, where students and amateur artists like to hang their paintings for sale in the summer, contains the Renaissance **Municipal Arsenal**, which now houses part of the National Museum's **Czartoryski Collection**, one of the best art exhibits in Poland. Highlights include Leonardo da Vinci's *Lady with an Ermine*, Raphael's *Portrait of a Young Man*, and Rembrandt's *Landscape with the Good Samaritan*. *Ul. Św. Jana 19, tel. 012/22–55–66. Admission: zł 10,000, free Fri. Open Fri. noon–5:30, Sat.–Tues. 10–3:30.*

Pass through the beautiful **Brama Floriańska** (Florian Gate), built around 1300, to ulica Floriańska, one of the streets laid out according to the town plan of 1257. The Gothic houses of the 13th-century burgesses still remain, although they were rebuilt and given Renaissance or neoclassical facades. Note on your left at No. 41 the **Dom Jana Matejki**, the family house of 19th-century painter Jan Matejko; it is now a museum of his work. While you examine his Romantic paintings, you can also admire the well-preserved interior of this 16th-century building. *Tel. 012/22–59–26. Admission: zł 10,000, free Fri. Open Wed., Sat., and Sun. 10–3:30; Fri. noon–5:30.*

Time Out **Jama Michalikowa** (ul. Floriańska 45) is a café with a perfectly preserved Art Nouveau interior; the walls are hung with drawings by late-19th-century customers, who sometimes had to pay their bills in kind. No smoking in the main room.

The house at ulica Floriańska 24, decorated with an emblem of three bells, was once the workshop of a bell founder, for whom, as you can tell from the number of churches, there was no doubt plenty of employment in medieval Kraków. The chains hanging on the walls of the house at No. 17 barred the streets to invaders when the city was under siege. On your right at No. 14 you will see the **Hotel pod Różą**, one of the city's oldest, where both Franz Liszt and Russian czar Al-

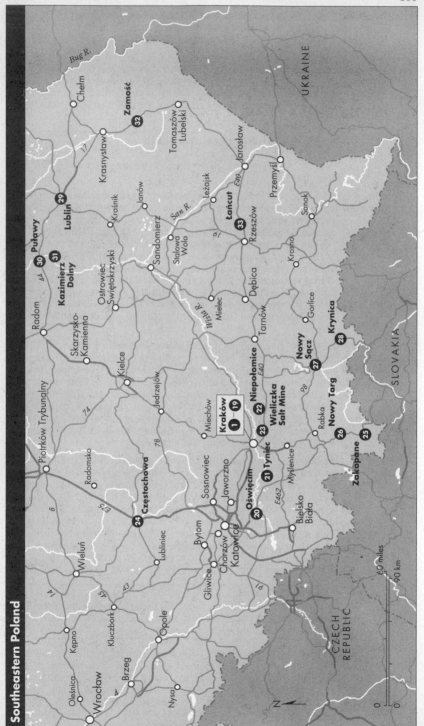

Southeastern Poland

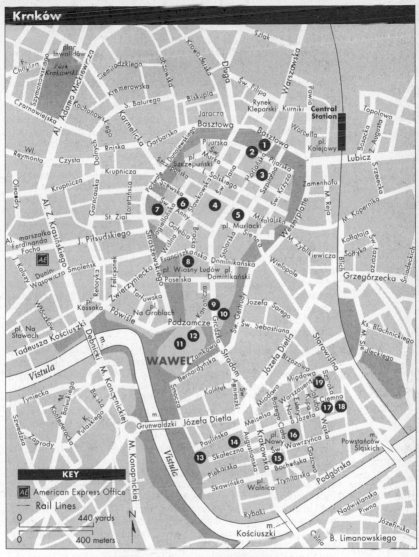

Kraków

KEY

AE American Express Office

— Rail Lines

| 0 | 440 yards |
| 0 | 400 meters |

N

Barbakan, **1**

Collegium
Juridicum, **9**

Collegium Maïus, **7**

Dom Jana Matejki, **3**

Franciscan Church and
Monastery, **8**

Kościół Bożego
Ciała, **16**

Kościół Mariacki, **5**

Kościół na Skałce, **13**

Kościół św.
Andrzeja, **10**

Kościół św.
Katarzyny, **14**

Municipal Arsenal, **2**

Pałac pod
Baranami, **6**

Rynek Główny, **4**

Stara Synagoga, **18**

Synagoga Wysoka, **17**

Synagoga R'emuh, **19**

Town Hall of
Kazimierz, **15**

Wawel Cathedral, **11**

Zamek Królewski, **12**

exander I stayed. And finally, at the left-hand corner as you enter the market square, stands the **Dom pod Murzynami** (Negroes' House), a 16th-century tenement decorated with two black faces—testimony to the fascination that citizens of the Age of Discovery had for Africa.

❹ Europe's largest medieval marketplace, the magnificent **Rynek Główny** (Main Market Square) measures 220 yards by 220 yards and is on a par with St. Mark's Square in Venice when it comes to size and grandeur. It even has the same plague of pigeons—although legend tells us that the ones here are no ordinary birds. They are allegedly the spirits of the knights of Duke Henry IV Probus, who in the 13th century were cursed and turned into doves.

The great square was not always so spacious. In an earlier period it also contained—in addition to the Renaissance **Sukiennice** (Cloth Hall), which now stands in splendid near-isolation in the middle—a Gothic town hall, a Renaissance granary, a large weigh house, a foundry, a pillory, and hundreds of traders' stalls. A few flower sellers under colorful umbrellas are all that remain of this bustling commercial activity. A pageant of history has passed through this square. From 1320 on, Polish kings came here on the day after their coronation to meet the city's burghers and receive homage and tribute in the name of all the towns of Poland. Albert Hohenzollern, the grand master of the Teutonic Knights, came here in 1525 to pay homage to Sigismund the Old, king of Poland. And in 1794 it was here that Tadeusz Kościuszko took his solemn vow to fight against czarist Russia in a national Polish insurrection.

❺ As you enter the Rynek from ulica Floriańska, the **Kościół Mariacki** (Church of Our Lady) is in front of you on the left. The first church was built on this site before the town plan of 1257, which is why it stands slightly askew from the main square; the present church, completed in 1397, was built on the foundations of its predecessor. You'll note that the two towers, added in the early 15th century, are of different heights. Legend has it that they were built by two brothers, one of whom grew jealous of the other's work and slew him with the "bloody sword," a symbol of Magdeburg law, which still hangs in the Sukiennice. From the higher tower, a strange bugle call rings out to mark the passing of each hour. It breaks off on an abrupt sobbing note to commemorate an unknown bugler struck in the throat by a Tartar arrow as he was playing his call to warn the city of imminent attack. The main feature of the Mariacki church is the magnificent wooden altarpiece with more than 200 carved figures, the work of the 15th-century artist Wit Stwosz, who for many years made his home in Kraków. The panels offer a detailed picture of medieval life, and Stwosz himself is believed to be represented in the figure in the bottom right-hand corner of the Crucifixion panel.

Passing the **statue of Adam Mickiewicz,** you now enter the **Sukiennice.** The Gothic arches date from the 14th century; but after a great fire in 1555, the upper part was rebuilt in Renaissance style. The inner arcades on the ground floor still hold traders' booths, now mainly selling local craft products; on the first floor, in a branch of the **National Museum,** you can view a collection of 19th-century Polish painting. *Al. 3 Maja 1, tel. 012/34–33–37. Admission: zł 20,000, free Thurs. Open Wed. and Fri.–Sun. 10–3:30, Thurs. noon–5:30.*

Emerging on the other side of the Sukiennice, you'll face the **Wieża Ratuszowa** (Town Hall Tower), all that remains of the 16th-century town hall, which was demolished in the early 19th century. The Tower now houses a branch of the Kraków History Museum and offers a panoramic view of the old city. *Admission: zł 10,000. Open June–Sept., Fri.–Wed. 9–3, Thurs. noon–5. Closed second weekend of every month.*

Time Out The **Sukiennice Café** (Rynek Główny 15), on the east side of the Cloth Hall, is the most traditional of Kraków's cafés. Its Art Nouveau decor includes fitted mirrors and wall lamps, marble-topped tables, and a no-smoking room with elaborate ceiling paintings.

On the corner of ulica Świętej Anny, opposite the Town Hall Tower, **❻** is the **Pałac pod Baranami** (Palace at the Sign of the Rams), comprising several Gothic houses converted into a Renaissance palace by Jost Decjusz, secretary to King Sigismund the Old. After World War II it was the home of the famed satirical cabaret *Piwnica pod Baranami*; returned to the Potocki family, who owned it in the 19th century, the building was damaged by fire and is now being converted to other uses.

The **Dom pod Jeleniami** (House at the Sign of the Stag) at No. 36 was once an inn where both Goethe (1790) and Czar Nicholas I (1849) found shelter. At No. 45 is the **Dom pod Orłem** (House at the Sign of the Eagle), where Tadeusz Kościuszko lived as a young officer in 1777; a little farther down the square, at No. 6, is the **Szary Dom** (Gray House), where he made his staff headquarters in 1794. In 1605, in the house at No. 9, the young Polish noblewoman Maryna Mniszchówna married the False Dymitri, the pretender to the Russian throne (these events are portrayed in Pushkin's play *Boris Godunov* and in Mussorgsky's operatic adaptation). At No. 16, in a 14th-century house that belonged to the Wierzynek merchant family, is a famous restaurant named for them. In 1364, during a "summit" meeting attended by the Holy Roman Emperor, one of the Wierzyneks gave an elaborate feast for the visiting royal dignitaries; this was the beginning of the house's reputation for haute cuisine.

Having admired the house on the square, now turn via ulica Świętej Anny into ulica Jagiellońska. On the corner of these two streets is **❼** the **Collegium Maïus**, the earliest existing building of the Jagiellonian University, founded by Kazimierz the Great in 1364 as the first university in Poland. By 1400 the original buildings had become overcrowded and were replaced with the Collegium Maïus, which has an arcaded courtyard with lecture rooms on the ground floor; the rooms on the upper level were originally for the fellows of the college. The Jagiellonian's most famous student, Nicolaus Copernicus, studied here from 1491 to 1495. To the left of the entrance is the **Stuba Communis** of the early scholars, which has a fine collection of pewter pots, a reminder of the hall's original function. The room is now used only for major university functions. Above the portal is the universitiy's motto: *Plus ratio quam vis* (Better reason than force).

Time Out **Wierzynek** (Rynek Główny 16), the famous restaurant, now has a ground-floor café that serves delicious cakes.

Turn left into ulica Gołębia, passing later university buildings at No. 13 (the **Collegium Physicum**) and No. 20 (the **Collegium Slavisticum**) and then through ulica Bracka and plac Wszystkich Świętych. Note **❽** here the mid-13th-century **Franciscan church and monastery** (among the earliest brick buildings in Kraków), before continuing on to ulica Grodzka and ulica Floriańska, on the other side of the square, which are Kraków's oldest streets.

Time Out | The **Tunis Bar** (plac Dominikański 1) is good for a quick and delicious lunchtime snack. A tiny white-tiled bar with black stools and tables, it is run by Tunisian youths in red tunics.

---

9 At ulica Grodzka 53 is the magnificent Gothic **Collegium Juridicum,** built in the early 15th century to house the university's lawyers. Be-
10 yond it, on the left, is the 11th-century fortified **Kościół św. Andrzeja** (Church of St. Andrew), one of Kraków's few well-preserved Romanesque structures (the interior, however, is Baroque); it was here that the inhabitants of the district took refuge during Tartar raids.

Now turn to your right, into the small garden in front of the Collegium Juridicum. The garden connects with ulica Kanonicza, named for the canons of the cathedral, who once lived here. Most of the houses date from the 14th and 15th centuries, although they were "modernized" in Renaissance or later styles. Pope John Paul II lived here in the **Chapter House** at No. 19 and, later, in the late 16th-century **Dean's House,** at No. 21.

Ulica Kanonicza leads to the foot of the **Wawel Hill,** a raised area of about 15 acres that formed a natural point for fortification on the flat Vistula Plain. During the 8th century a tribal stronghold had already been constructed here, and from the 10th century it held a royal residence and the seat of the bishops of Kraków. Construction
11 on **Wawel Cathedral** was begun in 1320, and the structure was consecrated in 1364. Lack of space for expansion on the hill has meant that the original austere structure was basically preserved, although a few Renaissance and Baroque chapels have been crowded around it. The most notable of these is the **Kaplica Zygmuntowska** (Sigismund Chapel), built during the 1520s by the Florentine architect Bartolomeo Bertecci and widely considered to be the finest Renaissance chapel north of the Alps.

From 1037, when Kraków became the capital of Poland, Polish kings were crowned and buried in the Wawel Cathedral. This tradition continued up to the time of the partitions, even after the capital had been moved to Warsaw. Later, during the 19th century, only great national heroes were honored by a Wawel entombment: Tadeusz Kościuszko was buried here in 1817; Adam Mickiewicz and Juliusz Słowacki, the great Romantic poets, were also brought back from exile to the Wawel after their deaths; Marshal Józef Piłsudski, the hero of independent interwar Poland, was interred in the cathedral crypt in 1935.

You may also visit the Cathedral treasury, archives, library, and museum. Among the showpieces in the library, one of the earliest in Poland, is the 12th-century Emmeram Gospel from Regensburg. After touring at ground level, you can climb the wooden staircase of the **Sigismund Tower,** which you enter through the sacristy. The tower holds the famous Sigismund bell, which was endowed in 1520 by King Sigismund the Old and is still tolled on all solemn state and church occasions.

12 The **Zamek Królewski** (Royal Castle) that now stands on the Wawel Hill dates from the early 16th century, when the Romanesque residence that stood on this site was destroyed by fire. King Sigismund the Old brought artists and craftsmen from all over Europe to create his castle; and despite Baroque reconstruction after another fire in the late 16th century, the fine Renaissance courtyard remains. After the transfer of the capital to Warsaw at the beginning of the 17th century, Wawel was stripped of its fine furnishings, and later in the century it was devastated by the Swedish wars. Under the Austrians in the 19th century, Wawel was turned into an army barracks. In 1911, a voluntary Polish society purchased the castle from the Austrian authorities and began restoration. Today you can visit the royal chambers on the first floor, furnished in the style of the 16th and 17th centuries and hung with the 16th-century Belgian arras that during World War II was kept in Canada. The Royal Treasury on the ground floor contains a somewhat depleted collection of Polish crown jewels; the most fascinating item displayed here is the *Szczerbiec*, the Jagged Sword used from the early 14th century onward at the coronation of Polish kings. The Royal Armory houses a collection of Polish and Eastern arms and armour; in the west wing is an imposing collection of Turkish embroidered tents. *Tel. 012/22 51–55. Admission: zł 25,000. Open Tues.–Sun. 10–3. Closed Mon. and day after holidays.*

From Wawel Hill, make your way via ulica Bernardyńska to the Vistula embankment, and turn left to the Pauline **Kościół na Skałce** (Church on the Rock). This is the center of the cult of St. Stanisław, bishop and martyr, who is believed to have been beheaded on the orders of the king in the church that stood on this spot in 1079—a tale of rivalry similar to that of Henry II and Thomas à Becket. Starting in the 19th century, this also became the last resting place for well-known Polish writers and artists; among those buried here are the composer Karol Szymanowski and the poet and painter Stanisław Wyspiański.

You are now on the edge of **Kazimierz,** a district of Kraków that was once a town in its own right, chartered in 1335 and named for its founder, Kazimierz the Great. After 1495, when they were expelled from Kraków by King John Albert, this was the home of Kraków's Jewish community. Walk up ulica Skałeczna from the Church on the Rock, passing on your left the fine 14th-century Gothic **Kościół świętej Katarzyny** (Church of St. Catherine). Turn right on ulica Krakowska onto plac Wolnica, in the middle of which stands the 15th-century **Town Hall of Kazimierz,** now the Ethnographic Museum, which displays a well-mounted collection of regional folk art. *Pl. Wolnica, tel. 012/66–28–63. Admission: zł 10,000, free Mon. Open Mon. 10–6, Wed.–Sun. 10–3.*

On the northeast corner of plac Wolnica is the 15th-century **Kościół Bożego Ciała** (Corpus Christi Church), which King Charles Gustavus of Sweden used as his headquarters during the Siege of Kraków in 1655. Make your way along ulica Bożego Ciała and turn right onto ulica Józefa. The late-16th-century **Synagoga Wysoka** (High Synagogue) stands on your left at No. 38. On the corner of ulica Szeroka is the **Stara Synagoga** (Old Synagogue), built in the 15th century and reconstructed in Renaissance style following a fire in 1557. It was here in 1775 that Tadeusz Kościuszko successfully appealed to the Jewish community to join in the national insurrection. Looted and partly destroyed during the Nazi occupation, it has now been rebuilt and houses the **Museum of the History and Culture of Kraków Jews.** *Tel. 012/22–09–62. Admission free. Open Mon.–Thurs., Sat., and Sun. 9–3; Fri. 11–6. Closed first weekend of month.*

There are two more synagogues on ulica Szeroka. The 16th-century **Synagoga R'emuh** at No. 40, still used for worship, is associated with the name of the son of its founder, Rabbi Moses Isserles, who is buried in the cemetery attached to the synagogue. Used by the Jewish community from 1533 to 1799, this is the only well-preserved Renaissance Jewish cemetery in Europe. (The so called **new cemetery** on ulica Miodowa, which contains many old headstones, was established during the 19th century.) On the other side of ulica Szeroka is the **Poper** or **Bocian Synagogue,** dating from 1620. Nearby, at ulica Jakuba 25, is the **Ajzyk Synagogue,** which dates from 1638, and at ulica Warschauera 8 is the **Kupa Synagogue,** built by subscription in 1590. Finally, on the corner of ulica Miodowa and ulica Podbrzezie is the 19th-century Reformed **Tempel Synagogue.**

Numbers in the margin correspond to points of interest on the Southeastern Poland map.

Tour 2: Kraków Environs

The Jewish community of Kazimierz came to an abrupt and tragic end during World War II. A ghetto was established here in March 1941, and its inhabitants were transported to their deaths in the concentration camp of **Auschwitz-Birkenau** (at least 1 million Jews and other so-called "undesirables" were killed here between 1941 and

⑳ 1945). The small town of **Oświęcim** (Auschwitz) lies 55 kilometers (35 miles) west of Kraków. The camp, with the cynical slogan *Arbeit Macht Frei* (Work Frees You) above its high iron gate, is preserved as a museum. You can reach Oświęcim by train or bus from plac Kolejowy in Kraków. *Oświęcim, ul. Więźniów Oświęcimia 20, tel. 0381/320–22. Open June–Aug., daily 8–7; Sept.–May, daily 8–6.*

⑪ Perched high on a cliff above the Vistula River 12 kilometers (8 miles) southwest of Kraków is the **Benedictine Abbey** at **Tyniec.** This fortified cloister had its own garrison from the 11th century onward. It was from here that the Confederates of Bar set off to raid Kraków in 1772, and as a result the abbey was destroyed by the Russian army later that year. In 1817 the Benedictine order was banned, and the monks disbanded. It was not until 1939 that the order recovered the land, and not until the late 1960s that it again became an abbey and the work of reconstruction began in earnest. From May to September recitals of organ music are held in the abbey church. You can travel to Tyniec by city Bus 112 from Kraków-Dębniki PKS bus station.

⑫ The **Niepołomice Forest** is also within easy reach, 25 kilometers (15 miles) east of Kraków. The town of **Niepołomice** is on the western edge of the forest and has a 14th-century hunting lodge and church built by Kazimierz the Great, who, like many other Polish kings of the period, liked to hunt in the forest. The animals—including bison—remain, and you may be lucky enough to see some of them as you stroll under the trees. Take a PKS bus or train from plac Kolejowy; on summer weekends Kraków city transport also runs special buses to Niepołomice from plac Kolejowy.

㉓ Twelve kilometers (7 miles) southeast of Kraków lies the **Wieliczka salt mine.** Salt has been mined at Wieliczka for a thousand years, and during the 11th century Wieliczka was owned by the Benedictines of Tyniec, who drew a large part of their income from its revenues. By the 14th century the salt was so prized that King Kazimierz the Great built city walls with 11 defense towers at Wieliczka to protect the mines from Tartar raids. There are historic galleries and chambers 150 yards below ground level, including underground lakes and underground chapels carved by medieval miners. Serious flooding in 1992 brought commercial salt production to a halt after a millennium and threatened to destroy the historic part of the mine, but the museum is now open again. To get to Wieliczka, take a PKS bus or train from plac Kolejowy or city Bus 103 from aleje Krasińskiego, changing to Bus 133 at Nowy Prokocim. *Wieliczka, ul. Daniłowicza 10, tel. 012/22–08–92. Open daily 8–4. Admission: zł 70,000 adults, zł 40,000 children.*

Another short journey from Kraków will take you to the **Ojców National Park,** the limestone gorge of the Prudnik River. The ridge above the gorge is topped by a series of ruined castles—the "eagles' nests"—that once guarded the trade route from Kraków to Silesia. The best-preserved of these is at **Pieskowa Skała,** which now houses a branch of the Wawel Museum Art Collection. There are also caves in the limestone rock with which many stories and legends are connected; Władysław the Short, a medieval Polish king, is supposed to have escaped his German pursuers here with the help of a spider, which spun its web over the mouth of the cave in which he was hiding. The gorge is at its best in autumn, when shades of gold and red stand out against the white limestone. PKS buses leave regularly from the bus station on plac Kolejowy. *Ojców. Admission: zł 10,000. Władysław the Short's cave open May–Sept., daily 8–7. Pieskowa Skała museum open Tues. noon–5:30, Wed.–Sun. 10–3:30.*

㉔ The pilgrims' town of **Częstochowa** lies 120 kilometers (70 miles) northwest of Kraków, across the Kraków plateau. Inside the 14th-century **Pauline monastery** at Jasna Góra (Hill of Light) is Poland's holiest shrine, the famous *Black Madonna of Częstochowa,* an early-15th-century painting of a dark-skinned Madonna and Child, the origins of which are uncertain (legend attributes the work to St. Luke). Pilgrims from all over Poland, many of them on foot, make their way to the shrine each August to participate in Marian devotions. The church and monastery were fortified during the 16th century, and 100 years later Jasna Góra held out against a Swedish siege for 40 days. It was here that the invading Swedish army was halted and finally driven out of the country. The Black Madonna's designation as savior of Poland dates from those turbulent days. The monastery was rebuilt in Baroque style during the 17th and 18th centuries, as was the interior of the Gothic church. The **Monastery Treasury** holds an important collection of manuscripts and works of art. Trains and PKS buses leave regularly from plac Kolejowy. *Treasury open daily 11–1 and 3–5.*

Tour 3: Zakopane and the Tatra Mountains ㉕ Nestled at the foot of the Tatra Mountains 3,281 feet above sea level, **Zakopane** is the highest town in Poland. Until the 19th-century Romantic movement started a fashion for mountain scenery, Zakopane was a poor and remote village. During the 1870s, when the Tatra Association was founded, people began coming to the mountains for their health and recreation, and Zakopane developed into Poland's leading mountain resort. At the turn of the century it was home to many writers, painters, and musicians. Stanisław Wyspiański based his best-known drama, *Wesele* (The Wedding, 1901), on his experiences here. Stanisław Witkiewicz ("Witkacy"), the artist and playwright, lived here and was responsible for creating the elaborate carved-wood architecture that he called the "Zakopane style." Many fine examples can still be seen on ulica Krupówki, Zakopane's main thoroughfare, or on ulica Kościuszki. The elaborate **Willa pod Jedlami,** designed by Witkiewicz and considered one of his most ambitious works, stands at ulica Koziniec 1; the architect's very first project was the **Willa Koliba** at ulica Kościeliska 18. Another interesting wooden villa, the **Willa Atma,** was home to the composer Karol Szymanowski in the 1920s; it is now a museum with mementos of his life and work. *Ul. Kasprusie 19, tel. 0165/140–32. Admission: zł 10,000. Open Wed., Thurs., Sat., and Sun. 10–4; Fri. 2–6.*

Around the corner and up the hill, on Zakopane's main street, the **Muzeum Tatrzańskie** (Tatra Museum) is also worth a visit; it has splendid collections of the flora and fauna of the Tatras and a section with mountain crafts. *Ul. Krupówki 10, tel. 0165/152–05. Admission: zł 10,000. Open Wed.–Sun. 9–3:30.*

Back down at the foot of the hill on ulica Kościeliska is the wooden **church of St. Clement,** the first church built in Zakopane, dating from the mid-19th century. The adjoining cemetery has a number of striking carved-wood memorials; Witkiewicz is buried here, as is Tytus Chałubiński, the founder of the Tatra Association. Farther up ulica Kościeliska, on the left, you can see a dozen or more 19th-century **wooden farmsteads,** which have been moved to this site and are being restored.

From the corner of ulica Krupówki and ulica Kościeliska you can walk down to the cable railway to **Gubałówka,** from which, on a clear day, you will have a fine view of the Tatras and of the town. You can return by the same route, or take the path along the ridge to Pałkówka, and from there back down into town, about 9 kilometers (5 miles).

Time Out   The **Terrace Café** on Gubałówka has fine views and good cakes and is an excellent place for sitting and watching life mosey by.

The **Dolina Kościeliska** (Kościeliska Valley) is about 9 kilometers (5 miles) southwest of Zakopane. Take a bus from the PKS bus station on ulica Kościuszki to **Kiry** (buses run frequently but are often so crowded that they do not stop to pick up passengers on the way back). The valley is in the **Tatra National Park,** which covers the entire mountain range in both Poland and Slovakia. Remember that you are not allowed to pick flowers here—which may be a temptation in spring, when the lower valley is covered with crocuses. The first part of the valley runs for roughly a mile through flat open pasture, before the stream that gave the Kościeliska its name begins to come down through steep, rocky gorges. You finally emerge at **Ornak,** 5½ kilometers (3½ miles) from the road, where there are splendid views. Horse-drawn carriages (on sleighs in winter) wait at the entrance to take visitors halfway up the valley (for about zł 200,000), but if you want to reach Ornak, you must make the last stage on foot.

Morskie Oko, about 30 kilometers (20 miles) southeast of Zakopane, is the largest and loveliest of the lakes in the High Tatras, 4,570 feet above sea level. The name means "Eye of the Sea," and an old legend claims that it has a secret underground passage connecting it to the ocean. The **Mięguszowiecki** and **Mnich** peaks appear to rise straight up from the water, and the depth of the lake makes it permanently deep blue. A small chalet beside the lake offers tea and light refreshment. Orbis in Zakopane runs a regular bus service to within 10 minutes' walk of the lake. If you feel more energetic, you can take a PKS bus from the bus station to Łysa Polana and follow the marked trail for 8 kilometers (5 miles).

Bukowina Tatrzańska, 13 kilometers (8 miles) northeast of Zakopane, can easily be reached by PKS bus from the bus station on ulica Kościuszki. The ridge-top path, parallel to the main road to Łysa Polana, affords spectacular views of the Tatra range and is a favored spot for winter sunbathing.

㉖ **Nowy Targ,** the unoffical capital of the Podhale region, is 24 kilometers (15 miles) north of Zakopane on the main road to Kraków; buses run every hour. It has been a chartered borough since the 14th century, when it stood on a crossing point of international trade routes, and it remains an important market center for the entire mountain region. It is worth visiting on Thursday, market day, when farmers bring their livestock in for sale in the streets, and a range of local products, including rough wool sweaters and sheepskin coats, are on sale. The White and Black Dunajec streams meet in Nowy Targ to form the Dunajec River, which then runs on through steep limestone gorges to Nowy Sącz (*see below*). Following the valley of the river (by car or PKS bus), you will come to Dębno, which has a tiny wooden church dating from the 15th century (it's believed to be the oldest wooden building in the Pohdale region); inside are medieval wall paintings and wood sculptures.

At Czorsztyn, 22 kilometers (14 miles) from Nowy Targ, you will see a ruined 14th-century castle high on the rocks above the Dunajec. Here the road moves farther away from the river; and you will have to make a detour if you also wish to see the split-level 14th-century Niedzica Castle farther down the gorge—where, according to local legend, the last descendant of the South American Incas lived during the 18th century. Alternatively, take the 15-kilometer (8-mile) raft trip (cost: zł 200,000) through the gorge, which affords a fine view of the castle. Rafts accommodating 12 passengers depart from the Czorsztyn dock; at the end of the trip you can catch one of the frequent local buses back to Czorsztyn.

Krościenko is another village that became a holiday resort during the late 19th century. It, too, has many Zakopane-style wooden structures. Nearby is the small spa of Szczawnica, which dates from the same period; you can stroll around in the high-vaulted pump rooms and sip the foul-tasting mineral waters. Nowy Sącz existed as a market town during the 13th century; a ruined 14th-century castle remains from this early period, as do the church on the northeast side of the market square (founded by King Władysław Jagiełło) and the 15th-century church and chapter house on the east side.

(28) Krynica, 32 kilometers (20 miles) south of Nowy Sącz, is a spa and winter-sports center in a high valley. The salutary properties of the mineral waters were recognized during the 18th century, and the first bathhouse (ul. Kraszewskiego 9) was built in 1807. Krynica was developed farther in classic spa style in the late 19th century: It has a tree-lined promenade through gardens, a pump room, and concert halls. The waters here taste no better than those in Szczawnica, but you can console yourself with the thought that they are the most concentrated mineral waters in Europe, with no fewer than 15 parts of solids per liter.

What to See and Do with Children

The Kraków Philharmonic (ul. Zwierzyniecka 1, tel. 012/22–94–77) organizes special Saturday-matinée concerts for children.

Every Polish child knows the legend of the fire-breathing dragon that once terrorized local residents from his Smocza Jama (Dragon's Den), a cave at the foot of Wawel Hill. The dragon threatened to destroy the town unless he was fed a damsel a week. In desperation the king promised half his kingdom and his daughter's hand in marriage to any man who could slay the dragon. The usual quota of knights tried and failed. But finally a crafty cobbler named Krak tricked the dragon into eating a lambskin filled with salt and sulfur. The dragon went wild with thirst, rushed into the Wisła River, and drank until it exploded. Krak the cobbler was made a prince and the town was named (or renamed) for him. The Smocza Jama is still there, however, and every 15 minutes smoke and flame belch out of it to thrill young visitors. A bronze statue of the dragon itself stands guard at the entrance. *Follow signs to Smocza Jama, below Thief's Tower on*

Wawel Hill near Vistula River. Admission: zł 10,000. Open May–Sept., Mon.–Thurs., Sat., and Sun. 10–3.

All Polish children who visit **Zakopane** have their photograph taken on the terrace at Gubałówka in a carriage drawn by four white mountain sheepdogs and driven by a man dressed in a white bearskin. They love it.

Off the Beaten Track

Kopiec Kościuszki. This mound on the outskirts of Kraków was built in tribute to the memory of Tadeusz Kościuszko in 1820, three years after his death. The earth came from battlefields on which he fought; soil from the United States was added in 1926. This is the best place from which to get a panoramic view of the city. Take Tram 1, 2, or 6 from plac Dominikański to the terminus at Salwator and then walk up aleje Waszyngtona to the mound.

Robert Jahoda's Printing Press. This little museum shows the history of printing and bookbinding in Kraków. *Ul. Gołębia 4, tel. 012/22–99–22. Admission: zł 10,000. Open daily 10–2. Closed first weekend of month.*

Shopping

Kraków has always been an interesting place for shopping, but here, as everywhere else in Poland, things are changing rapidly. Many of the craftsmen whose tiny shops made the Old City such a fascinating place in which to hunt for original purchases have now been driven out of business by high rents and taxes. But the streets off the Rynek have a few new shops selling the leather products that are a specialty of this region. Most shops in Kraków are open weekdays 10–6, Saturday 9–2.

In Kraków the **Sukiennice booths** on the main square are still a good place to look for regional tooled leatherwork (slippers, bags, and belts) or for the embroidered felt slippers made in the Podhale region. Rabbit-skin slippers are also a local specialty. **Craft boutiques** in the recently reconstructed arcade at ulica Stolarska 3–9 have more exciting (and expensive) handmade products; there is often a selection of beautiful leather, jewelry, and brasswork.

In Zakopane, leather and sheepskin products are local specialties, and you'll find them all over, along with socks, sweaters, and caps handknitted in white, gray, and black patterns from rough undyed wool. The best places to look are the Thursday **markets at Nowy Targ** (*see* Exploring Krákow and the South, *above*) and at **Zakopane** (Wednesday). The Zakopane market is held at the foot of ulica Krupówki, on the way to the Gubałówka cable railway. Street vendors, who work throughout the region on every day of the week, charge higher prices.

Sports and Outdoor Activities

Kraków The **Niepołomice Forest** and **Ojców National Park** (*see* Exploring Krákow and the South, *above*) in Kraków have extensive marked trails for hikers. If you want to jog in Kraków the **Planty,** a ring of gardens around the Old Town, makes an excellent 5-kilometer (3-mile) route and is easily accessible from most hotels. The pathways along the Vistula also provide a good route: West of the Dębiński Bridge, take the path on the right bank; east of the bridge, the one on the left bank.

Zakopane
Hiking The Gorczański, Pieniński, and Tatrzański national parks all offer excellent hiking territory. The routes are well marked; all national parks have maps at entrance points explaining distances, times, and degrees of difficulty of the trails. On the lower reaches of trails out of major tourist points (for example, Zakopane, Szczawnica, Krynica), walkers crowd the paths, but they soon thin out higher up.

Jogging In Zakopane, the **Droga pod Reglami,** which runs along the foot of the Tatra National Park, makes an excellent, relatively flat jogging route; it can be approached from various points in the town.

Skiing **Zakopane**—which acquired snow-making facilities in 1990—is still the region's major center for downhill skiing, although Krynica and Krościenko also have facilities. You'll find the most advanced runs at **Kasprowy Wierch** mountain, accessed via a cable lift from Łozienice (lower station, tel. 816/45–10; upper station, tel. 816/44–05). Chair lifts also bring skiiers to the peaks of **Butory Wierch** (lift at ul. Powstańców Śląskich, tel. 816/39–41) and **Nosal** (lift ul. Balzera, tel. 816/31–81).

The towns of **Szczawnica, Krościenko,** and **Krynica** are good bases for **cross-country skiing**; nearer to Kraków, **Rabka** also offers excellent trails.

Dining and Lodging

This is one of the few regions in Poland that offer extensive options for inexpensive bed-and-breakfast accommodations in private pensions. Pensions usually offer full board and hearty meals. For information in **Zakopane** check with the **Hotel Giewont** (ul. Kościuszki 1, tel. 816/20–11); in **Krynica** consult **Pensjonat Wisła** (Bulwary Dietla 1, tel. 0135/23–86). You can also look for signs in windows advertising POKOJE (rooms). Highly recommended restaurants and lodgings in a particular price category are indicated by a star ★.

Częstochowa
Dining and
Lodging **Orbis Patria Hotel.** This six-story hotel built in the 1980s provides a predictable Orbis standard of cuisine and accommodations. The rooms are brightly furnished and comfortable, the staff cheerful and friendly. *Ul. Popiełuszki 2, 42–200, tel. 034/24–53–59, fax 034/24–63–32. 109 rooms. No air-conditioning. Breakfast included. AE, DC, MC, V. $$*

Hotel Polonia. This was a comfortable hotel for wealthy business travelers when it opened at the turn of the century. The mahogany double doors to the bedrooms remain, along with potted palms in the windows and velvet curtains. Unfortunately, the fixtures are becoming a little shabby, and the high ceilings and windows make for drafts. But the hotel is clean and the beds comfortable. The dining room offers traditional Polish cooking; the potatoes come with a spoonful of melted lard, and almost all main courses feature pork. *Ul. Piłsudskiego 9, tel. 034/24–40–67, fax 034/65–11–05. 62 rooms, most with bath or shower. AE, DC, MC, V. $*

Kraków
Dining **Cracovia.** The enormous dining room of this 1960s hotel conveys a sense of mass production that fortunately is not apparent in the excellent, internationalized Polish cuisine. Try the *krem z pieczarek* (thick and creamy mushroom soup) followed by chateaubriand, one of the chef's specialties. The side salads are fresh and delicious: Recent selections included sweetened grated carrots, cucumbers in cream, and beets mixed with horseradish. *Al. Marszałka Ferdinanda Focha 1, tel. 012/66–88–00. Reservations advised. Jacket and tie advised. AE, DC, MC, V. $$$$*

Hawełka. Recently privatized and upgraded, this first-floor restau-

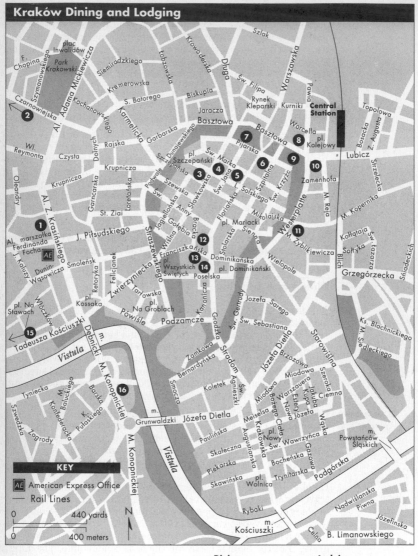

Kraków Dining and Lodging

KEY

AE American Express Office
— Rail Lines

0 ——— 440 yards
0 ——— 400 meters

Dining
Balaton, **14**
Cracovia, **1**
Francuski, **9**
Grand Hotel, **4**
Hawełka, **3**
Kurza Stopka, **13**
Pod Kopcem, **15**
U Pollera, **6**
Wierzynek, **12**

Lodging
Cracovia, **1**
Dom Turysty   PTTK, **11**
Europejski, **10**
Forum, **16**
Francuski, **7**
Grand Hotel, **4**
Holiday Inn, **2**
Hotel Pollera, **6**
Pod Różą, **5**
Warszawski, **8**

ımı ɛparkles with crystal and silver cutlery. Attentive waiters will advise in English on a range of traditional Polish dishes —the Hawełka's specialty. Try the fried eel in cream and dill sauce, or one of the excellent veal dishes. There is also an expansive wine list. *Rynek Główny 34, tel. 012/22–47–53 Reservations advised. Jacket and tie advised. AE, DC, MC, V. $$$$*

★ **Wierzynek.** Poland's most famous restaurant is in a fine 18th-century upper room on the Rynek, glittering with chandeliers and silver. It was here, after a historic meeting in 1364, that the king of Poland wined and dined the Holy Roman Emperor Charles IV, five kings, and a score of princes. Wierzynek is perhaps resting a little on its laurels these days, and the food may not really be any better than in other restaurants of its class, but the traditional Polish dishes—impressively served by armies of red-jacketed waiters—are very good. The kitchen excels in soups and game: Try the *żurek* (sour barley soup) followed by *zrazy*, small beef rolls filled with mushrooms and served with buckwheat. *Rynek Główny 15, tel. 012/22–98–96. Reservations required. Jacket and tie advised. AE, DC, MC, V. Closed public holidays. $$$$*

Francuski. After two years of renovations, the popular restaurant reopened in April 1992 under new management. The French and internationalized Polish cuisine is still first-rate, and the fin-de-siècle dining room remains an excellent place for a peaceful dinner in the shadow of the Old Town wall. *Ul. Pijarska 13, tel. 012/22–51–22. Reservations required. Jacket and tie advised. AE, DC, MC, V. $$$*

Grand Hotel. The restaurant in this renovated hotel is in a ground-floor room looking out onto an interior courtyard. The white paint and tablecloths make the ambience rather antiseptic, and the high ceiling over an (unused) minstrels' gallery gives the room a top-heavy look. The service is swift and efficient; the cuisine, international. Try the Grand Hotel cutlet: pork with ham and cheese, followed by one of the cream-filled gâteaux, a hotel specialty. *Ul. Sławkowska 5–7, tel. 012/21–72–55. Reservations advised. Jacket and tie advised. AE, DC, MC, V. Closed public holidays. $$$*

Pod Kopcem. The dining room in this hotel, in the building of the old Austrian barracks on St. Bronisława's Hill, has bare brick walls and brightly checked tablecloths. Alcoves and corners offer diners privacy. The cuisine is internationalized Polish, with a good selection of pork dishes. If you are really hungry try the *golonka* (knuckle of pork) with bread and a side salad. *Al. Waszyngtona, tel. 012/22–03–57. Reservations advised. Dress: casual but neat. AE, DC, MC, V. $$$*

Balaton. Kraków's Hungarian restaurant has dark wood paneling and trestle tables with benches, relieved by bright folk-weave rugs and embroideries on the walls. It is usually crowded, but the waitresses cope cheerfully. *Zupa gulaszowa* (hot spiced fish soup) is good for starters; follow it up with *placek ziemniaczany* (potato pancakes with pork stuffing). Good Hungarian wine is regularly available. *Ul. Grodzka 37, tel. 012/22–04–69. Reservations advised. Dress: casual but neat. AE, DC, MC, V. $$*

U Pollera. The large, high fin-de-siècle dining room, with a balcony from which the 19th-century owner inspected her staff's work, has a look of decayed grandeur. Recently repossessed by its prewar owner, however, this restaurant is on the way up. The chef from the newest Orbis hotel, the Forum, was lured here; the enormous crystal mirrors on the walls have been polished; and a complete redecoration is planned. The cuisine is eclectic but has enough traditional Polish items to satisfy anyone who wants to stick to native specialties. Chicken roasted with garlic and served with crispy potatoes is an excellent main course, and the chocolate gâteau for dessert is wonderfully light and creamy. *Ul. Szpitalna 30, tel. 012/22–16–21. Reservations advised. Jacket and tie advised. AE, DC, MC, V. $$*

Kurza Stopka. This small and rather dark restaurant specializes in chicken dishes, as its name ("Chicken's Claw") suggests. An unusual crisp and spicy *risotto paprykarz* (paprika risotto) served with a cool cucumber salad is one of the kitchen's specialties. This is the place for an informal and friendly dining experience, despite the din of sometimes large throngs of diners. *Pl. Wszystkich Świętych 9, tel. 021/22–91–96. No reservations. Dress: casual. AE, DC, MC, V. $*

Lodging
★ **Grand.** This early 19th-century hotel on the corner of ulica Solskiego in the Old Town was completely renovated—the work took 12 years—before reopening in 1990. An air of Regency elegance predominates, though some fine Art Nouveau stained-glass windows have been preserved on the first floor. The bedrooms, still reasonably sized despite some alterations, are decorated with Regency striped wallpaper and bedspreads; most of the furniture is period reproduction. The corridors are agreeably unpredictable, with alcoves and potted plants breaking the monotony at intervals. *Ul. Sławkowska 5–7, tel. 012/21–72–55, fax 012/21–83–60, telex 0326498. 50 rooms, 5 suites, all with bath. Facilities: restaurant. AE, DC, MC, V. $$$$*

Forum. Opened in 1988, this modern hotel has proved to be something of a disappointment. Although it commands spectacular views over the Wawel Castle, it is located on the right bank of the Vistula, adding 10 minutes to the traveling time to the Old City, while its immediate surroundings are slightly squalid. A four-story, bow-shaped structure on stilts, the Forum has rooms of good size with light and solidly comfortable furnishings; the bathrooms are particularly well appointed. One other plus: The Forum definitely has the best health and sports facilities in town. *Ul. Marii Konopnickiej 28, 30–302, tel. 012/66–95–00, fax 012/66–58–27. 265 rooms, 15 suites, all with bath. Facilities: restaurant, 2 bars, sauna, indoor pool, tennis courts. AE, DC, MC, V. $$$*

Francuski. This turn-of-the-century hotel is just inside the only remaining fragment of the town walls, within five minutes' walk of the main square. The Francuski reopened in 1991 after a comprehensive renovation that upgraded the bathrooms and fixtures without altering the hotel's basic character. The rooms are comfortable and furnished in updated period style; the entrance hall features a wide mahogany staircase and lush stained-glass windows. *Ul. Pijarska 13, tel. 012/22–51–22, fax 012/22–52–70. 36 rooms, 6 suites, all with bath or shower. Facilities: restaurant, café. AE, DC, MC, V. $$$*

Cracovia. Opened in 1964, this mammoth five-story hotel opposite the Błonie (Kraków Common) long provided the city's only luxury accommodations. Now, after 30 years of catering to tourist groups, it is beginning to show signs of strain and has become somewhat downscale. But the rooms, although rather small and standardized, are well appointed with dark, heavy furniture, and the staff members do their best to make you feel at home. Because of its size, it's one of the few hotels to consistently have space during the summer season. *Al. Marszałka Ferdinanda Focha 1, tel. 012/22–86–66, fax 012/21–95–86. 415 rooms, 10 suites, all with bath. Facilities: restaurant, bar. AE, DC, MC, V. $$*

Holiday Inn. This high-rise hotel, the first Holiday Inn in Eastern Europe, is 3 kilometers (2 miles) to the west of the city center in pleasant suburban surroundings on the far side of the Kraków Common. It provides standardized but comfortable and cheerfully decorated accommodations and has good parking facilities. Its clients are mainly tourists (including a good number of travelers on packaged tours). This hotel's proximity to open parkland and sports facilities makes it a good choice for those who want to combine sightseeing with a little exercise. *Ul. Koniewa 7, tel. 012/37–50–44, fax 012/37–59–38. 310 rooms with bath (reduced rates for single occupancy). Facilities: restaurant, solarium, sauna, indoor pool. AE, DC, MC, V. $$*

Pod Różą. One of Kraków's oldest hotels, the Pod Różą has seen many distinguished guests, including Czar Alexander I. Now, despite renovations in the 1980s, the upper floors are a little worse for wear: Although the guest rooms are large and have comfortable furniture, the paint is peeling and the plumbing is incredibly noisy. The lack of an elevator is not a terrible hardship, since the hotel has only four stories. If you don't mind the down-at-the-heels ambience, the Pod Różą does have some advantages: It stands on the beautiful ulica Floriańska, and the staff is very helpful. *Ul. Floriańska 14, tel. 012/22–93–99, telex 0325340, fax 012/21–75–13. 30 rooms, 1 suite, all with bath. Facilities: restaurant, casino. AE, DC, MC, V. $$*

Dom Turysty PTTK. This six-story 1960s building stands opposite Planty Park, facing the outer walls of the Bernadine convent in the Old Town. Its upper floors contain large, multiple-occupancy rooms that often house groups of students, who can be noisy. The rooms on the lower floors are comfortable though long, narrow, and fairly spartan (the double rooms have two beds head-to-foot along the wall). Nevertheless, the hotel is clean and conveniently located, with parking facilities for guests. *Westerplatte 15, tel. 012/22–95–66, fax 012/21–27–26. 51 doubles, 16 with bath; 78 singles, 9 with bath. Facilities: restaurant. AE, DC, MC, V. $*

Europejski. Although this late-19th-century hotel opposite the main railway station has been undergoing renovation for some time, the standard of accommodation is high in rooms where work has already been completed. All the rooms, even the older and somewhat shabby ones, are reasonably sized and comfortable. However, rooms facing the busy main street are noisy. *Ul. Lubicz 5, tel. 012/22–09–11, fax 012/22–89–25. 30 rooms, most with bath. Facilities: restaurant. AE, DC, MC, V. $*

Hotel Pollera. In 1990 Pollera was restored to the Kraków lawyer from whom it was compulsorily purchased in 1950. He is a descendant of the Poller for whom the hotel is named: an Austrian army officer who married a local girl and settled in Kraków during the early 19th century. The new owner and his eight children—all apparently involved in the business—are very eager to restore the hotel's reputation. The building's exterior has already had a face-lift; and the guest rooms, which had greatly deteriorated over the past 45 years, are also gradually being renovated and upgraded with private bathrooms. The fine Art Nouveau entrance hall, dominated by an imposing grand staircase and stained-glass window, is as elegant as ever. *Ul. Szpitalna 30, tel. 012/22–10–44, fax 012/22–13–89. 107 rooms, most with bath. Facilities: restaurant, some singles have TV. No tel. in rooms. AE, DC, MC, V. $*

Warszawski. This was a busy railway hotel when it was built in the late 19th century on a corner opposite Kraków's main station. Since then it has deteriorated. A lot of the original fixtures and furniture remain, and many of the rooms are enormous but tend to be dark and gloomy, with peeling paint and flaking plaster. Traffic noise can keep you awake in summer, when the windows are open. There is no restaurant, though a café next door offers breakfast. *Ul. Pawia 6, tel. 012/22–06–22. No air-conditioning. No TV or tel. in rooms. No credit cards. $*

Nowy Sącz
Dining and Lodging

Beskid. This standard, cube-shape Orbis hotel is a typical product of the mid-1960s. It commands good views while being conveniently located near the rail and bus stations in the town center. The rooms are rather small and drab but comfortable, brightened up with Podhale folk elements. The restaurant, which closes at 9 PM, emphasizes basic Polish cuisine. Breakfasts are delicious, featuring freshly baked rolls, white cheese mixed with chives, scrambled eggs cooked with chopped bacon, and a variety of jams and honey. *Ul. Limanowskiego 1, 33–330 Nowy Sącz, tel. 018/207–70, fax 018/221–44. 97 rooms, 34 with bath; 25 suites. Facilities: restaurant. No air-conditioning. No tel. in rooms. AE, DC, MC, V. $$*

Zakopane
Dining and Lodging

Kasprowy. This is not a convenient place to stay unless you have your own means of transportation: It's several kilometers outside of town and a 15-minute walk from the bus routes. However, the Kasprowy is a good option for skiiers: The lift to Butory Wierch is nearby, and there are beginners' slopes all around. Situated on the side of Gubałówka, this four-story hotel fits snugly into the hillside and has panoramic views of Mount Giewont and beyond. The rooms are comfortable and well furnished (those overlooking Giewont have a 25% markup), but the public areas have become a little shabby since the hotel was opened in 1974. The restaurant is large and light and has good views. Try the *Kotlet góralski* (highlander's cutlet), which is beef covered in finely chopped mushrooms. *Ul. Powstańców Śląskich, tel. 0165/140–11, fax 0165/157–00. 243 rooms, 12 suites, all with bath. Facilities: restaurant, shops. No air-conditioning. AE, DC, MC, V. $$$*

Gazda. Opened in 1975 opposite the post office in the center of town, this hotel is in a pleasantly solid, low-rise building. Outside, the stone figure of a farmer in full folk costume reinforces the local theme (*gazda* means farmer). The rooms are comfortably furnished in stripped pine and decorated in light, bright colors. As befits a hotel run by the peasant cooperative Gromada, the Gazda has the best food for miles around. The large, light dining room, outfitted with linen tablecloths and napkins, is usually full; the service is friendly and prompt. The menu always offers a wide choice, and portions are large. Recommended dishes include roast lamb, and, in season, the bilberry dessert pancakes. *Gromada, ul. Zaruskiego 2, tel. 0165/150–11, fax 0165/153–30. 64 rooms, 54 with bath. Facilities: restaurant. No air-conditioning. No TV or tel. in rooms. AE, DC, MC, V. $$*

Giewont. If you can, pick a room in this late-19th-century hotel with a view of the peak after which it is named, Mt. Giewont. The rooms are reasonably well furnished but vary greatly in size; it would be best to see the room before moving in. The dining room is high and galleried, decorated with crystal chandeliers and crisp white tablecloths on well-spaced tables. The game dishes are the best items on the menu; try the roast pheasant when it's in season. *Ul. Kościuszki 1, tel. 0165/120–11, fax 0165/120–13 (reservations via the Kasprowy). 48 rooms, 37 with bath. Facilities: restaurant. No air-conditioning. No tel. in rooms. AE, DC, MC, V. $$*

The Arts and Nightlife

The Arts

Kraków has a lively tradition in theater and music, although during the past few years the arts in Poland have fallen on hard times. You will still find interesting performances, however; check with the tourist office or the daily *Gazeta Krakowska* for details about what's on.

Zakopane has no regular theater, but performances of plays (by "Witkacy," for example) are occasionally staged in the summer; watch for posters on kiosks for announcements.

Film **Kijów** (al. Krasińskiego 34, tel. 012/22–77–67) is a large 1960s cinema in Kraków that is now showing mainly U.S. films, with subtitles. **Kultura** (Rynek Główny 27, tel. 012/22–32–65) occasionally shows Polish films.

Giewont (plac Zwycięstwa, tel. 0165/140–40) in Zakopane shows a variety of films, usually a little out of date.

Music In Kraków the local philharmonic—**Filharmonia im. Karola Szymanowskiego** (ul. Zwierzyniecka 1, tel. 012/22–94–77)—performs Friday and Saturday. Badly damaged by fire in 1991, the philharmonic hall was given a face-lift while being rebuilt. Chamber-music concerts, occasionally given in Wawel Castle, are well worth looking out for.

Occasional concerts (not only of music by Szymanowski) are given in Zakopane at the **Willa Atma** (ul. Kasprusie 19, tel. 0165/140–32). There is a festival of Szymanowski's music in September, when concerts are held at various points in the town.

Opera and The **Teatr im. Juliusza Słowackiego** (plac Św. Ducha 1, tel. 012/22–
Dance 43–64) provides a regular program of old opera and ballet favorites as well as dramatic performances.

Theater **Maszkaron** (Wieża Ratuszowa, tel. 012/21–50–16), a tiny theater in the cellar of the old Town Hall Tower, stages small-scale dramas against a bare-brick backdrop. The **Stary Teatr im. Heleny Modrzejewskiej** (plac Szczepański 1, tel. 012/22–85–66), a 19th-century theater named after Kraków's most famous actress—who ended her career in the United States as Helena Modjeska—stages some of the best productions in Poland; Andrzej Wajda still directs here when his political career permits.

Nightlife Much of the café and cabaret nightlife for which Kraków was renowned until recently has folded, but there are some signs of a revival.

With the exception of the bar and nightclub in the **Hotel Kasprowy** (ul. Powstańców Śąskich), Zakopane goes to bed early.

Bars The **"Bacchus" Drinks Bar** (ul. Solskiego 21), a refurbished and very expensive bar in the Old Town, is popular with a younger crowd. The **Grand Hotel Café** (ul. Sławkowska 5–7, entrance from ul. Solskiego) is a good place for a quiet evening drink.

Cabaret The cabaret at **Jama Michalika** (ul. Floriańska 45) is currently Kraków's best satirical and musical show, following the demise of the Pod Baranami cabaret. The **Hotel Cracovia** has a nightclub with more sophisticated floor shows, including strippers. The **Forum** also has a nightclub.

Casinos Kraków's first casino is on the first floor of the **Pod Różą** hotel (ul. Floriańska 14; open 1 PM–3 AM).

Lublin and the East

Lublin, the largest town in eastern Poland, is a good hub for exploring the villages and countryside of the eastern and southeastern parts of the country. Lublin's location protects it from Western commercial influences and gives the visitor an opportunity to peek at the old Poland—less prosperous and more traditional. Historically, Lublin lay in the heart of Poland and served as a crossroads for east and west. It was in Lublin in 1569 that the eastern duchy of Lithuania joined the kingdom of Poland by signing the Union of Lublin, thus creating the largest empire in Europe at the time. Following World War II, Poland's borders shifted west and Lublin found itself sitting near the Soviet border. Today's Eastern influence comes predominantly from the flood of Russian traders peddling everything from old car parts to champagne and caviar in the city's marketplace.

But this is not to imply that the changes sweeping across Poland have passed Lublin by. New freedoms have meant political opportunity for several enthusiastic, idealistic students at the Catholic University of Lublin. The newest of the town council members, these aspiring Lech Wałęsas are running city government in between lectures and exams. One of their most important projects will be leading the restoration of Lublin's chief monument, its walled Stare Miasto (Old Town). Located at the western end of Krakowskie Przedmieście, the quaint cobblestone streets of this district are filled with more rubble and debris from crumbling facades than tourists.

Despite its graying exterior and mild urban decay, Lublin is rich in parks, offering wild, lush greens in summer and golden yellows in autumn. Less than one hour away, visitors can enjoy a picnic on the palace grounds in Puławy or a walk along the banks of the Vistula River in the picturesque village of Kazimierz Dolny.

Important Addresses and Numbers

Tourist Information Lublin's main source of tourist information—**Centrum Informacji Turystycznej**—is in the Old Town (Krakowskie Przedmieście 78, tel. 081/244–12). **Orbis** (ul. Narutowicza 31/33, tel. 081/222–56 or 081/222–59) books train tickets and exchanges money. Other places to check are **Turysta Travel** (ul. Chopina 14, tel. 081/291–17) and **PTTK Hostels** (ul. Kościuszki 6, tel. 081/237–58).

In **Zamość** tourist information is provided by **Zamojski Ośrodek Informacji Turystycznej** (Rynek Wielki 13, tel. 084/22–92) and **Orbis Travel** (ul. Grodzka 18, tel. 084/30–01).

Emergencies **Police,** tel. 997. **Other emergencies,** tel. 999 or 330–92. **Medical emergencies:** For medical assistance go to the **Szpital Kliniczny** at ulica Staszica 16 or to **Szpital Kliniczny No. 4** at ulica Jaczewskiego 8. The emergency room—*Pogotowie Ratunkowe*—at ulica Weteranów 46A (tel. 081/330–92) is open 24 hours.

Late-Night Pharmacies Two pharmacies (*apteki*) in Lublin (ul. Bramowa 8, tel. 081/205–21, and Krakowskie Przedmieście 49, tel. 081/224–25) are open 24 hours.

Arriving and Departing by Train and Bus

Exploring the region around Lublin is best done by bus from either Dworzec PKS Główny in downtown Lublin or the Północy station.

By Train **Lublin Główny** (pl. Dworcowy), the town's main station, is about 4 kilometers (2½ miles) south of the city center. Frequent train service connects Lublin with Warsaw (2½ hours), Kraków (4½ hours), and Zamość (3 hours). Buses 13 and 158 connect the train station with the town center. Luggage storage is available for zł 10,000 a day per bag. The RUCH newsstand outside the station sells a great city map as well as local bus tickets.

By Bus Dworzec PKS Główny (al. Tysiąclecia 4), located just north of Stare Miasto near the castle, connects Lublin with cities to the west and south. Buses run regularly to Puławy (one hour), Kazimierz Dolny (1½ hours), Rzeszów (three hours), and Warsaw (three hours). Buses 5, 10, 35, 38, 154, and 161 connect the station with ulica Krakowskie Przedmieście. Luggage storage is available daily 6 AM–7 PM for zł 10,000 per day per bag. To find it, go outside the station and look for the PRZECHOWALNIA BAGAŻU sign. The Russian market right outside the station sells food and every other item imaginable but lures a somewhat seedy element that loiters in and around the terminal.

Located about 4 kilometers (2½ miles) southeast of the town center, Dworzec PKS Póplnocny (ulica Gospodarcza) connects Lublin with points east. Buses run frequently to Zamość (1¾ hours). You can reach the town center on Bus 155 or 159.

Getting Around

Most of Lublin's restaurants and hotels lie on or around ulica Krakowscie Przedmieście and its continuation to the west, aleja Racławickie. This route is anchored by the Stare Miasto in the east and the Catholic University in the west. The Majdanek concentration camp is a few kilometers southeast. If you don't mind walking, you can easily explore the entire city on foot.

By Bus Lublin's bus system is convenient for traveling in from the train station and out to Majdanek, but it's often crowded, and service has been reduced to just three main routes after midnight. Avoid traveling before 9 AM and between 3 PM and 5 PM to escape a crush of passengers. Plainclothes officers frequently patrol the bus system during rush hours, and ticket shirkers are fined $8. You can buy a ticket at the RUCH kiosks or anywhere you see a SPRZEDAŻ BILETÓW sign. Passengers are responsible for canceling their tickets on the bus; look for ticket punchers at the door.

By Taxi Taxi stands can be found near the bus and train stations, outside the Stare Miasto near Lublin Cathedral, and up and down ulica Krakowskie Przedmieście. The fares are reasonable: A trip from the train station to the outskirts of town should cost no more than $3.50, including a 5% tip. Radio taxis (tel. 919) are also available. Most cabs now have electronic meters showing the exact fare; though some confusingly still use older meters whose fares must be multiplied by 400, 500, or 600 (it varies from meter to meter). In either case, be sure the driver turns on the meter.

Exploring Lublin and the East

Numbers in the margin correspond to points of interest on the Southeastern Poland map.

㉙ The tourist attractions of **Lublin** are located in three distinct regions of the city. **Stare Miasto** (Old Town), a medieval walled city of cobblestone streets and crumbling architecture, is situated at the eastern end of Krakowskie Przedmieście, the main street. The Catholic and Marie Skłodowska-Curie universities and the adjacent Saxon Gardens are on the western edge of Lublin, off Aleja Racławickie. Majdanek, the second-largest Nazi concentration camp in Europe, lies several kilometers southeast of central Lublin.

At the eastern end of Krakowskie Przedmieście is **Brama Krakowska** (Kraków Gate), a Gothic and Baroque structure that served as the main entrance to medieval Lublin. Today it separates modern Lublin from the Stare Miasto. It houses the **Muzeum Lubelskie** (Lublin History Museum), which offers an overview of the area's history. *Pl. Łokietka 2, tel. 081/26–001. Admission: zł 10,000 adults, zł 5,000 students. Open Wed.–Sat. 9–4, Sun. 9–5.*

Part of Lublin's tremendous success as a medieval trading center stemmed from a royal decree exempting the city from all customs duties. As a result, huge fortunes were made, and the town's merchants were able to build the beautiful 14th- and 15th-century houses—complete with colorful frescoed facades and decorative moldings—that surround the **Rynek** (Market Square). The Rynek's trapezoidal shape, unusual for a market square, is the result of medieval builders adapting the construction of the town to the shape of the protective walls surrounding Lublin.

Filling the center of the Rynek is the reconstructed **Stary Ratusz** (Old Town Hall), built in the 16th century and rebuilt in neoclassical style in the 1780s by the Italian architect Domenico Merlini. Here a royal tribunal served as the seat of the Crown Court of Justice for Małopolska beginning in 1578. On Saturday the hall fills with young couples waiting to be married. Off the Rynek and down ulica Złota stands the **Dominican Church and Monastery,** dating from 1342, the jewel of Lublin's Old Town; the interior was renovated in Rococo style during the 17th century. Of the 11 chapels within, two are of particular note: **Firlej Chapel,** with its late-Renaissance architecture; and the **Tyszkiewski Chapel,** with its early Baroque decoration. Circling the walls above the chapels are paintings depicting the bringing of a piece of the True Cross on which Jesus was crucified to Lublin and the protection given the city through the ages by the relic. Unfortunately, this protection did not extend to the relic itself, which was stolen from the Dominican church in 1991. The church is often closed now, but try knocking on the monastery door to the right of the entrance to get someone to let you in. *Ul. Złota. Admission free. Open weekdays 9–noon and 3–6, Sat.–Sun. 3–6.*

Outside the Old City Wall and around the corner from Kraków Gate stands **Lublin Cathedral,** begun in 1625. The exterior of this Jesuit church is an example of Lublin Renaissance style—steep-pitched roofs, highly decorated gables, and elaborate patterned vaulting. Inside to the left of the Baroque high altar, a reproduction of the Black Madonna of Częstochowa is on display. You can reach the **Kaplica Akustyczna** (Acoustic Chapel) by a passage to the right of the high altar. Watch what you say here—the acoustics are so astounding that a whisper in one corner can be heard perfectly in another. Next to the chapel is the **treasury,** the only place to view what remains of the original illusionistic frescoes that decorated the church interior: The images were painted so skillfully that they appear almost three-dimensional. *Ul. Królewska. Admission to Acoustic Chapel and treasury: zł 5,000 adults, zł 2,000 students.*

During the late 14th century King Kazimierz the Great ordered the construction of **Lublin Castle,** as well as the defensive walls surrounding the city, to protect the wealthy trading center from foreign invasion. Most of the castle was rebuilt during the 19th century, when it was converted to a prison. Run at various times by the Russian czar, the Polish government, and the German Gestapo, the castle prison witnessed the largest number of deaths during World War II, when more than 10,000 political prisoners were murdered by the Nazis. The **Castle Museum** houses historical and ethnographic exhibits and an art gallery known for Jan Matejko's *Unia Lubelska* (1869), which depicts the signing of the Lublin Union by the king of Poland and Grand Duke of Lithuania exactly three centuries earlier. *Ul. Zamkowa 9, tel. 081/25-001. Admission: zł 10,000 adults, zł 5,000 students. Open Wed.-Sat. 9-4, Sun. 9-5.*

The hill behind the castle is the site of the **Old Jewish Cemetery,** destroyed during World War II by the German SS, which used the rubble from the headstones to pave the entranceway to Majdanek concentration camp (*see below*). The park at the base of the castle was the site of the Jewish ghetto, in which Nazis imprisoned the Jewish population of Lublin until April 1943, when they sent them to Majdanek. In the 16th century Lublin was a center of Jewish culture.

Reminders of World War II are never far away in Poland, and several kilometers southeast of Lublin at **Majdanek** lie the remnants of a **concentration camp** that was second in size only to Auschwitz. Established in July 1941, it grew to 1,235 acres, although the plan was to make it five times as large. Majdanek originally housed 5,000 Polish, Russian, and Ukrainian prisoners of war, who were later followed by citizens of 29 other countries, most of them Jewish. From 1941 to 1944, more than 360,000 people lost their lives here, either by direct extermination or through disease.

Standing at the camp entrance is one of two monuments designed for the 25th anniversary of the liberation of Majdanek. The **Monument of Struggle and Martyrdom** symbolizes the inmates' faith and hope; the **mausoleum** at the rear of the camp marks the death of that hope. Of the five fields constituting the original camp, only the gas chambers, watchtowers, and crematoria, as well as some barracks on Field Three, remain. The visitor center to the left of the entrance monument sells guidebooks in English. *Droga Męczenników Majdanka 76, tel. 081/42-647. Admission free. Open May-Sept. 15, Tues.-Sun. 8-6; Sept. 16-Apr., Tues.-Sun. 8-3. Closed day after holidays.*

The 18th-century **Puławy Palace,** 12 kilometers (7 miles) northwest ③⓪ of Lublin in the village of **Puławy,** is a wonderful place to spend an afternoon strolling through parks and gardens or enjoying a picnic lunch. The palace was originally the residence of the Czartoryski family, a patriotic, politically powerful clan. Prince Adam Czartoryski was one of the most educated men of his day and a great patron of art and culture. He attracted so many prominent Poles to Puławy that by the late 18th century it was said to rival Warsaw as a cultural and political capital. Today the yellow-and-white neoclassical building has become the home of a humble agricultural institute, and the site is best known for the beautiful English-style gardens and pavilions.

Set in a building modeled on the Vesta Temple in Tivoli, **Świątynia Sybilli** (Sybil's Temple) is Poland's first museum. Completed in 1809, it houses a collection of national relics that was started after the first partitioning of Poland in an effort to preserve remainders of the country's glorious past and traditions. The museum also contains a rotating selection from the Czartoryski Collection in Kraków. The **Palace Chapel,** built in 1803, is based on the Pantheon in Rome. It's located at ulica Piłsudskiego 10, outside the palace grounds (from the palace front, walk two blocks north on ulica Czartoryskich to ulica Piłsudskiego, and then left two blocks). *Admission to palace grounds free; to Sybil's Temple: zł 10,000 adults, zł 5,000 students. Open May-Nov., Tues.-Sun. 9-5.*

③① The small village of **Kazimierz Dolny,** perched on a steep, hilly bank of the placid Vistula River, seems to define the word "quaint." Its assortment of whitewashed facades and steeply pitched red-tiled roofs peeking out over the treetops strikes a harmonious balance with the surrounding forests and sandstone hillsides. The effect is so pleasing that Kazimierz Dolny has thrived for over a century as an artists' colony and vacation spot for city-weary tourists. Often referred to as the Pearl of the Polish Renaissance, Kazimierz Dolny prospered as a port town during the 16th and 17th centuries, but the partitioning of Poland left it cut off from the grain markets of Gdańsk. Thereafter the town fell into decline until it was rediscovered by painters and writers during the 19th century. Today nonartistic visitors can still enjoy the Renaissance architecture along the village's dusty cobblestone streets, or commune with nature on a hike through the nearby hills and gorges.

Two of the city's most powerful families, the Przybyłas and the Celejs, left behind ornate houses that stand out gaudily amid the whitewash of Kazimierz Dolny. Adorning the facades of the **Przybyła Brothers' House** on the southeast corner of the compact *Rynek* (market square) are the two-story bas-relief figures of St. Nicholas (left) and St. Christopher (right), the patron saints of the brothers. One block toward the river from these houses stands the **Celej House.** Embellished with griffins, dragons, and salamanders, it outdoes the Przybyła at least in terms of gaudy decoration. The Celej family departed long ago, and their former abode now houses the **Town Museum of Kazimierz Dolny,** which has many paintings depicting local Jewish life in the past. *Ul. Senatorska 11/13, tel. 0831/ 102–88. Admission: zł 10,000 adults, zł 5,000 students. Open May– Oct., Tues.–Sun.*

A covered passageway off ulica Senatorska leads up to the walled courtyard of the **Church and Monastery of the Reformati Order,** which stand on the southern hill overlooking Kazimierz Dolny. During the late 18th century an encircling wall was built to protect the monastery's buildings. A plaque inside the passageway memorializes the Nazis' use of the site as a house of torture during the occupation of Poland. The climb up to the courtyard is worthwhile just for the spectacular view of Kazimierz. You can also see the ruins of the 14th-century **Kazimierz Castle,** which served as a watchtower to protect the Vistula trade route, and **Góra Trzech Krzyży** (Three Crosses Hill), constructed in 1708 to commemorate the victims of a plague that ravaged the town.

㉜ For an easy day trip from Lublin, head to the fortified town of **Zamość,** 87 kilometers (54 miles) to the southeast. Here you can wander through a town kept marvelously intact since the Renaissance, with a grand central piazza, wide boulevards, neat rows of colorful houses, arcaded passages, and brightly painted facades. Physically, though, it could use a little updating for us finicky moderns; hundreds of houses have no running water or sanitation.

Zamość was conceived in the late 16th century as an outpost on the thriving trade route between Lublin and Lwów. The town thrived, and its strong fortifications spared it from destruction during the Swedish onslaught of the 17th century. The Polish victory over Lenin's Red Army near Zamość in 1920 helped clear the way for a restoration of the country's independence. World War II saw the town renamed Himmlerstadt and thousands of its residents deported or exterminated to make way for German settlers. The buildings are unscathed, but you may see something else in the eyes of older villagers.

Zamość's **Rynek** (marketplace) is a breathtaking arcaded piazza surrounded by the decorative facades of homes built by local merchants. Dominating the square is the impressive Baroque **town hall**, topped by a 164-foot spire. It's easy to imagine characters in period costumes making a grand entrance from its double staircase. Next door in the **Zamość Regional Museum** you can see regional artifacts, paintings of the Zamoyski clan, the town's founding family, and a scale model of Zamość. *Ul. Ormianska 24 tel. 084/64-94. Admission: zł 10,000 adults, zł 5,000 students. Open daily 10-5.*

Near the southwest corner of the Rynek is the **St. Thomas Collegiate Church,** one of Poland's most beautiful Renaissance churches. In the presbytery are four 17th-century paintings ascribed to Domenico Robusti, Tintoretto's son. The church is also the final resting place of Jan Zamoyski, buried in the appropriately named **Zamoyski Chapel** to the right of the high altar.

Beyond the church lies yet another Zamoyski-connected building, the **Zamoyski Palace,** which lost much of its decorative detail in renovation and restoration and now serves as a courthouse. Behind the palace, the **Arsenal Museum** houses a collection of Turkish armaments and rugs, as well as a model of the original town plan. *Admission: zł 10,000 adults, zł 5,000 students. Open daily 10-3:30.*

Near the northwest corner of the Rynek, behind the town hall, the **Old Academy** of Zamość was a distinguished center of learning during the 17th and 18th centuries and the third-largest university after those in Kraków and Vilnius (it's now a high school). Across ulica Akademicka from the academy is the town's oldest entrance, **Lublin Gate.** In 1588, Jan Zamoyski led the Austrian archduke Maximilian triumphantly into town through this gate, after defeating him in his attempt to seize the Polish throne from Sigismund III. He then bricked up the gate to commemorate his victory.

To explore what's left of the town's **fortifications,** head east from the Rynek down ulica Staszica to another Morando legacy, the **Lwów Gate and Bastion.** With defenses like these, three stories high and 20 feet thick, it's easy to understand why Zamość was one of the few places to escape ruin in the Swedish deluge. *Gate and bastion admission: zł 5,000. Open daily 10-4.*

A 10-minute walk south of the Rynek on ulica Moranda brings you to the **rotunda,** a monument to a tragic era in Zamość's history. From 1939 to 1944 this fortified emplacement served as an extermination camp where thousands of Poles, Jews, and Russians were brutally killed, some even burned alive. Now it serves as a memorial to the victims of Nazi terror in the region, and its museum details the town's suffering in the war. *Open Apr. 15-Sept. 30, daily 9-6; Nov. 1-Apr. 14, daily 10-5.*

Seventeen kilometers (10½ miles) northeast of the industrial and transit center of Rzeszów is the neo-Baroque **Łańcut Palace**, situated within an elegant and serene 76-acre natural reserve in the town of **Łańcut.** Built during the 16th century, the palace is one of the most grandiose aristocratic residences in Eastern Europe. In the 19th century it was willed to the Potocki family, who amassed an impressive art collection here. Count Alfred Potocki, the last owner, emigrated to Liechtenstein in 1944 as Russian troops approached, absconding with 11 train cars full of art objects and paintings. Much was left behind, however, and after the war a museum was established in the palace (which had survived intact). Today you can see the family collection of art and interior decorations, including Biedermeier, neoclassical, and Rococo furnishings. Of particular interest are the intricate wood-inlay floors, the tiny theater off the dining hall, and the hall of sculpture painted to resemble a trellis of grapevines. More than 40 rooms are open to the public, including the Turkish and Chinese apartments that reflect the 18th-century fascination with the Near and Far East. Outside, a moat and a system of bastions laid out like a five-point star separate the inner Italian and rose gardens from the rest of the park. The **Carriage Museum,** in the old coach house outside the main gates, contains more than 50 vehicles and is one of the largest museums of its kind in Europe. *Admission (to both museums): zł 12,000 adults, zł 6,000 students. Park open daily until sunset. Museums open Tues.–Sat. 8–2:30, Sun. 9–4.*

To return to Lublin, drive to Rzeszów and take Road 26 north; from here you can also conveniently travel on to Kraków, 152 kilometers (94 miles) to the west.

Sports and Outdoor Activities

Kazimierz Dolny Boat rides on the Vistula originate at ulica Puławska 6. The peaceful half-hour ride takes you south to **Janowiec** with its Firlej Castle ruins. Landlubbers may prefer to take one of the numerous marked trails, ranging in length from 2 to 6 kilometers (1 to 4 miles), and explore the rich landscape. All trails converge in the market square. Tourist tracks lead north (marked red) and south (marked green) along the river from the Rynek and lead down streets and cart paths, through orchards and quarries, by castles and granaries.

Lublin On hot summer days the residents of Lublin head for **Zalew Zemborzycki,** a man-made lake about 4 kilometers (2½ miles) south of central Lublin. Set in Las Dąbrowa (Oak Woods), the lake offers sailing and canoe rentals, as well as a great place to take a walk. To get there, take Bus 25 or 42 from Lublin Cathedral.

Dining and Lodging

Highly recommended restaurants and lodgings in a particular price category are indicated by a star ★.

Łańcut **Hotel Zamkowy.** The simple, cozy accommodations within this 18th-
Lodging century palace are somewhat anomalous for their 1970s decor. How-
★ ever, the comfortable rooms overlook the palace courtyard and allow you to peer into the museum beyond. Take a peaceful walk in the palace gardens at sunset, and wake up to the sound of birds and crickets. There are only 50 beds, so reservations are imperative. *Ul. Zamkowa 1, tel. 017/25–26–71. 23 rooms, some with bath. Facilities: restaurant, luggage storage. AE. $*

Lublin **Karczma Słupska.** Part of a chain of traditional Polish taverns, this
Dining local favorite near the Catholic University is a good choice for casual dining. Settle into a rustic, carved-wood booth and feast on such Polish specialties as sautéed carp and pork chop Lublin style. The food is delicious, though the service is slow even by Polish standards. *Al. Racławickie 22, tel. 081/388–13. Reservations not required. Dress: casual. No credit cards. $$*

Restauracja Europa. Located in the heart of central Lublin, the Europa is a classic Polish restaurant: A dark-paneled dining room, white tablecloths, and formal (but *slow*) service give this place traditional charm. A dinner of pork loin is filling and inexpensive; vegetarian meals are also available. *Krakowskie Przedmieście 29, tel. 081/220–12. Reservations advised. Dress: casual. No credit cards. $*

Dining and
Lodging
★

Unia Hotel. The six-story hotel is just off the main road, outside the Old Town. Most of the public spaces and guest rooms are fairly cramped, though each room has its own bathroom and television (not a given for this part of Poland). The small restaurant, decorated in a bland 1960s style, is one of the hotel's main assets—despite its dull looks, it's definitely the best dining room in Lublin. The menu features Polish and international cuisine, and the service is good (but don't expect the waiters to speak English). The mushroom soup makes an excellent appetizer; recommended main courses include beefsteak with french fries, roast duck, or the *de volaille* cutlet (rolled chicken stuffed with cheese). *Al. Racławickie 12, tel. 081/ 320–61, fax 081/330–21. Facilities: restaurant, conference room. AE, DC, MC, V. $$*

Victoria Hotel. This old hotel is large and well situated, within walking distance of all the Old Town's landmarks. The rooms are on the small side, but the service is efficient and friendly. The restaurant offers such traditional Polish specialties as *zupa ogórkowa* (cucumber soup) and cherry soup, in addition to fairly typical meat entrées such as roast pork, veal cutlet, and beef medallions with mashed potatoes. *Ul. Narutowicza 58–60, tel. 081/270–11, fax 081/290–26. 190 rooms. Facilities: restaurant. AE, DC, MC, V. $*

Lodging

Lublinianka Hotel. Built in the 19th century, this old hotel offers somewhat spartan accommodations in a handsome, cupola-tipped building. The rooms are large but don't have bathrooms—you have to use public ones at the end of the corridor. The location is an advantage, however: It's on the main street of the Old Town. *Krakowskie Przedmieście 56, tel. 081/242–61. 57 rooms, none with bath. AE, DC, MC, V. $*

PZMot Motel. A utilitarian concrete block situated near the center of town, the PZMot is efficiently run and offers clean and bright accommodations at a very fair price. Admittedly, singles here are no bigger than the bed, but many of the doubles come with their own bath or shower and the public bathrooms are clean. The management speaks a little English. The small restaurant serves simple Polish dishes. *Ul. Prusa 8, tel. 081/342–32 or 081/343–72. 64 rooms, some with bath. No credit cards. $*

Zamość
Dining

Restauracja Hetmańska. This popular tavern attracts local customers even at off-hours. Specialties include kiełbasa and applesauce. *Ul. Staszica 2. No credit cards. $*

Lodging

Hotel Renesans. Just two blocks east of the market square, this drab cement-block building clashes with its Renaissance surroundings. Rooms are small and characterless but clean. The hotel café serves breakfast. *Ul. Grecka 6, tel. 084/51–74. 120 beds. Facilities: café. No credit cards. $*

The Arts and Nightlife

For up-to-date information about movies, theater, and concerts in Lublin, consult the local papers, *Kurier Lubelski* and *Dziennik Lubelski*. Philharmonic tickets can be purchased at ulica Kapucyńska 7, Tuesday–Sunday noon–7. Theater tickets are available at **Centrum Kultury** (ul. Peowiaków 12), the home of all theater groups in Lublin. Student nightlife centers around Marie Skłodowska-Curie University's **Chatka Żaka Club** (ul. 1. Radziszewskiego 16, tel. 081/332–01). The club offers a cafeteria, bar, popular disco, and a cinema that often shows American movies.

Gdańsk and the Northeast

Gdańsk is the third-largest city in Poland and the capital of the northern province of Pomorze Gdańskie (East Pomerania). Linked with two smaller neighboring towns, Gdynia and Sopot, in an urban conglomerate called the Trojmiasto (Tri-City), Gdańsk is one of Poland's most exciting and vibrant cities. Formerly the "Free City" of Danzig, this Baltic port has changed hands many times in its 1,000 years of history, the Poles taking turns with the Teutonic Knights, the Prussians, and finally the Nazis.

A series of areawide street demonstrations in the early 1970s led to the first workers' strikes at the Lenin Shipyards. The government attempted to stifle the agitation by threatening to fire all of them and by bringing in soldiers (at least 40 people were killed in riots in the 1970s). But by 1980 the workers had organized enough to form Solidarność (Solidarity), which gained independent trade-union status the same year. Although it lost official government recognition a year later, after the government declared martial law, its members continued to meet secretly. After the communist government fell, in 1989, Solidarity leader Lech Wałęsa became president of Poland in the nation's first free elections since World War II.

Today the carefully restored city streets hum with activity; economic privatization has brought new cultural events and the opening of galleries and shops. The university's presence keeps the city young and on its toes. Keep an eye on this town—whether it produces more workers' strikes in Poland's still shaky economy or more artists and musicians, it's sure to remain at the forefront.

In the northeast of Poland, formerly part of East Prussia, lies a land of 1,000 lakes and 1,000-year-old forests (and thousands of mosquitoes). Hardly known to Western tourists, the Mazurian and Augustów-Suwałki lakes form an intriguing labyrinth of interconnecting rivers and canals, set in ancient forests teeming with birds and wild animals.

Important Addresses and Numbers

Tourist Information The main tourist information office in Gdańsk is the **Centralny Ośrodek Informacji Turystycznaj** (Heweliusza 27, tel. 058/31–43–55); **Orbis** (Heweliusza 22, tel. 058/41–00–00) also has a good selection of maps and brochures. Other tourist offices in the region include **Giżycko** (PT Centrum Mazur, tel. 0878/33–83); **Gdynia** (Orbis, ul. Świętojańska 36, tel. 058/20–00–70); **Malbork** (ul. Przedzamcze, tel. 055/32–59); and **Sopot** (Orbis, ul. Bohaterów Monte Cassino 49, tel. 058/51–26–15).

Emergencies **Gdańsk: police,** tel. 997; **ambulance,** tel. 999; **hospital,** tel. 058/41–00–00 (al. Zwyciestwa 46).

Late-Night Pharmacy In Gdańsk try the **Apteka** at Podwale Staromiejskie 89–90 for late-night service.

Arriving and Departing by Train, Bus, and Ferry

By Train The main rail station, **Gdańsk Główny** (Podwale Grodskie, tel. 058/31–00–51), has a 24-hour baggage check, a snack bar, and a traveler's lounge. Trains leave from here for Hel (two trains a day, 2½ hours), Warsaw (five trains a day, 4 hours), Kraków (five trains a day, 8 hours), Poznań (five trains a day, 4 hours), and Malbork (15 trains a day, 1 hour).

By Bus Located right next to the train station, the PKS bus station (ul. 3 maja, tel. 058/32–15 32) may prove useful to those who want to venture to small towns off the tracks; otherwise train service is more frequent and comprehensive.

By Ferry Ferries travel daily from Gdańsk to Oxelösund, Sweden; and to Helsinki. Fares range from about $30 to $60, depending on the season. You can book a ticket at the **Orbis** office in Hotel Hevelius (ul. Heweliusa 22, tel. 058/31–34–56) or at **Polish Baltic Shipping Co.** (ul. Przemysłowa 1, Gdańsk, tel. 058/43–18–87 or 43–69–78).

Getting Around

Unless you plan to spend time in outlying Gdańsk, you probably won't make use of its tram system. Although trams travel north to Sopot and Gdynia, it's much faster to take a train from Gdańsk Główny, the main station. They leave every 15 to 30 minutes until midnight, and tickets cost around zł 5,000 at any ticket window. Be sure to time-stamp your ticket in the yellow machine on the platform before getting on the train; if you're caught with a ticket that isn't stamped, you'll get a stern look at the very least, a fine at the worst. Gdańsk's Old Town and Main Town areas are easily walkable.

Exploring Gdańsk and the Northeast

Numbers in the margin correspond to points of interest on the Gdańsk and the Northeast map.

Gdańsk and Environs ❶ Gdańsk was almost entirely destroyed during World War II, the streets of its **Główne Miasto** (Main Town) have been lovingly restored and still retain their historical and cultural richness. Especially beautiful areas to explore are the **Długi Targ** (Long Market) and the tiny, shady **ulica Mariacka,** which host a vibrant and changing art-gallery scene; the waterfront walkway, which follows the Motława River; and the marketplace on the northern edge, where you can find everything from wild mushrooms to pirated Madonna tapes. North of Main Town, **Stare Miasto** (Old Town) actually contains many new hotels and shops, but several churches and the preserved Old Town Hall earn it its name. At the north end of Old Town sit the Gdańsk Shipyards and the monument to Solidarity; this site, which saw numerous workers' riots and much violence during the 1970s and '80s, has now settled back into its daily grind.

Built during the 15th through the 17th centuries, the **Dwór Artusa** (Artus Mansion) behind Neptune's Fountain on Długi Targ was named for King Arthur, who otherwise has no affiliation with the place (alas, there are no signs of Excalibur or Merlin). This and the other stately mansions on the Długi Targ are reminders of the wealthy traders and aristocrats who once resided in this posh district. The mansion's collection includes Renaissance furnishings, paintings, holy figures, and the world's largest Renaissance oven.

The largest brick church in the world, and the largest church in Poland, the **Kościół Najświętszej Marii Panny** (Church of Our Lady) on ulica Piwna holds 25,000 people. Also referred to in abbreviated form as *Kościół Mariacki*, this enormous 14th century church underwent major restoration after World War II, and 15 of its 22 altars have been relocated to museums in Gdańsk and Warsaw. The high-

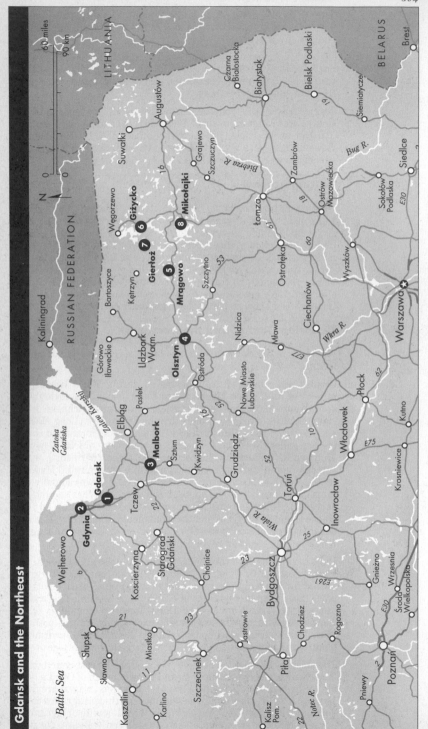

Gdańsk and the Northeast

light of a visit is climbing the hundreds of steps up the church tower. It costs zł 10,000 to make the climb, but it's cheaper and more inspirational than an aerobics class—and the view is sensational. The church also contains a 500-year-old, 25-foot-high astronomical clock that has only recently been restored to working order after years of neglect. It keeps track of the solar and lunar phases and features all of the signs of the zodiac—somewhat of an anomaly in a Catholic church. Two blocks west of the church on ulica Piwna, the **Wielka Zbrojownia** (Great Armory) is a good example of 17th-century Dutch Renaissance architecture. The ground floor is now a trade center, and the upper floors house an art school.

Three huge and somber crosses perpetually draped with flowers stand outside the gates of the **Stocznia Gdańska** (Gdansk Shipyards, ul. Jana z Kolną). Formerly named the Lenin Shipyards, this place gave birth to the Solidarity movement, which later became the first independent trade union under a communist government. The shipyards and the entire city also witnessed the long, violent struggle for autonomy that began as a series of impromptu street demonstrations in the early 1970s and blossomed into a nationwide political party that swept the country's first free elections in 1989. The crosses are only one part of the monument to Solidarity; other parts include plaques commemorating the struggle and a moving quotation by Pope John Paul II upon visiting the monument in 1987: "The Grace of God could not have created anything better; in this place, silence is a scream."

The shipyards monument clearly shows the fundamental link in the Polish consciousness between Catholicism and political dissent; another example is the **Św. Brygidy Church** (ul. Profesorka, near Old Town Hall), a few blocks north of the monument in Old Town. After the government declared martial law in 1981 in an attempt to force Solidarity to disband, members began meeting secretly here during masses. There is a statue of Pope John Paul II in the front.

The **Harbor Crane** is another item on Gdańsk's long list of superlatives. Built in 1444, it was medieval Europe's largest and oldest crane. Today it houses the **Maritime Museum**'s collection of models of the ships constructed in the Gdańsk Shipyards since 1945. At the museum ticket office, you can also buy tickets for tours of the *Soldek*, a World War II battleship moored nearby on the canal. *Ul. Szeroka. Admission: zł 25,000. Open Tues. and Fri. 10–5, Wed. and Thurs. 10–6, weekends 10–4. Closed day after holidays.*

The worthwhile **Muzeum Narodowe w Gdańsku** (National Museum in Gdańsk) is housed in the former Franciscan Monastery. Exhibits include 14th- to 20th-century art and ethnographic collections. Look for the changing exhibitions; the permanent displays of Gdańsk art and artifacts can hold your interest for only so long. *Ul. Toruńska 1, off ul. Okopowa, tel. 058/31–70–61. Admission: zł 15,000 adults, zł 5,000 students. Open Tues. and Sat. 11–5, Wed.–Fri. 9–3, Sun. 9–4. Closed day after holidays.*

The small **Museum Archeologiczne Gdańsku** (Gdańsk Archaeological Museum) features displays of Slavic tribal artifacts, including jewelry, pottery, boats, and bones. *Ul. Mariacka 25–26, tel. 058/31–50–31. Admission: zł 10,000 adults, zł 5,000 students.*

The historic entrance to the Old City is marked by the **Brama Wyżynna** (High Gate), off ulica Wały Jagiellońskie. This magnificent Renaissance gate, built in 1576, is adorned with the flags of Poland, Gdańsk, and the Prussian kingdom. As the king entered the city on his annual visit, he'd pass this gate first, then the **Brama Złota**

(Golden Gate), which dates from 1614 and combines characteristics of the Italian and Dutch Renaissance. Continuing east along ulica Długa reveals one of the city's most distinctive landmarks, the **Fontanna Neptuna**. Every day after dusk, this 17th-century fountain is illuminated, adding a romantic glow to the entire area. Around the fountain, vendors selling amber jewelry and souvenirs maintain a centuries-old tradition of trading at the **Długi Targ** (Long Market). Right at the water at the end of Długi Targ is the **Brama Zielona** (Green Gate). If you're a king and you're going to visit a city once a year, you might as well build a place to stay. So up went this gate (which doubled as a royal residence) in 1568. Unfortunately, the name no longer fits: The gate is now painted brown.

The former parish church of Gdańsk's Old Town, **Kościół św. Katarzyny** (St. Catherine's Church) is supposedly the oldest church in the city. Parts of it date to the 12th century, the tower was constructed in the 1480s, and the carillon of 37 bells was added in 1634. The 17th-century astronomer Jan Hevelius was buried in the presbytery of the church, below which lies what's left of the town's oldest Christian cemetery (10th century). On a small island in the canal, just north of the church, stands the **Wielki Młyn** (Great Mill). The largest mill in medieval Europe, it operated from the time of its completion in 1350 until 1945.

Although Gdańsk's original **Ratusz Główny** (Town Hall) was completely destroyed during World War II, a careful reconstruction of the exterior and interior now re-creates the glory of Gdańsk's medieval past. Inside the Town Hall, the **Muzeum Historii Miasta Gdańska** (Gdańsk Historical Museum) covers more than five centuries of Gdańsk's history in exhibits that include paintings, sculptures, and weapons. The Ratusz's tower provides a great view of the city. *Ul. Długa 47, tel. 058/31–97–22. Admission free. Open Tues.– Thurs. and weekends 10–4.*

The district of Oliwa, north of Gdańsk, is well worth visiting for its beautiful **cathedral.** Originally part of a Cistercian monastery, the church was erected during the 13th century. Like most other structures in Poland, it has been rebuilt many times, resulting in an interesting hodgepodge of styles from Gothic to Renaissance and Rococo. An amazing 18th-century organ graces the interior. The life's work of a Cistercian monk, the 6,300-pipe organ is decorated with angelic figures that move in time to the music. Demonstrations of the organ and a brief narrated church history are given almost hourly on weekdays in summer, less frequently on weekends and the rest of the year. Also of interest in Oliwa are the **art** and **ethnographic museums,** located in a beautiful park surrounding the cathedral. *Take train to Gdańsk-Oliwa or Tram 2 or 6 toward Sopot. Museums open Tues.–Thurs. and weekends 10–3.*

➋ The farthest north of the three cities—Gdańsk, Sopot, and Gdynia—that make up the tricity area, **Gdynia** has less to offer the visitor than its southern neighbors. In 1922 it was only a tiny fishing village, but by 1939 it had grown into one of the Baltic's biggest ports. In addition to the shipyards and docks that dominate this industrial area, Gdynia boasts a beautifully landscaped **promenade** and a **Muzeum Oceanograficzne-Akwarium Morskie** (Oceanographic Museum and Aquarium, al. Zjednoczenia 1, tel. 058/21–70–21. Admission zł 15,000 adults, zł 5,000 children. Open Tues.–Sun. 10–5). The aquarium, near the harbor, has tanks holding more than a thousand species of fish and is worth a visit. Opposite the Aquarium, a **Ship Museum** is housed in a World War II battleship, the *Błyskawica* (open May–mid-Oct., Tues.–Sun. 10–1 and 2–4). Continuing in the nautical vein, the town's **Naval Museum** (open Tues.–Sun. 10–4), south of the pier on Bulwar Nadmorski, traces the history of Polish sea life from Slavic times to the present.

❸ On the route between Gdańsk and Warsaw lies **Malbork**, the former German city of Marienburg. This quiet city has little to offer the visitor, but **Malbork Castle** is an amazing site and it alone warrants a stop. Built during the 13th century as the headquarters of the Teutonic Knights, the castle passed into Polish hands after the second Toruń Treaty in 1466 concluded the 13-year war between the Poles and the Order of Teutonic Knights. For the next three centuries, Malbork served as the royal residence for Polish kings during their annual visit to Pomerania. The castle was half destroyed during World War II, after which the building underwent a major renovation. Visitors can now view the wonderfully restored castle on a two-hour tour. Expect to pay about zł 30,000 per person for a tour in English or German; or pick up the English guidebook (sold outside the main entrance) and join one of the tours in Polish, which cost about ⅒ those for foreigners. Displays within the castle include an amber museum, 17th- and 18th-century china, glass, coins, paintings, and a large display of antique weapons and armor. *Tel. 055/33–64. Admission zł 45,000 adults, zł 35,000 children. Open May–Sept., Tues.–Sun. 9–4:30; Oct.–Apr., Tues.–Sun. 9–3.*

Olsztyn and the Mazury
❹ Since World War II **Olsztyn** has served as the Warmia and Mazury region's primary industrial center. The city is large and has a good number of hotels and restaurants ready to handle a large influx of summer tourists. Even so, you probably won't want to spend too much time here; Olsztyn is simply too gray and industrialized to offer much to the visitor. In just a few hours you can take in all its main sights, which are clustered near the Rynek. The Gothic **Brama Wysoka** (High Gate) marks the entrance to the Old Town and the main square. West of the square stands Olsztyn's **castle**, with its ethnographic and historical **museum** (open Tues.–Sun. 10–4). Once again Copernicus, that Renaissance man who got around northern Poland, is featured in a museum exhibit. He successfully directed the defense of the castle from 1516 to 1521 against the Teutonic Knights while serving as an administrator of Warmia province. Southeast of the square, **St. James Cathedral** dates from the 15th century.

To see yet another former fortress of the Teutonic Knights, catch a bus from Olsztyn to **Lidzbark Warmiński**. The well-preserved 14th-century **castle** survived World War II only because the local population refused to help the Germans demolish it. Inside the Gothic castle a **regional museum** (open Tues.–Sun. 10–4) features a strange mix of Gothic sculpture, icons, and modern Polish art.

❺ Normally one of the quieter spots in the Masurian lakes, **Mrągowo** fills with aspiring country-and-western performers here every July to attend the **Country Pikniky** (Country Picnic Festival) at the amphitheater on Lake Mamry. Would-be Dolly Partons and Willie Nelsons from all over the world turn out for this popular annual event. For information and tickets contact **Activ Holiday**, the only tourist office in town (ul. Ratuszowa 8, tel. 08984/32–20–21, open weekdays 8–8). It's about a three-hour bus trip from Olsztyn to Mrągowo.

❻ Because its historic buildings were destroyed in 1945, **Giżycko** lacks character. Nonetheless, this town at the intersection of Lake Niegocin and Lake Kisajno is one of the main Masurian lake resorts with a beach (of sorts) and some water-sports possibilities. Its tourist offices provide invaluable information for exploring the entire region.

7 In the Mazury Forest, **Gierłoż** is better known as **Wilczy Szaniec** (Wolf's Lair), the headquarters for Hitler's general staff during World War II. It was here on July 20, 1944, that an unsuccessful attempt was made on Hitler's life. During the war this amazing 27-acre military complex of massive concrete bunkers was completely concealed by a camouflage screen of vegetation that was changed according to the season. Beneath this screen lay the private bunkers of Hitler, Bormann, Göring, and Himmler; the SS operations rooms; a movie house; and a posh teahouse. Unfortunately, the ruins at Gierłoż are more of a tourist trap than an educational sight; an increasing number of gift and snack shops are popping up on the premises, yet the site lacks a museum. For zł 40,000 you can pick up a small pamphlet on the site, but that's about it for historical information. To reach Giertoż from Giżycko take a bus via Kętrzyn.

8 One of the more attractive Mazury resorts, **Mikołajki** is a quaint fishing village on the shores of Lake Tałty and Lake Mikołajskie. Boating is a popular activity at **Lake Śniardwy,** a larger lake just a few minutes' walk from the train station. Four kilometers (2½ miles) east of Mikołajki is the incredible nature preserve of Lake Łukajno, which is home to one of the last remaining wild-swan colonies.

Between the lakes of Beldany and Nidzkie, Ruciane-Nida is in the heart of the Pisz Forest. It's especially popular among nature enthusiasts, who come to hike through its pine forest. From Mikołajki you can hike the 22-kilometer (13½-mile) trail or make the trip on horseback or by ferry. Ruciane-Nida is also served by trains from Olsztyn. The PTTK tent campground is a 15-minute walk from the train station.

Dining and Lodging

Highly recommended restaurants and lodgings in a particular price category are indicated by a star ★.

Gdańsk
Dining
★

Pod Łososiem. The "Salmon," a historic Old Town inn that dates to 1598, is considered one of the best restuarants in Gdańsk. As the name suggests, fish is the specialty here: Salmon or smoked eel makes a fine appetizer, and flounder and grilled trout are highly recommended entrées. The menu also features wild fowl such as roast duck, pheasant, and goose. The dining area is warmly decorated with antique furniture, dark-wood paneling, and huge brass chandeliers; paintings of old Gdańsk adorn the walls. The service is also top-rate. *Ul. Szeroka 53–54, tel. 058/31–76–52. Reservations advised. Dress: casual but neat. AE, DC, MC, V. $$$*

Pod Wieżą. This elegant restaurant has a reputation for good meat dishes and generous portions. If they're on the menu when you visit, try the *zupa rybna* (fish soup), veal steak with mushroom sauce, or roast duck with apples and brown rice. The waiters generally speak English and German. *Ul. Piwna 51, tel. 058/31–39–24. Reservations advised. Dress: casual but neat. AE, DC, MC, V. $$$*

Kaszubska. The specialties here come from Kashubia, the lake region west of Gdańsk. Smoked fish dishes are highly recommended. *Ul. Kartuska 1, tel. 058/32–06–02. Reservations advised. Dress: casual. AE, DC, MC, V. $$*

Retman. This small, quaint restaurant offers good Polish and Continental cuisine. A clientele of mostly Germans and Danes linger over plates of schnitzel and chateaubriand in a candle-lit, wood-paneled locale on the water. *Ul. Stągiewna 1, tel. 058/31–41–14. Reservations advised. Dress: casual. AE, DC, MC, V. $$*

★ **Tawerna.** This well-established, well-touristed restaurant overlooking the river serves traditional Polish and Germanic dishes such as pork cutlets and seafood. Yes, it's touristy, but the food really is good. *Ul. Powroźnicza 19–20, off Długi Targ, tel. 58/31–92–48. Reservations advised. Dress: casual. AE, DC, MC, V. $$*

Zapraszamy. This is one of the few inexpensive restaurants that keep the doors open past 6 PM. It serves standard but fresh Polish fare like *kiełbasa* and *żurek* (creamy potato-and-sausage soup), and the staff will explain the menu to you in German or French if your Polish is hopeless. *Ul. św. Ducha 8–10. Dress: casual. No credit cards. $*

Lodging **Hewelius.** This large, modern, high-rise hotel is within walking distance of the Old Town. The rooms are spacious and blandly furnished, with all modern conveniences. *Ul. Heweliusza 22, tel. 058/31–56–31, fax 058/31–19–22. 250 rooms, most with bath. Facilities: restaurant, nightclub. AE, DC, MC, V. $$*

★ **Hotel Mesa.** This superb hotel near the train station was once part of the Communist-party headquarters. Now it's a small hotel run by a friendly Christian staff (don't worry, you don't have to say grace to stay here). The rooms are clean, well furnished, and each has a phone, color TV, and functioning shower. Finding a hotel of Mesa's quality in Poland seems too good to be true. The catch? With only eight rooms, it requires advance planning and reservations to book a room here in summer. *Wały Jageillońskie, tel. 058/31–80–52. 8 rooms, 4 with bath. Facilities: restaurant. Reservations advised. AE, MC. $$*

Marina. Built in 1982, this large high rise, popular with Western businesspeople, is one of Poland's newer hotels and probably Gdańsk's best. Upper floors have splendid views. *Ul. Jelitkowska 20, tel. 058/53–20–79, fax 058/53–04–60. 193 rooms with bath or shower. Facilities: restaurant, nightclub, indoor pool, tennis courts, bowling alley. AE, DC, MC, V. $$*

Posejdon. Though this modern hotel is a bit out of town, it is well equipped with leisure facilities. *Ul. Kapliczna 30, tel. 058/53–18–03, fax 058/53–02–38. 140 rooms with bath or shower. Facilities: solarium, sauna, indoor pool, disco. AE, DC, MC, V. $$*

Olsztyn **Orbis Novotel.** This standard 1970s hotel is typical of the kind found
Lodging in Poland. It is, however, the most comfortable lodging in the area, located in beautiful surroundings on the shores of Lake Ukiel. *Ul. Sielska 4A, tel. 089/27–60–81, fax 089/27–54–03. 98 rooms. Facilities: restaurant, pool. $$*

The Arts and Nightlife

The Arts Check with Orbis for details on opera and orchestral performances at Gdańsk's **National Opera and Philharmonic** (al. Zwycięstwa 15, tel. 058/41–46–42).

Nightlife The nightlife in Gdańsk is limited. There are, however, a few places worth mentioning. Discos and nightclubs are popping up all over; many of them optimistically advertise that they stay open until 4 or 6 in the morning, but a lot of them seem to lack the clientele to make it happen. **Bar Vinifera** (ul. Wodopoj 7, south of Hotel Hewelius) is a really small, really intimate wine bar with red lights and a smoky atmosphere that serves a variety of drinks to a mostly young crowd. **Klub Aktora** (ul. Mariacka 17) draws the artsy types of Gdańsk, including actors. Upbeat music plays on the stereo, and a casual crowd engages in heated discussions at low wooden tables. **The Scottish**

Bar (Chlebnicka 9–10), opposite the Kościół Mariacki, is hard to miss, with brightly colored tartans hanging from the second story. The Highland atmosphere is complemented by waiters clad in Scottish kilts.

Western Poland

Western Poland is comprised of three provinces: **Pomorza** (Pomerania) in the north, **Dolny Śląsk** (Lower Silesia) in the south, and **Wielkopolska** (Great Poland) sandwiched in between. Pomerania and Great Poland are a part of the flat, vast plain that extends north through Europe, and both are typified by smooth farmland, splotches of forest, and many lakes; there are opportunties here for walking, swimming, fishing, and hunting. The hills of Lower Silesia rise gently to the Karkoneaza mountains, where'll you'll find more energetic walking trails and resorts that lure skiers during winter. Wrocław and Poznań, two of western Poland's primary cities, attract crowds year-round for theater, music, and other cultural diversions.

Although the early Polish state had its origins in the west, the region has fallen (more than once) under German influence. The Poles of Greater Poland are affectionately mocked by their countrymen for having absorbed the archetypal German habits of cleanliness, order, and—to put the matter politely—thrift. Lower Silesia and Pomerania were intergrated with Poland only as recently as 1945, so don't be surprised if the west feels sober, restrained, and altogether more Germanic than anything else you'll find in modern Poland.

Important Addresses and Numbers

Tourist Information

Poznań: IT (Stary Rynek 77, tel. 061/52–61–56) sells excellent town maps; it's open weekdays 9–5, Saturday 10–2. **Orbis** (ul. Marcinkowskiego 21, tel. 061/53–20–52) sells train and bus tickets.

Szczecin: PTTK (al. Jedności Narodowej 49a, tel. 091/33–58–32). **Pomerania** (pl. Brama Portowa 4, tel. 091/34–72–08 or 091/34–28–61) can provide maps and brochures as well as information on a range of accommodations from hotels to private lodgings to campgrounds throughout the region; it's open in the summer, daily 8–4. **Orbis** (pl. Zwycięstwa 1, tel. 091/34–51–54) is primarily concerned with domestic and international train travel, though it has some local tourist information. The office is open daily 8–5.

Toruń: Orbis (ul. Żeglarska 31, tel. 056/261–30) has maps and pamphlets, an exchange desk, the occasional English-speaking staff person, and a complete train timetable for all cities. **PTTK** (pl. Rapackiego 2, tel. 056/249–26) is usually packed during peak travel periods; early in the morning or just before closing are the best times to avoid the crowds. The office is open weekdays 8–5, weekends 9–1.

Wrocław: Two **IT** offices offer general tourist information in English (Rynek 29, tel. 071/44–31–11; in PTTK office, Rynek 38, tel. 071/44–39–23). Both are open weekdays 9–5, Saturday 10–2. **Orbis** offers maps and information in English (Rynek 45, tel. 071/44–76–79).

Arriving and Departing by Plane

LOT offers daily flights from Warsaw to Strachowice Airport in the southwestern suburbs of **Wrocław**. Special LOT buses shuttle passengers from arriving flights to downtown Wrocław. For those flying out of Wrocław, a bus departs from the LOT office (ul. Józefa Piłsudskiego 77) for the airport one hour before each flight. City bus 106 will also take you the 10 kilometers (6 miles) from the city to the airport *For LOT flight information in Wrocław, tel. 071/33-17-44.*

Arriving and Departing by Train and Bus

By Train Trains run frequently from the modern **Poznań Główny** station to
Poznań Szczecin (three hours), Toruń (2½ hours), Wrocław (three hours), Kraków (eight hours), and Warsaw (4½ hours). International destinations include Berlin (5½ hours), Budapest (15 hours), and Paris (20 hours). The train station has a secure luggage-storage office, 24-hour post office, map store, snack bar, and a quiet café upstairs. From the central platform in front of the station, the best way into the city center is to take a bus up the long station approach road to ulica Św. Marcina and turn right, or take steps up to ul. Towarowa, turn back over the railway bridge, and keep walking (the city center and bus station are straight ahead).

Szczecin **Dworzec Główny** (ul. Kolumba, tel. 091/395) has service to and from the following cities: Warsaw (five hours), Gdańsk (six hours), Berlin (three hours), and the small towns along the Baltic coast. The station is just south of the city on the river; take Tram 3 to reach the city center.

Toruń The **PKP** train station (tel. 056/272-22) is located south of the city, across the Wisła River. Take Bus 22 (follow the little bus signs from the station) to reach the city center. There's daily service to and from Poznań (three hours), Gdańsk (four hours), Warsaw (three hours), and Kraków (nine hours).

Wrocław **Wrocław Główny PKP** connects Wrocław by rail to most major cities in Poland, with frequent service to and from Kraków (five hours), Warsaw (six hours), Gdańsk (seven hours), and Rzeszów (7½ hours). Trains also leave from here for many cities in Western and Eastern Europe: Dresden, Berlin, Prague, Budapest, and Frankfurt. The station is in the city center, a 30-minute walk south of the Rynek. It offers more services and all-night facilities than any other station in Poland, including a bus-ticket office, pharmacy, snack bar, and a movie theater. *Ul. Józefa Piłsudskiego, tel. 071/360-31, 360-32, or 360-33; reservations tel. 071/44-31-13.*

The **Wrocław Nadodrze** station is the hub for local routes to the east and southeast, including those going to Kluczbork, Kępno, Opole, Trzebnica, and Gniezno. *Pl. Powstańców Wielkopolskich.*

You might want to come to the **Wrocław Świebodzki** station just to admire the station building, which dates from 1848. Otherwise, you can catch local trains from here to Głogów, Węgliniec, Bogatynia, Legnica, and Jelenia Góra. *Pl. Orląt Lwowskich.*

By Bus The **Dworzec PKS** bus station (tel. 061/33-12-12) is on ulica
Poznań Towarowa 17-19, a short walk from the train station. Frequent bus service is available to and from Kornik, Łódź, and Gniezno.

Szczecin The **PKS** bus station (pl. Grodnicki, tel. 891/469-80) is right behind the train station. Check here for service to obscure towns along the Baltic coast. The bus to Gorzów takes two hours, the one to Międzyzdroje, 2½ hours.

Toruń Toruń's **PKS** bus station (ul. Dąbrowskiego, tel. 056/228-42) is located east of the medieval old town. Take local Bus 22 to and from the station.

Wrocław Diagonally opposite the main train station, **Dworzec Centralny PKS** (ul. Kościuszki 135, tel. 071/44–44–61 or 071/385–22) serves local routes, with frequent service to Jelenia Góra, Trzebnica, Częstochowa, Łódź, and the spas of Kudowa, Duszniki, and Polanica.

Exploring Western Poland

Numbers in the margin correspond to points of interest on the Western Poland map.

Tour 1:
Wrocław
and the Spa
Region
❶

Situated midway between Kraków and Poznań on the Odra River, **Wrocław,** the capital of **Dolny Śląsk** (Lower Silesia), dates to the 10th century, when the Ostrów Tumski islet on the Odra became a fortified Slav settlement. There are now some 100 bridges spanning the city's 90-kilometer (56-mile) network of slow-moving canals and tributaries, giving Wrocław its particular charm. Indeed, after Venice and St. Petersburg, Wrocław is the city with the third-largest number of bridges in Europe. The other overwhelming impression you get is of the extraordinary preponderance of young people—almost half the population is less than 30 years old—most of whom are students at one of the city's many institutions of higher learning.

Following the destruction that ravaged Wrocław during World War II, many of the city's historic buildings were restored. Wrocław's greatest architectural attractions are its many brick Gothic churches, the majority of which lie in or around **Stare Miasto** (Old Town) and **Ostrów Tumski.** This area is small enough to explore easily on foot.

The **Rynek** (marketplace) and the adjoining **plac Solny** (Salt Square) form the crux of Stare Miasto, which stretches between the Fosa Miejska moat and the Odra River. Wrocław's Rynek is almost as grand as Kraków's and bustles with almost as much activity.

The magnificently ornate **Ratusz** (Town Hall) is the heart of the Rynek. Mostly Gothic in style, with a dash of Renaissance and Baroque, the Ratusz was under continuous construction from the 13th to 16th century as Wrocław grew and prospered. In the center of the spired, pinnacled, and gabled **east facade** is a Renaissance **astronomical clock** from 1580. The **Gothic portal,** with reliefs of the Silesian eagle, the Bohemian lion, and the head of St. John, was the main entrance of the Ratusz until 1616. The lavish **south facade,** dating from the 15th to 16th century, will leave you awestruck with its delicately wrought sculptures, friezes, reliefs, and oriels. The simple **west facade** is worth a peek just to see the flat oriel dated 1504. Today the Ratusz houses the **Historical Museum of Wrocław.** *Admission: zł 10,000 adults, zł 5,000 children; free Wed. Open Wed.–Fri. 10–4, Sat. 11–5, Sun. 10–6.*

The Rynek itself is lined with colorful mansions, the grandest of which sit on the western side of the Rynek. Look for the **Pod Gryfami** (Griffin House), at No. 2, which dates from the 15th century. Its steep gable is decorated with reliefs of eagles, lions, and griffins.

One block east of the Rynek is the massive 14th-century, Gothic **St. Mary Magdalene's Church.** The 12th-century **Romanesque portal** on the church's south wall is considered the finest example of Romanesque architecture in Poland.

Of the many old houses around the Rynek, the two little **Jaś i Małgosia** (Hansel-and-Gretel) houses off the northwest corner of the Rynek are particularly appealing. Pass through the **Baroque arcade**

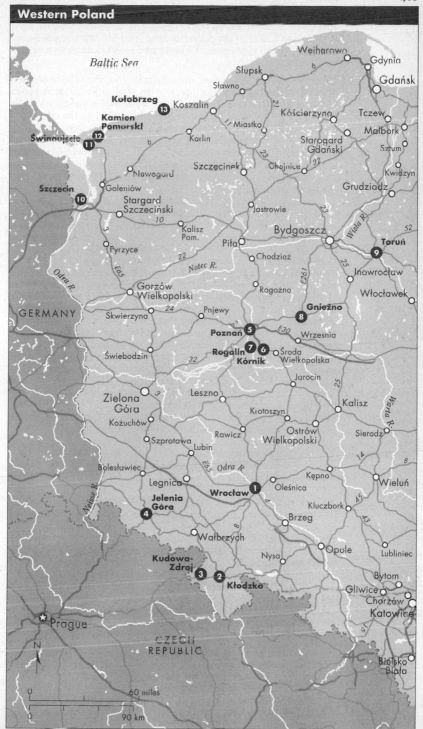

Baltic Sea

Weiherowo
Gdynia
Gdańsk
Słupsk
Sławno
Kościerzyna
Tczew
Malbork
Kołobrzeg
Koszalin
13
Kamien
Pomorski
Miastko
Starogard
Gdański
Sztum
Świnoujście
12
Karlin
Szczecinek
Chojnica
Kwidzyn
11
Nowogard
Grudziadz
Szczecin
Goleniów
10
Stargard
Szczeciński
Jastrowie
Bydgoszcz
Toruń
9
Inowrocław
Kalisz
Pom.
Piła
Włocławek
Pyrzyce
Chodzież
Notec R.
Rogoźno
Gorzów
Wielkopolski
Gnieżno
8
GERMANY
Skwierzyna
Pnjewy
Poznań
5
Wrzesnia
Rogalin
7
6
Środa
Wielkopolska
Świebodzin
Kórnik
Jarocin
Zielona
Góra
Leszno
Kalisz
Kożuchów
Krotoszyn
Ostrów
Wielkopolski
Sieradz
Szprotawa
Rawicz
Lubin
Bolesławiec
Odra R.
Kępno
Wieluń
Legnica
Wrocław
1
Oleśnica
Jelenia
Góra
4
Kluczbork
Brzeg
Wałbrzych
Kudowa-
Zdroj
Nysa
Opole
Lubliniec
3
2
Kłodzko
Bytom
Gliwice
Chorzów
Prague
Katowice
CZECH
REPUBLIC
Bielsko-
Biała

N

60 miles

90 km

Odra R.
Neisse R.
Warta R.
Wisła R.
E65
E30
E261

linking the houses to see the 14th-century brick **Church of St. Elizabeth,** which has been under reconstruction since fires ravaged it in 1975 and 1976. If the church is open, you can brave the 302-step climb to the top of the church's **tower** and look inside at its magnificent organ.

Head four blocks north along ulica Kuźnicza to reach the university district, which begins at the intersection of ulica Kuźnicza and ulica Uniwersytecka. The vast 18th-century **Wrocław University** was built between 1728 and 1741 by the emperor Leopold I on the site of the west wing of the former prince's castle. Behind the fountain and up the frescoed staircase is the magnificent assembly hall, **Aula Leopoldina.** The Aula is decorated with illusionist frescoes and life-size sculptures of great philosophers and patrons of learning. *Aula, pl. Uniwersytecki 1. Suggested admission: zł 10,000 adults, zł 5,000 students. Open daily 9–3:30.*

Time Out   **Café Uni** (pl. Uniwersytecki 11) is a great place to sip coffee and admire the 565-foot facade of the university. It has an outdoor patio and often hosts recitals.

Ostrów Tumski (Cathedral Island—although it's no longer an island) is the cradle of Wrocław and one of its oldest and most charming quarters. Its winding streets, beautiful bridges, and wonderful churches are nine blocks northwest of the Rynek. From the Rynek walk east on ulica Wita Stwosza and turn left on ulica świętej Katarzyny until you reach **Most Piastowy.** This bridge, which connects the left bank of the Odra with the Wyspa Piaskowa (Sand Island), was once part of the amber route, an ancient trade route that led from the Baltic down to the Adriatic. Across the bridge, you'll see a former Augustinian monastery used as Nazi headquarters during the war; the building is now the **University Library.** On Sand Island is the 14th-century **St. Mary's Church on the Sand.** Don't let the church's characterless exterior put you off. The interior was restored after World War II to its original Gothic appearance, with a lofty vaulted ceiling and brilliantly colored stained-glass windows.

Time Out   The **vegetable market,** in the market hall next to the church, is a great place to buy picnic supplies for lunching on the banks of Cathedral Island. *Open weekdays 8–6, Sat. 9–3.*

Behind St. Mary's, **Most Tumski** and **Most Młyński,** two gracefully designed and painted bridges, lead to Ostrów Tumski. After passing over Most Tumski, you'll reach a cluster of churches including **Sts. Peter and Paul Church,** which has no aisles. More impressive are the **Holy Cross** and **St. Batholomew's churches,** just beyond the **statue of Pope John XXIII** (1968). The two churches are housed in a rigid and forbidding building erected by Duke Henryk as his own mausoleum. The duke's Gothic sarcophagus has been moved to the Historical Museum (*see above*). On the lower level of the building lies the 13th-century St. Bartholomew's Church; on the upper level is the early 14th-century Church of the Holy Cross.

Straight down either ulica świętego Idziego or ulica Katedralna is the 13th-century **St. John's Cathedral,** with its two truncated towers. Its chancel is the earliest example of Gothic architecture in Poland. The cathedral houses the largest organ in the country, featuring 163 tones and 10,000 pipes. On the southern side of the cathedral is **St. Elizabeth's Chapel,** with an amazing fresco in its oval dome. The bust of Cardinal Frederick above the entrance, along with numerous other sculptures and frescoes, came from the studio of Bernini. The **Elector's Chapel,** in the northwestern corner of the cathedral, dates from the early 18th century and was designed by the great Baroque architect Johan von Erlach of Vienna. As these chapels are often closed, check at the sacristy for an update as well as for admission costs. To the left of the cathedral lies the **Archdiocesan Museum,** with its collection of rare and medieval Silesian sacred art. *Ul. Kanonia 12, tel. 071/22–17–55. Open daily 10–3.*

Tour 2: The **Kłodzko** region south of Wrocław is known for its spas, to which **The Spa** health seekers are drawn for mineral baths and libations. If you're **Region** already healthy enough, the region also offers good hiking in an unspoiled rural environment.

The cheapest way to get to the spa region is to take the train from Kraków and change in Kłodzko, so you're likely to change trains or buses here. There are two very small train stations; if you arrive at the one outside town, just follow the tracks 20 minutes to reach the central station, where most local trains depart. Trains from Wrocław reach Kłodzko in 1½ hours (cost: zł 45,000); service is not frequent, so be sure to check times.

2 The small town of **Kłodzko** is the gateway to almost all the spas of the region; it's definitely worth a short stop en route to Kudowa-Zdrój or Polanica-Zdrój (*zdrój* means spa). Kłodzko straddles the Nysa Kłodzka River and is dominated by the 40-acre **stronghold of Prussian king Frederick the Great.** The fortress looms over the city from Mt. Forteczna, one of the Table Mountains, and has a spectacular view. More than 4 acres of the fortress are open to the public, but the **underground tunnels and cellars** stretching for kilometers under the fortress and town are the most interesting part. Claustrophobes, beware; often you have to crawl on hands and knees. *Entrance beyond town hall. Fort admission: zł 20,000 adults, zł 10,000 children. Cave admission: zł 10,000 adults, zł 5,000 children. Fort open daily 9–6. Caves open daily 9–5.*

As you head into town from Dworzec PKS and Kłodzko Miasta PKP along ulica Grottgera and hit the Młynówka River, you'll cross a wonderful **Gothic bridge** lined with stone figures of saints. Continue up ulica Wita Stwosza to the **town hall.**

Time Out For a cool drink stop at **Pergrotaur Café,** on the terrace behind the town hall.

3 **Kudowa-Zdrój,** an aging European spa in a deep valley with curative mineral waters, is a good place to catch some Zs. (The quickest way to get to Kudowa is to take a train to Kłodzko and then a bus to Kudowa). Kudowa's rich past shows in its grand, decaying 19th-century mansions. It was a popular health resort as early as the 17th century and long attracted nobility, socialites, and such public figures as Winston Churchill. Now the pace of life here is slow and relaxed, and the most exercise you'll get is a stroll through the **English-style gardens** of the spa park. The *pijalnia* (pump room) at the park's main entrance is the largest in the region. Bring a glass to sample the waters. *Open weekdays 7–6, Sat. 9–6.*

Two kilometers (1¼ miles) away is the ghoulish Skull Chapel of Czermna, lined with thousands of human skulls and bones. You can get there by PKS bus from the main bus stop on ulica Maja 3, near the intersection of ulica Zdrojowa.

4 Approximately 50 kilometers (32 miles) west of Wrocław is the **Jelenia Góra** valley, with its main ski resorts of **Karpacz** and

Szklarska Poręba on the thickly wooded slopes of the **Karkonosze**, the highest range of the Sudety Mountains. The climate here is fairly severe, with heavy snowfalls, so skiing conditions are exceptionally good. Karpacz has a bobsled track and a chair lift up the slopes on **Mt. Śnieżka** (5,257 feet). While you're up here try and see the local curiosity in **Bierutowice**: a 13th-century wooden church that originally stood on Lake Wang in Norway. In 1841, Friedrich Wilhelm IV of Prussia brought it over lock, stock, and altar and erected it on the present site. Even now after more than 100 years, the Romanesque-cum-Viking elements carved on the doorpost look strangely alien here.

Tour 3:
Poznań
and Toruń
⑤

Situated halfway between Warsaw and Berlin, in the middle of the monotonously flat Polish lowlands, **Poznań** has been an east–west marketplace for more than 1,000 years. In the Middle Ages, merchants made a great point of bringing their wares here on St. John's Day (June 23), and the annual tradition has continued. (The markets have now been superseded by the important International Trade Fair, which has been held here since 1922.) Until the 13th century, Poznań was (on and off) the capital of Poland, and in 968 the first Polish bishopric was founded here by Mieszko I. It still remains the capital of the **Wielkopolska** (Great Poland) region.

Despite its somewhat grim industrial environs, Poznań has one of the country's most charming old towns; consider making the trek through western Poland if only to visit Poznań's majestic market square. Poznań may be only the fifth-largest city in Poland, but to a tourist it will feel larger than that. While the majority of sights are located near the Old Town's impressive Stary Rynek, other attractions are far off in the sprawling maze of ancilliary streets. Walking is not recommended here. Invest in some tram tickets and a city map with the transit routes marked; your feet will thank you.

Start your sightseeing in the **Stary Rynek** (Old Market Square), which engulfs the imposing, arcaded Renaissance **Ratusz** (Town Hall). (Poznań residents will proudly tell you it's the most splendid building in Poland.) Its clock tower is famous for the goats that appear every day at noon to butt heads before disappearing inside. Legend has it that the clock maker who installed the clock planned to give a party on the occasion. He ordered two goats for the feast, but the goats escaped and started fighting on the tower. The mayor was so amused by the event that he ordered the clock maker to construct a mechanism to commemorate the goat fight. The Ratusz now houses a **Museum of City History** that contains a room dedicated to Chopin, and a beautiful vaulted ceiling in the Great Hall. *Stary Rynek 1, tel. 061/52–56–13. Admission: zł 10,000 adults, zł 5,000 children. Open Sun.–Fri. 10–4.*

The tiny arcaded shopkeepers' houses by the town hall date to the mid-16th century. At No. 45 is the **Museum of Musical Instruments,** where you can see Chopin's piano and a plaster cast of the maestro's hands. *Stary Rynek 45, tel. 061/52–08–57. Admission: zł 10,000. Open Tues. and Sat. noon–6, Wed. and Fri. 10–4, Thurs. and Sun. 10–3.*

At No. 3 is the **Historical Museum,** which features temporary exhibitions on the history of Poznań and, recently, the Solidarity movement. *Stary Rynek 3, tel. 061/52–94–64. Admission free. Open Tues.–Sat. 10–6, Sun. 10–3.*

Just west of the Stary Rynek, on Góra Przemysława (Przemyslaw's Hill), is the neoclassical Przemysław Castle, which now houses the **Museum of Decorative Arts.** Among its holdings are unusual examples of wrought gold, Venetian glass, and Dutch porcelain; particularly interesting is its collection of woven sashes worn by Polish noblemen during the 18th century. The castle itself has been restored after being half destroyed during World War II. *Góra Przemysławu. Admission: zł 10,000 Open Tues. and Sat. noon-6, Wed. and Fri. 10-4, Thurs. and Sun. 10-3.*

Ostrów Tumski (Cathedral Island), an islet in the Warta River east of the Old Town, is the historic cradle of the town. This is where the Polanie tribe built their first fortified settlement and their first basilica in the 10th century. The present **Poznań Cathedral** was rebuilt after World War II in pseudo-Gothic style, but 10th- and 11th-century remains can be seen in some interior details. Located directly behind the main altar is the heptagonally shaped Golden Chapel, which is worth seeing for the sheer opulence of its Romantic-Byzantine style (1840). Within the chapel is the mausoleum of the first rulers of Poland, Mieszko I and Bolesław the Great.

Time Out **Eliksir** (Stary Rynek 61) is a cool and elegant café with white marble floors. Its tables afford fine views of the adjacent square.

For nature lovers and the sports-minded, the **Wielkopolski National Park** southwest of Poznań is a marvelous place for a day trip. It has 16 lakes set in pine forests full of many different types of birds and game. Lake Rusałka and Lake Strzeszynek have long beaches, tourist accommodations, and water-sports equipment for hire. Splendid legends abound here. At the bottom of Lake Góreckie, for example, there is supposed to be a submerged town, and on still nights if you're very lucky you can hear the faint ringing of the town bells, although it's probably nothing more eerie than the call of water birds.

❻ To see how the wealthy families of Poznań lived, take a trip to the countryside southeast of the city. In the old town of **Kórnik**, 20 kilometers (12 miles) away (accessible from Poznań by PKS bus) is an 18th-century neo-Gothic castle surrounded by a moat. It now houses a museum full of hunting trophies, rare books, and furnishings, as well as an enormous library of incunabula and rare books (more than 150,000 volumes including manuscripts by Mickiewicz and Słowacki). Be sure to look down while you're viewing the exhibits— you'll be walking on some truly magnificent wood-inlaid floors. The castle is surrounded by Poland's largest arboretum, with more than 2,000 varieties of trees and shrubs. *Admission: zł 20,000 adults, zł 10,000 children. Open Mar.-Nov., Tues.-Fri. and Sun. 9-3, Sat. 9-2. Closed day after holidays.*

❼ In nearby **Rogalin**, 12 kilometers (8 miles) west from Kórnik, an 18th-century Rococo palace lounges in a French-style park. Inside the palace an exhibit of folk and Impressionist art is on display. In the park are three 1,000-year-old oak trees more than 30 feet in diameter, named Lech, Czech, and Rus after the founding brothers of three Slavic nations. *Open Wed.-Fri. and Sun. 10-4, Sat. 10-6. Buses run by park at Rogalin, but service to Poznań is inconsistent.*

❽ The original capital of Poland, **Gniezno** owes this honor (according to myth) to some white eagles spotted nesting on the site by Lech, the legendary founder of the country, who named the town Gniezno (nesting site) and proclaimed the white eagle the nation's emblem. On a more historical note, King Mieszko I brought Catholicism to the Polish people during the 10th century and made Gniezno the seat of the country's first bishop, St. Wojciech. Lying along the Piast Route, Poland's historic memory lane running from Poznań to

Kruszwica, Gniezno is surrounded by towns whose monuments date to the origins of the Polish state. But the highlight of the area is the largest prehistoric fortified swamp settlement in Europe at Biskupin. In Gniezno itself, the cathedral, with the remains of the bishop, and the Museum of the Original Polish State attract some visitors to this small, industrial town today.

The first **cathedral** in Gniezno was built by King Mieszko I before AD 977. The 14th-century building is considered the most imposing Gothic cathedral in Poland. On the altar a silver sarcophagus, supported by four silver pallbearers, bears the remains of St. Wojciech (Adalbert), the first bishop of Poland. At the back of the church the famous 12th-century bronze-cast **Doors of Gniezno** have intricate bas-relief scenes depicting the life of St. Wojciech, a Czech missionary commissioned to bring Christianity to the Prussians in northeast Poland. Not everyone appreciated his message: He was killed by pagans. It is said that his body was ransomed from its murderers by its weight in gold, which the Poles paid ungrudgingly. *Cathedral open Mon.–Sat. 10–5, Sun. and holidays 1:30–5:30.*

Time Out Café Gnieznieńska (ul. Kaszarska 1A–1B), just off the Market Square, is a great place to relax after a morning of sightseeing.

Housed in a characterless concrete school building, the **Museum of the Original Polish State** shows multimedia exhibitions (in five languages, including English) on medieval Poland. *Ul. Kostrzewskiego. Open 10–5.*

Step back in time by wandering along the wood-paved streets and peering into the small wooden huts at the fortified settlement at **Biskupin,** about 30 kilometers (18½ miles) from Gniezno. This 100-acre Polish Pompeii is one of the most fascinating archaeological sites in Europe. It was discovered in 1933, when a local school principal and his students noticed some wood stakes protruding from the water during an excursion to Lake Biskupieńskie. The lake was later drained, revealing a settlement largely preserved over the centuries by the lake waters. Dating to 550 BC, the settlement was surrounded by defensive ramparts of oak and clay, and a breakwater formed from stakes that were driven into the ground at a 45° angle. A wooden plaque at the entrance to the settlement shows a plan of the original settlement. An English-language pamphlet is sold at the entrance. *Admission: zł 35,000 adults, zł 15,000 children. Open daily 8–6.*

⑨ Toruń, the birthplace of Nicolas Copernicus, is a beautiful medieval city, although pollution has been increasingly taking its toll. Fortunately, because Toruń was left relatively undamaged in World War II, most of its ancient buildings are still intact. The **Stare Miasto** (Old Town) brims with ancient churches, civic buildings, and residences.

The best place to start a tour of Toruń is at the birthplace of its most famous native son. The **Copernicus Museum** in the western half of the city, one block south of the Old Town Square, consists of two houses, one of which adjoins the house at ulica Kopernika 17, where Copernicus was born and lived until he was 17 years old. The rooms have been restored with period furnishings, some of which belonged to the Copernicus family. You can view his research equipment and exhibits associated with him and his findings. In addition, collections of stamps, badges, coins, and other trinkets pay homage to this stargazing Pole. For a small fee, you can view a scale model of Toruń while listening to a recorded dialogue (available in English) that tells the story of the city from its founding to the present. While the story is narrated, slides simultaneously flash on the wall behind the scene and lights direct your attention to relevant areas of the city. This entertaining and informative presentation provides you with a good feel for both the geography and the history of the city. *Ul. Kopernika 17. Admission: zł 20,000 adults, zł 10,000 children. Open Thurs.–Tues. 10–4.*

Time Out A few steps down from the museum at No. 3 ulica Ducha Świętego is the atmospheric café **Kawiarnia Pod Atlantem** (tel. 056/267–39). Waitresses in floor-length gowns serve decadent pastries and delicious *lody* (ice cream) at the antique, dark-wood booths and tables.

Walk one block north from the museum along ulica Ducha Świętego to reach the **Rynek Staromicjski** (Old Town Square), which is dominated by the 14th-century **Ratusz** (Town Hall), one of the largest buildings of its kind in northern Poland. There are 365 windows in the Ratusz, and the hall's four pinnacles are meant to correspond to the four seasons of the year. Concerts and poetry readings are occasionally held in the hall. Information on such events, as well as on all of the museums of Toruń, can be obtained at the office inside.

Built in 1274, the Ratusz's **tower** is the oldest in Poland, although it did receive some later Dutch Renaissance additions. For a small fee, you can go up into the tower for a spectacular view. You can see the entire city of Toruń from the top, including the central Polish plains stretching away across the Wisła River. Traces of the wall that once divided the Stare Miasto from the Nowe Miasto are still visible. In the square outside the Ratusz is a **statue of Nicolaus Copernicus.**

Located within the Ratusz is the **historical museum,** which houses a collection of fine works from the region's craftsmen. The collection includes painted glass, paintings, and sculptures. Look for the gingerbread molds, which have been used since the 14th century to create the delicious treats for which Toruń is famous. *In Ratusz, Rynek Staromiejski 1, tel. 056/270–38. Open Wed.–Sun. 10–4.*

Located in the building known as **Pod Gwiazdą** (House under the Stars), opposite the Ratusz, the **Far Eastern Art Museum** houses collections from China, India, Japan, Korea, and Vietnam. The house itself may, however, be the most interesting feature of the museum. Built in the 15th century, it was remodeled in the 17th century in the Baroque style by a wealthy Italian. Notice the carved-wood staircase. *Rynek Staromiejski 35, tel. 056/211–33. Open Fri.–Tues. 10–4.*

South of the Rynek on ulica Żeglarska is **St. John's Church,** built in the 13th–15th centuries. This is where Toruń's most famous native son, Copernicus, was baptized. Special care has been taken in recent years to preserve the church, and regional artists are painstakingly restoring the Gothic frescoes. The *tuba Dei,* a 15th-century bell in the church's tower, is one of the largest and most impressive in Poland.

In a pleasant park northeast of the Old Town, across the avenue called Wały Sikorskiego, stands the local **Ethnographic Museum,** one of the most interesting you'll find in Poland. Its collections include tools of the fisherman's trade—nets, rods, and boats—from Kashubia and other parts of northwestern Poland, folk architecture, and arts and crafts. Outside the museum are brightly decorated farmhouses that have been restored and filled with antique furnishings and art pieces. The grounds have been designed to replicate life in the Bydgoszcz region (west of Toruń) in the 19th and early 20th centuries. You can see 19th-century gardens and barns and an 1896 windmill removed from the nearby village of Wójtówka. *Wały Sikorskiego 19, tel. 056/280–91. Open May–Sept., Tues.–Sun. Closed day after holidays.*

Time Out Situated in a restored thatch-roof farmhouse on the north side of the Ethnographic Museum, **Kawiarnia u Damroki** offers phenomenal coffee and pastries, the likes of which have probably never been served inside a Polish farmhouse before. The entrance is on ulica Juliana Nowickiego.

Tour 4: Szczecin and the Coast ⑩ The large port of **Szczecin** is on the Odra River just 48 kilometers (30 miles) from the German border. Despite its somewhat industrial atmosphere, Szczecin's location and the overall friendliness of its inhabitants (maybe it's that healthy sea air) make it a pleasant stop on your way to Germany or the towns on the Baltic coast. Ruled by several countries over the centuries, Szczecin (or Stettin in German) finally ended up as part of Poland after the Potsdam Conference of 1945. Although not on the coast, Szczecin is separated from the Baltic Sea only by the Szczecin Lagoon (Zalew Szczecinski).

Szczecin was remodeled during the 19th century on the Parisian system of radiating streets and is particularly pretty in spring, when the avenues along the Odra River glow with flowering magnolias. Though it is no longer the most important German Baltic port, the city still carries many reminders of its Teutonic heritage, including the grandiose **Pomeranian Princes' Castle.** Originally built during the 13th and 14th centuries, the castle reached the height of its glory under a series of Pomeranian princes during the Renaissance. The past 300 years have not been kind to the castle, which fell into the hands of the Swedes, Prussians, and French only to be ruined by carpet bombing near the end of World War II. Today the reconstructed castle is a cultural center housing an art gallery, photographic exhibits, an opera hall, an open-air concert hall, a cinema, a café, and the musical department of the university. *Ul. Rycerska 1, tel. 091/34–78–35.*

Housed in a Baroque palace and in an annex that faces it across the street, the **National Museum** (three blocks northwest of the castle) is devoted mainly to art—older paintings, sculpture, and antiques (13th- to 16th-century Pomeranian), and some Polish pieces from the 17th century. The annex, devoted to modern Polish art, brings a welcome respite when you've seen one too many representations of the *Annunciation* or old pewter cups. It contains works by a diverse collection of internationally known artists—another way to gain insight into the culture of modern Poland. *Ul. Staromłyńska 27–28, tel. 091/33–60–53. Admission to both museums: zł 25,000. Open Tues. and Thurs. 10–5, Wed. and Fri. 9–3:30; weekends and holidays 10–4. Closed day after holidays.*

Most of Usedom Island (60 kilometers, or 37 miles, north of Szczecin) lies within Germany, but on its easternmost edge along the Świna ⑪ River is the Polish town of **Świnoujście,** a fishing port and popular health resort. Relatively quiet during the winter months, Świnoujście comes to life during the summer holidays, when Poles, Swedes, and Germans head for its sandy beaches and stroll along its long beachfront promenade, graced by rosebushes, flowers, and shrubs. Across the river, Wolin Island is another popular vacation destination.

A visit to Swinoujście in season affords the opportunity to mingle with Germans, Swedes, and Poles in a number of tourist-oriented restaurants and clubs. But don't rule it out of your itinerary during the off-season. Room prices drop, the town quiets down, and its beach and parks become exceedingly peaceful places to recuperate from museums and train stations for a few days.

Across the river from Świnoujście on the east bank of the Świna River, **Wolin Island** was first settled in the 8th century by a Slavic tribe known as the Wolinians. Ancient carved-wood idols standing about 10 feet tall along the beach are the only visible reminder of this pagan settlement destroyed by the Christian Poles during the 12th century. The **local museum** (open Tues.–Sun. 10–4) exhibits other relics of this settlement and is worth a stopover should you be traveling on the island's main road.

North of the city of Wolin, **Woliński National Park** contains beautiful pine forests and dunes; it is also a reserve for bison and wild swan. Świnoujście's train and bus station are actually on Wolin Island, but if you're coming from the town itself, the free ferry from the small port brings you to the island.

⑫ On the mainland 20 kilometers (12½ miles) east of Świnoujście sits the small town of **Kamień Pomorski.** Just as on Wolin Island, mysterious carved-wood idols can be found along its beaches, a reminder of the Slavic settlements that once existed here. The old walls that originally encircled the town are no longer complete, but portions have survived, including the gateway, Brama Wolińska, on the west end of the Rynek. Also on the Rynek is a well-preserved town hall, but the town's most impressive structure is its late-Romanesque cathedral, with a splendid Baroque organ. Free organ concerts take place in the cathedral every Friday night at 7 in summer, and there's even an International Organ Festival in June.

⑬ Every summer the coastal town of **Kołobrzeg** attracts thousands of vacationers, mostly Poles and Germans, to lie on its beaches and stroll along its promenade. Aside from the beach, there's not much else of interest; the **Collegiate Church of St. Mary** near the station was severely damaged during the war but has been fairly well reconstructed. At the western end of the beach stands **Pomnik Zaślubin,** a monument to "Poland's Reunion with the Sea" after World War II, not far from the lighthouse near the mouth of the Parsęta River.

Dining and Lodging

Highly recommended restaurants and lodgings in a particular price category are indicated by a star ★.

Poznań
Dining

Poznań. This hotel restaurant is large and slightly cavernous, though the tables are discreetly separated by banks of plants, and the food and service are considered by many to be the best in Poznań. The menu includes a range of Polish dishes common to western Poland; try the roast pork and potatoes with sour cream and dill. There is also a reasonable wine list. *Pl. Dąbrowskiego 1, tel. 061/33–20–81. Jacket and tie advised. Reservations advised. AE, DC, MC, V. $$–$$$*

Pod Koroną. This recently renovated restaurant on the edge of Poznań's Old Town specializes in traditional Polish dishes like pig's knuckle (*golonka*) cooked in beer and honey, or veal with bacon and prunes. There's also a range of lighter entrées—steak and grilled salmon, among them—and a good selection of desserts. *Ul. Zamkowa 7, tel. 061/52–20–47. Jacket and tie advised. Reservations advised. AE, DC, MC, V. $$*

Lodging **Merkury.** This five-story, glass-fronted hotel is a standard Orbis product from the 1960s. Identical brown doors lead from long corridors into nearly identical rooms, which either look out onto the noisy intersection by the rail station or onto a quieter courtyard at the back. Furnishings are in dark and somewhat gloomy shades but are well up to the usual Orbis standard of comfort. Besides the Merkury's excellent location, with easy access to the station and town center, the other big plus is the parking facilities. *Ul. Roosevelta 20, tel. 061/47–08–01, fax 061/47–31–41. 351 rooms, 42 suites. Facilities: restaurant, bar, café. AE, DC, MC, V. $$*

Dom Turysty PTTK. This hotel has only a small number of rooms, but its location, right at the center of the Old Town, makes it an attractive option—if you can get in. Rooms are comfortably furnished, with Polish folk elements, and the staff is friendly and well informed about the city and current cultural events. *Stary Rynek 91, tel. and fax 061/52–88–93. 18 rooms; 8 singles, 10 doubles, some with bath. Facilities: restaurant, café. AE, DC, MC, V. $*

Lech. This older hotel stands in the center of town, near the university, and is a good base for exploring Poznań by foot. Rooms are on the small side but comfortably and cheerfully furnished. There is no restaurant service apart from breakfast, and the hotel bar sometimes attracts a rather rowdy crowd in the evenings. *Ul. Św. Marcin 4, tel. 061/53–01–51, fax 061/53–08–80. 79 rooms; 34 singles, 44 doubles, 1 suite, all with bath. Facilities: bar. AE, DC, MC, V. $*

Szczecin **Restauracja Balaton.** Named for the largest lake in Hungary, Bala-
Dining ton specializes in Hungarian cuisine at reasonable prices. The goulash soup served with bread is especially tasty and filling. The service tends to be a little slow, but the rustic wood-paneled atmosphere helps to ease the wait. *Pl. Lotników 3, tel. 091/34–68–73. Reservations advised. Dress: casual. AE, DC, MC, V. $$*

Restauracja Chief. This quasielegant seafood restaurant, in the more modern area of town, is cleverly decorated with stuffed fish, lobsters, and turtles on the walls; aquariums with live fish and turtles fill the corners of the two main rooms. The courteous staff serves such fish dishes as halibut, as well as beef Stroganoff, and the mandatory pork cutlet. *Ul. Rajskiego 16, tel. 091/34–37–65. Reservations advised. Dress: casual. No credit cards. $*

Lodging **Neptun.** This hotel offers comfortable rooms, each outfitted with color TV, a large bathroom, and modern furniture. A favorite with German and Scandinavian businesspeople, the Neptun is one of the most cosmopolitan hotels in Szczecin. *Ul. Matejki 18, tel. 091/24–01–11, fax 091/22–57–01. Facilities: restaurant, 2 bars. AE, MC, V. $$*

Hotel Gryf. The best feature of this large, weathered hotel is its central location, in downtown Szczecin. A standard buffet breakfast, free to guests, partially makes up for the lack of decoration in the small but clean rooms. *Al. Wojska Polskiego 49, tel. 091/33–45–66, fax 091/33–40–30. 64 rooms, all with bath. Facilities: restaurant. AE, MC, V. $*

Hotel Pomorski. This is just your average inexpensive Polish hotel, but its central location makes it a good base for exploring Szczecin. The rooms (singles to quads) are nothing to rave about, but you'll survive. *Brama Portowa 4, tel. 091/33–61–51. 38 rooms, some with bath. No credit cards. $*

Toruń **Pod Kurantem.** Regional cuisine is featured in this attractive, old
Dining wine cellar. Slow service is the penalty for popularity. *Rynek Staromiejski 28. No tel. No reservations. No credit cards. $$$*

Zajazd Staropolski. This traditional Polish restaurant features excellent meat dishes and soups in a restored 17th-century interior. *Ul. Żeglarska 10–14, tel. 056/260–60. Reservations advised. Dress: casual but neat. AE, DC, MC, V. $$*

Hotel Helios Restaurant. As at most other Orbis hotel restaurants, the food here is good and moderately priced, with an emphasis on Polish and Continental dishes. A short walk from Rynek Staromiejski, this place isn't the most exciting hangout in town, but it's clean and has decent service. Some of its tastier items are the pork and veal cutlets and the omelets. *Ul. Kraszewskiego 1–3, tel. 056/235–65. Reservations advised. Dress: casual. AE, DC, MC, V. $*

★ **Restauracja Staromiejska.** This is one of the best deals in town. The new Italian owner renovated this restaurant's old wine cellar, restored the polished wood and stone floors, whitewashed the walls, and repaired the brick-ribbed, vaulted ceilings. Enjoy excellent pizza here as well as Polish fare. Coffee lovers will have to be dragged kicking and screaming out the door—an imported espresso-maker whips up one of the best cappuccinos east of Italy. The restaurant also has an extensive wine list. *Ul. Szczytna 2–4. No tel. No reservations. Dress: casual. No credit cards. $*

Lodging **Helios.** This friendly, medium-size hotel is situated in the city center and offers a good restaurant (albeit with slow service). *Ul. Kraszewskiego 1, tel. 856/250–33, fax 856/235–65. 140 rooms, all with bath or shower. Facilities: restaurant, sauna, nightclub, beauty parlor. AE, DC, MC, V. $$*

Hotel Polonia. A favorite of Polish families, this antiquated hotel is just across the street from the Municipal Theater near the Rynek. The friendly new owner is renovating the place, and he plans to put in Swiss furnishings. The rooms are large, with high ceilings—unusual for Polish hotels. *Pl. Teatralny 5, tel. 856/230–28. 46 rooms, some with bath. Facilities: restaurant. AE, MC, V. $$*

Kosmos. A functional 1960s hotel, Kosmos is beginning to show signs of wear and tear—from the shabby furniture to the somewhat dank rooms. It is situated near the river, in the city center. *Ul. Portowa 2, tel. 056/270–85. 180 rooms, most with bath or shower. AE, DC, MC, V. $*

Zajazd Staropolski. Cheaper than the Orbis hotels in Torun (Helios and Kosmos), this central hotel off Rynek Staromiejski is well maintained and has a friendly staff, most of whom speak either English or German. Many of the rooms have clean private baths and excellent showers. The hotel has a good, moderately priced restaurant, open until 10 PM. *Ul. Żeglarska 10–14, tel. 056/260–61, fax 056/253–84. 33 rooms, most with bath. Facilities: restaurant. AE, MC, V. $*

Wrocław **Dwór Wazów.** This beautifully decorated establishment in the heart
Dining of Wrocław is divided into two parts: restaurant–night club and
★ café–wine cellar. The restaurant offers a Polish and international menu. The *shashlik* (grilled beef and peppers) served with brown rice is particularly tasty. The service is discreet and professional; most waiters speak both English and German. The atmospheric Renaissance-style wine cellar is a good place for conversation or relaxation on a hot summer day. Try one of the Hungarian or Bulgarian reds, which are far better than the selection of French or Italian labels offered here. *Rynek 5, tel. 071/44–16–33. Reservations advised. Dress: casual but neat. AE, DC, MC, V. $$$*

Grunwaldzka. This is the place to try in Wrocław if you want a menu full of typical Polish fare. Heading the menu are *schabowy* (pork cutlet) with mashed potatoes and sauerkraut, fried liver with onions and rice, *zrazy wolowe* (stuffed and rolled beef), *kaszu* (buckwheat groats), and *golonka* (pig's knuckle). *Pl. Grunwaldzki 6, tel. 071/ 21–98–21. Reservations advised. Dress: casual. No credit cards. $$*

Lodging **Hotel Europejski.** Renovations in this hotel have been sporadic, leaving half old and half new. Though the refurbished rooms are up to Western standards, they have Western prices to match. The small and simple older rooms are more reasonably priced, and guests can still gawk at the exquisitely redone lobby. *Ul. Józefa Piłsudskiego 88, tel. 071/310–71. Facilities: restaurant. AE, MC, V. $$*

6 Bulgaria

Bulgaria, a land of mountains and seascapes, of austerity and rustic beauty, lies in the eastern half of the Balkan Peninsula. From the end of World War II until recently, it was the closest ally of the former Soviet Union and presented a rather mysterious image to the Western world. This era ended in 1989 with the overthrow of Communist party head Todor Zhivkov. Since then, Bulgaria has gradually opened itself to the West as it struggles along the path toward democracy and a free-market economy.

Endowed with long Black Sea beaches, the rugged Balkan Range in its interior, and fertile Danube Plains, Bulgaria has much to offer the tourist year-round. Its tourist industry is quite well developed and is being restructured to shield visitors from shortages of goods and services and the other legacies of rigid central planning.

The Black Sea coast along the country's eastern border is particularly attractive, with secluded coves and old fishing villages, as well as wide stretches of shallow beaches that have been developed into self-contained resorts. The interior landscape offers magnificent scenic beauty, and the traveler who enters it will find a tranquil world of forested ridges, spectacular valleys, and rural communities where folklore is a colorful part of village life.

Founded in 681, Bulgaria was a crossroads of civilization even before that date. Archaeological finds in Varna, on the Black Sea coast, give proof of civilization from as early as 4600 BC. Bulgaria was part of the Byzantine Empire from AD 1018 to 1185 and was occupied by the Turks from 1396 until 1878. The combined influences are reflected in Bulgarian architecture, which has a truly Eastern feel. Five hundred years of Muslim occupation and nearly half a century of communist rule did not wipe out Christianity, and there are many lovely, icon-filled churches to see. The 120 monasteries, with their icons and many frescoes, provide a chronicle of the development of Bulgarian cultural and national identity, and several merit special stops on any tourist's itinerary.

The capital, Sofia, is picturesquely situated in a valley near Mount Vitosha. There is much of cultural interest here, and the city has good hotels and restaurants serving traditional and international cuisines. Other main towns are Veliko Târnovo, the capital from the 12th to the 14th century and well worth a visit for the old, characteristic architecture; Plovdiv, southeast of Sofia, which has a particularly interesting old quarter; and Varna, the site of one of Europe's first cultural settlements and the most important port in Bulgaria.

Before You Go

When to Go

The ski season lasts from mid-December through March, while the Black Sea coast season runs from May to October, reaching its crowded peak in July and August. Fruit trees blossom in April and May; in May and early June the blossoms are gathered in the Valley of Roses (you have to get up early to watch the harvest); the fruit is picked in September, and in October the fall colors are at their best.

Summers are warm, winters are crisp and cold. The coastal areas enjoy considerable sunshine, though March and April are the wettest months inland. Even when the temperature climbs, the Black Sea breezes and the cooler mountain air prevent the heat from being overpowering.

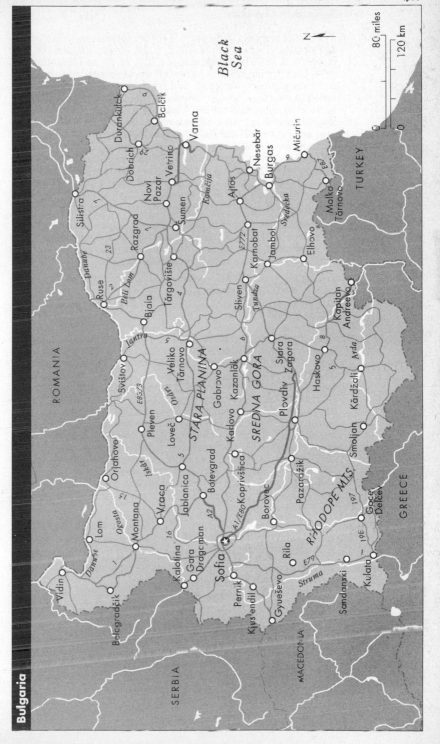

Bulgaria

Black Sea

ROMANIA

SERBIA

MACEDONIA

GREECE

TURKEY

80 miles
120 km

Vidin
Belogradčik
Lom
Danube
Ogosta
Montana
Vraca
Kalofina
Gara Dragoman
Orjahovo
Iskǎr
Pleven
Loveč
Jablanica
Botevgrad
Sofia
Pernik
Kjustendil
Gyueševo
Rila
Boroveč
Koprivštica
Pazardžik
STARA PLANINA
SREDNA GORA
Veliko Tǎrnovo
Gabrovo
Kazanlǎk
Karlovo
Plovdiv
Stara Zagora
Haskovo
RHODOPE MTS.
Smoljan
Kǎrdžali
Arda
Kapitan Andreevo
Goce Delčev
Sandanski
Kulata
Struma
E79
Svištov
E85/3
Osǎm
Jantra
Bjala
Ruse
Beli Lom
Danube
Silistra
Razgrad
Tǎrgovište
Šumen
Novi Pazar
Dobrich
Durankulak
Beličik
Varna
Verino
Kamčija
Ajtos
Nesebǎr
Burgas
Mičurin
Malko Tǎrnovo
Elhovo
Jambol
Karnobat
Sliven
Tundža
Sredečka
E772
E87
19E
197
E80
A2
A1/E80

Bulgarian Currency

The unit of currency in Bulgaria is the lev (plural leva), divided into 100 stotinki. There are bills of 1, 2, 5, 10, 20, 50, 100, and 200 leva; coins of 1, 2, and 5 leva; and coins of 1, 2, 5, 10, 20, and 50 stotinki. At press time (spring 1994), as part of efforts at economic reform, hard-currency payments for goods and services were no longer permitted. The only legal tender for commercial transactions and tourist services in Bulgaria is the lev. These services include air, train, and long-distance bus travel; all accommodations, from camping to hotels; and car rentals and Balkantourist package tours. You may import any amount of foreign currency, including traveler's checks, and exchange it at branches of the Bulgarian State Bank, commercial banks, Balkantourist hotels, airports, border posts, and other exchange offices, which quote their daily selling and buying rates. The rate quoted by the Bulgarian State Bank at press time was 57 leva to the U.S. dollar, and 85.5 leva to the pound sterling.

It is forbidden to either import or export Bulgarian currency. Unspent leva must be exchanged at frontier posts on departure before you go through passport control. You will need to present your official exchange slips to prove that the currency was legally purchased.

The major international credit cards are accepted in the larger stores, hotels, and restaurants.

What It Will Cost

Prices in Bulgaria have been low for years, but this is changing as the government tries to revive the economy and open it up to the West. If you choose the more moderate hotels, accommodations won't be very expensive. It is possible to cut costs even more by staying in a private hotel or private room in a Bulgarian house or apartment—also arranged by Balkantourist or other tourism companies—or by camping. The favorable cash exchange rate, linked to foreign-currency fluctuations, makes such expenses as taxi and public transport fares, museum and theater admission, and meals in most restaurants seem comparatively low by international standards. A little hard currency, exchanged at this rate, goes a long way. Shopping for imported and domestic wares in the duty-free shops also helps to keep travel expenses down. The following price list, correct as of spring 1994, can therefore be used only as a rough guide.

Sample Prices Trip on a tram, trolley, or bus, 3 leva; theater ticket, 20 leva–40 leva; coffee in a moderate restaurant, 5 leva–20 leva; bottle of wine in a moderate restaurant, 40 leva–100 leva.

Museums Museum admission is very inexpensive, ranging from 10 leva to 30 leva (less than 40¢).

Visas

All visitors need a valid passport. Those traveling in groups of six or more do not require visas, and many package tours are exempt from the visa requirement. Americans do not need visas when traveling as tourists. However, British and Canadian citizens require a visa for stays of up to 30 days in Bulgaria. For visa information and applications, contact the nearest Bulgarian consulate (*see also* Passports and Visas in Chapter 1).

Customs

You may import duty-free into Bulgaria 250 grams of tobacco products, plus 1 liter of hard liquor and 2 liters of wine. Items intended for personal use during your stay are also duty-free. Travelers are advised to declare items of greater value—cameras, tape recorders, etc.—so there will be no problems with Bulgarian customs officials on departure.

Language

The official language, Bulgarian, is written in Cyrillic and is very close to Old Church Slavonic, the root of all Slavic languages. English is spoken in major hotels and restaurants, but is unlikely to be heard elsewhere. It is essential to remember that in Bulgaria, a nod of the head means "no" and a shake of the head means "yes."

Staying in Bulgaria

Getting Around

By Car Main roads are generally well engineered, although some routes are
Road poor and narrow for the volume of traffic they have to carry. A large-
Conditions scale expressway construction program has begun to link the main
towns. Completed stretches run from Kalotina—on the Serbian border—to Sofia and from Sofia to Plovdiv. Highway tolls of some $20 total are paid at the border; be prepared for delays during the summer season at border points (open 24 hours) while documents are checked and stamped.

Rules of the Drive on the right, as in the United States. The speed limits are 50 or
Road 60 kph (31 or 36 mph) in built-up areas, 80 kph (50 mph) elsewhere, except on highways, where it is 120 kph (70 mph). The limits for a car towing a trailer are 50 kph (31 mph), 70 kph (44 mph), and 100 kph (62 mph), respectively. You must obtain a Green Card or Blue Card from your car insurance company, as recognized international proof that your car is covered by International Civil Liability (third-party) Insurance. You may be required to show one of these cards at the border. Balkantourist recommends that you also take out collision, or Casco, insurance. You are required to carry a first-aid kit, fire extinguisher, and breakdown triangle in the vehicle, and you must not sound the horn in towns. Front seat belts must be worn. The drinking-driving laws are extremely strict—you are expressly forbidden to drive after consuming any alcohol at all.

Parking Park only in clearly marked parking places. If you are in doubt, check with the hotel or restaurant.

Gasoline Stations are spaced at regular intervals on main roads but may be few and far between off the beaten track. All are marked on Balkantourist's free motoring map. At press time service stations were still selling unlimited quantities of fuel, supplies permitting, for leva (in spring 1994, 38¢ per liter, or $1.52 per gallon, for regular leaded). For motorist information contact the automobile club **Shipka**, located at 6 Sveta Sofia Street, Sofia (tel. 2/87-88-01 or 2/88-38-56).

Breakdowns In case of breakdown, telephone 146. The S.B.A. (Bulgarian Automobile Touring Association) trucks carry essential spares, but it's wise to carry your own spare-parts kit. Fiat, Ford, Volkswagen,

Peugeot, and Mercedes all have car-service operations in Bulgaria that offer prompt repairs by skilled technicians.

Car Rental The **Balkan Holidays/Hertz Rent-a-Car** organization has offices in most of the major hotels and at Sofia Airport (tel. 2/72–01–57). Its main headquarters in Sofia are at 41 Vitosha Boulevard (tel. 2/83–34–87 or 2/88–52–05). Rental cars and fly/drive arrangements can be prebooked through Balkantourist agents abroad. These agents can also provide you with a driver for a small extra charge. **Avis** (tel. 2/73–80–23), **Intercar** (tel. 2/79–14–77), and **Europe Car** (tel. 2/72–01–57) also have offices in Sofia.

By Train Buy tickets in advance at a ticket office—there is one in each of the major centers—and avoid long lines at the station. Trains are very busy; seat reservations are obligatory on expresses. All medium- and long-distance trains have first- and second-class carriages and limited buffet services; overnight trains between Sofia and Black Sea resorts have first- and second-class sleeping cars and second-class couchettes. From Sofia there are six main routes—to Varna and Burgas on the Black Sea coast, to Plovdiv and on to the Turkish border, to Dragoman and the Serbian border, to Kulata and the Greek border, and to Ruse on the Romanian border. The main line is powered by electricity. Plans to electrify the rest are under way.

By Plane **Balkanair** (Balkan Bulgarian Airlines) has regular services to Varna and Burgas, the biggest ports of the Black Sea. Book through Balkantourist offices; this can take time, however, and overbooking is not unusual. Group travel and air-taxi services are available through privately run Hemus Air and Air Via. Business flights to other destinations in the country are also arranged by Hemus Air.

By Bus The routes of the crowded buses are mainly planned to link towns and districts not connected by rail. Within the cities a regular system of trams and trolley buses operates for a single fare of 3 leva. Ticket booths, at most tram stops, sell single or season tickets; you can also pay the driver. The tourist information offices have full details of routes and times.

By Boat Modern luxury vessels cruise the Danube from Passau in Austria to Ruse. Hydrofoils link main communities along the Bulgarian stretches of the Danube and the Black Sea, and there are coastal excursions from some Black Sea resorts. A ferry from Vidin to Calafat links Bulgaria with Romania.

Telephones

Calls can be made from hotels or from public telephones in the post office in each major town or resort. Elsewhere there is a new system of international telephones—modern, direct-dial phones with no coin slots—that operate only with special cards paid for in leva. Directions for buying the cards are given, often in English, on the phones. There is no AT&T or MCI service as yet from Bulgaria.

Mail

Letters and postcards to the United States cost 10 leva, 7 leva to the United Kingdom.

Opening and Closing Times

Banks are open weekdays 9–3.

Museums are usually open 8–6:30 but are often closed on Monday or Tuesday.

Shops are open Monday–Saturday 9 AM–7 PM. Many shops are open on Sunday, as are most grocery stores.

National Holidays

January 1 (New Year's Day); March 3 (Independence Day); April 23 and 24 (Easter Sunday and Monday; the date is determined by the Eastern Orthodox church every year); May 1 (Labor Day); May 24 (Bulgarian Culture Day); December 24, 25, 26 (Christmas).

Dining

There is a choice of hotel restaurants with their international menus, Balkantourist restaurants, or the inexpensive restaurants and cafeterias run privately and by cooperatives. The best bets are the small folk-style restaurants that serve national dishes and local specialties. The word *picnic* in a restaurant name means that the tables are outdoors. Standards have improved, but food is still rarely served piping hot, and visitors should be prepared for loud background music.

Specialties Balkan cooking revolves around lamb and pork, sheep cheese, potatoes, peppers, eggplant, tomatoes, onions, carrots, and spices. Fresh fruit, vegetables, and salads are particularly good in season, and so are the soups. Bulgaria invented yogurt (*kiselo mleko*), with its promise of good health and longevity, and there are excellent cold yogurt soups (*tarator*) during the summer. Rich cream cakes and syrupy *baklava* are served to round out a meal.

Bulgarian wines are good, usually full-bodied, dry, and inexpensive. The national drink is *rakia*— plum or grape brandy *slivova* or *grosdova*—but vodka is popular, too. Coffee is strong and is often drunk along with a cold beverage, such as cola or a lemon drink. Tea is taken with lemon instead of milk.

Dress In Sofia, formal dress (jacket and tie) is customary at more expensive restaurants. Casual dress is appropriate elsewhere.

Ratings Prices are per person and include a first course, main course, dessert, and tip, but no alcohol.

Category	Cost
$$$$	over $10
$$$	$7–$10
$$	$4–$7
$	under $4

Credit Cards Increasingly, even restaurants in the moderate category are accepting credit cards, although the list of cards accepted may not always be posted correctly. Before you place an order, check to see whether you can pay with your card.

Lodging

There is a wide choice of accommodations, ranging from hotels— most of them dating from the '60s and '70s—to apartment rentals, rooms in private homes, hostels, and campsites. Although hotels are improving, they still tend to suffer from temperamental wiring and erratic plumbing, and it is a good idea to pack a universal drain plug, as plugs are often missing in hotel bathrooms. In moderate and inexpensive hotels, bathrooms often look unusual. Don't be surprised if strangely placed plumbing turns the entire bathroom into a shower. Due to power cuts in the winter, flashlights and other battery-powered utilities are strongly recommended.

Hotels Until recently, most hotels used by Western visitors were owned by Balkantourist and Interhotels. At press time (spring 1994) many of the government-owned or -operated hotels listed below were on the verge of privatization. The conversion is expected to take up to five years. Hotels may be closed for renovation for extended periods or may be permanently shut down. Visitors are strongly urged to contact hotels in advance to get the latest information. Some hotels were always privately run or run by municipal authorities or organizations catering to specific groups (Sipka for motorists, Orbita for young people, Pirin for hikers). Most have restaurants and bars; the large, modern ones have swimming pools, shops, and other facilities. Some coastal resorts have complexes where different categories of hotels are grouped, each with its own facilities.

Rented Accommodations Rented accommodations are a growth industry, with planned, modern complexes as well as picturesque cottages. Cooking facilities tend to be meager, and meal vouchers are included in the package. An English-speaking manager is generally on hand.

Private Accommodations Staying in private homes—arranged by Balkantourist—is becoming a popular alternative to hotels as a means of not only cutting costs but of offering increased contact with Bulgarians. There are one-, two-, and three-star private accommodations. Some offer a bed or bed-and-breakfast only; some provide full board. Three-star rooms are equipped with kitchenettes. Booking offices are located in most main tourist areas. In Sofia, contact **Balkantourist** at 27 Stambolijski Boulevard (tel. 2/88–52–56), or go to the private accommodations office at 37 Dondukov Boulevard.

Hostels Hostels are basic but clean and cheap. Contact **Orbita** (45a Stambolijski Blvd. Sofia, tel. 2/80–15–03 and at 48 Hristo Botev Blvd., Sofia, tel. 2/80–01–02).

Campsites There are more than 100 campsites, many near the Black Sea coast. They are graded one, two, or three stars, and the best of them offer hot and cold water, grocery stores, and restaurants. Balkantourist provides a location map.

Ratings Prices are for two people in a double room with half-board (breakfast and a main meal). You can pay in either Western or local currency, but if you pay in leva, you must show your exchange slips to prove that the money was changed legally.

Category	Sofia	Other Areas
$$$$	over $200	over $75
$$$	$75–$200	$55–$75
$$	$40–$75	$30–$55
$	under $40	under $30

Tipping To tip, round out your restaurant bill 3%–5%.

Sofia

Important Addresses and Numbers

Since late 1990, a national commission has been working to rename cities, streets, and monuments throughout the country. Names given in the following sections were correct as of spring 1994 but are subject to change.

Tourist Information
Balkantourist Head Office (tel. 2/4-33-31) is at 1 Vitosha Boulevard; the tourist and accommodations office (tel. 2/88-44-30 or 2/88-03-62) is at 37 Dondukov Boulevard. The organization also has offices or desks in all the major hotels. **Balkantour** is at 27 Stambolijski Boulevard (tel. 2/88-52-56). **Pirin** is located at 30 Stambolijski Boulevard (tel. 2/88-41-22).

Embassies
U.S. (1 Stambolijski Blvd., tel. 2/88-48-01). **U.K.** (65 Levski Blvd., tel. 2/88-53-61).

Emergencies
Police: Sofia City Constabulary (tel. 166), **ambulance** (tel. 150), **Fire** (tel. 160), **Doctor:** Clinic for Foreign Citizens (Mladost 1, 1 Eugeni Pavlovski St., tel. 2/7-43-91), **"Pirogov"** Emergency Hospital (tel. 2/5-15-31), **pharmacies** (tel. 178 for information about all-night pharmacies).

Arriving and Departing by Plane, Train, and Car

By Plane
All international flights arrive at Sofia Airport. For information on international flights, call 2/79-80-35 or 2/72-06-72; for domestic flights, tel. 2/72-24-14 or 2/88-13-94.

Between the Airport and Downtown
Bus 84 (nonstop) serves the airport. Fares for taxis taken from the airport taxi stand run about 50 leva–120 leva for the 9-kilometer (6-mile) ride into Sofia. Avoid the taxi touts; they tend to overcharge or to insist on payment in hard currency.

By Train
The central station is at the northern edge of the city. For information, call 2/3-11-11 or 2/59-71-97. The ticket offices in Sofia are in the underpass of the National Palace of Culture (1 Bulgaria Sq., tel. 2/59-71-97) or at the Rila International Travel Agency (5 Gurko St., tel. 2/87-07-77 or 2/87-59-35). There is a taxi stand at the station.

By Car
Heading to or from Serbia, the main routes are E80, going through the border checkpoint at Kalotina on the Niš-Sofia road, or E871 going through the checkpoint at Gyueshevo. Traveling from Greece, take E79, passing through the checkpoint at Kulata; from Turkey, take E80, passing through checkpoint Kapitan-Andreevo. Border crossings to Romania are at Vidin on E79 and at Ruse on E70 and E85.

Getting Around

By Bus
Buses, trolleys, and trams run fairly often. Buy a ticket from the ticket stand near the streetcar stop and punch it into the machine as you board. (Watch how the person in front of you does it.) For information, call 2/3-12-41 or 2/88-13-53.

By Taxi
Since private taxi drivers were given permission to operate in 1990, it has become easier to find cabs in Sofia. Hail them in the street or at a stand—or ask the hotel to call one. Daytime taxi rates (at press time) run 5–7 leva per kilometer, and 7.50–9 leva per kilometer after 10 PM. There is a 10-leva surcharge for taxis ordered by phone. To

order by phone, call 142, or 2/68–01–01 or 2/12–81. To tip, round out the fare 5%–10%.

By Rental Car You can rent a car, with or without driver, through Balkantourist, at the airport, and at hotel reception desks.

On Foot The main sites are centrally located, so the best way to see the city is on foot.

Guided Tours

Orientation Tours Guided tours of Sofia and environs are arranged by Balkantourist from either of the main Sofia offices or from Balkantourist desks at the major hotels. Among the possibilities are three- to four-hour tours of the principal city sights by car or minibus or a longer four- to five-hour tour that goes as far as Mount Vitosha.

Excursions Balkantourist offers 23 types of special-interest tours of various lengths, using Sofia as the point of departure. There are trips to the most beautiful monasteries, such as the Rila Monastery, 118 kilometers (74 miles) south of Sofia; to museum towns, such as Nesebâr and Koprivshtitsa; to sports areas and spas; to the Valley of Roses; and to other places of exceptional scenic or cultural interest.

Evening Tours Balkantourist has a number of evening tours, from a night out eating local food and watching folk dances to an evening at the National Opera.

Exploring Sofia

Sofia is set on the high Sofia Plain, ringed by mountain ranges: the Balkan Range to the north; the Lyulin Mountains to the west; part of the Sredna Gora Mountains to the southeast; and, to the southwest, Mount Vitosha, the city's playground, which rises 7,500 feet. The area has been inhabited for about 7,000 years, but the visitor's first impression is of a modern city with broad streets, light traffic, spacious parks, and open-air cafés. As recently as the 1870s it was part of the Turkish Empire, and one mosque still remains. Most of the city, however, was planned after 1880. There are enough intriguing museums and high-quality musical performances to merit a lengthy stay, but if time is short, you need only two days to see the main sights and at least one more day for Mount Vitosha.

Numbers in the margin correspond to points of interest on the Sofia map.

❶ **Ploshtad Sveta Nedelya** (St. Nedelya Square) is a good starting point for an exploration of the main sights. The south side of the square is **❷** dominated by the 19th-century **Tzarkva Sveta Nedelya** (St. Nedelya Church). Go behind it to find Vitosha Boulevard, a lively pedestrian street with plenty of stores, cafés, and dairy bars.

The first building along this boulevard, on the west side of the **❸** street, is the former Courts of Justice, now the **Natzionalen Istoricheski Musei** (National History Museum). Its vast collections, vividly illustrating the art history of Bulgaria, include priceless Thracian treasures, Roman mosaics, enameled jewelry from the First Bulgarian Kingdom, and glowing religious art that survived the years of Ottoman oppression. The courts are due to return to this location as soon as a new home is found for the National History Museum collection. *2 Vitosha Blvd., tel. 2/88–41–60. Open Tues.–Fri. and weekends 10:30–6:15.*

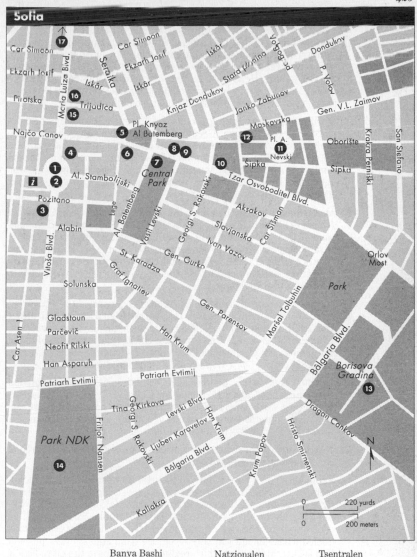

Sofia

Banya Bashi
Djamiya, **16**

Borisova Gradina, **13**

Hram pametnik
Alexander Nevski, **11**

Mavsolei Georgi
Dimitrov, **7**

Natzionalen
Archeologicheski
Musei, **6**

Natzionalen Dvoretz
na Kulturata **14**

Natzionalen
Etnografski Musei, **8**

Natzionalen
Istoricheski Musei, **3**

Natzionalna
Hudozheotvena
Galeria, **9**

Partiyniyat Dom, **5**

Ploshtad Sveta
Nedelya, **1**

Rotonda Sveti
Georgi, **4**

Tsentralen
Universalen
Magazin, **15**

Tsentralni Hali, **17**

Tzarkva Sveta
Nedelya, **2**

Tzarkva Sveta
Sofia, **12**

Tzarkva Sveti
Nikolai, **10**

Return to the northeast side of St. Nedelya Square, and in the courtyard of the Sheraton Sofia Balkan Hotel you will see the
④ **Rotonda Sveti Georgi** (Rotunda of St. George). Built during the 4th century as a Roman temple, it has served as a mosque and church, and recent restoration has revealed medieval frescoes. It is not open to the public. Head east to the vast and traffic-free Alexander
⑤ Batenberg Square, which is dominated by the **Partiyniyat Dom** (the former headquarters of the Bulgarian Communist party).

Facing the square, but entered via Alexander Stambolijski Boulevard, is the former Great Mosque, which now houses the
⑥ **Natzionalen Archeologicheski Musei** (National Archaeological Museum). The 15th-century building itself is as fascinating as its contents, which illustrate the culture of the different peoples who inhabited Bulgaria until the 19th century. *Tel. 2/88–24–06. Open Tues.–Sun. 10–noon and 2–6.*

⑦ On the next block to the east is the former **Mavsolei Georgi Dimitrov** (Georgi Dimitrov Mausoleum), which until 1990 contained the embalmed body of the first general secretary of the Bulgarian Communist party, who died in Moscow in 1949 and was known as the "Father of the Nation." His remains have been moved to the Central Cemetery, and there is talk of either converting the mausoleum into a museum or destroying it.

Across from the mausoleum is the former palace of the Bulgarian
⑧ czar, which currently houses the **Natzionalen Etnografski Musei** (National Ethnographical Museum), with displays of costumes, handicrafts, and tools that illustrate the agricultural way of life of the country people until the 19th century. *Alexander Batenberg Sq., tel. 2/88–42–09. Open Wed.–Sun. 10–noon and 1:30–5:30.*

⑨ In the west wing of the same building is the **Natzionalna Hudozhestvena Galeria** (National Art Gallery). It houses a collection of the best works of Bulgarian artists, as well as a foreign-art section that contains some graphics of famous artists. *1 Knyaz Al. Batemberg, tel. 2/88–35–59. Open Tues.–Sun. 10:30–6.*

⑩ Nearby stands the ornate Russian **Tzarkva Sveti Nikolai** (Church of St. Nicholas), erected 1912–14.

From here you'll enter Tzar Osvoboditel Boulevard, with its monument to the Russians, topped by the equestrian statue of Russian Czar Alexander II. It stands in front of the National Assembly. Behind the National Assembly, just beyond Shipka Street, you'll be confronted by the neo-Byzantine structure with glittering onion domes whose image you may recognize from almost every piece of tourist literature, and which really does dominate the city. This is
⑪ the **Hram-pametnik Alexander Nevski** (Alexander Nevski Memorial Church), built by the Bulgarian people at the beginning of this century as a mark of gratitude to their Russian liberators. Inside are alabaster and onyx, Italian marble and Venetian mosaics, magnificent frescoes, and space for a congregation of 5,000. Attend a service to hear the superb choir, and, above all, don't miss the fine collection of icons in the **Crypt Museum.** *Ploshtad Alexander Nevski, tel. 2/87–76–97. Admission: 20 leva. Open Wed.–Mon. 10:30–6:30.*

Cross the square to the west to pay your respects to the much older
⑫ **Tzarkva Sveta Sofia** (Church of St. Sofia), which dates to the 6th century, though remains of even older churches have been found during excavations. Its age and simplicity are in stark contrast to its more glamorous neighbor.

Return to Tzar Osvoboditel Boulevard and continue east to the
⑬ **Borisova Gradina** (Boris's Garden), with its lake and fountains,
woods and lawns, huge sports stadium, and open air theater. From
the park take Dragan Tsankov west (back toward St. Nedelya
Square) briefly, before going left on Patriarh Evtimij, toward Južen
Park. The formal gardens and extensive woodlands here are to be
extended as far as Mount Vitosha.

At the entrance to the park stands a large modern building, the
⑭ **Natzionalen Dvoretz na Kulturata** (National Palace of Culture), with
its complex of halls for conventions and cultural activities. Its underpass, on several levels, is equipped with a tourist information office,
shops, restaurants, discos, and a bowling alley. *1 Bulgaria Sq., tel.
2/5–15–01. Admission: 5 leva. Open 10:30–6:30. Closed Tues.*

Back at St. Nedelya Square, follow Knyaginya Maria-Luiza Boulevard to the train station. The large building on the right is the re-
⑮ cently refurbished **Tsentralen Universalen Magazin** (Central
Department Store). *2 Knyaginya Maria-Luiza Blvd. Open Mon.–
Sat. 8–8.*

Just beyond is a distinctive building, a legacy of Turkish domination,
⑯ the **Banya Bashi Djamiya** (Banja Basi Mosque); it is closed to visitors. Nearby you will see the Public Mineral Baths. Across the boul-
⑰ evard is the busy **Tsentralni Hali** (Central Market Hall), which is
closed for renovations until the end of 1994.

Time Out　If you're doing the full tour you'll need at least one refreshment stop.
There are several eateries on the northern length of Vitosha Boulevard; three of the best cafés are **Magura, Medovina,** and **One Dollar.**
A café huddles near the 14th-century church of **Sveta Petka Samard-
zijska** (St. Petka of the Saddles) in the underpass leading to the Central Department Store. Or take a break at a café in the underpass at
the National Palace of Culture or on St. Nedelya Square itself at the
Complex Roubin.

Off the Beaten Track

The little medieval church of **Boyana,** about 10 kilometers (6 miles)
south of the city center, is well worth a visit, as is the small, elegant
restaurant of the same name next door. The church itself is closed
for restoration, but a replica, complete with copies of the exquisite
13th-century frescoes, is open to visitors.

The **Dragalevci Monastery** stands in beechwoods above the nearby
village of Dragalevci. The complex is currently a convent, but you
can visit the 14th-century church with its outdoor frescoes. Shepherds can often be seen tending their flocks in the surrounding
woods. From here take the chair lift to the delightful resort complex
of **Aleko,** and another nearby chair lift to the top of Malak Rezen.
There are well-marked walking and ski trails in the area. Both
Boyana and Dragalevci can be reached by taking Bus 64.

Shopping

Gifts and　There are good selections of arts and crafts at the shop of the **Union**
Souvenirs　of Bulgarian Artists (6 Tzar Osvoboditel Blvd.) and at the **Bulgarian
Folk Art Shop** (14 Vitosha Blvd.). You will find a range of souvenirs
at **Sredec** (7 Lege St.), **Souvenir Store** (7 Stambolijski Blvd.), and
Prizma Store (2 Tzar Osvoboditel Blvd). If you are interested in furs
or leather, try 4 **Slavjanska St.,** 7 **Car Kalojan St.,** or 2 **Tzar**

Osvoboditel Blvd. For recordings of Bulgarian music, go to the **National Palace of Culture** (*see* Exploring Sofia, *above*).

Shopping Districts The latest shopping center is in the underpass below the modern **National Palace of Culture,** where stores sell fashions, leather goods, and all forms of handicrafts. The pedestrians-only area along **Vitosha Boulevard** features many new, privately owned shops. The colorful small shops along **Graf Ignatiev Street** also merit a visit.

Department Stores Sophia's biggest department store is the newly renovated **Central Department Store** (2 Knyaginya Maria-Luiza Blvd.).

Dining

Eating in Sofia can be enjoyable and even entertaining if the restaurant has a nightclub or folklore program. Be prepared to be patient and make an evening of it, as service can be slow at times. Or try a *mehana*, or tavern, where the atmosphere is informal and the service sometimes a bit quicker. For details and price-category definitions, *see* Dining in Staying in Bulgaria, *above*. Highly recommended restaurants in a particular price category are indicated by a star ★.

$$$$ **Club Restaurant of the Hunting and Fishing Union.** Here you can choose from an excellent menu of game, fish, and fowl. *31–33 Vitosha Blvd., tel. 2/87–94–65. Reservations essential. Dress: casual but neat. AE, DC, MC, V.*

Coop-35 Vitosha. Continental cuisine is served in a friendly, homey atmosphere that makes it a good choice for both business dinners and more intimate dining. *Dragalevci District, 1 Narcis St., tel. 2/67–11–84. Reservations advised. Dress: casual but neat. No credit cards.*

Dionyssos Vip. This club and restaurant above the Central Department Store (Zum), opposite the Sheraton Hotel, provides a rich selection of international and Bulgarian cuisines spiced with a three-hour floor show. *2 Knyaginya Maria-Luiza Blvd., tel. 2/81–37–26. Reservations advised. Dress: casual but neat. DC, MC, V.*

Krim. This Russian restaurant serves the best beef Stroganoff in town. *17 Slavyanska St., tel. 2/87–01–31. Reservations advised. Dress: casual. AE.*

$$$ **Berlin.** German food is the specialty in this sophisticated restaurant in the Serdika Hotel. *2 Yanko Sakazov Blvd., tel. 2/44–12–58. Reservations accepted. Dress: casual. AE, DC, MC, V.*

★ **Budapest.** This place enjoys a reputation as one of the best restaurants in Sofia for good food, wine, and live music. As the name suggests, Hungarian food takes center stage. *145 G.S. Rakovski St., tel. 2/87–37–50. Reservations accepted. Dress: casual but neat. No credit cards.*

Havana. Cuban food is featured in this popular restaurant near the center of town. *27 Vitosha Blvd., tel. 2/80–05–44. Reservations accepted. Dress: casual. AE, DC, MC, V.*

$$ **Boyansko Hanche.** Local and national specialties are the main features in this restaurant and folklore center, 6 miles from downtown (take Bus 63, 64, or 107). *Near Bojanska church, tel. 2/56–30–16. Reservations accepted. Dress: casual but neat. AE, DC, MC, V.*

Phenyan. This place is known for its Far Eastern ambience and Chinese specialties. *24 Assen Zlatarov St., tel. 2/44–34–36. Reservations accepted. Dress: casual but neat. DC, MC, V.*

Ropotamo. With its central location and reasonable prices,

Ropotamo is a good bet for visitors on a budget. *63 Trakia Blvd., tel. 2/72-25-16. No reservations. Dress: casual. AE, DC, MC, V.*

Rubin. This eating complex in the center of Sofia has a snack bar and an elegant restaurant that serves Bulgarian and international food. A full meal can sometimes push the cost into the $$$ bracket. *4 St. Nedelya Sq., tel. 2/87 45-04. Reservations advised. Dress: casual but neat. AE, DC, MC, V.*

Vodeničarski Mehani. The English translation is "Miller's Tavern," which is appropriate, since it's made up of three old mills linked together. It is at the foot of Mount Vitosha and features a folklore show and a menu of Bulgarian specialties. *Dragalevci District (Bus 64), tel. 2/67-10-21. Reservations advised. Dress: casual but neat. AE, DC, MC, V.*

$ **Party Club.** This restaurant features international and Chinese cuisines. *3 Vasil Levski Blvd., tel. 2/81-05-44. Reservations accepted. Dress: casual. AE, DC, MC, V.*

Zheravna. Candlelight, stone walls, and wood tables set the scene for Zherzavna's country cuisine. *26 Levski Blvd., tel. 2/87-21-86. No reservations. Dress: casual. No credit cards.*

Zlatnite Mostove. This restaurant on Mount Vitosha has live music in the evenings. *Vitosha District, 19 km (12 mi) from the city center. Reservations accepted. Dress: casual. No credit cards.*

Lodging

The following hotels maintain a high standard of cleanliness and are open year-round unless otherwise stated. If you arrive in Sofia without reservations, go to Interhotels Central Office (4 Sveta Sofia St.), Balkantourist (37 Dondukov Blvd.), Bureau of Tourist Information and Reservations (35 Eksarh Josif St.), the National Palace of Culture (1 Bulgaria Sq.), or the central rail station. For details and price-category definitions, *see* Lodging in Staying in Bulgaria, *above.* Highly recommended lodgings in a particular price catergory are indicated by a star ★.

$$$$ **Novotel Europa.** This member of the French Novotel chain is near the train station and isn't far from the center of the city. *131 Knyaginya Maria-Luiza Blvd., tel. 2/3-12-61. 600 rooms with bath. Facilities: 2 restaurants, cocktail bar, coffee shop, shops. AE, DC, MC, V.*

★ **Sheraton Sofia Hotel Balkan.** The former Grand Hotel Balkan has recently been done up to Sheraton standards. It is now a first-class hotel with a central location that is hard to match. It also has excellent restaurants. *1 St. Nedelya Sq., tel. 2/87-65-41. 188 rooms with bath. Facilities: 3 restaurants, fitness center, whirlpool, nightclub, bars. AE, DC, MC, V.*

★ **Vitosha.** There is a distinct Oriental flavor to this towering, trim Interhotel, which is not surprising since it was designed by the Japanese. It is hard to match the range of services and activities available here. The Vitosha also has a superb Japanese restaurant. *100 James Boucher Blvd., tel. 2/6-25-11. 454 rooms with bath. Facilities: 5 restaurants, 6 bars, shopping and business center, tennis courts, sauna, fitness center, pool, nightclub, casino. AE, DC, MC, V.*

$$$ **Grand Hotel Sofia.** This five-story, centrally located Interhotel conveys an atmosphere of relative intimacy, compared with some of its larger rivals in the capital. *4 Narodno Sobranie Sq., tel. 2/87-88-21. 204 rooms with bath. Facilities: 3 restaurants, coffee shop, folk tavern, nightclub, cocktail bar, and shops. AE, DC, MC, V.*

Park Hotel Moskva. The pleasant park setting makes up for the fact that this hotel is not as centrally located as other comparable hotels. The excellent Panorama restaurant is hidden away on the rooftop. *25 Nezabravka St., tel. 2/7–12–61 or 2/83–32–15. 390 rooms with bath. Facilities: 4 restaurants, coffee shop, cocktail bar, nightclub, shops. AE, DC, MC, V.*

Rodina. Sofia's tallest building is not far from the city center and boasts the latest in modern facilities. *8 Tzar Boris III Blvd., tel. 2/ 5–16–31. 536 rooms with bath. Facilities: 3 restaurants, coffee shop, cocktail bar, shops, summer and winter gardens, pool, gym, nightclub. AE, DC, MC, V.*

$$ **Bulgaria.** Despite its central location, this small hotel is quiet and a bit old-fashioned. *4 Tzar Osvoboditel Blvd., tel. 2/87–19–77, 2/88– 22–11, or 2/87–01–91. 85 rooms, some with bath or shower. Facilities: restaurant, tavern, coffee shop, cocktail bar. AE, DC, MC, V.*

Deva-Spartak. This small hotel is located behind the National Palace of Culture. It offers excellent sports facilities. *Valdo Georgiev St., tel. 2/66–12–61. 16 rooms with bath. Facilities: restaurant, indoor and outdoor swimming pools, Spartak sports complex, shop. No credit cards.*

Hemus. This is a smaller place near the Vitosha Hotel. Guests can take advantage of the facilities of its larger neighbor while saving money for the casino or nightclub. *31 Cherni Vrah Blvd., tel. 2/6– 39–51 or 2/66–13–19. 240 rooms, most with bath or shower. Facilities: restaurant, folk tavern, nightclub, shops. AE, DC, MC, V.*

Pliska-Cosmos. Part of the Balkan Airlines hotel chain, the Pliska-Cosmos, located at the entrance to Sofia, has been renovated. *87 Tzarigradsko Shose Blvd., tel. 2/71–281. 200 rooms with shower. Facilities: restaurant, cocktail bar, shops, casino. DC, MC, V.*

Rila. A convenient, central downtown location makes this establishment a low-cost alternative to the Sheraton. *6 Kaloyan St., tel. 2/ 88–18–61. 120 rooms with bath or shower. Facilities: restaurant, folk tavern, coffee shop, art gallery, fitness center. AE, DC, MC, V.*

$ **Serdika.** The centrally located Serdika has an old Berlin-style restaurant that serves German specialties. *2 Yanko Sakazov Blvd., tel. 2/44–34–11. 140 rooms, most with shower. DC, MC, V.*

The Arts and Nightlife

The Arts The standard of music in Bulgaria is high, whether it takes the form of opera, symphonic, or folk music, which has just broken into the international scene with its close harmonies and colorful stage displays. Contact Balkantourist or the **Concert Office** (2 Tzar Osvoboditel Blvd., tel. 2/87–15–88) for general information.

You don't need to understand Bulgarian to enjoy a performance at the **Central Puppet Theater** (14 Gourko St., tel. 2/88–54–16) or at the **National Folk Ensemble** (check with the tourist office for details).

There are a number of fine-art galleries: The art gallery of the **Sts. Cyril and Methodius International Foundation** has a collection of Indian, African, Japanese, and Western European paintings and sculptures (Alexander Nevski Sq., tel. 2/88–49–22; open Wed.–Mon. 10:30–6). The art gallery of the **Union of Bulgarian Artists** has exhibitions of contemporary Bulgarian art (6 Shipka St., tel. 2/44– 61–15; open daily 10:30–6). **City Art Gallery** (1 Gen. Gurko, tel. 2/ 87–21–81) has permanent exhibits of 19th-century and modern Bulgarian paintings as well as changing exhibits by contemporary artists.

The Odeon, Serdika, and **Vitosha cinemas** show recent foreign films in their original languages with Bulgarian subtitles.

Nightlife Gamblers can try their luck at the casino in the **Vitosha Hotel** (100
Casino James Boucher Blvd., tel. 2/62–41–51), at the **Sheraton Sofia Hotel** (1 St. Nedelya Sq., tel. 2/82–65–43), or at **Pliska–Cosmos** (87 Tzarigradsko Shose, tel. 2/71–281).

Discos There is a disco, a nightclub, and a bowling alley at the **National Palace of Culture** (1 Bulgaria Sq.). Other choices are **Orbylux,** known as the classiest disco in town (76 James Boucher Blvd., tel. 2/66–89–97); **Angel** (centrally located at Narodno Sobranie Sq.); and **Sky Club,** a big, two-tier disco (63 Hristo Botev Blvd., tel. 2/54–81–40).

Nightclubs The following hotel bars have floor shows and a lively atmosphere: **Bar Sofia** (Grand Hotel Sofia, 1 Narodno Sobranie Sq., tel. 2/87–88–21); **Bar Variety Ambassador** (Vitosha Hotel, 100 James Boucher Blvd., tel. 2/6–25–11); **Bar Variety** (Park Hotel Moskva, 25 Nezabravka St., tel. 2/7–12–61); **Bar Fantasy** (Sheraton Sofia Hotel Balkan, 1 St. Nedelya Sq., tel. 2/87–65–41).

The Black Sea Golden Coast

Bulgaria's most popular resort area attracts visitors from all over Europe. Its sunny, sandy beaches are backed by the easternmost slopes of the Balkan Range and by the Strandja Mountains. Although the tourist centers tend to be huge state-built complexes with a somewhat lean feel, they have modern amenities. Sunny Beach, the largest of the resorts, with more than 100 hotels, has plenty of children's amusements and play areas; baby-sitters are also available.

The historic port of Varna is a good center for exploration. It is a focal point of land and sea transportation and has museums, a variety of restaurants, and some nightlife. The fishing villages of Nesebâr and Sozopol are more attractive. Lodgings tend to be scarce in these villages, so private accommodations, arranged on the spot or by Balkantourist, are a good option. Whatever resort you choose, all offer facilities for water sports and some have instructors. Tennis and horseback riding are also available.

Tourist Information

There is a Balkantourist office in most towns and resorts.

Albena (tel. 05722/21–52 or 05722/23–12).
Burgas (1 Gani-Ganev St., tel. 056/4–81–11).
Nesebâr (18 Yana Luskova St., tel. 0554/28–55).
Sunny Beach (tel. 0554/69–01, 0554/23–12, or 0554/23–15).
Sveti Konstantin (tel. 052/82–10–45).
Varna (main office, 3 Moussala St., tel. 052/22–55–24 or 052/22–22–72; private accommodations office, 3 Kniaz Boris I Blvd.).
Golden Sands (tel. 052/85–54–07).

Getting Around

Buses make frequent runs up and down the coast and are inexpensive. Buy your ticket in advance from the kiosks near the bus stops. **Cars** and **bicycles** can be rented; bikes are particularly useful for get-

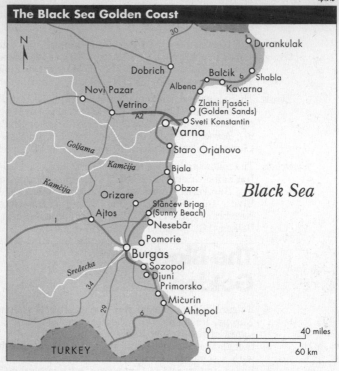

The Black Sea Golden Coast

N

Durankulak

Dobrich

Balčik

Shabla

Novi Pazar

Albena

Kavarna

Vetrino

A2

Zlatni Pjasâci
(Golden Sands)

Sveti Konstantin

Varna

Goljama

Staro Orjahovo

Kamčija

Bjala

Kamčija

Obzor

Black Sea

Orizare

Slănčev Brjag
(Sunny Beach)

Ajtos

Nesebâr

Pomorie

Burgas

Sredecka

Sozopol

Djuni

Primorsko

Mičurin

Ahtopol

TURKEY

0 _____ 40 miles

0 _____ 60 km

ting around such sprawling resorts as Sunny Beach. A **hydrofoil** service links Varna, Nesebâr, Burgas, and Sozopol. A regular **boat** service travels the Varna–Sveti Konstantin (St. Konstantin)–Golden Sands–Albena–Balčik route.

Guided Tours

A wide range of excursions are arranged from all resorts. There are bus excursions to Sofia from Golden Sands, Sveti Konstantin, Albena, and Sunny Beach; a one-day bus and boat trip along the Danube from Golden Sands, Sveti Konstantin, and Albena; and a three-day bus tour of Bulgaria, including the Valley of Roses, departing from Golden Sands, Sveti Konstantin, and Albena. All tours are run by Balkantourist (*see* Tourist Information, *above*, or check with your hotel information desk).

Exploring the Black Sea Golden Coast

Varna **Varna,** Bulgaria's third-largest city, is easily reached by rail (about 7½ hours by express) or road from Sofia. If you plan to drive, allow time to see the Stone Forest (Pobiti Kammani) just off the Sofia-Varna road between Devnya and Varna. The unexpected groups of monumental sandstone tree trunks are thought to have been formed when the area was the bed of the Lutsian Sea. There is plenty to see in the port city of Varna. The ancient city, named Odessos by the Greeks, became a major Roman trading center and is now an important shipbuilding and industrial city. The main sights can be linked by a planned walk.

Begin with the **Archeologicheski Musei,** one of the great—if lesser known—museums of Europe. The splendid collection includes the world's oldest gold treasures from the Varna necropolis of the 4th millennium BC, as well as Thracian, Greek, and Roman treasures and richly painted icons. *41 Osmi Primorski Polk Blvd., tel. 052/23–70–57. Open Tues.–Sun. 10–6.*

Near the northeastern end of Osmi Primorski Polk Boulevard are numerous shops and cafés; the western end leads to Mitropolit Simeon Square and the monumental **cathedral** (1880–86), whose lavish murals are worth a look. Running north from the cathedral is Vladislav Varnenchik Street, with shops, movie theaters, and eateries. Opposite the cathedral, in the City Gardens, is the **Old Clock Tower,** built in 1880 by the Varna Guild Association. On the south side of the City Gardens, on Nezavisimost Square, stands the magnificent Baroque **Stoyan Bucharov National Theater.**

Leave the square to the east and walk past the Moussala Hotel. The **tourist information office** is at 3 Moussala Street (tel. 052/22–55–24). Nearby, on the corner of Kniaz Boris I Boulevard and Shipka Street, are the remains of the **Roman fortress wall** of Odessos. Kniaz Boris I Boulevard is another of Varna's shopping streets. At No. 44 you can buy handcrafted souvenirs from one of the outlets of the Union of Bulgarian Artists.

Walk south along Odessos Street to Han Krum Street. Here you'll find the Holy Virgin Church of 1602 and the substantial remains of the **Roman Thermae**—the public baths, dating from the 2nd to the 3rd century AD. Buy the excellent English guidebook here to get the most out of your visit.

Not far from the baths, moving west, is old Dräzki Street, recently restored and comfortingly lined with restaurants, taverns, and coffeehouses.

Head toward the sea and November 8 Street. The old prison building at No. 5 houses the **Archaeological Museum** (open Tues.–Sun. 10–5). Continue to Primorski Boulevard and follow it, with the sea on your right, to No. 2 for the **Naval Museum** (tel. 052/24–06; open daily 8–6:30), with its displays of the early days of navigation on the Black Sea and the Danube. The museum is at the edge of the extensive and luxuriant **Marine Gardens,** which command a wide view over the bay. In the gardens there are restaurants, an open-air theater, and the fascinating **Copernicus Astronomy Complex** (tel. 052/82–94; open weekdays 8–noon and 2–5) near the main entrance.

Sveti Konstantin Eight kilometers (5 miles) north along the coast from Varna is **Sveti Konstantin,** Bulgaria's oldest Black Sea resort. Small and intimate, it spreads through a wooded park near a series of sandy coves. Warm mineral springs were discovered here in 1947, and the five-star **Grand Hotel Varna,** the most luxurious on the coast, offers all kinds of hydrotherapy under medical supervision (*see* Dining and Lodging, *below*).

In contrast to the sedate atmosphere of Sveti Konstantin is lively **Zlatni Pjasâci** (Golden Sands), a mere 8 kilometers (5 miles) to the north, with its extensive leisure amenities, mineral-spring medical centers, and sports and entertainment facilities. Just over 4 kilometers (2 miles) inland from Golden Sands is **Aladja Rock Monastery,** one of Bulgaria's oldest, cut out of the cliff face and made accessible to visitors by sturdy iron stairways.

From Sveti Konstantin, if time permits, take a trip 16 kilometers (10 miles) north to **Balčik.** Part of Romania until just before World War

II, it is now a relaxed haven for Bulgaria's writers, artists, and scientists. On its white cliffs are crescent-shaped tiers populated with houses, and by the Balčik Palace, the beautiful **Botanical Gardens** are dotted with curious buildings, including a small Byzantine-style church.

Albena, the newest Black Sea resort, is located between Balčik and Golden Sands. It is well known for its long, wide beach and clean sea. The most luxurious among its 35 hotels is the **Dobrudja,** with extensive hydrotherapy facilities.

Slânčev Brjag Another popular resort, this time 36 kilometers (22.5 miles) south of Varna, is **Slânčev Brjag** (Sunny Beach). It is enormous and especially suited to families because of its safe beaches, gentle tides, and facilities for children. During the summer there are kindergartens for young vacationers, children's concerts, and even a children's discotheque. Sunny Beach has a variety of beachside restaurants, kiosks, and playgrounds.

Nesebâr is 5 kilometers (3 miles) south of Sunny Beach and accessible by regular excursion buses. It would be hard to find a town that exudes a greater sense of age than this ancient settlement, founded by the Greeks 25 centuries ago on a rocky peninsula reached by a narrow causeway. Among its vine-covered houses are richly decorated medieval churches. Don't miss the frescoes and the dozens of small, private, cozy pubs all over Nesebâr.

Continue traveling south along the coast. The next place of any size is **Burgas,** Bulgaria's second main port on the Black Sea. Burgas is rather industrial, with several oil refineries, though it does have a pleasant **Maritime Park** with an extensive beach below.

For a more appealing stopover, continue another 32 kilometers (20 miles) south to **Sozopol,** a fishing port with narrow cobbled streets leading down to the harbor. This was Apollonia, the oldest of the Greek colonies in Bulgaria. It is now a popular haunt for Bulgarian and, increasingly, foreign writers and artists who find private accommodations in the rustic Black Sea–style houses, so picturesque with their rough stone foundations and unpainted wood slats on the upper stories. The area is also famous for the Apollonia Arts Festival, held each September.

Ten kilometers (6 miles) farther south is the vast, modern resort village of **Djuni,** where visitors can stay in up-to-date cottages, in the modern Monastery Compound, or in the Seaside Settlement. The wide range of amenities—cafés, folk restaurants, a sports center, shopping center, yacht club, and marina—make this another attractive vacation spot for families.

Dining and Lodging

For details and price-category definitions, *see* Dining and Lodging in Staying in Bulgaria, *above*. Gradually, even restaurants in the moderate category are beginning to accept credit cards. Check with a restaurant before ordering. Highly recommended restaurants and lodgings in a particular price category are indicated by a star ★.

Albena **Bambuka** (Bamboo Tree). This open-air restaurant serves interna-
Dining tional and Bulgarian cuisines and seafood. *Albena Resort, tel. 5772/ 24–04. No credit cards. $$*

Lodging **Dobrudja Hotel.** This is a big, comfortable hotel with a mineral-water health spa. *Albena Resort, tel. 5722/20–20. 272 rooms with bath. Facilities: restaurants, nightclub, coffee shops, cocktail bars,* *shops, indoor and outdoor swimming pools, fitness center, hydro-therapy. DC, MC, V. $$*

Burgas **Starata Gemia.** The name of this restaurant translates as "old boat,"
Dining appropriate for a beachfront restaurant featuring fish specialties.
39 Aleksandrovsku St., tel. 056/45708. No credit cards. $$

Lodging **Bulgaria.** The Bulgaria is a high-rise Interhotel in the center of
town. It features its own nightclub, with floor show and a restaurant
set in a winter garden. *21 Aleksandrovska St., tel. 56/4–28 20. 200
rooms, most with bath or shower. DC, MC, V. $$*

Slânčev Brjag **Hanska Šatra.** Situated in the coastal hills behind the sea, this com-
Dining bination restaurant and nightclub has been built to resemble the
tents of the Bulgarian khans of old. It has entertainment well into
the night. *4.8 km (3 mi) west of Slânčev Brjag, tel. 0554/2811. No
credit cards. $$*
Ribarska Hiza. This lively beachside restaurant specializes in fish
and has music until 1 AM. *Northern end of Slânčev Brjag Resort, tel.
0554/2437. No credit cards. $*

Lodging **Burgas.** Large and comfortable, this hotel lies at the southern end of
the resort. *Slânčev Brjag Resort, tel. 0554/23–58. 250 rooms with
bath or shower. Facilities: restaurant, 2 pools, sports hall, coffee
shop, cocktail bar. AE, DC, MC, V. $$*
★ **Globus.** Considered by many to be the best in the resort, this hotel
combines a central location with modern facilities. *Slânčev Brjag
Resort, tel. 0554/22–45. 100 rooms with bath or shower. Facilities:
indoor pool, restaurant, sports hall, coffee shop, cocktail bar. AE,
DC, MC, V. $$*
Kuban. Near the center of the resort, this large establishment is
just a short stroll from the beach. *Slânčev Brjag Resort, tel. 0554/
23–09. 216 rooms, most with bath or shower. Facilities: restaurants,
coffee shops. AE, DC, MC, V. $$*
Čajka. This hotel offers the best location at a low cost. *Slânčev Brjag
Resort, tel. 0554/23–08. 36 rooms, some with bath or shower. No
credit cards. $*

Sveti **Bulgarska Svatba.** This folk-style restaurant with dancing is on the
Konstantin outskirts of the resort; charcoal-grilled meats are especially recom-
Dining mended. *Sveti Konstantin Resort, tel. 052/861283. No credit cards.
$$*
Manastirska Izba. Centrally located, this eatery is a modest but
pleasant restaurant with a sunny terrace. *Sveti Konstantin Resort,
tel. 0568/6–11–77. No credit cards. $$*

Lodging **Grand Hotel Varna.** This Swedish-built hotel has a reputation for be-
★ ing the best hotel on the coast. It is set just 139 meters (150 yards)
from the beach and offers a wide range of hydrotherapeutic
treatments featuring the natural warm mineral springs. *Sveti
Konstantin Resort, tel. 0528/6–14–91. 325 rooms with bath. Facilities: 3 restaurants, nightclub, 2 swimming pools, sports hall, tennis
courts, bowling alley, coffee shops, cocktail bars, shops. AE, DC,
MC, V. $$$*
Čajka. Čajka means "sea gull" in Bulgarian, and this hotel has a
bird's-eye view of the entire resort from its perch above the north-
ern end of the beach. *Sveti Konstantin Resort, tel. 052/861332. 130
rooms, most with bath or shower. No credit cards. $$*

Varna **Odessa.** This hotel-restaurant offers patio seating with good views
Dining of the activity on Slivnitza Boulevard. The Shopska salad and cheese
omelet make a good combo. Avoid the overpriced drinks. Menus are
printed in English. *Slivnica Blvd. 1, no tel. No credit cards. $$*

Orbita. Don't come here for the ambience (it's a dark room with tables) but to experience the typical Eastern European food in vast quantities. This cheap hole-in-the-wall is extremely popular with the locals, who come here for the lentil soup, grilled kebabs with potatoes, and Bulgarian sausage in a pot. *Czar Osvoboditel 25, in Hotel Orbita, off Knjaz Boris I, tel. 052/22–52–75. No credit cards. $$*

Horizont. This restaurant in Seaside Garden near the Delphinerium has a good selection of seafood as well as a view of the Black Sea from its outside tables. It's not too busy during the day, but at night the live music draws a crowd. *Morskaya Gradina, tel. 052/88–60–26. No credit cards. $*

Lodging **Černo More.** One of the best things about this modern Interhotel is
★ the panoramic view from the 22nd floor; another is the modern facilities. *33 Slivnitza Blvd., tel. 052/23–21–15. 230 rooms with bath or shower. Facilities: 3 restaurants, ground-floor café with terraces, nightclub, cocktail bar. AE, DC, MC, V. $$$*

Inland Bulgaria

Inland Bulgaria is not as well known to tourists as the capital and the coast, but an adventurous traveler, willing to put up with limited hotel facilities and unreliable transportation, will find plenty to photograph, paint, or simply savor. Wooded and mountainous, the interior is dotted with attractive "museum" villages (entire settlements listed for preservation because of their historic cultural value) and ancient towns; the folk culture is a strong survivor from the past, not a tourist-inspired re-creation of it. The foothills of the Balkan Range, marked Stara Planina ("old mountains") on most maps, lie parallel with the lower Sredna Gora Mountains, with the verdant Valley of Roses between them. In the Balkan Range is the ancient capital of Veliko Târnovo; south of the Sredna Gora stretches the fertile Thracian Plain and Bulgaria's second-largest city, Plovdiv. Between Sofia and Plovdiv is the enchanting old town of Koprivshtitsa. To the south, in the Rila Mountains, is Borovec, first of the mountain resorts. A round-trip covering all these towns, with a side excursion to Rila Monastery, could be made in four or five days, although more time is recommended.

Tourist Information

Plovdiv (34 Bulgaria Blvd., tel. 032/5–38–48, 032/22–25–60, or 032/55–28–07).
Veliko Târnovo (1 Vasil Levski St., tel. 062/2–02–36).

Getting Around

Rail and bus services cover all parts of inland Bulgaria, but the timetables are not easy to follow and there are frequent delays. Your best bet is to rent a car. You may also prefer to hire a driver; Balkantourist can arrange this.

Guided Tours

Organized tours set out from Sofia, each covering different points of interest. Check with your Sofia hotel information desk or with Balkantourist for specific information.

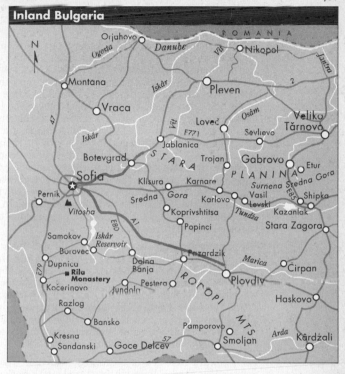

Inland Bulgaria

Exploring Inland Bulgaria

Koprivshtitsa

Koprivshtitsa, one of Bulgaria's showpiece villages, is set amid mountain pastures and pine forests, about 3,000 feet up in the Sredna Gora Range. It is 105 kilometers (65 miles) from Sofia, reached by a minor road south from the Sofia–Kazanlak expressway. Founded during the 14th century, it became a prosperous trading center with close ties to Venice during the National Revival period 400 years later. The architecture of this period, also called the Bulgarian Renaissance, features carved woodwork on broad verandas and overhanging eaves, brilliant colors, and courtyards with studded wooden gates. Throughout the centuries, artists, poets, and wealthy merchants have made their homes here, and many of the historic houses can be visited. The town has been well preserved and revered by Bulgarians as a symbol of freedom since April 1876, when the rebellion that led, two years later, to the end of Turkish occupation ignited.

Return to the main road and turn right. After 15 kilometers (9 miles) you'll reach **Klisura** and the beginning of the **Rozova Dolina** (Valley of Roses). Here the famous Bulgarian rose water and attar, or essence, are produced. Each May and June, the entire valley is awash in fragrance and color. After another 17 kilometers (11 miles), turn at the village of Karnare and take the winding scenic road north over the Balkan Range to the town of Trojan. A few miles away, you'll see the **Trojan Monastery,** built during the 1600s in the heart of the mountains. Trojan Monastery Church was painstakingly remodeled during the 19th century, and its icons, wood carvings, and frescoes are classic examples of National Revival art. Back at Trojan, continue north on the mountain road until it meets highway E771, where you turn right for Veliko Târnovo, 82 kilometers (50 miles) away.

Veliko Târnovo **Veliko Târnovo,** a town of panoramic vistas, rises up against steep mountain slopes through which the River Jantra runs its jagged course. During the 13th and 14th centuries, this was the capital of the Second Bulgarian Kingdom. Damaged by repeated Ottoman attack, and again by an earthquake in 1913, it has been reconstructed and is now a museum city of marvelous relics. The town warrants two or three days of exploration, but even in a short visit some sights should not be missed. Ideally, you should begin at a vantage point above the town in order to get an overview of its design and character. Next, seek out **Tszarevec** to the west (Carevec on some maps), protected by a river loop. This is where medieval czars and patriarchs had their palaces. The area is under restoration, and steep paths and stairways now provide opportunities to view the extensive ruins of the Patriarchite and the royal palace. In summer there is a spectacular sound-and-light show, presented at night, that can be seen from the surrounding pubs.

The prominent feature to the south is **Baldwin's Tower,** the 13th-century prison of Baldwin of Flanders, onetime Latin emperor of Constantinople. Nearby are three important churches: the 13th-century **church of the Forty Martyrs,** with its Târnovo school frescoes and two inscribed columns, one dating to the 9th century; the **church of Saints Peter and Paul,** with vigorous murals both inside and out; and, across the river, reached by a bridge near the Forty Martyrs, the restored **church of Saint Dimitrius,** built on the spot where the Second Bulgarian Kingdom was launched in 1185.

Back toward the center of town, near the Yantra Hotel, is Samovodene Street, lined with restored crafts workshops—a fascinating place to linger in and a good place to find souvenirs, Turkish candy, or a charming café. On nearby Rakovski Street are a group of buildings of the National Revival period. One of the finest is **Hadji Nikoli,** a museum that was once an inn. *17 Georgi Sava Rakovski, tel. 62/2–17–10 for opening times.*

Moving east from Veliko Târnovo toward Varna on E771, you can go back farther in time by visiting the ruins of the two capitals of the First Bulgarian Kingdom in the vicinity of **Šumen** (spelled Shoumen in some English translations). The first ruins are the fortifications at **Pliska,** 23 kilometers (14 miles) southeast of Šumen, and date from 681. At **Veliki Preslav,** 21 kilometers (13 miles) southwest of Šumen, there are ruins from the second capital that date from 893 to 927. The 8th- to 9th-century **Madara Horseman,** a bas-relief of a rider slaying a lion, appears 18 kilometers (11 miles) east of town on a sheer cliff face.

If you leave Veliko Târnovo by E85 and head south toward **Plovdiv,** you can make three interesting stops en route. The first, near the industrial center of Gabrovo—interesting in itself for its House of Humor Museum—is the museum village of **Etur,** 8 kilometers (5 miles) to the southeast. Its mill is still powered by a stream, and local craftsmen continue to be trained in traditional skills. The second is the **Shipka Pass,** with its mighty monument on the peak to the 200,000 Russian soldiers and Bulgarian volunteers who died here in 1877, during the Russian-Turkish Wars. The third is **Kazanlak,** at the eastern end of the Valley of Roses, where you can trace the history of rose production, Bulgaria's oldest industry. Here, in early June, young rose pickers dress in traditional costumes for rose parades and other carnival processions. There is also a highly decorated replica of a Thracian tomb of the 3rd- or 4th-century BC, set near the original, which remains closed for preservation.

Plovdiv From Kazanlak, take the road west through the **Valley of Roses** to either Vasil Levski or Karlovo, another Rose Festival town. Then turn south for **Plovdiv,** Bulgaria's second-largest city, one of the oldest cities in Europe as well as a major industrial center. The old town, on the hillier southern side of the Marica River, is worth a visit.

Begin at the **National Ethnographical Museum** in the House of Arghir Koyumdjioglu, an elegant example of National Revival style that made its first impact in Plovdiv. The museum is filled with artifacts from that important period. *2 Čomakov St. Open Tues.–Sun. 9–noon and 1:30–5.*

Below the medieval gateway of Hissar Kapiya are the attractive **Georgiadi House,** on Starina Street, and the steep, narrow **Strumna Street,** lined with workshops and boutiques, some reached through little courtyards. Follow Saborna Street westward to its junction with the pedestrians-only Kniaz Alexander I Street; here you'll find the remains of a **Roman stadium.** Nearby, the **Kapana District** has many restored and traditional shops and restaurants. Turn east off Kniaz Alexander I Street and walk to the fine hilltop **Roman Amphitheater,** sensitively renovated and frequently used for dramatic and musical performances. On the other side of the old town, toward the river, is the **National Archaeological Museum,** which holds a replica of the 4th-century BC Panagjuriste Gold Treasure, the original of which is in Sofia. *1 Suedinie Sq., Open Tues.–Sun. 9–12:30 and 2–5:30.*

Travel west along the E80 Sofia Road. At Dolna Banja, turn off to **Borovec,** about 4,300 feet up the northern slopes of the Rila Mountains. This is an excellent walking center and winter-sports resort, well equipped with hotels, folk taverns, and ski schools. The winding mountain road leads back to Sofia, 70 kilometers (44 miles) from here, past Lake Iskar, the largest in the country.

On the way back to Sofia you should consider a visit to the **Rila Monastery,** founded by Ivan of Rila during the 10th century. Cut across to E79, travel south to Kočerinovo, and turn east to follow the steep forested valley past the village of Rila. The monastery has suffered so frequently from fire that most of it is now a grand National Revival reconstruction, although a rugged 14th-century tower has survived. The atmosphere in this mountain retreat, populated by many storks, is still heavy with a sense of the past—although part of the complex has been turned into a museum and some of the monks' cells are now guest rooms. The visitor can see 14 small chapels with frescoes from the 15th and 17th centuries, a lavishly carved altarpiece in the new Assumption church, the sarcophagus of Ivan of Rila, icons, and ancient manuscripts—a reminder that this was a stronghold of art and learning during the centuries of Ottoman rule. It is well worth the detour of 120 kilometers (75 miles)—or a special trip from Sofia.

Dining and Lodging

For details and price-category definitions, *see* Dining and Lodging in Staying in Bulgaria, *above.* In the moderate hotels and restaurants, check to see whether your credit card will be accepted.

Koprivshtitsa **Djedo Liben Inn.** This attractive folk restaurant with cocktail bar
Dining and nightclub is built in the traditional style of the area—with half-

timbered, high stone walls. The menu reflects similar attention to traditional detail. *Tel. 997184/21–09. No credit cards. $$*

Lodging **Barikadite.** This small hotel is located on a hill 15 kilometers (9 miles) from Koprivshtitsa. *Tel. 997184/20–91. 20 rooms with shower. Facilities: restaurant, nightclub, cocktail bar. No credit cards. $*
Koprivshtitsa. This good-value hotel is popular with Bulgarians themselves and is just over the river from the center of town. *Tel. 997184/21–18. 30 rooms. No credit cards. $*

Plovdiv **Pldin.** This is an attractive folk restaurant in the center of town. A
Dining video presentation in the lobby highlights the city's past. *3 Knyaz Tseretelev St., tel. 032/23–17–20. AE, DC, MC, V. $$$*
Alafrangite. This charming folk-style restaurant is located in a restored 19th-century house with wood-carved ceilings and a vine-covered courtyard. *17 Nektariev St., tel. 032/22–98–09 or 032/26–95–95. No credit cards. $$*
Filipopoli. This is an elegant folk-style restaurant with a menu that combines traditional Bulgarian, Greek, and international cuisines (including seafood), served by candlelight with the accompaniment of a jazz piano. Try the rich salads and *chushka byurek*. *56 Stamat Matanov St., tel. 032/22–52–96. Reservations accepted. No credit cards. $$*
Rhetora. This coffee bar is in a beautifully restored old house near the Roman amphitheater in the old part of the city. *8A G. Samodoumov St., tel. 032/22–20–93. No credit cards. $$*

Lodging **Novotel Plovdiv.** The large, modern, and well-equipped Novotel is across the river from the main town, near the fairgrounds. *2 Zlatju Boyadjiev St., tel. 032/55–51–71 or 032/5–58–92. 322 rooms with bath. Facilities: restaurant, folk tavern, nightclub, cocktail bar, sports hall, swimming pools, shop. AE, DC, MC, V. $$$*
Trimontium. This centrally located Interhotel built in the 1950s is comfortable and ideal for exploring the old town. *2 Kapitan Raico St., tel. 032/2–34–91. 163 rooms with bath or shower. Facilities: restaurant, cocktail bar, folk tavern, shop. AE, DC, MC, V. $$$*
Marica. This is a large, modern hotel that offers a less expensive alternative to its neighbor, the Novotel. *5 Vazrazhdane St., tel. 032/55–27–35. 171 rooms with bath or shower. Facilities: restaurant, bar. AE, MC, DC, V. $*

Veliko **Boljarska Izba.** In the center of the busy district just north of the
Târnovo river, this place is a folk tavern. *Dimiter Blagoev St., no tel. No cred-
Dining it cards. $$*

Lodging **Veliko Târnovo.** Located right in the middle of the most historic part of the town, this modern Interhotel boasts some of the best facilities for this class of hotel. *2 Emile Popov St., tel. 062/3–05–71. 195 rooms with bath or shower. Facilities: 2 restaurants, cocktail bar, coffee shop, disco, sports hall, indoor pool, shops. AE, DC, MC, V. $$$*
Yantra. The Yantra has some of the best views in town, looking across the river to Tsaravec. *1 Velchova Zavera Sq., tel. 062/2–03–91. 60 rooms, most with shower. Facilities: restaurant, coffee shop, bar. DC, MC, V. $$*
Etur. This moderate-size hotel, with an address near the more expensive Veliko Târnovo, makes it a good base for sightseeing within town. *I. Ivailo St., tel. 062/2–18–38. 80 rooms, most with shower. Facilities: restaurant, coffee shop, bar. AE, DC, MC, V. $*

7 Romania

Romania is not an easy place to visit as a tourist, but it is perhaps the most beautiful country in Eastern Europe. Its natural tourist attractions are varied, from the summer resorts on the Black Sea coast to the winter ski resorts in the rugged Carpathian Mountains; but perhaps even more surprising are the numerous medieval towns and traditional rural villages that are among the most unspoiled and unchanged in Europe.

The overthrow of the Ceaușescu regime in December 1989 started a continuing process of reform toward a Western-style democracy and market economy. Shortages are easing, and the range of available goods and services is increasing, although rising prices have hit many Romanians hard. But the many problems and inefficiencies that tourists may encounter are often outweighed by the traditional hospitality that the Romanian people are free to express since the 1989 revolution.

Comparable to the state of Oregon in size, Romania is made up of the provinces of Walachia, Moldavia, and Transylvania and borders Ukraine, Moldova, Bulgaria, Serbia, and Hungary. With a population of 23 million, Romania is a "Latin Island" in a sea of Slavs and Magyars. Its people are the descendants of the Dacian tribe and of the Roman soldiers who garrisoned this easternmost province of the Roman Empire. Barbaric invasions, struggles against the Turks, the Austro-Hungarian domination of Transylvania, and a strong French cultural influence have endowed them with a rich heritage to add to a folk culture that survives to this day.

Bucharest, with its wide, tree-lined avenues, Arcul de Triumf, and lively café life, was once known as the Paris of the East. Transylvania, a region wrapped in myth, is home to a sizable minority of Hungarians and a small minority of Germans with their own folk traditions and distinctive building styles. This area has long been a favorite with tourists because of the real and fictional sites associated with Dracula. Many enchanting Orthodox monasteries, including some of medieval origin that sport colorful frescoes on their outside walls, characterize the remote and mountainous region of Moldavia.

To the northeast of Bucharest lies the Danube Delta, a watery wilderness populated by fishermen (many of Ukrainian origin) and visited by hundreds of rare bird species. The Carpathian mountain ranges, which form a crown in the center of the country, offer the double pleasure of skiing during the winter and hiking during the summer. The unattractive effects of industrialization are generally confined to the cities, with life in the countryside remaining picturesquely simple. Horse and cart is a popular means of transportation, horse-drawn plows a common sight, and folk costume everyday wear in the northern regions of Maramures and Bukovina.

Romania is a bargain for package tourists. Prepaid package holidays to ski, spa, and seaside resorts offer the best available standards at a very reasonable cost. Independent travelers, however, often pay much more overall for their visit and find wide variations in quality. The country is now in the throes of privatization of its state monopolies, including its tourism industry. Much chaos has resulted from restructuring, and visitors may experience continual changes in prices, amenities, and the quality of services. Nevertheless, conditions for visitors are constantly improving. More and better restaurants, refreshment facilities, and shops are opening in many of the larger towns.

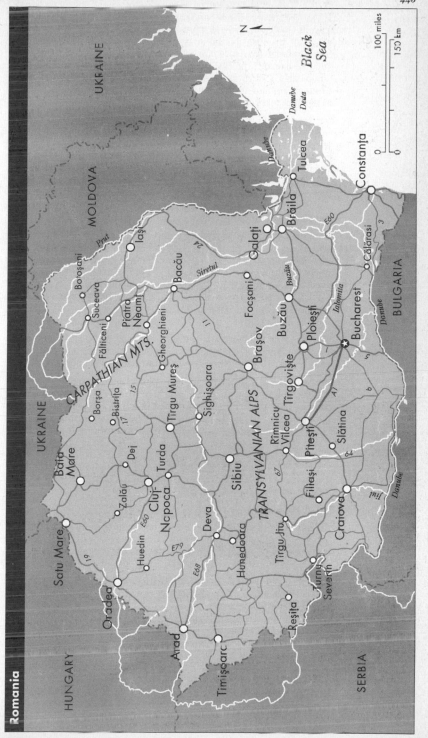

Romania

448

If you are traveling independently, you may wish to take some food supplies with you. Vegetarians are warned that there is a limited range of produce available, especially in winter. However, most towns now have private markets where local farmers sell produce at very reasonable prices. Bread is usually available in Bucharest (shop early!), but it is often hard to find in the smaller towns. Dairy products remain in short supply, though cheese can usually be found at peasant markets.

Visitors should use water purification tablets or boil their tap water, since hepatitis is a danger in Romania. Alternatively, drinking-water fountains in most towns provide natural spring water, and bottled mineral water is available in many restaurants. All visitors should bring an emergency supply of toilet paper, a full first-aid kit, a flashlight for poorly lit streets and corridors, and, in summer, insect repellent. Since medical facilities do not meet Western standards, it is best to take along your own vitamins and medication (including needles and syringes for injections).

Romania enjoyed a period of comparative prosperity during the 1970s, but it is currently the poorest country in Europe after Albania. Petty theft is a widespread problem, although the streets are fairly safe at night. Romanians still have limited experience in dealing with foreigners and are sometimes envious of Westerners' wealth. Their efforts on your behalf may charm you, but they could also be cheating you. Tips, gifts, and even bribes are often expected, but use discretion or you may be regarded as patronizing.

Tourists nowadays may roam much as they wish, and many enjoy "discovering" old churches and buildings, museums, and crafts workshops, or wandering through the beautiful countryside.

Romania is likely to remain underexplored until its serious economic difficulties are resolved, but in the meantime, the package tourist is still assured a good price, while the intrepid independent traveler will experience a part of Europe rich in tradition, one that has largely escaped the pressures and complexities of modern times.

Before You Go

When to Go

Bucharest, like Paris, is at its best during the spring. The Black Sea resorts open in mid- to late May and close at the end of September. Winter ski resorts in the Carpathians are now well developed and increasingly popular, while the best time for touring the interior is late spring to fall.

The Romanian climate is temperate and generally free of extremes, but snow as late as April is not unknown, and the lowlands can be very hot in midsummer.

Romanian Currency

The unit of currency is the leu (plural lei). There are coins of 1, 3, 5, 10, 20, 50, and 100 lei. Bank notes come in denominations of 200, 500, 1,000, and 5,000 lei. The Romanian currency is expected to continue to drop sharply in value, causing frequent price rises; costs are therefore best calculated in hard currency. At press time (spring 1994) the official exchange rate was approximately 1,420 lei to the dollar and 2,120 to the pound sterling. The price of a pack of Western cigarettes rose from 450 lei in 1993 to 2,000 lei in 1994, but because of exchange-rate inflation, the "real" cost rose only from 93¢ to $1.40. Prices of basic items, artificially low from communism, are gradually being increased.

Because of high inflation, upon your arrival check to make sure that low-denomination notes and coins are still in use. There is no longer an obligatory currency exchange, and an increasing number of licensed exchange offices (*casă de schimb*) have been competing to offer rates far higher than official rates, almost equal to those available on the illegal and risky black market. Retain your exchange receipts, as you may need to prove that your money was changed legally. Except for air tickets, foreigners must pay in lei by law, though hard currency is widely accepted. The financial police (*garda financiară*) are useful if you experience difficulty. You may not import or export lei.

Credit Cards Major credit cards are welcome in a number of major hotels and their restaurants but are not accepted in most shops and independent restaurants.

What It Will Cost

Prices of hotels and restaurants can be as high as those in Western Europe as far as the independent traveler is concerned. Those with prepaid arrangements, however, may enjoy reductions of about 30% in some cases.

Sample Prices Museum admission usually costs less than 50¢, a bottle of imported beer in a restaurant around $1.50, and a bottle of good local wine in a top restaurant around $6. A 1-mile taxi ride will cost around 60¢.

Visas

All visitors to Romania must have a visa, obtainable from Romanian embassies abroad or at border stations (for those with prepaid arrangements, the cost of the visa is often included). Send the visa fee ($31), a stamped, self-addressed envelope, and your passport to the relevant office: in the **United States,** Embassy of Romania, 1607 23rd Street, NW, Washington DC 20008, tel. 202/387–6902, fax 202/232–4748; or Romanian Consulate, 573–577 3rd Avenue, New York, NY 10016, tel. 212/682–9122, fax 212/972–8463; in **Canada,** Romanian Consulate, 111 Peter Street, Suite 530, Toronto, Ontario M5V 2H1, tel. 416/585–5802, fax 416/585–4798; Romanian Consulate, 1111 Street Urbain, Suite M-09, Montreal, Quebec H2Z 1Y6, tel. 514/876–1793, fax 514/876–1796; Embassy of Romania, 655 Rideau St., Ottawa, Ontario K1N 6A3, tel. 613/789–3709, fax 613/789–4365; in the **United Kingdom,** Consular Section of the Romanian Embassy, 4 Palace Green, London W8, tel. 0171/937–9667, fax 0171/937–8069.

Customs

You may bring in 2 cameras, 20 rolls of film, 1 small movie camera, 2 rolls of movie film, a typewriter, binoculars, a radio/tape recorder, a small television set, a bicycle, a stroller for a child, 200 cigarettes, 2 liters of liquor, and 4 of wine or beer. Gifts are permitted, though you may be charged duty for some electronic goods. Camping and sports equipment may be imported freely. Declare video cameras, personal computers, and expensive jewelry on arrival.

Souvenirs and gifts may be taken out of Romania, provided their value does not exceed 50% of the currency you have changed legally—so keep your receipts. In addition, you may export five paintings from the Plastic Artists' Union.

There is an increasing number of tempting antiques shops in Bucharest. Sales clerks may encourage you to make purchases, but exporting antiques is difficult and risky. It is possible to obtain export licenses for some items from the Patrimonium office (Calea Victoriei 118, 5th Floor, tel. 01/6592070; open weekdays 12:30–3:30), but the process is very time-consuming and there is no guarantee that you'll succeed. If you are considering buying an antique, ask the shop owner to obtain a license for you before making a commitment.

Language

Romanian sounds pleasantly familiar to anyone who speaks a smattering of French, Italian, or Spanish. French is widely spoken and understood in Romanian cities. Romanians involved with the tourist industry, in all hotels and major resorts, usually speak English.

Staying in Romania

Getting Around

By Car An adequate network of main roads cover the country, though the
Road great majority are still a single lane wide in each direction. Some
Conditions roads are badly potholed, and a few have not been paved. Progress may be impeded by convoys of farm machinery or slow-moving trucks, by horses and carts, or by herds of animals. Night driving can be dangerous: Roads and vehicles are either poorly lit or not lit at all.

Rules of the Driving is on the right, as in the United States. Speed limits are 60
Road kph (37 mph) in built-up areas and 80–90 kph (50–55 mph) on all other roads. Driving after drinking any alcohol whatsoever is prohibited. Police are empowered to levy on-the-spot fines. Vehicle spot checks are frequent, but police are generally courteous to foreigners. Road signs are the same as those in Western Europe.

Gasoline Gas stations are scarce and usually found on main roads at the edge of towns. They sell *regular* (90-octane), *premium* (98-octane), and *motorina* (diesel), but rarely unleaded gas. Prices remain well below those in Western Europe, but shortages sometimes cause waits of several hours. Gas coupons for foreigners—and the privilege of jumping to the front of the line—have been phased out. The Automobil Clubul Roman (*see* Breakdowns, *below*) and tourist offices can provide visitors with a useful Tourist and Motor Car Map that pinpoints the location of each gas station.

Breakdowns **Automobil Clubul Roman** (ACR, Str. Take Ionescu 27, Bucharest, tel. 01/6502595, fax 01/3120434) offers mechanical assistance in case of breakdowns and medical and legal assistance at fixed rates in case of accidents. (It also arranges bus and driving tours, as well as advance hotel bookings.) For breakdowns, call 927 in Bucharest and 12345 elsewhere. Spare parts are scarce, so carry extras. Thefts of parts from vehicles under repair are frequent.

Car Rentals A number of international car-rental companies have opened offices in Bucharest and other major towns. **Hertz** is in the former ACR building (Str. Cihoski 2, Bucharest, tel. 01/6114365, and also at Bucharest's Otopeni Airport, tel. 01/6795284). **Europcar** is in the

ONT Carpați building (B-dul. Magheru 7, tel. 01/6131540, fax 01/3120915).

By Train Romanian Railways (CFR) operates *expres, accelerat, rapide,* and *personal* trains; if possible, avoid the *personal* trains because they are very slow. Trains are inexpensive and often crowded, with carriages in need of repair. First class is worth the extra cost. A *vagon de dormit* (sleeper) or cheap *cușeta*, with bunk beds, is available for longer journeys. It is always advisable to buy a seat reservation in advance, but you cannot buy the ticket itself at a train station more than one hour before departure. If your reserved seat is already occupied, it may have been sold twice. If you're in Bucharest and want to buy your ticket ahead of time, go to the Advance Booking Office, Strada Brezoianu 10, tel. 01/6132642/3/4 or, for international reservations, go to CFR International (B-dul I.C., Brătianu 44, tel. 1/6134008). You will be charged a small commission, but the process is less time-consuming than buying your ticket at the railway station.

By Plane Tarom operates daily flights to major Romanian cities from Bucharest's Baneasa Airport. During the summer, additional flights link Constanța with major cities, including Cluj and Iași. Be prepared for delays and cancellations. Prices average $90 round-trip. External flights can be booked at the central reservations office, Strada Brezoianu 10, and at some major hotels. For domestic flights go to Piața Victoriei 1, tel. 01/6594185

By Bus Bus stations, or *autogara*, are usually located near train stations. Buses are generally crowded and far from luxurious. Tickets are sold at the stations up to two hours before departure.

By Boat Regular passenger services operate on various sections of the Danube; tickets are available at the ports.

Telephones

All large Romanian towns can be dialed directly, and international direct dialing is slowly being introduced in Bucharest. The system is stretched, and you may have to order and wait a long time for nonlocal calls. It is less expensive to telephone from the post office than from hotels. Post offices have a waiting system whereby you order your call and pay at the counter. When your call is ready, the name of the town or country you are phoning is announced, together with the number of the cabin you should proceed to for your call. Private business services are opening in large towns, offering phone, fax, and telex facilities. Coin-operated telephones at roadsides, airports, and train stations may work only for local calls.

Telephone numbers in Bucharest, and area codes throughout Romania, changed in 1994. The area code for Bucharest is now 01, and telephone numbers in the city now have 2, 3, 6, or 7 as a prefix. Long-distance calls should now be prefixed with a 0 followed by the new area code for the country. For information dial the relevant area code, then 11515; in Bucharest it is 931 (A–L) and 932 (M–Z). Your hotel's front desk or a phone book will be much more helpful.

Mail

The central post office in Bucharest is at Calea Victoriei 37 and is open Monday–Thursday 7:30 AM–7 PM, Friday–Saturday 8 AM–2 PM. The telephone section is open 24 hours a day.

Postal Rates Rates are increasing regularly in line with inflation, so check before you post.

Opening and Closing Times

Banks are open weekdays 9 to 12:30 or 1. Licensed exchange (schimb) bureaus are usually open weekdays and Saturday mornings, though private bureaus could have other hours.

Museums are usually open from 10 to 6, but it's best to check with local tourist offices. Most museums are closed on Monday, and some are also closed on Tuesday.

Shops are generally open Monday–Friday from 9 or 10 AM to 6 or 8 PM and close between 1 and 3, though some food shops open earlier. Many shops are closed on Saturday afternoons.

National Holidays January 1; January 2; April 17 (Easter Monday); May 1; December 1, December 25 and 26.

Dining

Shortages have eased and poor standards have now improved sufficiently for the better hotels and restaurants to offer reasonable cuisine and menu choices. Elsewhere, expect poorly cooked dishes based on pork or beef. Vegetables and salads may be canned or pickled. Traditional Romanian main courses are not always offered, but you might try *gustare*, a platter of hot or cold mixed hors d'oeuvres, or *ciorbă*, a soup stock that is slightly spicy and sour. Overcharging is a hazard outside the bigger restaurants with printed menus. You can insist on seeing the prices, but small establishments may genuinely not have a menu prepared for just one or two dishes.

Mealtimes Outside Bucharest and the Black Sea and Carpathian resorts, many restaurants stop serving by 9 PM, although an increasing number have begun to stay open until 11 PM or later. Restaurants usually open at midday.

Precautions The far less expensive *bufet expres*, *lacto vegetarian* snack bars, and *autoservire* cannot be recommended, but creamy cakes are available at the better *cofetarie* (coffee shops). Romanian coffee is served with grounds; instant coffee is called *nes*. You may want to bring your own coffee creamer, as milk is in short supply.

Dress There are no dress rules as such, but Romanians themselves usually wear smart, informal clothes for an expensive evening out. Casual dress is appropriate elsewhere.

Ratings Prices are per person and include first course, main course, and dessert, plus wine and tip. Because high inflation means local prices change frequently, ratings are given in dollars, which remain reasonably constant. Your bill will be in lei.

Category	Cost
$$$$	over $12
$$$	$9–$12
$$	$5–$9
$	under $5

Lodging

Prepaid arrangements through travel agencies abroad often benefit from discounted prices. Some schemes, such as fly-drive holidays, give bed-and-breakfast accommodation vouchers (these cannot be bought in Romania). Most places take vouchers; in deluxe hotels, you have to pay a little extra. Otherwise, book accommodations directly with hotels or through tourism agencies. Some agencies deal only with their local areas; those spawned from the formerly monolithic national tourism office (ONT)—the *agenția de turism*—and from the former youth tourism bureau, now known as the *Biroul de Turism și Tranzacții* (BTT), offer nationwide services. Avoid the cheap and often cheerless hotels used by many Romanians. Rooms in private homes can be booked through many of the ONT offices and are a good alternative to hotels. Private citizens come to railway stations and offer spare rooms in their homes, but use discretion and be prepared to bargain. Inexpensive accommodations such as pensions or hostels are almost nonexistent, and student hostels are not available to foreigners.

Hotels The star system of hotel classification is just being introduced in Romania. Instead, you will encounter Deluxe categories A and B, First-class categories A and B, and so on. Deluxe A is equivalent to five-star or Very Expensive, Deluxe B to four-star or Expensive, first-class A to three-star or Moderate, and first-class B to two-star or Inexpensive. Standards of facilities, including plumbing and hot water, may not be good even in the top hotels, and decline rapidly through the categories. Ask at the front desk when hot water will be available. In principle, at least, all hotels leave a certain quota of rooms that remain unoccupied until 8 PM for unexpected foreign visitors.

Rentals A few delightfully rustic cottages may be rented at such ski resorts as Sinaia and Predeal. Details are available from Romanian tourist offices abroad (*see* Important Addresses and Numbers in Bucharest, *below*).

Camping There are more than 100 campgrounds in Romania; they provide an inexpensive way of exploring the country, but standards vary. The best ones are at Brașov, Cluj, Sibiu, and Suceava, which also offer reasonable bungalow accommodations. They all have showers with hot water at least some of the time. The worst of these have no running water apart from a natural spring and very unpleasant toilets. Rates vary. Campsites are usually clean and comfortable but are only for use during the summer. Details are available from Romanian tourist offices abroad.

Ratings The following hotel price categories are for two people in a double room. Guests staying in single rooms are charged a supplement. Prices are estimates for high season. Because of inflation, ratings are given according to hard-currency equivalents—but you must pay in lei. (Note that hotels may insist on your buying lei from them to pay your bill, unless you can produce an exchange receipt to prove that you changed your money legally.)

Category	Bucharest	Black Sea Coast/Transylvania
$$$$	over $200	over $80
$$$	$125–$200	$50–$80
$$	$70–$125	$30–$50
$	under $70	under $30

Tipping A 12% service charge is added to meals at most restaurants. Elsewhere, a 10% tip is welcome and is expected by taxi drivers and porters.

Bucharest

Important Addresses and Numbers

Tourist Information The main **Romanian National Tourist Office (ONT)** is located at 7 Boulevard General Magheru (tel. 01/6145160) and deals with all inquiries related to tourism (open weekdays 8–8 and weekends 8–2). There are ONT offices at Otopeni Airport, open 24 hours, and at the Gara de Nord, open 8–8 Monday–Saturday. ONT is currently being broken up and privatized, so its office signs in most Romanian towns now read *Agenţia de Turism.* The **Biroul de Turism şi Tranzacţii** (BTT) at Bulevardul Nicolae Bălcescu 21 (tel. 01/6133841) also has branches nationwide.

For information before your trip, write or call **in the United States** (573 3rd Ave., New York, NY 10016, tel. 212/697–6971); **in the United Kingdom** (17 Nottingham Street, London W1M 3RD, tel. 0171/224–3692).

Arriving and Departing by Plane, Train, and Car

By Plane All international flights to Romania land at Bucharest's Otopeni Airport (tel. 01/6333137), 16 kilometers (9 miles) north of the city.

Between the Airport and Downtown Bus 783 leaves the airport every 30 minutes between 7 AM and 10 PM, stopping in the main squares before terminating in Piata Unirii. The journey takes an hour and costs 20¢. Your hotel can arrange transport by car from the airport. Taxi drivers at the airport seek business aggressively and charge outrageously in dollars. Note that the "official" fare is in lei, the equivalent of about $12 with tip, so bargain.

By Train There are five main stations in Bucharest, though international lines operate from Gara de Nord (tel. 01/952). For tickets and information, go to the Advance Booking Office (Str. Brezoianu 10, tel. 01/6132642). For international trains, go to CFR International (B-dul I.C. Brătianu 44, tel. 01/6134008).

By Car There are three main access routes into the city—E70 west from the Hungarian border, E60 north via Braşov, and E70/E85 south to Bulgaria. Bucharest has poor signposting and many tortuous one-way systems: *Unde este centrul* (**oon**-day **yes**-tay **tchen**-trul)? or "Where is the town center?" is essential vocabulary.

Getting Around

Bucharest is spacious and sprawling. Though the old heart of the city and the two main arteries running the length of it are best explored on foot, long, wide avenues and vast squares make some form of transportation necessary. New tourist maps are being printed and can be found in bookstores; they may also be available at tourism agencies and hotels. It is generally safe on the streets at night, but watch out for vehicles and hidden potholes.

By Subway Four lines of the subway system are now in operation. Change is available from kiosks inside stations, and you may travel any distance. The system closes at 1 AM.

By Tram, Bus, and Trolley Bus These are uncomfortable, crowded, and infrequent, but service is extensive. A ticket valid for two trips of any length can be purchased from kiosks near bus stops or from tobacconists; validate your ticket when you board. There are also day and week passes *(abonaments)*, but more expensive *maxi taxis* (minibuses that stop on request) and express buses take fares on board. The system shuts down at midnight.

By Taxi Hail in the street, or phone 01/953—they speak English. The price should be around 40¢ per kilometer, charged in lei.

Guided Tours

A wide variety of tours are promised for 1995 from the growing number of competing tourism agencies, many of which maintain desks in the larger hotels. Tours range from sightseeing in the city—by car with your own driver, if you prefer—to weekend excursions to the Danube Delta or the monasteries of Bukovina.

Exploring Bucharest

The old story goes that a simple peasant named Bucur settled on the site upon which the city now stands. True or not, the name Bucureşti was first officially used only in 1459, by none other than Vlad Ţepeş, the real-life Dracula (sometimes known as Vlad the Impaler for his bloodthirsty habit of impaling unfortunate victims on wooden stakes). Two centuries later, this citadel on the Dimboviţa (the river that flows through Bucharest) became the capital of Walachia, and after another 200 years, it was named the capital of Romania. The city gradually developed into a place of bustling trade and gracious living, with ornate and varied architecture, landscaped parks, busy, winding streets, and wide boulevards. It became known before the Second World War as the Paris of the Balkans, but its past glory is now only hinted at.

The high-rise Intercontinental Hotel now dominates the main crossroads at Piaţa Universităţii; northward, up the main shopping streets of Bulevardul Nicolae Bălcescu, Bulevardul General Magheru, and Bulevardul Ana Ipătescu, only the occasional older building survives. However, along Calea Victoriei, a flavor of Bucharest's grander past can be savored, especially at the former royal palace opposite the Romanian senate (formerly Communist party headquarters) in Piaţa Revoluţiei. Here one also sees reminders of the December 1989 revolution, including the slow restoration of the domed National Library, gutted by fire, and bullet holes on walls nearby. Modest, touching monuments to the more than 1,000 people killed in the revolution can be found here, and Piaţa Universităţii has a wall still festooned with protest posters.

South along Calea Victoriei is the busy Lipscani trading district, a remnant of the old city that sprawled farther southward before it was bulldozed in Nicolae Ceauşescu's megalomaniacal drive to redevelop the capital. Piaţa Unirii is the hub of his enormously expensive and impractical vision, which involved the forced displacement of thousands of people and the demolition of many houses, churches, and synagogues. Cranes now stand eerily idle above unfinished tower blocks with colonnaded, white marble frontages. They flank a lengthy boulevard leading to the enormous, empty, and unfinished Palace of the People, second in size only to the Pentagon. With such a massive diversion of resources, it is not surprising that Bucharest is potholed and faded, and suffers shortages and erratic services. But happily, the city continues to offer many places of historic interest, as well as cinemas, theaters, concert halls, and an opera house.

Numbers in the margin correspond to points of interest on the Bucharest map.

Historic A tour of this city should start at its core, the **Curtea Veche** (old
Bucharest Princely Court) and the Lipscani District. The Princely Court now
❶ houses **Muzeul Curtea Veche-Palatul Voievodal,** a museum exhibiting the remains of the palace built by Vlad Ţepeş during the 15th century. One section of the cellar wall presents the palace's history from the 15th century onward. You can see the rounded river stones used in the early construction, later alternating with red brick, and later still in plain brick. Prisoners were once kept in these cellars, which extend far into the surrounding city; a pair of ancient skulls belonging to two young *boyars* (aristocrats), decapitated at the end of the 17th century, will interest some. *Str. Iuliu Maniu 31. Admission charged. Open Tues.–Sun. 10–6.*

❷ The **Biserica din Curtea Veche** (Curtea Veche Church), beside the Princely Court, was founded during the 16th century and remains
❸ an important center of worship in the city. Nearby, **Hanul lui Manuc** (Manuc's Inn), a renovated 19th-century inn arranged in the traditional Romanian fashion around a courtyard, now houses a hotel and restaurant. Manuc was a wealthy Armenian merchant who died in Russia by poisoning—at the hand of a famous French fortune-teller who, having forecast Manuc's death on a certain day, could not risk ruining her reputation. The 1812 Russian-Turkish Peace Treaty was signed here.

Nearby, **Lipscani** is a bustling area of narrow streets, open stalls, and small artisans' shops that combine to create the atmosphere of a bazaar. At Strada Selari 11–13, you'll find glassblowers hard at work; glassware is sold next door. In Hanul cu Tei, off Strada Lipscani, are many galleries, crafts boutiques, and gift shops. On
❹ Strada Stavreopolos, a small but exquisite **Biserica Ortodoxă** (Orthodox church) combines late-Renaissance and Byzantine styles with elements of the Romanian folk-art style. Go inside to look at the superb wood and stone carving and a richly ornate iconostasis, the painted screen that partitions off the altar. Boxes on either side of the entrance contain votive candles—for the living on the left, for the "sleeping" on the right.

Time Out Down the road, at Strada Stavreopolos 3, is the **Carul cu Bere,** serving half-liter tankards of beer, appetizers, and Turkish coffee.

❺ At the end of the street is the **Muzeul Naţional de Istorie** (Romanian History Museum), which contains a vast collection of exhibits from Neolithic to modern times. The Treasury, which can be visited and paid for separately, has a startling collection of objects in gold and precious stones—royal crowns, weapons, plates, and jewelry—dating from the 4th millennium BC through the 20th century. Opposite
❻ the Treasury is a full-size replica of **Columna Traiană** (Trajan's Column; the original is in Rome), commemorating a Roman victory over Dacia in AD 2. *Calea Victoriei 12. Admission charged. Treasury open Tues.–Sun. 10–5, last ticket at 4 PM. Museum open Wed.–Sun. 10–4.*

Turning north along the Calea Victoriei, you'll pass a military club
❼ and academy before reaching the pretty little **Creţulescu Church** on your left. Built in 1722, the church and some of its original frescoes were restored during the 1930s. Immediately north is a massive

building, once the royal palace and now the Palace of the Republic.

⑧ The **Muzeul de Artă al României** (National Art Museum) is housed here, with its fine collection of Romanian art, including works by the world-famous sculptor Brâncuşi. The foreign section has a wonderful Brueghel collection and is well worth a visit. *Str. Stribei Voda 1. Museum admission charged. Open Wed.–Sun. 10–6.*

Opposite the palace, in Piaţa Revoluţiei, was the former headquarters of the Romanian Communist party. Before the revolution in December 1989, no one was allowed to walk in front of this building. During the uprising the square was a major site of the fighting that destroyed the National Library, parts of the Palace, and the Cina

⑨ restaurant next to the **Ateneul Român** (Romanian Athenaeum Concert Hall). The Ateneul, dating from 1888, with its Baroque dome and Greek columns, survived the upheavals and still houses the George Enescu Philharmonic Orchestra.

Time Out The cafeteria of the **Hotel Bucureşti** on Calea Victoriei has excellent cakes.

Follow Calea Victoriei as far as the Piaţa Victoriei. Opposite is the

⑩ **Muzeul de Ştiinţe Naturale "Grigore Antipa"** (Natural History Museum), with its exceptional butterfly collection and the skeleton of the dinosaur *Dinotherium gigantissimum. Şoseaua Kiseleff 1. Admission charged. Open Tues.–Sun. 10–5.*

Next door, in an imposing redbrick building, is the impressive

⑪ **Muzeul Iăranalui Român** (Museum of the Romanian Peasant). Reopened in 1993, this museum has a fine collection of costumes, icons, carpets, and other artifacts from rural life, including two 19th-century wooden churches. *Şoseana Kiseleff 3. Admission charged. Open Tues.–Sun. 10–6.*

Şoseaua Kiseleff, a pleasant tree-lined avenue, brings you to the

⑫ **Arcul de Triumf,** built in 1922 to commemorate the Allied victory in World War I. Originally constructed of wood and stucco, it was rebuilt during the 1930s and carved by some of Romania's most talented sculptors.

Still farther north lies Herăstrău Park, accommodating the fascinat-

⑬ ing **Muzeul Satului Romanesc** (Village Museum), as well as Herăstrău Lake. The museum is outstanding, with more than 300 authentic, fully furnished peasants' houses, representing folk styles taken from all over Romania. *Şoseaua Kiseleff 28. Admission charged. Open winter, daily 8–4; summer, daily 10–7.*

Shopping

Gifts and New private shops are beginning to bring extra style and choice to
Souvenirs Bucharest, but note the astonishing customs restrictions (*see* Customs in Before You Go, *above)* that prohibit exporting even bric-a-brac. Keep receipts of all purchases, regardless of their legal export status. The **Apollo gallery,** in the National Theater building next to the Intercontinental Hotel, and the galleries in the fascinating **Hanul cu Tei** off Strada Lipscani sell art that you may legally take home with you.

Market The main food market is in Piaţa Amzei, open seven days a week and best visited during the morning. It sells a limited variety of cheese, fruit, and flowers. If you decide to visit outlying flea markets such as Piaţa Obor, take a guide to avoid being hassled and ripped off.

Bucharest

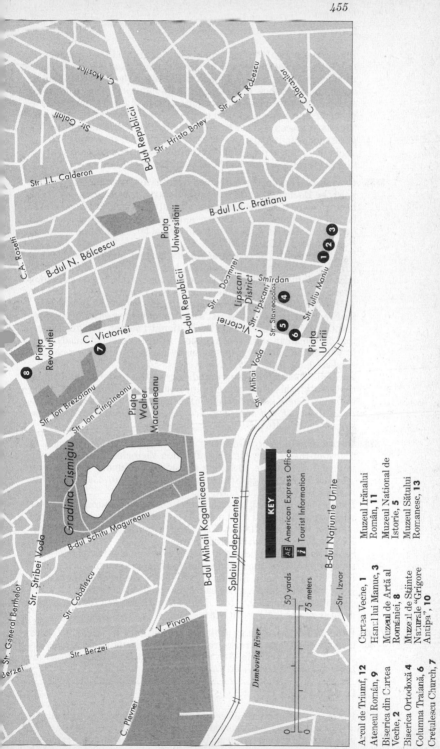

KEY

AE American Express Office

i Tourist Information

0   55 yards

0   75 meters

Arcul de Triumf, **12**

Ateneul Român, **9**

Biserica din Curtea
Veche, **2**

Biserica Ortodoxă **4**

Columna Traiană, **6**

Crețulescu Church, **7**

Curtea Veche, **1**

Hanul lui Manuc, **3**

Muzeul de Artă al
României, **8**

Muzeul de Știinte
Naturale "Grigore
Antipa", **10**

Muzeul Iranului
Român, **11**

Muzeul National de
Istorie, **5**

Muzeul Satului
Romanesc, **13**

Dining

The restaurants of the Continental, Bucureşti, and Intercontinental hotels are all recommended for a reasonable meal in pleasant surroundings. Some, like the **Balada,** at the top of the Intercontinental, offer a folklore show or live music. Although prices are not unreasonable, it is possible to rack up quite a total. Many restaurants have no menu, and waiters' recommendations can be expensive. Also note that most places will serve wine only by the bottle and not by the glass. For details and price-category definitions, *see* Dining in Staying in Romania, *above.* Highly recommended restaurants in a particular price category are indicated by a star ★.

$$$$ **Casa Doina.** Recently refurbished, this historic restaurant, popular with the Bucharest elite between the wars, is once again one of the best in town. It serves Romanian and international cuisines in a relaxing atmosphere. In summer you can enjoy the terrace, which backs onto Kiseleff Park. *B-dul. Kiseleff 4, tel. 01/6176715. Reservations advised. AE, DC, MC, V.*

Hotel Bucureşti. The restaurant in this modern hotel sometimes has a loud band playing in the evenings, but the air-conditioning makes it comfortable, and it is one of the few places where you can enjoy good, genuine Romanian cuisine. *Calea Victoriei 63–81, tel. 01/ 155850 or 01/154640. Reservations not necessary. AE, DC, MC, V.*

La Premiera. One of Bucharest's most popular restaurants is conveniently located at the back of the National Theater. The good selection of Romanian and French cuisine includes excellent salads, even in winter. In summer, you can enjoy La Premiera's terrace. *Str. Arghezi 9, tel. 01/3124397. Reservations advised. AE, DC, V.*

Rapsodia. Located on the ground floor of the modern Hotel Intercontinental, this is a quiet, elegant restaurant with a pianist in the evenings. There is a wide choice of authentic Romanian and international dishes. *B-dul Nicolae Bălcescu 4–6. Reservations not necessary. AE, DC, MC, V.*

$$$ **Bistrot Pierrot.** A new German-run restaurant is in the basement of a turn-of-the-century building off Calea Victoriei. It serves mainly international cuisine, including a good-value Sunday brunch amid intimate surroundings. *Str. Occidentului 44, tel. 01/6596155. Reservations advised. AE, DC, MC, V.*

Brâdet. This informal, privately run Lebanese restaurant is popular with expatriates and diplomats. It's east of the city center in the pleasant Cotroceni district. *Str. Carol Davilla 60, tel. 01/6386014. Reservations advised. No credit cards.*

Select Restaurant. Located in the pleasant primavera district, this restaurant offers good Romanian food at reasonable prices in a friendly atmosphere. Fish lovers will enjoy the locally caught sturgeon; the *mici* (small, spicy sausages) is also worthwhile. You can eat outside in summer. *Aleea Alexandru 18, tel. 01/6792177. Reservations advised. No credit cards.*

$$ **Dong Hai.** One of many Chinese restaurants in Bucharest, this
★ large, well-decorated restaurant in the Lipscani district serves authentic Chinese cuisine. *Str. Blánari 14, tel. 01/6156494. Reservations not necessary. No credit cards.*

Lodging

Hotels in Bucharest are often heavily booked during the tourist season. If you don't have reservations, the ONT office will be of help in suggesting available alternatives. For details and price-category definitions, *see* Lodging in Staying in Romania, *above*. Highly recommended lodgings in a particular price category are indicated by a star ★.

$$$$ **Holveția.** Bucharest's first privately constructed hotel since World War II, the Helveția has established itself as one of the capital's best establishments since opening in mid-1993. This is a small, quiet hotel with an emphasis on individual service and comfort. It is located a little north of the city center but is easily accessible by metro or taxi. *Str. Uruguay 29, tel. 01/3110566, fax 01/3110567. 30 rooms with bath. Facilities: restaurant, bar, café. AE, DC, MC, V.*

★ **Intercontinental.** Designed principally for business clients, the Intercontinental offers American-style accommodations in the city's tallest building. Each room is air-conditioned and has a balcony. *B-dul N. Bălcescu 4–6, tel. 01/6140400, fax 01/3120486. 423 rooms with bath. Facilities: fitness center, sun terrace, pool, nightclub, minicasino, 7 bars and restaurants. AE, DC, MC, V.*

$$$ **Ambassador.** The 13-story Ambassador was built in 1937 and enjoys a fine central location. Although a little shabby, its rooms are comfortably furnished. The restaurant is not recommended, but there is a good café. *B-dul General Magheru 6–8, tel. 01/6159080, fax 01/3121239. 233 rooms with bath. Facilities: restaurant, café. AE, DC, MC, V.*

Bucureşti. The city's largest hotel has an excellent central location and spacious, pleasantly furnished rooms. Its modern ambience is complemented by the vast range of facilities. *Calea Victoriei 63–81, tel. 01/6155850, fax 01/3120927. 402 rooms with bath. Facilities: 2 pools, health club, sauna, cafeteria, restaurant. AE, DC, MC, V.*

Capitol. The circa 1900 Capitol is situated in a lively part of town near the Cişmigiu Gardens. In days gone by, it was the stomping ground of Bucharest's mainstream artists and writers. Today the Capitol is modernized and offers comfortable rooms—though the literati have long since moved on. *Calea Victoriei 29, tel. 01/6139440. 70 rooms with bath. Facilities: restaurant. No credit cards.*

★ **Continental.** This small, turn-of-the-century hotel recalls Bucharest's more gracious past. Furnishings are traditional, but rooms have air-conditioning. It is excellently located in the city center, just north of the lively Lipscani district. *Calea Victoriei 56, tel. 01/6145348, fax 01/3120134. 53 rooms with bath. Facilities: restaurant, coffee shop, bar. AE, DC, MC, V.*

Flora. The modern Flora, situated on the outskirts of the city near Herăstrău Park, offers its cosmopolitan clientele top facilities for geriatric (antiaging) treatment. The sun terraces are havens of relaxation. Most guests stay in this quiet, restful hotel for at least two weeks. *B-dul Poligrafiei 1, tel. 01/6184640, fax 01/3128344. 155 rooms with bath. Facilities: pool, spa-care unit, health club, sauna, restaurant. AE, DC, MC, V.*

Lebada. This pleasant hotel overlooks a lake on the southeast outskirts of Bucharest. *Str. Biruintei 3, tel. 01/6243000, fax 01/3128041. Facilities: restaurant, outdoor terrace, bar, outdoor pool, sauna. AE, DC, MC, V.*

Lido. Conveniently located in the center of the city, this prewar hotel has recently been privatized and renovated to offer comfortable rooms and good facilities, including an outdoor swimming pool and terrace. *B-dul Magheru 5, tel. 01/6144930, fax 01/3126544. 92 rooms with bath. Facilities: restaurant, bar, nightclub, outdoor pool. AE, DC, MC, V.*

Parc. Located near Herăstrău Park and the Flora Hotel, the Parc is modern and within easy reach of the airport; many guests stay here before moving on to the Black Sea resorts. There's a good restaurant that provides music every evening. *B-dul Poligrafiei 3, tel. 01/ 6180950, fax 01/3128419. 314 rooms with bath. Facilities: restaurant, pool, sauna, tennis. AE, DC, MC, V.*

★ **Triumf.** This comfortable hotel is set on its own grounds slightly outside the city center near the Arcul de Triumf. Formerly the President, it used to serve only the communist elite. The more expensive rooms are miniapartments. *Şoseaua Kiseleff 12, tel. 01/6184110, fax 01/3128411. 98 rooms, 49 with bath. Facilities: restaurant, bar, tennis court. AE, DC, V.*

The Arts and Nightlife

The Arts You can enjoy Bucharest's lively theater and music life at prices well below those in the West. Tickets can be obtained directly from the theater or hall or from your hotel (for a commission fee). Performances usually begin at 7 PM (6 in winter). **Opera Română** (The Opera House, B-dul Mihail Kogălniceanu 70) has some good productions, but don't expect to find the same quality prevalent in Prague or Budapest. The George Enescu Philharmonic Orchestra holds concerts at the **Ateneul Român** (Romanian Athenaeum on Piaţa Revoluţiei) or at the more modern **Studioul de Concerte al Radioteleviziunii** (Radio Concert Hall, Str. General Berthelot 62–64). The **Teatrul de Operetă** (Operetta House) is now located at the **Teatrul National** (National Theater, B-dul N. Bălcescu 2), which also offers serious drama. For lighter entertainment, try the **Teatrul de Comedie** (Comedy Theater, Str. Mandinesti); despite the language barrier, there is often enough spectacle to ensure a very good evening's entertainment. **Teatrul Tăndărică** (The Tandarica Puppet Theater, Calea Victoriei 50) has an international reputation, and the **Teatrul Evreesc de Stat** (State Jewish Theater, Str. Barasch 15) stages Yiddish-language performances. Don't miss the fine folkloric show at the **Rapsodia Română Artistic Ensemble** (Str. Lipscani 53). The **Cinematica Romana** (Str. Eforie 5) runs a daily program of old, undubbed American and English films.

Nightlife Increasing numbers of bars and restaurants stay open late. Coffee shops, however, are usually closed after 8 PM.

Cafés Cafés with outdoor terraces remain a feature of the city. Try the **Lido** or, in winter, the excellent indoor **Ana Café** (Str. Aviator Radu Beller 6), just north of Piaţa Dorobanţi.

Nightclubs The **Lido, Ambassador,** and **Intercontinental** hotels have nightclubs with floor shows, and many others are popping up as well. **Vox Maris,** at the corner of Calea Victoriei and Bulevardul Mihail Kogălniceanu, and **Club A,** on Str. Blănari, are among several late-night discos. **Şarpele Roşu** (Str. Icoanei Piaţa Galaţi), or "Red Snake," has a pleasant, bohemian atmosphere, with Gypsy bands playing until 3 AM.

The Black Sea Coast and Danube Delta

The southeastern Dobrogea region, only 45 minutes by air from Bucharest, 210 kilometers (130 miles) by road, is one of the major focal points of Romania's rich history. Within a clearly defined area are the historic port of Constanţa; the Romanian Riviera pleasure coast; the renowned Murfatlar vineyards; Roman, Greek, and earlier ruins; and the Danube Delta, one of Europe's leading wildlife sanc-

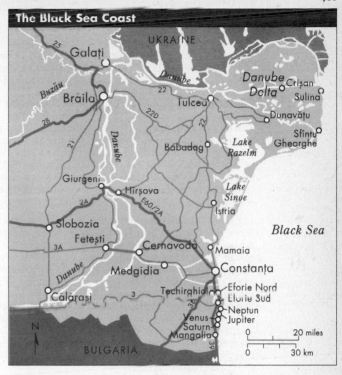

The Black Sea Coast

UKRAINE

Galați

Buzău

Brăila

Danube

Tulcea

Danube Delta

Crișan

Sulina

Dunavățu

Sfintu Gheorghe

Bábadag

Lake Razelm

Giurgeni

Hîrșova

Lake Sinoe

Istria

Slobozia

Fetești

Cernavoda

Mamaia

Black Sea

Medgidia

Constanța

Călărași

Danube

Techirghiol

Eforie Nord

Eforie Sud

Neptun

Jupiter

Venus

Saturn

Mangalia

BULGARIA

0   20 miles

0   30 km

N

---

tuaries. The rapid development of the Black Sea resorts and increasing interest in the delta region mean that tourist amenities (such as hotels and restaurants) and train, bus, and plane connections are good.

Tourist Information

Constanța. Societatea Comercială Litoral (B-dul Tomis 69, tel. 041/617181, fax 041/611429). **BTT** (Hotel Tineretului, B-dul Tomis 20–26, tel. 041/515262, fax 041/516624).

Mamaia. Societatea Comercială Mamaia (Hotel București, tel. 041/531025).

Tulcea. Societatea Comercială Deltarom (Hotel Delta, Str. Isaccei 2, tel. 040/614720, fax 040/616260). **BTT** (Str. Babadag Bloc B1, tel. 040/612496, fax 040/61684).

Getting Around

By Bus Bus trips from the Black Sea resorts and Constanta to the Danube Delta, the Murfatlar vineyards, Istria, and the sunken city of Adamclisi are arranged by tourism agencies.

By Car Rental cars, with or without drivers, are available through Societatea Comercială Litoral (formerly ONT) offices, hotels, and specialized agencies.

By Boat Regular passenger and sightseeing boats operate along the middle and southern arms of the Danube Delta. Motorboats are available for hire, or rent one of the more restful fishermen's boats.

Guided Tours

Tours always involve some hours on the road, so it is better to go for more than one day. The **Societatea Comercială Litoral** has the most tour experience. Try trips to the Bukovina monasteries, the Prahova Mountains, or, especially, the Danube Delta.

Exploring the Black Sea Coast and Danube Delta

Tulcea, the main town of the Danube Delta, is the gateway to the splendors of the region. Built on seven hills and influenced by Turkish styles, this former market town is now an important sea and river port, as well as the center of the Romanian fish industry. The **Muzeul Deltei Dunării** (Danube Delta Museum) provides a good introduction to the flora, fauna, and way of life of the communities in the area. *Str. Progresului 32. Admission charged. Open daily 10–6.*

The **Delta Dunării** (Danube Delta) is Europe's largest wetlands reserve, covering 2,681 square kilometers (1,676 square miles), with a sprawling, watery wilderness that stretches from the Ukrainian border to a series of lakes north of the Black Sea resorts. It is Europe's youngest land—more than 43.7 square meters (47 square yards) are added each year by normal silting action. As it approaches the delta, the great Danube divides into three streams. The northernmost branch forms the border with Ukraine, the middle arm leads to the busy port of Sulina, and the southernmost arm meanders gently toward the little port of Sfintu Gheorghe. From these channels, countless canals widen into tree-fringed lakes, reed islands, and pools covered with water lilies; there are sand dunes and pockets of lush forest.

More than 80% of the delta area is water. Over 300 bird species visit the area; 70 of these species come from as far away as China and India. The delta is a natural stopover for migratory birds, but the most characteristic bird is the common pelican, the featured star of this bird-watchers' paradise. Fishing provides most of the area's inhabitants, many of whom are of Ukrainian origin, with a livelihood. One of the most common sights are the long lines of fishing boats strung together to be towed by motorboats to remote fishing grounds. Smaller communities, such as Independenţa on the southern arm and Crišan on the middle arm, rent out the services of a fisherman and his boat to foreigners. The waters here are particularly rich in catfish, perch, carp, and caviar-bearing sturgeon.

There are good roads to the Black Sea resorts from Tulcea that take you to **Babadag** via the strange, eroded Măcin Hills. It was here, according to local legend, that Jason and his Argonauts cast anchor in their search for the mythical golden fleece. Farther south is **Istria,** an impressive archaeological site founded in 6 BC by Greek merchants from Miletus. There are traces of early Christian churches and baths and even residential, commercial, and industrial districts. A useful English-language booklet, available on the spot, will help make sense of the remains of several cultures.

Istria lies only 60 kilometers (37 miles) from **Mamaia,** the largest of the Black Sea resorts. Mamaia is situated on a strip of land bordered by the Black Sea and fine beaches on one side and the fresh waters of the Mamaia Lake on the other. All the resorts along this stretch of the coast have modern high-rise apartments, villas, restaurants, nightclubs, and discos. There are cruises down the coast to Mangalia and along the new channel linking the Danube with the Black Sea near Constanţa. Sea-fishing expeditions can also be arranged for early risers, with all equipment provided. These resorts offer everything necessary for a complete vacation by the sea.

Constanţa is Romania's second-largest city and is only a short ride by trolley bus from Mamaia. With a polyglot flavor characteristic of so many seaports, Constanţa is steeped in history. The famous Roman poet Ovid was exiled here from Rome in AD 8, probably for his part in court scandals and for the amorality of his poem *Ars amandi (The Art of Making Love)*. A city square has been named in his honor and provides a fine backdrop for a statue of him by the sculptor Ettore Ferrari. Behind the statue, in the former town hall, is one of the best museums in Europe, the **Muzuel Naţional de Istorie şi Arheologie** (National History and Archaeological Museum). Of special interest here are the statuettes of *The Thinker* and *The Seated Woman*, from the Neolithic Hamangian culture (4000 to 3000 BC). Collections from the Greek, Roman, and Daco-Roman cultures are generally outstanding. *Piaţa Ovidiu 12. Admission charged. Open Tues.–Sun. 10–6.*

Near the museum is **Edificiu Roman cu Mozaic,** a Roman complex of warehouses and shops from the 4th century AD, including a magnificent mosaic floor measuring over 6,510 square meters (21,000 square feet) (Piaţa Ovidiu 1). Not far away are the remains of the Roman baths from the same period. The **Parcul Arheologic** (Archaeology Park) on Boulevard Republicii contains items dating from the 3rd and 4th centuries AD and from a 6th-century tower. Modern-day attractions include an **Acvariul,** or aquarium (Str. Februarie 16), and **Delfinariul,** the dolphinarium (B-dul Mamaia 265), which offers aquatic displays by trained dolphins.

A string of seaside resorts lie just south of Constanţa. **Eforie Nord** is an up-to-date thermal treatment center. A series of resorts built during the 1960s are named for the coast's GrecoRoman past— **Neptun, Jupiter, Venus,** and **Saturn.** Not in any way typically Romanian, these resorts offer good amenities for relaxed, seaside vacations. The old port of **Mangalia** is the southernmost resort.

Most of the old Greek city of **Callatis** lies underwater now, but a section of the walls and the remains of a Roman villa are still visible.

There are regular excursions from the seaside resorts to the **Columna Traiană** (replica of Trajan's Column), the **Podgoriile Murfatlar** (Murfatlar vineyards) for wine tastings, and the ruins of the Roman town at **Tropaeum Trajani.**

Dining and Lodging

For details and price-category definitions, *see* Dining and Lodging in Staying in Romania, *above*. Travelers are advised not to rely on credit cards in this region since many resorts are not yet equipped to accept them.

Constanţa **Cazinou.** A turn-of-the-century former casino situated close to the
Dining aquarium, the Cazinou is decorated in an ornate 20th-century style; there's an adjoining bar by the sea. Seafood dishes are the house specialties. *Str. Februarie 16, tel. 041/617416. Reservations advised. No credit cards. $$$$*

Lodging **Continental.** Older, slightly less luxurious, but larger than the Palace, the Continental is conveniently situated near the open-air archaeological museum in the downtown area. *B-dul Republicii 20, tel. 041/15660. 140 rooms with bath. AE. $$$*

Palace. Located near the city's historic center, the large and gracious old Palace has recently been renovated. It has a good restaurant and a terrace overlooking the sea and the tourist port of Tomis. *Str. Remus Opreanu 5–7, tel. 041/14696. 132 rooms with bath. Facilities: restaurant. $$$*

Crişan **Lebăda.** This is a comfortable hotel from which to make fishing trips
Lodging into the more remote parts of the delta. *Sulina Canal, mile 14.5, tel. 040/14720. 74 rooms with bath. Facilities: restaurant, currency exchange. $$*

Mamaia **Satul de Vacanţa.** This holiday village is an attractive complex of tra-
Dining ditional Romanian buildings, built in styles from all over Romania and featuring many small restaurants that serve local specialties. *$–$$$*
Insula lui Ovidiu. This is a reed-thatched complex of rustic-style buildings with lively music every evening. A relaxed, informal atmosphere provides a good setting for delicious seafood dishes. *Lake Siurghiol. No tel. Reservations not necessary. $$*

Lodging **Rex.** One of King Carol's former residences, this is the largest and grandest of all the hotels in Mamaia. An outdoor swimming pool, an excellent restaurant, a bar, and a cafeteria are among its facilities. *Tel. 041/31595, fax 041/62292. 102 rooms with bath. AE, DC, MC, V. $$$$*
Ambasador, Lido, and **Savoy.** Among the many modern hotels, these three are all newly built and moderately priced. They are grouped in a horseshoe around open-air pools near the beach at the north end of the resort. Contact them through the Societatea Comercială Mamaia (*see* Tourist Information, *above*). *$$*

Tulcea **Delta.** A large, modern hotel on the banks of the Danube, the Delta
Lodging currently has a mixed reputation. Amenities include a restaurant, bar, and cafeteria. *Str. Isaacei 2, tel. 040/14720, fax 040/16260. 117 rooms with bath. $$*

Venus **Dana.** This is a new, privately run three-star hotel at the popular
Lodging Venus resort. All rooms have balconies and showers. *Venus Resort, tel. 041/31503, fax 041/31465. 110 rooms with shower. Facilities: restaurant, terrace, shop, currency office. $$$*

Transylvania

Transylvania, Romania's western province, offers travelers the chance to explore some of Europe's most beautiful and unspoiled villages and rural landscapes. The Carpathian Mountains, which separate Transylvania from Wallachia and Moldavia, Romania's other two regions, shielded the province from the Turks and Mongols during the Middle Ages. Germans and Hungarians settled in Transylvania during this period, building many wonderful castles, towns, and churches. Since the 1980s many ethnic Germans have emigrated, but Transylvania, which was ruled by Hungary until 1920, is still home to a large Hungarian minority and to many of Romania's 2 million ethnic Gypsies. Many of Romania's most beautiful tourist spots can be found in Transylvania, but the lack of amenities outside of the main towns makes traveling difficult. Although private entrepreneurs are developing tourism, hotels and restaurants of a reasonable standard are often difficult to find. One solution is to base yourself in a major town like Sibiu, Cluj, or Braşov and take day trips into the countryside. Another option is to join a guided tour.

Tourist Information

Braşov **Nouvelles Frontières** (Piaţa Sfatului 4, tel. 068/151173). This French tourist agency organizes tours, makes hotel and plane reservations, and provides guides and other services.
Cluj. **Cluj County Tourism Office** (Str. Şincai 2, tel. 064/117778).
Tarom (Piaţa Mihai Viteazul 11, tel. 064/130234).
Sibiu. **Tarom** (Str. Nicolae Bălcescu 10, tel. 069/411157).

Getting Around

By Bus Bus trips to Transylvania are arranged by an increasing number of tourism agencies in Bucharest, Budapest, the Hungarian capital, and larger Transylvanian towns such as Braşov and Cluj. There is an extensive network of local bus services in the region, but buses are often crowded, uncomfortable, and slow and should be used only for short distances if at all.

By Car Travel by car is perhaps the best way to explore Transylvania's rich rural life. Rental cars, with or without drivers, are available through tourism offices and major hotels. Hitchhiking is also common in Romania. Many Romanians cannot afford cars, and in remote areas they often rely on this form of transport. It is customary to contribute to gas costs in return for a ride.

By Plane There are regular flights from Bucharest to Cluj, Sibiu, and other major Transylvanian towns. Traveling by plane is a good option for those with limited time, given the slowness of train and bus services and the relatively inexpensive cost of air travel.

By Train Many Transylvanian towns are on international train routes, making train travel a good way to explore the region. Cluj, for example, can be reached by overnight train from both Bucharest and Budapest. Try to travel by *expres* or *accelerat* services, as otherwise you may find that it takes several hours to cover just a couple of hundred kilometers.

Guided Tours

The Romanian National Tourist office (ONT) and the Romanian Automobile Club (ACR) in Bucharest organize tours in Transylvania, as do an increasing number of private companies.

Exploring Transylvania

Wooded mountains provide a scenic backdrop to the medieval town of **Braşov,** the gateway to Transylvania for those starting their journey in Bucharest. Braşov, known as Kronstadt to the Saxon merchants who settled in the city during the 13th century, keen to exploit trade routes with Turkey and the Orient, is the first town one reaches after crossing the Carpathian Mountains on the A1 road from Bucharest or by train from the capital. Like many Romanian cities, Braşov underwent heavy industrialization during the communist period. Thankfully, however, much of the historic part of the city remains intact. Good amenities and the town's proximity to **Poiana Braşov,** Romania's best ski and mountain resort, and **Dracula's Castle** at **Bran** make it a popular tourist destination. The **Black Church,** the largest church between Vienna and Istanbul, dominates the old part of the town. Begun during the 14th century, this Lutheran church has an impressive collection of medieval Oriental carpets, donated by those who were successful in trade with the

East. The church backs onto **Piaţa Sfatului,** a splendid medieval square, with a **Romanian Orthodox Church** at No. 3, a museum in the 15th-century former town hall in the middle, and several pleasant cafés and restaurants. To the east of the square, toward **Mount Timpa** with its cable car, one can see remnants of the old city wall and its seven towers built to protect the town from Turkish invasion. From the **Panoramic** restaurant at the top of the cable car, you can enjoy fantastic views of Braşov and the surrounding countryside.

Leaving Braşov you can either turn westward, following the spectacular **Fagaraş** range, the highest point of the Carpathians, toward the town of **Sibiu** or head northwest to **Sighişoara.** Along the road to Sighişoara you will find some of Transylvania's most enchanting villages. During the 12th and 13th centuries, Romania's Hungarian kings offered Saxon craftsmen land in return for settling in the region and defending it against raiders. Many villages have fortified churches, where entire communities retreated when Turkish or Mongol horsemen marauded Transylvania. Sadly, with the departure of ethnic Germans to Germany since the 1980s, many villages have fallen into disrepair. However, you can still find impressive fortified churches at **Homorod, Rupea,** and **Saschiz.**

Sighişoara's towers and spires can be seen from quite a distance before you reach this enchanting place. Towering above the modern town is a medieval **citadel** and town that must be among the loveliest and least spoiled in Europe. Walking up from the city center, one enters the citadel through the 60-meter-tall **clock tower,** which dates from the 14th century. The clock still works, complete with rotating painted wooden figures, one for each day of the week. The tower houses the town's **History Museum,** which includes some moving photographs of the 1989 revolution that led to the execution of dictator Nicolae Ceauşescu and his wife, Elena. From the wooden gallery at the top of the tower, you can look out over the town with its terracotta roofs and painted houses. Opposite is a small ocher-colored house where the father of Vlad Ţepes, better known as **Dracula,** once lived. It is now a pleasant restaurant. Behind the restaurant, walking uphill along narrow, cobbled streets lined with faded pink, green, and ocher houses, you'll come to a covered staircase. This leads to a 14th-century **Gothic church** and a leafy, ivy-filled **German cemetery,** a testament to the town's settlers, which extends over the hilltop beyond the city walls.

Cluj, once the capital of Hungarian-ruled Transylvania and known as Kolozsvar to Hungarians, is some 170 kilometers (105 mi) northwest of Sighişoara. Nearly a quarter of Cluj's 320,000 inhabitants are ethnic Hungarians, and this elegant Habsburg city enjoys a rich cultural life, with good theaters, galleries, and concert halls. **Piaţa Unirii,** the main square, is dominated by **St Michael's,** a 14th-century Roman Catholic church with a huge 19th-century spire. In front of it is an imposing statue of **Matthias Corvinus,** the son of a Romanian prince, who became one of Hungary's greatest kings (1458–90). On the east side of the square is the **Art Museum,** which has regular exhibitions as well as an interesting permanent collection. To the west of the square at Str. Memorandumului 21 is the **Ethnographic Museum,** which has one of Romania's best collections of costumes and carpets. To the south you'll find **Babes-Bolyai University,** one of the finest colleges in Romania, while to the east, in the adjoining Piaţas Victoriei and Stefan Cel Mare, you'll find the imposing **Romanian Orthodox Cathedral** (1921–33), a neo-Byzantine building with a huge cupola, as well as the local branch of the **Romanian National Theater** and the **Opera House.**

Sibiu is 165 kilometers south of Cluj and 145 kilometers (90 mi) west of Braşov. Sibiu, known as Hermannstadt to the Germans who founded the city in 1143, was the Saxons' main town in Transylvania. Like Sighişoara and Dı aşov, the town still has a distinctly German or Central European feel to it even though there are few ethnic Germans left. The old part of the town centers around the magnificent **Piaţa Mare** (Great Square) and **Piaţa Mica** (Small Square), with their painted 17th-century town houses. In Piaţa Mare is the **Roman Catholic church,** a splendid high-Baroque building, as well as the **Brukenthal Museum.** This museum, housed in the palace of its founder, Samuel Brukenthal, Habsburg governor from 1777 to 1787, has one of the most extensive collections of silver, paintings, and furniture in Romania. It also has an annex around the corner on Str. Mitropoliei. Next to Piaţa Mica you'll find the **Lutheran Cathedral,** a massive 14th- to 15th-century edifice with a simple, stark interior in total contrast to the Roman Catholic church just a couple of hundred meters away. On the outskirts of the town you'll find a large Gypsy community and the ornate homes of their self-proclaimed leaders **King Cioba** and **Emperor Iulian.** Many Gypsy women wear traditional clothes—brightly colored long, flowing skirts and head scarves.

Dining and Lodging

Braşov Dining

Stradivari. This is a new Italian-owned establishment with both a pizzeria and a more expensive restaurant that serves pasta and seafood dishes. *Piaţa Sfatului 1, tel. 068/151165. No credit cards. Closed Wed. Pizzeria: $. Restaurant: $$$*

Marele Zid China Restaurant. The "Great Wall," a large privately run restaurant with a pleasant decor and ambience, serves reasonably priced Chinese food. *Piaţa Sfatului, tel. 068/144089. No credit cards. $$*

Gustari. This simple, bistro-type restaurant serves traditional Romanian dishes such as sour soups (*ciorbă*), fried cheese (*caşcaval pane*), and pancakes (*clătite*). It is open from 9 AM to 9 PM. *Piaţa Sfatului 14, tel. 068/150857. No credit cards. $*

Timpa. A new self-service restaurant located on the pedestrian mall, a couple of minutes from Piaţa Sfatului, Timpa serves hot and cold dishes—including pizza, excellent salads, and vegetarian offerings even in winter. This is the best place to have a quick and inexpensive snack or light meal. *Str. Republicii. No credit cards. Closed Sun. $*

Lodging

Aro Palace. Architecturally a typical communist-era hotel built in the 1950s, the Aro Palace lacks charm but is comfortable, has good facilities, and is conveniently located in the center of town near the main tourist attractions. *Bdul Eroilor 27, tel. 068/142840, fax 068/150427. 586 places in 15 suites, 30 single and 262 double rooms with bath. Facilities: 2 restaurants, garden restaurant, outdoor swimming pool, barber, currency exchange, parking. AE, DC, MC, $$$*

Coroana. This turn-of-the-century two-star hotel, formerly known as the Postăvarul, has seen better days. Though shabby, the rooms are clean and spacious and the hotel is well located a few minutes' walk from Piaţa Sfatului with its many restaurants, cafés, and tourist attractions. *Str. Republicii 62, tel. 068/144330, fax 068/141505. 319 places in single and double rooms or apartments with bath. Facilities: indoor and outdoor restaurants, parking, currency exchange. AE, MC, V. $$*

Cluj
Dining and Lodging

Transylvania. Formerly the Belvedere, the Transylvania is a modern, seven-story hotel situated on top of Cetățuia Hill just 15 minutes' walk from the city center. It is clean, warm in winter, and offers many facilities including two inexpensive but good restaurants. The hotel lacks charm but has excellent views of the town and the surrounding countryside. *Str. Călărași 1, tel. 064/134466, fax 064/136910. 156 rooms with bath and satellite TV. Facilities: 2 restaurants, nightclub, barber and beauty salon, sauna, gym, swimming pool, conference halls, tourist information and exchange office, garage and parking. AE, DC, MC, V. $$$$*

Casa Alba. This is a small, privately run hotel in a pleasant residential district on Cetățuia Hill, not far from the Transylvania hotel. It also has one of the town's best restaurants, which is open to nonresidents. *Str. Racovița 22, tel. 064/132315. 18 rooms with bath. Facilities: restaurant, bar, parking. $$$*

Continental. Located in the central square with views of St. Michael's Cathedral, this turn-of-the-century hotel is down-at-heel but has managed to preserve some of its former elegance. *Str. Napoca 1, tel. 064/111441, fax 064/111152. 91 places in single or double rooms with bath. Facilities: 2 restaurants, currency exchange. $$$*

Sibiu
Dining and Lodging

Împăratul Romanilor. This turn-of-the-century hotel, conveniently situated in the town center, is considered by many to be Romania's best provincial hotel. Rooms are attractively decorated with paintings and locally made furniture. The restaurant, open to nonresidents, is the best eatery in Sibiu, with a lively floor show and discotheque on weekends. *Str. Nicolae Bălcescu 4, tel. 069/416490, fax 069/413278. Facilities: restaurant and breakfast room, currency exchange, antiques shop. AE, DC, MC, V. $$$*

Bulevard. Located at the end of Str. Nicolae Bălcescu, this hotel is a little dingy but offers comfortable accommodations at moderate prices and a reasonable restaurant. *Piața Unirii 2, tel. 069/412140. 129 rooms with bath. Facilities: 2 restaurants, parking, bar. $$*

Sighișoara
Dining

Casa Vlad Dracul. Located in a house where the father of Vlad Țepes, better known as Dracula, once lived, this pleasant bar and restaurant is the best place in town for a meal. On the first floor you can drink draft beer from a tankard and sit at wooden tables. Upstairs, you'll find a cozy restaurant with fittingly Gothic-style furniture that serves good soups and traditional Romanian dishes. It has an early closing, however—9 PM. *Str. Cositorarilor 5, tel. 065/771596. $$*

Lodging

Steaua. This 19th-century hotel has seen better days. Though the lobby is shabby, the rooms are spacious and clean and the staff is helpful. The restaurant serves traditional Romanian dishes and is reasonably priced. *Str. 1 Decembrie 12, tel. 065/771954. 121 places with shower or bath. Facilities: restaurant, bar, parking, nightclub. $*

Vocabulary

Czech Vocabulary

	English	Czech	Pronunciation
Basics	Please.	Prosím.	**pro**-seem
	Thank you.	Děkuji.	**dyek**-oo-yee
	Thank you very much.	Děkuji pěkně.	**dyek**-oo-yee **pyek**-nyeh
	You're welcome (it's nothing).	Není zač.	**neh**-nee **zahtch**
	Yes, thank you.	Ano, děkuji.	**ah**-no **dyek**-oo-yee
	Nice to meet you.	Těší mě.	**tye**-shee myeh
	Pardon me.	Pardon.	**par**-don
	Pardon me (formal)	Promiňte.	**pro**-meen-teh
	I'm sorry.	Je mi líto.	yeh mee **lee**-to
	I don't understand.	Nerozumím.	**neh**-rohz-oom-eem
	I don't speak Czech very well.	Mluvim česky jen trochu.	**mloo**-vim **ches**-ky yen **tro**-khoo
	Do you speak English?	Mluvte anglicky?	**mloo**-vit-eh ahng-**glit**-ski
	Yes/No	Ano/ne	**ah**-no/neh
	Speak slowly, please.	Mluvíte pomalu, prosím.	**mloov**-teh poh-**mah**-lo **pro**-seem
	Repeat, please.	Opakujte, prosím.	**oh**-pahk-ooey-teh **pro**-seem
	I don't know.	Nevím.	**neh**-veem
Questions	What . . . What is this?	Co . . . Co je to?	**tso** yeh toh
	When . . . When will it be ready?	Kdy . . . Kdy to bude hotové?	**g'dih** toh **boo**-deh **hoh**-toh-veh
	Why . . . Why is the pastry shop closed?	Proč . . . Proč je cukrárna zavřená?	protch yeh tsu-**krar**-na za-v'zhe-nah
	Who . . . Who is your friend?	Kdo . . . Kdo je váš přítel?	**g'doh** yeh vahsh **pshec**-tel

This material is adapted from the Living Language™ *Fast & Easy series (Crown Publishers, Inc.). Fast & Easy "survival" courses are available in 15 different languages, including Czech, Hungarian, Polish, and Russian. Each interactive 60-minute cassette teaches more than 300 essential phrases for travelers. Available in bookstores, or call 800/733-3000 to order.*

How . . . How do you say this in Czech?	Jak . . . Jak se to řekne česky?	yak seh toh **zhek**-neh **ches**-kee
Which . . . Which train goes to Bratislava?	Který . . . Který vlak jede do Bratislavy?	k'**tair**-ee vlahk **yeh**-deh doh **bratislavee**
What do you want to do?	Co chcete dělat?	tso kh'**tseh**-teh **dyeh**-laht
Where are you going?	Kam jdete?	kahm **dyeh**-teh
What is today's date?	Kolikátého je dnes?	**ko**-li-kah-**teh**-ho yeh d'nes
May I?/I'd like permission (to do something)	S dovolením, prosím.	s'**doh**-voh-leh-**neem pro**-seem
May I . . . ?	Smím . . . ?	smeem
May I take this?	Smím si to vžít?	**smeem** see toh v'**zheet**
May I enter?	Smím vstoupit?	smeem v'**sto**-pit
May I take a photo?	Smím fotografovat?	smeem **fo**-to-gra-fo-vaht
May I smoke?	Smím kouřit?	smeem **ko**-zhit

Numbers	Zero	Nula	**noo**-la
	One	Jeden, jedna, jedno	ye-**den**, **yed**-nah, **yed**-no
	Two	Dva, dvě	dvah, dvyeh
	Three	Tři	tshree
	Four	Čtyři	ch'**ti**-zhee
	Five	Pět	pyet
	Six	Šest	shest
	Seven	Sedm	**sed**-oom
	Eight	Osm	**oh**-soom
	Nine	Devět	**deh**-vyet
	Ten	Deset	**deh**-set
	Eleven	Jedenáct	yeh-deh-**nahtst**
	Twelve	Dvanáct	dvah-**nahtst**
	Thirteen	Třináct	tshree-**nahtst**
	Fourteen	Čtyrnáct	ch't'r-**nahtst**
	Fifteen	Patnáct	paht-**nahtst**
	Sixteen	Šestnáct	shest-**nahtst**
	Seventeen	Sedmnáct	**sed**-oom-**nahtst**
	Eighteen	Osmnáct	**oh**-soom-**nahtst**
	Nineteen	Devatenáct	deh-**vah**-teh-**nahtst**
	Twenty	Dvacet	**dvaht**-set
	Twenty-one	Dvacet jedna	**dvaht**-set **yed**-nah
	Twenty-two	Dvacet dva	**dvaht**-set dvah
	Twennty-three	Dvacet tři	**dvaht**-set tshree
	Thirty	Třicet	**tshree**-tset
	Forty	Čtyřicet	ch'**ti**-zhee-tset
	Fifty	Padesát	**pah**-deh-**saht**
	Sixty	Šedesát	**sheh**-deh-saht
	Seventy	Sedmdesát	**sed**-oom-deh-saht
	Eighty	Osmdesát	**oh**-soom-deh-saht
	Ninty	Devadesát	deh-**vah**-deh-saht

	100	Sto	sto
	1,000	Tisíc	**tee**-seets
Common Greetings	Hello/Good morning.	Dobrý den.	**dob**-ree den
	Good evening.	Dobrý večer.	**dob**-ree ve-chair
	Goodbye.	Na shledanou.	Na **sled**-ah-noh
	Title for married woman (or unmarried older woman)	Paní	**pah**-nee
	Title for young and unmarried woman	Slečno	**sletch**-noh
	Title for man	Pané	**pan**-eh
	How do you do?	Jak se vám daří?	yak seh vahm **dah**-zhee
	Fine, thanks. And you?	Děkuji, dobře. A vám?	**dyek**-oo-yee **dobe**-zheh a vahm
	How do you do? (informal)	Jak se máte?	yak se **mah**-teh
	Fine, thanks. And you?	Děkuji, dobře. A vy?	**dyek**-oo-yee **dobe**-zheh ah vee
	What is your name?	Jak se jmenujete?	yak se **men**-weh-teh
	My name is . . .	Jmenuji se . . .	**ymen**-weh-seh
	I'll see you later.	Na shledanou brzo.	na **sled**-ah-noh **b'r**-zo
	Good luck!	Mnoho štěstí!	m'**no**-ho **shtyes**-tee
Directions	Where is	Kde je	g'deh yeh
	Excuse me. Where is the . . . ?	Promiňte, prosím. Kde je . . . ?	**pro**-meen-teh **pro**-seem g'deh yeh
	Excuse me. Where is Wencaslas Square?	Promiňte, prosím. Kde je Václavské náměstí?	**pro**-meen-teh **pro**-seem g'dch yeh **vat**-slav-skeh **nahm**-yes-tee
	Where is the bus stop?	Kde je autobusová zastávka?	g'deh yeh ow-to-boos-oh-vah zah-**stahv**-kah
	Where is the subway station, please?	Kde je stanice metra, prosím?	g'deh je stah-nit-seh **mch**-trah **pro**-seem
	Where is the rest room?	Kde jsou toalety, prosím?	g'deh so twa-**leh**-tee **pro**-seem
	Go	Jděte	**dye**-teh
	On the right	Napravo	**na**-pra-vo

One the left	Nalevo	**na**-leh-vo
Straight ahead	Rovně	**rohv**-nyeh
At (go to) the end of the street	Jděte na konec ulici	**dye**-teh na **ko**-nets **oo**-lit-si
The first left	První ulice nalevo	**per**-vnee **oo**-lit-seh **na**-leh-vo
Near	Blízko	**bleez**-ko
It's near here.	Je to blízko.	yeh to **bleez**-ko
Turn	Zahnete	**zah**-hneh-teh
Go back.	Jděte zpátky.	**dye**-teh z'**paht**-ky
Next to	Vedle	ved-**leh**
It's very simple.	To je velmí jednoduché.	to yeh **vel**-mee **yed**-no-doo-kheh

Shopping	Money	Peníze	pen-**ee**-zeh
	Where is the bank?	Kde je banka?	g'deh yeh **bahn**-ka
	I would like to change some money.	Chtěla bych si vyměnit peníze.	kh'**tyel**-ah bikh see vih-myen-it pen-**ee**-zeh
	140 crowns	Sto čtyřicet korun	sto ch'**ti**-zhee-tset koh-**roon**
	17 crowns	Sedmnáct korun	sed-oom-**nahtst** koh-**roon**
	1,100 crowns	Tisíc sto korun	**tee**-seets sto koh-**roon**
	3,000 crowns	Tři tisíce korun	tshree **tee**-see-tse koh-**roon**
	Please write it down.	Napište to, prosím.	**nah**-peesh-tye toh **pro**-sim
	What would you like?	Co si přejete?	tso see **pshay**-eh-teh
	I would like this.	Chtěl bych tohle.	kh'**tyel** bikh **toh**-hleh
	Here it is.	Tady to je.	**tah**-dee toh yeh
	Is that all?	To je všechno?	toh yeh **vshekh**-no
	Thanks, that's all.	Děkuji. To je všechno.	**dyek**-oo-yee toh yeh **vshekh**-no
	Do you accept traveler's cheques?	Přijímáte cestovni šeky?	**pshee**-yee-**mah**-teh **tses**-tohv-nee **shek**-ee
	Credit cards?	Kredit Karty?	**cre**-dit **kar**-tee
	How much?	Kolik?	**ko**-lik
	Department store	Obchodní dům	**ohb**-khod-nee **doom**
	Grocery store	Potraviny	**poh**-trah-**vin**-ee
	Pastry shop	Cukrárna	tsoo-**krar**-na

Dairy products shop	Mlekárna	mleh-**kar**-na
The butcher	Řeznictví	**zhez**-nitst-vee
I would like a loaf of bread and rolls.	Chtěla bych chléb a rohlíky.	kh'**tyel**-ah bikh khleb ah roh-hleck-ee
Milk	Mléko	mleh-koh
A half kilo of this salami	Půl kilo tohoto salámu	**pool** kee-lo **toh**-ho-toh sah-**lah**-moo
This cheese	Tento sýr	**ten**-toh seer
A kilo of apples	Kilo jablek	**kee**-lo **yah**-blek
Give me six cucumbers.	Dejte mi šest okurek.	**day**-teh mee shest **oh**-koo-rek
Three kilos of pears.	Tři kila hrušek.	tshree **kee**-la h'**roo**-shek
Clothing	Oděvy	oh-**dyeh**-vee
Women's clothing	Dámské odévy	**dahm**-skeh oh-**dyeh**-vee
Men's clothing	Pánské odévy	**pahn**-skeh oh-**dyeh**-vee
Souvenirs	Upomínkové předměty	oo-poh-**meen**-koh-veh pshed-**myeh**-tee
Toys and gifts	Hračky a dárky	h'**rahtch**-kee ah **dar**-ky
Jewelry and perfume	Bižutérie a voňavky	**bizh**-oo-teh-ree-yeh ah **voh**-nyahv-kee
At the Hotel Room	Pokoj	**poh**-koy
I would like . . .	Chtěl (Chtěla) bych . . .	kh'**tyel** (kh'**tyel**-ah) bikh
I would like a room.	Chtěl (Chtěla) bych pokoj.	kh'**tyel** (kh'**tyel**-ah) bikh **poh**-koy
For one person	Pro jednu osobu	pro **yed**-noo oh-so-boo
For two people	Pro dvě osoby	pro dveh **oh**-so-bee
For how many nights?	Na kolik nocí?	na **ko**-lik **note**-see
For tonight	Na dnešní noc	na **dnesh**-nee notes
For two nights	Na dvě noci	na dveh **note**-see
For a week	Na týden	na **tee**-den
Do you have a different room?	Máte jiný pokoj?	ma-teh **yee**-nee **poh**-koy
With a bath	S koupelnou	s'**ko**-pel-noh
With a shower	Se sprchou	seh sp'**r**-kho
With a toilet	S toaletou	s'twa-**leh**-to

	The key, please.	Klíc, prosím.	kleech **pro**-seem
	How much is it?	Kolik to stojí?	**ko**-lik toh **stoy**-ee
	One hundred crowns	Sto korun	sto ko-**roon**
	Seven hundred crowns	Sedm set korun	**seh**-doom set ko-**roon**
	My bill, please.	Účet, prosím.	**oo**-chet **pro**-seem
Dining Out	Café	Kavárna	ka-**vahr**-na
	Restaurant	Restaurace	res-toh-**vrat**-seh
	A table for two	Stůl pro dva	stool pro dvah
	Waiter, the menu, please.	Pane vrchní! Jídelní lístek, prosím.	**pah**-neh **verkh**-nee **yee**-dell-nee **lis**-tek **pro**-seem
	The wine list, please.	Líst vin, prosím. (or, vinny listek).	leest vin **pro**-seem **vin**-nee **lis**-tek
	The main course	Hlavní jídlo	**hlav**-nee **yid**-lo
	What would you like?	Co si přejete?	tso see **psheh**-yeh-teh
	What would you like to drink?	Co se přejete k pití?	tso seh **psheh**-yeh-teh k'**pit**-ee
	Can you recommend a good wine?	Můžete doporučit dobré víno?	**moo**-zheh-teh **doh**-por-oo-cheet **dohb**-zheh **vi**-noh
	Wine, please.	Víno, prosim.	**vi**-noh **pro**-seem
	Pilsner beer	Plzeňské pivo	**pil**-zen-skeh **piv**-oh
	What's the specialty of the day?	Jaká je dnešní specialitá?	**ya**-ka yeh **dnesh**-nee spet-sya-lih-**tah**
	Do you have strawberry ice cream?	Máte jáhodovou zmrzlinu?	**ma**-teh **ya**-ho-doh-voh zmer-**zlee**-noo
	I didn't order this.	Tohle jsem neobjednal.	**toh**-hleh sem **neh**-ob-yed-nahl
	That's all, thanks.	Děkuji, to je všechno.	**dyek**-oo-yee to yeh **vsheh**-khno
	The check, please.	Učet, prosím.	**oo**-chet **pro**-seem
	Is the tip included?	Je záhrnuto zpropítně?	yeh **za**-her-noo-toh **zpro**-peet-nyeh
	Enjoy your meal.	Dobrou chut'.	**doh**-broh khoot
	To your health!	Na zdraví!	**na** zdrah-vee
	Fork	Vidlička	**vid**-litch-ka
	Knife	Nůž	noozh
	Spoon	Lžíce	l'**zheet**-seh

Napkin	Ubrousek	oo-bro-sek
A cup of tea	Šálek čaje	shah-lek tcha yeh
A bottle of wine	Láhev vína	lah-hev vi-nah
One beer	Jedno pivo	yed-noh piv-oh
Two beers, please.	Dvě piva, prosím.	dveh piv-ah pro-seem
Salt and pepper	Sůl a pepř	sool ah pepsh
Sugar	Cukr	tsook-rr
Bread, rolls, and butter	Chléb, rohlíky a máslo	khleb roh-hlee-ky ah mah-slo
Black coffee	Černá káva	chair-na kah-va
Coffee with milk	Káva s mlékem (or, Bílá káva)	kah-va s mleh-kem bee-la kah-va
Tea with lemon	Čaj se citrónem	tchai se tsi-tro-nem
Orange juice	Pomerančový džus	po-mair-ahn-cho-vee dzhoos
Another (masc., fem., neuter)	Ještě jeden (ještě jednu, ještě jedno)	yesh-tyeh ye-den (yesh-tyeh yed-nu, yesh-tyeh yed-no)
More	Ještě	yesh-tyeh
I'd like more mineral water.	Chtěl bych ještě minerálku.	kh'tyel bikh yesh-tyeh min-eh-rahl-ku
Another napkin, please.	Ještě jeden ubrousek, prosím.	yesh-tyeh jeh-den oo-bro-sek, pro-seem
More bread and butter	Ještě chléb a máslo	yesh-tyeh khleb ah mah-slo
Not too spicy	Ne příliš ostré	neh pshee-leesh oh-streh
I like the meat well done.	Chci maso dobře upečené (or, Chci propečené).	kh'tsee mah-so dobe-zheh oo-petch-en-eh kh'tsee pro-petch-en-eh
One beer. Cold, please.	Jedno pivo. Chlazené, prosím.	yed-no piv-oh khlah-ze-ne pro-seem
May I exchange this for . .	Mohl bych tohle vyměnit za . . .	mole bikh to-hleh vee-myen-it zah
Telling Time What time is it?	Kolik je hodin?	ko-lik yeh ho-din
Midnight	Půlnoc	pool-nohts
It is noon.	Je poledne.	yeh po-led-neh
Morning	Ráno, dopoledne	rah-no, doh-po-led-neh

Afternoon	Odpoledne	**ohd**-po-led-**neh**
Evening	Večer	**veh**-chair
Night	Noc	nohts
It is 9:00 AM.	Je deset hodin dopoledne.	yeh **deh**-set **ho**-din **doh**-po-led-neh
It is 1:00 PM.	Je jedna hodina odpoledne.	yeh yed-**na ho**-din-ah **ohd**-po-led-**neh**
It is 3 o'clock.	Jsou tři hodiny.	so tshree **ho**-din-y
It is 5 o'clock.	Je pět hodin.	yeh pyet **ho**-din
5:15	Pět patnáct	pyet paht-**nahtst**
7:30	Sedm třicet	**sed**-oom **tshree**-tset
9:45	Devět čtyřicet pět	**deh**-vyet **ch'ti**-zhee-tset **pyet**
Now	Teď'	tedj
Later	Později	poh-**zdyay**-ee
Immediately	Hned	h'ned
Soon	Brzo	b'r-zo

Days of the Week	Monday	Pondělí	**pon**-dye-lee
	Tuesday	Úterý	**oo**-teh-ree
	Wednesday	Středa	**stshreh**-da
	Thursday	Čtvrtek	**ch't'v'r**-tek
	Friday	Pátek	**pah**-tek
	Saturday	Sobota	**so**-boh-ta
	Sunday	Neděle	**neh**-dyeh-leh

Months	January	Leden	**leh**-den
	February	Únor	**oo**-nor
	March	Březen	**b'zhe**-zen
	April	Duben	**doo**-ben
	May	Květen	**k'vyet**-en
	June	Červen	**chair**-ven
	July	Červenec	**chair**-ven-ets
	August	Srpen	**s'r**-pen
	September	Září	**zah**-zhee
	October	Říjen	**zhee**-yen
	November	Listopad	**list**-o-pahd
	December	Prosinec	**pro**-sin-ets

At the Airport	Airport	Letiště	**leh**-tish-tyeh
	Where is customs?	Kde je celnice?	g'deh yeh **tsel**-nit-seh
	Where is the passport control?	Kde je pasová kontrola?	g'deh je **pah**-so-vah kon-**trol**-ah
	The baggage claim	Zavazadla	**zah**-vah-**zahd**-lah
	Where are the international departures?	Kde jsou mezinárodní odlety?	g'deh soh **meh**-zee-**nah**-rohd-nee **ohd**-leh-tee
	Arrivals	Přílety	**pshee**-leh-tee

Where are the taxis?	Kde jsou taxíky?	g'deh so tak-seek-ee
Where is the exit?	Kde je východ?	g'deh yeh vec-khohd
Is there a subway?	Je tady metro?	yeh tah-dee meh-tro
Is there a bus?	Je tady autobus?	yeh tah-dee out-oh-boos
Stop here, please!	Zastavte tady, prosím!	zah-stahv-teh tah-dee pro-seem
What is the fare to downtown?	Kolik to stojí do středu města?	ko-lik toh stoy-ee doh st'shreh-doo myes-tah
Have a good trip!	Šťastnou cestu!	sht'shast-no tsest-oo

At the Train Station	Train station	Nádraží	nah-drah-zhee
	I'd like a ticket, please.	Chtěl bych lístek, prosím.	kh'tyel bikh list-ek pro-seem
	A one-way ticket	Jednoduchý lístek	yed-no-dookh-nee list-ek
	A return ticket	Zpáteční lístek	zpah-tetch-nee list-ek
	A local train	Osobní vlak	oh-sobe-nee vlahk
	An express train	Rychlík	rikh-leek
	Do you have a timetable?	Máte jízdní řád?	mah-teh yeezd-nee zhahd
	Is there a dining car?	Je ve vlaku jídelní vůz?	yeh veh vlah-koo yee-dell-nee vooz
	A sleeping car	Spací vůz	spa-tsee vooz
	Where is this train going?	Kam jede tenhle vlak?	kahm jeh-deh ten-h-leh vlahk
	What time does the train leave for . . . ?	V kolik hodin odjíždí vlak do . . . ?	v'ko-lik ho-din ohd-ycezh-dee vlahk doh
	What time does the train arrive from . . . ?	V kolik hodin přijíždí vlak z . . . ?	v-ko-lik ho-din pshee-yeezh-dee vlahk z
	From what platform does the train leave?	Z kterého nástupiště vlak odjíždí?	z'k'tair-ay-ho nah-stoo-pish-tyeh vlahk ohd yeezh-dee
	The train arrives at 2:00 PM.	Vlak přijíždí ve čtyrnact hodin.	vlahk pshee-ycezh-dee veh ch'tr-nahtst ho-din
	The train is late.	Vlak ma zpoždění.	vlahk mah z'poh-zhdyeh-nee

Can you help me, please?	Mohl byste mi pomoci, prosím?	**mole** bis-teh mee **poh**-moh-tsee **pro**-seem
Can you tell me, please?	Mohl byste mi říci, prosím?	**mole** bis-teh mee zhee-tsee **pro**-seem
I've lost my bags.	Ztratila jsem zavazadla.	z'**tra**-tih-lah sem zah-vah-zahd-lah
My money	Peníze	**peh**-nee-zeh
My passport	Pas	pahss
I've missed my train.	Zmeškal jsem vlak.	z'**mesh**-kahl sem vlahk

At the Post Office	Post office	Pošta	**po**-shta
	Stamps, please.	Známky, prosím.	**znahm**-kee **pro**-seem
	For letters or for postcards?	Na dopisy nebo na pohlednice?	na **doh**-pis-ee **neh**-bo poh-**hled**-nit-seh
	To where are you mailing the letters?	Kam posíláte dopisy?	kahm poh-see-**lah**-teh **doh**-pis-ee
	To the United States	Do Spojených Států	doh **spoy**-en ikh **stah**-too
	Airmail	Letecky	**leh**-tet-skee
	The telephone directory	Telefonní seznam	te-le-**fon**-nee **sez**-nahm
	Where can I go to make a telephone call?	Odkud mohu telefonavat?	**ohd**-kood **moh**-hoo te-le-**fo**-no-**vaht**
	A telephone call	Telefonní rozhovor	te-le-**fon**-nee **rohz**-ho-vor
	A collect call	Hovor na účet volaného	**ho**-vor na **oo**-chet voh-lah-**neh**-ho
	What number, please?	Jaké číslo, prosím?	**yah** -keh **chee**-slo **pro**-seem
	May I speak to Mrs. Newton, please.	Mohl bych ja mluvit s paní Newtonovou, prosím.	**mole** bikh ya **mloo**-vit **spah**-nee **new**-ton-oh-voh **pro**-seem
	The line is busy.	Je obsázeno.	yeh ob-**sah**-zen-**oh**
	There's no answer.	Nehlásí se.	**neh**-hlah-see seh
	Try again later.	Zkuste to poszději.	**zkoo**-steh toh po-**zdyay**-ee
	May I leave a message, please?	Mohla bych nechát vzkaz, prosím?	**moh**-hla **bikh neh**-khaht v'**zkahz** **pro**-seem

Hungarian Vocabulary

English	Hungarian	Pronunciation
Common Greetings Hollo (good day).	Jó napot./Jó napot kivánok.	yoh nuh-poht/yoh nuh-poht kee-vah-nohk
Good-bye.	Viszontlátásra.	vee-sohnt-lah-tahsh-ruh
Hello/Good-bye (informal).	Szervusz.	ser-voos
Good morning.	Jó reggelt kivánok.	yoh reg-gelt kee-vah-nohk
Good evening.	Jó estét kivánok.	yoh esh-tayt kee-vah-nohk
Ma'am	Asszonyom	uhs-sohn-yohm
Miss	Kisasszony	keesh-uhs-sohny
Mr./Sir	Uram	oor-uhm

To address someone as Mrs., add the suffix "né" to the last name. Mrs. Kovács is then "Kovácsné." To address someone as Mr., use the word "úr" after the last name. Mr. Kovács is then "Kovács úr."

English	Hungarian	Pronunciation
Good morning, Mrs. Kovács/ Mr. Kovács	Jó reggelt, Kovácsné/ Kovács úr.	yoh reg-gelt koh-vahch-nay/ koh-vahch oor
How are you?	Hogy van?	hohdge vuhn
Fine, thanks. And you?	Jól vagyok, köszönöm. És maga?	yohl vuhdge-ohk ku(r)-su(r)-nu(r)m aysh muh-guh
What is your name?	Hogy hívják?	hohdge heev-yahk
What is your name (informal)?	Hogy hívnak?	hohdge heev-nuhk
My name is . . .	(Name) vagyok.	vuhdge-ohk
Good luck!	Jó szerencsét!	yoh se-ren-chayt
Polite Expressions Please	Kérem szépen	kay-rem say-pen
Thank you.	Köszönöm.	ku(r)-su(r)-nu(r)m
Thank you very much.	Nagyon szépen köszönöm.	nuhdge-ohn say-pen ku(r)-su(r)-nu(r)m
You're welcome.	Kérem szépen.	kay-rem say-pen
You're welcome (informal).	Szivesen.	scc-vesh-en
Yes, thank you.	Igen, köszönöm.	ee-gen ku(r)-su(r)-nu(r)m
No, thank you.	Nem, köszönöm.	nem ku(r) su(r)-nu(r)m
Pardon me.	Bocsánat.	boh-chah-nuht

I'm sorry (sympathy, regret).	Sajnálom.	**shuhy**-nahl-ohm
I don't understand.	Nem értem.	nem **ayr**-tem
I don't speak Hungarian very well.	Nem beszélek jól magyarul.	nem **bess**-ayl-ek yohl **muh**-dgeuhr-ool
Do you speak English?	Beszél angolul?	be-sayl **uhn**-gohl-ool
Yes/No	Igen/Nem	ee-gen/nem
Speak slowly, please.	Kérem, beszéljen lassan.	**kay**-rem **bess**-ay-yen **luhsh**-shuhn
Repeat, please.	Ismételje meg, kérem.	**eesh**-may-tel-ye meg **kay**-rem
I don't know.	Nem tudom.	**nem** too-dohm
Here you are (when giving something).	Tessék.	**tesh**-shayk
Excuse me (what did you say)?	Tessék?	**tesh**-shayk

Questions What is . . . What is this?	Mi . . . Mi ez?	**mee** ez
When . . . When will they be ready?	Mikor . . . Mikor lesznek készen?	**mee**-kor **less**-nek **kayss**-en
Why . . . Why is the pastry shop closed?	Miért . . . Miért van zárva a cukrászda?	**mee**-aryt vuhn **zahr**-vuh uh **tsook**-rahss-duh
Who . . . Who is your friend?	Ki . . . Ki a barátod?	**kee** uh **buh**-raht-ohd
How . . . How do you say this in Hungarian?	Hogy . . . Hogy mondják ezt magyarul?	**hohdge mohnd**-yahk ezt **muh**-dgeuhr-ool
Which . . . Which train goes to Esztergom?	Melyik . . . Melyik vonat megy Esztergomba?	**mey**-eek **voh**-nuht **medge ess**-ter-gohm-buh
What do you want to do?	Mit akar csinálni?	**meet** uh-kuhr **chee**-nahl-nee
What do you want to do (informal)?	Mit akarsz csinálni?	**meet** uh-kuhrss **chee**-nahl-nee
Where are you going?	Hova megy?	**hoh**-vuh medge
Where are you going (informal)?	Hova mész?	**hoh**-vuh mayss
What is the date today?	Hanyadika van ma?	**huh**-nyuh-deek-uh vuhn muh

May I?	Szabad?	**suh**-buhd
May I take this?	Szabad ezt elvenni?	**suh**-buhd ezt el-ven-nee
May I come in?	Szabad bejönni?	**suh**-buhd be-yu(r)n-nee
May I take a photo?	Szabad fényképezni?	**suh**-buhd **fayn**-kayp-ez-nee
May I smoke?	Szabad dohányozni?	**suh**-buhd **doh**-hahn-yohz-nee

Directions	Where	Hol	hohl
	Excuse me, where is the . . . ?	Bocsánat, hol van a . . . ?	**boh**-chah-nuht **hohl** vuhn uh
	Excuse me, where is Castle Hill?	Bocsánat, hol van a vár?	**boh**-chah-nuht **hohl** vuhn uh **vahr**
	Where is the toilet?	Hol van a toálet (WC)?	**hohl** vuhn uh **toh**-ah-let (**vay**-tsay)
	Where is the bus stop?	Hol van a buszmegallo?	**hohl** vuhn uh **booss**-meg-ahl-loh
	Where is the subway station?	Hol van a metro?	**hohl** vuhn uh **met**-roh
	Go	Menjen	**men**-yen
	To the right	Jobbra	**yohb**-bruh
	To the left	Balra	**buhl**-ruh
	Straight ahead	Egyenessen előre	**edge**-en-esh-shen e-lu(r)-re
	At the end of the street	Az utca végén	uhz **oot**-suh **vay**-gayn
	The first left	Az első balra	uhz **el**-shu(r) **buhl**-ruh
	Near	Közel	**ku(r)z**-el
	It's near here.	Közel van ide.	**ku(r)z**-el vuhn **ee**-de
	Turn	Forduljon	**fohr**-dool-yohn
	Go back.	Menjen vissza.	**men**-yen **vees**-suh
	Next to . . .	. . . mellett	. . . **mel**-lett
	Next to the post office	A pósta mellett	uh **pohsh**-tuh **mel**-lett
	It's very simple.	Nagyon egyszerű.	**nuhdge**-ohn **edge**-ser-ew

At the Hotel	Room	Szoba	**soh**-buh
	I would like . . .	Kérek . . .	**kay**-rek
	I would like a room.	Kérek egy szobát.	**kay**-rek edge **soh**-baht
	For one person	Egy személyre	edge **sem**-ay-re

For two people	Két személyre	**kayt sem**-ay-re
For how many nights?	Hány éjszakára?	**hahny**-suhk-ah-ruh
For tonight	Ma éjszakára	**muh ay**-suhk-ah-ruh
For two nights	Két éjszakára	**kayt ay**-suhk-ah-ruh
For a week	Egy hétre	**edge hayt**-re
Do you have a different room?	Van egy másik szoba?	vuhn **edge mahsh**-eek **soh**-buh
With a bath	Fürdőszobával	**fewr**-du(r)-soh-bah-vuhl
With a shower	Zuhanyal	**zoo**-huhn-yuhl
With a toilet	WC-vel	**vay**-tsay vel
The key, please.	Kérem a kulcsot.	**kay**-rem uh **koolch**-oht
How much is it?	Mennyibe kerül?	**men**-yee-be **ker**-ewl
My bill, please.	Kérem a számlát.	**kay**-rem uh **sahm**-laht

At the Restaurant

Café	Kávéház	**kah**-vay-hahz
Restaurant	Étterem	**ayt**-ter-rem
Where is a good restaurant?	Hol van egy jó étterem?	hohl vuhn **edge yoh ayt**-ter-rem
Reservation	Rezerváció	re-zer-vah-tsee-oh
Table for two	Asztal két személyre	**uhss**-tuhl kayt **sem**-ay-re
Waiter	Pincér	**peen**-sayr
Waitress	Pincérnő	**peen**-sayr-nu(r)

(Waiters and waitresses are more likely to respond to the request "Kérem" (**kay**-rem), which means "please.")

I would like the menu, please.	Kérem az étlapot.	**kay**-rem uhz **ayt**-luhp-oht
The wine list, please.	Kérem a borlapot.	**kay**-rem uh **bohr**-luhp oht
The beverage list, please.	Kérem az itallapot.	**kay**-rem uhz **ee**-tuhl-luhp-oht
Appetizers	Előételek	**el**-u(r)-ay-tel-ek
Main course	Főétel	**fu(r)**-ay-tel
Dessert	Deszert	**dess**-ert
What would you like to drink?	Mit tetszik inni?	meet **tet**-seek **een**-nee
A beer, please.	Egy sört kérek.	**edge** shurt **kay**-rek
Wine, please.	Bort kérek.	**bohrt kay**-rek

The specialty of the day	A mai ajánlat	uh muh-ee uhy-ahn-luht
What would you like?	Mit tetszik parancsolni?	meet tet-sook puh-ruhn-chohl-nee
Can you recommend a good wine?	Tudna ajánlani egy finom bort?	tood-nuh uhy-ahn-luhn-ee edge fee-nohm bohrt
I didn't order this.	Ezt nem rendeltem.	ezt nem ren-del-tem
That's all, thanks.	Ez minden, köszönöm.	Ez meen-den ku(r)-su(r)-nu(r)m
The check, please.	Kérem szépen a számlát.	kay-rem say-pen uh sahm-laht
Is the tip included?	Benne van a borravallo?	ben-ne vuhn uh bohr-ruh-vuhl-loh
Breakfast	Reggeli	reg-gel-ee
Lunch	Ebéd	e-bayd
Supper	Vacsora	vuh-chohr-uh
Bon appetit.	Jó étvágyat.	yoh ayt-vahdge-uht
To your health!	Egészségére!	e-gayss-shayg-ay-re
Fork	Villa	veel-luh
Knife	Kés	kaysh
Spoon	Kanál	kuh-nahl
Napkin	Szalvéta	suhl-vay-tuh
Cup of tea	Téa	tay-uh
Bottle of wine	Üveg bor	ew-veg bohr
Ice	Kis jég	keesh yayg
Salt and pepper	Só és bors	shoh aysh bohrsh
Sugar	Cukor	tsoo-kohr
Soup	Leves	le-vesh
Salad	Saláta	shuhl-ah-tuh
Vegetables	Zöldség	zu(r)ld-shayg
Beef	Marhahús	muhr-huh-hoosh
Chicken	Csirke	cheer-ke
Bread	Kenyér	ken-yayr
Black coffee	Fekete kávé	fe-ke-te kah-vay
Coffee with milk	Tejeskávé	tey-esh-kah-vay
Tea with lemon	Téa citrommal	tey-uh tseet-rohm-muhl
Orange juice	Narancslé	nuh-ruhnch-lay
Mineral water	Ásványvíz	ahsh-vahn'y-veez
Another	Még egy	mayg ed'y

I'd like some more mineral water.	Kérek még egy ásványvízet.	**kay**-rek **meyg** ed'y **ahsh**-vahny-veez-et
I'd like some more bread and butter.	Kérek még kenyeret és vajat.	**kay**-rek mayg **ken**-yer-et aysh **vuhy**-uht
Is it very spicy?	Nagyon erős ez?	**nuhdge**-ohn e-ru(r)sh ez
May I exchange this?	Ezt kicserélhetem?	ezt **kee**-che-rayl-het-em

Numbers	Zero	Nulla	**nool**-luh
	One	Egy	edge
	Two	Kettő	**ket**-tu(r)
	Three	Három	**hah**-rohm
	Four	Négy	naydge
	Five	Öt	u(r)t
	Six	Hat	huht
	Seven	Hét	hayt
	Eight	Nyolc	nyohlts
	Nine	Kilenc	**kee**-lents
	Ten	Tíz	teez
	Eleven	Tizenegy	**teez**-en-edge
	Twelve	Tizenkettő	**teezen**-ket-tu(r)
	Thirteen	Tizenhárom	**teez**-en-hah-rohm
	Fourteen	Tizennégy	**teez**-en-naydge
	Fifteen	Tizenöt	**teez**-en-u(r)t
	Sixteen	Tizenhat	**teez**-en-huht
	Seventeen	Tizenhét	**teez**-en-hayt
	Eighteen	Tizennyolc	**teez**-en-nyohlts
	Nineteen	Tizenkilenc	**teez**-en-kee-lents
	Twenty	Húsz	hooss
	Twenty-one	Huszonegy	**hooss**-ohn-edge
	Twenty-two	Huszonkettő	**hooss**-ohn-ket-tu(r)
	Thirty	Harminc	**huhr**-meents
	Forty	Negyven	**nedge**-ven
	Fifty	Ötven	**u(r)t**-ven
	Sixty	Hatvan	**huht**-vuhn
	Seventy	Hetven	**het**-ven
	Eighty	Nyolcvan	**nyohlts**-vuhn
	Ninty	Kilencven	**kee**-lents-ven
	One Hundred	Száz	sahz
	One Thousand	Ezer	e-zer

Telling Time	What time is it?	Hány óra van?	**hahny oh**-ruh vuhn
	Midnight	Éjfél	**ay**-fayl
	It is 1:00 AM.	Hajnali egy óra van.	**huhy**-nuhl-ee **edge oh**-ruh vuhn
	It is 2:00 AM.	Hajnali két óra van.	**huhy**-nuhl-ee **kayt oh**-ruh vuhn
	It is 9:00 AM.	Reggel kilenc óra van.	**reg**-gel **kee**-lents **oh**-ruh vuhn
	10:00 AM	Reggel tíz óra	**reg**-gel **teez oh**-ruh
	It is noon.	Dél van.	**dayl** vuhn

It is 1:00 PM.	Délután egy óra van.	**dayl**-oo-tahn **edge** oh-ruh vuhn
It is 6:00 PM.	Délután hat óra van.	**dayl**-oo-tahn **huht** oh-ruh vuhn
7:00 PM	Este hét óra	**esh**-te **hayt** oh-ruh
8:00 PM	Este nyolc óra	**esh**-te **nyolts** oh ruh
Minute	Perc	perts
3:20 PM	Délután három óra húsz perc	**dayl**-oo-tahn **hah**-rohm oh-ruh hooss perts
8:30 AM	Reggel nyolc óra harminc perc	**reg**-gel **nyohlts** oh-ruh **huhr**-meents perts
Early morning	Hajnal	**huhy**-nuhl
Morning	Reggel	**reg**-gel
Before noon	Délelött	**dayl**-el-u(r)t
Afternoon	Délután	**duyl**-oo-tahn
Evening	Este	**esh**-te
Night	Ejszaka	ay-suhk-uh
Now	Most	mohsht
Later	Később	**kay**-shu(r)b
Immediately	Mindjárt	**meen**-dyahrt
Soon	Majd	muhyd

Days of the Week	Monday	Hétfő	**hayt**-fu(r)
	Tuesday	Kedd	ked
	Wednesday	Szerda	**ser**-duh
	Thursday	Csütörtök	**chew**-tur-tu(r)k
	Friday	Péntek	**payn**-tek
	Saturday	Szombat	**sohm**-buht
	Sunday	Vasárnap	**vuh**-shahr-nuhp

Months	January	Január	**yuh**-noo-ahr
	February	Február	**feb**-roo-ahr
	March	Március	**mahr**-tsee-oosh
	April	Április	**ah**-pree-leesh
	May	Május	**mah**-yoosh
	June	Június	**yoo**-nee-oosh
	July	Július	**yoo**-lee-oosh
	August	Augusztus	**ow**-goost-oosh
	September	Szeptember	**sep**-tem-ber
	October	Október	**ohk**-toh-ber
	November	November	**noh**-vem-ber
	December	December	**de**-tsem-ber

Shopping	Money	Pénz	paynz
	Where is the bank?	Hol van a bank?	hohl vohn uh **buhnk**

I would like to change some money.	Szeretnék pénzt beváltani.	Se-ret-nayk paynzt be-vahl-tuh-nee
140 forints	Száznegyven forint	Sahz-nedge-ven foh-reent
1,100 forints	Ezeregyszáz forint	e-zer-edge-sahz foh-reent
Please write it down.	Kérem írja fel.	kay-rem eer-yuh fel
How can I help you?	Tessék parancsolni?	tesh-shayk puh-ruhn-chohl-nee
I would like this.	Ezt kérem.	ezt kay-rem
Here it is.	Tessék itt van.	tesh-shayk eet vuhn
Would you care for anything else?	Más valamit?	mahsh vuh-luh-meet
That's all, thanks.	Mást nem kérek, köszönöm.	mahsht nem kay-rek ku(r)-su(r)-nu(r)m
Would you accept a traveler's check?	Elfogadják az utazási csekket?	el-foh-guhd-yahk uhz oot-uhz-ahsh-ee chek-ket
Credit cards?	Hitelkártya?	hee-tel-kahr-tyuh
How much?	Mennyi?	men-nyee
Department store	Áruház	ah-roo-hahz
Bakery	Pékség	payk-shayg
Pastry shop	Cukrászda	tsook-rahz-duh
Grocery store	Élelmiszerbolt	ayl-el-mees-er-bohlt
Butcher's shop	Hentes	hen-tesh
I would like a loaf of bread.	Kérek egy kenyeret.	kay-rek edge ke-nyer-et
Bottle of white wine	Üveg fehérbor	ew-veg fe-hayr-bohr
I would like 30 dekagrams of cheese.	Kérek harminc deka sajtot.	kay-rek huhr-meents de-kuh shuhy-toht
Give me six apples.	Tessék adni hat almát.	tesh-shayk uhd-nee huht uhl-maht
. . . and a kilo of grapes	. . . és egy kiló szőlőt	aysh edge kee-loh su(r)-lu(r)t
Clothing	Ruha	roo-huh
Woman's clothing	Nőiruha	nu(r)-ee-roo-huh
Toys and gifts	Játék és ajándék	yah-tayk aysh uh-yahn-dayk

	Folk art and embroideries	Népművészet és kézimunka	**nayp**-mew-vays-et **ayah kay-zoo-**moon kuh
The Post Office	Post office	Pósta	**pohsh**-tuh
	Where is the post office?	Hol van a pósta?	**hohl** vuhn uh **pohsh-tuh**
	Some stamps, please.	Bélyegeket kérek.	**bay**-yeg-ek-et **kay-rek**
	For letters or postcards?	Levélre vagy képeslapra?	le-**vayl**-re vuhdge **kay**-pesh-luhp-ruh
	Where are you sending them?	Hova küldi?	**hoh**-vuh **kewl**-dee
	To the United States	Az Egyesült Államokba	uhz **edge**-esh-ewlt **ahl**-luhm-ohk-buh
	Airmail	Légipósta	**lay**-gee-pohsh-tuh
	Telephone directory	Telefonkönyv	**te**-le-fohn-ku(r)nyv
	Where can I telephone?	Hol lehet telefonálni?	hohl **le**-het **te**-le-fohn-ahl-nee
	Telephone call	Telefonhívás	**te**-le-fohn-heev-ahsh
	What number, please?	Melyik telefonszámat kéri?	me-**yeek te**-le-fohn-sahm-uht **kay**-ree
	The line is busy.	A vonal foglalt.	uh **voh**-nuhl **fohg**-luhlt
	There's no answer, try again later.	Nincs válasz, tessék később próbálni.	**neench vah**-luhs **tesh**-shayk **kay**-shu(r)b **proh**-bahl-nee
	May I speak to . . . ?	Beszélhetek . . . ?	be-**sayl**-he-tek
	May I leave a message?	Hagyhatok üzenetet?	**huhdge**-huh-tohk ew-ze-net-et
The Airport	Where is customs?	Hol van a vám?	hohl vuhn uh **vahm**
	Where is the passport control?	Hol van az útlevélellenőrzes?	hohl vuhn uhz **oot**-le-vayl-**el**-len-ur-zesh
	Where does the baggage arrive?	Hol érkeznek a csomagok?	hohl **ayr**-kez-nek uh **choh**-muhg-ohk
	Where is the departures wing?	Hol van az indulási oldal?	hohl vuhn uhz **een**-dool-ahsh-ee **ohl**-duhl
	Where is the arrivals wing?	Hol van az érkezési oldal?	hohl vuhn uhz **ayr**-kez-ay-shee **ohl**-duhl
	Where is a taxi?	Hol van a taxi?	hohl vuhn uh **tuhx**-ee

Where is the exit?	Hol van a kijárat?	hohl vuhn uh **kee**-yahr-uht
Is there a subway or a bus here?	Van itt metro vagy autobusz?	vuhn eet **met**-roh **vuhdy ow**-toh-boos
Stop here, please.	Kérem szépen, álljon meg itt.	**kay**-rem **say**-pen **ahl**-yohn meg eet
What is the fare to the Parliament?	Mennyi az ár a Parlementig?	**men**-yee uhz ahr uh **puhr**-le-men-teeg
What is the fare?	Mennyi a viteldíj?	**men**-yee uh **vee**-tel-dee

The Train Station

I would like a ticket, please.	Egy jegyet kérek.	edge **yedge**-et **kay**-rek
A return ticket First class	Egy retur jegy Első osztályú	edge **re**-toor yedge **el**-shu(r) **ohs**-tahy-oo
Do you have a timetable?	Van itt menetrend?	vuhn eet **me**-net-rend
Is there a dining car?	Van étkezőkocsi?	vuhn **ayt**-kez-u(r)-koh-chee
Sleeping car	Hálókocsi	**hah**-loh-koh-chee
Where is this train going?	Hova megy ez a vonat?	**hoh**-vuh medge ez uh **voh**-nuht
When does the train leave for Pécs?	Mikor indul a vonat Pécsre?	**mee**-kohr **een**-dool uh **voh**-nuht **paych**-re
When does the train arrive from Pecs?	Mikor érkezik a vonat Pécsröl?	**mee**-kohr **ayr**-kez-eek uh **voh**-nuht **paych**-ru(r)l
The train is late.	A vonat késik.	uh **voh**-nuht **kay**-sheek
Can you help me, please?	Tudna segíteni?	**tood**-nuh she-geet-e-nee
Can you tell me . . . ?	Meg tudna mondani . . . ?	meg **tood**-nuh **mohn**-duh-nee
I've lost my bags.	Elvesztettem a csomagjaimat.	el-ves-tet-tem uh **choh**-muhg-yuh-ee-muht
I've lost my money.	Elvesztettem a pénzemet.	el-ves-tet-tem uh **paynz**-em-et
I've lost my passport.	Elvesztettem az útlevélemet.	el-ves-tet-tem uhz **oot**-le-vayl-em-et
I've missed my train.	Lekéstem a vonatot.	le-**kaysh**-tem uh **voh**-nuht-oht

Polish Vocabulary

English	*Polish*	*Pronunciation*
Basics Please (or "You're welcome").	Proszę.	**pro**-sheh
Thank you.	Dziękuję.	dzhen-**koo**-yeh
Thank you very much.	Dziękuję bardzo.	dzhen-**koo**-yeh **bahr**-dzoh
You're quite welcome.	Proszę bardzo.	**pro**-sheh **bahr**-dzoh
It's nothing.	Nie ma za co.	**nye** mah **zah** tso
Yes, please.	Tak, proszę.	**tahk**, **pro**-sheh
No, thank you.	Nie, dziękuję.	**nye**, dzhen-**koo**-yeh
Nice to meet you.	Miło mi poznać.	**mee**-wo mee **poh**-znahch
Excuse me.	Przepraszam.	psheh-**prah**-shahm
Excuse me, sir/madam.	Przepraszam pana/ panią	psheh-**prah**-shahm **pahn**-ah/ **pahn**-yohn
I'm sorry.	Przykro mi.	**pshee**-kroh mee
I don't understand.	Nie rozumiem.	**nyeh** rohz-**oo**-myehm
I don't speak Polish very well.	Nie mówię dobrze po polsku.	nyeh **moohv**-yeh **dohb**-zheh po-**pohl**-skoo
Do you speak English?	Czy pan (pani) mówi po angielsku?	**chee** pahn (**pahn**-ee) **moo**-vee po-ahn-**gyel**-skuu
Yes/no	Tak/nie	**tahk**/nye
Speak slowly, please.	Proszę mówić wolniej.	**proh**-sheh **moo**-veech **vohl**-nyay
Repeat, please.	Proszę powtórzyć.	**proh**-sheh pof-**too**-zheech
I don't know.	Nie wiem.	nye-**vyehm**
Questions What . . . What is this?	Co . . . Co to jest?	**tsoh** toh **yest**
When . . . When will they be ready?	Kiedy . . . Kiedy one będą gotowe?	kye-dee **ohn**-yeh **bend**-ohn goh-**toh**-veh
Why . . . Why is the pastry shop closed?	Dlaczego . . . Dlaczego cukiernia jest zamknięta?	dlah-**cheh**-goh tsoo-**kyehr**-nyah yest zahm-**kniehn**-tah
Who . . . Who is that?	Kto . . . Kto to jest?	**tkoh** to **yest**
How . . . How do you say this in Polish?	Jak . . . Jak to powiedzieć po polsku?	**yahk** to poh-**vyehd**-zhehch po **pohl**-skoo

Which . . . Which train goes to Gdansk?	Który . . . Który pociąg jedzie do Gdańska?	**ktoo**-ree **poh**-chohnk **yeh**-dzheh doh **gdayn**-skah
What do you want to do?	Co chcesz robić?	**tsoh** kh'tsehsh **roh**-beech
Where are you going?	Dokąd idziesz?	**doh**-kont **eed**-zhyesh
Where is the toilet?	Gdzie jest toaleta?	**gdzhyeh** yest toh-ah-**lyet**-ah
What is today's date?	Którego jest dzisiaj?	ktoo-**reh**-goh yest **dzee**-shahy
May I?	Czy mogę?	**chee mohg**-eh
May I take this?	Czy mogę to wziąć?	**chee mohg**-eh toh **vzhyonch**
May I enter?	Mogę wejść?	**mohg**-eh vayhshch
May I take a photo?	Czy mogę zrobić zdjęcie?	**chee mohg**-eh **zroh**-beech **zdyehn**-chyeh
May I smoke?	Czy mogę zapalić?	**chee mohg**-eh zah-**pahl**-eech
Good luck!	Wszystkiego najlępszego!	fshist-**kyeh**-goh nahy-lyehp-**shyeh**-go

Common Greetings	Hello/Good morning	Dzień dobry	**dzhehn dohb**-ree
	Good evening	Dobry wieczór	**dohb**-ree **vyeh**-choor
	Goodbye	Do widzenia	doh vee-**dzehn**-yah
	Good night	Dobranoc	doh-**brah**-nohts
	To a woman; Ms.	Pani	**pahn**-ee
	To a man; Mr.	Panu	**pahn**-oo
	To a couple or mixed group of adults	Pánstwu	**pahn'**-stvoo
	How are you (formal)?	Jak się pan (pani) ma?	**yahk** sheh pahn (**pahn**-ee) mah
	Thanks, I'm fine, and you?	Dziękuję, dobrze, a pan (pani)?	**dzehn**-koo-yeh, **dohb**-zheh, a pahn (**pahn**-ee)
	Thanks, not bad, and you?	Dziękuję, nieźle, a pan (pani)?	**dzehn**-koo-yeh, **nyeh**-zhleh, a pahn (**pahn**-ee)
	How are you (informal, singular/plural)?	Cześć, jak się masz/macie?	**chehshch, yahk** sheh **mahsh/mah**-cheh
	What's new?	Co słychać?	tso **swikh'**-ahch

What's your name?	Jak się pan (pani) nazywa?	**yahk** sheh **pahn** (**pahn**-ee) nah-**ziv**-ah
My name is . . .	Nazywam się . . .	nah-**ziv**-ahm sheh
What is your (formal) first name?	Jak pan (pani) ma na imię?	**yahk** pahn (**pahn**-ee) mah nah **eem**-yeh
What is your (informal) first name?	Jak masz na imię?	**yahk** mahsh nah **eem**-yeh
See you later.	Do zobaczenia.	**doh** zoh-bah-**chen**-ya

Directions	Where	Gdzie	gdzhyeh
	Excuse me, . . .	Przepraszam, . . .	psheh-**prah**-shahm
	Where is the bus stop?	Gdzie jest przystanek autobusowy?	**gdzhych** yest pshee-**stahn**-ehk a'oo-toh-boo-**soh**-vee
	Where is the train station?	Gdzie jest dworzec kolejowy?	**gdzheh** yest **dvoh**-zhets koh-lay-**oh**-vee
	Where is the theater?	Gdzie jest teatr?	**gdzheh** yest teh-**ah**-tr
	Where is the bathroom?	Gdzie jest łazienka?	**gdzheh** yest wah-**zhen**-ka
	Please go there.	Proszę iść tam.	**proh**-sheh **eeshch** tahm
	To the right/left.	Na prawo/lewo.	nah **prah**-voh/ **lyeh**-voh
	Straight ahead.	Prosto.	**proh**-stoh
	At the end of the street	Na końcu ulicy	nah **kon'**-tsoo oo-**lee**-tsee
	The first left	Pierwsza na lewo	**pyehr**-fshah na **lyeh**-voh
	Near	Blisko	**blee**-skoh
	It's near here.	To jest blisko stąd.	toh yest **blee**-skoh stohnt
	It isn't far.	Niedaleko stąd.	nyeh-dah-**lyeh**-koh stohnt
	Turn	Proszę skręcić	**proh**-sheh **skren**-cheech
	Go back	Proszę wrócić	**proh**-sheh **vroo**-cheech
	Next to	Obok	**oh**-bohk
	It's very simple.	To bardzo proste.	to **bahr**-dzoh **proh**-steh

Numbers	Zero	Zero	**zeh**-roh
	One	Jeden	**yeh**-den

Two	Dwa	**dvah**
Three	Trzy	**tchee**
Four	Cztery	**chteh**-ree
Five	Pięć	**pyehnch**
Six	Sześć	**shayshch**
Seven	Siedem	**shyeh**-dem
Eight	Osiem	**oh**-shyem
Nine	Dziewięć	**dzhyeh**-vyehnch
Ten	Dziesięć	**dzhyeh**-shehnch
Eleven	Jedenaście	yed-en-**ah**-shcheh
Twelve	Dwanaście	dvah-**nah**-shcheh
Thirteen	Trzynaście	tchee-**nah**-shcheh
Fourteen	Czternaście	chtehr-**nah**-shcheh
Fifteen	Piętnaście	pyent-**nah**-shcheh
Sixteen	Szesnaście	shehs-**nah**-shcheh
Seventeen	Siedemnaście	sheh-dem-**nah**-shcheh
Eighteen	Osiemnaście	oh-shem-**nah**-shcheh
Nineteen	Dziewiętnaście	dzhyeh-vyehnt-nah-shcheh
Twenty	Dwadzieścia	dvah-**dzheh**-shchah
Twenty-one	Dwadzieścia jeden	dvah-**dzheh**-shchah **yeh**-den
Twenty-two	Dwadzieścia dwa	dvah-**dzheh**-shchah dvah
Twenty-three	Dwadzieścia trzy	dvah-**dzheh**-shchah tchee
Thirty	Trzydzieści	tchee-**dzheh**-shchee
Forty	Czterdzieści	chtehr-**dzheh**-shchee
Fifty	Pięćdziesiąt	pyehnch-**dzheh**-shont
Sixty	Sześćdziesiąt	shehshch-**dzheh**-shont
Seventy	Siedemdziesiąt	shyeh-dem-**dzheh**-shont
Eighty	Osiemdziesiąt	oh-shem-**dzheh**-shont
Ninety	Dziewięćdziesiąt	dzhyeh-vyent-dzheh-shont
Hundred	Sto	stoh
Thousand	Tysiąc	**tee**-shonch

Telling Time	What time is it?	Która godzina?	**ktoo**-rah goh-**dzhee**-nah
	It's noon.	Jest południe.	yest poh-**wood**-nyeh
	Midnight	Północ	**poow**-nohts
	It's 8:00 AM.	Jest ósma.	yest **oos**-ma
	It's 9:00 AM.	Jest dziewiąta.	yest dzhyeh-**wyon**-ta
	It's 10:00 AM.	Jest dziesiąta.	yest dzhyeh-**shyon**-ta
	Before noon	Przed południem	pshet poh-**woo**-dnyem

Afternoon	Po południem	poh poh-**woo**-dnyem
11:00 AM	Jedenasta przed południem	ye-den-ah-stah pshet poh-**woo**-dnyem
2:00 PM	Druga po południu	**droo**-gah poh poh-**woo**-dnyoo
It's 8:00 PM (20:00).	Jest dwudziesta.	yest dvoo-**dzhyeh**-stah
11:00	Jedenasta	yeh-den-**ah**-stah
Four o'clock (16:00)	Godzina szesnasta	goh-**dzheen**-ah sheh-**nah**-stah
At what time?	O której?	oh-**ktoo**-ray
At four (16:00).	O szesnastej.	oh-shehs-**nah**-stay
8:10	Dziesięć po ósmej	**dzyeh**-shaynch poh-**oos**-may
7:50	Za dziesięć ósma	zah **dzheh**-shaynch **oos**-mah
It's 8:30 ("half to," colloquial)	Jest pół do dziewiątej.	yest **poow** doh dzheh-**vyon**-tay
Now	Teraz	**teh**-rahs
Later	Później	**poozh**-nyay
Immediately	Natychmiast	nah-**tikh**'-myahst

At the Hotel	I (m/f) would like to reserve a room.	Chciałbym (Chciałabym) zamówić pokój.	**kh'chow**-bim kh'chow-**ah**-bim zah-**moo**-veech **poh**-kooy
	For one person	Jednoosobowy	yed-noh-oh-soh-**boh**-vee
	For two people	Dwuosobowy	dvoo-oh-soh-**boh**-vee
	For how many days?	Na ile dni?	nah **ee**-leh dnee
	For today	Na dzisiaj (or, Na dziś)	na **dzhih**-sheye (na **dzheesh**)
	For two days	Na dwa dni	na dvah dnee
	For two days and two nights	Na dwie doby	na dwyeh **doh**-bee
	For a week	Na tydzień	na **tih**-dzhayn
	Is there another room?	Czy jest jakiś inny pokój?	chee yest yah kcesh **een**-ee **poh**-kooy
	With a bath	Z łazienką	zwah-**zhen**-koh
	With a shower	Z prysznicem	spree-**shnee**-tsem
	With a toilet	Z toaletą	stoo-ah-**lyeh**-toh
	The key, please.	Proszę o klucz.	**proh**-sheh o **klyuch**

How much is it?	Ile to kosztuje?	**ee**-leh to kosh-**too**-yeh
My bill, please.	Proszę o rachunek.	**proh**-sheh o rah-**kh'oo**-nek
Dining Out Where is a good restaurant?	Gdzie jest dobra restauracja?	gdzheh yest **doh**-brah rest-ow-**rah**-tsya
Café, snack bar	Bar szybkiej obsługi	bahr **sheep**-kay ohp-**swoog**-ee
Restaurant	Restauracja	rest-ow-**rah**-tsya
A table for two	Stolik na dwie osoby	**stoh**-leek na dvyeh oh-**soh**-bee
The menu, please.	Proszę menu.	**proh**-sheh **men**-yoo
The wine list, please.	Proszę kartę win.	**proh**-sheh **kahr**-teh **veen**
Appetizers	Przystawki	pshee-**stahf**-kee
The main course	Drugie danie	**droo**-gyeh **dahn**-yeh
Dessert	Deser	**deh**-ser
What will you have to drink?	Czego się pan (pani) napije?	**cheh**-goh sheh pahn (**pahn**-ee) nah-**pee**-yeh
A beer, please.	Proszę piwo.	**proh**-sheh **pee**-voh
The specialty of the day	Danie gotowe	**dahn**-yeh goh-**toh**-veh
What would you like?	Czego pan (pani) sobie życzy?	**cheh**-go pahn (**pahn**-ee) **soh**-byeh **zhee**-chee
I (m/f) didn't order this.	Ja tego nie zamówiłem/ zamówiłam.	yah **teh**-goh nyeh zah-moo-**vee**-wem/ zah-moo-**vee**-wahm
That's all, thanks.	Dziękuję, to wszystko.	dzhen-**koo**-yeh, to **fshees**-tkoh
The check, please.	Proszę rachunek.	**proh**-sheh rah-**kh'oon**-ehk
Is the tip included?	Czy napiwek jest wliczony?	**chee** nah-**pee**-vehk yest vlee-**chohn**-ee
Breakfast	Śniadanie	shnya-**dahn**-iyeh
Lunch	Obiad	**oh**-byat
Supper	Kolacja	koh-**lah**-ts'yah
Bon appétit!	Smacznego!	smahch-**neh**-goh
To your health!	Na zdrowie!	na **zdroh**-v'yeh
Fork, knife, spoon	Widelec, nóż, łyżka	vee-**deh**-lets, noosh, **wizh**-ka
Napkin	Serwetka	ser-**vyet**-kah

A cup of tea, please.	Proszę herbatę.	**proh**-sheh kh'er-**bah**-teh
A bottle of wine, please.	Proszę butelkę wina.	**proh**-sheh boo-**tehl**-keh
Some ice, please.	Proszę trochę lodu.	**proh**-sheh **trokh'**-eh **loh**-doo
Salt and pepper	Sól i pieprz	soow ee pyehpsh
Sugar	Cukier	**tsoo**-kyehr
Soup	Zupę	**zoo**-peh
Lettuce	Sałatę	sah-**wah**-teh
Vegetables	Jarzyny	yah-**zhin**-ee
Beef	Wołowina	voh-woh-**veen**-a
Broiled chicken	Kurczę z rusztu	**koor**-cheh **zroo**-shtoo
Bread and butter	Chleb i masło	kh'lyep ee **mahs**-woh
Black coffee	Czarną kawę	**chahrn**-ohn **kah**-veh
Coffee with milk	Kawę z mliekem	**kah**-veh **zmlyeh**-kem
Tea with lemon	Herbaté z cytryną	kh'ehr-**bah**-teh **ststrin**-ohn
Orange juice	Sok pomarańczowy	sohk poh-mah-rahn-**choh**-vee
Mineral water	Wodę mineralną	**voh**-deh mee-nehr-**ahl**-nohn
Another	Inny, inna, inne	**een**-nee, **een**-nah, **een**-neh
More	Jeszcze	**yehsh**-cheh
More mineral water, please.	Proszę jeszcze wody mineralnej.	**proh**-sheh **yesh**-cheh **voh**-dee mee-nehr-**ahl**-nay
Another napkin, please.	Proszę inną serwetkę.	**proh**-sheh **een**-ohn sehr-**vyeht**-keh
More bread and butter, please.	Proszę jeszcze chleb i masło.	**proh**-sheh **yesh**-cheh kh'lyep i **mahs**-woh
Not too spicy.	Nie za ostre.	nyeh zah **ohs**-treh
May I exchange this for . . . ?	Czy mogę to zamienić na . . . ?	chee **mohg**-geh to zah-**my'en**-eech nah
Shopping Money	Pieniądze	pen-**yohn**-dzeh
Where is the bank?	Gdzie jest bank?	gdzheh yest bahnk

I (m/f) would like to change some money.	Chciałbym (Chciałabym) wymienić pieniąze.	kh'chow-beem (kh'chow-ah-beem) vee-myeh-neech pen-yohn-dzeh
Polish currency unit	Złoty	zwoh-tee
15,000 złoty	Piętnaście tysięcy złoty	pyent-nah-shcheh tee-shehn-tsee zwoh-tee
Please write it down.	Proszę napisać.	proh-sheh nah-pee-sahtch
How can I help you?	Czym mogę służyć?	cheem mohg-eh swoo-zheech
I (m/f) would like this.	Chciałbym (Chciałabym) to.	kh'chow-beem (kh'chow-ah-beem) toh
Here it is.	Proszę bardzo.	proh-sheh bahr-dzoh
Is that all?	Czy to wszystko?	chee toh fshee-stkoh
Thanks, that's all.	To wszystko, dziękuję.	toh fshee-stkoh, dzhen-koo-yeh
Do you accept credit cards?	Czy państwo akceptujecie karty kredytowe?	chee pahn-stfoh ahk-tsep-too-yeh kahr-tee kreh-dee-toh-veh
Traveler's checks	Czeki podróżne	cheh-kee poh-droozh-neh
How much?	Ile?	ee-leh
Department store	Dom Handlowy	dohm hahn-dloh-vee
Bakery	Piekarnia	pyeh-kahr-ny'a
Pastry or confectioner's shop	Cukiernia	tsoo-kyehr-ny'a
Grocery store	Sklep spożywczy	sklehp spoh-zhif-chee
The butcher's	Sklep mięsny	sklehp myehn-snee
Liquor store	Sklep monopolowy	sklehp moh-noh-poh-loh-vee
Pharmacy	Apteka	ahp-ty'e-kah
I'd like a loaf of bread.	Proszę bochenek chleba.	proh-sheh boh-kh'en-ek kh'leh-ba
A bottle of white wine	Butelkę białego wina	boo-tell-keh byah-weh-go vee-nah
A kilo of this cheese	Kilo tego sera	kee-loh teh-go seh-ra
Clothing	Odzież	oh-dzhyesh

Women's clothing	Odzież damska	oh-dzhyesh dahm-vku
Souvenirs and crystal	Pamiątki i kryształy	pah-**myohnt**-kee ee kree-**shtahl**-ee
Amber and silver jewelry	Bursztyny i srebrna biżuteria	boor-**shteen**-ee ee sre-burr-na bee- zhoor-**tehr**-y'a

Days of the Week	Monday	Poniedziałek	poh-nyeh-**dzhyu**-wek
	Tuesday	Wtorek	**ftohr**-ek
	Wednesday	Środa	**shroh**-da
	Thursday	Czwartek	**chvahr**-tek
	Friday	Piątek	**pyohn**-tek
	Saturday	Sobota	soh-**boh**-ta
	Sunday	Niedziela	nyeh-**dzhy'e**-la

Months	January	Styczeń	**stich**-ehn
	February	Luty	**loo**-tee
	March	Marzec	**mah**-zhets
	April	Kwiecień	**kvy'eh**-chehn
	May	Maj	mahy
	June	Czerwiec	**cher**-vyets
	July	Lipiec	**lee**-pyets
	August	Sierpień	**sher**-pyehn
	September	Wrzesień	**vzheh**-shehn
	October	Październik	pahzh-**dzhehr**-neek
	November	Listopad	lee-**stoh**-paht
	December	Grudzień	**groo**-dzhehn

The Airport	Airport	Lotnisko	loht-**nees**-koh
	Where is customs?	Gdzie jest odprawa celna?	gdzheh yest ot-**prahv**-ah **tsel**-nah
	Where is passport control?	Gdzie jest odprawa paszportowa?	gdzheh yest ot-**prahv**-ah pahsh-port-**oh**-vah
	The baggage claim	Odbiór bagażu	**ohd**-byoor bah-**gah**-zhoo
	Departures	Odloty	ohd-**loh**-tee
	Arrivals	Przyloty	pshee-**loh**-tee
	Where are the taxis?	Gdzie są taksówki?	gdzheh sohn tahk-**soof**-kee
	Where is the exit?	Gdzie jest wyjście?	gdzheh yest **veey**-shcheh
	Is there a tram?	Czy jest tu tramwaj?	**chee** yest too **trahm**-vahy
	A bus?	Czy autobus?	**chee** a'oo **toh**-boos
	Please stop (here).	Proszę się tu zatrzymać.	**proh**-sheh sheh too zah-**tchee**-mahch
	Have a good trip!	Szczęśliwej podróży!	shchehn-**shlee**-vay poh-**droo**-zhee

The Train Station	I'd like a ticket, please.	Proszę bilet.	**proh**-sheh **bee**-let
	A round-trip ticket	Bilet powrotny	**bee**-let poh-**vroht**-nee
	First class	Pierwsza klasa	**pyehr**-fshah **klah**-sah
	A reserved seat	Bilet z miejscówką	**bee**-let zmyeh-**tsoof**-kohn
	What is the schedule?	Jaki jest rozkład jazdy?	**yah**-kee yest rohs-kwat **yahz**-dee
	Is there a dining car?	Czy jest wagon restauracyjny?	**chee** yest **vah**-gohn rehs-ta'oo-rah-**tseey**-nee
	A sleeping car	Wagon sypialny	**vah**-gohn see-**pyal**-nee
	Where is this train going?	Dokąd ten pociąg jedzie?	**doh**-kohnt ten **poh**-chohnk **yeh**-dzheh
	What time does the train leave for . . .	O której godzinie odjeżdża pociąg do . . .	oh **ktoo**-ray goh-**dzhee**-ny'e ohd-**yehzh**-dzha **poh**-chohnk doh
	What time does the train arrive from . . .	O której godzinie przyjeżdża pociąg z . . .	oh **ktoo**-ray goh-**dzhee**-ny'e pshee-**yezh**-dzhah **poh**-chohnk z
	The train is late.	Pociąg jest spóźniony.	**poh**-chohnk yest spoozh-**nyoh**-nee
	Can you help me, please?	Czy pan (pani) może mi pomóc?	**chee** pan (**pahn**-ee) **moh**-zheh mee **poh**-moots
	Can you tell me, please . . . ?	Proszę mi powiedzieć . . . ?	**proh**-sheh mee poh-**vyehd**-zhy'ech
	I've (m/f) lost my bags.	Zgubiłem (Zgubiłam) swój bagaż.	zgoo-**bee**-wem (zgoo-**bee**-wahm) svooy **bah**-gahzh
	My money	Moje pieniądze.	**moh**-yeh pen-**yohn**-dzeh
	My passport	Mój paszport	mooy **pash**-port
	I've (m/f) missed the train.	Spóźniłem (Spóźniłam) się na pociąg.	spoozh-**nee**-wem (spoozh-**nee**-wam) sheh na **poh**-chohnk
The Post Office	Post office	Poczta	**poch**-tah
	Some stamps, please.	Proszę znaczki pocztowe.	**proh**-sheh **znach**-kee pohch-**toh**-weh
	For letters	Na listy	nah **lees**-tee
	For postcards	Na kartki pocztowe	nah **kahrt**-kee poch-**toh**-veh

Where to?	Dokąd?	doh-kohnt
To the United States.	Do Stanów Zjednoczonych.	do **stahn**-oof zyed-noh-**chohn**-eekh'
Airmail letter	List lotniczy	leest loht-**nce**-chee
Telephone directory	Książka telefoniczna	**kshyohn**-zhkah tel-eh-**foh-neech** nuh
Public telephone	Automat telefoniczny	a'oo-**toh**-maht tel-eh-foh-**neech**-nee
An international phone call, please.	Międzynarodową rozmovę telefoniczną, proszę.	myen-dzee-nah-roh-**doh**-wohn roh-**moh**-veh tel-eh-foh-**neech**-nohn, **proh**-sheh
Information, please.	Informację, proszę.	een-fohr-**mah**-tsy'e, **proh**-sheh
Could you connect me to this number?	Proszę mnie połączyć z tym numerem?	**proh**-sheh mnyeh poh-**wohn**-cheech steem noo-**meh**-rem
What number?	Jaki numer?	**yah**-kee **noo**-mer
The line is busy.	Telefon zajęty.	teh-**leh**-fon zah-**yen**-tee
There's no answer.	Nikt nie odpowiada.	neekt nye ot-poh-**vyah**-dah
Try again later.	Proszę spróbować później.	**proh**-sheh sproo-**boh**-vatch poozh nyay

Index

Abrahámhegy, 275
Academy of Fine
 Arts, 231
Academy of Sciences,
 224
Accident and health
 insurance, 15–16
Acoustic Chapel, 386
Acvariul, 461
Adam Mickiewicz
 Museum of
 Literature, 340
Aggtelek, 293
Agricultural Museum,
 232
Air travel, 24–27, 28
Bulgaria, 420, 423
Czech Republic, 47,
 48, 98, 128, 129
Hungary, 200, 201,
 208–209, 288
Poland, 325, 326,
 333–334, 363–364,
 400–401
Romania, 447, 450,
 463
Slovakia, 153, 154,
 160, 173, 181
Ajzyk Synagogue, 372
Aladja Rock
 Monastery, 433
Albena, 434–435
Aleš Art Gallery, 107
Alexander Nevski
 Memorial Church,
 426
All Saints Chapel, 82
All Saints' Church,
 118
American Express, 8,
 9
Andrássy Út, 229–232
Angel Pharmacy
 Museum, 306
Anniversary
 Monument, 297
Aquincum, 259
Archaeological
 Museum (Varna), 433
Archaeology Park,
 461
Archbishop's Palace,
 77
Archdiocesan
 Museum, 405

Archeologicheski
 Musei, 433
Arcul de Triumf, 453
Arpád Bridge, 223
Arsenal Museum, 389
Art galleries, 77, 79,
 82–83, 107, 166, 167,
 214, 231–232, 236,
 255–256, 261, 263,
 296, 307, 310,
 312–313, 341, 343,
 344, 346, 350, 365,
 393, 426
Art Gallery, 231
Art Museum
 (Gdańsk), 396
Artus Mansion, 393
Astronomical Clocks,
 65–66, 395, 402
Aszó fő, 273, 282
Attila József
 Memorial Museum,
 280
Augsburg Evangelical
 Church, 343
Augustine monastery,
 105
Aula Leopoldina, 404
Auschwitz-Birkenau,
 372
Austerlitz, 140
Avas Church, 276

Babadag, 460
Babes-Bolyai
 University, 464
Baby-sitting, 21, 200
Badacsony, 275, 282
Balaton Museum, 277
Balaton Pantheon,
 270
Balatonakali, 274,
 282
Balatonbéreny, 278
Balatonboglár, 279
Balatonfenyves, 278
Balatonföldvár, 280
Balatonfüred, 270,
 272, 283–284
Balatongyörök, 276,
 284
Balatonlelle, 279
Balatonmáriafürdő,
 278, 284
Balatonrendes, 275

Balatonszárszó, 280
Balatonszemes, 279
Balatonszentgyořgy,
 278
Balatonszepezd, 274
Balatonudvari, 274
Balčik, 433–434
Baldwin's Tower, 438
Ballhouse, 309
Banja Basi Mosque,
 427
Bank transfers, 8–9
Banská Bystrica,
 189–190, 191
Barbakan (Kraków),
 365
Barbakan (Warsaw),
 341
Bardejov, 184, 191
Baryczka Mansion,
 340
Batthyány Palace,
 215
Beaches, 274, 275,
 433, 434
Béla Bartók Concert
 Hall, 310
Belvedere Palace, 346
Benedictine Abbey at
 Tyniec, 372
Beskydy range, 130
Bethlehem Chapel, 67
Bezerédy Palace, 307
Bicycling, 4, 50, 156,
 202, 264, 281, 329
Bierutowice, 406
Bishop's House, 289
Bishop's Palace, 310
Black Church, 463
Black Sea Coast and
 Danube Delta,
 458–462
guided tours, 460
hotels, 461–462
restaurants, 461–462
sightseeing, 460–461
tourist information,
 459
transportation, 459
Black Sea Golden
 Coast, 431–436
guided tours, 432
hotels, 434–436
restaurants, 434–436
sightseeing, 432–434

tourist information, 431

transportation, 431-432

Black Tower, 107

Blood Spring, 274

Blue Chapel, 279

Boat travel, 160, 201, 209, 269, 420, 447, 459

Boating and sailing, 50, 156, 204, 281, 329, 390

Bocian Synagogue, 372

Bocskai Muzeum, 297

Bohemia, 97-127

arts and nightlife, 127

emergencies, 97

guided tours, 98-99

hotels, 120-126

pharmacies, 97-98

restaurants, 101, 102, 105, 109, 111, 112, 114, 118, 120-126

shopping, 119-120

sightseeing, 99-119

sports/outdoor activities, 120

tourist information, 97

transportation, 98

Bohemian Chancellery, 82

Boris's Garden, 427

Borovec, 439

Botanical Gardens, 345, 434

Boyana, 427

Braşov, 463, 465

Bratislava, 159-172

arts and nightlife, 170-171

embassies, 160

emergencies, 160

English-language bookstores, 160

excursions, 171-172

guided tours, 161

hotels, 169-170

pharmacies, 160

restaurants, 165, 168-169

shopping, 168

sightseeing, 161-167

tourist information, 159

transportation, 160-161, 172

travel agencies, 160

Bretfeld Palace, 72

Breweries, 113-114

Brewery Museum, 114

Bridges, 70, 107, 165, 212, 218, 219, 223, 224, 225, 227

Brno, 129, 135, 137-140, 143-144, 145, 146

Brukenthal Museum, 465

Bucharest, 450-458

arts and nightlife, 458

guided tours, 451

hotels, 456-458

restaurants, 452, 453, 456

shopping, 453

sightseeing, 451-453

tourist information, 450

transportation, 450-451

Buda Hills, 218-222, 260

Budapest, 206-258

arts and nightlife, 254-258

currency exchange, 208

embassies, 207

emergencies, 207-208

English-language bookstores, 208

English-language periodicals, 208

English-language radio, 208

guided tours, 211

hotels, 249-254

lost and found, 208

pharmacies, 208

restaurants, 216, 222, 225, 227, 233, 242-249

shopping, 237-239

sightseeing, 211-236

spas and thermal baths, 240-241

sports and fitness, 239-242

tourist information, 207

transportation, 208-210

Budapest Historic Museum, 214

Budapest Zoo, 233, 236-237

Bugac Prairie, 298

Bulgaria, 416-440. *See also* Sofia, Black Sea Golden Coast, Inland Bulgaria

business hours, 420-421

climate, 416

costs, 418

currency, 418

customs, 419

holidays, national, 421

hotels, 421-422

language, 419

mail, 420

passports, 10, 11, 12

restaurants, 421

telephones, 420

tipping, 422

transportation, 419-420

visas, 418

Bulgarian Communist Party, former headquarters, 426

Burgas, 434, 435

Bus travel, 27, 28

Bulgaria, 420, 423, 431, 436

Czech Republic, 47, 48, 56, 98, 128, 129

Hungary, 201, 209-210, 269, 288, 304

Poland, 326-327, 334, 335, 348, 364, 384, 385, 393, 401-402

Romania, 447, 451, 459, 463

Slovakia, 154, 160, 161, 173, 174, 182

Business hours, 50, 155-156, 203, 328, 336, 420-421, 448

Buzsák, 279

Cairn of Peace, 140

Callatis, 461

Calvinist College, 293

Cameras, film, camcorders, and laptops, 14

Camping, 50, 156, 206, 260, 329, 360, 422, 449

Capuchin Chapel, 165-166

Capuchin Church, 219, 222

Car rentals, 17–18, 45, 152, 199, 324, 420, 424, 446–447

Car travel, 27, 28–29
Bulgaria, 419–420, 423, 424
Czech Republic, 47, 48, 56, 98, 128
Hungary, 201–202, 209, 210, 269, 288, 304
Poland, 325–326, 327, 334, 364
Romania, 446–447, 450, 459, 463
Slovakia, 154, 160, 173, 174, 181–182

Cardiac Hospital, 270

Carriage Museum, 390

Cash machines, 9

Castle Church, 133

Castle District, 75–77

Castle Hill, 211–218, 261

Castle Museum (Lublin), 386–387

Castle Theater, 214–215

Castles
Czech Republic, 77, 79–82, 101, 102–103, 104, 105, 106, 107, 115, 116, 118, 119, 132, 134, 135, 139
Hungary, 232, 276, 280, 289, 291, 293, 308, 309
Poland, 337, 340, 370, 375, 388, 397, 407, 410
Romania, 463
Slovakia, 165, 167, 171, 188

Cathedral (Szombathely), 310

Cathedral Church of St. John, 342

Cathedral Island (Poznań), 407

Cathedral Island (Wrocław), 404

Cathedral of St. Elizabeth, 186–187

Cathedral of St. Wenceslas, 141

Cathedral of Saints Peter and Paul, 138

Catherine Cave, 140

Catholic Church, 274, 275

Catholic Parish Church, 261

Caves, 140, 215, 274, 293, 373

Cegléd, 297

Celej House, 388

Cemeteries, 69, 297, 347, 348, 371–372, 387

Cemetery Hill, 279

Ceremony Hall, 69

Červený Kameň, 171

České Budějovice, 106–107, 121

Český Krumlov, 105, 119, 121, 127

Český Sternberk, 102–103

Cézár House, 307

Chain Bridge, 212, 224

Chalice House, 117

Chapel of St. Catherine, 164

Chapel of St. John the Evangelist, 166

Chapel of St. Wenceslas, 80

Chapel of the Holy Cross, 79

Chapel of the Holy Virgin, 130

Chapter Houses, 306, 370

Charles Bridge, 70–75

Cheb, 110–111, 121–122

Cheb Castle, 111

Cheb Museum, 111

Chernin Palace, 76

Children
attractions for, 83–84, 119, 142, 167, 177, 236–237, 348, 375–376
traveling with, 20–21, 200

Chopin Memorial, 345

Chopin Society, 344

Chronology of Eastern Europe, 31–38

Church and Convent of the Poor Clares, 164

Church and Monastery of the

Reformati Order, 388

Church of Mary, 107–108

Church of Mary Magdelene, 110

Church of Our Lady (Kraków), 368

Church of Our Lady of Perpetual Help at the Theatines, 72–73

Church of Our Lady of Victories, 73

Church of St. Andrew, 370

Church of St. Anne, 222

Church of St. Bartholemew, 114

Church of St. Catherine, 371

Church of St. Clement, 374

Church of St. Dimitrius, 438

Church of St. Elizabeth, 404

Church of St. Giles, 67

Church of St. John Nepomuk, 77

Church of St. Mary Magdelene, 217

Church of St. Maurice, 141

Church of St. Nicholas (Kecskemét), 297

Church of St. Nicholas (Prague), 66

Church of St. Nicholas (Sofia), 426

Church of St. Nicholas of the Old Town, 66

Church of St. Procopius, 73

Church of St. Sofia, 426

Church of Saints Peter and Paul, 438

Church of the Discalced Carmelites, 342

Church of the Forty Martyrs, 438

Church of the Holy Cross (Brno), 138

Church of the Holy Cross (Jihlava), 130

Church of the Holy
Cross (Slovakia),
183
Church of the Holy
Ghost, *138*
Church of the Holy
Trinity, *161*
Church of the Most
Sacred Heart, *84*
Church of the Sisters
of the Blessed
Sacrament, *341*
Church of the
Visitation Sisters,
344
Church on the Rock,
371
Churches. *See also*
Monasteries;
Mosques;
Synagogues
Bulgaria, *424, 426,
427, 433, 438*
Czech Republic, *64,
66, 67, 71–72, 73,
76, 77, 79–83, 84,
99, 101, 106,
107–108, 109, 110,
111, 114, 118, 130,
132, 133, 138, 141*
Hungary, *215–216,
217, 210, 222, 225,
226, 228–229, 234,
235, 261, 262, 263,
272, 273, 274, 277,
278, 280, 289, 291,
292, 295, 297, 298,
307, 310, 313*
Poland, *341, 342, 343,
344, 345, 368, 369,
370, 371, 372, 374,
375, 386, 388, 389,
393, 395, 396, 402,
404–405, 406, 408,
409*
Romania, *452, 463,
464*
Slovakia, *161, 164,
166, 172, 183–184,
185, 188, 189–190*
Cistercian Church,
292
Citadel, *262*
Citadella, *219*
City Hall (Köszeg),
309
City Hall (Sopron),
305
City Museum, *117,
166, 189, 309*

Clam-Gallas Palace,
67
Climate, *5–7, 150,
197, 321, 410, 444*
Clock Tower, *189, 404*
Cloth Hall, *368*
Cluj, *464, 466*
Coin production, *101*
Colleges/universities,
*291, 294–295, 296,
297, 344, 369, 389,
404, 464*
Collegiate Church of
St. Mary, *411*
Collegium Juridicum,
369
Collegium Maĩus, *369*
Constanta, *461–462*
Contra Aquincum,
225
Copernicus
Astronomy Complex,
433
Copernicus Museum,
408–409
Corpus Christi
Church, *371*
Cost of traveling, *10,
44, 151, 198,
322–323, 418, 445*
Council House, *297*
Country Picnic
Festival, *397*
County Council Hall,
291
County Hall, *295*
Credit cards, *31, 421,
445*
Crețulescu Church,
452
Crypt Museum, *426*
Crypt of the
Habsburg Palatines,
214
Csontváry Múzeum,
312
Currency
Bulgarian, *418*
Czech, *44*
exchange, *9*
Hungarian, *197–198*
money, *8–9*
Polish, *322*
Romanian, *444–445*
Slovak, *151*
Curtea Veche Church,
452
Customs and duties,
*12–13, 45, 152,
198–199, 323, 419,*

445–446
Czapski Palace,
343–344
Czartoryski
Collection, *365*
Czech National
Gallery, *82–83*
Czech National
Museum, *62*
Czech Republic,
40–146. See also
Bohemia; Moravia;
Prague
business hours, *50*
car rentals, *45*
climate, *43*
cost of traveling, *44*
currency, *44*
customs/duties, *12,
45*
festivals/seasonal
events, *43*
health concerns, *45*
holidays, national, *50*
hotels, *52–53*
languages, *45*
mail, *49*
packing essentials,
43–44
passports/visas, *10,
11, 12, 44–45*
publications, *46–47*
rail passes, *46*
restaurants, *51–52*
shopping, *50*
sports/outdoor
activities, *50–51*
student/youth travel,
46
telephones, *49*
tipping, *49–50*
tourist information,
42–43
transportation, *47–49*
Częstochowa, *373, 377*
Czorsztyn, *375*

Danube Bend,
258–268
emergencies, *259*
hotels, *265–268*
pharmacies, *259*
restaurants, *265–268*
shopping, *264*
sightseeing, *259–264*
sports and fitness,
264
tourist information,
258–259
transportation, *259*

Danube Bend
(continued)
travel agencies, 259
Danube bridges,
233–235
Danube Delta,
460–461
Danube Delta
Museum, 460
Deaf and Blind
Institute, 345
Dean's House, 370
Dębno, 375
Debrecen, 294–296,
299–300
Delfinariul, 461
Déri Museum, 296
Devín, 167
Dietrichstein Palace,
138
Diósgyőr, 293
Disabled travelers,
hints for, 21–22
Discounts, air travel,
25–26, 325
Dr. Lajos Smidt
Museum, 310
Dolní Věstonice, 135,
142
Dominican Church
and Monastery, 386
Dominican Church
(Sopron), 307
Dominican Church
(Warsaw), 341
Dom Jana Matejko,
365
Downtown Pest,
223–229
Dracula's Castle, 463
Dragalevci
Monastery, 427
Drechsler Palace, 230
Duties, 12–13, 45,
152, 198–199, 323,
419, 445–446
Dvořák Museum,
115–116

Eastern Pest,
233–235
Eastern Slovakia,
180–192
emergencies, 181
hotels, 190–192
pharmacies, 181
restaurants, 187,
190–192
sightseeing, 182–190
sports, 190

tourist information,
181
transportation,
181–182
Edificiu Roman cu
Mozaic, 461
Eforie Nord, 461
Eger, 288, 289,
301–302
Eger Castle, 289
Elector's Chapel, 405
Elizabeth Bridge,
218, 219, 223
Embassies, 55, 152,
207, 224, 333, 423
Emergencies
Bulgaria, 423
Czech Republic, 55,
97, 128
Hungary, 207–208,
259, 269, 288
Poland, 333, 363, 384,
392
Slovakia, 160, 173,
181
Endre Nemes
Múzeum, 312
Erdődy Palace, 307
Estates Theater, 62
Esterházy Summer
Mansion, 276
Esztergom, 262, 265
Esztergom Cathedral,
262
Eszterházy Palace,
307
Ethnographic
Museum (Cluj), 464
Ethnographic
Museum (Gdańsk),
396
Ethnographic
Museum (Warsaw),
343
Ethnographic
Museum, (Western
Poland), 409–410
Etur, 438

Far Eastern Art
Museum, 409
Father Popieluszko's
Church, 348
Femina cinema, 347
Fenékpuszta, 277
Fenyves (Pinewood
Park), 280
Ferenc Erkel Theatre,
234
Ferenc Hopp Museum

of Eastern Asiatic
Arts, 231
Ferenc Medgyessy
Memorial Museum,
296
Ferenczy Museum,
261
Ferries, 27–28, 167,
274, 325–326, 327,
393. See also Boat
travel
Festetics Palace, 277
Fire Tower, 304–305
Firlej Chapel, 386
Fishermen's Bastion,
216
Fishing, 50–51, 156
Florian Gate, 365
Fontanna Neptuna,
396
Fonyód, 279, 284–285
Fool's Castle, 280
Fortresses, 116, 219,
225, 262, 280, 405,
433, 438
Franciscan Church
(Bratislava), 166
Franciscan Church
(Budapest), 226
Franciscan Church
(Szolnok), 297
Franciscan Church
and Monastery
(Kraków), 369
Františkovy Lázně,
111–112, 122
Franz Liszt Academy
of Music, 230
Franz Liszt Memorial
Museum, 231
Freedom Square, 137
Freud, Sigmund, 142

Garden of Ruins
(Lake Balaton), 274
Garden of Ruins
(Szombathely), 310
Gardens, 73, 74, 75,
84, 115, 140, 167,
223, 263–264, 295,
343, 345, 405, 427,
433, 434
Gay and lesbian
travelers, hints for,
23
Gazi Khassim Pasha
Inner City Parish
Church, 311
Gdańsk and the
Northeast, 392–400

arts and nightlife,
399–400
emergencies, 392
hotels, 398–399
pharmacy, 392
restaurants, 398–399
sightseeing, 393–398
tourist information,
392
transportation,
392–393
Gdańsk
Archaeological
Museum, 395
Gdańsk Historical
Museum, 396
Gdańsk Shipyards,
395
Gdynia, 396–397
Gellért Hill, 219
General's House, 306
Georgiadi House, 439
Georgi Dimitrov
Mausoleum, 426
Georhikon Farm
Museum, 277
Gestapo
Headquarters, 345
Ghetto Museum, 123
Gierloź, 398
Giźycko, 397–398
Gniezno, 407–408
Goat Church, 306
Golden Eagle
Pharmacy Museum,
215
Golden Gate, 395–396
Golden Sands, 433
Golden Unicorn
Pharmacy, 309
Golf, 51, 87, 203–204,
239
Gray House, 369
Great Armory, 395
Great Church, 295
Great Fish Pond,
293–294
Great Forest, 296
Great Plain, 293–298
Great Ring Road,
233–235
Great Synagogue,
227–228
Greek Church, 261
Greek Orthodox
Church, 225
Green Gate, 396
Griffin House, 402
Gubalówka, 374
Gyöngyös, 289

Gyula, 298

Hadji Nikoli, 438
Hajdúszoboszló, 296,
302–303
Hansel-and-Gretel,
402
Harbor Crane, 395
Harrachov, 119
Health and fitness
clubs, 239–240, 350
Health concerns,
14–15, 152
Helikon Library, 277
Hercules Villa, 259
Heroes' Gate, 309
Heroes' Square, 231
Héviz, 277, 285
High Gate (Gdańsk),
395
High Gate (Olsztyn),
397
High Synagogue
(Kraków), 371
High Synagogue
(Prague), 68
High Tatras, 172–180
arts and nightlife,
180
emergencies, 173
guided tours, 174
hotels, 178–180
pharmacies, 173
restaurants, 176,
178–180
shopping, 177
sightseeing, 174–176
sports, 177–178
tourist information,
173
transportation,
173–174
Hiking, 51, 120,
156–157, 177, 190,
264, 329, 377
Historical Museum
(Poznań), 406
Historical Museum of
Wrocław, 402
Hlohovec, 135
Holidays, national,
50, 156, 203, 421,
448
Holy Cross Chapel
(Balatongyörök),
276–277
Holy Cross Church,
(Warsaw), 344
Holy Cross Church
(Wrocław), 404

Holy Trinity Column,
306
Homes,
historic/traditional,
Bulgaria, 439
Czech Republic, 63,
141–142
Hungary, 270, 275,
277, 278, 280, 289,
291, 305–306
Poland, 340, 368, 369,
370, 373, 388, 393,
402
Slovakia, 164, 165,
185, 188, 189
Horse racing, 351
Horseback riding, 5,
204, 240, 264, 281
Hortobágy, 293, 294,
299, 303
Horváth House, 270
Hotels. *See* under
specific areas
House at the Good
Shepherd, 165
House at the Sign of
the Eagle, 369
House at the Sign of
the Stag, 369
House of Culture, 279
House on Soles, 278
House under the
Stars, 403
Houses of Parliament,
223–224
Hradčany, 75–77
Hungarian Museum
of Commerce and
Catering, 217
Hungarian National
Archives, 217
Hungarian National
Gallery, 214
Hungarian National
Museum, 227
Hungarian Royal
Chamber, 164
Hungarian Television
Headquarters, 224
Hungary, 194–315.
See also Budapest;
Danube Bend; Lake
Balaton; Northern
Hungary and the
Great Plain;
Transdanubia
business hours, 203
car rentals, 199
climate, 197
cost of traveling, 198

Hungary *(continued)*
currency, *197–198*
customs and duties, *198*
disabled travelers, hints for, *200*
holidays, national, *203*
hotels, *205–206*
language, *199*
mail, *203*
packing essentials, *197*
passports/visas, *11, 12, 198–199*
restaurants, *204–205*
shopping, *203*
sports/outdoor activities, *203–204*
student/youth travel, *199*
telephones, *202–203*
tipping, *203*
tourist information, *196–197*
transportation, *200–202*
traveling with children, *200*
Hunyady Mansion, *280*
Hus Jan, *65, 103*

Imperial Sanatorium, *109*
Imperial Spa, *110*
Inland Bulgaria, *436–440*
guided tours, *436*
hotels, *439–440*
restaurants, *439–440*
sightseeing, *437–439*
tourist information, *436*
transportation, *436*
Inner City Parish Church, *225*
Inner Lake, *272*
Insurance, *15–17, 18*
Istria, *460*
Italian Court, *101*

Jagiellonian University, *369*
Jan Hus Monument, *65*
Jan Matejko, family house of, *365*
Janos Hill, *237*
Janowiec, *390*

Janské Lázně, *119*
Javorina, *177*
Jedlinka, *185*
Jelenia Góra, *405–406*
Jesuit Church (Bratislava), *166*
Jesuit Church (Warsaw), *342*
Jesuit College, *164*
Jesuit School, *106*
Jewish Cemetery, *347*
Jewish Ghetto, *68–69*
Jewish Historical Institute and Museum, *346–347*
Jewish Town Hall, *68*
Jewish Warsaw, *346–347*
Jihlava, *130, 144*
Jogging, *87, 240, 350, 377*
Josefov, *68–69*
József Egry Memorial Museum, *275*
Jurisics Castle, *309*

Kafka, Franz, *65, 66, 73, 83*
Kafka's Grave, *84*
Kamień Pomorski, *411*
Kampa Gardens, *74*
Kampa Island, *74*
Kampinoski National Park, *348*
Kapana District, *439*
Karlovy Vary, *108–110, 119, 122–123, 127*
Karlsbad, *108–110*
Kassák Muzeum, *236*
Kazanlak, *438*
Kazanowski Palace, *342*
Kazimierz, *371*
Kazimierz Castle, *388*
Kazimierz Dolny, *387–388, 390*
Kecskemét, *297*
Kékestető, *289*
Keleti (East) Railway Station, *234*
Keszthely, *277, 285*
Kežmarok, *183–184, 191*
Kiliántelep, *274*
King Baths, *222*
Kinský Palace, *64–65*
Kiry, *374*
Kiscelli Museum, *236*

Kisfaludy Lookout Tower, *276*
Kiskőrös, *297–298*
Kiskunfélegyháza, *297*
Klariský Church, *164*
Klisura, *437*
Klodsko, *405*
Klucznikowska Mansion, *340*
Kmetty Museum, *261*
Kolobrzeg, *411*
Komorní Hůrka Volcano, *111–112*
Konopiště, *102, 123*
Kopiec Kościuszki, *376*
Koprivshtitsa, *437, 439–440*
Kórnik, *407*
Kőröshegy, *280*
Kościeliska Valley, *374*
Košice, *186–187, 191*
Kossuth Museum, *297*
Kőszeg, *308, 313*
Kotnov Castle, *104*
Kővágóörs, *274*
Kraków and the South, *363–383*
arts and nightlife, *382–383*
emergencies, *363*
guided tours, *364*
hotels, *377–382*
pharmacies, *363*
restaurants, *365, 369, 370, 374, 377–382*
shopping, *376*
sightseeing, *365–375*
sports/outdoor activities, *376–377*
tourist information, *363*
transportation, *363–364*
Kraków Gate, *385–386*
Kraków Philharmonic, *375*
Krasinski Palace, *341*
Krkonoše range, *119*
Króscienko, *375*
Krumlov Castle, *106*
Krynica, *375*
Kudowa-Zdrój, *405*
Kupa Synagogue, *372*
Kutná Hora, *99, 101–102, 123*

Labyrinth of Buda
Castle, *215*
Lajos Kossuth
University, *296*
Lake Balaton,
268–287
emergencies, *269*
guided tours, *269*
hotels, *281–287*
restaurants, *272, 273,*
276, 281–287
sightseeing, *270–281*
sports and fitness,
281
tourist information,
268–269
transportation, *269*
Lake Héviz, *277*
Lake Śniardwy, *398*
Lakes, *277, 374, 390,*
398, 460
Łańcut, *389–390*
Łańcut Palace, *389*
Languages
Bulgarian, *419*
Czech and Slovak, *45,*
152
Hungarian (Magyar),
199
Polish, *323–324*
Romanian, *446*
Łazienki Park, *345*
Lázně I, *110, 127*
Lednice Castle, *135,*
142
Lennon Peace Wall,
74
Lesser Quarter, *71–72*
Letna Gardens, *84*
Levoča, *188–189*
Liberation Memorial,
219
Liberty Bridge, *219*
Liberty Square, *224*
Libraries, *76, 118,*
164, 214, 277, 295,
341, 404
Lidice, *114–115*
Lidzbark Warmiński,
397
Lipscani, *452*
Litoměřice, *117–118,*
124
Little Balaton,
277–278
Little Castle, *101*
Little Town, *71–72*
Little White Horse,
104
Lobkovitz Palace, *83*

Loreto Church, *76*
Lublin and the East,
383–391
arts and nightlife,
391
emergencies, *384*
hotels, *390–391*
pharmacies, *384*
restaurants, *390–391*
sightseeing, *385 390*
sports/outdoor
activities, *390*
tourist information,
384
transportation,
384–385
Lublin Castle, *386*
Lublin Cathedral, *386*
Lublin Gate, *389*
Lublin History
Museum, *386*
Ludwig Museum, *214*
Luggage, *8*
Lutheran Cathedral,
465
Lutheran Church, *228*
Lutheran Museum,
228
Lwów Gate and
Bastion, *389*
Lyceum, *291*

Macocha abyss, *140*
Madara Horseman,
438
Mail, sending and
receiving, *49, 155,*
203, 328, 420, 447
Main Market Square,
368
Main Town, *393*
Maisel Synagogue, *69*
Majdanek, *387*
Malá Strana, *70–75*
Malá Strana Bridge
Towers, *71*
Malbork Castle, *397*
Maltese Square, *73*
Mamaia, *460–461,*
462
Mangalia, *461*
Margaret Bridge, *223*
Margaret Island,
222–223
Margit Kovács
Museum, *262*
Mariánské Lázně,
112–113, 124–125,
127
Marine Gardens, *433*

Maritime Museum,
395
Maritime Park, *434*
Market Square, *386*
Marosvásárhely
Musical Fountain,
223
Martinic Palace, *77*
Máta, *294*
Mátra, *289*
Mátra Museum, *289*
Mátrafüred, *289*
Matthias Church,
215–216
Mátyás Király
Múzeum, *262*
Mausoleum
(Majdanek), *387*
Mausoleum (Pécs),
313
Mazury, *397–398*
Medical services,
14–15, 45
Medieval Synagogue,
217
Mělník, *118–119, 125*
Memorial Cross, *261*
Memorial Garden,
295
Memorial Museum
(Balatonrendes and
Ábrahámhegy), *275*
Memorial Museum
(Kiskőrös), *298*
Michael's Gate, *163*
Mikolajki, *398*
Mikulov Castle, *134,*
144
Military
Amphitheatre, *236*
Military Museum, *77*
Millennial Monument,
231
Minaret, *292*
Miniature golf, *281*
Mining museum, *312*
Minorite Church
(Eger), *292*
Minorite Church
(Moravia), *130*
Mintner's Chapel, *101*
Mirbach Palace, *166*
Mirów, *337*
Mirror Gallery, *277*
Miskolc, *293*
Modra, *171*
Monasteries, *74, 76,*
105, 113, 139, 369,
373, 386, 388, 427,
433, 437, 439

Monastery of Staré
Brno, *139*
Money, *8–9*
Eastern European
currency, *44, 151,
197–198, 322,
444–445*
Monument of
Struggle and
Martydom, *387*
Monument to the
Heroes of the
Warsaw Ghetto, *347*
Monument to the
Heroes of the
Warsaw Uprising,
341
Monuments, *65, 74,
114–115, 167, 231,
261, 297, 306, 307,
337, 342, 347, 376,
387, 388, 395, 411,
452*
Moravia, *127–146*
arts and nightlife,
145–146
emergencies, *128*
hotels, *143–145*
pharmacy, *128*
restaurants, *132, 135,
140, 143–145*
shopping, *142*
sightseeing, *129–142*
sports/outdoor
activities, *143*
tourist information,
128
transportation,
128–129
Moravian Karst,
129–130, 140, 142
Moravian Museum,
138
Moravský Krumlov,
142
Morskie Oko, *374*
Morzin Palace, *72*
Mosques, *311, 427*
Mt. Śnieżka, *406*
Municipal Arsenal,
365
Municipal Art Gallery
(Szombathely), *310*
Municipal Gallery
(Bratislava), *166*
Municipal Gallery
(Danube Bend), *261*
Municipal Grand
Circus, *233*
Municipal House, *63*

Muranów, *337*
Murfatlar Vineyards,
461
Museum of Applied
and Decorative Arts,
235
Museum of Artistic
Handicrafts, *165*
Museum of the
Badacsony State
Farm, *275–276*
Museum of Christian
Art, *263*
Museum of the City,
106
Museum of City
History, *406*
Museum of Clocks,
165
Museum of Decorative
Arts, *406–407*
Museum of
Ethnography, *224*
Museum of Fine Arts,
231–232
Museum of the
History and Culture
of Kraków Jews, *371*
Museum of Hunting,
345
Museum of the
Hussite Movement,
103
Museum of Local
History, *293*
Museum of Military
History, *217*
Museum of Music
History, *217*
Museum of Musical
Instruments, *406*
Museum of National
Literature, *76*
Museum of the
Original Polish
State, *408*
Museum of Recent
History, *214*
Museum of the
Romanian Peasant,
453
Museum of the Slovak
National Uprising,
189
Museum of the Tatras
National Park, *175,
177*
Museum of Weapons
and Fortifications,
163–164

Museums
Bulgaria, *424, 426,
433, 438, 439*
Czech Republic, *62,
68, 76, 77, 82–83,
101, 103, 106, 111,
112, 114, 115, 116,
117, 133, 134, 135,
138, 140, 142*
Hungary, *214, 215,
217, 218, 224, 227,
231–232, 236,
261–262, 263, 272,
273, 275–276, 277,
279, 280, 281, 289,
291, 293, 295, 296,
297, 298, 306, 307,
309, 310, 311,
312–313*
Poland, *340, 341, 343,
344, 345, 346–347,
348, 365, 368, 371,
372, 373–374,
386–387, 388, 389,
390, 395, 396, 397,
402, 405, 406–407,
408, 409, 410, 411*
Romania, *452, 460,
461*
Slovakia, *163–164,
165, 166, 167, 171,
175, 177, 184–185,
188, 189*
Muzeul Curtea
Veche-Palatul
Voievodal, *452*
Muzeum Marii
Skłodowskiej-Curie,
341

Nagyberek State
Farm, *278*
Nagy Templom, *291*
National
Archaeological
Museum, *426, 439*
National Art Gallery,
426
National Art
Museum, *453*
National
Ethnographical
Museum, *426, 439*
National Gallery, *77*
National History and
Archaeological
Museum, *461*
National History
Museum, *424*
National Jewish

Museum, 228
National Museum
(Kraków), 368
National Museum
(Szczecin), 410
National Museum in
Gdańsk, 395
National Museum of
Warsaw, 344
National Palace of
Culture, 427
National Puppet
Theater, 231
National War
Memorial, 231
Natural History
Museum, 453
Naval Museum
(Gdańsk), 397
Naval Museum
(Varna), 433
Negro House
(Warsaw), 340
Negroes' House
(Kraków), 368
Nelahozeves, 115–116
Nesebär, 434
New Cemetery,
371–372
New Library, 113
New Synagogue, 298
New Town (Warsaw),
337
New Town Square,
341
Nicholas Prison, 187
Niedzica Castle, 375
Niepołomice Forest,
372, 376
Nine-Arched Bridge,
294
North Buda, 219–222
Northern Bohemia,
114–119
Northern Hungary
and the Great Plain,
287–303
emergencies, 288
hotels, 299–303
pharmacies, 288
restaurants, 292–293,
299–303
shopping, 299
sightseeing, 289–298
tourist information,
288
transportation, 288
Northern Moravia,
140–142
Nowy Sącz, 375, 382

Nowy Targ, 374–375
Nyíregyháza, 288
Nyugati (West)
Railway Station, 235

Óbuda, 235–236
Óbuda Local History
Museum, 230
Óbuda Parish Church,
235
Oceanographic
Museum and
Aquarium, 396
Ohrada Hunting
Lodge, 107
Ojców National Park,
373, 376
Old Academy, 389
Old Castle, 276
Old Clock Tower, 433
Old Jewish Cemetery
(Lublin), 387
Old Jewish Cemetery
(Prague), 69
Old-New Synagogue,
68
Old Powder Tower,
341
Old Princely Court,
476
Old Synagogue
(Kraków), 371
Old Synagogue
(Szeged), 298
Old Town Bridge
Tower, 70
Old Town
(Bratislava), 163
Old Town (Gdańsk),
393
Old Town (Lublin),
385
Old Town (Prague),
59, 62–67
Old Town (Toruń),
408
Old Town (Warsaw),
337
Old Town (Western
Bohemia), 108
Old Town (Wrocław),
402
Old Town Hall,
(Bratislava), 166
Old Town Hall
(Brno), 137
Old Town Hall
(Lublin), 386
Old Town Hall
(Prague), 65

Old Town Square
(Prague), 63–64
Old Town Square
(Toruń), 409
Old Town Square
(Warsaw), 337, 340
Older travelers, hints
for, 22–23
Olomouc, 130,
140–141, 144–145
Olsztyn, 397–398, 399
Open-air
Ethnographic
Museum, 261–262
Open-air Museum of
Ethnography, 273
Opera House
(Budapest), 230, 254
Opera House
(Warsaw), 343, 361
Ornak, 374
Ornamental Palace,
297
Orthodox Church,
452
Orvényes, 274
Ostrogski Palace, 344
Outer Lake, 272
Owl Castle, 280

Packing essentials,
7–9, 151, 197, 322
Pałac Potockich, 342
Palace at the Sign of
the Rams, 369
Palace Chapel, 387
Palace of Culture and
Science, 348
Palace on the Lake,
345
Palaces
Bulgaria, 427
Czech Republic,
64–65, 67, 72, 73,
76, 77, 83, 138
Hungary, 212, 215,
230, 277, 291, 297,
307
Poland, 341, 342–343,
344, 345, 346, 369,
387, 389, 407
Slovakia, 163,
166–167, 183, 190
Palatinus Baths, 223
Palme House, 233
Paragliding, 177
Parish Church
(Balatonberény), 278
Parish Church
(Balatonszemes), 280

Parish Church
(Keszthely), *277*
Parish Church
(Slovakia), *189–190*
Parish Church
(Tapolca), *276*
Park Colonnade, *109*
Parks, *84, 174–177,*
189, 190, 232–233,
296, 343, 345, 348,
365, 373, 374, 407,
411, 434, 461
Park Ujazdowski, *345*
Passports, *10–12,*
44–45, 152, 198, 323
Patika Múzeum, *326*
Pauline Monastery,
373
Pécs, *310–313, 314*
Pécs Cathedral, *313*
Pethó Hall, *232*
Pethó House, *277*
Petőfi, Sándor, *297*
Petřín, *84–85*
Petržalka gardens,
167
Pezinok, *171*
Pharmacies, *55,*
97–98, 160, 181, 259,
288, 333, 363, 384,
392, 423
Pharmacy museums,
163
Pieskowa Skała, *373*
Pilsner-Urquell
Brewery, *113–114*
Pinkas Synagogue, *69*
Pioneer Railway, *237*
Písek Bridge, *107,*
125
Planty, *365, 376*
Plovdiv, *438, 439, 440*
Plzen, *113–114, 125*
Poland, *317–414. See*
also Gdańsk;
Prague; Kraków;
Lublin; Warsaw;
Western Poland
business hours, *328*
car rentals, *324*
climate, *321*
cost of traveling,
322–323
currency, *322*
customs and duties,
323
festivals, *321–322*
hotels, *331–332*
language, *323–324*
mail, *328*

packing essentials,
322
passports/visas, *10,*
11, 12, 323
publications, *325*
rail passes, *324*
restaurants, *329–330*
shopping, *328–329*
sports/outdoor
activities, *329*
student/youth travel,
324–325
telephones, *327*
tipping, *328*
tourist information,
321
transportation,
325–327
Polish Army Museum,
344–345
Polish Communist
Party, former
headquarters, *344*
Pomeranian Princes'
Castle, *410*
Pomnik Zaślubin, *411*
Poncichter wine
quarter, *308*
Pope John Paul II,
395
Poper Synagogue, *372*
Poprad, *174–175, 178*
Postal Museum
(Balatonszemes), *280*
Postal Museum
(Budapest), *229*
Powązki, *348*
Powder Tower, *63*
Poznań, *406–408,*
411–412
Poznań Cathedral,
407
Praga, *337*
Prague, *53–96*
arts and nightlife,
94–96
embassies, *55*
emergencies, *55*
English-language
bookstores, *55*
guided tours, *57–58*
hotels, *62, 92–94*
pharmacy, *55*
restaurants, *63, 66,*
67, 69, 72, 74,
75–76, 87–92
shopping, *85–86*
sightseeing, *58–83*
sports and fitness,
86–87

tourist information,
54–55
transportation,
56–57
travel agencies, *55*
Prague Castle, *77,*
79–82
Prešov, *186, 192*
Příbor, *142*
Primates' Palace,
166–167
Protestant Church
(Budapest), *226*
Protestant Church
(Slovakia), *183–184*
Provost's House, *291*
Przybyła Brothers'
House, *388*
Publications
for disabled
travelers, *22*
English-language
bookstores, *55, 160,*
208, 333
on Czech Republic,
46–47
on Eastern Europe,
24
on Poland, *325*
on Slovakia, *153, 173*
traveling with
children, *20*
Puławy Palace, *387*
Punkva Cave, *140*

Rác Baths, *219*
Radziwiłł Palace,
342–343
Rail passes, *18–19,*
152–153, 324
Railroads, *229, 234,*
237
Red Chapel, *279*
Red Church, *295–296*
Red Rock Castle, *171*
Reduta, *167*
Reformed Cemetery,
297
Reformed Church
(Balatonudvari), *274*
Reformed Church
(Cegléd), *297*
Reformed Church
(Zánka), *274*
Reformed College
(Cegléd), *297*
Reformed College
(Debrecen), *294–295*
Regional House
Museum, *279*

Restaurants. See
under specific areas
Révfülöp, *274*
Rhody House, *185*
Rila Monastery, *439*
Robert Jahoda's
Printing Press, *376*
Rogalin, *407*
Roman Amphitheater,
236, 439
Roman Archaeology
Museum, *306*
Roman Bath, *236*
Roman Catholic
Church (Sibiu), *465*
Romanesque Church,
273
Roman Fortress Wall,
433
Romania, *442–466*.
See also Bucharest,
Black Sea Coast and
Danube Delta
business hours, *448*
climate, *444*
currency, *444–445*
customs, *445–446*
holidays, national,
448
hotels, *448–449*
language, *446*
mail, *447*
passports and visas,
10–11, 12, 445
restaurants, *448*
telephones, *447*
tipping, *450*
transportation,
446–447
Romanian
Athenaeum Concert
Hall, *453*
Romanian History
Museum, *452*
Romanian Orthodox
Cathedral, *464*
Romanian Orthodox
Church, *464*
Rosenberg Castle, *105*
Rotunda (Lublin), *389*
Rotunda of St.
George, *426*
Round Church, *270*
Royal Castle
(Kraków), *370–371*
Royal Castle
(Warsaw), *337, 340*
Royal Palace
(Budapest), *212*
Royal Palace (Prague

Castle), *81*
Royal Palace
(Slovakia), *190*
Royal Route, *342–346*
Róza Szegedy House,
275
Rožmberk nad
Vltavou, *105*
Rudas Baths, *219*
Ruins/excavations,
*225, 236, 259–260,
273, 277, 306, 433,
438, 439, 460, 461*
Rynek (Lublin), *386*
Rynek (Poznań), *406*
Rynek (Wrocław), *402*
Rynek (Zamość), *389*

Sacred Heart Church,
308
St. Alexander's
Church, *345*
St. Anne's Chapel,
141
St. Anne's Church,
342
St. Barbara
Cathedral, *99, 101*
St. Barbara's Chapel,
190
St. Bartholomew
(Gyöngyös), *289*
St. Bartholomew's
Church (Wrocław),
404
St. Bridigy Church,
395
St. Catherine's
Church, *396*
St. Catherine's
Rotunda, *133*
St. Egidius (Giles)
Church, *184*
St. Elizabeth Church,
310
St. Elizabeth's
Chapel, *404–405*
St. Emerich's Church,
308–309
St. Florian Chapel,
222
St. George's Basilica,
82
St. George's Convent,
82
St. Ignace Church,
130
St. Jacob's Church,
118
St. James Cathedral,

397
St. James Church
(Bohemia), *101*
St. James Church
(Jihlava), *130*
St. James Church
(Köszeg), *308*
St. James Church
(Levoča), *188*
St. James Church
(Telč), *132*
St. John Nepomuk,
sarcophagus of,
81
St. John's Cathedral,
404
St. John's Church,
409
St. Ladislas Church,
273
St. Martin-in-the-
Wall, *67*
St. Martin's
Cathedral, *164*
St. Mary Magdalene's
Church, *402*
St. Mary's Church,
341
St. Mary's Church on
the Sand, *404*
St. Mary's Column,
307
St. Michael's Chapel,
187
St. Michael's Church,
464
St. Nedelya Church,
424
St. Nicholas
Cathedral, *172*
St. Nicholas Church
(Cheb), *111*
St. Nicholas Church
(Prague), *71–72*
St. Nicholas Church
(Znojmo), *133*
St. Roch Chapel, *234*
St. Stephen's Basilica,
228–229
St. Stephen's
Cathedral, *118*
St. Thomas Collegiate
Church, *389*
St. Vitus Cathedral,
79
St. Vitus Church, *106*
St. Wenceslas Chapel,
118
St. Wenceslas Church,
133

Saints Peter and Paul
Church, *404*
Sala Terrena, *310*
Salt mine, *372*
Salt Square, *402*
Šariš Icon Museum,
184–185
Sárospatak, *293*
Saxon Gardens, *343*
Scene of Fire, *75*
Schönborn Palace, *73*
Schwarzenberg
Palace, *77*
Segner House, *164*
Sejm, *345*
Semmelweis Hospital,
234
Semmelweis Museum
of Medical History,
218
Serbia Orthodox
Church, *292*
Serbian Orthodox
Cathedral, *261*
Serbian Orthodox
Church (Budapest),
226
Serbian Orthodox
Museum, *261*
Sgraffitóház, *309*
Shipka Pass, *438*
Ship Museum, *396*
Shopping. *See* under
specific areas
Sibiu, *465, 466*
Sighişoara, *464, 466*
Sigismund Chapel,
370
Sigrismund Tower,
370
Siófok, *281, 285–286*
Sixt House, *63*
Skiing, *51, 120, 143,
157, 177–178, 289,
329, 377, 427*
Slavín Memorial, *167*
Slavkov, *140*
Slovak National
Gallery, *167*
Slovak National
Museum, *165*
Slovak National
Theater, *167*
Slovak National
Uprising, *161, 189*
Slovak Paradise, *189,
190*
Slovak Pedagogical
Library, *164*
Slovak Philharmonic

Orchestra, *167,
170–171*
Slovakia, *148–192*.
See also Bratislava;
The High Tatras;
Eastern Slovakia
business hours,
155–156
car rentals, *152*
cost of traveling, *151*
currency, *151*
customs and duties,
11, 152
festivals/seasonal
events, *150–151*
health concerns, *152*
holidays, national,
156
hotels, *158*
languages, *152*
mail, *155*
packing essentials,
151
passports and visas,
10, 11, 152
publications, *153*
rail passes, *152–153*
restaurants, *157–158*
shopping, *156*
sports/outdoor
activities, *156–157*
student/youth travel,
153
telephones, *155*
tipping, *155*
tourist information,
150
transportation,
153–155
Small Carpathian
Museum, *171*
Small Fortress, *116*
Small Reformed
Church, *295*
Small Square, *66*
Smokovec, *175, 179*
Soccer, *87, 351*
Sofia, *423–431*
arts and nightlife,
430–431
embassies, *423*
emergencies, *423*
guided tours, *424*
hotels, *429–430*
restaurants, *427,
428–429*
shopping, *427–428*
sightseeing, *424–427*
tourist information,
423

transportation,
423–424
Sopron, *304, 314*
Southern Bohemia,
99, 101–108
Southern Moravia,
130, 132–135
Soviet Embassy, *346*
Sozopol, *434*
Spa Museum, *112*
Spas and thermal
baths
Bulgaria, *427, 433*
Czech Republic, *108,
110, 111–113*
Hungary, *219, 222,
232–233, 240–241,
270, 277, 296, 298*
Poland, *375, 405*
Romania, *461*
Slovakia, *185*
Spectator sports, *87,
351*
Špilberk Castle, *139*
Špindleru[dt]v Mlýn,
119, 125–126
Spiš Castle, *188–189*
Spiš Museum, *188*
Sports, fitness, and
outdoor activities,
*50–51, 86–87, 120,
143, 156–157, 177,
190, 203–204,
239–242, 281, 329,
350–351, 390*
Star Castle, *278*
Staszic Palace, *344*
State Jewish Museum,
68
State Lavender and
Medicinal Herb
Farm, *273*
State Theater, *187*
Statue of Adam
Mickiewicz, *368*
Statue of Cardinal
Stefan Wyszyński,
344
Statue of George
Washington, *232*
Statue of Nicholas
Copernicus, *344, 409*
Statue of Pope John
XXIII, *404*
Statue of Prince of
Savoy, *212*
Statue of Raoul
Wallenberg, *299*
Statue of St.
Wenceslas, *59*

Statues, *59, 70–71,*
212, 223, 225, 231,
232, 234, 235, 273,
292, 296, 299, 306,
341, 344, 368, 404,
426, 464
Sternberg Palace, *77*
Stone Valley, *274*
Storno House, *305*
Strahov Library, *76*
Strahov Monastery,
76
Štrbské Pleso, *175,*
177, 179–180
Student and youth
travel, *19–20, 46,*
153, 199, 324–325
Subway Museum, *233*
Subways/metro, *57,*
210, 450
Šumen, *438*
Sunny Beach, *434,*
435
Sveti Konstantin,
433–434, 435
Svidnik, *185, 186*
Swimming, *87, 120,*
177, 190, 223, 264,
296, 350
Swinoujście, *410–411*
Sybil's Temple, *387*
Synagoga R'emuh,
371
Synagogues, *68, 69,*
217, 227–228, 297,
298, 307, 371, 372
Szántóclpuszła, *281*
Szczawnica, *375*
Szczecin, *410, 412*
Széchenyi Baths, *232*
Széchenyi Mansion,
280–281
Széchenyi National
Library, *214*
Szeged, *298*
Szent Tamás Hill, *263*
Szentendre, *260–262,*
265–267
Szigliget, *276*
Szlichtyngowska
Mansion, *340*
Szobor Park, *237*
Szolnok, *297*
Szombathely,
309–310, 314–315

Tabán, *218*
Tabán Parish Church,
218
Tábor, *103–104, 126*

Talenti Mansion, *340*
Tapolca, *276, 286*
Tatra Mountains,
373–374
Tatra Museum,
373–374
Tatra National Park,
374
Tatranská Lomnica,
175, 176, 180
Taxis, *57, 161, 200,*
210, 334, 335–336,
385, 423–424, 451
Telč, *130, 132, 145*
Telefónia museum,
215
Telephones, *10, 29,*
49, 155, 202–203,
327, 420, 447
Tempel Synagogue,
372
Tennis, *51, 87, 157,*
241–242, 281
Teplá, *113*
Theaters, *62, 95,*
145–146, 167, 171,
187, 214–215, 225,
234, 235, 237,
254–256, 296, 341,
361–362, 383, 433,
458
Theresa Town Parish
Church, *235*
Theresienstadt,
116–117, 119
Thermae Maiores, *236*
Three Crosses Hill,
388
Three Crosses Square,
345
Thun-Hohenstein
Palace, *72*
Thurzo House, *188,*
189
Tihany Abbey, *272*
Tihany Historical
Museum, *272–273*
Tihany Peninsula,
272–274, 286–287
Tipping, *49–50, 155,*
203, 328, 422, 450
Toboggan slide, *265*
Tokaj, *293*
Tököly Palace, *183*
Tomb of Gül Baba,
222
Tomb of the Unknown
Soldier, *343*
Toruń, *406, 408–410,*
412–413

Tour groups, *2–5,*
150, 196–197, 321
Tourist offices, *2,*
54–55, 150, 159, 173,
181, 196, 207,
258–259, 268–269,
288, 303–304, 321,
333, 363, 384, 392,
400, 423, 431, 436,
450, 459, 463
Tours, guided, *4–5,*
57–58, 98–99, 161,
174, 211, 269, 336,
364–365, 424, 432,
436, 451, 460, 463
Towers, *63, 65, 70, 71,*
107, 117, 141, 166,
187, 189, 219, 225,
276, 279, 304–305,
308, 341, 368–369,
370, 409
Town Castle
(Moravia), *132*
Town Hall
(Bardejov), *184*
Town Hall (Bohemia),
106
Town Hall (Gdańsk),
396
Town Hall
(Kazimierz), *371*
Town Hall
(Kecskemét), *297*
Town Hall (Levoča),
188
Town Hall (Olomouc),
141
Town Hall (Poznań),
406
Town Hall (Toruń),
409
Town Hall (Wrocław),
402
Town Hall (Zamość),
389
Town Hall Towers, *65,*
368–369
Town Museum of
Kazimierz Dolny,
388
Tőzsér Gyüjtémeny,
296–297
Trade Unions'
Holiday Home, *279*
Trade Unions'
Sanatorium, *270*
Train travel, *5, 27,*
28. See also
Railroads
Bulgaria, *420, 423*

Train travel
(continued)
Czech Republic,
47–48, 56, 98, 128,
129
Hungary, *201, 209,*
269, 288, 304
Poland, *326, 334, 364,*
384, 392–393, 401
Romania, *447, 450,*
463
Slovakia, *154, 160,*
173, 174, 182
Trajan's Column, *452*
Transdanubia,
303–315
hotels, *313–315*
restaurants, *310, 312,*
313–315
sightseeing, *304–313*
tourist information,
303–304
transportation, *304*
Transport Museum,
232
Transylvania,
462–466
guided tours, *463*
hotels, *465–466*
restaurants, *465–466*
sightseeing, *463–465*
tourist information,
463
transportation, *463*
Travel agencies, *22,*
23, 55, 160, 259, 333
Třeboň Castle, *104,*
126
Trinity Chapel, *216*
Trip-cancellation and
flight insurance, *16*
Trnava, *172*
Trojan Monastery,
437
Tszarvec, *438*
Tugendhat Haus, *140*
Tulcea, *460, 462*
Týn Church, *64*
Tyszkiewski Chapel,
386

Ujazdowski Park, *348*
Umschlagplatz, *347*
Underground
Railway, *229*
University of
Economics, *226*
University Church,
226
University Church of

John the Baptist, *172*
University Library,
404
Urbans' Tower, *187*

Vác, *263*
Vácrátóti Arborétum,
263–264
Vajdahunyad Castle,
232
Vak Bottyán
Múzeum, *263*
Valcum, *277*
Valkoun House, *72*
Valley of Roses, *437,*
439
Valtice Castle,
134–135, 145
Varna, *432–433,*
435–436
Városliget, *232–233*
Vasarely Museum, *312*
Veliki Preslav, *438*
Veliko Târnovo, *438,*
440
Velké Karlovice, *145*
Veltrusy Castle and
Gardens, *115*
Veszprém, *287*
Victorian Church, *109*
Vidám Park, *233, 237*
Vidám Concert Hall,
225
Villa Bertramka, *85*
Villa Tugendhat, *140*
Village Museum, *453*
Visas, *10–12, 44–45,*
152, 198, 323, 419,
445
Visegrád, *262,*
267–268
Vocabulary, *467–497*
Vojanovy Sady, *74*
Vonyarcvashegy,
276–277
Votive Church, *298*
Vranov Castle, *132*
Vřídlo, *108–109*
Vrtba Palace and
Gardens, *73*

Wallenberg, Raoul,
299
Wallenstein Chapel,
81
Wallenstein Gardens,
75
Warhol Family
Museum of Modern
Art, *190*

Warsaw, *332–362*
arts and nightlife,
360–362
business hours, *336*
currency exchange,
333
embassies, *333*
emergencies, *333*
English-language
bookstores, *333*
guided tours, *336*
hotels, *356–360*
pharmacies, *333*
restaurants, *340, 342,*
343, 344, 345, 347,
351–356
shopping, *349–350*
sightseeing, *336–348*
sports and fitness,
350–351
tourist information,
333
transportation,
333–336
travel agencies, *333*
Warsaw Historical
Museum, *340*
Warsaw University,
344
Water sports, *204,*
264, 281, 329
Wawel Cathedral,
370
Wawel Hill, *370*
Well House, *270*
Wenceslas Square, *59*
Western Bohemia,
108–114
Western Poland,
400–414
hotels, *411–414*
restaurants, *404, 405,*
407, 408, 409, 410,
411–414
sightseeing, *402–411*
tourist information,
400
transportation,
400–402
Wieliczka salt mine,
372
Wielkopolski National
Park, *407*
Wilanów Palace, *346*
Wine Country,
171–172
Wine industry, *134,*
171–172, 273, 274,
275–276, 279,
292–293, 308, 461

Wine Museum, 186, 813

Wolf's Lair, 398

Wolin Island, 411

Woliński National Park, 411

Wrocław, 402, 404–405, 413–414

Wrocław University, 404

Xantus Lookout Tower, 279

Zachęta Gallery, 343

Zakopane, 373–376, 382

Zalew Zemborzycki, 390

Zamość Regional Museum, 389

Zamoyski Chapel, 389

Zamoyski Palace, 389

Zánka, 274

Ždiar, 177

Zichy Mansion, 236

Žilina, 192

Znojmo, 133–134, 145

Zoological Park (Warsaw), 337

Zoos, 83, 107, 233, 296, 337

Zsolnay Fountain, 311

Zsolnay Mausoleum, 311

Zsolnay Museum, 311

Zsolnay Porcelain Factory, 311

Zygmunt Bell, 340

Zygmunt Column, 337

Personal Itinerary

Departure *Date*

Time

Transportation

Arrival *Date*   *Time*

Departure *Date*   *Time*

Transportation

Accommodations

Arrival *Date*   *Time*

Departure *Date*   *Time*

Transportation

Accommodations

Arrival *Date*   *Time*

Departure *Date*   *Time*

Transportation

Accommodations

Personal Itinerary

Arrival *Date*   *Time*

Departure *Date*   *Time*

Transportation

Accommodations

Arrival *Date*   *Time*

Departure *Date*   *Time*

Transportation

Accommodations

Arrival *Date*   *Time*

Departure *Date*   *Time*

Transportation

Accommodations

Arrival *Date*   *Time*

Departure *Date*   *Time*

Transportation

Accommodations

Personal Itinerary

Arrival *Date* *Time*

Departure *Date* *Time*

Transportation

Accommodations

Arrival *Date* *Time*

Departure *Date* *Time*

Transportation

Accommodations

Arrival *Date* *Time*

Departure *Date* *Time*

Transportation

Accommodations

Arrival *Date* *Time*

Departure *Date* *Time*

Transportation

Accommodations

Personal Itinerary

Arrival	Date	Time
Departure	Date	Time

Transportation

Accommodations

Arrival	Date	Time
Departure	Date	Time

Transportation

Accommodations

Arrival	Date	Time
Departure	Date	Time

Transportation

Accommodations

Arrival	Date	Time
Departure	Date	Time

Transportation

Accommodations

Personal Itinerary

Arrival	*Date*	*Time*
Departure	*Date*	*Time*
Transportation		
Accommodations		

Arrival	*Date*	*Time*
Departure	*Date*	*Time*
Transportation		
Accommodations		

Arrival	*Date*	*Time*
Departure	*Date*	*Time*
Transportation		
Accommodations		

Arrival	*Date*	*Time*
Departure	*Date*	*Time*
Transportation		
Accommodations		

Personal Itinerary

Arrival *Date*   *Time*

Departure *Date*   *Time*

Transportation

Accommodations

Arrival *Date*   *Time*

Departure *Date*   *Time*

Transportation

Accommodations

Arrival *Date*   *Time*

Departure *Date*   *Time*

Transportation

Accommodations

Arrival *Date*   *Time*

Departure *Date*   *Time*

Transportation

Accommodations

Addresses

Name _____ *Name* _____

Address _____ *Address* _____

_____ _____

Telephone _____ *Telephone* _____

Name _____ *Name* _____

Address _____ *Address* _____

_____ _____

Telephone _____ *Telephone* _____

Name _____ *Name* _____

Address _____ *Address* _____

_____ _____

Telephone _____ *Telephone* _____

Name _____ *Name* _____

Address _____ *Address* _____

_____ _____

Telephone _____ *Telephone* _____

Name _____ *Name* _____

Address _____ *Address* _____

_____ _____

Telephone _____ *Telephone* _____

Name _____ *Name* _____

Address _____ *Address* _____

_____ _____

Telephone _____ *Telephone* _____

Name _____ *Name* _____

Address _____ *Address* _____

_____ _____

Telephone _____ *Telephone* _____

Name _____ *Name* _____

Address _____ *Address* _____

_____ _____

Telephone _____ *Telephone* _____

Addresses

Name	Name
Address	Address
Telephone	Telephone
Name	Name
Address	Address
Telephone	Telephone
Name	Name
Address	Address
Telephone	Telephone
Name	Name
Address	Address
Telephone	Telephone
Name	Name
Address	Address
Telephone	Telephone
Name	Name
Address	Address
Telephone	Telephone
Name	Name
Address	Address
Telephone	Telephone
Name	Name
Address	Address
Telephone	Telephone

Escape to ancient cities and exotic

islands *with CNN Travel Guide, a*

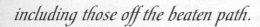

wealth of valuable advice. Host Valerie Voss will take you

to all of your favorite destinations,

including those off the beaten path.

Tune into your passport to the world.

CNN TRAVEL GUIDE
SATURDAY 10:00 PMᴘᴛ   SUNDAY 8:30 AMᴇᴛ

The only guide to explore a Disney World® you've never seen before:

The one for grown-ups.

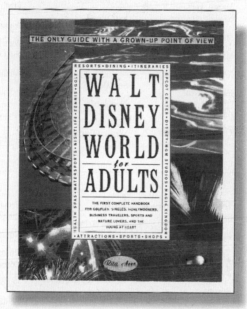

0-679-02490-5 $14.00 ($18.50 Can)

This is the only guide written specifically for the millions of adults who visit Walt Disney World® each year <u>without</u> kids. Upscale, sophisticated, packed full of facts and maps, *Walt Disney World® for Adults* provides up-to-date information on hotels, restaurants, sports facilities, and health clubs, as well as unique itineraries for adults. With *Walt Disney World® for Adults* in hand, you'll get the most out of one of the world's most fascinating, most complex playgrounds.

At bookstores everywhere, or call **1-800-533-6478**.

Fodor's

Fodor's Travel Guides

Available at bookstores everywhere, or call 1–800–533–6478, 24 hours a day.

U.S. Guides

Alaska

Arizona

Boston

California

Cape Cod, Martha's Vineyard, Nantucket

The Carolinas & the Georgia Coast

Chicago

Colorado

Florida

Hawaii

Las Vegas, Reno, Tahoe

Los Angeles

Maine, Vermont, New Hampshire

Maui

Miami & the Keys

New England

New Orleans

New York City

Pacific North Coast

Philadelphia & the Pennsylvania Dutch Country

The Rockies

San Diego

San Francisco

Santa Fe, Taos, Albuquerque

Seattle & Vancouver

The South

The U.S. & British Virgin Islands

USA

The Upper Great Lakes Region

Virginia & Maryland

Waikiki

Walt Disney World and the Orlando Area

Washington, D.C.

Foreign Guides

Acapulco, Ixtapa, Zihuatanejo

Australia & New Zealand

Austria

The Bahamas

Baja & Mexico's Pacific Coast Resorts

Barbados

Berlin

Bermuda

Brittany & Normandy

Budapest

Canada

Cancún, Cozumel, Yucatán Peninsula

Caribbean

China

Costa Rica, Belize, Guatemala

The Czech Republic & Slovakia

Eastern Europe

Egypt

Euro Disney

Europe

Florence, Tuscany & Umbria

France

Germany

Great Britain

Greece

Hong Kong

India

Ireland

Israel

Italy

Japan

Kenya & Tanzania

Korea

London

Madrid & Barcelona

Mexico

Montréal & Québec City

Morocco

Moscow & St. Petersburg

The Netherlands, Belgium & Luxembourg

New Zealand

Norway

Nova Scotia, Prince Edward Island & New Brunswick

Paris

Portugal

Provence & the Riviera

Rome

Russia & the Baltic Countries

Scandinavia

Scotland

Singapore

South America

Southeast Asia

Spain

Sweden

Switzerland

Thailand

Tokyo

Toronto

Turkey

Vienna & the Danube Valley

Special Series

Fodor's Affordables

Caribbean

Europe

Florida

France

Germany

Great Britain

Italy

London

Paris

**Fodor's Bed &
Breakfast and
Country Inns Guides**

America's Best B&Bs

California

Canada's Great
Country Inns

Cottages, B&Bs and
Country Inns of
England and Wales

Mid-Atlantic Region

New England

The Pacific
Northwest

The South

The Southwest

The Upper Great
Lakes Region

The Berkeley Guides

California

Central America

Eastern Europe

Europe

France

Germany & Austria

Great Britain &
Ireland

Italy

London

Mexico

Pacific Northwest &
Alaska

Paris

San Francisco

**Fodor's Exploring
Guides**

Australia

Boston &
New England

Britain

California

The Caribbean

Florence & Tuscany

Florida

France

Germany

Ireland

Italy

London

Mexico

New York City

Paris

Prague

Rome

Scotland

Singapore & Malaysia

Spain

Thailand

Turkey

Fodor's Flashmaps

Boston

New York

Washington, D.C.

Fodor's Pocket Guides

Acapulco

Bahamas

Barbados

Jamaica

London

New York City

Paris

Puerto Rico

San Francisco

Washington, D.C.

Fodor's Sports

Cycling

Golf Digest's Best
Places to Play

Hiking

The Insider's Guide
to the Best Canadian
Skiing

Running

Sailing

Skiing in the USA &
Canada

USA Today's Complete
Four Sports Stadium
Guide

**Fodor's Three-In-Ones
(guidebook, language
cassette, and phrase
book)**

France

Germany

Italy

Mexico

Spain

**Fodor's
Special-Interest
Guides**

Complete Guide to
America's National
Parks

Condé Nast Traveler
Caribbean Resort and
Cruise Ship Finder

Cruises and Ports
of Call

Euro Disney

France by Train

Halliday's New
England Food
Explorer

Healthy Escapes

Italy by Train

London Companion

Shadow Traffic's New
York Shortcuts and
Traffic Tips

Sunday in New York

Sunday in San
Francisco

Touring Europe

Touring USA:
Eastern Edition

Walt Disney World and
the Orlando Area

Walt Disney World
for Adults

**Fodor's Vacation
Planners**

Great American
Learning Vacations

Great American
Sports & Adventure
Vacations

Great American
Vacations

Great American
Vacations for Travelers
with Disabilities

National Parks and
Seashores of the East

National Parks
of the West

**The Wall Street
Journal Guides to
Business Travel**

At last, a guide for Americans with disabilities that makes traveling a delight

This guide lists hundreds of attractions, hotels, restaurants, and other destinations, and it includes:

- descriptions of attractions, hotels, restaurants, and other destinations
- Up-to-date information on ISA-designated parking, level entranceways, and accessibility to pools, lounges, and bathrooms

Fodor's At bookstores everywhere, or call **1-800-533-6478**